Healthcare Law and Ethics

Seventh Edition

Bonnie F. Fremgen, PhD

Commercial Product Management: Katrin Beacom and Stephen Heasley
Content Development: Laura Horowitz
Content Producer: Maria Reyes
Product Marketing: Brooke Imbornone
Rights and Permission: Jenell Forschler and Chandan Kumar
Cover image: Stock Studio 4477/Shutterstock.

Please contact www.AskPearsonSupport.com with any queries on this content. Pearson puts care into the creation of our products. Our learning materials undergo content reviews to minimize bias and ensure the content is inclusive, accurate, and relevant. Please use this link to report instances of bias and inaccuracies: https://www.pearson.com/report-bias.html You can learn more about Pearson's commitment to accessibility at https://www.pearson.com/us/accessibility.html

Copyright © 2025, 2020, 2016, 2012 by Pearson Education, Inc. 221 River Street, Hoboken, NJ 07030. This digital publication is protected by copyright, and permission should be obtained from the publisher prior to any prohibited reproduction, storage in a retrieval system, or transmission in any form or by any means, electronic, mechanical, photocopying, recording, or otherwise except as authorized for use under the product subscription through which this digital application is accessed. For information regarding permissions, request forms and the appropriate contacts within the Pearson Education Global Rights & Permissions department, please visit https://www.pearson.com/global-permission-granting.html.

PEARSON and ALWAYS LEARNING are exclusive trademarks in the U.S. and/or other countries owned by Pearson Education, Inc. or its affiliates.

Acknowledgments of third-party content appear on the appropriate page within the text. Unless otherwise indicated herein, any third-party trademarks that may appear in this work are the property of their respective owners and any references to third-party trademarks, logos or other trade dress are for demonstrative or descriptive purposes only. Such references are not intended to imply any sponsorship, endorsement, authorization, or promotion of Pearson's products by the owners of such marks, or any relationship between the owner and Pearson Education, Inc. or its affiliates, authors, licensees or distributors.

Library of Congress Cataloging-in-Publication Data Names: Fremgen, Bonnie F., author. Title: Healthcare law and ethics / Bonnie F Fremgen. Other titles: Medical law and ethics Description: Seventh edition. | Hoboken, NJ : Pearson, [2025] | Preceded by Medical law and ethics / Bonnie F. Fremgen. Sixth edition. 2020. | Includes bibliographical references and index. | Summary: "Healthcare Law and Ethics is aimed at the nonlawyer health professional who must be able to cope with multiple legal and ethical issues. This text is appropriate for those studying in a college or university who are working toward careers in the allied health field in a variety of settings, such as medical offices, hospitals, clinics, laboratories, rehabilitation facilities, and skilled-nursing facilities. Because most allied healthcare professionals work either with or for a physician, it is important to understand the physician's responsibilities and duties to the patient. Included are examples of common legal and ethical issues that affect those working in the healthcare field. A wide range of topics are discussed, such as the legal system, professional liability and medical malpractice, public duties of the physician, the medical record, and ethical and bioethical issues. The intent is to help healthcare professionals to better understand our ethical obligation to ourselves, our patients, and our employers"-- Provided by publisher. Identifiers: LCCN 2024007462 (print) | LCCN 2024007463 (ebook) | ISBN 9780138322243 (paperback) | ISBN 0138322244 (paperback) | ISBN 9780135334638 (ebook) Subjects: MESH: Legislation, Medical | Ethics, Medical | Bioethical Issues | United States Classification: LCC KF3821 (print) | LCC KF3821 (ebook) | NLM W 32.5 AA1 | DDC 344.7304/1--dc23/eng/20240516 LC record available at https://lccn.loc.gov/2024007462 LC ebook record available at https://lccn.loc.gov/2024007463

2 2024

Pearson

ISBN-10: 0-13-832224-4
ISBN-13: 978-0-13-832224-3

To my children, who have always been my inspiration for ethical behavior.
And a special thanks to my husband for his continual support and help.

Contents

Preface   vi

A Letter to the Student from the Author   viii

About the Author   ix

Reviewers   x

1   Introduction to Healthcare Law, Ethics, and Bioethics   1
Introduction   2
Why Study Law, Ethics, and Bioethics?   2
Healthcare Law   5
Ethics   7
Models for Examining Ethical Dilemmas   15
What Ethics Is Not   17
Bioethics   18
The Role of Ethics Committees   19
Quality Assurance Programs   19
Medical Etiquette   20

PART 1   THE LEGAL ENVIRONMENT

2   The Legal System   26
Introduction   27
The Legal System   27
Sources of Law   29
Classification of Laws   31
The Court Systems   39
The Trial Process   40

3   Essentials of the Legal System for Healthcare Professionals   48
Introduction   48
Practice Acts   49
Licensure   51
Accreditation of Healthcare Institutions   56
Standard of Care   56
Confidentiality   58
Telehealth   58
Statute of Limitations   59
Good Samaritan Laws   59
Respondeat Superior   60
Scope of Practice   61
Risk Management   62

4   Working in Today's Healthcare Environment   69
Introduction   70
Delivery of Healthcare   70

Types of Healthcare Practices   77
Types of Healthcare Practitioners   79
The Delegation of Duties   84

PART 2   THE HEALTHCARE ENVIRONMENT

5   The Patient Relationship   90
Introduction   90
Provider's Rights and Responsibilities   91
Professional Practice Responsibilities   92
Patient's Rights and Responsibilities   97
Consent   100
Advance Directives   104

6   Professional Liability and Medical Malpractice   113
Introduction   114
Professional Negligence and Medical Malpractice   115
The Tort of Negligence   116
Fraud   120
Office of the Inspector General   122
Defense to Malpractice Suits   123
Professional Liability   125
Alternative Dispute Resolution   130
Liability of Other Health Professionals   131
Tort Reform   134
Guidelines for Malpractice Prevention   135

7   Public Duties of the Healthcare Professional   142
Introduction   143
Public Health Records and Vital Statistics   143
Controlled Substances Act and Regulations   151
Protection for the Employee and the Environment   156

8   Workplace Law and Ethics   163
Introduction   164
Professionalism in the Workplace   164
Discrimination in the Workplace   165
Privacy and the Workplace   165
Cultural Considerations in Healthcare Practice   165
Effective Hiring and Managing Practices   168
Federal Regulations Affecting Professionals   170
Equal Employment Opportunity and Employment Discrimination   170
Employee Health and Safety   175
Compensation and Benefits Regulations   178
Consumer Protection and Collection Practices   181

9 The Medical Record 188
  Introduction 189
  Purpose of the Medical Record 189
  Contents of the Medical Record 190
  Ownership of the Medical Record 194
  Confidentiality and the Medical Record 195
  Retention and Storage of Medical Records 197
  Electronic Health Records 198
  Personal Health Record 200
  Loss of Medical Records 201
  Reporting and Disclosure Requirements 201
  Use of the Medical Record in Court 201

10 Patient Confidentiality and HIPAA 208
  Introduction 209
  Confidentiality 209
  Privacy Act of 1974, Amended in 1988 210
  Health Insurance Portability and Accountability
    Act of 1996, Updated in 2013 211
  Ethical Concerns with Information Technology 224
  Pending Updates to HIPAA 227

PART 3 HEALTHCARE ETHICS

11 Ethical and Bioethical Issues in Healthcare 234
  Introduction 235
  Ethical Standards and Behavior 236
  Codes of Ethics 237
  Bioethical Issues 239
  The Ethics of Biomedical Research 245

12 Ethical Issues Related to the Beginning of Life 254
  Introduction 255
  Fertility Treatments and Assisted Reproductive
    Technology 255
  Contraception and Sterilization 259
  Abortion 262
  Genetic Disorders 266
  Wrongful-Life Suits and Safe Haven Laws 269

13 Ethical Issues Related to the End of Life 277
  Introduction 278
  Legal Definition of Death 278
  Ethical Issues in Caring for Terminally Ill Patients 281
  Stages of Grief 286
  Quality-of-Life Issues 287
  Ethical Dilemmas 292

14 Ethical Issues in Healthcare Trends 298
  Introduction 299
  Selected Issues in the Current Healthcare System 299
  Diversity and Equity in Healthcare 305
  Ethical Issues Regarding Selected Advances in
    Healthcare 313

APPENDIX A: Codes of Ethics 320

APPENDIX B: Case Citations 322

Glossary 324
Index 330

Preface

Advanced practice providers, nurses, and allied health professionals have always been important members of the healthcare team. This team awareness is even more critical in today's healthcare environment because physicians do not practice medicine alone. Therefore, the text discusses healthcare law and ethics as it relates to all healthcare professionals.

The seventh edition has been named *Healthcare Law and Ethics* to reflect its focus on the entire healthcare team. New examples and content cover many more healthcare disciplines such as advance practice providers (nurse practitioners and physician assistants), nurses, medical assistants, physical therapists, occupational therapists, respiratory therapists, and emergency medical personnel, among others. Chapter introductory cases have been updated to cover current issues such as hospitals being shut down by ransomeware attacks and abortion after the *Dobbs v. Jackson Women's Health Organization* decision. Reviewers from a variety of healthcare disciplines have helped to round out the content.

Healthcare Law and Ethics is written in straightforward language that is aimed at the nonlawyer health professional who must be able to cope with multiple legal and ethical issues. This text is appropriate for those studying in a college or university who are working toward careers in nursing or the allied health field in a variety of settings, such as healthcare offices, hospitals, clinics, laboratories, rehabilitation facilities, and skilled nursing facilities. Because most healthcare professionals work either with or for a physician or advanced practice provider, it is important to understand their responsibilities and duties to the patient. Therefore, they are covered in this book. Included are examples of common legal and ethical issues that affect those working in the healthcare field. A wide range of pertinent topics are discussed, such as the legal system, professional liability and medical malpractice, public duties of the healthcare team, the medical record, telehealth, and ethical and bioethical issues. The intent is to help healthcare professionals to better understand our ethical obligation to ourselves, our patients, and our employers.

Many legal cases are cited throughout the text to demonstrate the history of the law as it pertains to subjects such as patient confidentiality, managed care, federal regulations affecting the employee, death and dying, and abortion. In some examples, the cases may seem old, but because we as a country have a legal system based on case law, these laws are still pertinent today. A legal icon (scales of justice) appears in the margin to indicate legal case citations. A special feature called Med Tips provides quick information about law and ethics. These brief scenarios and hints help to maintain interest in this vital subject. Each chapter includes glossary terms highlighted in bold on first reference, extensive end-of-chapter exercises, and at least one actual practice case.

Chapter Structure

- **Learning Objectives.** These include an overview of the basic knowledge discussed within the chapter and can be used as a chapter review.

- **Key Terms.** Important vocabulary terms are listed alphabetically at the beginning of each chapter and printed in bold the first time they are defined in the text.

- **Introduction.** Each chapter begins with an introductory statement that reflects the topic of the chapter.

- **Review Challenge.** A selection of short answer, matching, and multiple-choice questions are included to test the student's knowledge of the chapter material.

- **Case Study.** The case studies are based on real-life occurrences and offer practical application of information discussed within the chapter. These are included to stimulate and draw upon the student's critical thinking skills and problem-solving ability.

- **Critical Thinking Exercise.** These exercises at the end of each chapter challenge the student to answer the question "What would you do if . . ." relating to many current healthcare and legal dilemmas in today's environment.

- **Bibliography.** These useful resources provide further information on the topics included within the chapter.

Special Features

- **Med Tip.** Med Tips are placed at strategic points within the narrative to provide helpful hints and useful information to stimulate the student's interest in the topic.

- **Legal Case Citations.** Discipline-specific cases are used throughout the text to illustrate the topic under discussion. The cases reflect the many healthcare disciplines, including that of the physician, that come together in the care of the patient. Although this book is not meant to be a law book, the cases cited are meant to emphasize the importance of the law for the students.

- **Points to Ponder.** Thought-provoking questions give students an opportunity to evaluate how they might answer some of the tough, healthcare related ethical dilemmas encountered in today's society. These questions can also be used for critical debate among students during a class activity.

- **Discussion Questions.** These end-of-chapter questions encourage a review of the chapter contents.

- **Put It into Practice.** These engaging activities appear at the end of each chapter. They provide a clinical correlation with the topics discussed in the chapter and stimulate the student's own contemplation of legal and ethical issues that are apparent in everyday life.

- **Web Hunt.** This end-of-chapter Internet activity encourages the student to access the multitude of healthcare resources available through this medium.

- **Appendices.** Codes of Ethics are included in Appendix A; the case citations used throughout the book are listed in Appendix B.

- **Additional Examination Review Questions.** These and additional helpful resources are included in the significantly updated Instructor's Resource Manual.

What's New in the Seventh Edition?

The seventh edition of *Healthcare Law and Ethics* has been thoroughly updated, starting with the new title. New sections and information in this edition include the following:

- **Chapter 2** Content on how to interpret case citations.

- **Chapter 3** Increased coverage of practice acts and licensure for advanced practice providers and nurses, and the scope of practice and licensure for allied health professionals such as respiratory therapists, phlebotomists, and medical assistants.

- **Chapter 4** Additional information on types of healthcare insurance, and greatly expanded information on advanced practice providers and nurses.

- **Chapter 5** All new content on duty to tell the truth and expanded content on patient's rights and responsibilities.

- **Chapter 6** Updated examples of fraud in healthcare settings and expanded content on liability of health professionals including physician assistants, nurses, dental assistants, laboratory technicians, paramedics, pharmacists, and physical therapists, among others.

- **Chapter 7** New case study on child abuse; expanded coverage on intimate partner violence, animal bites, the use of electronic prescribing of controlled substances (EPCS), and the opioid crisis; and a new section on substance misuse by healthcare personnel, which includes a table on warning signs.

- **Chapter 8** An entire new section on cultural considerations in healthcare practice; new coverage on the employment status of travel nurses; and updated content on the Family and Medical Leave Act.

- **Chapter 9** A new case study on a ransomware attack at a hospital; a primary focus on electronic health records instead of manual charting; expanded coverage on HIPAA regarding the ownership of the medical record; and a new section on challenges with using electronic health records.

- **Chapter 10** Expanded coverage on penalties for noncompliance with HIPAA and examples of sanctions against companies that violated HIPAA; new sections on clinical decision support systems and the Privacy Rule when providing home care; and a brief section on the pending updates to HIPAA.

- **Chapter 11** A new case study on COVID-19 vaccine line jumpers; expanded coverage of organ donation, organ trafficking, and transplant rationing; and updated content on end-of-life issues and medical aid-in-dying.

- **Chapter 12** A new case study on a woman who needs a therapeutic abortion; expanded coverage on fertility treatments, assisted reproductive technology, and surrogacy; expanded treatment on contraception, including emergency contraception, and involuntary sterilization; new content on abortion law after the *Dobbs v. Jackson Women's Health Organization* decision; and expanded coverage on genetic disorders, savior siblings, wrongful life lawsuits, and safe haven laws.

- **Chapter 13** Updated content on the legal definition of death including cardiopulmonary death and death by neurologic criteria (brain death); new content on the Brittany Maynard case on assisted suicide, arguments for and against euthanasia, and the right to refuse treatment; updated content on the stages of grief, including mentions of the models by Worden, Bowlby and Parkes, and the Dual Process Model; and new sections on the dying person's bill of rights, pain management in the terminally ill, and the domains of palliative care.

- **Chapter 14** New section on systemic problems in healthcare, including the cost of healthcare, the lack of providers, and resource allocation; new section on examples of situations with ethical implications including maternal morbidity, healthcare-associated infections, multidrug-resistant organisms, and the opioid crisis; new section on diversity and equity in healthcare including disparities in healthcare, social determinants of health, health literacy, food insecurity, and healthcare for patients with disabilities (hearing loss, deafness, vision disorders, intellectual disabilities, physical disabilities), and older adults; and a new section on ethical issues regarding advances in healthcare including telehealth, use of robotics, concierge healthcare, and artificial intelligence.

A Letter to the Student from the Author

There is a lot of information in this book, some that you will use as soon as you begin your career in healthcare. Hopefully, some material and tips will be usable as soon as you read them. You are working in a field that is full of people: patients of all ages, hospital and healthcare facilities with a variety of caregivers, and numerous fellow employees. If you remember one thing from this letter to you, remember to care. You and your skills—and your caring—are the gifts that you give to your patients. Now, read on and prepare for that Ah-Ha! moment when you realize that you are doing what you should be doing.

It's a natural tendency to read some of the case examples in this book and think that they must be fictional, as no well-trained healthcare professional would ever be so negligent. However, the short ethics cases at the beginning of each chapter are indeed based on real cases, many of them drawn from the author's experience.

Throughout the book, there are numerous examples of actual legal cases that usually resulted in suffering for patients as well as for providers and other healthcare professionals. The cases discussed are not meant to focus on particular healthcare disciplines, nor to exclude any disciplines. And these cases are not meant to frighten but, rather,

to alert all of us to the potential risks to patients when healthcare professionals are not diligent about the care they provide. Do not memorize the case citations, but rather try to understand the circumstances and why the case was included in this book.

I have a great respect for *all* the disciplines mentioned in this book. My intent is to prepare students to promote good patient care as well as to protect themselves and their employers from lawsuits.

The law is dynamic and often is revised as changes take place in society. An example is the Healthcare Insurance Portability and Accountability Act (HIPAA). It has had an impact on all types of healthcare organizations. This textbook is not meant to be a study of the law, but rather to introduce students to the impact that law and ethics have on their professional lives.

Finally, our goal as teachers is to help our students learn how to judge themselves and their actions. Because you won't have us with you in the workplace, we want you to be able to evaluate your own actions in light of their ethical and legal impact on others.

I wish you the very best in your healthcare career.

—Bonnie F. Fremgen

About the Author

Bonnie F. Fremgen, PhD, is a former associate dean of the Allied Health Program at Robert Morris College and was vice president of a hospital in suburban Chicago. She has taught medical law and ethics courses as well as clinical and administrative topics. She has broad interests and experiences in the healthcare field, including hospitals, nursing homes, and physicians' offices. She currently has two patents on a unique circulation-assisting wheelchair. She is the author of *Medical Terminology: A Living Language*, also published by Pearson.

Dr. Fremgen holds a nursing degree as well as a master's in healthcare administration. She received her PhD from the College of Education at the University of Illinois. She has performed postdoctoral studies in medical law at Loyola University Law School in Chicago.

Dr. Fremgen has taught ethics at the University of Notre Dame, South Bend, Indiana; University of Detroit, Detroit, Michigan; and Saint Xavier University, Chicago, Illinois.

Source: Courtesy of Bonnie F. Fremgen

Reviewers

Seventh Edition Reviewers

Arameh Anvarizadeh, BS, MA, OTD, OTR/L, FAOTA
Associate Professor of Clinical Occupational Therapy
Chan Division of Occupational Science and Occupational Therapy
University of Southern California
Los Angeles, California

Gayl M. Anglin, PhD
Chair, Health Programs
Trident University International
Portland, Maine

Margaret-Ann Carno, RN, MBA, MJ, PhD, PNP-AC/PC, CNE, FAAN, ATSF
Professor of Clinical Nursing and Pediatrics
Director of RN to BS Completion Program
School of Nursing
University of Rochester
Rochester, New York

Mark Jaffe, BA, MHSA, DPM
Associate Professor
NSU's Halmos College of Arts and Sciences
Department of Biological Sciences
Farquhar Honors College
Nova Southeastern University
Fort Lauderdale, Florida

Teandra Knapp, ADN, BS, JM
Boise, Idaho

Leonard Mascaro, AAS, NRP
Instructor, Commonwealth Training Associates
Director of Operations, Guardian Medical Services
Linden, Virginia

Danielle Mills, PT, EDPT, EdD
Vice Provost
Carrington College
Los Vegas, Nevada

Darlene Moretti, MSN, RN, RRT
Director of Nursing
Memorial Regional Hospital
Hollywood, Florida

Sixth Edition Reviewers

- **Dawn Bell,** Rhodes State College, Lima, Ohio
- **Kenneth Campbell,** Chicago State University, Chicago, Missouri
- **Liz Cooper,** Midwest Technical Institute, Springfield, Missouri
- **Abimbola Farinde,** Columbia Southern University, Orange Beach, Alabama
- **Ann Fiest,** Youngstown State University, Girard, Ohio
- **Angela Fleming,** Florida Technical College, Orlando, Florida
- **Pamela Giannone,** Indian River State College, Fort Pierce, Florida
- **Stefanie Goodman,** Ivy Tech Community College of Indiana—Marion, Marion, Indiana
- **Cheryl Goretti,** Quinebaug Valley Community College, Killingly, Connecticut
- **Christy Lee,** Southwest Virginia Community College, Richlands, Virginia
- **Vicki Lemaster,** The Southern Baptist Theological Seminary, Louisville, Kentucky
- **Christine Malone,** Everett Community College, Everett, Washington
- **Deborah Rouse,** Coastal Pines Technical College, Waycross, Georgia
- **Kristiana Routh,** Institute of Medical and Business Careers, Erie, Pennsylvania
- **Sharon Runyon,** Sullivan University, Lexington, Kentucky
- **Mary Zulaybar,** ASA College, New York, New York

Previous Edition Reviewers

- **Diana Alagna,** Program Director—Medical Assisting, Stone Academy, Waterbury, Connecticut
- **Rosana Darang,** Bay State College, Boston, Massachusetts
- **Amy DeVore,** Butler County Community College, Butler, Pennsylvania
- **Candace Lynn Doyle,** Midlands Technical College, West Columbia, South Carolina

- **Gail High,** YTI Career Institute—Altoona Campus, Altoona, Pennsylvania

- **Lisa Huehns,** Instructor—Allied Health, Lakeshore Technical College, Cleveland, Wisconsin

- **Cecelia Jacob,** Southwest Tennessee Community College, Memphis, Tennessee

- **Ana M. Linville,** University of Texas at Brownsville/Texas Southmost College, Brownsville, Texas

- **Michelle Lovings,** Missouri College, Brentwood, Missouri

- **Sharon Nelson,** Program Director—Allied Health, Columbus Technical College, Columbus, Georgia

- **Lorraine Papazian-Boyce,** Colorado Technical University Online, Hoffman Estates Illinois

- **Mary Lou Pfeiffer,** Fellow, Senior Faculty in the Honors College; Adjunct Professor—Religious Studies, Florida International University, Miami, Florida

- **Peter Joshua Richards,** Coordinator—Health Information Management/Medical Assisting, Black Hawk College, Moline, Illinois

- **Starra Robinson,** Program Director and Practicum Coordinator—Medical Assisting, Stanly Community College, Locust, North Carolina

- **Donna M. Rowan,** Harford Community College, Bel Air, Maryland

- **Andrew Rucks,** Adjunct Instructor—Healthcare Ethics, American International College, Springfield, Massachusetts

- **George W. Strothmann,** Sanford Brown Institute, Fort Lauderdale, Florida

- **Lori Warren Woodard,** Spencerian College, Louisville, Kentucky

- **Mindy Wray,** ECPI—Greensboro Campus, Greensboro, North Carolina

Introduction to Healthcare Law, Ethics, and Bioethics

Key Terms

Advanced practice providers
Amoral
Applied ethics
Bioethicists
Bioethics
Comparable worth
Cost/benefit analysis
Due process
Duty-based ethics
Ethics

Healthcare ethics
Healthcare etiquette
Indigent
Justice-based ethics
Laws
Litigious
Medical practice acts
Morality
Precedent

Principle of autonomy
Principle of beneficence
Principle of justice
Principle of nonmalfeasance
Quality assurance
Rights-based ethics
Sexual harassment
Utilitarianism
Virtue-based ethics

Learning Objectives

After completing this chapter, you will be able to:

1.1 Define the key terms.

1.2 Describe the similarities and differences between laws and ethics.

1.3 Discuss the reasons for studying law, ethics, and bioethics.

1.4 Describe how to apply the three decision-making models discussed in this chapter.

1.5 Explain why ethics is not *just* about the sincerity of one's beliefs, emotions, or religious viewpoints.

The Case of Jeanette M. and the Phone Call

Jeanette, an 80-year-old widow, called her primary care provider early one morning reporting shortness of breath. She spoke to the office receptionist who asked if she was having any other difficulty. Jeanette said no. The receptionist said she would give the message to the doctor.

The doctor's office was extremely busy that October day giving out flu shots. The receptionist immediately became busy answering telephone calls and admitting a long line of patients waiting for their annual flu shot. The telephone message from Jeanette was left unnoticed on the front office desk for several hours and was then placed in the physician's electronic record with other messages.

Jeanette became so exhausted from her shortness of breath that she fell asleep. When she awoke in the afternoon, she could not catch her breath. She called her neighbor and just said, "Help." Paramedics arrived at Jeanette's home shortly after the neighbor called 911 and found Jeanette to be unresponsive. She was taken to the local emergency department where she was diagnosed and treated for pneumonia and congestive heart failure. The emergency care team tried to determine who her personal physician was, but Jeanette had no personal belongings or medical information with her. She never regained consciousness and she died that evening.

When the neighbor went over to Jeanette's home that evening to feed the cat, she noticed the light on the phone's answering machine. The doctor had returned Jeanette's call at 5:00 PM. She apologized for not calling sooner.

1. Do you believe that this case presents a legal or an ethical problem or both?

2. In your opinion, is *anyone* at fault for Jeanette's death?

3. Is the physician at fault? Is anyone on the physician's staff at fault?

4. What could have been done to prevent this problem?

I long to accomplish a great and noble task, but it is my chief duty to accomplish humble tasks as though they were great and noble. The world is moved along, not only by the mighty shoves of its heroes, but also by the aggregate of the tiny pushes of each honest worker.

—Helen Keller

Introduction

Healthcare professionals encounter healthcare dilemmas that are not experienced by the general population. They are faced with individual choices that must, of necessity, always take into consideration the common good of all patients. Healthcare–ethical decisions have become increasingly complicated with the advancement of healthcare science and technology. The topics of healthcare law, ethics, and bioethics, while having specific definitions, are interrelated. One cannot deliver healthcare in any setting without an understanding of the legal implications for both the practitioner and the patient. Healthcare ethics is an **applied ethics**, meaning that it is a practical application of moral standards that are meant to benefit the patient. Therefore, the healthcare practitioner must adhere to certain ethical standards and codes of conduct. **Bioethics**, a branch of applied ethics, is a field resulting from modern healthcare advances and research. Many healthcare practitioners, patients, and religious organizations believe that advances in bioethics, such as cloning, require close examination, control, and even legal constraints.

Ethics experts explain that ethical behavior is that which puts the common good above self-interest. However, this textbook is not here to tell you *what* to think; it is here to tell you *to* think.

One teacher of healthcare law and ethics clearly stated, "Our primary goal is to teach students to think independently and become sensitive to the risks and issues that pervade the field." The ultimate goal in teaching this topic is to enable students to understand complex public healthcare policy from legal and ethical perspectives, regardless of personal beliefs. We want our students to be able to conduct themselves in a manner that is ethical, legal, and exemplary. We know you are learning when you begin to examine both (or *all*) sides of any issue.

Why Study Law, Ethics, and Bioethics?

Without a moral structure for their actions, people would be free simply to pursue their own self-interests. In many cases, people would behave in a moral fashion within the constraints and framework of their culture and religious beliefs. However, upon closer examination, it is clear that in a society where people live and act without the constraints and limitations imposed by moral standards and laws, a state of hostility could arise in which only the interests of the strong would prevail. The words *justice* and *injustice* would have little meaning. We all believe we know the difference between right and wrong. We may firmly believe that even when decisions are difficult to make, we would intuitively make the right decision. However, there is ample proof in medical malpractice cases that, in times of stress and crisis, people do not always make the correct ethical decisions. Because what is illegal is almost always unethical, it is important to have a basic understanding of the law as it applies to the healthcare world.

Med Tip

We must always remember that our primary duty is to promote good patient care and to protect our patients from harm.

We should also understand that we live in a **litigious** society in which people have become excessively inclined to sue healthcare practitioners. In addition, healthcare agencies, hospitals, nursing homes, and manufacturers of medical products and equipment are all at risk of being sued by patients and their families. In fact, in our society anyone can sue anyone else. Lawsuits take a great toll in terms of stress, time, and money for all parties involved. While being sued does not indicate guilt, nevertheless it can affect the reputation of a person or an institution even if that person or institution is judged to be innocent in a court of law.

Med Tip

A basic understanding of law and ethics can help protect you and your employer from being sued.

Another reason for studying ethics and the law is that people often convince themselves that what they are doing is not wrong. For example, plagiarism, which is using someone else's words or ideas, may be both unethical and illegal, depending on the circumstances. It's understandable that an author who has worked hard to write a book would not want another author to use their written material without permission and proper credit. In fact, lawsuits have been won when plagiarism is proven to have occurred. In this case, plagiarism is both illegal and unethical. But what happens when students have someone else do their work, or if they lift passages from a book and then claim the words as their own? Is this also illegal and unethical? It may be both.

A student entering the healthcare field is held to a high standard. Strong ethical values can begin with something as simple as turning in honest papers. There have been numerous examples of people lying on their job resume by embellishing duties and achievements in past jobs, stretching employment dates to cover gaps between jobs, inflating salaries, and even omitting criminal convictions. Many healthcare employers are sensitive to this problem and use consulting firms to perform background checks on potential employees. These background checks can uncover unethical and illegal acts.

Healthcare is based on the professional skills of many persons, including physicians, nurse practitioners, physician assistants, nurses, medical assistants, radiology technicians, pharmacists, surgical technologists, phlebotomists, reimbursement specialists and coders, pharmacy technicians, and a multitude of other allied health professionals. The healthcare team, composed of these professionals, with the addition of healthcare administrators, often must decide on critical issues relating to patient needs. In some cases, the decisions of these professionals are at odds with one another. For example, when an obstetrician withholds resuscitation attempts on a newborn with severe congenital anomalies, such as one born without a brain (anencephalic), they may be acting in opposition to the law in many states and the ethics of many people. Do nurses have an ethical responsibility to override this order if they believe it to be wrong? Is there a better way to handle such an ethical dilemma without the patient's suffering in the process? It is generally understood that nurses and other allied health professionals carry out the orders of their employer/provider. However, as illustrated in the case of the newborn with anencephaly, in some situations, confusion arises about what is the right thing to do. In the Jeanette M. case at the beginning of the chapter, does the physician's receptionist have any responsibility for the physician's delay in returning the patient's call?

It is generally accepted that some behavior, such as killing, is always wrong. But even this issue has been in the news when, as Hurricane Katrina roared through New Orleans in 2005, several critically ill hospital patients who could not be moved, and would certainly die, were allegedly given a lethal injection of morphine by a doctor and two nurses. In 2007, a grand jury determined not to indict the physician and cleared her of all accusations. There have been 194 Katrina-related claims filed by a Louisiana state agency that manages malpractice lawsuits. There is a concern, resulting from this case, that prosecutions against hospitals and healthcare staff could prevent doctors from helping in times of a disaster. As a result, two state laws were passed in 2008 protecting healthcare staff during states of emergency.

Med Tip

A study of law, ethics, and bioethics can assist the healthcare professional in making a sound decision based on reason and logic rather than on emotion or a "gut feeling."

Ethics asks difficult questions, such as "How should we act?" and "How should we live?" The answers to such questions are often subjective and can change according to circumstances, so it is realistic to ask, "Why study ethics?" The short answer is that, in spite of the many gray areas of ethics, we are expected to take the right action when confronted with an ethical dilemma. We must consider the consequences of wrongdoing. We must learn how to think about the ethics of an action and then how to translate those thoughts into action. So, even if the "right thing" isn't always clear, we can prepare our minds to think about an action and to see how the experiences of others can influence our own actions. The important thing is to be able to think and then take action!

Of course, not all illegal or unethical cases end up with a lawsuit or in a court of law. However, brief descriptions of actual court cases are sprinkled throughout the text to illustrate the topics that are discussed in the chapter. These cases alert us to the variety of situations that have negatively affected the careers of physicians and other healthcare professionals as well as the patients who were harmed.

Med Tip

The reason we want to do the ethical thing is *not* because we could be named in a lawsuit but because we would not want poor care for anyone, including our family and ourselves.

While studying ethics, ask yourself the following questions. Do you know what you would do in each of the following situations? Do you know whether you are exposing yourself to a lawsuit? The ethics and legalities of these types of situations will be addressed in this book (see chapters listed after each scenario).

- A fellow student says, "Sure, I stole this book from the bookstore, but the tuition is so high that I figured the school owed me at least one book." What do you do? (Chapter 1, "Introduction to Healthcare Law, Ethics, and Bioethics")
- An orderly working in a skilled nursing facility is left alone in the dining room in charge of a group of older adult residents who are finishing their dinner. One of the residents does not want to eat but wishes to go back to his own room, which he cannot find by himself. The orderly has been instructed never to leave patients alone. Because he cannot leave the dining room full of patients, nor can he allow the one resident to find his own room, the orderly locks the dining room door. The resident claims he has been falsely imprisoned. Is he correct? (Chapter 2, "The Legal System")
- You are drawing a specimen of blood from Fatima, who says that she doesn't like having blood drawn. In fact, she tells you that the sight of blood makes her "queasy." While you are taking her blood specimen, she faints and hits her head against the side of a cabinet. Are you liable for Fatima's injury? If you are not liable, do you know who is? (Chapter 3, "Essentials of the Legal System for Healthcare Professionals")
- You are a recently hired registered nurse working in the office of an internist. You have agreed to answer the phone calls in the physician's office while the receptionist is having lunch. A patient calls and says he must have a prescription refill order for blood pressure medication called in right away to his pharmacy because he is leaving town in 30 minutes. He says that he has been on the medication for 4 years and that he is a personal friend of the physician. No one except you is in the office at this time. What do you do? (Chapter 4, "Working in Today's Healthcare Environment")
- Terry O'Rourke, a 25-year-old female patient of Dr. Singh, refuses to take her medication to control diabetes and is not following her dietary plan to control the disease. After repeated attempts to help this patient, Dr. Singh has decided that she can no longer provide care for Terry. The office staff has been advised not to schedule Terry for any more appointments. Is there an ethical or legal concern (or both) regarding this situation? Is there anything else that either Dr. Singh or her staff should do to sever the patient's relationship with Terry? (Chapter 5, "The Physician–Patient Relationship")
- You drop a sterile packet of gauze on the floor. The inside of the packet is still considered sterile; however, the policy in your office is to re-sterilize anything that drops on the floor. This is the last sterile packet on the shelf. The chances are very slight that any infection would result from using the gauze within the packet. What do you do? (Chapter 6, "Professional Liability and Medical Malpractice")
- The pharmaceutical salesperson has just brought in a supply of nonprescription vitamin samples for the providers in your practice to dispense to their patients. All the other staff members take samples home for their families' personal use. They tell you to do the same because the samples will become outdated before the providers can use all of them. It would save you money. What do you do? Is it legal? Is it ethical? (Chapter 7, "Public Duties of the Healthcare Professional")
- You feel a slight prick on your sterile glove as you assist Dr. Whelan on a minor surgical procedure. Dr. Whelan has a quick temper, and he will become angry if you delay the surgical procedure while you change gloves. As there was just a slight prick and the patient's wound is not infected, will it

hurt to wear the gloves during the procedure? Who is at fault if the patient develops a wound infection? Is this a legal and/or ethical issue? (Chapter 8, "Workplace Law and Ethics")

- A patient calls to ask you to change her diagnosis in her healthcare record from R/O (rule out) bladder infection to "bladder infection" because her insurance will not pay for an R/O diagnosis. In fact, she tested negative for an infection, but the provider placed her on antibiotics anyway. What do you do? Is this legal? Is it ethical? (Chapter 9, "The Medical Record")

- A physician from another office steps into your office and asks to see the chart of a neighbor whom he believes may have an infectious disease. He states that the neighbor is a good friend and that she will not mind if he reviews her healthcare l chart. Is it legal for you to give the chart to this physician? (Chapter 10, "Patient Confidentiality and HIPAA")

- A local hospital was attempting to arrange liver transplants for several patients. At the same time that a liver became available from an organ donor, it was learned that a prominent local politician also needed a new liver. The politician was moved to the head of the line for the available liver. What are the ethics of giving a scarce liver to a prominent politician ahead of other patients who have been waiting for some time? What are your thoughts about the statement "People should not be punished just because they are celebrities"? (Chapter 11, "Ethical and Bioethical Issues in Healthcare")

- You are a registered nurse, and your neighbor's 18-year-old daughter has just given birth to a baby boy. The neighbor is concerned that neither she nor her daughter can take care of this baby. She asks you what you can suggest. Is it a violation of ethics to tell her about the Safe Harbor Law? (Chapter 12, "Ethical Issues Related to the Beginning of Life")

- An 82-year-old widow is rushed to the hospital in the middle of the night with a massive heart attack. She is in need of emergency treatment that requires the services of a special surgical team. It takes almost 2 hours to gather the entire team as they had all left for the day. This patient has a good chance of recovering if the procedure is done within 6 hours after the heart attack occurs. But, as soon as the surgical team is together and the operating room is ready, another patient, a 45-year-old woman, is brought into the emergency department in need of the same procedure to save her life. It is agreed that the 45-year-old woman will receive the treatment first, but the procedure takes longer than expected. This procedure could not be performed on the widow because the 6-hour "window of opportunity" to do the procedure had passed. The younger woman lives, and the older widow dies the next day. Is the decision on who will receive the procedure first an ethical or legal one, or both? (Chapter 13, "Ethical Issues Related to the End of Life")

- Robert, who is 78 years old and Deaf, walks into a very busy hospital emergency department. The receptionist asks Robert what his problem is but, getting no response, hands Robert a form to complete. The receptionist then asks Robert if he has any allergies they should know about when they examine him. He does not understand this question. Frustrated, Robert turns around and walks back out the door and gets in a cab to go home. After a 30-minute cab trip, the driver tells Robert he is home but gets no response. Robert had died of a heart attack during the ride. What could/should have been done to prevent this from happening? (See discussion of Deaf Culture in Chapter 14, "Ethical Issues in Healthcare Trends.")

These situations, and others like them, are addressed throughout this text.

Healthcare Law

Laws are rules or actions prescribed by an authority such as the federal government and the court system that have a binding legal force. Healthcare law addresses legal rights and obligations that affect patients and protect individual rights, including those of healthcare employees. For example, practicing medicine without a license, Medicaid fraud, and patient rape are violations of healthcare laws that are always illegal and immoral or unethical.

It is easy to become confused when studying law and ethics, because, while the two are different, they often overlap. Some illegal actions may be quite ethical—for example, exceeding the speed limit when rushing an injured child to the hospital. Of course, many unethical actions may not be illegal, such as cheating on a test. Law and ethics both exist in everyday life and, thus, are difficult to separate. An insurance company denying payment for a life-saving heart transplant on a 70-year-old male is not illegal in most cases, but it may well be unethical.

Med Tip

In general, an illegal act, or one that is against the law, is almost always unethical. However, an unethical act may not be illegal. For instance, a physician traveling on a plane does not have a legal obligation to come forward when an announcement is made requesting a doctor to assist with an emergency. But it may be an unethical action if the passenger dies without the help of an available doctor.

There is a greater reliance on laws and the court system, as our society and healthcare system have become more complex. In fact, some physicians and **advanced practice providers** (e.g., nurse practitioners, certified nurse midwives, and physician assistants) have been practicing a form of healthcare called "defensive medicine." This means that they may order unnecessary tests and procedures in order to protect themselves from a lawsuit because then they can say "I did everything that I could to treat the patient." This type of preventive medicine is not only costly but also may put the patient through needless and uncomfortable tests and procedures. In some cases, physicians may even avoid ordering tests or procedures that may carry a risk for the patient because they do not want to take a chance that a lawsuit may result if the patient outcome is poor.

The law provides a yardstick by which to measure our actions, and it punishes us when our actions break the laws. Many of the actions punishable by law are considered morally wrong, such as rape, murder, and theft. The problem with measuring our actions using only the law, and not considering the ethical aspects of an issue, is that the law allows many actions that are morally offensive, such as lying and manipulating people. Laws against actions such as adultery, which most people agree are immoral, exist, but they are rarely enforced. Some situations involving interpersonal relationships between coworkers, such as taking credit for someone else's work, are difficult to address with laws. Other work issues such as lying on job applications, padding expense accounts, and making unreasonable demands on coworkers are usually handled on the job and are typically not regulated by laws.

A further caution about relying on the law for moral decision-making: The requirements of the law often tend to be negative. The standards of morality, on the other hand, are often seen to be positive. The law forbids us to harm, rob, or defame others; but in most states, it does not require us to help people. Morality would tell us to give aid to the drowning victim even if the law does not mandate that we do so.

Many people believe that something is wrong, or unethical, only if the law forbids it. Conversely, they reason that if the law says it's all right, then it is also ethical. Unfortunately, these people believe that until the law tells them otherwise, they have no ethical responsibility beyond the law. Finally, laws are often reactive and may lag behind the moral standards of society; slavery is the most obvious example. Sexual harassment and racial discrimination existed as moral problems long before laws were enacted to suppress this behavior.

There are a multitude of laws, including criminal and civil statutes (laws enacted by state and federal legislatures) as well as state medical practice acts that affect healthcare professionals. **Medical practice acts**, established in all 50 states by statute, apply specifically to the way medicine is practiced in a particular state. These acts define the meaning of the "practice of medicine" as well as the requirements and methods for licensure. They also define what constitutes unprofessional conduct in that particular state. While the laws vary from state to state, the more common items of unprofessional conduct include the following:

- Practicing medicine without a license
- Impaired judgment because of addiction or mental illness
- Conviction of a felony
- Violation of patient privacy
- Incompetence or negligence
- Insufficient record-keeping
- Allowing an unlicensed person to practice medicine
- Physical abuse of patients
- Healthcare fraud

- Prescribing medication in excessive amounts
- Patient abandonment

As we study law and ethics as they relate to healthcare, we will frequently use court cases to illustrate points. For our purposes it is not necessary to memorize the specifics of a lawsuit such as the legal citation that has been decided in a court of law. But it is important to keep in mind that unless a decided case is overturned in an appeals court, it is considered to have established a **precedent**. This means that the decision of the case acts as a model for any future cases in which the facts are the same.

Ethics

Healthcare law addresses rights and obligations that affect patients and protect their rights; ethics also addresses issues that affect patients and their rights. **Ethics** is the branch of philosophy related to morals, moral principles, and moral judgments. Ethics is often about making choices. A more practical explanation from ethics experts tells us that ethical behavior is that which puts the common good above self-interest. Ethics is concerned with the obligation of what we "should" or "ought to" do. **Morality** is the quality of being virtuous or practicing the right conduct. People are said to be **amoral** if they are lacking or indifferent to moral standards. However, the terms *ethics* and *morality* are used interchangeably by many people.

Ethics, as part of philosophy, uses reason and logic to analyze problems and find solutions. Ethics, in general, is concerned with the actions and practices that are directed at improving the welfare of people in a moral way. Thus, the study of ethics forces us to use reason and logic to answer difficult questions concerning life, death, and everything in between. In modern terms, we use words such as *right, wrong, good,* and *bad* when making ethical judgments. In other cases, people refer to issues or actions that are *just* and *unjust* or *fair* and *unfair*.

Healthcare ethics concerns questions specifically related to the practice of healthcare. This branch of ethics is based on principles regulating the behavior of healthcare professionals, including practitioners such as physicians, nurses, and allied health professionals. It also applies to patients, relatives, and the community at large.

Med Tip

Ethics always involves people. This includes patients, healthcare professionals, other caregivers, and the general public.

Ethics is meant to take the past into account, but also to look to the present and future and ask, "What should I do now?" and "What will be the outcome?" Unfortunately, using moral views based only on those of parents and peers can lead to radical subjectivism that can make ethical discussion of issues such as euthanasia, abortion, or cloning difficult, if not impossible. Many of our beliefs are based on emotions—for example, we believe that something is wrong if we feel guilt when we do it. While most healthcare practitioners, other than physicians, will not be required to make life-and-death decisions about their patients, it is still important for everyone to develop their own personal value system. Whenever you are involved in an ethical dilemma, you must analyze actions and their consequences for all concerned parties. Law also does this by directing actions into "legal" and "illegal" human actions. Ethical issues are not so easily divided into two categories such as "right" and "wrong."

As we study ethics, we will also analyze various actions and their effects. When following a moral line of reasoning it is advisable to carefully take apart the issues, restate them in your own words, and offer an interpretation, and even a criticism, of them.

Med Tip

Remember that ethics always involves formal consideration of the interests of others in deciding how to act or behave. In fact, some philosophers believe that almost every decision to do anything is an ethical decision.

Theories of Ethics

Basic questions relating to the study of ethics have been the subject of much debate and analysis, particularly among philosophers. Various philosophers have defined ethics under several categories, such as utilitarianism, natural rights, or rights-, duty-, justice-, and virtue-based ethics. A division is often made between *teleological* and *deontological* theories in ethics. A teleological theory asserts that an action is right or wrong depending on whether it produces good or bad consequences. Utilitarianism (described below) is an example of this theory. Deontological ethical theory asserts that at least *some* actions are right or wrong and, thus, we have a duty or obligation to perform them or refrain from performing them, without consideration of the consequences. Duty-based ethics (also described below) is an example of deontological theory. These ethical theories are the basis for many of our country's regulations, such as the Occupational Safety and Health Act (OSHA), and the norms of our society.

Utilitarianism

Utilitarianism is an ethical theory based on the guiding principle of the greatest good for the greatest number of people. This ethical theory is concerned with the impact of actions, or final outcomes, on the welfare of society as a whole. In other words, the "rightness" or "wrongness" of an act is determined solely by its consequences. This view looks at what would satisfy the interests, wants, and needs of *most* people. Additionally, utilitarianism is a consequences-based ethical theory that follows the premise that the ends (consequences) justify the means (methods for achieving the ends). For example, in the case of limited financial resources, money would be spent in a way to benefit the greatest number of people. In this respect, utilitarianism is considered to be an efficient allocation of resources. In a professional context, a **cost/benefit analysis** justifies the means of achieving a goal. In other words, if the benefit of a decision outweighs the cost (financial or otherwise) of achieving a goal, then the means to obtain the goal would be justified. A problem arises when utilitarianism, or cost/benefit analysis, is used for making ethical decisions, because when a decision benefits *most* people, *some* people will inevitably "fall through the cracks." This could result in serious consequences if a person is denied treatment and eventually suffers and/or dies because of this denial.

The United States Medicare system, in which persons over the age of 65 and other qualified individuals receive healthcare benefits, is one example of utilitarianism. Congress has limited amounts of funds to allocate for healthcare coverage and uses those funds to cover older adults and others, such as people with disabilities, under the federal government Medicare Act. However, not *all* people require the benefit. In the case of Medicare, for example, not all older adults need to have healthcare coverage provided for them by this act, because some are wealthy and can afford their own coverage, or because they are still working and covered by their employer's insurance. On the other hand, there are people with low incomes who are not yet 65, and are not **indigent** (impoverished) enough to qualify for Medicaid, a state government program, but still require some type of healthcare insurance.

Another example of utilitarianism occurs when there is a limited supply of donor organs. Under a utilitarianism approach, patients with the most immediate need (and who would benefit the most) would receive the organ. Using this approach for organ distribution, terminally ill or older persons with a limited lifespan would not be the first to receive a scarce resource such as a new heart. A weakness of the utilitarianism approach to moral reasoning is that it is impossible to quantify all the variables. Therefore, it can result in a biased allocation of resources, ignoring the rights of some vulnerable people such as those who are young, sick, disabled, or older who lack representation or a voice.

Rights-Based Ethics

Rights-based ethics, or a natural rights ethical theory, places the primary emphasis on a person's individual rights. This ethical theory states that rights belong to all people purely by virtue of their being human. Under our rights-based democracy, all Americans have the right to freedom of speech. Some employees have the right to **due process**, which entitles them to a fair hearing in the case of dismissal from their jobs. In the previous example of limited donor organs, using a rights-based ethical approach, every patient needing a donor organ would have the same right to receive the available organ.

The strength of rights-based ethics is a strong attempt to protect the individual from injury. Laws such as OSHA (Occupational Safety and Health Act) benefit society as a whole because everyone in the workplace is protected by this act. The downside to this approach is that there can be incidents of individualistic selfish behavior that is independent of the outcomes (consequences). For example, unions protect their membership while excluding the rights of the non-union members of society.

Duty-Based Ethics

Duty-based ethics focuses on performing one's duty to various people and institutions such as parents, employers, employees, and customers (patients). This line of moral reasoning follows the belief that our actions should be universal, which means that everyone would act the same way under the same set of circumstances. For example, Americans have some duties, adhering to adhere to laws enforced by government authorities. Duties also arise from our own actions. Therefore, we have a duty to keep promises, not to lie, and to make reparations to those whom we have harmed. These reparations include compensation for any damage to another person. An example is the financial compensation a healthcare practitioner would make if they caused harm to a patient.

One of the problems encountered with this moral line of reasoning is the mandate to do things out of a sense of duty regardless of the consequences. In addition, we may hear conflicting opinions about what our "duty" or responsibility is in particular circumstances. If your employer asks you to do something that you are sure is wrong or unethical, you have a duty not to perform the action. (You will come across some malpractice cases later in the text that demonstrate this.) However, this violates your duty to your employer. Most religions have statements that address one's duty as a member of that faith or religion. However, many people do not accept their faith's beliefs concerning issues such as birth control or working on the Sabbath, but they do adhere to other doctrines of their religion. Many people claim that a sense of duty is not enough when dealing with ethical dilemmas. Rules do not always work. And people from different cultures may have a different sense of what "duty" means.

Justice-Based Ethics

Justice-based ethics is based on an important moral restraint called "the veil of ignorance." The philosopher John Rawls believed that all social contracts, such as who should receive a scarce organ donation, should be handled so that no one would know the gender, age, race, health, number of children, income, wealth, or any other arbitrary personal information about the recipient. This "veil of ignorance," meaning we would not *see* the recipients of our choices, would allow the decision-makers (such as Congress or healthcare experts) to be impartial in their decisions. The so-called "veil of ignorance" means that no one person is advantaged or disadvantaged. In effect, the "least well off" person would then have the same chance for scarce resources and justice as the wealthier and more educated. Rawls, who equated justice with fairness, assumed that people have a self-interest when forming social contracts such as who will receive healthcare. The justice-based model of ethics infers that every citizen should have equal access to healthcare. For example, children with genetic diseases that would require large financial resources deserve good care simply as a matter of justice. Proponents of justice-based ethics believe insurance premium rates and risk should be spread over all members of the nation such as in a federal single-payer system like Medicare.

Opponents of this theory believe it is unfair for the healthy to subsidize the unhealthy. Furthermore, under the current gigantic healthcare system and extensive media coverage, it is impossible to have the "veil of ignorance" that is demanded by this ethical model.

Justice, according to John Rawls (Rawlsian Justice), requires the following:

- Using a democratic and fair approach to others
- Maintaining a fair distribution of benefits and burdens
- Protecting the interests of the weak or powerless
- Allocating resources fairly

Virtue-Based Ethics

A moral virtue is a character trait that is morally valued. The emphasis of **virtue-based ethics** is on persons and not necessarily on the decisions or principles that are involved. Most people agree that virtues, such as fairness and honesty, are just good habits. Other examples of virtues and good character traits are integrity, trust, respect, empathy, generosity, truthfulness, and the ability to admit mistakes.

Virtue-based ethics, or seeking the "good life," is our legacy from the philosopher Aristotle. According to him, the goal of life, for which we all aim, is happiness. He believed that happiness is founded not solely on what we gain in life, but also on who we are. For example, the joy of being a healthcare professional cannot be present without having the traits or virtues that make one a good physician, nurse, medical assistant, technologist, or other healthcare professional. These virtues include perseverance, integrity, compassion, and trust. Aristotle's theory is considered inadequate by many because it does not take into account the consequences of an action, as in utilitarianism, or the rights of others, as in rights-based ethics. In addition, there are some who believe that people might take advantage of someone who is too trusting.

Comparing the Five Theories of Ethics

While each of these five ethical theories can have positive outcomes and are useful in certain circumstances, no one ethical theory or system is perfect. Ethical standards that relate to the healthcare professions are set and defined by professional organizations such as the American Medical Association. All professional disciplines, such as nursing and medical assisting, have their own organizations and standards of guiding ethical codes of conduct. Codes of ethics are discussed more fully in Chapter 5.

In general, people believe an action is wrong or unethical if it

- causes emotional or physical harm to someone else,
- goes against their deepest beliefs,
- makes a person feel guilty or uncomfortable about a particular action,
- breaks the law or traditions of their society, or
- violates the rights of another person.

Because no one ethical theory is perfect, the healthcare community and healthcare professionals use a combination of many theories to determine the correct action to take.

See Table 1.1 for a comparison of the strengths and weaknesses of the five ethical theories.

Table 1–1 Strengths and Weaknesses of Five Ethical Theories

Theory	Strengths	Weaknesses
Utilitarianism The greatest good for the greatest number	• Encourages efficiency and productivity • Consistent with profit maximization—getting the most value (benefit) for the least cost • Looks beyond the individual to assess impact of the decision on all who are affected	• Virtually impossible to quantify all variables • Can result in biased allocations of resources, especially when some who are affected lack representation or voice • Can result in ignoring the rights of some people to achieve a utilitarian outcome
Rights-Based Ethics Individual's rights to be protected	• Protects the individual from injury; consistent with rights to freedom and privacy	• Can encourage individualist, selfish behavior that, if misinterpreted, may result in anarchy
Duty-Based Ethics Based on absolute moral rules	• Absolute rules or principles help us determine what our duty is toward others. • Determines what our duty is to one another • A mandate for respect and impartiality	• Hard to identify who should determine the rules and principles of moral behavior • May tend to treat people as a means to an end
Justice-Based Ethics Fair distribution of benefits and burdens	• A democratic approach • Based on a "veil of ignorance" • No one person is advantaged or disadvantaged.	• Some believe it is unfair for the healthy to subsidize the unhealthy.
Virtue-Based Ethics Based on belief that we have a duty or responsibility to others	• Exemplifies the premise that our actions are universal • Virtuous behavior includes perseverance, courage, integrity, compassion, humility, and justice.	• Concern that people can be taken advantage of if they are too complacent or trusting

Principles or Values That Drive Ethical Behavior

Most people have established, throughout their lifetime, their own set of principles or values that drive their ethical behavior. Benjamin Franklin included in his list of virtues such things as cleanliness, silence, and industry. In today's world, we don't think of these things as virtues; they are assumed by many people to be a part of everyday life.

Med Tip
One should not perform an action that might threaten the dignity or welfare of another individual.

However, in today's fast-paced healthcare environment, it is important to slow down enough to consider some of the most respected virtues. Some of these virtues include beneficence, empathy, fidelity, gentleness, holistic care, humility, justice, perseverance, responsibility, sanctity of life, tolerance, and work.

- *Beneficence*—The action of helping others and performing actions that would result in benefit to another person. It cautions all those working in the healthcare field to do no harm to anyone. In fact, when we prevent harmful actions from happening to our patients, we are using this virtue to its fullest extent (Figure 1.1).
- *Empathy*—An objective awareness of the feelings, emotions, and behavior of another person. (Also called compassion.)
- *Fidelity*—Loyalty and faithfulness to others. Fidelity implies that you will perform your duty. You must use caution when practicing fidelity. A strict adherence to a sense of duty or loyalty to an employer does not mean that you must perform actions that are wrong or harmful to your patients.
- *Gentleness*—A mild, tenderhearted approach to other people. Gentleness goes beyond compassion because it can exist in the absence of a person's pain and suffering. A gentle approach to patient care is considered by patients to be one of the most welcome virtues. All people have the ability to demonstrate gentleness.
- *Holistic care*—A comprehensive total care approach to a patient including physical, emotional, and spiritual care.
- *Humility*—Acquiring an unpretentious and humble manner. Humility is considered to be the opposite of vanity. It has been said that honesty and humility are siblings. This means that to be truly humble, you

Figure 1–1 Beneficence: helping others

Source: val lawless/Shutterstock

must be entirely honest with yourself. Humility requires that you recognize your own limits. Vanity and a sense of self-importance have no place in healthcare. When mistakes are made, they must be reported so that corrections can take place. It takes a humble—and honest—person to admit mistakes.

- *Justice*—Fairness in all your actions with other people. It means that you must carefully analyze how to balance your behavior to be fair to all. Justice implies that the same rules will apply to everyone. This means that as healthcare workers, we cannot demonstrate favoritism with our patients or our coworkers. The four cardinal virtues are justice, temperance, prudence, and courage. Of these four, only justice is considered to be an absolute good. To emphasize this point, the philosopher Immanuel Kant said, "If legal justice perishes, then it is no longer worthwhile for men to remain alive on this earth."

- *Perseverance*—Persisting with a task or idea even against obstacles. This virtue implies a steady determination to get the job done. For example, it takes perseverance to complete your education. This is an outstanding virtue for a healthcare worker to have. It implies that you will finish the job even if it is difficult.

- *Responsibility*—A sense of accountability for your actions. Responsibility implies dependability. A sense of responsibility can become weakened when you are faced with peer pressure. Healthcare professionals must be able to "answer" or be accountable for their actions. Taking responsibility is a sign of maturity.

- *Sanctity of life*—The sacredness of human life. All human beings must be protected. This means that you may have to become an advocate for people who cannot speak out for themselves, such as children and some older adults.

- *Tolerance*—A respect for those whose opinions, practices, race, religion, and nationality differ from your own. Tolerance requires a fair and objective attitude toward opinions and practices with which you may or may not agree.

- *Work*—An effort applied toward some end goal. Work, if performed well, is clearly a virtue that almost everyone enters into at one time or another. In its broadest sense, work is part of our everyday existence that includes activities such as studying, child rearing, home maintenance, gardening, hobbies, and religious activities. The work you do to earn a living can be performed with pride or can be performed poorly and grudgingly. The most satisfying work involves achieving a goal that you believe is worthwhile and worthy of our talent.

Source: The Metaphysics of Morals, Mary J. Gregor, Cambridge University Press,1991

Med Tip

Not all patients are easy to care for. Many patients do not feel well or may be saddened by a diagnosis. All patients have a right to our respect and understanding.

Interpersonal Ethics

The expectation of employees in the workplace is that they will be treated ethically with respect, integrity, honesty, fairness, empathy, sympathy, compassion, and loyalty. Professional healthcare employees are no different in their expectation of receiving such treatment.

Med Tip

Remember to treat each person, whether patient or coworker, the way you wish to be treated.

- *Respect* implies the ability to consider and honor another person's beliefs and opinions. This is a critical quality for a healthcare worker because patients come from a variety of racial, ethnic, and religious backgrounds. Coworkers' opinions must also be respected, even if contrary to one's own.

- *Integrity* is the unwavering adherence to your principles. People with integrity are dedicated to maintaining high standards. For example, integrity means that healthcare professionals will wash their hands between each patient contact even when no one is looking. Dependability, such as being on time for work every day, is a key component of integrity. Integrity is so important that many professions include a statement regarding this quality in their code of ethics. For example, the Pharmacy Technician Code of Ethics states that the pharmacy technician "supports and promotes honesty and integrity in the profession, which includes a duty to observe the law, maintain the highest moral and ethical conduct at all times, and uphold the ethical principles of the profession."

Source: Pharmacy Technician Code of Ethics

Integrity includes the following:

- Doing the right thing even when nobody is looking
- Showing concern for others
- Using ethically acceptable behavior
- Fairness
- Accepting responsibility for one's actions

- *Honesty* is the quality of truthfulness, no matter what the situation. Healthcare professionals must have the ability to admit an error and then take corrective steps. Anyone who carries out orders for a provider has a duty to notify the provider of any error or discrepancy in those orders.
- *Fairness* is treating everyone the same. It implies an unbiased impartiality and a sense of justice. This is a particularly important characteristic for supervisors.
- *Empathy* is the ability to understand the feelings of others without actually experiencing their pain or distress. Acting in this caring way expresses sensitivity to patients' or fellow employees' feelings.
- *Sympathy*, on the other hand, is sharing someone's feelings, including feeling sorry for them or pitying them. Most people, including patients, react better to empathetic listeners than to sympathetic ones.
- *Compassion* is the ability to have a gentle, caring attitude toward patients and fellow employees. Any illness, and in particular a terminal illness, can cause fear and loneliness in many patients. A compassionate healthcare professional can help to ease this fear.
- *Loyalty* is a sense of faithfulness or commitment to a person or persons. Employers expect loyalty from their employees. This loyalty should be granted unless the practice of your employer is unethical or illegal. For example, it is never appropriate to recommend that a patient seek the services of another physician unless instructed to do so by your employer. By the same token, employees expect loyalty, or fair treatment, from their employer.

Med Tip

Loyalty to your employer does *not* mean hiding an error that has been committed by that employer or by a physician. If you're not sure, ask.

Additionally, there are specific issues that affect the workplace, such as privacy, due process, sexual harassment, and comparable worth.

- *Privacy*, or confidentiality, is the ability to safeguard another person's confidences or information (Figure 1.2). Violating patient confidentiality is both a legal and an ethical issue that carries penalties. Employees have a right to expect the contents of their personnel records to be held in confidence by their employer. By the same token, it is inappropriate for employees to discuss the personal lives of their colleagues in the professional setting.
- *Due process* is the entitlement of employees of the government and public companies to have certain procedures followed when they believe their rights are in jeopardy. The Fourteenth Amendment acts to prevent the state's deprivation or impairment of "any person's life, liberty, or property without due process of the law" (The Fourteenth Amendment Acts). The Fifth Amendment also restricts the federal government from depriving individuals of these rights without due process of the law. In a work environment, this means that employees of the government and public companies accused of an offense are entitled to a fair hearing in their defense. Due process is also a protection guaranteed to healthcare workers as it relates to their state certification, license, or registration to practice. To remove a person's license to practice their profession is the same as removing a person's livelihood. Thus, the removal of this documentation is not to be taken lightly. If there are allegations

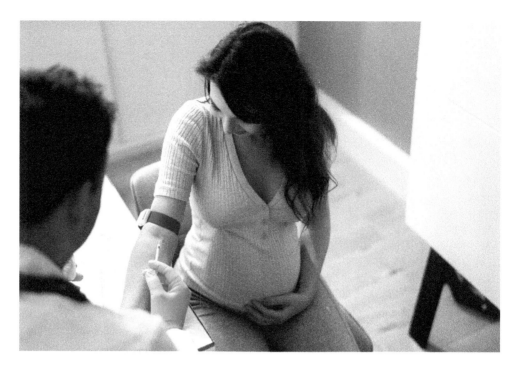

Figure 1–2 Healthcare workers should respect the privacy of their patients

Source: Andrey_Popov/Shutterstock

(accusations) made claiming that a healthcare worker, such as a medical technologist, nurse, or physician, has committed malpractice, then that person's right to defend themself and right to due process must be protected. This means that the person must receive a notice of the charges, an investigation of the allegations, and a hearing if enough evidence is found. If these allegations are proven to be false, then the individual must not be penalized.

- *Sexual harassment*, or gender harassment, is defined in the Equal Employment Opportunity Commission guidelines, which are part of Title VII of the Amended Civil Rights Act of 1964:

  Unwelcome sexual advances, requests for sexual favors, and other verbal or physical conduct of a sexual nature constitute sexual harassment when (1) submission to such conduct is made either explicitly or implicitly a term or condition of an individual's employment; (2) submission to or rejection of such conduct by an individual is used as the basis for employment decisions affecting such individual; or (3) such conduct has the purpose or effect of interfering with an individual's work performance or creating an intimidating, hostile, or offensive working environment. People of all genders working in the healthcare field have reported sexual harassment.

Med Tip

Any type of gender harassment is seen as one person exerting power over another.

- *Comparable worth*, also known as pay equity, is a theory that extends equal pay requirements to all persons who are doing equal work. The principle of fairness and justice dictates that work of equal value performed by people in the workplace should be rewarded with equal compensation. However, research demonstrates that there is a wage gap, with some estimates as high as 36 percent, because of the undervaluation of work performed by women. This results in injustice; equals are not treated equally. Because pay scales are the same for everyone in many of the healthcare professions, the situation is not as intense as it is in the business world. However, employers and supervisors who are involved in the hiring process must be committed to providing equal pay for equal work.

While it is important to reflect on the previous concepts, many ethical topics relating to the healthcare field fall into categories of common sense. Examples that might fall into the category of a "common sense" approach to ethics include the following:

- Avoid harming others.
- Respect the rights of others.
- Do not lie or cheat.

- Keep promises and contracts.
- Obey the law.
- Help those in need.
- Be fair.
- Reinforce these imperatives in others.

Models for Examining Ethical Dilemmas

The decision-maker must always be objective when making ethical decisions. It is critical to examine all the facts of a given situation by gathering as much information or data as possible. Alternative solutions to the problem must be assessed if they are available. All sides of every issue should be studied before ethical decisions are made. The following are three decision-making models that can be helpful when resolving ethical issues: the Blanchard-Peale three-step ethics model, a seven-step decision model, and Dr. Bernard Lo's three-step clinical model.

The Blanchard-Peale Three-Step Ethics Model

Kenneth Blanchard and Norman Vincent Peale in their book *The Power of Ethical Management* advise the use of a three-step model when evaluating an ethical dilemma. The steps are to ask yourself each of the following three questions: *Is it legal? Is it balanced? How does it make me feel?*

1. *Is it legal?*   When applying the Blanchard-Peale three-step model, if the situation is clearly illegal, such as inflicting bodily harm on another, then the matter is also clearly unethical, and you do not have to progress to the second question. However, if the action is not against the law, then you should ask yourself the second question.

2. *Is it balanced?*   This question helps to determine if another person or group of people is negatively affected by the action. In other words, is there now an *imbalance* so that one person or group suffers or benefits more than another as a result of your action? For example, in the case of a scarce resource such as donor organs, does one group of people have greater access?

3. *How does it make me feel?*   This final question refers to how the action will affect you emotionally. Would you be hesitant to explain your actions to a loved one? How would you feel if you saw your name in the paper associated with the action? Can you face yourself in the mirror?

If you can answer the first two questions with a strong "Yes" and the final question with a strong "Good," then the action is likely to be ethical.

For example, student cheating is clearly unethical. By using the three-step ethics model, we have an even clearer idea of why it is unethical to look at even one answer on another student's test. We ask the three questions:

1. *Is it legal?*   Yes, as far as we know there is no law against cheating.

2. *Is it balanced?*   No, it is not. This question is where the model really helps us. One group or person (in this case the cheater) does have an advantage over another group or person. In addition, the grades will be skewed for the entire class, because the person who cheated will receive a higher grade than the one actually earned.

3. *How does it make me feel?*   Remember that we have to live with ourselves. The philosopher Thomas Aquinas said, "We become what we do," meaning that if we lie, we become a liar. Or in this case, if we cheat, we become a cheater.

Med Tip

The Blanchard-Peale three-step ethics model is a quick way to check yourself when you are uncomfortable about an ethical decision. Use it often!

Analysis is the ability to carefully take apart issues, restate them in your own words, and offer an interpretation, and even criticism, of them. The following two models require careful analysis of the problem.

A Seven-Step Decision Model

A number of seven-step decision-making models have been developed. Here is a typical seven-step model:

1. *Determine the facts by asking the following questions:*

   What do we need to know?

   Who is involved in the situation?

   Where does the ethical situation take place?

   When does it occur?

2. *Define the precise ethical issue.*

   For example, is it a matter of fairness, justice, morality, or individual rights?

3. *Identify the major principles, rules, and values.*

   For example, is this a matter of integrity, quality, respect for others, or profit?

4. *Specify the alternatives.*

   List the major alternative courses of action, including those that represent some form of compromise. This may be a choice between simply doing or not doing something.

5. *Compare values and alternatives.*

   Determine if there is one principle or value, or a combination of principles and values, that is so compelling that the proper alternative is clear.

6. *Assess the consequences.*

   Identify short-term, long-term, positive, and negative consequences for the major alternatives. The short-term gain or loss is often overridden when long-term consequences are considered. This step often reveals an unanticipated result of major importance.

7. *Make a decision.*

   The consequences are balanced against one's primary principles or values. Always double-check your decision.

This seven-step decision model forces us to closely examine the facts before we make an ethical decision. This model is helpful when making a decision that has many subdecision questions to examine. For example, "Who should the physician treat first?" "Should I look at the exam paper of the person sitting next to me?" or even "What career choice should I make?" Obviously, some of these decisions require a quicker response, while others, such as the selection of a career, require more time and research. This model can be used to examine all of the end-of-chapter cases in this textbook.

The Lo Three-Step Clinical Model

Bernard Lo, MD, author of *Resolving Ethical Dilemmas: A Guide for Clinicians*, has developed a clinical model for decision-making to ensure that no important considerations relating to patient care are overlooked. He believes this approach can be used to help resolve important patient care issues, such as when to proceed with life-sustaining interventions (e.g., cardiopulmonary resuscitation [CPR] or kidney dialysis). His model also includes the patient's preferences and viewpoints:

1. *Gather information.*

   a. If the patient is competent, what are their preferences for care?

   b. If the patient lacks decision-making capacity, have they provided advance directives for care?

   c. If the patient lacks decision-making capacity, who should act as a surrogate?

   d. What are the views of the healthcare team?

   e. What other issues complicate the case?

2. *Clarify the ethical issues.*

   a. What are the pertinent ethical issues?

   b. Determine the ethical guidelines that people are using.

   c. What are the reasons for and against the alternative plans of care?

3. *Resolve the dilemma.*

    a. Meet with the healthcare team and with the patient or surrogate.

    b. List the alternatives of care.

    c. Negotiate a mutually acceptable decision.

Dr. Lo emphasizes that patients should play an active role in decisions about their care. Everything should be done to ensure that the patient has been well informed by providing information in an easy-to-understand way. This model cautions the healthcare team to seek the patient's decision on advance directives. He requires that the entire healthcare team—including medical students, nurses, social workers, and all others who provide direct care for the patient—be involved in the decisions. These caregivers should voice any moral objections they have to the proposed care. Finally, the patient's best interests must always be protected. This model is more commonly used in a hospital or clinic setting.

In Summary

All the ethical decision-making models that were presented provide valuable guidance. Do the following when dealing with ethical dilemmas:

1. Make sure you know and understand the issue/issues.

2. Consider all the facts and alternatives for action.

3. Evaluate all alternatives: Ask is it legal, is it fair, and is it balanced?

4. Carefully select the best alternative.

5. Move ahead and act on your decision.

Med Tip

When following a moral line of reasoning, it is always advisable to examine all of the facts rather than to predetermine what should be done.

What Ethics Is Not

Ethics is not just about how you feel, the sincerity of your beliefs, or your emotions; nor is it only about religious viewpoints. Feelings such as in the statement "I feel that capital punishment is wrong" are not sufficient when making an ethical decision. Others may feel that capital punishment is right in that it helps to deter crime. All people have feelings and beliefs. However, ethics must be grounded in reason and fact. In this respect, law and ethics are similar. For example, a statement such as "I feel that cheating is wrong" doesn't tell us why you believe it is wrong to cheat. A better statement reflecting ethics would be, "I think cheating is wrong because it gives one student an unfair advantage over another student." That "advantage" may mean that one person may be hired rather than another simply because the grades were the deciding factor.

The sincerity with which people hold their beliefs is also not an adequate reason when making an ethical decision. For example, Hitler sincerely believed that he was right in exterminating more than 6 million Jewish people, 250,000 people with disabilities, and at least 250,000 Roma people. His sincerity did not make him right.

Emotional responses to ethical dilemmas are not sufficient either. Emotions may affect why people do things they wouldn't normally do in calmer situations. However, we should not let our emotions dictate how we make ethical decisions. You may have helplessly watched a loved one die a slow death from cancer, but your emotions should not cloud the issue of euthanasia and cause you to kill your ill patients.

Ethics is not just about religious beliefs. Many people associate ideas of right and wrong with their religious beliefs. While there is often an overlap between ethics and what a religion teaches as right and wrong, people can hold very strong ethical and moral beliefs without following any formal religion.

Ultimately, we study ethics to assist us in providing compassionate and competent care to all our patients.

Med Tip

Your determination of what is ethical or moral can have serious consequences in human action. If you know it's wrong, don't do it!

Bioethics

Bioethics, also known as biomedical ethics, is one branch of applied, or practical, ethics. It refers to moral dilemmas and issues prevalent in today's society as a result of advances in healthcare and healthcare research. Bioethics is the study of the ethical problems arising from scientific advances, especially in biology and healthcare. The term *bio*, meaning life, combined with *ethics* relates to the moral conduct of right and wrong in life-and-death issues. Ethical problems in the biological sciences, including research on animals, all fall under the domain of bioethics. Some of the bioethical issues discussed in this text include the allocation of scarce resources such as transplant organs, beginning-of-life issues, cloning, harvesting embryos, concerns surrounding death and dying, experimentation and the use of human subjects, who owns the right to body cells, and dilemmas in the treatment of catastrophic disease.

Bioethics uses a form of moral analysis to assist in determining the obligations and responsibilities relating to unique issues in modern healthcare. In healthcare today, decision-makers are required to carefully examine facts, identify the moral challenges, and then look carefully at all alternatives. There are four basic principles that can serve as guidelines when confronting bioethical dilemmas. They are the principles of autonomy, beneficence, nonmalfeasance, and justice.

1. The **principle of autonomy** means that people have the right to make decisions about their own lives. The concept of "informed consent" is included in this principle. It means that patients must be informed and understand what they are told before they can provide consent for treatment. They must be told what the treatment involves, the risks involved, the chance for success, and the alternatives.

2. The **principle of beneficence**, or the principle of doing good, means that we must not harm patients while we are trying to help them. This principle recognizes that medical science must do what is best for each individual patient. If there are risks involved, then the principle of autonomy must be invoked so that decisions are made in conjunction with the patient's wishes.

3. The **principle of nonmalfeasance** is based on the Latin maxim *Primum non nocere*, which means "First, do no harm." This is a warning to all members of the healthcare professions. Nonmalfeasance completes the principle of beneficence because we are now asking the healthcare profession to not only do good for the patient, but also to do no harm in the process. In some cases, the risks of a treatment may outweigh the benefits. For example, when a surgeon removes a pregnant patient's cancerous uterus to save her life, her unborn child will not live. The principle of nonmalfeasance causes the healthcare provider to stop and think before acting.

4. Finally, the **principle of justice** warns us that equals must be treated equally. The same treatments must be given to all patients whether they are rich, poor, educated, uneducated, able-bodied, or disabled.

These four bioethical principles are guidelines for physicians and healthcare professionals to use when patients are unable to provide their personal wishes. For example, there have been cases of "wrongful life" in which a fetus is delivered too soon before development is complete. Many of these infants, if they survive, may have severe disabilities. Physicians may be requested by parents to "do nothing" to resuscitate or save their undeveloped child. Issues such as these weigh heavily upon the shoulders of all healthcare professionals. Having a set of guidelines, such as the previous four principles, to follow has helped in some of the decision-making.

Bioethicists, specialists in the field of bioethics, give thought to ethical concerns that often examine the more abstract dimensions of ethical issues and dilemmas. For example, they might ask, "What are the social implications of surrogacy?" Bioethicists are often authors, teachers, and researchers. This branch of ethics poses difficult, if not impossible, questions for the healthcare practitioner. Examples of some of the difficult ethical and bioethical situations that face the healthcare professional are listed under "Points to Ponder" at the end of this chapter.

The Role of Ethics Committees

Hospitals, as well as other healthcare organizations and agencies, have active ethics committees that examine ethical issues relating to patient care. This type of oversight committee consists of a variety of members from many healthcare fields as well as other disciplines, including physicians, nurses, clergy, psychologists, ethicists, lawyers, healthcare administrators, and family and community members. The ethics committee can serve in an advisory capacity to patients, families, and staff for case review of difficult ethical issues, especially when there is a lack of agreement as to what is in the patient's best interests. They also develop and review health policies and guidelines regarding ethical issues such as organ transplantation. After examining the facts surrounding the ethical issue, the committee often determines a recommendation based on predetermined criteria. These criteria might include the severity of the patient's condition, the age of the patient, and the chance for ultimate recovery.

The ethics committee may examine issues such as when hospitalization or treatment needs to be discontinued for a patient. For example, a hospital ethics committee will assist in determining the best action to take for a terminally ill patient who is on a respirator. In some cases, the committee may be asked to examine if a patient received the appropriate care.

Ethics committees have tremendous power in today's healthcare environment. Patients are holding their doctors and hospitals to a high standard of care. While it is necessary for the committee meetings to be confidential in order to protect the patient's privacy, nevertheless, there should be a strong set of policies that govern how the meetings are conducted.

Unfortunately, in some cases, members of an ethics committee will never see or talk to the patient whose life and care they are discussing. Mistakes can be made when a group of people makes a judgment without reviewing all the facts.

Med Tip

It has been suggested that ethics committees make an effort to have disabled people represented on their committee either as a member or as a resource person to represent the viewpoint of disabled patients.

Quality Assurance Programs

In addition to ethics committees, most hospitals and healthcare agencies have a quality assurance (QA) program. These programs were established in the early 1960s as a response to the increasing demand from the public for accountability in quality healthcare. **Quality assurance**, also known as **QA**, s gathering and evaluating information about the services provided, as well as the results achieved, and comparing this information with an accepted standard.

Quality assessment measures consist of formal, systematic evaluations of overall patient care. After the results of the evaluations are compared with standard results, any deficiencies are noted and recommendations for improvements are made (Figure 1.3). Types of issues that are reviewed by a QA committee include the following:

- Patient complaints relating to confidentiality
- Errors in dispensing medications

Figure 1–3 Quality assurance committee meeting

Source: Shutterstock

- Errors in labeling of laboratory specimens
- Adverse reactions to treatments and/or medications
- Inability to obtain venous blood on the first attempt
- Safety and monitoring practices for radiology and laboratory areas
- Infection control

Medical Etiquette

There are certain rules of medical etiquette, or standards of professional behavior, that physicians and advance practice providers follow in their relationships and conduct with patients and other professionals. These are general points of behavior and are not generally considered to be healthcare ethics issues. For instance, physicians may expect that their telephone calls to fellow physicians will be taken promptly and that they will be seen immediately when visiting a physician's office. This courtesy is extended to physicians and advanced practice providers because they are often consulting about patients with other providers. However, ethical issues are present when one physician overlooks or "covers up" the medical deficiencies of another physician.

In addition, physicians should be referred to as "Doctors" unless they request to be called by their first name. The same courtesy is required for the patient. Some patients, especially older adults, might prefer to be addressed by their surname (with Ms., Miss, Mrs., or Mr.). Many nurses and allied health professionals prefer to be addressed in this manner also. There are allied health professionals who have decades of experience and do not wish to be addressed by either the patient or physician by their first name.

Med Tip

"All that is necessary for evil to triumph is for good men to do nothing."—Edmund Burke, Irish-born British statesman, orator, and author (1729–1797)

Chapter 1 Review

Points to Ponder

1. Should an alcoholic patient, who may die of liver disease, be eligible for an organ transplant?

2. Should a patient who has attempted suicide be allowed to refuse a feeding tube?

3. Should prisoners be eligible to receive expensive healthcare therapies for illnesses?

4. Is assisting with suicide ever ethically justified?

5. Should healthcare personnel suggest other treatment modes or suggest the patient request a consultation with another physician?

6. Under what circumstances should you report a colleague or physician who is physically, psychologically, or pharmacologically impaired?

7. Is experimentation on human subjects ever justified?

8. When, if ever, should you disclose a patient's health condition to the family?

9. Should parents be allowed to refuse medical treatment, such as chemotherapy, for their child?

10. If you are an employee in a healthcare office with access to healthcare records, should you protect your friend by telling him that you know that his partner has tested positive for syphilis?

These questions, and others like them, are addressed throughout this textbook.

Discussion Questions

1. In the case of Jeanette M. at the beginning of the chapter, what additional training for taking telephone messages should the receptionist have had?

2. Discuss the difference between the terms *legal* and *moral*.

3. Give an example for each of the following: a healthcare ethics dilemma, a bioethics situation, and a medical–legal problem.

4. Determine whether the ten questions under "Points to Ponder" are ethical issues, legal issues, or both.

5. Describe five ethical situations that you may face in the profession you intend to follow.

Review Challenge

Short Answer Questions

1. Why do we study law, ethics, and bioethics?

_____

_____

_____

_____

_____

2. What is the purpose of the Medical Practice Acts?

_____

_____

_____

_____

_____

3. What are five theories of ethics?

_____

_____

_____

_____

_____

4. What are ten virtues that drive ethical behavior?

_____

_____

_____

_____

_____

5. What are the three steps of the Blanchard-Peale Model?

   a. _____

   b. _____

   c. _____

6. What is bioethics?

   _____

   _____

   _____

   _____

   _____

7. What is the role of an ethics committee?

   _____

   _____

   _____

   _____

   _____

8. Discuss what's wrong with the following rationalizations for unethical behavior:

   a. "Everybody does it!"

   b. "It's not *really* illegal."

   c. "No one will find out."

   d. "My employer will protect me."

   e. "It's not wrong to do it just this once."

Matching

Match the responses in column B with the correct term in column A.

COLUMN A

_____   1. healthcare etiquette

_____   2. ethics

_____   3. applied ethics

_____   4. laws

_____   5. healthcare ethics

_____   6. beneficence

_____   7. veil of ignorance

_____   8. three-step ethics model

_____   9. R/O

_____   10. gut feeling

COLUMN B

a. justice-based

b. decision based on emotion

c. binding rules determined by an authority

d. principle of doing good

e. standards of professional behavior

f. practical application of moral standards

g. rule out a diagnosis

h. moral conduct to regulate behavior of healthcare professionals

i. branch of philosophy

j. Kenneth Blanchard and Norman Vincent Peale's approach to ethics

Multiple Choice

Select the one best answer to the following statements:

1. A problem that occurs when using a duty-based approach to ethics is _____.

   a. the primary emphasis on a person's individual rights

   b. determining the greatest good for the greatest number of people

   c. the conflicting opinions regarding what our responsibility is

   d. remembering the three-step model approach to solving ethical dilemmas

   e. understanding the difference between what is fair and unfair

2. Moral issues that occur as a result of modern medical technology are covered under what specific discipline?

   a. law

   b. healthcare

   c. philosophy

   d. bioethics

   e. none of the above

3. When trying to solve an ethical dilemma, it is necessary to
   _____.

   a. do what everyone else is doing

   b. use logic to determine the solution

   c. do what we are told to do by others

   d. base the decision on religious beliefs only

   e. allow our emotions and feelings to guide us

4. The three-step approach to solving ethical dilemmas is based on
   _____.

   a. asking ourselves how our decision would make us feel if we
      had to explain our actions to a loved one

   b. asking ourselves if the intended action is legal

   c. asking ourselves if the intended action results in a balanced
      decision

   d. a, b, and c

   e. none of the above

5. A utilitarian approach to solving ethical dilemmas might be used
   when _____.

   a. allocating a limited supply of donor organs

   b. trying to find a just decision in which everyone will benefit

   c. finding a decision based on a sense of duty toward another
      person

   d. assuring everyone has a right to healthcare

   e. none of the above

6. An illegal act is almost always _____.

   a. hidden

   b. unethical

   c. performed with the full knowledge of the healthcare worker

   d. obvious

   e. all of the above

7. A practical application of ethics is _____.

   a. philosophy

   b. the law

   c. illegal

   d. applied ethics

   e. b and d

8. An employee who is entitled to a fair hearing in the case of a
   dismissal from a job is an example of _____.

   a. duty-based ethics

   b. utilitarianism

   c. rights-based ethics

   d. justice-based ethics

   e. c and d

9. Laws that affect the healthcare professions _____.

   a. often overlap with ethics

   b. have a binding force

   c. are always fair to all persons

   d. are determined by a governmental authority

   e. a, b, and d

10. Modern laws _____.

    a. may allow some unethical acts such as lying on job applications

    b. are interpreted by some people to require no ethical
       responsibility beyond what the law requires

    c. are not used as a type of yardstick for group behavior

    d. a and b only

    e. a, b, and c

Discussion Cases

1. Analyze the following case using the five theories of ethics
   discussed in this chapter.

   *It has become necessary to ration a vaccine for a contagious
   disease. There is only enough vaccine available to cover
   75 percent of the U.S. population. It is necessary to
   determine an appropriate method for doing this.*

   a. Utilitarianism:

      _____

      _____

   b. Rights-based ethics:

      _____

      _____

   c. Duty-based ethics:

      _____

      _____

   d. Justice-based ethics:

      _____

      _____

   e. Virtue-based ethics:

      _____

      _____

2. Using the three-step ethics model (Blanchard-Peale),
   analyze the following case:

   *A student knows that two other students who sit next to
   each other in class are cheating on exams because they talk
   about it after class. Is this an ethical dilemma? What, if
   anything, should the student do?*

   a. _____

   b. _____

   c. _____

Put It Into Practice

Talk to someone who is currently working in the healthcare field that you are working in or plan to enter. Ask them for a definition of healthcare ethics. Then compare it with the textbook definition. Does it match? Discuss with that person an ethical dilemma that they have faced and handled.

Web Hunt

Search the website of the American Medical Association for their Code of Medical Ethics (**https:// code-medical-ethics.ama-assn.org/**). Select **Search Ethics Opinions**. Read one of the opinions and decide whether you agree with it.

Critical Thinking Exercise

What would you do if you are in charge of passing out patient medications and a fellow employee asks you for an aspirin from your medication cart for his headache?

Bibliography

Beauchamp, T.L., & Childress, J.F. (2019). *Principles of biomedical ethics* (8th ed.). Oxford University Press.

Blanchard, K., & Peale, N. (1988). *The power of ethical management.* William Morrow.

Boatright, J.R., & Smith, J. (2016). *Ethics and the conduct of business* (8th ed). Pearson

DeGrazia, D., Mappes, T., & Ballard, J. (2010). *Biomedical ethics* (7th ed). McGraw-Hill.

Jervis, R. (2010). Katrina case alleges negligence. *USA Today* (January 11), 1A.

Levine, C. (2011). *Taking sides: Clashing Views on Bioethical Issues* (14th ed). McGraw-Hill.

Lo, B. (2019). *Resolving ethical dilemmas: A guide for clinicians* (6th ed). Lippincott Williams & Wilkins.

Nossiter, A. (2007). Grand jury won't indict doctor in hurricane deaths. *New York Times* (July 25), A10.

Valinoti, A. (2009). Exam-room rules: What's in a name? *New York Times* (December 15), D5.

Vaughn, L. (2019). *Bioethics: Principles, issues, and cases* (4th ed.). Oxford University Press.

Veatch, R. Haddad, A.M., & English, D.C. (2014). *Case studies in biomedical ethics* (2nd ed.). Oxford University Press.

Part 1

The Legal Environment

Chapter 2   The Legal System

Chapter 3   Essentials of the Legal System for Healthcare Professionals

Chapter 4   Working in Today's Healthcare Environment

The Legal System

Learning Objectives

After completing this chapter, you will be able to:

2.1 Define the key terms.

2.2 Discuss why an understanding of the legal profession is necessary for the healthcare professional.

2.3 Describe the sources of law.

2.4 Describe the steps for a bill to become a law.

2.5 Discuss the difference between civil law and criminal law, explaining the areas covered by each.

2.6 List six intentional torts and give examples of each.

2.7 List examples of criminal actions that relate to the healthcare worker.

2.8 Discuss the difference between a felony and a misdemeanor.

2.9 Describe the types of courts in the legal system.

2.10 Explain the trial process.

2.11 Discuss why an expert witness might be used during a lawsuit.

Key Terms

Administrative law
Assault
Battery
Beyond a reasonable doubt
Breach
Breach of contract
Case law
Checks and balances
Civil law
Class action lawsuit
Closing arguments
Common law
Competent
Consideration
Constitutional law
Contract law
Criminal law
Defamation of character

Defendant
Deposition
Discovery
Embezzlement
Expert witness
Expressed contract
False imprisonment
Felony
Fraudulent
Implied contract
Indictment
Intentional torts
Invasion of privacy
Jurisdiction
Libel
Litigation
Malpractice
Misdemeanor

Negligence
Plaintiff
Pleadings
Preponderance of evidence
Probate court, or estate court
Prosecutor
Public law
Regulations
Slander
Statutes
Subpoena
Summary judgment
Tort
Tort law
Unintentional torts
Waive

The Case of Jacob and the Diseased Leg

Jacob is an outstanding quarterback on his high school football team who has been offered a college scholarship when he graduates. Unfortunately, Jacob was injured during a late summer practice just before his senior year. He suffered a compound fracture of the fibula in his lower leg. Because the fracture broke through his skin, he required a surgical repair to align or set the bone and close the skin. Dr. Chambliss, an orthopedic surgeon, kept Jacob in the hospital for three days and ordered intravenous antibiotics to be administered. When he was discharged from the hospital, Jacob was told to come in for an office visit once a week for six weeks.

At six weeks, Jacob's parents took him into the surgeon's office for his cast removal, and except for a slightly inflamed and draining area around his stitches, Jacob's broken bone seemed to be healing. After his cast was removed, Jacob was told to wait for a few minutes while the surgeon went across the hall to check on another patient. Dr. Chambliss removed her gloves, washed her hands in Jacob's exam room, and then went across the hall to examine another patient, Sylvia. The doors between the exam rooms were left open, and Jacob's parents could see and hear Dr. Chambliss examining Sylvia's infected leg. They could tell that Dr. Chambliss did not replace her gloves. She told Sylvia that she was glad to see that her osteomyelitis (a serious bone infection) was almost better, and she told her to come back in another week.

Dr. Chambliss then came back into Jacob's room, without gloves, and examined Jacob's leg more carefully. She was concerned about the inflammation around the incision site and told the parents to keep the area clean and dry. She wrote Jacob a prescription for an oral antibiotic and said he could start to put a little weight on his leg. When Jacob came back the following week, his leg was grossly infected with a large abscess. Jacob had to have further surgery to drain the abscess. The pathology report of tissue specimens from Jacob's leg determined that he had developed osteomyelitis. This infection took several months to heal. The delay in his recovery meant that Jacob was unable to play football that fall and lost his chance at a college scholarship. Jacob's parents asked Dr. Chambliss to provide them with the results of the tissue test. They then sued Dr. Chambliss for negligence.

1. What obvious mistake did Dr. Chambliss make?
2. Did Jacob or his parents contribute in any way to his condition?
3. What could all of the involved parties have done to prevent this situation from occurring?

Introduction

Healthcare professionals must have a good understanding of the legal system for a variety of reasons. The advanced state of medical technology creates new legal, ethical, moral, and financial problems for the consumer and the healthcare practitioner. Today's healthcare consumer demands more of a partnership with the physician and the rest of the healthcare team. Patients have become more aware of their legal rights. Court cases and decisions have had a greater impact than ever on the way healthcare professionals practice business in the medical field. It's important to remember that while laws do protect an individual's rights, they are made for the protection of society as a whole. Laws tell us how we must conduct ourselves during interactions with other people as well as in business transactions, such as in providing healthcare services.

Med Tip

Every effort should be made to provide quality of care for patients that will not only help them recover their health but will also avoid lawsuits.

The Legal System

The U.S. legal system has one federal legal system and 50 separate and unique state systems. For example, the federal government administers the U.S. Tax Court and the U.S. Bankruptcy Court. The state governments administer courts such as traffic and small claims courts. State governments also administer medical licensing acts. The majority of criminal cases originate in state courts. Most states have at least three court levels: trial, appellate, and supreme. The jurisdiction of a particular court refers to the subject matter of a particular case, territory the case occurred in, or the people that a court has lawful authority over. An appellate court has the authority to review a decision made by a lower court, such as a trial court.

The court system is only one part of the government, however. In establishing a federal government, the U.S. Constitution separated the government's power into three branches: legislative, executive, and judicial. Each branch complements the others but does not take on the power of the other branches. The separation between the three branches created a system of **checks and balances** and was designed by the framers of the Constitution so that no one branch could have more power than another branch. See Figure 2.1 for an illustration of the branches of the U.S. government.

The legislative branch, referred to as Congress, is the lawmaking body. It is composed of members of the Senate and House of Representatives and is responsible for passing legislation into law. The executive branch (consisting of the president of the United States, their cabinet, and various advisers) administers and enforces the law. The judicial branch (consisting of judges and the federal courts, including the Supreme Court) interprets the laws. Congress has the power to make laws, but the president has the power to veto these laws, although Congress can then override the veto with a two-thirds majority vote. The president can appoint all federal and Supreme Court judges, but Congress must confirm appointments. The judicial branch can review legislation and interpret the laws passed by Congress and the

Figure 2–1 Branches of U.S. government

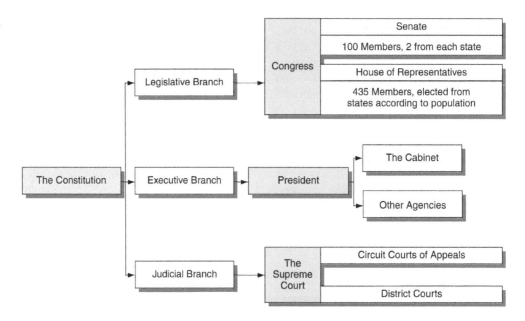

Figure 2–2 Separation of powers in the federal legal system

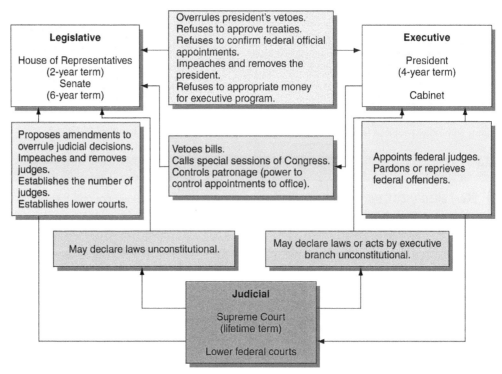

president, but the president must enforce the law. Congress can, in many instances, pass new laws to replace laws that are deemed unconstitutional by a judicial decision. See Figure 2.2 for an illustration of the separation of powers.

The states all have their own constitutions, which in many respects mirror the U.S. Constitution. The state constitutions likewise establish legislative, executive, and judicial branches within each state. See Figure 2.3 for an illustration of the federal court system.

Med Tip

Federal law is administered the same in all states. However, individual states may vary on how they interpret and implement laws relegated to the states. Therefore, interpretation of legal acts for allied health professionals varies greatly from state to state.

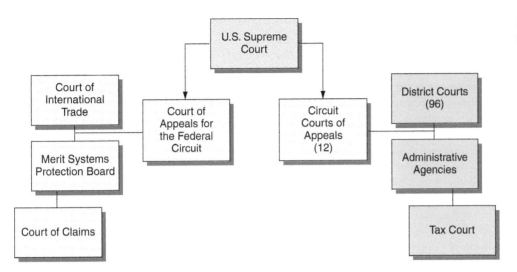

Figure 2–3 Federal court structure

Sources of Law

All laws—those enforceable rules prescribed by a government authority—must come from somewhere. Let's say that you are pulled over and given a ticket for driving 70 miles an hour, when the speed limit is only 55. You obviously broke a law. But where did that law come from? Did someone just walk down the highway and put up signs saying how fast they thought you should drive? Of course not. The speed limit, like all other laws, originated from a government body authorized to establish rules. These rules fall into four different categories: constitutional, statutory, regulatory, and common (or case) law.

Constitutional Law

The U.S. Constitution is the country's highest judicial authority. It sets up the government, defines the government's power to act, and sets limits on the government's power (e.g., individual rights such as the right to free speech). It takes precedence over all state laws and the state constitutions.

Constitutional law derives from both the U.S. Constitution and the constitutions of the individual states. It is the body of laws that define the role, powers, and structure of entities that fall within the three branches of government—legislative, executive, and judicial—as defined by the U.S. Constitution and the state constitutions.

It is important to realize that the Constitution only addresses the relationship between individuals and their government; it does not apply to the relationship between private entities, whether they are individuals or businesses.

Statutory and Regulatory Law

Statutes are laws passed by legislative bodies, either Congress or a state legislature. This is called statutory or legislative law. Congress and the state legislatures have the authority to pass laws because in setting up our form of government, the Constitution authorized legislatures to make laws. Statutory law consists of ever-changing rules and regulations created by the U.S. Congress, state legislatures, local governments, or constitutional lawmakers. These statutes are the inviolable rights, privileges, or immunities secured and protected for each citizen by the U.S. Constitution. They include written codes, bills, and acts (also called regulations).

Legislatures sometimes authorize agencies to make laws. The legislature does this by passing a statute, called enabling legislation. This statute creates an agency and authorizes it to pass laws regarding specific issues. For instance, the Food and Drug Administration is a federal agency that can pass rules governing the sale of food and drugs. The rules or laws made by agencies are called **regulations**.

Statutes begin as bills submitted by legislators at the state or federal level. The first step is taken when the bill is introduced in either of the two legislative houses, the Senate, or the House of Representatives. If the bill does not "die" (fails to be acted upon) in one of the houses, it then goes to a committee for discussion and consideration. (Note that vast majority of all bills die before they reach a committee.) The committee studies the bill and may hold a hearing to gain more facts about the bill. This first committee issues a report, including a recommendation to either pass or fail the bill. The bill then goes back to the house (Senate or House of Representatives) in which it originated, where a discussion and vote takes place. After the bill passes in one house, it becomes an act. The act is then sent to the other house, where it goes through the same steps as it did as a bill. The act can always be amended by the second house, which results in its being returned to the originating house for a discussion and vote on the amendment. There may be a reconciliation conference between members of both houses to settle any discrepancies between the two versions.

If the second house passes the act (or if both houses pass the reconciled version), then the heads of each house—Speaker of the House of Representatives and the president pro tem of the Senate (the vice president of the United States, in the case of a federal act)—sign it. The act is then sent to the chief executive, who is, in the case of a federal act, the president, and for a state act, the governor. The act becomes a law if it is signed by the chief executive or if it is not vetoed within 10 days. If vetoed, the bill goes back for an override vote. A presidential veto can be overridden by a two-thirds majority of both houses of Congress. After this complicated process, the act is referred to as a public law or statute.

Med Tip

A public law is designated by the initials PL, and the five or six digits that follow indicate the Congress that passed the law and which piece of legislation the law was in that Congress. For example, a new law is issued with a public law number, such as PL 94-104, which indicates that it was the 94th Congress that passed the law (the first two or three digits) and the 104th piece of legislation in that Congress.

Laws that are passed by city governments are called municipal ordinances. Federal laws have precedence over state laws; state laws have precedence over city or municipal laws. In other words, a state or city may make laws and regulations that expand rights more than the federal law, but cannot take rights away. For example, the use of marijuana is illegal at the federal level, but its use is legal in many states.

Common Law (or Case Law)

The final source of law is common law. Unlike the laws established by legislative bodies (statutory laws), common law is made by judges when they apply previous court decisions to current cases. This means it is based on the judicial interpretation of previous laws, leading to a common understanding of how a law should be interpreted. Thus, **common law**, as established from a court decision, may explain or interpret the other sources of law. Because common law evolves on a case-by-case basis, it is also called **case law**. For instance, the way a case is argued and settled and any written statements from the judge at the conclusion of the case may explain or elaborate on what a provision of the constitution, a statute, or a regulation means. In addition to interpreting the other sources of law, common law defines other legal rights and obligations. For example, a physician's obligation to use reasonable care in treating a patient (i.e., not to commit medical malpractice) is a legal obligation created from actual court decisions.

Common law (or case law) based on decisions made by judges was a legal concept originally established by English courts in the twelfth century and brought to America by the early colonists. The only state that doesn't follow English common law is the state of Louisiana, which bases its law on early French law. Common law is based on precedent, the ruling in an early case that is then applied to subsequent cases when the facts are the same. Each time common, or judge-made, law is applied, it must be reviewed by the court to determine if it is still justified and relevant or has not been overturned by existing laws. As a result of this constant review of common law, many laws have been changed (or updated) over the years. The ultimate arbiter, or interpreter, of common law is the state supreme court or, if the law involves a federal question, the U.S. Supreme Court. The legal principle of stare decisis, or "let the decision stand," comes to us from the precedence of basing decisions on similar past case decisions.

Med Tip

Taken literally, *stare decisis* means to abide by, or adhere to, decided cases.

Case Citations

Selected legal cases are used in this textbook to illustrate various legal principles. At the end of each case summary is a citation, such as *Moon Lake Convalescent Center v. Margolis*, 433 N.E.2d 956 (Ill. App. Ct. 1989). This citation, similar to a street address, tells you where you can find this case among the many sets of reported cases (called *reporters*) in the library. Most case citations end with information in parentheses, such as (Ill. App. Ct. 1989), which tells you what court (the Illinois Appellate Court) decided the case and the year (1989) of the decision, but you do not need that information when you are trying to locate a particular case in the library. The small *v.* between the litigants' names stands for "versus." The components of a case citation include the following:

- The italicized case name—usually the name of the plaintiff and the defendant. In our example, *Moon Lake Convalescent Center* is the defendant and *Margolis* is the plaintiff.
- The name of the reporter(s) where the case is published (Northeast Reporter, 2d series).
- The volume number(s) of the reporter(s) where the case is published (433).
- The page number of the volume where the case begins (956).
- The year the case was decided (1989).
- For federal Court of Appeals cases, there is a designation of the circuit; for federal District Court cases, it includes the state and judicial district where the court is located; for state cases, there is an indication of the state if it is not apparent from the name of the reporter (Illinois Appellate Court).

Therefore, our example case between Moon Lake Convalescent Center and Margolis is found in volume 433 of the Northeast Reporter, 2d series, on page 956.

- Abbreviations for other reporters (books) are:
- A (Atlantic Reporter)
- P (Pacific Reporter)
- U.S. (United States Reporter)
- F.Supp. (Federal Supplement)
- F (Federal Reporter)
- NE (Northeast Reporter)
- NW (Northwest Reporter)
- NYS (New York Supplement)
- So (Southern Reporter)
- SW (Southwestern Reporter)

Most reporters have been published in two or more series, such as 2d, meaning second series. You do not need to memorize the names of the reporters. The abbreviations for them are found at the beginning of most of the legal research publications that you will use. As you do research within your own state, you will become familiar with the abbreviations that are most commonly used. Legal research can be done through a law library or via the Internet from Lexis-Nexis, which is a subscription service used by law firms and libraries.

Classification of Laws

Laws are classified as private and public. Private (or civil) laws can be divided into six categories: tort, contract, property, inheritance, family, and corporate law. Only tort and contract law are discussed here, as they most often affect healthcare professionals. Public law can be divided into four categories: criminal, administrative, constitutional, and international law. This chapter discusses criminal and administrative law.

Civil (Private) Law

Civil law concerns relationships either between individuals or between individuals and the government. It involves all the law that is not criminal law, although the same conduct may violate criminal and civil law. For instance, murder is a crime that the government prosecutes in order to punish the **defendant**— the person being sued in a court of law—by inflicting a prison term or even death, while the surviving family members can sue the person in a civil suit for wrongful death and receive compensation for their loss. Civil law cases generally carry a monetary damage or award as compensation for harm or injury. An individual can sue another person, a business, or the government. Some civil law cases include divorce, child custody, vehicle crashes, slander, libel, and trespassing.

Civil law includes tort law and contract law. **Tort law** covers private or civil wrongful acts that result in harm to another person or that person's property. A tort can result in money damages having to be paid. **Contract law** includes enforceable promises and agreements between two or more persons to do, or not do, a particular action. Healthcare employees are most frequently involved in cases of civil law, in particular, tort and contract law. Most medical malpractice lawsuits fall within the category of the civil law of torts. See Figure 2.4 for the components of civil law.

In a civil law case, there must be a **preponderance of evidence**, meaning the fact of the issue is more probable than not, in order to receive a determination of guilty. This means that it is more likely than not that the incident did occur.

Med Tip

In many cases, civil law matters are handled and settled outside of the courtroom.

Tort Law

A **tort** is a civil injury, or wrongful act, that is committed against another person or property, resulting in harm, and is compensated by monetary damages. To sue for a tort, a patient must have suffered a mental or physical injury that was caused by the physician or the physician's employee. A tort case is tried before either a judge or a jury. In certain cases, in which a jury trial has been waived, a "bench trial" may take place in which the trial is held before a judge sitting without a jury. Torts can be either intentional or unintentional, and the patient may recover monetary damages. In order to recover damages, there must be "fault" on the part of the defendant.

Med Tip

Under tort law, if a wrongful act has been committed against another person and there is no harm done, then there is no tort. However, in healthcare practice, every wrongful act or error must be reported because patients may experience a resulting harm sometime later than when the tort occurs.

Figure 2–4 Components of civil law

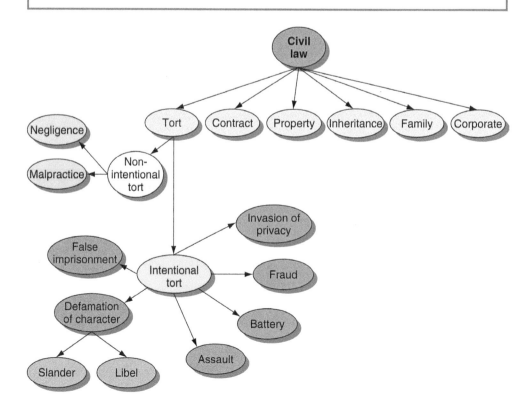

Table 2–1 Intentional Torts

Tort	Description	Example
Assault	Threat of bodily harm to another; there does not have to be actual touching (battery) for an assault to take place	Threatening to harm a patient or to perform a procedure without the informed consent (permission) of the patient
Battery	Actual bodily harm to another person without permission; referred to as unlawful touching or touching without consent	Performing surgery or a procedure without the informed consent (permission) of the patient
False imprisonment	Violation of the personal liberty of another person through unlawful restraint	Refusing to allow a competent patient to leave an office, hospital, or healthcare facility when they request to leave
Defamation of character	Damage caused to a person's reputation through spoken or written word	Making a negative statement about another physician's ability
Fraud	Deceitful practice that deprives another person of their rights	Promising a miracle cure
Invasion of privacy	Unauthorized publicity of information about a patient	Allowing personal information about a patient to become public without the patient's permission

INTENTIONAL TORTS

Intentional torts occur when a person has been intentionally or deliberately injured by another. Intentional torts include assault, battery, false imprisonment, defamation of character, fraud, and invasion of privacy. Table 2.1 provides a description and example of each.

ASSAULT

No healthcare professional would knowingly perform a tort against a patient or any other person. However, even a trained professional can make a mistake if they are not aware of what constitutes a "wrongful act" under these torts. For example, for a tort of **assault**, it is sufficient for the patient to just fear that they will be hurt or has an "imminent apprehension of bodily harm." So, if a healthcare professional threatens a patient by saying, "If you don't lie still, we will have to hold you down," and the patient believes this will cause them injury or harm, this is considered a tort of assault. Shaking your fist in a patient's face in a threatening manner can also be considered assault.

BATTERY

The tort of **battery** requires bodily harm or unlawful touching (touching without the consent of the patient) and not just the fear of harm. No procedure, including drawing blood for a laboratory test, can be performed without the patient's knowledge and consent. When a patient offers an arm or rolls up a sleeve for the phlebotomist, this constitutes a form of consent (implied) for the procedure. When a surgeon has a patient sign an informed consent for a specific surgical procedure, then it is considered battery if the surgeon does anything to the patient that is not listed on the informed consent form. (This does not include emergency life-saving procedures such as CPR.) For example, if, during surgery for a hysterectomy (removal of the uterus), a surgeon notes that the patient's appendix is inflamed, the surgeon cannot remove the appendix unless this procedure was stated on the consent form. The surgeon would have to complete the surgery for the hysterectomy and then, after the patient is awake, discuss the need for surgical removal of the appendix.

Often assault and battery occur together. Other examples of battery include hitting a patient or forcing competent patients to do anything against their wishes, such as having therapy or getting out of bed.

FALSE IMPRISONMENT

False imprisonment in healthcare occurs when a healthcare professional, or a person hired by that professional, takes an action to confine a patient. There have been cases in which patients were not allowed to leave a room or building when they wished, and had no reasonable means of escape, resulting in a tort of false imprisonment in which the patient (**plaintiff**, the person bringing an action into litigation) won the case. This occurred in a Texas case in which the patient, who was assessed as being competent, was detained against his will from leaving a nursing home (*Big Town Nursing Home v. Newman*, 461 S.W.2d195, Tex. Civ. App. 1970).

A more common situation occurs when a patient wishes to leave a hospital against medical advice (AMA). In this case, the patient is asked to sign a statement that says they are leaving against the advice of the physician. There have also been a few cases of false imprisonment resulting from hospitals trying to hold patients until their bills were paid (*Williams v. Summit Psychiatric Ctrs.*, 363 S.E.2d 794, Ga. App. 1987). However, no such cases have been reported in the last few years because hospitals now understand that this practice is unacceptable.

DEFAMATION OF CHARACTER

Making false and/or malicious statements about another person constitutes **defamation of character** if the person can prove damages. Defamation can be in two forms: slander or libel. According to *Black's Law Dictionary*, **slander** (oral defamation) is speaking false and malicious words concerning another person that brings injury to their reputation. There are four recognized exceptions that require no proof of actual harm to a person's reputation in order to recover damages for slander: accusing a person of a crime; accusing someone of a "loathsome" disease, such as a sexually transmitted disease; using words against a person's business or profession; and calling a woman unchaste. **Libel** is, in general, any publication in print, writing, pictures, or signs that injures the reputation of another person. Healthcare practitioners are protected against an accusation of libel when complying with a law to report disease or cases of abuse. The amount and degree of such protection varies depending on the laws and regulations in their jurisdictions. See Chapter 7, "Public Duties of the Healthcare Professional."

FRAUD

Fraudulent practices consist of attempts to deceive another person. For example, making a statement to a cancer patient that "Dr. Wu is a miracle worker; she'll have you feeling better in no time" is a false promise because there are too many variables when dealing with cancer. However, a more common type of medical fraud consists of false billing practices such as the following:

- *Coding up:* Billing an insurance company or government agency for a diagnosis with a higher compensation rate than the actual diagnosis, especially relating to Medicare and Medicaid
- *Phantom billing:* Submitting bills for services, treatments, procedures, or drugs that were never performed or given.
- *Double billing:* Billing both Medicare (or Medicaid) AND a private insurance company for the same services; or when two providers bill for the same services to the same patient at the same time.

Under the Medicare-Medicaid Anti-fraud and Abuse Amendments, physicians are prohibited from accepting kickbacks, or payments of any kind, for the referral of Medicare and Medicaid patients. In some cases, physicians have received kickbacks from medical technology companies for using their products on patients. This is considered a criminal offense under the anti-fraud law and could result in a large penalty and even imprisonment.

Embezzlement, a form of fraud, is the illegal appropriation of property, usually money, by a person entrusted with its possession. It can occur in a physician's or dentist's office when an office manager has total control over the business financials without proper oversight, reconciliation, or separation of duties and responsibilities. To embezzle means to willfully take another person's rightly owned property or funds. For control purposes, more than one person should receive payments, issue receipts for payments, audit the accounts, and deposit the money.

INVASION OF PRIVACY

An **invasion of privacy** can occur at any time during a patient's treatment, even after the patient has granted permission to allow publicity. For example, in the case of allowing photographs or videotapes to be taken, the patient may cancel the permission at any time. In *Estate of Berthiaume v. Pratt*, an invasion of privacy case was tried after a patient with cancer of the larynx died. The deceased patient had allowed his physician to take several photographs that were to be used for the healthcare record but not for publication. A few hours before the hospitalized patient died, the surgeon and a nurse attempted to take more photographs in spite of the patient's indication he did not want this done and his wife's protests. The wife sued the surgeon for assault because he had moved the patient's head during the photo taking as well as invasion of privacy. An appeals court found in favor of the plaintiff and stated that taking photographs in spite of the patient's protests was an invasion of his legal rights to privacy (*Estate of Berthiaume v. Pratt*, 365 QA.2d 792, Me. 1976).

UNINTENTIONAL TORTS

Unintentional torts, such as negligence, occur, for example, when the patient is injured as a result of the healthcare professional's not exercising the ordinary standard of care. The term *standard of care* means that the professional must exercise the type of care that a "reasonable" person would use in a similar circumstance.

Morrison v. MacNamara illustrates the standard of care issue. In this case, MacNamara, a technician, took a urethral smear from the patient, Morrison, while the patient was standing. Morrison fainted, hit his head, and permanently lost his sense of smell and taste. An expert witness from Michigan testified that the national standard of care for taking a urethral smear requires the patient to sit or lie down. Thus, the court found in favor of the patient (*Morrison v. MacNamara*, 407 A.2d 555, D.C. 1979). Standard of care is discussed more fully in Chapter 3.

An unintentional tort exists when a person had no intent of bringing about an injury to the patient. Healthcare professionals can be sued for a variety of situations, but most lawsuits relate to the unintentional tort of negligence.

Negligence is the failure or omission to perform professional duties to an accepted standard of care, such as a "reasonable person" would do. In other words, negligence occurs when a person's actions fall below a certain level of care. Negligence can involve doing something carelessly or failing to do something that should have been done. It can also involve doing something reckless such as performing a procedure without adequate training. Physicians and other healthcare professionals usually do not knowingly indulge in acts that are negligent, so negligence usually falls within the classification of unintentional tort. Malpractice, which is misconduct or demonstration of an unreasonable lack of skill, relates to a professional skill such as medicine or the law. **Malpractice** is a particular type of negligence that can be thought of as "professional negligence." While anyone can be accused of being negligent, only professionals can be sued for malpractice. Examples of professionals who are sued for malpractice include physicians, nurses, lawyers, accountants, pharmacists, and physical therapists.

Negligence and malpractice are similar in that both relate to wrongdoing. In medical malpractice, negligence is considered the predominant theory of liability. You can only be sued for malpractice if you are negligent in something done within your professional capacity. The topics of negligence and malpractice are discussed further in Chapter 6.

Some actions that are considered unintentional or negligent torts include:

- Failure to document or communicate correctly
- Failure to adequately assess or monitor a patient's condition
- Failure to maintain a safe environment
- Failure to dispense the correct medication
- Failure to document in a timely manner
- Failure to follow policies and procedures

Med Tip

Remember that it is easier to prevent negligence than it is to defend it.

Contract Law

Contract law addresses a **breach**, or neglect, of a legally binding agreement between two parties. The agreement or contract may relate to insurance, sales, business, real estate, or services such as healthcare.

A contract consists of a voluntary agreement, written or verbal, that two parties enter into with the intent of benefiting each other. Something of value, which is termed **consideration**, is part of the agreement. In the medical profession, the consideration might be the performance of an appendectomy for a specific fee. An agreement would take place between the two parties that would include the offer ("I will perform the appendectomy") and the acceptance of the offer ("I will allow you to perform the appendectomy"). Therefore, a surgeon who has consent to perform a hysterectomy on a patient may not perform an appendectomy at the same time unless there is consent from the patient for both procedures.

In order for the contract to be valid (legal), both parties must be **competent**. The concerned party (patient) must be of legal age, mentally competent, and not under the influence of drugs or alcohol at the time the contract is entered into. If there is a question as to whether an individual is mentally competent, this must be adjudicated in a court of law. Consent must be given freely without undue influence of fraud, duress, or misrepresentation of another.

TYPES OF CONTRACTS

A contract can be either expressed or implied. An **expressed contract** is an agreement that clearly states all the terms. It can be entered into verbally or in writing.

> ## Med Tip
> Most contracts are enforceable, even if verbal.

Each state identifies certain types of contracts that must be in writing. The sale of property, mortgages, and deeds are required to be in writing by most state statutes.

There are state statutes and federal laws regarding contracts that relate to the medical profession, such as needing a signed permit to receive a vaccine. For example, if a third party (such as an insurance company) agrees to pay a patient's bill, a contract must be put in writing and signed by the third party. A copy of this document should be kept in the patient's chart or file. If physicians agree to allow their patients to pay bills in four or more installments, the interest (if any) must be stated in writing (Truth in Lending Act of 1969, discussed in Chapter 8).

An **implied contract** is one in which the agreement is inferred from signs, inaction, or silence. For example, when a patient explains their symptoms to the physician, and the physician then examines the patient and prescribes treatment, a contract exists, even though it was not clearly stated, and both parties must follow through on the implied agreement. This can cause problems for both parties if there is not a clear understanding of the implied contract. For example, a New York court found an implied contract to pay for medical services existed when a physician listened to a patient describe his symptoms over the telephone (*O'Neill v. Montefiore Hosp.*, 202 N.Y.S.2d, 436, App. Div. 1960). An implied contract can exist when a patient brought into an emergency department clearly needs and receives immediate treatment.

> ## Med Tip
> Breach of contract refers to the failure, without legal excuse, to perform any promise or to carry out any of the terms of a contract.

TERMINATION OF THE CONTRACT

A **breach of contract** occurs when either party fails to comply with the terms of the agreement. For example, if a physician refuses to perform a medical procedure they had agreed to perform, the physician has breached the contract. If a patient does not pay an agreed-upon fee, then the patient breached the contract with the physician.

The termination of a contract between patient and physician generally occurs when the treatment has ended and the fee has been paid. However, issues may arise that cause premature termination of a contract. It should be noted that both physicians and patients have the right to terminate the contractual agreement. A breach of contract occurs when one of the parties that entered into the contract does not keep their promise as, for example, when a patient refuses to pay a bill. A physician may be liable for breach of contract if they promised to cure a patient and then failed to do so. The breach of contract can occur even if there was no negligence on the part of the physician.

When terminating a contract, physicians should be careful that they are not charged with abandonment of the patient. To protect against an abandonment charge, any letter from the physician to the patient should indicate the date their services will be terminated. A copy of this letter to the patient should be placed in the patient's record. In addition, there should be a notation in the patient's chart that a notification of termination letter was sent. It is also a good idea to use U.S. Postal Service certified mail and include "signature required" when the letter is sent and to ask for proof of delivery, keeping those receipts with the patient's records. That extra step should the case go to court is vital. See Chapter 5 for a complete discussion of abandonment. Some of the reasons for premature termination of a medical contract are the following:

- Failure to follow instructions
- Missed appointments
- Failure to pay for service
- Statement from the patient (verbally or in writing) that they are seeking the care of another physician (e.g., the patient's insurance may have changed and the physician may not be covered by the new insurance, or the patient may have relocated)

Class Action Lawsuit

A **class action lawsuit** can be filed by one or more people on behalf of a larger group of people who are all affected by the same situation. For example, class action lawsuits are commonly filed in product liability or pharmaceutical cases in which a large number of people are negatively affected by the same product, such as cigarettes. In March 2000, a group of women in Florida filed a class action lawsuit against a group of physicians who failed to get informed consent before subjecting the women to random medical experimentation.

Public Law

Public law concerns relationships between individuals and the government as well as relationships between individuals that are of concern to society as a whole. Within public law, criminal law and administrative law are most likely to have application to medical practice.

Criminal Law

Criminal law is a branch of public law that deals with offenses against the state. These laws are created by the government to protect the public as a whole from the harmful acts of others. The purpose of criminal law is to define socially intolerable conduct that is punishable by law. No citizen of the United States can bring a criminal lawsuit against another person because these are offenses against society as a whole. A criminal act is one in which a person or institution commits an illegal act or a failure to act. Criminal law requires evidence **beyond a reasonable doubt**, which is evidence with an almost absolute certainty that a person did commit a crime. It is a higher standard than the mere preponderance of evidence required in civil law. In a state crime, a local prosecutor in the District Attorney's office will bring about a criminal action against the accused person. In a federal crime, it will be a federal prosecutor who brings about this action.

In a criminal case, the government (the state government in most cases) brings the suit against a person or group of people accused of committing a crime within the boundaries of the state, resulting in a fine, imprisonment, or both if the defendant is found guilty. Federal criminal offenses include illegal actions that cross state lines—kidnapping, treason, or other actions that affect national security. Crimes involving crossing the borders of the United States (e.g., illegal transport of drugs and any illegal act against a federally regulated business, such as a bank) are also federal criminal offenses.

Criminal acts fall into two categories: felony and misdemeanor. A **felony** carries a punishment of death or imprisonment in a state or federal prison for more than one year. These serious crimes include murder, rape, robbery, larceny, arson, burglary, tax evasion, and practicing medicine without a license. A **misdemeanor** is a less serious offense. Misdemeanors include traffic violations, disturbing the peace, and minor theft. A misdemeanor carries a punishment of fines or imprisonment in jail for up to a year. See Figure 2.5 for an illustration of the felony case process and Figure 2.6 for an illustration of the misdemeanor case process.

A physician's license may be revoked by the state licensing board if the physician is convicted of a crime. Criminal cases in the healthcare field have included revocation of a license for violating narcotics laws, sexual misconduct, income tax evasion, counterfeiting, and murder.

Figure 2–5 Felony case process

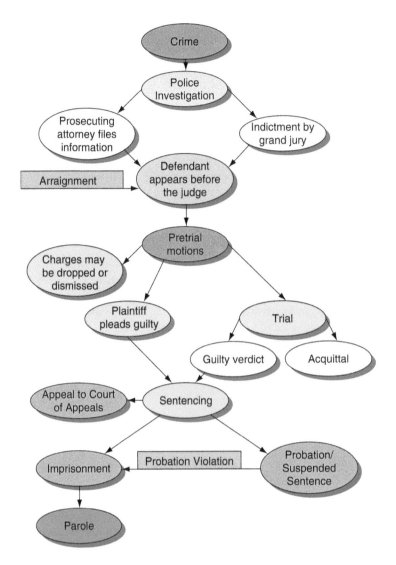

Administrative Law

Administrative law, another branch of public law, covers regulations that are set by government agencies. In the healthcare field, federal and state agencies, under authorization from Congress or state legislatures, have created a multitude of rules and regulations. Violations of these regulations may constitute criminal or civil violations. However, in most cases, they are civil law violations. Examples of entities that are covered under administrative law include licensing boards for physicians, nurses, and allied health professionals; workers' compensation programs; and the Department of Health and Human Services. Wide-ranging healthcare-related regulations include the following:

- Licensing and supervision of prescribing, storing, and dispensing controlled substances
- Health department regulations, including reporting requirements of certain communicable diseases
- Regulations against homicide, infanticide, euthanasia, assault, and battery
- Regulations against fraud
- Internal Revenue Service regulations that are healthcare related

Healthcare professionals are more involved in areas of administrative law than in any other source of law. The penalties for violations of this category of law include fines, sanctions, and revocation or termination of licenses.

Med Tip

When faced with difficult ethical or legal dilemmas, remember that your hard-earned license or certification can be revoked if you make the wrong decision.

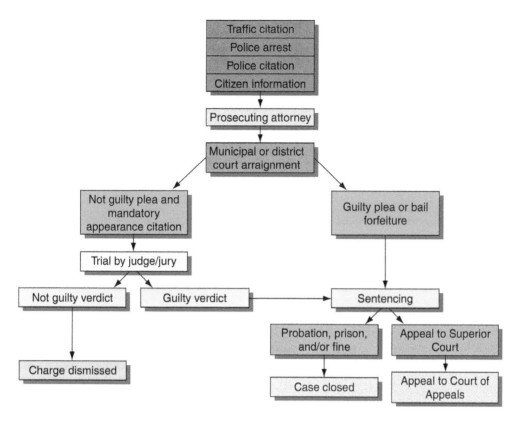

Figure 2–6 Misdemeanor case process

The Court Systems

There are two court systems in the United States: state and federal. Each system has specific responsibilities that may be either exclusive, meaning that only that particular court can hear a case, or concurrent, meaning both courts have the power to hear the case. Which court hears the case depends on the plaintiff's choice, provided both courts have jurisdiction to hear the case. For a criminal case, this depends on the type of crime and where the criminal action occurred. For example, a bank robbery that took place in Alabama will usually be tried by a federal court in that state. In a civil case, the type of court used depends on where the incident occurred and the type of lawsuit.

Types of Courts

The federal court system has **jurisdiction**, or power to hear a case, when one of the following conditions is present:

- The dispute relates to a federal law or the U.S. Constitution
- The U.S. government is one of the parties involved in the dispute
- Different states' citizens are involved in the dispute and the case involves over $75,000
- Citizens of another country are involved in a dispute with a U.S. citizen and the case involves over $75,000
- The disputed activity occurred in international waters

If the case does not involve one of these situations, it must be tried in state court. However, even if one of these situations exists, the case may still be heard in state court unless Congress has prohibited state courts from hearing the case, such as with a kidnapping that takes place across state lines. Cases involving a federal crime, bankruptcy law, and patent law must be heard in federal court. Cases involving divorce, child custody, and probate must be heard in state court.

The court system is divided into three levels. The levels for the federal court system are district (or municipal), court of appeals (or circuit courts), and the U.S. Supreme Court. A case is tried at the lowest level court first. If that court's decision is appealed, or challenged, then the next higher court may examine the decision.

The state courts, from lower to higher, are divided into district or municipal trial courts, state court of appeals, and the state's highest court for final appeals. The lower state courts hear cases such as small claims and traffic violations.

Physicians may have to take a patient who has a delinquent account to small claims court. Physicians may authorize their office manager, bookkeeper, or other office assistant to appear in court for the hearing. The clerk of a small claims court can provide information on the requirements and procedures relating to this type of lawsuit.

Probate court, or **estatecourt**, handles cases involving estates of the deceased. A physician may have to contact the county court recorder for information about filing a claim for payment from the estate of a deceased patient.

Med Tip

It is always advisable to seek payment for all healthcare services that have been provided to dying or deceased patients. Failure to seek payment may be thought of as an indication of guilt or negligence over a patient's treatment or death.

The Trial Process

In a trial, the judicial process is designed to determine certain facts by hearing evidence, determine which facts are relevant, apply relevant principles of law, and then pass a judgment. A grand jury hearing is the first step in some cases.

The Grand Jury

The federal government and many states use the grand jury process. A grand jury is typically made up of 12 to 23 private citizens and hears evidence about a criminal case in order to determine whether the case has enough merit to be heard in court. Thus, a grand jury can serve as a filter to prevent cases from being heard when there is insufficient evidence. The grand jury hearings are held in private, and the defendant may or may not appear to speak before the grand jury. The defendant can be a physician, a nurse, a representative of the healthcare facility (employer), and/or other healthcare providers. The grand jury can ask to see documents relating to the investigation and speak with witnesses. After hearing all the evidence and deliberating among themselves, the grand jury votes on whether they should move the **indictment**, a written legal charge against the defendant, to a trial court.

The Procedure

When two parties are unable to solve a dispute by themselves, it may result in **litigation**, a dispute or lawsuit that is tried in court. A physician may be the plaintiff (the person bringing an action into litigation), or the defendant (the person accused of the alleged wrongdoing). A plaintiff can be a patient, the patient's family, or anyone else who has a right to be compensated under the law because of the injury the patient (plaintiff) is said to have received. A **prosecutor** brings a criminal lawsuit on behalf of the government.

Subpoena

Discovery is the legal process by which facts are discovered before a trial begins. A court of law may need to subpoena a person or records. A **subpoena** is a written command from the court for a person or documents to appear in court. In some cases, a **deposition** can be taken, meaning that the person's statement is recorded with witnesses present, and the person may not be required to appear in court. The deposition is submitted by an attorney during the court case. A subpoena *duces tecum*, a Latin phrase meaning "under penalty, take with you," is a court order requiring a witness to appear in court and to bring certain records or other material to a trial or deposition. There is a penalty for failure to appear or present documents if subpoenaed by the court. A person or documents may also be produced in court on a voluntary basis, thus not requiring a subpoena. (Subpoena *duces tecum* is explained more fully in Chapter 9.)

A subpoena must be sent by registered mail or hand-delivered (served) to the person who is being requested to appear in court, that is, the person who is named on the subpoena. Unless requested to do so, an assistant cannot accept a subpoena on behalf of a physician without their knowledge; otherwise, the subpoena is considered "not served." The physician may delegate the responsibility to an assistant to accept a subpoena on their behalf, but this practice is not encouraged. If there are any questions, it is always a good idea to consult with an attorney if you are served a subpoena. Failure to comply with the subpoena's requests to appear in court or produce documents is regarded as "contempt of court" and is punishable by harsh fines.

Settling out of Court

Not all lawsuits end up in court. In many situations, attorneys for both sides work out a settlement, or agreement, between the parties, so there is no need for a trial. This is called *settling out of court*.

Summary Judgment

A request may be made by an attorney on either side for a summary judgment to take place in a civil lawsuit. A **summary judgment** is a decision made by the court (judge) in response to a motion that declares there is no necessity for a trial because there is no dispute as to the material facts. Any person who is involved in a civil action can request, through their attorney, a summary judgment by the judge if they believe there is no issue of law involved in the case. When the evidence supporting the position of one of the parties involved in the lawsuit is very clear from the onset, there may be no need for a trial to take place. Summary judgment is a procedural device that can assist in bringing a controversy to quick closure without a trial. It can result in a win for one side of the case and is based on **pleadings** (formal written statements) alone.

Trial

If the parties are unable to settle the dispute or if there is no summary judgment, a trial may be held. A court case can be tried before a judge only or before a judge and jury of the defendant's peers. Both parties (defendant and plaintiff) in the case may **waive**, or give up, their right to a jury trial or may request a jury trial.

JURY SELECTION

If a jury is requested, then 6 to 12 people are selected from a large pool of potential jurors. The jurors are most commonly summoned from a list of residents of a particular region, registered voters, or driver's license holders. The judge and attorneys for both sides of the case (plaintiff and defendant) question the potential jurors to find an impartial jury. After the final selection of jurors is made, the case is ready to begin.

OPENING STATEMENTS

A trial begins with opening statements made by the attorneys for both sides of the case that describe the facts they will attempt to prove during the case.

PRESENTATION OF EVIDENCE AND EXAMINATION OF WITNESSES

The plaintiff's attorney then questions the first witness. A witness is generally someone who has knowledge of the circumstances of the case and can testify, under oath, as to what happened. This witness can then be cross-examined (asked questions) by the defendant's attorney. After all of the plaintiff's witnesses have been examined and cross-examined, the defendant's attorney (defense counsel) presents witnesses for the defense side of the case. The plaintiff's attorney then has an opportunity to cross-examine the defense witnesses. At any time during the trial, as appropriate and approved by the judge, items such as documents, photos, or telephone records may be entered into evidence. When this portion of the case has been completed, and after any additional witnesses are called and cross-examined, both sides "rest their case," which means that all the evidence and witnesses they plan to present have been entered and/ or examined.

Med Tip

The U.S. legal system is based on the premise that all persons are innocent until proven guilty. Because the plaintiff is claiming that the defendant violated a law, the burden of proof is placed upon the plaintiff to prove that the defendant is liable.

CLOSING ARGUMENTS AND VERDICT

Attorneys for both the plaintiff and the defendant then present summaries of the evidence or summaries of their case, called **closing arguments**. In a jury trial, the judge instructs the jury on the areas of law that affect the case. The jury is then excused and taken to another room so they can deliberate, examine the evidence presented, and come to a conclusion, or verdict. If the trial has been conducted in front of a judge without a jury, then the judge makes a decision based on the evidence presented and the law. In a civil case, if the judge or jury finds in favor of the plaintiff, then the defendant is typically ordered to pay the plaintiff a monetary award. In a criminal case, if the defendant is found guilty, the judge sentences the defendant with a fine and/or a prison sentence. In some cases, if the state statutes allow it, the death penalty may be applied. If the defendant wins in either a civil or criminal case, the case is over unless an appeal is made. A plaintiff or defendant may appeal the decision to a higher court. Ultimately, a case can be appealed to the highest court, either in the state or, in a federal case, the U.S. Supreme Court. See Figure 2.7 for an illustration of a civil trial procedure.

Med Tip

A judgment of not guilty, or not liable as in a malpractice case, does not mean that the defendant did not commit the crime or perform the misconduct. It only means that, based on the evidence presented, the plaintiff failed to prove it to a jury.

Figure 2–7 The procedure for a civil trial

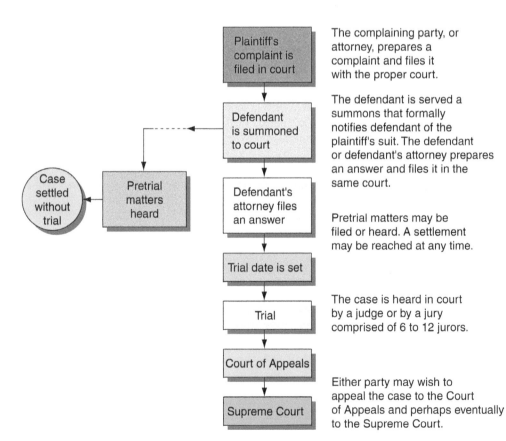

Plaintiff's complaint is filed in court

The complaining party, or attorney, prepares a complaint and files it with the proper court.

Defendant is summoned to court

The defendant is served a summons that formally notifies defendant of the plaintiff's suit. The defendant or defendant's attorney prepares an answer and files it in the same court.

Case settled without trial

Pretrial matters heard

Defendant's attorney files an answer

Pretrial matters may be filed or heard. A settlement may be reached at any time.

Trial date is set

Trial

The case is heard in court by a judge or by a jury comprised of 6 to 12 jurors.

Court of Appeals

Supreme Court

Either party may wish to appeal the case to the Court of Appeals and perhaps eventually to the Supreme Court.

Standards of Proof

When deciding a case in a court of law, there are several different levels of proof that are required depending on how serious society considers the crime to be. In a civil case, the court will generally look at a "preponderance of evidence." This is evidence that, as a whole, shows that the fact sought to be proved is more probably true than not. This means that the burden of proof in a civil case will place greater weight on evidence that is more credible and convincing. This does not mean that the cases will be decided on a greater number of witnesses, but rather on a greater weight of all the evidence.

In juvenile abuse cases, the court tends to use "clear and convincing evidence." This means that there is a reasonable certainty of the truth. "Clear and convincing evidence" or proof, requires more than a "preponderance of evidence" or proof, as in a civil case, and less than proof "beyond a reasonable doubt," as in a criminal case. In criminal trials, a judge or jury must find the defendant guilty "beyond a reasonable doubt," which means that the facts when proven must establish guilt.

Expert Witness

An **expert witness** is a person called as a witness in a case in which the subject matter is beyond the general knowledge of most people in the court or on the jury. In cases related to healthcare, this person, usually a healthcare professional, has special knowledge or experience not only about the facts of a case but also about the professional conclusions that are drawn from the facts. The testimony of the expert witness should assist the jury or judge in evaluating the facts in a particular case. In a medical malpractice suit, an expert witness often is called to testify as to what the standard of care for a patient is in a similar circumstance and locality. An expert witness in a medical malpractice suit involving a physician is generally a physician. In cases involving nurses, an expert witness is often a nurse.

Expert witnesses, who are generally paid a fee, may use visual aids such as charts, photos, X-rays, models, and diagrams. They do not testify about the actual facts of the case, but clarify points of knowledge that may not be readily understood by all present. Physicians and nurses often serve as expert witnesses to describe the standard of care in a community when another physician or nurse is being sued for negligence. For example, an expert witness on the topic of DNA may be called to testify in a paternity case.

Testifying in Court

If you are called to testify in court, remember the following:

- Always tell the truth.
- Be professional. People are judged by their appearance as well as by their behavior in court. An attorney can offer further advice on this.
- Act with poise, dignity, and seriousness. The opposing attorney may try to make the witness nervous by asking difficult questions.
- Do not answer a question you do not understand. Simply ask the attorney to repeat the question or state, "I don't understand the question."
- Just present the facts surrounding the case. Do not give any information that is not requested. Do not insert your opinion. "The patient was shouting" is stating a fact; "He was angry" is your opinion.
- Do not memorize your testimony ahead of time. You will generally be allowed to take some notes with you to refresh your memory concerning such things as dates.

Med Tip

Keep in mind that a lawsuit can take years to come to closure. The mean age for a lawsuit from beginning to settlement is three to five years. Every necessary step should be taken to avoid a lawsuit in the first place.

Appellate Court System

The U.S. legal system at both the state and federal levels has a built-in appeals process for decisions that need to be reviewed. If the losing party in a lawsuit believes that the case was handled improperly or unfairly, the party can "appeal" to a higher court of law to have the decision corrected or changed in its favor. The appellate court, or higher court, reviews the written transcripts of the original trial. This court will examine the evidence to determine if, in its opinion, the ruling was correct and fair. The appellate court does not retry the case but acts as a reviewing court. After reading the transcripts from the case, the judge affirms the original decision, reverses it, or modifies it.

Chapter 2 Review

Points to Ponder

1. Why do I have to know how a bill becomes a law?
2. Why is common law important?
3. How can I avoid a lawsuit?
4. Can I restrain a person against their will if I know it is for their own good?
5. Can I be sued if I make a statement to a patient about a mistake a physician has made?

6. What should I do if I see a physician or another healthcare employee make an error?
7. Can I be sued if I discuss a patient with a friend who is a nurse at another hospital?
8. What do I do if I am subpoenaed?

Discussion Questions

1. Discuss the significance of common laws for the healthcare professional.
2. Explain what is meant by the statement, "It is easier to prevent negligence than it is to defend it."
3. Differentiate between common law and statutory law.

4. Explain what the numbering system in public law means.
5. What is meant by *burden of proof*?
6. What is a subpoena and who can accept it?

Review Challenge

Short Answer Questions

1. How can embezzlement be prevented?

_____

_____

_____

_____

2. What is the difference between libel and slander?

_____

_____

_____

_____

3. What are some of the reasons for termination of a medical contract?

_____

_____

_____

_____

4. What is an expert witness and why might one be used during a lawsuit?

_____

_____

_____

5. What is the difference between a felony and a misdemeanor? Give an example of each.

_____

_____

_____

_____

6. What is a subpoena _duces tecum?_

_____

_____

_____

_____

7. What is a class action lawsuit? Give an example of one.

_____

_____

_____

_____

8. What is the role of the appellate court within the court system?

_____

_____

_____

_____

Matching

Match the responses in column B with the correct term in column A.

COLUMN A

_____ **1.** breach

_____ **2.** deposition

_____ **3.** plaintiff

_____ **4.** defendant

_____ **5.** felony

_____ **6.** misdemeanor

_____ **7.** waive

_____ **8.** tort

_____ **9.** subpoena

_____ **10.** precedent

COLUMN B

a. order for a person or documents to appear in court

b. person who is being sued

c. give up the right to something

d. law that covers harm to another person

e. earlier ruling applied to present case

f. failure

g. person who sues another party

h. less serious crime such as a traffic violation

i. oral testimony to be used in court

j. serious crime such as practicing medicine without a license

Multiple Choice

Select the one best answer to the following statements.

1. Sources of law include all of the following except

  a. regulatory law.

  b. executive law.

  c. statutory law.

  d. common law.

  e. constitutional law.

2. Subpoena _duces tecum_ means

  a. "let the master answer."

  b. "under penalty, take with you."

  c. "let the decision stand."

  d. "the thing speaks for itself."

  e. "the thing has been decided."

3. _Stare decisis_ means

  a. "let the master answer."

  b. "under penalty, take with you."

  c. statutory law has been invoked.

  d. constitutional law has been invoked.

  e. "let the decision stand."

4. Administrative law covers all of the following except

  a. health department regulations.

  b. licensing of prescription drugs.

  c. Internal Revenue Service regulations.

  d. fraud.

  e. All of the above are covered under administrative law.

5. The person who brings the action into litigation is called a(n)

  a. attorney.

  b. plaintiff.

  c. defendant.

  d. judge.

  e. juror.

6. A court order that requires a witness to appear in court with certain records is called a
   a. deposition.
   b. discovery.
   c. subpoena *duces tecum*.
   d. *res judicata*.
   e. waiver.

7. The common law of the past that is based on a decision made by judges is called
   a. civil law.
   b. constitutional law.
   c. case law.
   d. criminal law.
   e. statutory law.

8. The threat of doing bodily harm to another person—stating, for example, "If you won't allow us to continue this procedure, we will have to tie your hands"—is
   a. assault.
   b. battery.

   c. fraud.
   d. invasion of privacy.
   e. All of the above

9. Standard of care refers to the care that
   a. a reasonable person would use.
   b. is ordinary care.
   c. a prudent person would use.
   d. healthcare professionals in all specialties must practice.
   e. All of the above

10. Removing one's clothing in order to allow the physician to perform a physical examination is a(n)
   a. invasion of privacy.
   b. defamation of character.
   c. implied contract.
   d. abandonment.
   e. None of the above is correct.

Discussion Cases

1. Analyze *"The Case of Jacob and the Diseased Leg"* (found at the beginning of the chapter) using the three-step ethics model (Blanchard-Peale).

   a. _____
      _____
   b. _____
      _____
   c. _____
      _____

2. Using Figure 2.7, explain the procedure for a civil trial.
   _____
   _____
   _____
   _____
   _____
   _____

3. Adam Green is an orderly in the Midwest Nursing Home. His supervisor, Nora Malone, has asked him to supervise the dining room while 20 residents eat their evening meal. Bill Heckler is an 80-year-old resident who is very alert and ambulatory. He tells Adam that he doesn't like the meal that's being served, and he wants to leave the dining room and go back to his own room. Adam is quite busy, as he must oversee the behaviors of several patients who are confused. He's concerned that patients might choke on their food or otherwise harm themselves. Adam becomes impatient with Bill and tells him that he cannot leave the room until everyone is finished eating. Adam then locks the dining room door. Bill reports to the nursing home administrator that he was unlawfully detained. He then hires an attorney, who brings forth a charge of false imprisonment.

   a. Was Adam's action justified?
      _____
      _____

   b. In your opinion, was this a case of false imprisonment?
      _____
      _____

   c. What could Adam have done to defuse the situation?
      _____
      _____

   d. Do the nursing home administrator and Nora Malone have any legal responsibility for Adam's action?
      _____
      _____

Put It Into Practice

Give an example of a violation of each of the six torts mentioned in this chapter (assault, battery, false imprisonment, defamation of character, fraud, and invasion of privacy) as it might affect your particular area of healthcare specialization.

Web Hunt

Search the website of the National Institutes of Health (**www.nih.gov**). What types of information and services does this site offer?

Critical Thinking Exercise

What would you pick if you had a choice between having a legal system that never punishes an innocent person but often lets the guilty go free, or a system that sometimes punishes the innocent but never frees the guilty? Do you have a better solution?

Bibliography

Aiken, T. 2023. *Legal and ethical issues in health occupations* (5th ed.). Elsevier.

Beaman, N., Routh, K.D., Papazian-Boyce, L., Maly, R., & Nguyen, J.. 2017. *Pearson's comprehensive medical assisting: Administrative and clinical competencies* (4th ed.). Pearson

Garner, B. 2019. *Black's law dictionary* (11th ed.). Thomson Reuters.

Hall, M., & Orentlicher, D.. 2020. *Health care law and ethics in a nutshell* (4th ed.). West Academic Publishing.

Posgar, G.D. 2019. *Legal and ethical issues for health professionals.* Jones and Bartlett.

Schmallager, F. 2018. *Criminal justice today: An introductory test for the 21st century* (15th ed.). Pearson.

Venes, D. 2021. *Taber's cyclopedic medical dictionary* (24th ed.). F.A. Davis Company.

Essentials of the Legal System for Healthcare Professionals

Learning Objectives

After completing this chapter, you will be able to:

3.1 Define all key terms.

3.2 List the basic characteristics of state medical practice acts, advanced provider practice acts, and allied health scopes of work.

3.3 Describe the process of licensure for physicians, advanced practice providers, nurses, and selected allied health professionals.

3.4 Discuss what the term *standard of care* means for physicians, advance practice providers, and nurses and what it means for someone in your profession.

3.5 Describe the importance of the discovery rule as it relates to the statute of limitations.

3.6 Discuss the importance of the phrase *respondeat superior* as it relates to the physician.

Key Terms

Accreditation

Bonding

Confidentiality

Discovery rule

Endorsement

Good Samaritan laws

Guardian ad litem

Incident report

Mutual recognition model

Prudent person rule

Reciprocity

Respondeat superior

Revoke

Risk management

Scope of practice

Standard of care

Statute of limitations

The Joint Commission

Tolling

The Case of Latoya and the Patient Receiving Physical Therapy

Latoya is in training to become a physical therapist (PT). Dr. B., the head of the Physical Therapy Department, has told her that she helps the patients too much. Many times he has said, "You can't go home with the patients. They must learn to care for themselves." Nearing the end of her program, Latoya is doing very well in all her studies, but she fears that Dr. B. will not give her a good performance evaluation unless she can better prepare the patients for independence.

One of her patients, a 72-year-old-woman recovering from a stroke, is adamant in her refusal to walk with either a walker or a cane. She insists on remaining in her wheelchair because she is afraid of falling. Latoya is sympathetic toward this patient's fears.

She remembers seeing a patient fall during a physical therapy session resulting in a fractured vertebra (bone) in her spine. The woman was subsequently bedridden for several weeks while she recovered. In addition, a statement that Latoya heard in one of her classes, *primum non nocere*, meaning "first, do no harm," has always influenced her behavior. Latoya is reluctant to force her patient to do something she doesn't want to do.

1. In your opinion, is Dr. B. placing too much pressure on a student?

2. Is this a legal or ethical problem, or both?

3. Who should Latoya talk to about her dilemma?

Introduction

It is important that all healthcare professionals realize how the law impacts the practice of healthcare. The physician has a responsibility to respect the conditions of licensure. Healthcare employees *must* understand their obligations to their employer and to the patients they serve.

Practice Acts

Medical Practice Acts

Each state has statutes that govern the practice of medicine in that state. These are called medical practice acts and are meant to protect the health and safety of the general public. The acts were originally established in a limited number of states to protect the general public from *quackery*, or persons practicing medicine without a legitimate education and training. Each state legislature establishes a state medical board that has the authority to control the licensing of physicians. While some slight differences exist from state to state, in general, these practice acts define who must be licensed to perform certain procedures. These acts also specify the requirements for licensure; the duties of the licensed physician; grounds on which the license may be revoked, or taken away; and reports that must be made to the government or other appropriate agencies. Medical practice acts also define the penalties for practicing without a license. These state acts seek to protect patients from harm caused by persons who are not qualified to practice medicine. Therefore, each state licensing board has the authority to grant a medical license to qualified individuals as well as to revoke or take away that license for cause and to fine, reprimand, and censure the physician (Figure 3.1).

Med Tip

Every state has a state board set up to handle issues relating to physician registration. The title for these boards varies from state to state (e.g., state board of registration or state board of medical examiners). However, the functions are similar for all state boards.

State licensing boards receive complaints about physicians from a variety of sources: patients; other physicians; employees, including hospital employees; the media; and insurance companies. The board has the authority to investigate each complaint, but cannot prosecute the physician. However, the board may access records that relate to each incident, including patient hospital records, individual physician medical records, and insurance reimbursement records. The board may declare the name of the physician but is obligated to keep a patient's name confidential. The board cannot provide the information to a court unless presented with a court order.

A physician who moves to another state must obtain a license to practice in that state also. The physician may be required to pass another state's medical examination, or the physician may receive reciprocity or endorsement from the state.

Figure 3–1 Physician discussing test results with patient
Source: Shutterstock

While medical practice acts vary from state to state, they generally provide for the establishment of a medical examining board, also called a state board of registration or state board of examiners, that has authority to license physicians and

1. establish the baseline for the practice of medicine in that state;
2. determine the prerequisites for licensure;
3. forbid the practice of medicine without a license; and
4. specify the conditions for license renewal, suspension, and revocation.

Scope of Practice for Physician Assistants

The physician assistant (PA) scope of practice varies by state and usually includes providing primary care (evaluating and diagnosing), treatment (including performing procedures) and follow-up; prescribing medications; and performing health promotion and preventive care. PAs work under the supervision of a qualified physician. Their area of practice may change depending on their medical specialty and the policies of the healthcare facility.

Med Tip

It is important to know and understand the scope of practice for the state in which you work.

Nurse Practitioner Practice Acts

Practice acts for nurse practitioners vary widely from state to state. The scopes of practice for NPs can allow them to assess patients, order tests, interpret results, make diagnoses, prescribe medication, and order treatments. The various scopes of practice can be categorized as full practice, reduced practice, and restricted practice:

- *Full practice* states allow NPs to perform the full scope of practice without a collaborating or supervising physician. Some states require NPs to have a specific amount of time in supervised practice before allowing full practice. Full practice states include most western states (but not California), New York, and all of New England, as well as Maryland, Delaware, Florida, and Alaska.
- *Reduced practice* states allow NPs to perform some of their scope of practice without physician supervision. They may not be allowed to prescribe certain types of medications or they may need to be part of a practice that includes physicians, even though they see their own patients. Reduced practice states include the states from Pennsylvania to Wisconsin and the southern states of Arkansas, Louisiana, Mississippi, and Alabama.
- *Restricted practice* states require NPs to work under the supervision of a physician for the entire scope of practice. Some states allow a wider scope of practice as the NP becomes more experienced. Restricted practice states include California, Texas, Missouri, the Carolinas, Virginia, and Georgia.

Nurse Practice Acts

The practice of nursing is regulated at the state level through a nurse practice act (NPA). An NPA is a series of state statutes that define the scope of practice, standards for education programs, licensure requirements, and grounds for disciplinary actions. The law provides a framework for establishing nursing actions in the care of patients. Laws set the boundaries for and maintain a standard of nursing practice. For the RN, the provisions of NPAs are quite similar from state to state. Greater variation exists in the scope of practice for the licensed practical nurse (LPN) and licensed vocational nurse (LVN).

Each state's NPA is enforced and administered by a state board of nursing (BON), though some states use other titles for this regulatory board. BONs were established some 100 years ago to standardize the education of nurses, establish standards for safe nursing practice, and issue licenses to protect the public from unprepared, unsafe practitioners. BONs also act as a forum for citizens to report and discuss concerns regarding nursing services they have received. In this way, BONs continue to work toward their goal of protecting public health.

Scope of Practice for Allied Health Professionals

Allied health professionals represent a wide range of professions including, but not limited to, physical therapists, occupational therapists, speech-language pathologists, respiratory therapists, audiologists, dietitians, phlebotomists, and medical assistants. Most of the allied health disciplines have their own governing bodies and practice acts. A few are covered here:

- Physical therapists (PTs) and physical therapy assistants (PTAs) are governed by the American Physical Therapy Association (APTA) and the Federation of State Boards of Physical Therapy (FSBPT). Each state has its own practice act, most of which are based on the Model Practice Act for Physical Therapy (MPA). Physical therapists help individuals recover from injuries, manage chronic conditions, and improve their physical function. They assess patients; plan treatment; rehabilitate patients through exercise, activities, and education; injury prevention; and pain management.

- Occupational therapists (OTs) and occupational therapy assistants (OTAs) are governed by the American Occupational Therapy Association (AOTA). Each state has its own practice act, most of which are based on the Model Occupational Therapy Practice Act. The practice of occupational therapy includes evaluating factors affecting activities of daily living (ADLs) in both home and work environments; instrumental activities of daily living (IADLs), health management, sleep and rest, work, play, and social participation; methods for identifying interventions; and selecting interventions to promote or enhance ADLs and IADLs.

- Respiratory therapists (RTs), according to the American Association for Respiratory Care (AARC), practice under the general direction of a physician and execute orders from physicians and advanced practice providers. The National Board for Respiratory Care (NBRC) credentials RTs in seven specific areas. RTs collect diagnostic information, assess patients, apply therapeutics and assess their effectiveness, manage patients with acute and chronic diseases, and provide emergency care.

- Phlebotomists are trained to draw blood from patients for diagnostic testing, blood donation, or research. In some places, phlebotomists may have additional responsibilities, such as administering intravenous (IV) medications or performing more specialized procedures. Some states require phlebotomists to be trained and certified; others do not. The American Society of Phlebotomy Technicians (ASPT) provides opportunities for ongoing education.

- Medical assistants work under the supervision of licensed healthcare professionals (such as physicians or nurses). It's important to note that the specific tasks and responsibilities a medical assistant can perform may vary based on their level of education, training, certification, and state regulations. Some states may have more stringent requirements and may allow medical assistants to take on more clinical responsibilities, while others may limit their scope of practice to administrative tasks and basic clinical duties. Medical assistants may have administrative duties, such as scheduling appointments, managing office supplies, or maintaining EHRs. They can have clinical duties, such as taking patient histories, collecting laboratory specimens, and assisting with patient mobility and transfers. In addition, they may provide infection control, maintain equipment and instruments, and help with patient education.

Licensure

Licensure of Physicians

The board of examiners in each state may grant licensure through examination, endorsement, or reciprocity.

Examination

Each state offers its own examination for licensure. Some states also accept or endorse the National Board of Medical Examiners (NBME) licensing examination, usually taken before the end of medical school, for licensure. Within the United States, the official medical licensing exam is the Federal Licensing Examination (FLEX). The license is issued to those who pass the examination, graduate from an accredited school, and complete an internship. Successful completion of these criteria entitles one to set up private practice as a general practitioner.

The U.S. Medical Licensing Examination (USMLE), which was introduced in 1992, is a single licensing examination for graduates from accredited medical schools that allows them to practice medicine. In addition to successfully passing the examination (written and oral), the applicant is required by most states to do the following:

- Provide proof that they have completed the professional education as required by their state
- Provide proof of the successful completion of an approved internship/residency program
- Provide information about any past convictions and history of drug or alcohol abuse
- Have obtained an age of majority, generally 21 years old
- Be of good moral character
- Be a U.S. citizen or have evidence of filing a declaration of intent to become a citizen (some states have dropped this requirement)
- Be a resident of that state

Endorsement

Endorsement means an approval or a sanction. A state may grant a license by endorsement to applicants who have successfully passed the NBME exam. In fact, most physicians in the United States are licensed by endorsement. Any medical school graduate who is not licensed by endorsement is required to pass the state board examination.

Reciprocity

Physicians must satisfy the licensure requirements of any and all states in which they practice. In some cases, the state to which the physician applies for a license will accept the state licensing requirements of the state from which the physician already holds a license. In that case, the physician will not have to take another examination. This practice of cooperation by which a state grants a license to practice medicine to a physician already licensed in another state is known as **reciprocity**. Reciprocity is automatic if a reciprocity agreement exists between the states where the current license is held and licensure is being sought and if the requirements of the agreement are satisfied. For instance, some states require a physician to be licensed for a certain number of years before qualifying for reciprocity.

Registration

It is necessary for physicians to maintain their license by periodic reregistration or renewal either annually or biannually. In addition to paying a fee to renew their license, in almost all states, physicians are required to complete a prescribed number of hours of continuing medical education (CME) units to ensure that they remain current in their field of practice. While state requirements differ for renewal of a medical license, they generally include (1) attending approved workshops, courses, and seminars; (2) completing self-instruction modules; (3) teaching other health professionals; and (4) reading a variety of approved medical literature. Generally, physicians in different states may consult with each other without being licensed in each other's state.

Revocation and Suspension of Licensure

A state may **revoke** a physician's license for cases of severe misconduct, including unprofessional conduct, commission of a crime, or personal incapacity to perform one's duties. Unprofessional conduct involves behavior that fails to meet the ethical standards of the profession, such as inappropriate use of drugs or alcohol, gross immorality, or falsifying records. Crimes may include Medicare/Medicaid fraud, rape, murder, larceny, and narcotics convictions. Personal incapacity often relates to a physical or mental incapacity that prevents the physician from performing professional duties. Professional incompetence, such as malpractice or negligence, can also result in revocation of a medical license.

Practicing Medicine Without a License

No physician wishes to have a license expire for failure to renew or have their license revoked for inappropriate behavior. A physician cannot legally practice medicine without this license.

> ### Med Tip
> Remember that if a physician continues to practice medicine without renewal of their license, under the law, it is considered practicing medicine without a license.

Licensure of Physician Assistants

The National Commission of Certification of Physician Assistants (NCCPA) certifies physician assistants (PAs) in the United States. The certifications reflect the standards for "clinical knowledge clinical reasoning and other medical skills and professional behaviors" required of PAs.

Students who have graduated from a PA program accredited by the Accreditation Review Commission on Education for the Physician Assistant (ARC-PA) or its predecessors can take the Physician Assistant National Certifying Examination® (PANCE) for certification. After passing PANCE, PAs are issued NCCPA certification and can use the PA-C designation until the certification expiration date (approximately two years). PAs must be recertified periodically by taking the Physician Assistant National Recertifying Exam (PANRE).

After receiving NCCPA certification, PAs must become licensed by the state in which they will practice. Each state has a board of medical examiners that issues licenses to PAs and approves registration agreements between physicians and PAs.

Licensure of Nurse Practitioners

Following the completion of their education, nurse practitioners are required to pass a national certification examination specific to their chosen specialty. This examination evaluates their clinical knowledge and competence in delivering patient care. Additionally, many jurisdictions mandate ongoing continuing education to ensure NPs stay abreast of evolving healthcare practices and technologies.

Nurse practitioners are certified by a number of credentialing organizations, depending on their specialty. For example, the American Academy of Nurse Practitioners Certification Board (AANPCB) certifies Family Nurse Practitioners, Emergency Nurse Practitioners, and Adult-Gerontology Primary Care Nurse Practitioners. The American Nurses Credentialing Center (ANCC) certifies Family Nurse Practitioners, Adult-Gerontology Nurse Practitioners, and Psychiatric Nurse Practitioners. The Pediatric Nursing Certification Board also certifies Pediatric Nurse Practitioners

After being certified, NPs must become licensed by the state in which they will practice. Licensure requirements vary by jurisdiction, but they generally include submitting proof of education, clinical training, and certification, along with an application and associated fees. Background checks and verification of professional references may also be part of the licensure process. Regular renewal and compliance with state-specific regulations are essential to maintain licensure and uphold the highest standards of patient care.

Licensure of Nurses

Licensure allows a nurse the legal privilege to practice nursing as defined in the state's NPA. Through the process of licensure, each state's board of nursing (BON) ensures the provision of safe nursing care to the public. Typically, BONs oversee licensure through the following activities:

- Establishing and monitoring educational standards for nursing education programs
- Defining professional standards
- Examining and renewing the licenses of duly qualified applicants
- Investigating violations of the NPA
- Sanctioning (to the point of initiating prosecution against) those who violate the NPA
- Holding disciplinary hearings for possible suspension or revocation of a license
- Establishing and overseeing diversity programs in some states

Each BON oversees the administration of a licensure examination that measures the competencies needed to perform safely and effectively as a newly licensed, entry-level nurse. The National Council of State Boards of Nursing (NCSBN) has developed two licensure examinations, the National Council

Licensure Examination for Registered Nurses (NCLEX-RN®) and the National Council Licensure Examination for Practical Nurses (NCLEX-PN®), for state and territory BONs to implement as part of their requirements for licensure. The NCSBN also offers two additional examinations: the National Nurse Aide Assessment Program and the Medication Aide Certification Examination.

National Council of State Boards of Nursing

The NCSBN provides leadership to advance regulatory excellence for public protection. The membership of the NCSBN includes BONs in the 50 states, the District of Columbia, and four U.S. territories (Guam, Virgin Islands, American Samoa, and the Northern Mariana Islands). Four states (California, Georgia, Louisiana, and West Virginia) have separate BONs for RNs and LPNs/LVNs.

The NCSBN offers a number of services that support member BONs. It is responsible for developing the licensure and assessment exams mentioned earlier. In addition, the NCSBN offers continuing education opportunities via its e-learning community.

Nurse Licensure Compact

The **mutual recognition model** of nurse licensure allows a nurse to have a single license that confers the privilege to practice in other states that are part of the Nurse Licensure Compact. Monitoring the nurse's license and taking any needed disciplinary actions are the responsibilities of the state that issues the license. It is similar to the driver's license model: A single license to drive is issued in the individual's state of primary residency, but this license also gives the individual the privilege to drive in other Driver License Compact states.

Med Tip

When practicing in a mutual recognition state, nurses are held accountable for following the laws and rules of the state in which they are practicing, not the state that issued the license.

To achieve mutual recognition, each state must enact legislation or regulations authorizing the Nurse Licensure Compact. States that enter the compact also adopt administrative rules and regulations for implementation of the compact. More than 30 states are currently part of the compact.

Credentialing

Although a nursing license grants the legal privilege to practice, credentialing is the formal identification of professionals who meet predetermined standards of professional skill or competence. The American Nurses Credentialing Center (ANCC), a subsidiary of the American Nurses Association (ANA), provides credentialing programs to certify nurses in specialty practice areas and accredits providers of continuing nursing education and nursing specialty organizations.

Federal organizations, such as The Joint Commission and the Centers for Medicare and Medicaid Services, and federal guidelines affect the standards of care the nurse is held accountable for practicing. Individual healthcare agencies must implement policies, procedures, and job descriptions to ensure that the nurses they employ follow all applicable regulations and guidelines. The nurse needs to know the employing institution's policies and procedures and the specific job descriptions of the licensed and unlicensed nursing personnel. The purpose of knowing the standards of care is to protect both the patient and the nurse.

The impact of laws and standards on nurses is profound. The professional nurse is held accountable for many standards and statutes. Knowledge of the laws that regulate and affect nursing practice enables the nurse to practice within current legal principles and be aware of their legal obligations and responsibilities.

Nursing Students

Each NPA addresses the duties and responsibilities of nursing students in that state. Typically, this includes language that allows nursing students the privilege to practice nursing without a license while engaged in the clinical practicum of an approved nursing education program under the supervision of qualified faculty. Nursing students have the ultimate responsibility (accountability for their actions that includes the obligation to answer for an act done and to repair any injury one may have caused) for their own actions. Guidelines for clinical performance for nursing students typically include the following:

1. Provide safe nursing care.

2. Understand program and facility policies and procedures before undertaking any clinical assignment.

3. Demonstrate knowledge about the patient's condition, interventions, medications, and treatments.

4. Perform care only to the highest level of nursing knowledge; if you are unprepared for a clinical assignment, inform your instructor.

5. Seek help before beginning a procedure about which you are unsure; if the instructor is not readily available, allow the staff nurse to perform the intervention.

Nursing students are held accountable to the same standard of care as licensed nurses. Nursing faculty members are held accountable for appropriate assignments and supervision of students.

Med Tip

Student nurses do NOT practice on a faculty member's license. The only individual who can legally practice on a license is the individual whose name appears on the license.

Certified Nursing Assistants

Certified nursing assistants (CNAs) are healthcare professionals who provide hands-on healthcare to patients in healthcare settings under the supervision of a registered nurse (RN), or licensed practical nurse (LPN). CNAs assist patients with bathing, dressing, and other ADLs.

While requirements differ by state, prospective CNAs need to complete a state-approved CNA program at an accredited institution. Approved programs meet the standards set forth by the state and other governing bodies, ensuring that a student receives the proper knowledge and skills to become licensed and provide patient care. Upon program completion, students need to check their state's certification requirements to make sure they have fulfilled them all such as a minimum number of CNA training/clinical hours. They will need to submit a CNA certification application, pay any applicable fees, and complete fingerprinting and background checks.

Licensure of Allied Health Professionals

Licensing of allied health professionals varies by state. In most states, to obtain a license, the following requirements exist:

- ***PTs*** must have graduated from an approved program that includes clinical training, pass the National Physical Therapy Examination (NPTE), pass a jurisprudence exam and criminal background check, and apply for licensure in the state in which they will practice. As of 2016, all PTs entering the profession must obtain a doctorate of physical therapy (DPT).

- ***OTs*** must have a bachelor's degree in a related field and complete a doctoral degree (as of 2021) from an accredited institution. They must complete supervised clinical fieldwork, pass the National Board for Certification in Occupational Therapy (NBCOT) exam and a background check, and apply for licensure in the state in which they will practice.

- ***RTs*** must have at least an associate degree and then attend a respiratory therapy program that includes clinical experience and is accredited by The Commission on Accreditation for Respiratory Care (CoARC). RTs are typically required to pass the National Board for Respiratory Care (NBRC) examinations, such as the Certified Respiratory Therapist (CRT) and the Registered Respiratory Therapist (RRT) exams. The CRT is typically the entry-level certification, and the RRT is an advanced level certification.

- ***Phlebotomists*** must be licensed or certified to practice in some states; in other states, licensing is not required. Many phlebotomists attend a phlebotomy training program at a community college or medical training institution. Common certifying organizations include the National Phlebotomy Association (NPA), the American Society of Clinical Pathology (ASCP), and the National Healthcareer Association (NHA).

- *Medical assistants* often pursue formal education programs, such as a diploma or certificate program, and may become certified through organizations like the American Association of Medical Assistants (AAMA) or the American Medical Technologists (AMT). Certification can demonstrate competency and expand the scope of practice for medical assistants in some cases.

Continuing education is required by most states for most allied health professionals. Providers must complete continuing education credits to maintain their certification or license. These credits help ensure that allied health professionals stay current with best practices and any changes in their field.

Accreditation of Healthcare Institutions

Accreditation is a voluntary process in which an agency is requested to officially review healthcare institutions such as hospitals, nursing homes, and educational programs to determine competence. This is accomplished by sending in an objective third party, such as **The Joint Commission**, to examine the policies and procedures of the organization being accredited. The accreditation process can be rigorous and generally requires an onsite examination of the program under review. The institution or program must demonstrate that it maintains high standards of care, as set by the reviewing body, for patients and education of its participants. Accreditation of healthcare agencies and institutions became especially important with the advent of Medicare. The federal government stopped surveying hospitals providing care for Medicare patients and allowed The Joint Commission to perform this function. If an institution loses its accreditation, it also loses the ability to provide for Medicare patients.

The Joint Commission, established in 1952, accredits such organizations as all types of hospitals, including psychiatric, long-term care facilities; managed care organizations such as HMOs; visiting nurse associations (VNAs); and clinical laboratories. The Joint Commission emphasizes the use of qualitative standards and looks for compliance with outcome measures such as those found in quality assurance (QA) programs (see Chapter 1 for QA programs). A Joint Commission survey team visits the organization for an onsite inspection every three years. Upon successful completion of the accreditation process, an institution may display signage that it is accredited by The Joint Commission.

Other organizations that provide accreditation for the healthcare profession are the Commission on Accreditation of Allied Health Education Programs (CAAHEP) and Accrediting Bureau of Health Education Schools (ABHES). Both CAAHEP and ABHES provide accreditation for programs in allied health professions such as medical assisting, emergency medical technicians (EMTs), physician assistants and respiratory therapists, to name a few. Many other allied health professions also have accreditation programs.

Standard of Care

Standard of care refers to the ordinary skill and care that all healthcare practitioners such as physicians, nurses, and allied health professionals must use, as determined by their state license or certification and that a "reasonable" person would use in a similar circumstance. This level of expertise is that which is commonly used by other practitioners in the same specialty when caring for patients.

Med Tip

The term *reasonable* is a broad, flexible word to make sure the decision is based on the facts of a particular situation rather than on abstract legal principles. It can mean fair, rational, or moderate. Reasonable care has been defined as "that degree of care a person of ordinary prudence (the so-called reasonable person or reasonable healthcare professional) would exercise in similar circumstances."

The standard of care for particular professions has changed somewhat over the years. For instance, in a Louisiana case, the court concluded that because doctors and nurses are both members of the medical profession, they should both be held to the same high standard of professional competence (*Norton v.*

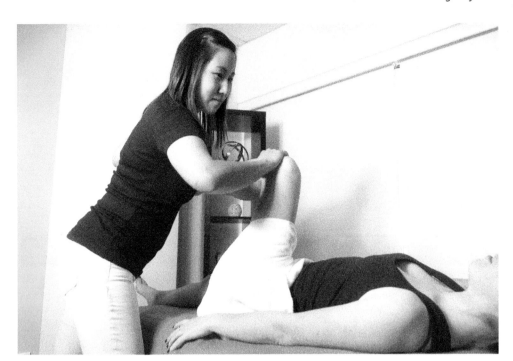

Figure 3–2 Standard of care applies to all healthcare professionals
Source: Lopolo/Shutterstock

Argonaut Ins. Co., 144 So.2d 249, La. App. 1962). However, in a later case, the court recognized that "situations could arise in which a doctor would be considered negligent in his performance of some task where he failed to act to the best of his ability as a physician, while a nurse, performing the same task in the same manner, could be acting to the best of her ability as a nurse" (*Thompson v. Brent*, 245 So.2d 751, La. App. 1971).

While physicians are not obligated to treat everyone (except in the case of an emergency), once a physician accepts a patient for treatment, they enter into the physician–patient relationship (contract) and must provide a certain standard of care (see Figure 3.2). This means that the physician must provide the same knowledge, care, and skill that a similarly trained physician would provide under the same circumstances. The law does not require the physician to use extraordinary skill, only reasonable, ordinary care and skill. The physician is expected to perform the same acts that a "reasonable and prudent" physician would perform. This standard also requires that a physician not perform any acts that a "reasonable and prudent" physician would not.

Physicians are expected to exhaust all the resources available to them when treating patients and not expose patients to undue risk. If they violate this standard of care, they could be liable for negligence.

Nursing, as a profession, has a responsibility to self-regulate by defining the practice of nursing, researching and developing the practice, establishing standards of practice, and providing for the education and credentialing of nurses. The ANA, the largest professional nursing organization, has established Standards of Clinical Nursing Practice, which address both standards for nursing care and standards for professional performance. Standards of practice are also available for various nursing specialties, including pediatric nursing, nurse anesthesia practice, critical care nursing, and psychiatric nursing.

The Prudent Person Rule

The **prudent person rule**, also called the "reasonable person standard," means that a healthcare professional, usually a physician, must provide information to a patient that a reasonable, prudent person would want before they make a decision about treatment or refusal of treatment. In general, a reasonable, prudent person would want to know the following:

- The diagnosis
- The risks and potential consequences of the treatment, excluding any remote or improbable outcomes (This information should include the success and failure rates of the healthcare provider and/or institution.)

- The expected benefits of the treatment or procedure
- Potential alternative treatments
- The prognosis if no treatment is received
- That an acceptable standard of care is followed
- The amount of pain to expect
- The costs

In general, the provider discusses these issues with the patient; however, ancillary healthcare professionals may be present during these conversations. The patient should always be treated in terms of what a "reasonable, prudent person" would want. Unfortunately, not all patients are provided the same courtesy.

Confidentiality

Confidentiality refers to keeping private all information about a person (patient) and not disclosing it to a third party without the patient's written consent. The duty of medical confidentiality is an ancient one. The Hippocratic Oath states, "What I may see or hear in or outside the course of the treatment . . . which on no account may be spread abroad, I will keep to myself, holding such things shameful to speak about." This duty seeks to respect the patient's privacy, and it also recognizes that if the physician does not keep information confidential, patients may be discouraged from revealing useful diagnostic information to their physician.

According to the Medical Patient's Rights Act (also called the Patient's Rights Act), a law passed by Congress in 1996, all patients have the right to have their personal privacy respected and their medical records handled with confidentiality. Information such as test results, patient histories, and even the fact that the person is a patient, cannot be passed on to another person without the patient's consent. No information can be given over the telephone without the patient's permission. No patient records can be given to another person or physician without the patient's written permission, unless a court has subpoenaed it.

In short, any information that is given to a physician by a patient is considered confidential, and it may not be given to an unauthorized person unless specifically required by the law. Information should be communicated only on a need-to-know basis. (See Chapter 10 for a more detailed discussion of confidentiality and the Health Insurance Portability and Accountability Act of 1996, or HIPAA.)

Med Tip

Be especially careful about discussing anything relating to a patient within earshot of others. A comment such as, "Did Ms. Jones come in for her pregnancy test?" can result in a breach-of-confidentiality lawsuit against the physician. And NEVER post anything about any patient on social media.

In addition, it is an employee's duty to refrain from discussing their employer's personal life with patients and coworkers.

Telehealth

Telehealth regulations vary by state and healthcare specialty. It is essential for physicians, advanced practice providers, nurses, and allied health providers to be aware of and comply with the specific regulations that apply to their practice. They must have the appropriate state or regional license to practice telehealth both in their own location and in the patient's location. As with in-person interactions, informed consent is required, as is adherence to privacy regulations such as HIPAA. The same standards of care and documentation are required for telehealth visits. Telehealth providers should have an emergency plan in place in the event of an emergency during the telehealth visit.

Statute of Limitations

The **statute of limitations** refers to the period of time that a patient has to file a lawsuit. The court will generally not hear a case that is filed after the time limit has run out. This time limit varies from state to state, but typically is one to three years. The only exception is that there is no statute of limitations for murder and some other criminal cases. One of the purposes of the statutes is to prevent potential plaintiffs from "sitting on their rights" while the memories surrounding the controversy grow dim or witnesses die or move away. In addition, the statutes allow potential defendants to go on with their lives without worrying about a lawsuit that could be filed relating to some long-ago occurrence.

The statute of limitations, or the time period, however, does not always start "running" at the time of treatment. It begins when the problem is discovered or should have been discovered, which may be some time after the actual treatment. This is known as the **discovery rule**. In *Teeters v. Currey*, the plaintiff sued her doctor, alleging that as a result of Dr. Currey's negligence in performing surgery to sterilize Teeters, she gave birth to a premature child with severe complications several years later. Teeters brought an action for malpractice, and Currey argued the statute of limitations. The court found in favor of the defendant, Currey. However, Teeters successfully appealed and the case was remanded back to the lower court. The court adopted the "discovery doctrine" under which the statute does not begin to run until the injury is, or should have been, discovered (*Teeters v. Currey*, 518 S.W.2d 512, Tenn. 1974).

In some cases, the statute of limitations is *tolled*, or stops running. **Tolling**, or running, of the statute of limitations means that time has not expired, even if it is past the usual two- to three-year time frame, such as two to three years after reaching the age of majority for a child. For instance, most states say that the statute of limitations does not begin to run until the injured person reaches age 18. So, when a minor is injured, the minor may sue years after learning of the injury. While generally the court will appoint a *guardian ad litem*, an adult to act in the court on behalf of a child in litigation, the child does not have to sue through the *guardian ad litem*. Children may wait until they reach adulthood before suing an obstetrician and their healthcare assistants 18 years (plus the statute of limitations period, which varies slightly in each state) after a birth injury has occurred, assuming the parents hadn't already sued.

Med Tip

The statute of limitations is a state law that varies by state.

Good Samaritan Laws

Good Samaritan laws are state laws that can protect healthcare professionals and ordinary citizens who treat victims of an accident or medical emergency from liability and legal consequences. The emergency aid covered under this law must be given at the scene of the accident or emergency. These laws exist in most states to encourage such aid. However, with the possible exception of Vermont, there is no *legal* duty to assist a stranger in a time of distress. But the law does state that those who volunteer to help must exercise reasonable care and skill in rendering such aid. This law protects those professionals who do offer aid, outside of their work environment, in good faith, without gross negligence. "Good faith" is an abstract quality that is best defined as being faithful to one's duty or obligation. It is an honest belief that a person can provide aid to an emergency victim with no intention to defraud that victim. Under this law, emergency care must be provided without an expectation of payment.

The protection under this law has limits, which can vary from state to state. If an emergency provider performed an action that was grossly negligent and acted in a way that a reasonable person would know would harm the victim, the law's protection would be withdrawn and a lawsuit could then take place. This can be difficult to determine, however. For example, an older person with osteoporosis who receives chest compressions during cardiopulmonary resuscitation (CPR) might sustain fractured ribs that puncture their lungs. A reasonable person would also have provided CPR in the same manner with the same result. In this case, the emergency care would be covered under the Good Samaritan law even though the victim received an injury to their lungs.

Figure 3–3 Allied health bystanders assisting at the scene of an accident

Source: Corepics VOF/Shutterstock

Some states have provided additional protection under this law. For example, the Ohio Good Samaritan law extends protection to emergency medical technicians (EMTs) during ambulance runs. Because these laws vary from state to state, it is vital that every healthcare professional knows and understands the Good Samaritan laws in their own state.

Someone responding in an emergency situation is only required to act within the limits of acquired skill and training. For example, a nursing assistant would not be expected, or advised, to perform advanced emergency treatment that is considered within the scope and practice of a physician or nurse.

Even though trained healthcare professionals are generally not under a legal obligation to offer aid to an emergency victim, some believe they do have an ethical obligation. Their personal ethics set the guidelines for care provided in emergency situations. The statute of limitations applies when filing a case under this law, with the time period starting to run when the injury occurs or is identified by the victim.

Med Tip

The Good Samaritan laws do not protect physicians or their employees from liability while practicing their profession in their work environment. The laws are meant to encourage healthcare professionals to assist with emergencies outside of the work setting. Always check on the coverage of the Good Samaritan Law in your own state (Figure 3.3).

Respondeat Superior

Respondeat superior is a Latin phrase meaning, "let the master answer." Under the principle of *respondeat superior*, an employer is liable for acts of the employee within the scope of employment. What this means for physicians is that they are liable for negligent actions of the employees working for them even though the employer's conduct may be without fault. The employee's wrongful action must be within the scope of their employment. This means that the employer has assumed the right and obligation to control the employee's performance of duties.

Med Tip

Even though the doctrine of *respondeat superior* mainly refers to the employer, in all states both the physician and the employee may be liable.

In effect, when a physician delegates certain duties to staff employees—nurses, physician assistants, and medical assistants—the ultimate liability for the correct performance of those duties rests with the physician. For example, in the case of *Thompson v. Brent*, a medical assistant removed a cast from Thompson's arm with an electrically powered saw, known as a Stryker saw. While sawing through the cast, the medical assistant cut the plaintiff's arm, causing a scar almost the length of the cast and the width of the saw blade. The court held that even though the medical assistant was negligent in the use of the saw, the physician was liable for the assistant's actions under the doctrine of *respondeat superior* (*Thompson v. Brent*, 245 So.2d 751, La. Ct. App. 1971).

In similar cases, the courts have consistently found both the employer *and* the healthcare employee negligent. In the case of Goff v. Doctors General Hospital, the court held that the nurses who attended a mother in labor, and who knew that she was bleeding excessively, were negligent in failing to report the circumstances so that prompt measures could be taken to safeguard her life; she died at the hospital (*Goff v. Doctors General Hospital*, 333 P.2d 29, Cal. Ct. App. 1958).

In some cases, the hospital may also incur liability under this doctrine. The best known case in which a nurse failed to bring the condition of the patient to the doctor's attention was Darling v. Charleston Community Memorial Hospital. This case involved a minor patient who sued a hospital and a physician for allegedly negligent medical and hospital treatment, which resulted in the amputation of the patient's right leg below his knee. On November 5, 1960, the 18-year-old plaintiff broke his leg while playing football. At the hospital emergency room, his leg was set and placed in a cast, and he was hospitalized. He complained of great pain in his toes, which became swollen, dark, and eventually cold and insensitive. Over the next few days, the physician relieved the pressure in the cast by "notching" the cast and cutting it three inches above the foot. On November 8, the physician split both sides of the cast, cutting the patient's leg as the cast was removed. Blood and seepage were observed coming from the leg as the cast was removed. The plaintiff was eventually transferred to another hospital on November 19 under the care of a specialist. After several attempts to save the plaintiff's leg, it was finally amputated eight inches below the knee. The plaintiff's attorney contended that it was the nurses' duty to routinely check on the patient's leg circulation and that it was the hospital's duty to have a staff of qualified nurses at each patient's bedside who could detect leg gangrene and notify the medical team. If the physician failed to act, it was the duty of the nurse to then advise hospital authorities so that medical action could be taken. In this famous case, the court found liability existed on the part of all three: the physician, the hospital, and the nurse (*Darling v. Charleston Community Mem. Hosp.*, 211 N.E. 2d 253, 1965).

Employee's Duty to Carry Out Orders

Healthcare employees have a duty to interpret and carry out the orders of their employer/physician. They are expected to know basic information concerning procedures and drugs that may be used. The nurse or other healthcare professional has a duty to clarify the physician's orders when they are ambiguous or erroneous. If the procedure or drug appears to be dangerous for the patient, the healthcare professional has a duty to decline to carry out the orders and should immediately notify the physician. In the case of Cline v. Lund, a hospital was held liable for the death of a patient because a nurse failed to check the patient's vital signs every 30 minutes as ordered by the physician. The nurse also failed to notify the physician when the patient's condition became life threatening (*Cline v. Lund*, 31 Cal. App.3d 755, 1973).

Med Tip

Healthcare workers have a duty to be assertive and question orders that they believe are erroneous or appear to be harmful to the patient. They also have a duty to refuse to carry out orders that violate their own practice acts.

Scope of Practice

Every employee in a healthcare setting must clearly understand and work within the scope of practice for their discipline. **Scope of practice** refers to the activities a healthcare professional is allowed to perform as indicated in their licensure, certification, and/or training. This means that a nurse can legally, through licensure, provide care and treatment to patients that a medical assistant is not licensed or certified to perform. For example, in some states a nurse may be permitted to renew medical prescriptions, with the physician's knowledge and authority, to a pharmacy over the telephone. A medical assistant is not licensed to do this. A trained and certified medical assistant can draw a sample of blood from a patient and perform certain tests on the sample, such as drawing a sample of blood from a patient and performing a CLIA waived testing on the sample, such as a blood count. However, a nurse's aide is typically not qualified or certified to perform these procedures.

It is imperative that employees understand and practice within the guidelines of their profession. However, the physician/employer also has a responsibility to instruct members of the healthcare team to perform activities that are within their respective scope of practice.

In addition, a physician/employer must clearly designate a chain of command for the healthcare team, assigning a person to oversee the functions of the healthcare team. In some cases, the physician assumes this duty. However, a nurse manager may also be designated for this role. In some healthcare offices, medical assistants can assume this function due to the intensive administrative portion of their training. Each employee must understand the chain of command so that when a question occurs regarding patient treatment or procedure, there is a clear route for obtaining the correct answer. A clear chain of command provides a "fail-safe" mechanism so that no employees are left to make decisions that they are unqualified to make.

Med Tip

All employees must understand that there are limits to their authority when it comes to healthcare decisions. The ultimate decision always rests with the physician, provided it does not violate their professional practice.

Employer's Duty to Employees

Physicians/employers have a responsibility to provide a safe environment for their employees and staff. However, accidents and unforeseen incidents do happen while performing work-related tasks, such as theft, fires, auto accidents, and injuries from falls. Most physicians have liability insurance to cover any injuries or thefts occurring on the owner's grounds and within the buildings. They may also bond employees who handle money. **Bonding** is a special type of insurance made with a bonding company that covers employees who handle financial statements, records, and cash. If the employee embezzles (steals) money from the physician/employer, the physician can then recover the loss up to the amount of the bond.

Some physicians also carry liability insurance to cover an employee who has an automobile accident while conducting work-related business, such as making a bank deposit, for the employer.

Just as employers have a duty to provide a safe work environment, the employee has a duty to the employer to maintain this safe environment. Healthcare workers are, by the very nature of their work, surrounded with equipment and drugs that could be dangerous if misused. For example, employees must use caution when handling electrical equipment with multiple cords. Yanking an electrical cord out of the wall instead of gently pulling it out at the wall socket can result in an electric spark to occur. Even a simple act such as wiping up a spill on the floor can cause an injury if a "Wet Floor" sign is not posted. Most physicians' offices and all hospitals have a multitude of medications, including narcotics, that must be kept locked up at all times.

Risk Management

Risk management is a practice used to control or minimize the incidence of problem behaviors that might result in injury to patients and employees and ultimately to liability for the physician/employer. A key factor in risk management is to identify problem behaviors and practices in an organization such as a hospital or healthcare office. A plan of action is then put into practice to eliminate these problem behaviors. Risk management factors include environmental issues such as wet floors, improper grounding of electrical equipment, and poor security. Risk factors that affect employees include poor record keeping, improper storage of drugs and needles, improper follow-up for patient care, and abandonment of patients. Corrective actions for these factors are often addressed in updated policies and procedures

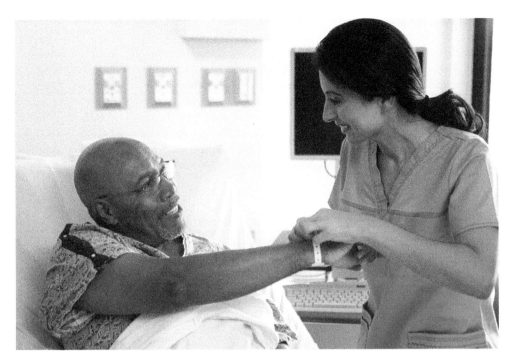

Figure 3–4 Occupational therapist verifies patient ID before beginning a therapy session
Source: Shutterstock

books and employee handbooks. Many offices and hospitals employ risk managers whose sole job is to oversee the practices and behaviors that might harm patients and even result in malpractice suits. But everyone in a healthcare institution—not just the risk manager—is responsible for risk management.

A fundamental element of risk management is patient identification. Before every interaction, healthcare providers must identify the patient using two identifiers. According to The Joint Commission, acceptable patient identifiers include the patient's name, telephone number, or date of birth; an assigned identification number; or another person-specific identifier. If the patient is wearing an identification band, that can be used as part of the identification process (see Figure 3.4).

Two of the most frequent accidental errors in healthcare are patient falls and medication errors. It is often difficult to know which patients may need assistance. Therefore, it is wise to prevent a possible problem by making sure that every patient is carefully observed when walking or moving in or out of bed or a wheelchair. A nurse or trained caregiver should always assist patients who are unsteady, frail, older, or have recently had surgery.

When performing medication administration, all medication orders must be checked for accuracy three times: once when selecting the medication; once prior to preparing the medication; and once more before administering the medication. This is known as the Triple Check method (or the Three Checks). In addition, the correct route of administration, as well as the time of dispensing the medication, must be recorded.

Medication errors have occurred for a variety of reasons, including the following:

- Inaccurate identification of patients
- Transcription errors when placing the drug name and dose into the patient's chart
- Failure to consider potential drug interactions and patient allergies
- Failure to double-check the dosage before administering a medication
- Administering the incorrect medication or dosage
- Administering a drug through the wrong route, or too early or late
- Administering an experimental medication without obtaining informed consent from the patient
- Illegible handwriting when charting

Med Tip

Remember the "Seven Rights" for administration of medications: right patient, right drug, right dose, right route, right time, right reason for the drug, and right documentation into the patient's chart.

Incident Report

One means of documenting problem areas within a hospital or other healthcare facility is the **incident report**. This report, using a form developed by the individual facility, should be completed whenever there is an unusual occurrence such as a fall, error in medication dispensing, needle stick, fire, or a patient or employee complaint. An incident report can be completed by anyone who observed or became aware of an unusual occurrence or incident such as an employee, manager, or healthcare provider. The purpose of the report is to document exactly what happened, when it happened, and what was done about the incident. The goal of using an incident report immediately after the situation happened is to accurately recall what happened as well as to prevent another incident. The incident report is not always part of the medical record; some facilities keep them separate.

Chapter 3 Review

Points to Ponder

1. If a patient who suffers from cirrhosis tells me in confidence that she has started drinking again, what should I do?

2. Does *respondeat superior* mean that I am fully protected from a lawsuit? Why or why not?

3. Does the Medical Practice Act in my state allow a registered nurse to prescribe birth control pills for patients? Why or why not?

4. What are the benefits for me to become a licensed or certified member of my profession?

5. What are the standards of care for patients I am responsible for and are they the same standards as my physician/employer are held to?

6. Am I protected by Good Samaritan laws if I perform CPR on a patient in a hospital emergency room waiting area and the patient dies?

7. Am I protected from a lawsuit if I have reported a medical emergency to my supervisor that I did not believe I was capable of handling?

8. If an injury occurred four years ago, am I protected from a lawsuit if the statute of limitations is two years in my state?

Discussion Questions

1. A patient collapses on the floor in your department (office) and you must administer CPR. If the patient is injured when you administer CPR, are you protected from a malpractice suit under the Good Samaritan laws?

2. Describe the process Clover Williams might use to become licensed to practice nursing when she moves from Chicago to New York.

3. Describe what *reasonable and prudent* means as it relates to standard of care.

Review Challenge

Short Answer Questions

1. What are some of the obligations an employee has to their employer as discussed in this chapter?

_____

_____

_____

_____

_____

2. Does the doctrine of *respondeat superior* always protect the employee? Explain why or why not.

_____

_____

_____

_____

_____

3. When does the "discovery rule" begin to "run"?

_____

_____

_____

_____

_____

4. What is the purpose of The Joint Commission?

_____

_____

_____

_____

_____

5. Explain the difference between endorsement and reciprocity for licensure.

_____

_____

_____

_____

_____

6. What does "standard of care" mean and why is it important?

_____

_____

_____

_____

_____

7. Explain the "prudent person rule" as it relates to the patient.

_____

_____

_____

_____

_____

8. Who or what determines the length of time for the statute of limitations?

_____

_____

_____

_____

_____

Matching

Match the responses in column B with the correct term in column A.

COLUMN A

_____ **1.** endorsement

_____ **2.** *guardian ad litem*

_____ **3.** revoked

_____ **4.** *respondeat superior*

_____ **5.** statute of limitations

_____ **6.** discovery rule

_____ **7.** reciprocity

_____ **8.** standard of care

_____ **9.** Good Samaritan Laws

_____ **10.** nonrenewal of license

COLUMN B

a. begins at the time the injury is noticed or should have been noticed

b. ordinary skill that healthcare practitioners use

c. "let the master answer"

d. court-appointed representative

e. law to protect the healthcare professional

f. period of time that a patient has to file a lawsuit

g. sanction

h. when a medical license is taken away

i. practicing medicine without a license

j. one state granting a license to a physician in another state

Multiple Choice

Select the one best answer to the following statements.

1. According to the Medical Patient's Rights Act, patient information

  a. may be given over the telephone without the patient's consent.

  b. must be communicated on a need-to-know basis.

  c. can always be given out to another physician.

  d. other than test results, cannot be given out to a relative.

  e. can never be given out to a third party.

2. The term for a court-appointed person to represent a minor or unborn child in litigation is

  a. *respondeat superior.*

  b. advanced directive.

  c. *guardian ad litem.*

  d. durable power of attorney.

  e. living will.

3. Standard of care refers to

   a. ordinary skill.

   b. type of care given to patients by other practitioners in the same locality.

   c. only the care given by the physician.

   d. a, b, and c

   e. a and b only

4. The statute of limitations varies somewhat from state to state but is typically

   a. ten years.

   b. five years.

   c. one to three years.

   d. There is no limitation.

   e. none of the above

5. *Respondeat superior* means that

   a. a healthcare employee can act independently of the employer.

   b. the healthcare employee is never found negligent by the courts.

   c. the employer is liable for the actions of the employee.

   d. healthcare employees have a duty to carry out the orders of their employers without question.

   e. all of the above

6. A process by which a physician in one state is granted a license to practice medicine in another state is

   a. endorsement.

   b. reciprocity.

   c. statute of limitations.

   d. revocation.

   e. suspension.

7. Patients' rights to have their personal privacy respected and their medical records handled with confidentiality is covered in the

   a. statute of limitations.

   b. rule of discovery.

   c. FLEX act.

   d. Medical Patient's Rights Act.

   e. Good Samaritan laws.

8. The prudent person rule refers to

   a. the needs of a medical assistant.

   b. the information that a reasonable patient would need.

   c. the type of employee that a physician would wish to hire in their office.

   d. the credentials for a malpractice attorney.

   e. None of the above is correct.

9. When a physician places an ambiguous order, the healthcare professional

   a. has a duty to carry out the order.

   b. can decline to carry out the order.

   c. should immediately notify the physician.

   d. b and c only

   e. None of the above is correct.

10. Both physicians and employees are

   a. liable in a lawsuit.

   b. have the same responsibility to protect patients' confidentiality.

   c. operate under a standard of care.

   d. must be trained to perform a procedure before attempting it.

   e. all of the above

Discussion Cases

1. Analyze the case at the beginning of this chapter, *"The Case of Latoya and the Physical Therapy Patient,"* by answering the following question:

   a. How can Latoya balance the benefits and harm of encouraging her patients to do something they do not want to do?

2. You are a phlebotomist drawing a specimen of blood from Emma Helm, who says she doesn't like having blood drawn. In fact, she tells you that the sight of blood makes her "queasy." You attempt to make her feel relaxed by quietly talking to her as you help her onto a chair in the hospital laboratory. While you are taking her blood specimen, she faints and hits her head against the side of a cabinet.

   a. Are you liable for Emma's injury? Why or why not?

   b. If you are not liable, do you know who is?

   c. Is Emma Helm at fault for her accident? Why or why not?

d. What might you do to prevent this type of injury from happening?

_____

_____

3. Jessica, a registered nurse (RN), and her husband were finally leaving on their vacation trip. They pull up to a red light as it is about to change to green. They watch in horror as a large truck, moving fast down a hill, is unable to stop before crashing into a van carrying a mother and her child. The van is thrown into the air and lands in a small park. Jessica runs over to offer aid. She finds a semiconscious woman in the driver's seat and an unconscious 4-year-old boy in the back seat strapped in his car seat. The mother asks Jessica if Christopher is all right before she slips into unconsciousness. Christopher is unconscious and not breathing, with his head down and chin touching his chest. He has a gash bleeding on the side of his head caused by his tricycle flying over the backseat during the crash.

A truck driver, who had also stopped to give help, yells in the window at Jessica, "Don't move him!" Jessica knows that she has to get Christopher's breathing started. Even though the truck driver is still yelling at her not to move the boy, with her index finger she gently lifts his head an inch up off his chest. Christopher, still unconscious, starts breathing immediately. Jessica stops the bleeding on his head by applying pressure using a clean handkerchief from her husband. Emergency help arrives 10 minutes later.

a. In your opinion, even though Jessica knew that, in most cases, an injured victim should not be moved, did she do the right thing by moving Christopher's chin up so he could breathe?

_____

_____

b. Was Jessica covered by the Good Samaritan Act, or was she held to a higher standard because she had a nursing license?

_____

_____

c. Would Jessica have been covered by the Good Samaritan Act if Christopher had not started breathing when she moved his head and he had suffered further injury from the movement?

_____

_____

d. Was Jessica, an RN, legally required to stop and provide aid? Was she ethically obligated to stop and provide aid?

_____

_____

e. In your opinion, is it always a good idea to stop and give assistance at an accident site before medical help arrives?

_____

_____

Put It Into Practice

Search the newspapers in your area for an article relating to medical malpractice or healthcare ethics issues. Discuss whether the standard of care was violated in the situation discussed in the newspaper.

Web Hunt

Using a search engine, find out about the Good Samaritan laws in your state.

Critical Thinking Exercise

What would you do if you were just certified in CPR last week and a woman collapsed in front of you on a very crowded bus? She does not appear to be breathing. No one on the bus does anything. You are worried that you will do something wrong and might even hurt her with chest compressions. Besides— everyone will be looking at you.

Bibliography

Badasch, S., & D. Chesebro. (2015). *Health science fundamentals* (2nd ed.). Pearson.

Beaman, N., Routh, K.S., Papazian-Boyce, L., et al. (2017). *Pearson's comprehensive medical assisting: Administrative and clinical competencies* (4th ed.). Pearson.

Brotherton, S., Kao, A., & Crigger, B.J. (2016). Professing the values of medicine: The modernized AMA *Code of Medical Ethics. JAMA*, 316(10):1041–1042. DOI:10.1001/jama.2016.9752

Cross, N., & D. McWay. (2022). *Stanfield's introduction to the health professions,* (8th ed.). Jones & Bartlett Learning.

Federation of State Medical Boards (FSMB). (2023). *About physician licensure.* https://www.fsmb.org/.

Garner, B.A. (2019). *Black's law dictionary* (11th ed.). Thomson Reuters.

National Council of State Boards of Nursing (NCSBN). (2024). Exams for the real world of nursing. https://ncsbn.org/nclex .page

Nurse Journal. (2023). Nurse practitioner practice authority: A state-by-state guide. https://nursejournal.org/nurse-practitioner/ np-practice-authority-by-state/

The Joint Commission. (2022). *Two patient identifiers—understanding the requirements.* https://www.jointcommission.org/standards/ standard-faqs/home-care/national-patient-safety-goals-npsg/ 000001545/#:~:text=Acceptable%20identifiers%20may%20 be%20the, of%20a%20unique%20patient%20identifier.

Venes, D. (2021). *Taber's cyclopedic medical dictionary* (24th ed.). F. A. Davis.

Working in Today's Healthcare Environment

Key Terms

Associate practice
Capitation rate
Certification
Conscience clause
Copayment
Corporation
Delegation
Diagnostic related groups (DRGs)
Exclusive provider organization (EPO)
Fee splitting

Fixed-payment plan
Gatekeeper
Group practice
Health Care Quality Improvement Act (HCQIA)
Health maintenance organization (HMO)
Indigent
Licensure
Managed care organization (MCO)
Medicaid

Medicare
Partnership
Per diem
Preferred provider organization (PPO)
Primary care provider (PCP)
Prospective payment system
Registration
Sole proprietorship
Solo practice
Third-party payers

Learning Objectives

After completing this chapter, you will be able to:

4.1 Define all key terms.

4.2 Describe how healthcare is paid for and delivered in the United States today.

4.3 State the differences between Medicare and Medicaid.

4.4 Discuss the similarities and differences among health maintenance organizations (HMOs), preferred provider organizations (PPOs), and exclusive provider organizations (EPOs).

4.5 Differentiate between physician-owned practices and professional corporations.

4.6 Identify the specialties of physicians.

4.7 List three categories of licensed nurses and describe their educational requirements.

4.8 Identify the various types of allied health professionals.

4.9 Describe the five A's of delegation.

The Case of Marion and the Pacemaker

Marion is a 92-year-old patient who weighs 78 pounds. She has had poor eating habits for at least 20 years. In addition, Marion had been a heavy smoker all her life and suffered frequent respiratory problems. During the past two years she has become quite forgetful, has suffered a broken hip as a result of a fall out of bed, and has been treated for pneumonia. In spite of Marion's protests, she is admitted to a nursing home. However, she quickly adjusts to her new home and likes the care and the attention that she receives.

During her third week in the nursing home, Marion develops a cough, high temperature, and respiratory problems. She is hospitalized with a diagnosis of pneumonia. The attending physician suggests that, in addition to treatment for pneumonia, Marion will also need to have a pacemaker inserted to regulate her heartbeat.

Marion clearly explained to her family her wishes not to receive extraordinary measures to prolong her life. She also signed a living will indicating her wishes. After thoughtful discussions with other family members, Marion's daughters tell the physician that they do not want to put their confused mother through the surgical procedure and the pain while recovering from the surgery. Further, they are concerned that their mother will not survive an anesthetic and surgical procedure in her frail condition.

The physician seems to be understanding of this decision. He says that he will place into Marion's chart their request not to have the pacemaker inserted. However, others on the healthcare team take the daughters aside on several occasions to tell them that this is not a dangerous procedure and that they should sign a permit for surgery. The healthcare team members make the daughters feel that they are not acting in their mother's best interests by not signing the surgical permit. Marion returns to the nursing home without a pacemaker. She lives another four years without any cardiac problems.

1. Were the other members of the healthcare team carrying out their responsibility as licensed healthcare professionals or were they overstepping their role?

2. Were Marion's daughters acting in the best interests of their mother in opposing the proposed pacemaker surgery?

3. What should happen when a physician agrees with the family members and the nursing staff does not?

Introduction

Today's healthcare professionals are immersed in an ever-changing environment. The use of for-profit health insurance companies, in the United States, the advent of managed care, a variety of medical practice arrangements, and a multitude of healthcare specialty areas have resulted in the continual need to understand healthcare law. Unfortunately, because of the rise in the number of malpractice suits, some primary care providers (PCPs) are protecting themselves by ordering multiple testing procedures, some of which might not be needed. In addition, many patients no longer want older, more conservative approaches to testing and diagnosis—and the newer tests may be more expensive.

As demonstrated in the chapter-opening case, all healthcare professionals need to pay attention to the wishes of their patients. And in circumstances where the patient has given family members or others authority to make a healthcare decision on their behalf, healthcare professionals must respect the patient's wishes. They also should use care not to place their own opinions ahead of the decisions made by physicians and other healthcare professionals in consultation with the patient. However, ethical dilemmas arise when the healthcare professional's moral and religious beliefs conflict with their role in healthcare. There are no easy, or perfect, answers to these dilemmas.

Delivery of Healthcare

The growth rate of the older adult population and the remarkable technological discoveries and applications, such as heart and kidney transplants and mobile mammogram units, are just a few of the developments that have caused a rapid expansion of the healthcare system. In addition, insurance companies, through managed care plans—such as **health maintenance organizations**, also known as HMOs, which stress preventive care and patient education—and government legislation have significantly impacted the way healthcare is delivered. Healthcare has also undergone major changes since 1965 when Medicare and Medicaid became law.

The United States spent over 4 trillion dollars on healthcare in 2021; However, this does not mean that everyone who lives in the United States is receiving good care, or even any care. We, as a nation, are far from the top in life expectancy at birth. With rising healthcare costs, many who live in the United States are concerned about the cost of services and access to healthcare. An ongoing critical issue is the crisis in health insurance coverage as many people do not have adequate insurance.

Health Insurance

Health insurance includes all forms of insurance against financial loss resulting from illness or injury. The U.S. private health insurance market was valued at 1.6 trillion dollars in 2022. The most common type of health insurance covers hospital care. Relatively new types of insurance are the fixed-payment plans. These are offered by organizations that operate their own healthcare facilities or that have made arrangements with a hospital or healthcare provider within a city or region. The **fixed-payment plan** offers subscribers (members) complete medical care in return for a fixed monthly fee. HMOs, for example, base their operations on fixed prepayment plans.

Insurance companies and other **third-party payers**, such as HMOs, recognize that persons who are well covered by medical insurance have no incentive to economize. Insurers, however, want to keep their costs for reimbursement as low as possible. Physicians may want to order more tests to avoid malpractice suits.

Patients want adequate tests and complete care. Keeping these differing viewpoints in mind, who then decides on the allocation of the health resources?

There are many types of insurance coverage in the United States. Healthcare is paid for in many complex ways by a variety of entities, some of which are listed below.

1. ***Employer-sponsored health insurance.*** Some employers provide group health insurance plans as part of their benefits package, usually to full-time employees only. Some also cover the families of employees. Most employer plans cover all employees, regardless of prior medical conditions. The Consolidated Omnibus Budget Reconciliation Act (COBRA) allows certain employees and their dependents to continue their employer-sponsored health insurance coverage for a limited period after leaving their job, experiencing a qualifying event (such as divorce or death of the employee), or having reduced work hours.

2. ***Government programs.*** Medicare is a federal health insurance program primarily for individuals over the age of 65 and those with end-stage renal disease. Medicaid is a joint state and federal program for low-income individuals and families as well as for people with disabilities. The income guidelines for Medicaid are very low, which means many working people struggle to find affordable health insurance. The Children's Health Insurance Program (CHIP) covers children in low-income families who do not qualify for Medicaid. Medicare and Medicaid are discussed in more detail in the following section.

3. ***Individual and family plans.*** Some individuals and families purchase health insurance through the Health Insurance Marketplace (the federal program of state-specific alternatives). Others purchase insurance directly from companies outside of the Marketplace. Individual and family plans can be very expensive, although ones bought through the Health Insurance Marketplace may be subsidized.

4. ***Veterans Health Administration.*** Veterans of the U.S. military may be eligible for healthcare services through the Veterans Affairs (VA) system.

5. ***Indian Health Service (IHS).*** American Indians and Alaska Natives may access healthcare services throughout the IHS, which provides medical care to eligible individuals the IHS offers healthcare services that respect the cultural traditions and values of their patient populations.

In the first three types of insurance, there is a complex array of options. Medicare and Medicaid recipients can choose from a variety of insurance providers within those programs. Employer-sponsored group plans can change periodically when employers seek a new, lower-cost plan or their insurer changes coverage. Both employer group plans and individual/family plans come with deductibles and co-pays (which are the responsibility of the patient to pay on top of their monthly premiums). But even with all of these options, in 2022, over 27 million Americans lack health insurance, many because they cannot afford even the most basic plans, even though they make too much money to qualify for Medicaid.

Federal Programs

Medicare

Medicare is the federal program that provides healthcare coverage for three groups of people: persons age 65 and over; disabled persons who are entitled to Social Security benefits or Railroad Retirement benefits; and patients with end-stage renal disease of any age (see Figure 4.1). The Medicare program is managed by the Centers for Medicare & Medicaid Services (CMS).

As a result of the rising costs of the Medicare program, a rationing of healthcare under Medicare has occurred.

Per the Medicare.gov website, in 2024, in addition to the patients' monthly premium for Part A (hospitalization coverage), they are required to pay a $1,632 deductible. After the deductible is paid, the patient's portion of hospital stays is as follows:

- Days 1–60: $0 after meeting Part A deductible.
- Days 61–90: A $408 coinsurance amount each day.
- After day 90: An $816 coinsurance amount each day while using 60 lifetime reserve days.

After using up all of lifetime reserve days, the person pays all costs (https://www.medicare.gov/coverage/inpatient-hospital-care).

Figure 4–1 A Medicare
health insurance card

Source: M.Shores/Alamy Stock Photo

These cost-saving devices result in a fixed allocation of healthcare services for many older adults who will not use a hospital or nursing home facility because they cannot afford the deductible payment. In many states, Medicare recipients cannot afford to also pay for supplemental insurance to cover costs not covered under Medicare.

Medicare patients have a right to appeal care that may be denied under existing Medicare rules and regulations. As a result of a court case, new rules by the Department of Health and Human Services for HMOs went into effect in August 1997. In the case of *Grijalva v. Shalala* (Donna Shalala was secretary of the department when the suit was filed), an Arizona court found that a 71-year-old Medicare patient was denied the right to appeal when her request for home healthcare was refused by her HMO. The judge ruled that the Department of Health and Human Services, which oversees Medicare, was at fault for failing to force HMOs to follow federal law that mandates allowing appeals when there are denials for treatment. Under the current rules, a Medicare patient in an HMO may appeal when there are denials for treatment (*Grijalva v. Shalala*, 946 F. Supp. 747, Ariz. 1996).

Med Tip

In 2006, Medicare added Part D, which helps cover the cost of outpatient prescription medications. But deductibles and co-pays still apply, and the high costs of medications for patients has meant that some older and disabled patients resort to splitting pills in two or skipping them entirely. In some cases, people with low income, who are older, or who have a disability have gone hungry in order to pay for their life-saving medications.

Diagnostic Related Groups

Another method of rationing healthcare was implemented in 1983, when Medicare instituted a hospital payment system—**diagnostic related groups**, also known as DRGs—that classifies each Medicare patient by illness. DRGs, now used for all patients, are designations that categorize diagnoses and treatments into groups that are used to identify reimbursement conditions. There are currently nearly 1,000 illness categories of medical conditions under the DRG system.

Hospitals receive a preset sum for treatment of an illness category, regardless of the actual number of "bed days" of care used by the patient. This method of payment provides a further incentive to keep costs down. However, it has also discouraged the treatment of severely ill patients because of the high costs associated with their care. In addition, patients are often discharged before they are ready to take care of themselves. This has resulted in hospital readmissions and, in some extreme cases, deaths that could have been prevented if the patient had remained under hospital supervision a few days longer.

Meaningful Use

The Health Information Technology for Economic and Clinical Health (HITECH) Act of 2009 has revolutionized the healthcare industry in the United States. These legislative and regulatory initiatives were introduced to promote the adoption and meaningful utilization of electronic health records (EHRs) to improve the quality, safety, and efficiency of healthcare delivery. Meaningful use, a pivotal component of the HITECH Act, refers to the use of certified EHR technology in a manner that improves patient care, enhances safety, and engages patients. It provides financial incentive for medical practices and corporations to use certified EHRs

1. in a meaningful manner, such as e-prescribing;
2. for electronic exchange of health information to improve quality of healthcare; and
3. to submit clinical quality and other measures for monitoring.

Medicaid

Medicaid is a federal program implemented by each state, with the federal government paying a percent of Medicaid expenditures, which varies by state. Enacted at the same time as Medicare, it provides financial assistance to states for insuring certain categories of the poor and **indigent** (a person without funds). There is a growing concern that Medicare and Medicaid operate at cross purposes, as they serve some of the same beneficiaries, and that better coordination of the two programs is needed. Cases of abuse and fraud are reported within both programs. For example, there are cases of physicians and others employed in the healthcare field submitting bills for reimbursement under these two programs for patients they have never treated.

Individual states enact their own legislation to direct the way funds such as Medicaid are spent. Ethical dilemmas surface as patients on Medicaid find they have little or no access to funds within their own state. For example (and this does unfortunately happen), hospitals have gotten themselves into trouble for discharging a patient too early. Hospitals have been found guilty for negligently discharging patients because adequate discharge planning was not implemented.

Medicaid patients in long-term-care facilities are required under the law to use their own excess income to help pay for their care. This means that they must use up their own income before Medicaid will assist them. This has proved to be a burden for married couples because it may impoverish the spouse as well as the patient. Some states have enacted laws in which the spouse may separate their financial resources from the patient's. In other words, the total amount of resources is divided in half so as not to leave the patient's spouse without a home or other resources. Some states offer nursing homes a **per diem**, or daily rate, payment for a patient's care. Other states may use a **prospective payment system** in which the payment amount or reimbursement for care is known in advance.

Managed Care

Managed care is a method for restructuring the healthcare system, including delivery of a broad range of services, financing of care, and purchasing. Managed care provides incentives to keep costs of healthcare down by using an administrative structure to manage the enrolled population of patients. The managed care movement is known for its goal of offering healthcare at lower costs and decreasing the amount of unnecessary medical procedures. Managed care provides a mechanism for a **gatekeeper**, such as a primary care provider or insurance company, to approve all patient referrals and nonemergency services, hospitalizations, or tests before they can be provided. **Primary care providers** (also known as PCPs, act in a gatekeeper capacity because they are responsible for the patient's healthcare and any referrals to other providers or services. However, patients can select any provider or specialist to treat them.

Med Tip

One of the fundamental principles of managed care is "managed choice." Patients have a choice about their medical care but only within certain parameters that are determined by the managed care organizations (MCOs).

Managed care organizations, also known as MCOs, pay for and manage the medical care a patient receives. One of the means an MCO uses to manage costs is to shift some of the financial risk back onto the physicians, advanced practice providers, and hospitals—when the costs go up, their income from the MCO goes down. This mechanism poses many ethical dilemmas. MCOs offer a variety of financial incentives, including bonuses to physicians for reducing the number of tests, treatments, and referrals to hospitals and specialists. These incentives can create a conflict of interest for physicians.

The offer of financial inducements to physicians who order fewer tests and hospitalizations for their patients is a widely discussed concern. Many fear that physicians may withhold services from patients in order to increase their own profits. Some of the reasons for these concerns are that MCOs attempt to limit the following:

- Choice of physician or other healthcare provider
- Treatments a physician or other healthcare provider can order
- Number and type of diagnostic tests that can be ordered
- Number of days a patient can stay in the hospital for a particular diagnosis
- Choice of hospitals
- Medications a physician or other healthcare provider can prescribe
- Referrals to specialists
- Choice of specialists
- Ordering of a second opinion for diagnosis and treatment

The managed care movement—with the implementation of health maintenance organizations (HMOs), preferred provider organizations (PPOs), and exclusive provider organizations (EPOs)—sought to bring healthcare costs under control by monitoring healthcare and hospital usage.

- **Health maintenance organization**, also known as an HMO—a type of managed care plan in which a range of healthcare services are made available to plan members for a predetermined fee (the **capitation rate**) per member, by a limited group of providers (such as physicians and hospitals). HMOs use a physician as the PCP to manage and control the enrolled patient's healthcare. This capitation rate replaced the former "fee-for-service" rate, which was considered to be more costly. The HMO places the PCP at some financial risk if there are excessive medical expenses involved in the patient's care.

- **Preferred provider organization**, also known as a PPO—a plan in which the patient uses a healthcare provider (physician or hospital) who is under contract with the insurer for an agreed fee in order to receive **copayment** from the insured. PPOs differ from HMOs in two main areas: (1) A PPO is a fee-for-service program not based on a prepayment or a fixed monthly fee paid to the healthcare provider for providing patient services (capitation rate) as with an HMO—physicians and hospitals designated as PPOs are reimbursed for each medical service they provide; and (2) PPO members are not restricted to certain designated physicians or hospitals.

- **Exclusive provider organization**, also known as an EPO—a new managed care plan that is a combination of HMO and PPO concepts. In an EPO, the selection of providers is limited to a defined group, but the providers are paid on a modified fee-for-service (FFS) basis. Unlike a PPO, there is no insurance reimbursement if nonemergency service is provided by a non-EPO provider.

Telehealth

Telehealth is the use of technology to deliver services when the practitioner and client are in different physical locations. The growth of the use of telehealth by healthcare teams was accelerated by the COVID-19 pandemic, which started in the United States in 2020. Physicians, APRNS, nurses, and allied health professionals used platforms such as Zoom for patient visits.

Occupational therapists, in particular, have made ample use of telehealth to deliver services to patients. Both the American Occupational Therapy Association (AOTA) and the World Federation of Occupational Therapists (WFOT) endorse the use of telehealth. Telehealth may be used to assess patients, determine and provide interventions, consult with patients or other providers, and for monitoring patients. Third-party payers have established definitions aligned with telehealth service models. The CMS expanded eligibility for OT practitioners to provide e-visits through telehealth to Medicare beneficiaries during the COVID-19 pandemic.

To provide telehealth services, a healthcare provider needs to understand the rules, considerations and reimbursement. For example, the technology used needs to be HIPAA compliant. Telehealth can be just audio to expand access to care in those areas where internet connections are not available, however not all services can be provided by audio per the Centers for Medicare & Medicaid. For Medicare patients, there is a specific list of telehealth services that can be provided. It is up to the healthcare provider to know what services can and cannot be provided by telehealth. This information changes frequently. Regulations of interstate licensure also change frequently. Documentation for reimbursement and for prescribing controlled substances need to be understood before engaging in telehealth services.

Med Tip

If you are tasked with providing telehealth services, make sure you know the regulations about telehealth in your organization and state.

Ethical and Legal Considerations

Ethical Dilemmas in Managed Care

Managed care, including Medicare and Medicaid, has many flaws. Because the basis for a managed care approach is an economic one of cost containment, those who know how to use the system will fare better. Patients who are well educated and/or have a high income may receive better care than patients who are not. For example, some Medicare patients may be able to carry a supplemental health insurance policy to cover the items, such as prescription medications and long-term care, that are not fully covered under Medicare. Other ethical considerations and questions concerning managed care include the following:

- Some physicians and other healthcare providers will not accept patients who are on Medicare. They are concerned that the reimbursement is not sufficient to treat patients who may require a great deal of care as they age.
- Many believe it is difficult, if not impossible, to provide a decent minimum standard of care or treatment to everyone under the managed care concept.
- Are all the families and patients who agree to a managed care contract at the closest clinic fully informed of the consequences of trying to obtain healthcare elsewhere?
- Is a bait-and-switch approach being used by the MCO in which the patient is lured into joining a managed care plan only to realize that only minimal services are provided in such areas as rehabilitation or long-term care?
- Are the patient's interests being sacrificed to the bottom line? In other words, does a profit for the MCO become more important than the patient?
- Do wealthy patients have better access to care and treatment?

Medicare and Medicaid laws prohibit physicians and other healthcare providers from referring their patients to any service, such as physical therapy or dialysis centers, in which they may have a financial ownership or interest. In addition, physicians and other healthcare providers must be cautious that their patient charges do not violate Medicare's fee-for-service reimbursement rule.

Managed care poses the question of how to maximize the services available to the maximum number of people. This ideal equity approach would bring access to healthcare for all at an appropriate level. This would result in a relationship between access, cost, and quality of care. However, changing any one of these three elements (access, cost, or quality of care) impacts the other two areas. For example, if we provide more access to care without increasing the cost, then quality will be negatively affected. If there is a proposal to increase quality and access to care, then there will be an increase in cost. In the current healthcare system, the public perception is that managed care has sacrificed quality and access for cost.

In spite of the potential problems with managed care, it is not an inherently unethical system of healthcare. Under this system, monitoring and control of the excessive use of testing and surgical procedures have improved. In addition, a reputable MCO can provide better preventive programs and healthcare screening for early detection of disease. It can also reduce the unnecessary testing, treatments, and hospitalizations that were present under the old fee-for-service system.

Conscience Clause

Because many employees in a variety of healthcare settings have religious or moral objections to assisting with certain procedures, such as sterilization and abortion, several states have enacted legislation called a **conscience clause**. These clauses state that hospitals may choose not to perform sterilization procedures and that physicians and hospital personnel cannot be required to participate in such procedures or be discriminated against for refusing to participate. In 1979, a Montana nurse-anesthetist was awarded payment (damages) from a hospital that violated the Montana conscience clause. The hospital had fired her for refusing to participate in a tubal ligation (*Swanson v. St. John's Lutheran Hosp.*, 579 P.2d 702, Mont. 1979).

On the other hand, there have been situations in which employees do not wish to leave their work setting even though they are morally unable to assist with sterilization or abortion procedures. In one New Jersey case, a court held that a hospital could transfer a nurse from the maternity ward to the medical-surgical staff because the nurse refused to assist in sterilization or abortion procedures. The court ruled that the transfer was not illegal because the nurse did not lose her seniority and it did not alter her pay (*Jeczalik v. Valley Hosp.*, 434 A.2d 90, N.J. 1981).

There are numerous examples of healthcare providers and patients clashing over the right to refuse to give treatment if it violates a person's beliefs. This conflict stimulates bitter debate over religious freedom versus patients' rights. Patients claim their rights are being ignored. Healthcare workers claim they are victims of religious discrimination when they are discharged or fired for refusing to provide service or care to patients. For example, a Chicago ambulance driver refused to transport a woman who was having an abortion, a Texas pharmacist refused to fill a prescription for a rape victim who was seeking the morning-after pill, and a California fertility clinic refused to give assistance to a gay woman who was requesting artificial insemination. Some respiratory therapists have objected to removing terminally ill patients from ventilators; gynecologists have declined to prescribe birth control pills; and some anesthesiologists have refused to provide anesthetics in sterilization procedures or to participate in executions.

Patient advocates claim that there is a long tradition in healthcare that healthcare professionals have an ethical, as well as a professional, responsibility to place the patient's needs first. Believers in a "right of conscience" or the "conscience clause" in medicine believe that U.S. citizens should not be forced to violate their moral and religious values. This debate is not new. Oregon's law in 1994 to legalize physician aid-in-dying allows doctors and nurses to decline to participate.

Med Tip

Do not share your views on politics, religion, or sexual or gender orientation with patients in the medical office or hospital.

Many such conflicts are quietly and informally handled. In some cases, an employee will seek a position elsewhere; in others, a coworker will step in to assist with a procedure, usually without the patient's even knowing of the change. The ethical dilemma facing both patients and healthcare workers becomes critical during an emergency. This is especially difficult in poor or rural areas where there are few options for care. There is currently no perfect solution, legal or otherwise, to this problem.

The Ethics of Fee Splitting

Fee splitting occurs when one physician offers to pay another physician for the referral of patients. Fee splitting has long been considered unethical and is a basis for professional discipline. The payment of a referral fee is also considered a felony in states such as Alaska, New Mexico, Vermont, and California. However, the most prohibitive statements against accepting a fee for referrals are at the federal level. The Medicare and Medicaid programs both contain anti-fraud and abuse provisions. These provisions declare that anyone who receives or pays any money, directly or indirectly, for the referral of a patient for service under Medicare or Medicaid is guilty of a felony punishable by five years' imprisonment, a $25,000 fine, or both.

Health Care Quality Improvement Act of 1986

Congress passed the **Health Care Quality Improvement Act**, also known as HCQIA, in response to a growing concern about medical malpractice. The act provides for peer review of physicians by other physicians and healthcare professionals. The act also provides protection from lawsuits (liability) that whistleblowers may face when they report issues of potential malpractice.

Types of Healthcare Practices

In the early part of the twentieth century, the main form of medical practice was the solo practice set up by a family practitioner within a designated town or geographic area. According to the American Medical Association, today, 49 percent work in physician-owned practices. The rest work fully or partially for a hospital, or health system. Over the years, the practice of medicine and the legal environment have changed. Few physicians make house calls any longer, but patients expect to be able to reach their physicians on a 24-hour basis.

Other forms of healthcare practice have become popular, including some that meet patient needs for around-the-clock coverage and some that provide the opportunity for a group of physicians and other healthcare providers to share insurance premium costs, staff, and facilities investments.

Physician-Owned Practices

There are may ways for physicians and advanced practice providers to set up their businesses.

- **Solo practices** are those where a professional practices alone. This is a common type of practice for dentists. However, physicians generally enter into agreements with other physicians to provide coverage for each other's patients and to share office expenses.

- **Sole proprietorship** is a type of solo practice in which one physician may employ other physicians and pay them a salary. However, the sole proprietor of the medical practice is still responsible for making all the administrative decisions. The physician–owner pays all expenses and retains all assets. The owner is responsible and liable for the actions of all the employees.

- **Partnerships** are a legal agreement to share in the business operation of a medical practice (Figure 4.2). A partnership may exist between two or more physicians. In this legal arrangement, each partner becomes responsible for the actions of all the other partners. This responsibility includes debts and legal actions unless otherwise stipulated in the partnership agreement. It is always advisable to have partnership agreements in writing. A document or "certificate of doing business as partners" is registered in the local county clerk's office. In addition, all the partners in the group share in the liabilities, even if only a few of the members are responsible for incurring them.

- **Associate practices** are legal agreements in which physicians agree to share a facility and staff but not the profits and losses. They do not generally share responsibility for the legal actions of each other, as in a partnership. The legal contract of agreement stipulates the responsibilities of each party. The physicians act as if their practice is a sole proprietorship.

- **Group practices** consist of three or more physicians who share the same facility (office or clinic) and practice medicine together. This is a legal form of practice in which the physicians share all

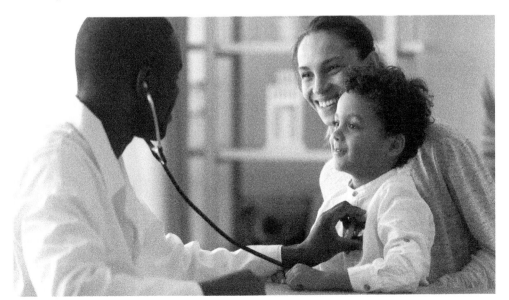

Figure 4–2 Pediatrician working in a partnership practice

Source: fizkes/Shutterstock

expenses and income, personnel, equipment, and records. A physician may be a member of a group practice as a partner or as an employee. Some areas of medicine frequently found in group practice are anesthesiology, rehabilitation, obstetrics/gynecology, radiology, and pathology. The membership of a group practice can be quite large, and thus it may be a difficult setting to work in for those who prefer to work alone. A group practice can be designated as an HMO or as an independent practice association (IPA). Group practices have grown rapidly during the last decade, and large groups of more than 100 doctors are not uncommon. A large group practice often forms a legal professional corporation.

Med Tip

Healthcare providers are moving away from solo practice and forming partnerships or corporations to better serve patient needs, share the costs of insurance, and, in the case of corporations, provide legal protection.

Professional Corporations

During the 1960s, state legislatures passed laws (statutes) allowing professionals—for example, physicians and lawyers—to incorporate. A **corporation** is managed by a board of directors. There are legal and financial benefits to incorporating the practice.

Professional corporation members are known as shareholders. Some of the benefits that can be offered to employees of a corporation include medical expense reimbursement, profit sharing, pension plans, and disability insurance. These fringe benefits may not always be taxable to the employee and are generally tax deductible to the employer. While a corporation can be sued, the individual assets of the members cannot be touched (as they can in a solo practice). In some cases, a physician in solo practice will take legal steps to incorporate in order to provide some protection of assets. A corporation will remain until it is dissolved. Other forms of practice, such as the sole proprietorship, end with the death of the owner. Today, most medical practices are corporations (Figure 4.3). Table 4.1 describes the types of medical practice along with the advantages and disadvantages of each.

Med Tip

Remember that in all forms of practice, the physician is responsible for the actions of all of their employees except for nurse practitioners.

Figure 4–3 Hospital owned by a healthcare system

Source: Shutterstock

Table 4–1 Types of Medical Practices

Type of Practice	Advantages for Physicians	Disadvantages for Physicians
Solo practice (only one physician)	Physician retains independence; simplicity of organization; physician retains all assets.	Difficulty raising capital; sole responsibility for liability and management functions; inadequate coverage of patients' needs; practice may die with the owner
Sole proprietorship	Physician retains all assets; autonomy; physician hires other physicians to provide assistance.	Pays all expenses; responsible for all liability
Partnership	Legal responsibility is shared among partners; work, assets, and income are shared.	Partners may have personality differences; all partners are liable for actions of the other partners.
Associate practice	Work is shared.	Legal responsibility is not shared by all members.
Group practice	All expenses and income are shared; all equipment and facilities are shared.	Income may not be as great as when a physician practices alone; possible personality clashes among members
Single specialty	Expenses and staff are shared.	Possible competition among specialists within the group
Corporation	Protection from loss of individual assets; many fringe benefits offered; corporation will remain until it is dissolved.	Income may not be as great as in other forms of practice.

Types of Healthcare Practitioners

There are specific requirements for all healthcare professionals, including licensure, certification, and registration as well as a means of establishing competency. In addition, programs for educating healthcare professionals may seek accreditation through such organizations as the The Joint Commission. (See more about The Joint Commission in Chapter 3.)

Licensure, generally issued at the state level, is a mandatory credentialing process that allows an individual to legally perform certain skills. As dictated by law, there is usually a requirement to pass certain tests and exhibit the ability to perform certain skills. For example, nurses and pharmacists must graduate from an accredited educational program and pass a national examination that shows competency in their chosen healthcare field. Licensed personnel including registered nurses, licensed practical nurses, and pharmacists are licensed in the state in which they practice. Licensed healthcare professionals can place their license in jeopardy, or can even lose their license to practice their profession, if they abuse drugs or alcohol, steal from their employer or patients, lie about their education and training, or commit a criminal act.

Certification is a voluntary credentialing process usually offered by a private professional organization, such as a school, college, or other accreditation body. Certification indicates that the health professional has met the standards set by the certification entity. The individual programs will have requirements to adequately perform certain skills. Certified, but not licensed, personnel include physician assistants or registered/certified medical assistants, certified medical transcriptionists, laboratory technicians, and ultrasound technologists.

The American Association of Medical Assistants (AAMA), founded in 1956, is a key association in the field of medical assisting. This organization is responsible for the medical assistants' certification process. Certification indicates that a candidate has met the standards of the AAMA by achieving a satisfactory test result. A certificate, or legal document, is issued to a person who has successfully passed the examination.

Registration indicates that a person whose name is listed on an official record or register has met certain requirements in their particular profession. The registry list of names can be accessed by healthcare providers to determine if a potential employee has met certain requirements. For example, registered nurses' names are listed in the registry of the state in which they hold a license. The American Medical Technologists (AMT) association provides oversight for the registration and testing of medical assistants, medical technologists, and phlebotomists. This association in cooperation with the AMT Institute for Education (AMTIE) has developed a continuing education (CE) program and recording system. The AMT, a nonprofit certifying body, provides a Registered Medical Assistant (RMA) certification for medical assistants who meet the eligibility requirements and who can prove their competency to perform entry-level skills through written examination. The RMA is awarded to candidates who pass the AMT certification examination.

Non-physician health professionals cannot practice outside of their own licensure, scope of practice and expertise. If one acts outside the area of their competency and the patient is injured as a result, that healthcare professional is liable for a charge of malpractice or, in other terms, medical negligence. If found to have committed malpractice, the healthcare professional could be fined and/or lose their license or certification. For example, it is against the law for a licensed practical nurse (LPN) or medical assistant to prescribe medications; this function lies only within the domain of a physician, nurse practitioner, or physician assistant. A phlebotomist is not licensed to discuss the results of a patient's laboratory tests with the patient; only certain healthcare providers are licensed to interpret and discuss this information with the patient.

Physicians

Of the 14 million people employed in the healthcare system, there are approximately 1 million physicians, of which only 250,000 practice primary care (family medicine, internal medicine, obstetrics, and pediatrics). By the year 2030, there will be a significant demand for more primary care physicians. The majority of physicians work in specialty fields such as anesthesiology, endocrinology, neurology, or a surgical specialty. Many physicians now work in salaried staff positions in hospitals, as members of group practices, for a corporate-sponsored medical care firm, or for community clinics.

Currently, 23 specialty boards are covered by the American Board of Medical Specialists. Included among these specialties are the American Board of Allergy and Immunology, American Board of Anesthesiology, American Board of Emergency Medicine, American Board of Internal Medicine, American Board of Surgery, and American Board of Urology. The specialty boards seek to improve the quality of medical care and treatment by encouraging physicians to further their education and training. The board evaluates the qualifications of candidates who apply and pass an examination. The physicians who pass the board review become certified as diplomats. As board-certified physicians, they may be addressed as either diplomats or fellows, a designation they can use after their name—for instance, Keesha Williams, MD, Diplomat of the American Board of Pediatrics.

The American College of Surgeons also confers a fellowship degree upon applicants who have completed additional training and submitted documentation of 50 surgical cases during the previous three years. A successful candidate becomes a Fellow of the American College of Surgeons (FACS). The American College of Physicians offers a similar fellowship and entitles the applicant to become a Fellow of the American College of Physicians (FACP) in a nonsurgical area.

Due to the dramatic advances in medicine over the past two decades, there continues to be an interest in specialization among physicians. A description of some of the more common medical and surgical specialties is found in Table 4.2.

Med Tip

It's important that the physician's support staff, including advanced practice providers, nurses, certified medical assistants, and technicians, understand the different medical specialty categories because they are often the ones who respond to patients' questions regarding these specialties.

The designation doctor (Dr.) is the proper way of addressing—verbally or in writing—someone who holds a doctoral degree of any kind. In the medical field, the title of doctor indicates that a person is qualified to practice medicine within the limits of the degree received; in other fields, the title means that a person has attained the highest educational degree in that field. Several designations for doctor are listed in Table 4.3.

Med Tip

The term *doctor* comes from the Latin word *docere*, meaning "to teach."

Table 4–2 Medical and Surgical Specialties

Medical Specialty	Description
Adolescent medicine	Treats patients from puberty to maturity (ages 11 to 21)
Allergy and immunology	Treats abnormal responses or acquired hypersensitivity to substances with medical methods such as testing and desensitization
Anesthesiology	Deals with administration of both local and general drugs to induce a complete or partial loss of feeling (anesthesia) during a surgical procedure
Bariatric medicine	Focuses on the causes, prevention, and treatment of obesity
Cardiology	Treats cardiovascular disease (of the heart and blood vessels)
Dermatology	Treats injuries, growths, and infections to the skin, hair, and nails
Emergency medicine	Focuses on the ability and skills to quickly recognize, prioritize (triage), and treat acute injuries, trauma, and illnesses
Endocrinology	Branch of medicine involving diagnosis and treatment of conditions and diseases of the endocrine glands
Family practice	Primary care provider who treats the entire family regardless of age and gender
Geriatric medicine	Focuses on the care of diseases and disorders of older adults
Hematology	Specializes in blood and blood-forming tissues
Hospitalists	Specializes in caring for patients while they are in the hospital; usually trained in internal medicine or family medicine
Infection control	Focuses on the prevention of infectious disease by maintaining medical asepsis, practicing good hygiene, and promoting immunizations
Internal medicine	Primary care provider who treats adults who have healthcare problems
Nephrology	Specializes in pathology of the kidney, including diseases and disorders
Neurology	Treats the nonsurgical patient who has a disorder or disease of the nervous system
Nuclear medicine	Specializes in the use of radioactive substances for the diagnosis and treatment of diseases such as cancer
Obstetrics and gynecology	Obstetricians treat pregnant patients through prenatal care, labor, delivery, and the postpartum period; gynecologists provide medical and surgical treatment of diseases and disorders of the female reproductive system; both are considered primary care providers
Oncology	Treats benign tumors and cancer-related tumors
Ophthalmology	Treats disorders of the eye
Orthopedics	Specializes in the prevention and correction of disorders of the musculoskeletal system
Otorhinolaryngology (ENT)	Specializes in medical and surgical treatment of the ear (otology), nose (rhinology), and throat (laryngology)
Pathology	Specializes in diagnosing abnormal changes in tissues that are removed during surgery or an autopsy
Pediatrics	Primary care provider who specialize in the care and development of children
Physical medicine/ rehabilitative medicine	Treats patients after they have suffered an injury or disability
Preventive medicine	Focuses treatment on the prevention of both physical and mental illness or disability
Psychiatry	Specializes in the diagnosis and treatment of patients with mental, behavioral, or emotional disorders
Radiology	Specializes in the study of tissue and organs based on X-ray visualization
Rheumatology	Treats disorders and diseases characterized by inflammation of the joints, such as arthritis
Surgery	Corrects illness, trauma, and deformities using an operative procedure
Surgical Specialty	**Description**
Cardiovascular	Surgically treats the heart and blood vessels
Colorectal	Surgically treats the lower intestinal tract (colon and rectum)
Cosmetic/plastic surgery	Surgically reconstructs underlying tissues
Hand	Surgically treats defects, traumas, and disorders of the hand
Neurosurgery (CNS)	Surgically intervenes for diseases and disorders of the central nervous system
Oral (periodontics/ orthodontics)	Treats disorders of the jaws and teeth by means of incision and surgery as well as tooth extraction; treats malocclusion (misalignment) of teeth
Orthopedic	Surgically treats musculoskeletal injuries and disorders, congenital deformities, and spinal curvatures
Thoracic	Surgically treats disorders and diseases of the chest

Table 4–3 Designations and Abbreviations for Doctors

Designations	Abbreviations
Doctor of Chiropractic	DC
Doctor of Dental Medicine	DMD
Doctor of Dental Surgery	DDS
Doctor of Education	EdD
Doctor of Medicine	MD
Doctor of Optometry	OD
Doctor of Osteopathy	DO
Doctor of Philosophy	PhD
Doctor of Podiatric Medicine	DPM

Advanced Practice Providers

Physician Assistants

Physician assistants (PAs) assist the physician in the primary care of the patient. They have education similar to a master's level program, and they must work or have internship experience and pass an accreditation exam. Most PAs work independently and have their own patient caseloads, while operating within the scope of work determined by the state in which they practice.

Nurse Practitioners and Other Advanced Practice Nurses

Nurse practitioners (NPs) have either a master's or doctoral degree along with advanced clinical training and licensure. In some states NPs can practice independent of physician oversight; in other states, a collaborative practice agreement with at least one physician is required. Nurse practitioners can have their own patient panel and work in a wide variety of settings including hospitals, clinics, public healthcare departments, urgent care sites, and private practices. There are other advance practice registered nurses, or APRNs, including Certified Nurse Midwives, Clinical Nurse Specialists, Certified Registered Nurse Anesthetists, and Pediatric Nurse Practitioner. The scope of practice of these other APRNs depends upon education and licensure. Scope of practice is determined at the state level.

Nurses

Registered Professional Nurses (RN), Licensed Practice Nurses (LPNs) and Licensed Vocational Nurses (LVN), have undergone education and training as prescribed by the state which they practice and passed a licensing exam administered by the National Council of State Boards of Nursing. Nursing is the largest of all the healthcare professions with about 5.2 million registered nurses (RNs).

The practice of nursing encompasses a wide array of skills, tasks, and responsibilities. Nursing involves the collaborative care of patients of all ages, both sick and well, in settings ranging from home care to schools to hospitals. Nurses promote health, prevent illness, educate patients, and care for those who are sick, disabled, or dying. They are advocates, participate in research, and help shape public policy. (See Table 4.4 for a description of types of nurses.)

Allied Health Professionals

Accreditation agencies for allied health educational programs for programs such as medical assisting, emergency medical technician (EMT), anesthesiology assistant, and medical illustration include the Commission on Accreditation of Allied Health Education Programs (CAAHEP) and the Accrediting Bureau of Health Education Schools (ABHES). This accreditation, which is voluntary, requires that the educational facilities maintain particular standards that usually include an internship. (See Table 4.5 for a description of allied health occupations.) Professions such as PT and OT have their own accrediting agencies.

Table 4–4 Types of Nurses

Type of Nurse	Description	Key Responsibilities
Licensed practical nurse (LPN)/ Licensed vocational nurse (LVN)	LPNs and LVNs support the care of patients while working under the supervision of an RN, APRN, or physician.	• Check and document vital signs, looking for improvement or deterioration • Perform basic nursing functions such as changing bandages • Ensure the comfort of patients • May administer medications
Registered nurse (RN)	RNs have an associate or bachelor's degree in nursing, have passed the NCLEX test for certification, and are the backbone of healthcare in the United States.	• Perform physical exams and take health histories • Provide health promotion and education • Administer medications and other interventions • Coordinate care in collaboration with the healthcare team
Advanced practice registered nurse (APRN)	APRNs have a master's or doctoral degree. They provide primary and preventive healthcare. There are many specialist roles, including: • Nurse practitioner (NP) • Certified nurse-midwife (CNM) • Clinical nurse specialist (CNS) • Certified registered nurse anesthetist (CRNA)	• NPs diagnose and treat patients, prescribe medication. • CNMs provide gynecological care and deliver babies. • CNSs treat patients with various physical and mental health problems. • CRNAs administer anesthetics for surgical and medical procedures.

Table 4–5 Selected Allied Health Professions

Occupation	Description
Certified Medical Assistant (CMA)	Duties are grouped into two categories: administrative and clinical; works in a variety of healthcare settings including physicians' offices and clinics; must pass a national certification exam
Certified Medical Transcriptionist (CMT)	Types dictation recorded by a physician or surgeon; must pass a certification exam; works in medical records departments in hospitals and other healthcare facilities
Certified Professional Coder (CPC)	Evaluates medical orders using the Healthcare Common Procedure Coding System (HCPCS) and ICD-10-CM coding manuals used for billing purposes
Dental Assistant	Works under the supervision of a dentist to prepare the patient for treatment, take dental X-rays, and hand instruments to the dentist
Dental Hygienist	Works directly with the dental patient to clean teeth, take X-rays, and discuss results of the patient's dental exam with the dentist
Electrocardiograph Technologist	Operates electrocardiograph (ECG) machines to record and study the electrical activity of the heart
Emergency Medical Technician (EMT) / Paramedic	Provides emergency care and transports injured patients to a medical facility; works for ambulance service or a hospital; paramedics are have more education and are certified to provide advanced medical procedures such as endotracheal intubation, manual defibrillation, and administering drugs through intravenous access
Laboratory or Medical Technologist (MT)	Performs laboratory analysis, directs the work of laboratory personnel, and maintains quality assurance standards for all equipment; also referred to as clinical laboratory scientist
Medical Records Technician	Skilled in health information technology; maintains medical records in healthcare institutions and medical practices
Occupational Therapist (OT)	Provides treatment to people who are physically, mentally, developmentally, or emotionally disabled in the area of personal care skills with the goal to restore the patient's ability to manage activities of daily living

Table 4–5 *(Continued)*

Occupation	Description
Occupational Therapy Assistant (OTA)	Help patients develop, recover, and improve activities of daily living, working under the direction of an OT
Pharmacy Technician	Prepares and dispenses patient medications
Phlebotomist	Draws blood from patients; certification is required in some states
Physical Therapist (PT)	Provides exercise and treatment of diseases and disabilities of the bones, joints, and nerves through massage, therapeutic exercises, heat and cold treatments, and other means
Physical Therapy Assistant (PTA)	Provides limited physical therapy to patients, working under the direction of a PT
Registered Medical Assistant (RMA)	This allied professional generally works in an ambulatory healthcare setting; must have at least five years of experience and on-the-job training or a medical assisting degree
Respiratory Therapist (RT)	Evaluates, treats, and cares for patients who have breathing abnormalities
Social Worker	Provides services and programs to meet the special needs of the ill, physically and mentally challenged, and older adults
Speech and Language Pathologist (SLP)	Work to prevent, assess, diagnose, and treat speech, language, social communication, cognitive communication, and swallowing disorders
Surgical Technician	Trained in operating room procedures and assists the surgeon during invasive surgical procedures
Ultrasound Technologist	Uses inaudible sound waves to outline shapes of tissues and organs
X-Ray Technologist (radiologic technologist)	Uses medical equipment to create images of patients' bodies

Med Tip

Patients often refer to anyone wearing scrubs, a white laboratory coat, or a white uniform as "doctor" or "nurse." Always correct patients and tell them exactly what your position is. If you are a student, be sure to wear an identifying badge so that you will not be asked to perform an action outside of your scope of practice.

The Delegation of Duties

The **delegation** of duties in healthcare is the transfer of responsibility for a patient's care from one healthcare team member who is in charge of the patients or medical unit to another team member. The ability to delegate or transfer an obligation to perform care to a patient does not free the person doing the delegation from a duty to see that the care is correctly performed.

The five rights of delegation, and questions to ask yourself about each one, are as follows:

1. *Right task*: Is the task to be delegated within the person's scope of practice?
2. *Right circumstances*: Do the circumstances allow for delegation of the task?
3. *Right person*: Is this the right person, or would another qualified person be better to delegate to?
4. *Right direction/communication*: Is the direction provided correct?
5. *Right supervision/evaluation*: Is the follow up after the task is completed appropriate?

Chapter 4 Review

Points to Ponder

1. What impact will managed care have upon your career as an allied health professionals?

2. What type of practice does your physician/employer have? If it is not a solo practice, what are the other specialties involved in the practice?

3. What are the advantages of forming a corporation?

4. Why is it important to include the medical specialty and initials indicating a particular degree or license after a physician's name?

5. What should you say if a patient refers to you as "doctor" or "nurse" even though your degree is in another discipline?

6. How should healthcare plans balance the interests of all the enrolled patients with the interests of a patient who has special medical needs and extraordinary expenses?

7. In the interest of maintaining a successful practice, should a physician refuse to provide care for patients who are uninsured or minimally insured?

8. Consider the question of ethics that arises when we ask ourselves if we are reducing unnecessary tests, as the HMOs and others believe we should, or if we are limiting tests for patients who really need them.

Discussion Questions

1. Discuss your role as a nurse or allied health professional in relation to the physician and advanced practice providers.

2. Discuss the impact that managed care is likely to have on your career in healthcare.

3. What can be done to ensure that MCOs provide ethical care for all patients?

4. Discuss "managed choice" as described in this chapter. Is there a choice?

Review Challenge

Short Answer Questions

1. What are the differences between Medicare and Medicaid?

_____

_____

_____

_____

_____

2. Describe the five rights of delegation.

_____

_____

_____

_____

_____

3. Explain the differences between HMOs and PPOs.

_____

_____

_____

_____

_____

4. Explain the titles for the following abbreviations:

DPM _____

OD _____

DO _____

DMD _____

MD _____

DC _____

5. Explain the titles for the following abbreviations:

NP _____

CMT _____

CMA _____

RT _____

PT _____

OTA _____

PA _____

RMA _____

6. Explain the differences between licensure, certification, and registration.

_____

_____

_____

_____

_____

7. What is the purpose of a conscience clause?

_____

_____

_____

_____

_____

8. What is the concept of Meaningful Use?

_____

_____

_____

_____

_____

9. Explain the difference between a per diem payment system and a prospective payment system.

_____

_____

_____

_____

_____

Matching

Match the responses in column B with the correct term in column A:

COLUMN A

_____   1. HMO

_____   2. EPO

_____   3. PPO

_____   4. solo practice

_____   5. associate practice

_____   6. sole proprietorship

_____   7. corporation

_____   8. third-party payer

_____   9. Medicaid

_____   10. Medicare

COLUMN B

a. preferred provider organization

b. physicians agree to share expenses of a facility

c. health maintenance organization

d. managed by a board of directors

e. financial assistance for older adults

f. exclusive provider organization

g. one physician may employ others

h. financial assistance for the indigent

i. physician practices alone

j. insurance company

Multiple Choice

Select the one best answer to the following statements.

1. Under this plan, a healthcare provider is paid a set amount based on the category of care provided to the patient.

   a. AMA

   b. DRG

   c. ANA

   d. HHS

   e. UNOS

2. Medicare patients who are members of HMOs may now, by law,

   a. not make any deductible payment.

   b. select any physician they wish.

   c. appeal a denial of treatment.

   d. have all their nursing home expenses paid.

   e. none of the above

3. A type of managed care in which the selection of providers is limited to a defined group who are all paid on a modified fee-for-service basis is a(n)

   a. exclusive provider organization.

   b. group practice.

   c. preferred provider organization.

   d. health maintenance organization.

   e. sole proprietorship.

4. A legal agreement in which physicians agree to share a facility and staff but not the profits and losses is a(n)

   a. solo practice.

   b. sole proprietorship.

   c. partnership.

   d. associate practice.

   e. none of the above.

5. The advantage of a corporation is that it

   a. offers protection from loss of individual assets.

   b. may offer fringe benefits.

   c. will remain in effect after the death of a member.

   d. offers the opportunity for a large increase in income.

   e. a, b, and c only

6. A physician who is board certified may be addressed as

   a. diplomat.

   b. fellow.

   c. partner.

   d. associate.

   e. a and b only

7. MCOs are able to manage costs by

   a. shifting some financial risk back to the physicians.

   b. shifting some financial risk back to the hospitals.

   c. using a fee-for-service payment method.

   d. a and b only.

   e. a, b, and c

8. This federal legislation provides healthcare for indigent persons and is administered by individual states.

   a. Medicare

   b. Medicaid

   c. HMO

   d. PPO

   e. COBRA

9. The managed care system

   a. has a gatekeeper to determine who will receive medical treatments.

   b. provides a mechanism for approval for all nonemergency services.

   c. provides care for a fixed monthly fee.

   d. includes HMOs, PPOs, and EPOs.

   e. all of the above

10. Which of the following is not a registered nurse?

    a. NP

    b. LPN

    c. CNA

    d. CNM

    e. b and c

Discussion Cases

1. Ryan McCall is Dr. Williams's office assistant. He has received professional training as both a medical assistant and an LPN. He is handling all the phone calls while the receptionist is at lunch. A patient calls and says he must have a prescription refill for Valium, an antidepressant medication, called in right away to his pharmacy because he is leaving for the airport in 30 minutes. He says that Dr. Williams is a personal friend and always gives him a small supply of Valium when he has to fly. No one except Ryan is in the office at this time. What should he do?

   a. Does Ryan's medical training qualify him to issue this refill order? Why or why not?

   b. Would it make a difference if the medication requested were for control of high blood pressure that the patient critically needs on a daily basis? Why or why not?

   c. If Ryan does call in the refill and the patient has an adverse reaction to it while flying, is Ryan protected from a lawsuit under the doctrine of *respondeat superior*?

   d. What is your advice to Ryan?

2. Allison G. has asked her doctor to prescribe a "morning-after" pill to prevent a pregnancy from taking place. Her doctor, Dr. Oberlin, tells her that he cannot prescribe this pill, which has the ability to abort a pregnancy, based on his own moral beliefs and conscience. Allison tells his medical assistant, Amy, that she thinks it is very wrong of Dr. Oberlin to impose his religious beliefs upon his patients. She says that he should not have become a physician if he could not separate his personal values from patient care.

a. In your opinion, what should Amy say to the patient?

_____

_____

b. Should Dr. Oberlin let his patients know what his religious beliefs are when they become his patient? Why or why not?

_____

_____

c. Is there an ethical or legal problem with Dr. Oberlin's action?

_____

_____

3. Joaquin tells his father that he wishes to study to be a Physician Assistant (PA). He says, "It's a great field. I can work independently and do almost everything the doctor does without having the high cost of malpractice insurance."

a. Is Joaquin's statement to his father correct?

_____

_____

b. What does a PA do?

_____

_____

c. Will Joaquin work independently of a physician if he becomes a PA?

_____

_____

Put It Into Practice

Interview one or more older adults and ask about their health insurance needs. Do they have difficulty with the paperwork required by the insurance company? Ask what could be done to make this a less difficult task.

Web Hunt

Discuss the type of information that is available on the website for the American Medical Association (**www.ama-assn.org**).

Critical Thinking Exercise

What would you do if you are processing billing statements for patients and notice that your physician/employer has entered patient charges for relatively minor procedures that were never done?

Bibliography

American Medical Association. (2021). AMA analysis shows most physicians work outside of private practice. https://www.ama-assn.org/press-center/press-releases/ama-analysis-shows-most-physicians-work-outside-private-practice. Accessed 9/12/2023.

Beaman, N., Routh, K.S., Papazian-Boyce, L., et al. (2017). _Pearson's comprehensive medical assisting: Administrative and clinical competencies_ (4th ed.). Pearson.

Cross, N., & McWay, D. (2022). _Stanfield's introduction to health professions_ (8th ed.). Jones & Bartlett Learning.

Fremgen, B., & Frucht, S. (2019). _Medical terminology: A living language_ (7th ed.). Pearson.

Hall, M., & Orentlicher, D. (2020). _Healthcare law and ethics in a nutshell._ West Academic Publishing.

Health Resources & Services Administration (HRSA). (2022). _Primary care workforce projections._ https://bhw.hrsa.gov/data-research/projecting-health-workforce-supply-demand/primary-health

Montoya, D.F., Chehal, P.K., & Adams, E.K. (2020). Medicaid managed care's effects on costs, access, and quality: An update. _Annual Review of Public Health_, 41:537-549. https://www.annualreviews.org/doi/10.1146/annurev-publhealth-040119-094345

Namburi, N. & Tadi, P. (2023). _Managed care economics._ StatPearls. https://www.ncbi.nlm.nih.gov/books/NBK556053/

Telehealth.HHS.gov. (2023). _Telehealth policy._ https://telehealth.hhs.gov/providers/telehealth-policy

Telehealth.HHS.gov. (2023). _Billing for telehealth._ https://telehealth.hhs.gov/providers/billing-and-reimbursement

Part 2

The Healthcare Environment

Chapter 5   The Patient Relationship

Chapter 6   Professional Liability and Medical Malpractice

Chapter 7   Public Duties of the Healthcare Professional

Chapter 8   Workplace Law and Ethics

Chapter 9   The Medical Record

Chapter 10   Patient Confidentiality and HIPAA

The Patient Relationship

Learning Objectives

After completing this chapter, you will be able to:

5.1 Define the key terms.

5.2 Describe the rights and responsibilities of physicians and advanced practice providers.

5.3 Describe the duties of all healthcare professionals.

5.4 Describe the rights and responsibilities of patients.

5.5 Describe the difference between consent and implied consent.

5.6 Outline the various components of advance directives.

Key Terms

Abandonment

Advance directive

Against medical advice (AMA)

Agent

Consent

Do not resuscitate (DNR)

Durable power of attorney

Implied consent

In loco parentis

Incompetent patient

Informed (or expressed) consent

Living will

Medical orders for life-sustaining treatment

Minor

Noncompliant patient

Parens patriae authority

Patient Self-Determination Act (PSDA)

Privileged communication

Proxy

Uniform Anatomical Gift Act

The Case of David Z. and Amyotrophic Lateral Sclerosis

David, who has lived with a diagnosis of ALS for 20 years, is now hospitalized in a private religious hospital on a respirator. He spoke with his physician before he became incapacitated and asked that he be allowed to die if the suffering became too much for him. The physician agreed that, while he would not give David any medications to assist a suicide, he would discontinue David's respirator if asked to do so. David has now indicated through a prearranged code of blinking eye movements that he wants the respirator discontinued. David had signed his living will before he became ill, indicating that he did not want extraordinary means keeping him alive.

The nursing staff has alerted the hospital administrator about the impending discontinuation of the respirator. The administrator tells the physician that this is against the hospital's policy. She states that once a patient is placed on a respirator, the family must seek a court order to have them removed from this type of life support. In addition, it is against hospital policy to have any staff members present during such a procedure. After consulting with the family, the physician orders an ambulance to transport the patient back to his home, where the physician discontinues the life support.

1. What were the primary concerns of the hospital?

2. What was the physician's primary concern?

3. When should the discussion about the patient's future plans have taken place with the hospital administrator?

Introduction

The relationship between the patient and their primary healthcare provider impacts the entire healthcare team. The relationships between nurses and allied health professionals and their patients are equally important. All healthcare professionals who interact with the patient must understand their responsibilities to both the patient and the provider.

In order for a good patient relationship to exist, both the provider and the patient must agree to form a contract for services. After a physician or advanced practice provider has agreed to treat a patient, the

Figure 5–1 The provider–patient relationship spans all ages

Source: michaeljung/Shutterstock

patient can expect that the provider will do so for as long as necessary (Figure 5.1). In order to receive proper treatment, the patient must confide truthfully in the provider. Failure to do so may result in serious consequences for the patient, and the provider is not liable if the patient has withheld critical information. Healthcare personnel who work closely with physicians and advanced practice providers, such as nurses and medical assistants, must keep in mind that the provider–patient relationship is one to be closely guarded. Any patient information that is either overheard or read is always to be considered confidential.

Provider's Rights and Responsibilities

Physicians (and advance practice providers, depending on the state in which they practice) have the right to select the patients they wish to treat. They also have the right to refuse service to patients. From an ethical standpoint, most providers treat patients who need their skills. This is particularly true in cases of emergency.

Providers in physician-owned practices may also state the type of services they will provide, the hours their offices will be open, and where they will be located. The provider has the right to expect payment for all treatment provided, and a provider can withdraw from a relationship if the patient is noncooperative or refuses to pay bills when able to do so.

Providers have the right to take vacations and time off from their practice and to be unavailable to care for their patients during those times. It is legally prudent for providers to arrange for coverage during an absence. In most cases, other providers will cover for them and take care of their patients. Providers should notify their patients when they will be unavailable.

Some providers now charge for services such as answering after-hours phone calls and filling out insurance forms. Many physicians feel that the large increases in their malpractice insurance premiums and the tighter regulations by HMOs have forced them to charge for services that they previously performed without charge.

Clearly, a provider's first responsibility is to be professionally competent. In addition, a provider must treat all patients with the same standards regardless of race, gender, sexual orientation, or religion. While a provider has the right to accept or decline to establish a professional relationship with any person, once that relationship is established, the provider has certain responsibilities. For example, federal law and many state laws prohibit hospitals from giving physicians "kickbacks" of money or other benefits in return for referring patients. In 2021, in *United States v. Beauchamp et al.*, 14 people associated with Forest Park Medical Center in Texas were sentenced to a combined 74 years in federal prison and ordered to pay $82 million in restitution. Ten more people pleaded guilty prior to the trials. The defendants were

Table 5–1 Examples of Duties of Licensed Healthcare Professionals

Conflict of interest	No healthcare team member should place their own financial interests above the patient's welfare.
Professional courtesy	Historically, there is an unwritten practice among many physicians that they would not charge each other for professional services. However, this practice has lost favor because many physicians are concerned about the lack of documentation when seeing a fellow physician free of charge.
Reporting unethical conduct of other physicians	Healthcare providers should report any unethical conduct by other providers.
Second opinions	Healthcare providers should recommend that patients seek a second opinion whenever necessary.
Sexual conduct	It is unethical for the healthcare providers to engage in sexual conduct with a patient during the provider–patient relationship.
Treating family members	Healthcare providers should not treat members of their families except in an emergency.

Source: American Medical Association. 2016. *Code of medical ethics: Current opinions on ethical and judicial affairs.* Chicago: American Medical Association.

all part of a scheme to induce doctors to steer patients with good insurance coverage to Forest Park. They included a hospital administrator, six physicians, a chiropractor, and a nurse, among others.

Providers have many duties upon entering the practice of medicine. Examples of duties for the licensed healthcare professionals are described in Table 5.1.

Professional Practice Responsibilities

Healthcare practice responsibilities include such commonplace routines as effective hand hygiene techniques before touching any patient (Figure 5.2). While this may seem to be an issue that hardly needs to be stated, nevertheless, there are serious ethical, legal, and economic implications when healthcare personnel ignore these sensible routines. It is estimated that 400,000 hospitalized patients experience some sort of preventable harm each year and that 100,000 people die each year due to medical errors.

Med Tip

Failure to practice correct hand hygiene is considered to be a medical error when it results in patient infection. All healthcare professionals must hold themselves to the same high standards regarding diligent hand hygiene.

Figure 5–2 Practicing good hand hygiene is critical for everyone on the healthcare team

Source: racorn/Shutterstock

Many fail-safe approaches have been instituted by healthcare professionals to prevent errors. For instance, performing surgery at the wrong site, such as the right knee instead of the left knee, is rare. But to prevent this type of injury to the patient, the American Academy of Orthopedic Surgery urges all its members to sign their initials directly on the site to be operated upon before the surgery. In order to help the healthcare staff avoid medical errors, patients can be of assistance. Patients, their primary care physicians, and their surgeons should all be aware of the plan of action before beginning any surgical procedure.

Duties During a Medical Emergency

A physician cannot ethically or legally turn away a patient who is in an emergency situation. If the physician is unable to adequately treat the patient, then they must call for emergency assistance from emergency medical services (a 911 call). For instance, allergy specialists may be unable to give life-saving medications to a stroke victim, because the medications won't be available in their offices. However, allergy specialists can handle patients who are in respiratory distress as well as, or better than, some other healthcare specialists. It is especially important to remember that patients cannot be turned away from a hospital or physician's office if they are indigent or uninsured.

Duty to Treat Indigent Patients

In U.S. hospitals, there has been, in the past, a "dumping crisis" of indigent patients who lack healthcare insurance. There are many stories of deaths occurring after a patient has been shuffled from a private hospital emergency department to a public hospital that accepts indigent patients. While the hospital treatment may not be to blame for the death, the long delay in treatment while the patient is being transferred might. The Comprehensive Omnibus Budget Reconciliation Act (COBRA) contains an amendment (EMTALA) that prohibits "dumping" patients from one facility to another. It is now a federal offense to do this. (See EMTALA discussion in Chapter 8.) This amendment does not mandate treatment, but it does require a hospital to stabilize a patient during an emergency situation.

Does a physician have a duty to treat a patient who is unable to pay? According to the Council on Ethical and Judicial Affairs of the AMA, a physician has the right to select which patients to treat. However, physicians do not have the same freedom to drop patients once they have agreed to treat them. The healthcare professional has the right to earn a living and charge for services, but from an ethical standpoint, a physician cannot abandon any patient, even in a nonemergency situation. Abandonment might expose the patient to dangers because of lack of oversight of medications and treatment.

Duty Not to Abandon a Patient

Once a provider has agreed to take care of a patient, this is considered to be a contract that may not be terminated improperly. Physicians may be charged with **abandonment** of the patient if they do not give formal notice of withdrawal from the case. In addition, the physician must allow the patient sufficient time to seek the services of another physician. This does not mean the physician may never withdraw from a case. Physicians may decide they can no longer accept responsibility for the medical treatment of a patient because the patient refuses to come in for periodic checkups or take prescribed medications and treatments. They may even offer referral suggestions. Abandonment could occur if the physician does not give enough notice to the patient so that other arrangements for medical care can be made. There is *no one single* definition of abandonment.

Med Tip

There are occasions, such as during vacations, when a provider will ask another provider to "cover" or take charge of their patients. This is not considered to be abandonment.

Abandonment is considered to be a civil wrong or tort. It can be considered to be a breach of contract and even negligence. The courts have found the physician–patient relationship to be that of a contract when they enter into a mutual agreement. The physician agrees to diagnose and treat the patient until the relationship is over. The patient agrees to pay the physician for these services. If the physician, who has already agreed to this mutual contract, does not allow the patient to make an appointment for treatment, then abandonment may exist.

Abandonment with negligence occurs when the physician terminates the relationship in an unreasonable way as compared with the way other physicians would act in the same circumstances. For example, if a physician refused to see a patient for follow-up care after a surgical procedure because the patient or the patient's insurance company did not pay the bill, the physician could be liable for damages due to negligence and abandonment.

The most common types of abandonment include the following:

- Refusal to treat a patient
- Delayed treatment
- Insufficient or lack of correct treatment
- Withdrawal of treatment without notice

It is a frustration for providers when patients do not comply with the treatment plan. Patients can also be frustrated when they do not experience a cure after following their provider's treatment plan. The patient may then terminate the provider–patient relationship by not making any more appointments to see the provider. However, providers and their office staffs must be vigilant about maintaining the relationship until it is terminated in a formal manner such as a letter sent from the provider to the patient by certified mail with proof of delivery.

Med Tip

Sending a letter by certified mail is the best method providers can use to protect themselves from a charge of abandonment when they have to sever a relationship with a patient.

Abandonment does not apply just to the physician–patient relationship. Licensed healthcare providers, such as dentists, podiatrists, physician assistants, and nurse practitioners, are all subject to this principle. There are difficult situations relating to abandonment that arise when healthcare personnel have started to provide emergency care such as CPR. For example, once emergency medical technicians (EMTs) have started to give treatment, they may not stop until someone else of equal or greater training takes over for them or the patient dies. In fact, all persons who administer CPR are taught to continue to provide this procedure until someone else of equal or greater training relieves them or they cannot perform CPR any longer.

Hospitals are also liable for abandonment, especially in emergency situations. In some cases, an emergency patient may have to be transferred to another hospital that can better handle their care, such as a hospital that has a burn unit. However, an emergency patient must be stabilized, often with intravenous medications, before being transferred to another facility.

The Noncompliant or Incompetent Patient

A **noncompliant patient** is one who is unable to, or refuses to, cooperate with the recommendations of a healthcare professional. This person may be unable to afford to take prescribed medications or to carry out a portion of their healthcare plan that is under their control.

An **incompetent patient** is one who is determined to be unable to provide for their own needs and protection. This status must be provided by a court of law.

A patient who is nonadherent and also incompetent presents a special concern for physicians and hospitals. Hospitalized patients who are nonadherent may discharge themselves **against medical advice**, also known as AMA, but incompetent patients pose a unique problem because they may not be able to understand the need for treatment and may even pose a threat to another person. In this case, a physician will submit an emergency application to a judge, who can then order an emergency hospital admission for the patient. Most states require that within 72 hours of the emergency hospital admission a formal (due process) hearing be held. At this hearing, the patient's medical condition is evaluated along with the loss of any of their rights. A decision may be made to either allow the patient to return home or to continue to be hospitalized. Additional hearings are held as long as the incompetent patient is hospitalized.

> **Med Tip**
>
> Note that abbreviations used for the American Medical Association (AMA) and against medical advice (AMA) are the same. Be careful not to confuse the two.

Duty to Properly Identify Patients

Many medical errors occur because the patient was not properly identified. It is necessary to identify the patient using two patient identifiers, such as having them state their name AND their date of birth, or examining other identification such as a medical wristband. Be especially careful with patients who have hearing loss or are Deaf, those who have dementia, those with whom you don't share a common language, and older patients who may not understand when you call them by name. Use interpreter services when necessary. There have been cases of incorrect patients in the emergency department (ED) waiting area going in for treatment because they didn't properly hear the name that was called. It's always wise to ask to examine some identification, such as a driver's license or medical wristband. Some healthcare offices take the patient's photo for their records.

> **Med Tip**
>
> If an error is made, such as not properly identifying the correct patient, report it immediately. Then seek to correct the situation. You may save a life.

Duty to Respect Confidentiality

Providers, nurses, and allied health professionals should use a low voice when speaking to patients over the telephone or when speaking about patients to other staff members within hearing distance of any patients in the waiting room. Ideally, a glass enclosure should be present at the front desk in all waiting rooms to separate the receptionist from the patients and provide an additional aid for patient confidentiality. The sign-in sheet or patient register should be designed so those patients who are signing in or registering cannot view other patients' names. More about respecting confidentiality is discussed in Chapter 10, Patient Confidentiality and HIPAA.

Duty to Tell the Truth

The duty to tell the truth is a fundamental principle in healthcare ethics and practice. Healthcare providers, including physicians, advance practice providers, nurses, and allied health professionals, are entrusted with the well-being and lives of their patients. The duty to tell the truth for healthcare providers is not only an ethical imperative but also a legal requirement. Upholding this duty is essential to maintaining patient trust, respecting patient autonomy, and reducing legal liabilities. Healthcare providers must recognize the ethical and legal foundations that underpin truth-telling and navigate the challenges in delivering information with empathy and transparency. In doing so, they fulfill their responsibility to prioritize the well-being and rights of their patients.

> **Med Tip**
>
> Honest and transparent communication fosters trust between healthcare providers and patients, and patients are more likely to follow treatment plans and engage in shared decision-making when they trust their healthcare team.

Upholding the duty to tell the truth is a reflection of the ethical and professional integrity of healthcare providers. It demonstrates their commitment to the well-being and rights of their patients. The ethical foundations of the duty to tell the truth include the following:

- *The principle of beneficence* requires healthcare providers to act in the best interests of their patients. Truth-telling is integral to this principle because withholding information or providing false information can undermine the patient's autonomy and ability to make informed decisions about their care. The American Medical Association's (AMA) Code of Medical Ethics states that physicians have an obligation to "share information with patients and to facilitate their understanding of that information."

- *Autonomy* is a fundamental ethical principle that underscores the importance of respecting a patient's right to make decisions about their own healthcare. This principle is covered in the Patient Self-Determination Act (PSDA) in the United States, which mandates that healthcare providers inform patients of their rights to make healthcare decisions and execute advance directives. Honesty and truth-telling are essential for patients to exercise their autonomy effectively.

- *Veracity* is the ethical principle that emphasizes truthfulness and honesty. It is a core component of the trust relationship between healthcare providers and patients. The American Nurses Association's (ANA) Code of Ethics for Nurses explicitly states that nurses have a duty to "be honest and provide comprehensive, accurate, and objective information."

Complying with the duty to tell the truth reduces legal liability for healthcare providers. In cases of medical malpractice or negligence, courts often consider whether the healthcare provider communicated effectively with the patient. The legal foundations of the duty to tell the truth include the following:

- *Informed consent* is a legal doctrine that requires healthcare providers to disclose all relevant information to patients before obtaining their consent for treatment. The landmark legal case of Canterbury v. Spence (1972) in the United States established the precedent that patients have the right to be informed about the risks, benefits, and alternatives to a proposed treatment. Failure to provide accurate information can lead to legal liabilities.

- *The Health Insurance Portability and Accountability Act (HIPAA)* places legal obligations on healthcare providers to protect the privacy and security of patients' health information. While it focuses primarily on confidentiality, it indirectly reinforces the duty to tell the truth. Patients must trust that healthcare providers will not withhold information or provide false information about their health status.

- *State laws:* In addition to federal laws like HIPAA, state laws often govern the duty to tell the truth in healthcare. For instance, many states have laws that require healthcare providers to inform patients of a positive HIV diagnosis. Failure to do so can result in legal consequences.

Med Tip

One of the pillars of healthcare ethics and practice is the responsibility to speak the truth.
Healthcare professionals have both a legal and ethical obligation to tell the truth to their patients.
This criterion must be met for informed consent.

One of the most infamous ethical violations in the history of healthcare was the Tuskegee Syphilis Study, conducted by the United States Public Health Service from 1932 to 1972. In this study, African American men with syphilis were not informed of their diagnosis and were denied treatment. This egregious breach of the duty to tell the truth not only violated ethical principles but also led to significant legal and policy changes, including the establishment of the National Research Act and the Belmont Report.

While the duty to tell the truth is clear in theory, healthcare providers may face challenges in practice. Some examples of these challenges are the following:

- Delivering difficult or life-altering diagnoses can be emotionally challenging for healthcare providers. However, ethical guidelines emphasize the importance of providing such information in a compassionate and supportive manner.

- Different cultures may have varying expectations and norms regarding the disclosure of healthcare information. Healthcare providers must navigate these cultural differences while upholding ethical and legal standards. In some cases, healthcare providers may consider withholding information to protect a patient's emotional well-being. Even in these situations, doctors and advanced practice providers should speak with ethics committees or seek legal advice to be sure that suppressing information is justified.

Patient's Rights and Responsibilities

Many organizations have lists of patient rights, including the American Medical Association (Patient Rights | AMA-Code [ama-assn.org]) and the National Institutes of Health (Patient Bill of Rights | Clinical Center Home Page [nih.gov]). Most such bills of rights have common elements, including that patients have the right to

- courtesy, dignity, respect;
- safe, timely, responsive attention to their needs;
- receive complete information from their physician about their diagnosis and the benefits, risks, and costs of appropriate treatments or no treatment;
- give informed consent before procedures;
- ask questions about their health status, treatment, or care, and have their questions answered;
- make decisions about their care and have those decisions respected;
- have their confidentiality and privacy respected;
- get a second opinion;
- obtain copies of their medical records;
- be advised of conflicts of interest their physician might have; and
- continuity of care.

The patient has the right to approve or give consent—permission—for all treatment (described fully in the next section). In giving consent for treatment, patients reasonably expect that their provider, nurse, or allied health professional will use the appropriate standard of care in providing care and treatment—this means that they will use the same skill that other professionals use in treating patients with the same ailments in the same geographic locality. (Standard of care is discussed in more detail in Chapter 3.)

The patient's right to privacy prohibits the presence of unauthorized persons during physical examinations or treatments. This right has long been established. In a precedent-setting 1881 case, the plaintiff, a poor woman named Mrs. Roberts, sued Dr. DeMay for bringing in a third party, by the name of Scattergood, to assist him while she was in labor. Mrs. Roberts claimed that Scattergood "indecently, wrongfully, and unlawfully" laid hands on her and assaulted her. Even though Mrs. Roberts thought Scattergood was a physician, which he was not, he was present without her permission. The court found in the plaintiff's favor and awarded her damages for the "shame and mortification" she suffered (*DeMay v. Roberts*, 9 N.W. 146, Mich. 1881). While this is a very old case, nevertheless, the message is appropriate for today. Privacy is an important right for all patients.

Med Tip

Reasonable care under the law is the degree of care that a prudent person would exercise (use) in a given or similar circumstance.

Additionally, patients have the right to be informed of the advantages and potential risks of treatment—including the risk of not having the treatment. They also have the right to refuse treatment. Some members of religious groups, such as Jehovah's Witnesses and Christian Scientists, do not wish to receive blood transfusions or other types of healthcare treatment. Physicians may not treat them against their wishes. However, in the case of a minor child, the court may appoint a guardian who can give consent for the child's procedure.

Med Tip

Know that, for some diseases, there have been false positives or false negatives in laboratory reports. The patient has a right to ask for a second opinion from another doctor or laboratory.

Today's healthcare consumer is better informed about medicine and treatments than ever before due to an abundance of literature, television programming, podcasts, social media, and information available on the Internet. However, wise consumers will not self-medicate or offer their medications to family members and friends for their use. Healthcare personnel must carefully question all patients/consumers about over-the-counter (OTC) medications they may be taking. Many OTC medications, such as aspirin, can have a negative interaction with prescribed medications. Dietary supplements such as herbs and vitamins should also be declared by the patient. The consumer must alert the healthcare staff to any allergies and adverse reactions to medications.

In addition to the patient's rights, the patient also has certain obligations. Patients are expected to follow their physician's instructions. They must make follow-up appointments to monitor their treatment and medication use if requested by their physician. Patients must be absolutely honest with the physician about such issues as past medical history; family medical history; and tobacco, drug, and alcohol use. Finally, patients and parents of minor children are expected to pay the physician for healthcare services When in the hospital, patient responsibilities include the following:

- Providing accurate and complete information
- Following the treatment plans as recommended
- Reporting unexpected changes in your condition
- Informing your provider and hospital staff when you have questions
- Informing your provider or nurse when you are having pain
- Being considerate of other patients
- Respecting property of others and of the hospital
- Knowing your rights and responsibilities
- Requesting your visitors to follow the rules and regulations relating to patient care or conduct

Healthcare consumers must be honest with their providers about prescriptions they may be taking that were prescribed by other doctors. Every patient/consumer should carry a small card listing all medication names and dosages in the event the names are needed for a patient history or in an emergency situation. They should ask questions about their medications and the treatments they are receiving. If they do not understand what they are told, then they should be persistent with the physician or healthcare professional until they do understand the instructions.

Confidentiality

Patients expect that their healthcare team will keep all information and records about their treatment confidential. In fact, HIPAA provides that all patients have the right to have their personal privacy respected and their medical records handled with confidentiality. No information, test results, patient histories, or even the fact that the patient is a patient, can be transmitted to another person without the patient's consent. A breach of confidentiality is both unethical and illegal. See Chapter 9 for a detailed discussion of confidentiality when using electronic transmission of patients' healthcare information as mandated by HIPAA.

Med Tip

Remember that no patient information can be given over the telephone without that person's permission.

Privileged communication refers to confidential information that has been told to a provider (or attorney) by the patient. The provider–patient relationship is considered to be a protected relationship and, as such, keeps the holder of this information from being forced to disclose it on a witness stand.

Patients are generally assumed to have the following rights:

- To obtain information concerning their diagnosis, treatment, risks, and alternatives to treatment
- To receive information about pain and pain relief
- To receive a comparable level of care as other patients
- To take part in decisions concerning their care

- To refuse treatment and to be informed of the medical risks of refusal
- To get a second opinion
- To receive a clear explanation of their care and what they will need when they leave the hospital
- To compose an advance directive

The Patient Care Partnership

The American Hospital Association created "The Patient Care Partnership" to help patients better understand what they have a right to expect during their hospital stay. The criteria include the following:

- *High-quality hospital care:* provide the care you need with skill, compassion, and respect.
- *A clean and safe environment:* the use of policies and procedures to avoid mistakes in your care.
- *Involvement in your care:* discussing your treatment plan; getting information about past illnesses, surgeries, hospital stays, and allergies; understanding your healthcare goals and values; and understanding who should make decisions when you cannot.
- *Protection of your privacy:* respect for the confidentiality of the sensitive information about your health and healthcare.
- *Preparing you and your family for help when leaving the hospital:* help with identifying sources of follow-up care.
- *Help with your billing and filing insurance claims.*

Source: © Used with permission of *American Hospital Association*

Rights of Minors

A **minor** is a person who has not reached the age of maturity, which in most states is 18. In most states, minors are unable to give consent for treatment except in special cases involving pregnancy, request for birth control information, abortion, testing and treatment for sexually transmitted diseases, problems with substance abuse, and a need for psychiatric care. The courts have held that the consent of a minor to medical or surgical treatment is not sufficient. The physician must secure the consent of the parents or someone standing in for the parents (*in loco parentis*) or run the risk of liability. There are exceptions to the requirement of parental consent, as shown in Table 5.2.

In some cases, the state must take over the care for minors who cannot care for themselves. The principle of *parens patriae* **authority** occurs when the state takes responsibility from the parents for the care and custody of minors under the age of 18. This principle may also occur when persons are mentally incompetent to take care of themselves. If the child is removed from their parents, then two rights must be protected through due process: the rights of the child and the rights of the parents. It is not a simple matter for the state to remove a child from the custody of the parents. The state must prove that the parents are neglecting the child or are not capable of caring for the child. Then a hearing must take place in juvenile court.

Mature minors and emancipated minors are considered competent and can provide consent for other types of treatment as well. The varying degrees of minors' competency are described in Table 5.2.

Table 5-2 Classification of Minors' Competencies

Classification	Definition
Minor	A person under the age of 18 (termed infant under the law). The signature of a parent or legal guardian is needed for consent to perform a medical treatment in nonemergency situations.
Mature minor	A person judged to be mature enough to understand the physician's instructions. Such a minor may seek medical care for treatment of drug or alcohol abuse, contraception, sexually transmitted diseases, and pregnancy.
Emancipated minor	A person from age 15 to under the age of 18 who is either married, in the military, or self-supporting and no longer lives under the care of a parent. Parental consent for medical care is not required. Proof of emancipation (for example, marriage certificate) should be included in the medical record.

Consent

Consent is the voluntary agreement that a patient gives permitting a medically trained person to touch them, examine them, and perform a treatment. The two types of consent, informed consent and implied consent, are discussed in the following sections.

The Doctrine of Informed Consent

Informed—or expressed—consent means that the patient agrees to the proposed course of treatment after having been told about the possible consequences of having or not having certain procedures and treatments (Figure 5.3). The patient's signature on the consent form indicates that the patient understands the limits or risks involved in the pending treatment or surgery as explained by the physician. The goal of informed consent is to protect patients' rights to decide for themselves about their own healthcare treatment. In addition, informed consent is meant to disclose information to the patient so that he or she can make a reasoned decision.

The physician, physician assistant, or nurse practitioner who is solely responsible for providing information to the patient, must carefully explain that in some cases the treatment may even make the patient's condition worse. The doctrine of informed consent requires the provider to explain the following in understandable language:

* The patient's diagnosis, if known
* The nature and purpose of the proposed treatment or procedure
* The advantages and risks of treatment
* The alternative treatments available to the patient, regardless of their cost and whether they will likely be covered by the patient's insurance
* Potential outcomes of the treatment
* What might occur, both risks and benefits, if treatment is refused

In 2018, the Pennsylvania Supreme Court, in *Shinal v. Toms*, ruled that obtaining informed consent cannot be delegated by the provider.

Figure 5–3 Patient signs a consent form

Source: Shutterstock

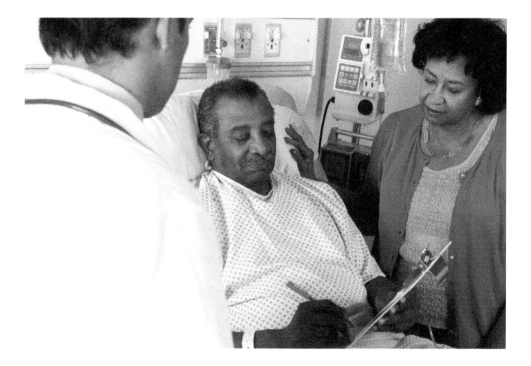

Med Tip

It is important to remember that many patients do not understand medical terminology. They may not admit that they either do not understand or cannot hear the instructions. It is the healthcare professional's duty to make sure that the patient is fully informed.

In addition, the provider must be honest with the patient and explain the diagnosis, the purpose of the proposed treatment, and the probability that the treatment will be successful. The purpose of this explanation is that the patient can then make a knowledgeable decision about whether to go ahead with the treatment or procedure. In an emergency situation in which the patient cannot understand the explanation or sign a consent form, the person providing the care is protected by law (Figure 5.4).

Med Tip

Patients who are Deaf or hard of hearing must be given their instructions in writing or through an interpreter. Every effort should be made to make sure the patient understands the same information that would be given to a hearing patient.

According to recent studies, some providers have withheld options for treatment from their patients. A University of Chicago research study found that 29 percent of the 1,144 surveyed physicians would have problems referring a patient to another doctor for some legal procedures. In some cases, such as for contraceptives or end-of-life issues such as withholding chemotherapy, they had ethical problems making the referral. The advice to patients is to be aware that they may not get all the information about treatments they are legally due.

In a case in Alaska, the court determined that the physician did not fulfill his duty to disclose the risks of breast-reduction surgery when he failed to warn the patient about the risk of scarring. In answer to the patient's questions, the physician said that she shouldn't worry and she would be happy with the results. The patient wasn't happy; she sued the physician and won (*Korman v. Mallin*, 858 P.2d 1145, Alaska 1993).

Is it difficult to know if or when the patient is fully informed? There are two standards to use to determine whether patients understand what they are being told. The first standard is based upon what the provider tells the patient. Many courts will use a "reasonable physician standard," meaning that the

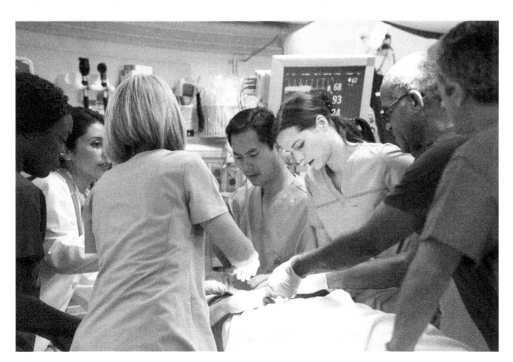

Figure 5–4 In emergencies, the provider is protected by law

Source: Shutterstock

physician or provider must tell the patient what a "reasonable physician in the same specialty" would tell them under the same circumstances. This allows for a type of mass-produced consent form for many treatments and surgical procedures. However, in addition to having a patient sign this mass-produced consent form, the physician must also explain the procedure, risks, and alternatives. The second standard is "the reasonable patient standard," which means that the patient must receive the information that other patients receive but, in addition, must be provided the opportunity to communicate questions to the physician. Nurses and allied health professionals cannot replace the physician or provider in obtaining a signed informed consent form. However, they are in an ideal situation in either the office or hospital to alert the physician when they believe that the patient is confused about the procedure.

Med Tip

In many cases, patients will be more comfortable discussing their fears with a trusted caregiver rather than with their physician. These patient fears must then be conveyed to the physician exactly as they were expressed, and documented in the patient chart, even if a consent form has been signed.

It is very difficult to fully inform a patient about all the things that can go wrong with a treatment. However, the physician must make a reasonable attempt to do so in order for the patient to make an informed decision about treatment.

The *Canterbury* decision is a classic example of two crucial components of informed consent: patients *granting consent* because they have the right to control what is done to their bodies and insisting on *information* so they can make an intelligent decision. For patients to be able to consent in an intelligent manner, they must be given information by the physician that a "reasonable person" in the patient's situation would wish to receive. As such, the amount of information is not based on what the physician believes is relevant but on what the patient believes they need to hear. The "reasonable person standard" was used in a 1959 case, *Canterbury v. Spence*. Nineteen-year-old Jerry Canterbury, who suffered from back pain, underwent a surgical procedure to treat a suspected ruptured vertebral disk. On the day following surgery, he fell off the hospital bed while he was trying to urinate and subsequently became paralyzed from the waist down. Emergency surgery reversed some of his paralysis, but he continued to have urological problems. Canterbury sued both the physician (Spence) and the hospital, claiming that he was not fully warned about the risk of falling out of bed and of paralysis. The physician based his defense on a therapeutic privilege claim that he did not think the disclosure of the risk of falling out of bed was necessary. The judge in the district court ordered a directed verdict and told the jury that they must find in favor of the hospital and physician. Upon appeal, a higher court sent the case back to the lower court so that a jury could hear the evidence and make a decision. The court was not clear on whether the fall or the surgery had caused the patient's paralysis. The court also declared that a physician cannot use the therapeutic privilege to justify withholding information the patient requires to make an informed decision. In an unusual decision, the jury also found in favor of the hospital and physician (*Canterbury v. Spence*, 464 F.2d 772, D.C. 1972).

Med Tip

Except in emergency situations, the process of obtaining consent cannot be delegated by the physician to someone else. If the emergency involves risk to the patient's life or the patient is unable to communicate, consent may be implied under the rationale that the patient would have consented to emergency treatment.

Except in cases of emergency, all patients must sign a consent form before undergoing a surgical procedure. This signed form indicates that the patient has been instructed concerning the risks associated with the procedure. If, after the physician has carefully explained the treatment, the patient acknowledges understanding the explanation and risks and signs the consent form, then, generally, there is some protection from lawsuits. However, patients have sued and won cases in which they were presented the risks of a procedure and signed the form, and then the treatment failed.

Procedures in which an informed consent form should be signed include the following:

- All medical procedures
- Organ donation
- Radiological therapy, such as radiation treatment for cancer, including radiological imaging procedures requiring IV contrast
- Electroconvulsive therapy
- Experimental procedures
- Chemotherapy
- Any procedure with more than a slight risk of harm to the patient

In some circumstances—such as procedures involving reproduction, and major surgical procedures—state laws require that the patient sign an informed consent form. This signed document represents a legal statement in which the patient certifies that the risks, benefits, and alternatives to treatment have been thoroughly explained. The document is an indication that the informed patient enters the treatment of their own free will and not by means of coercion. It is always important to ask the patient to sign an "Informed Consent to Treatment" form before administering any treatment. If there is a language barrier, the healthcare team is obligated to provide a translator service for the consenting process.

Certain categories of patients are judged to be incapable of giving informed consent. These include minors (other than emancipated minors), those with intellectual disabilities, persons who do not understand English or the language of the physician transmitting the information and have no interpreter present, and emergency patients who are unconscious.

Implied Consent

A physician should obtain written consent before treatment whenever possible. However, the law may assume or "imply" a patient's consent. Implied consent can be difficult to interpret because it is based on another person's interpretation. **Implied consent** occurs when patients indicate by their behavior that they are accepting of the procedure. The patient's nonverbal communication may indicate an implied consent for treatment or examination. Because consent means to give permission or approval for something, when a patient is seen for a routine examination, there is implied consent that the physician will touch the person during the examination. Therefore, the touching required for the physical examination would not be considered the crime of battery.

In a case from 2016, *Allen v. Harrison*, the patient, Teresa Allen, swallowed a small nail. The emergency department physician she saw (John Harrison) used X-ray to confirm the presence of the nail and then recommended that Allen eat a high-fiber diet until the nail passed on its own. A few days later, after severe vomiting, Allen went to a different hospital where emergency surgery was performed to remove the nail from her intestine, and she was treated for a perforated and infected bowel. She then required two additional surgeries for complications. The Oklahoma Supreme Court found that the physician failed to let the patient know that there were other treatment options. The court said that the physician should have discussed the alternatives to the recommended treatment, even if he didn't recommend them.

Med Tip

Both expressed and implied consent should be an informed consent. This means that patients must know, or be informed, about what they are providing consent for, except in the case of implied consent for a patient with a medical emergency who is unable to receive information or respond.

Exceptions to Consent

There are exceptions to the informed consent doctrine that are unique to each state. Some of the more general exceptions include the following:

- A physician need not inform a patient about risks that are commonly known. For example, physicians need not tell patients that they could choke swallowing a pill.

- A physician who believes the disclosure of risks may be detrimental to the patient is not required to disclose them. For instance, if a patient has a severe heart condition that may be worsened by an announcement of risks, the physician should not disclose the risks.
- If the patient asks the physician not to disclose the risks, then the physician is not required to do so.
- A physician is not required to restore patients to their original state of health and, in some cases, may be unable to do so.
- A physician may not be able to elicit a cure for every patient.
- A physician cannot guarantee the successful results of every treatment.

Refusal to Grant Consent

Adult patients who are conscious and considered to be mentally capable have a right to refuse any medical or surgical treatment. The refusal must be honored no matter what the patient's reasoning: concern about the success of the procedure, lack of confidence in the physician, religious beliefs, or even mere whim. Failure to respect the right of refusal could result in liability for assault and battery. In *Erickson v. Dilgard*, the hospital requested the court to authorize a blood transfusion over the patient's objection. The court held in favor of the patient who refused a blood transfusion, even though the refusal could have resulted in the patient's death (*Erickson v. Dilgard*, 252 2d 705, N.Y.S. 1962). The hospital and healthcare personnel have a responsibility to use reasonable care to protect the patient from touching (assault and battery) when consent has not been granted.

Advance Directives

An **advance directive** is a written statement in which a person states the type and amount of care they wish to receive during a terminal illness and as death approaches. Advance directives include living wills, durable powers of attorney, and organ donation directives. These self-determination documents provide protection for both the patient and the physician. Patients obtain assurance that their healthcare wishes will be followed at the point in time when they are unable to express their intent, and physicians have an assurance that they are acting within the guidelines for care set by their patients.

In some cases, an advance directive may name another person as **proxy** to make decisions for the patient when the patient can no longer do so. All states have enacted legislation empowering a patient to appoint a healthcare proxy. Table 5.3 contains a brief summary of advance directives.

The Patient Self-Determination Act

The **Patient Self-Determination Act**, also known as PSDA, enacted by Congress in 1991, requires healthcare institutions, including hospitals, nursing homes, and others, to provide information to adult patients about advance directives that they may create. (The law requiring that advance directive information be provided to patients applies to institutions but not to individual physicians.) Advance directives

Table 5–3 Advance Directives

Type	Description
Living will	A legal document that a person drafts before becoming incompetent or unable to make healthcare decisions.
Durable power of attorney for healthcare	A legal document that empowers another person (proxy) to make healthcare decisions for an incompetent patient. It goes into effect after the person becomes incompetent and only pertains to healthcare decisions.
Uniform Anatomical Gift Act	All states have some form of this law. It allows persons 18 years or older and of sound mind to make a gift of any part of their body for purposes of medical research or transplantation.
Do not resuscitate (DNR) order	This is an order placed into a person's medical chart or medical record. It indicates that the person does not wish to be resuscitated if breathing or heartbeat stops.

may be written well before the person becomes ill or hospitalized. After a patient is admitted to a health-care institution, advance directives should be placed in the patient's file.

Living Will

A **living will** allows patients to set forth their intentions in advance as to their treatment and care. This document contains the patient's desires in the case of a catastrophic situation in which they may be incompetent or unable to voice wishes concerning medical treatment. A patient may request that life-sustaining treatments and artificial nutritional support, such as tube feedings, either be used or not be used to prolong life. The patient may also request that no extraordinary medical treatment, such as being placed on a respirator (ventilator), be given. In this case, the physician puts a **do not resuscitate**, also known as DNR, order in the patient's medical chart in either the hospital or nursing home. This means that CPR cannot be used if the person's heart and breathing stop. This living will document gives patients the legal right to direct the type of care they wish to receive when death is imminent.

Some state statutes specifically note what conditions need to be present in order for a living will to go into effect. For example, Ohio follows the Modified Rights of the Terminally Ill Act, which states that the person must be terminally ill and/or in a state of permanent unconsciousness. The patient must be in a state that is irreversible, untreatable, and incurable with the prospect of imminent death. This type of regulation protects patients from having their living will implemented when, for example, they are briefly unconscious following surgery or a mild stroke.

Ideally, this process is discussed in the physician's office with patients when they are capable of making these decisions. Other family members or significant others can also be part of the discussion and decision process. The living will document must be signed by the patient and witnessed by another person. One copy should be kept in the patient's record. Many patients ask their attorneys to also retain a copy. See Figure 5.5 for a sample of a living will document.

Figure 5–5 Sample living will

Declaration:
This declaration is made this _____ day of _____ (month, year)
I, _____ being
of sound mind, willfully and voluntarily make known my desires that my moment of death [shall not be artificially] postponed.

If at any time I should have an incurable and irreversible injury, disease, or illness judged to be a terminal condition by my attending physician who has personally examined me and has determined that my death is imminent except for death-delaying procedures, I direct that such procedures that would only prolong the dying process be withheld or withdrawn, and that I be permitted to die naturally with only the administration of medication, sustenance, or the performance of any medical procedure deemed necessary by my attending physician to provide me with comfort care.

In the absence of my ability to give directions regarding the use of such death-delaying procedures, it is my intention that this declaration shall be honored by my family and physician as the final expression of my legal rights to refuse medical or surgical treatment and accept the consequences from such refusal.

Signed _____

Date _____

City, County, and State of Residence _____

The declarant is known to me personally and I believe him or her to be of sound mind. I saw the declarant sign the declaration in my presence, or the declarant acknowledged in my presence that he or she had signed the declaration, and I signed the declaration as a witness in the presence of the declarant. I did not sign the declarant's signature above for or at the direction of the declarant. At the date of this instrument, I am not entitled to any portion of the estate of the declarant according to the laws of intestate succession or to the best of my knowledge and belief, under any will of declarant or other instrument taking effect at declarant's death or directly financially responsible for declarant's medical care.

Witness _____

Date _____

Witness _____

Date _____

Durable Power of Attorney

The **durable power of attorney**, when signed by the patient, allows an **agent** (also called a proxy) or representative designated by the patient to act on behalf of the patient. If the durable power of attorney is for healthcare only, then the agent may only make healthcare-related decisions on behalf of the patient. (A broader power of attorney may permit the agent to make financial and other types of decisions for the patient.)

Because the power of attorney is "durable," the agent's authority continues even if the patient is physically or mentally incapacitated. This document is in effect until canceled by the patient. A copy of the durable power of attorney should also be kept with the patient record. Both a living will and a durable power of attorney for healthcare are recommended for all people. See Figure 5.6 for a sample of a durable power of attorney for healthcare document.

Medical Orders for Life-Sustaining Treatment

Medical orders for life-sustaining treatment, also called **MOLST**, is a document that outlines a patient's preferences for medical interventions in the event of a life-threatening situation. Unlike advance directives or living wills, MOLST is a physician's order, providing specific medical instructions that must be honored by healthcare professionals. This form is typically utilized for individuals with serious illnesses or frail health, helping to ensure that their wishes are respected during emergency medical situations.

The MOLST form includes details about cardiopulmonary resuscitation (CPR), intubation, and other life-sustaining treatments. It is designed to facilitate communication between patients, their families, and healthcare providers, fostering a shared understanding of the patient's goals of care. This proactive approach enables individuals to express their preferences in advance, avoiding potential misunderstandings during critical moments.

The MOLST is especially valuable for patients with terminal conditions, providing them with a voice in their end-of-life care. It serves as a guide for healthcare professionals, offering clear instructions about the level of intervention a patient desires. By honoring these medical orders, healthcare providers can align their care with the patient's values, enhancing the quality of life and ensuring dignity in the face of serious illness.

Uniform Anatomical Gift Act

The **Uniform Anatomical Gift Act** enacted by Congress allows persons 18 years or older and of sound mind to make a gift of any or all body parts for purposes of organ transplantation or medical research. The statute includes two specific safeguards. First, a physician who is not involved in the transplant must determine the time of death. Second, no money is allowed to change hands for organ transplantation.

The donor carries a card that has been signed in the presence of two witnesses. In some states, the back of the driver's license has space to indicate the desire to be an organ donor, with space for a signature.

If a person has not indicated a desire to be a donor, the family may consent on the patient's behalf. Generally, if a member of the family opposes the donation of organs, then the physician and hospital do not insist on it, even if the patient signed for the donation to take place. See Chapter 11 and Figure 11.3 for more information on organ donation.

Frequently Asked Questions about Advance Directives

Questions that are frequently asked about advance directives include the following:

- *To whom should the advance directives be given?* Copies of the advance directives should be given to the personal physician, close relatives, and a close friend. In addition (as noted earlier), a copy should be placed in the medical chart if the patient is hospitalized or in a nursing home.

Power of Attorney made this _____ day of _____ (month), _____(year)

1. I, _____
(insert name and address of principal) hereby appoint

_____
(insert name and address of agent) as my attorney-in-fact (my "agent") to act for me and in my name (in any way I could act in person) to make any and all decisions for me concerning my personal care, medical treatment, hospitalization, and healthcare and to require, withhold, or withdraw any type of medical treatment or procedure, even though my death may ensue. My agent shall have the same access to my medical records that I have, including the right to disclose the contents to others. My agent shall also have full power to make a disposition of any part or all of my body for medical purposes, authorize an autopsy, and direct the disposition of my remains.

2. The powers granted above shall not include the following powers or shall be subject to the following rules or limitations (here you may include any specific limitations you deem appropriate, such as your own definition of when life-sustaining measures should be withheld; a direction to continue food and fluids or life-sustaining treatment in all events; or instructions to refuse any specific types of treatments that are inconsistent with your religious beliefs or unacceptable to you for any other reasons, such as blood transfusion, electroconvulsive therapy, amputation, psychosurgery, voluntary admission to a mental institution, etc.).

_____
_____
_____

(The subject of life-sustaining treatment is of particular importance. For your convenience in dealing with that subject, some general statements concerning the withholding of life-sustaining treatment are set forth below. If you agree with one of these statements, you may initial that statement, but do not initial more than one): _____ (initialed) I do not want my life to be prolonged nor do I want life-sustaining treatment to be provided or continued if my agent believes the burdens of the treatment outweigh the expected benefits. I want my agent to consider the relief of suffering, the expense involved, and the quality as well as the possible extension of my life in making decisions concerning life-sustaining treatment.
_____ (initialed) I want my life to be prolonged, and I want life-sustaining treatment to be provided or continued unless I am in a coma that my attending physician believes to be irreversible, in accordance with reasonable medical standards at the time of reference. If and when I have suffered irreversible coma, I want life-sustaining treatment to be withheld or discontinued.
_____ (initialed) I want my life to be prolonged to the greatest extent possible without regard to my condition, the chances I have for recovery, or the cost of the procedures.

3. This power of attorney shall become effective on _____ (insert a future date or event in your lifetime, such as a court determination of your disability, when you want this power to first take effect).

4. This power of attorney shall terminate on _____ (insert a future date or event, such as a court determination of your disability, when you want this power to terminate prior to your death).

5. If any agent named by me shall die, become incompetent, resign, refuse to accept the office of agent, or be unavailable, I name the following (each to act alone and successively, in the order named) as successors to such agent:

_____
_____
_____

6. I am fully informed as to all the contents of this form and understand the full import of this grant of powers to my agent. Signed _____ (principal) The principal has had an opportunity to read the above form and has signed the form or acknowledged his or her signature or mark on the form in my presence. _____ (witness) Residing at: _____

Figure 5–6 Sample power of attorney

- *Where should advance directives be stored?* They should be kept with the patient's personal papers in the home or nursing home setting. It is not recommended that they be stored in a safety deposit box, as they will not be accessible in an emergency.

- *How can the advance directive be changed or amended?* Any revisions can be made by drawing through the outdated statement in the original document. After a revision is made, it should be dated and signed. An amended copy should be given to the personal physician, family member, and friend.

- *Can the advance directive be revoked?* People can revoke their documents by destroying them and asking anyone holding a copy to do the same. Ideally, the request to destroy the advance directive should be sent in writing to all those who hold a copy.

- *What does the law say about advance directives?* As described earlier, a federal law, the Patient Self-Determination Act (PSDA), was passed in 1991. Congress has strongly supported a person's right to self-determination before becoming incompetent or unable to do so.

Med Tip

It is recommended that all persons place in writing their wishes about what type of treatment they should receive if they become incompetent. The advance directive should be specific about treatments such as CPR, tube feedings, and the use of a ventilator. Many organizations use the Five Wishes advance directive document, which is easy to understand and is available in many languages.

Chapter 5 Review

Points to Ponder

1. Does it surprise you to find out that physicians have the right to select the patients they wish to treat?

2. Can a physician receive a payment from a hospital for referring patients to that particular institution? Why or why not?

3. If a deceased relative signed a statement (Uniform Anatomical Gift Act) requesting that any or all body parts be used for organ transplantation or medical research, can a family member overturn that statement?

4. Do you believe that it is appropriate for a physician to report the unethical conduct of a fellow physician?

5. Do you think that physicians should treat their own family members? Why or why not?

6. Can a nurse obtain consent from a patient for a surgical procedure if the physician is extremely busy handling an emergency case?

7. What can you say to your patient's employer who calls to find out if the employee's medical condition has improved?

Discussion Questions

1. Explain what it means when one physician "covers" for another.

2. Describe the three of the advance directives that a patient can use. When are they appropriate?

3. Brittany Gillen is being treated by Dr. Liu after having fallen off a ladder at work. Her employer calls to find out how Brittany is doing. Can Dr. Liu discuss Britanny's progress with her employer? Why or why not?

Review Challenge

Short Answer Questions

1. What might happen if a physician ignores a patient's refusal to grant consent?

2. A woman opens her mouth for the nurse practitioner to examine her throat. Is this a form of consent? If so, what form of consent is this?

3. A 4-year-old child opens his mouth for the physician assistant to examine his throat. In your opinion, has the child granted consent?

4. A physician makes the following statement to Sarah: "Your blood pressure is only slightly elevated. This blood pressure medication is guaranteed to reduce your blood pressure a few points." In your opinion, is this a safe comment to make? Explain your answer.

5. Why does a patient need to know the consequences of NOT having a procedure or treatment?

6. Why is a durable power of attorney called "durable"?

7. You are working in a nursing home as a nurse's aide, but your long-term goal is to become a nurse. You have become very skilled in performing CPR due to an excellent educational program. As you are about to move a patient to her bed, she stops breathing and has no pulse. You immediately begin CPR as you have been trained. A nurse in the room with you says that you must stop because the woman has a DNR order. You have been taught that once you begin CPR you must continue until you no longer can continue. What do you do?

8. You are in an externship in a physician's office in the final two weeks of a medical assisting program. Just as a patient is brought into the office, he collapses in front of you, stops breathing, and has no pulse. You call for help because you are afraid that, even though you have been trained in CPR, you have never performed it on a patient. It would take several minutes for someone else to begin CPR. Please comment.

Matching

Match the responses in column B with the correct term in column A.

COLUMN A

_____   1. gent

_____   2. minor

_____   3. standard of care

_____   4. implied consent

_____   5. privileged communication

_____   6. informed consent

_____   7. exception to consent

_____   8. right to be informed

_____   9. durable power of attorney

_____   10. abandonment

COLUMN B

a. commonly known risks

b. consent granted by inference

c. document that allows an agent to represent a patient

d. same skill that is used by other physicians

e. representative acts on patient's behalf

f. withdrawing medical care without notice

g. person under 18 years of age

h. a patient's bill of rights

i. knowledgeable consent

j. confidential information

Multiple Choice

Select the one best answer to the following statements.

1. A patient rolling up a sleeve to have a blood sample taken is an example of
   a. standard of care.
   b. informed consent.
   c. implied consent.
   d. advance directive.
   e. agent.

2. A condition in which a patient understands the risks involved by not having a surgical procedure or treatment performed is known as
   a. standard of care.
   b. informed consent.
   c. implied consent.
   d. advance directive.
   e. agent.

3. The Uniform Anatomical Gift Act is applicable for
   a. persons up to the age of 18.
   b. persons 18 years of age and older.
   c. persons who are intellectually disabled.
   d. very few people.
   e. the purpose of selling organs.

4. Which of these refers to a physician using the same skill that is used by other physicians in treating patients with the same ailment?
   a. privileged communication
   b. informed consent
   c. implied consent
   d. standard of care
   e. none of the above

5. The physician's rights include
   a. the right to decline to treat a new patient.
   b. the ability to receive payment from hospitals for referring patients.
   c. the right to protect fellow physicians who are guilty of a deception.
   d. the right to publish confidential information about a patient if it is in the physician's best interest.
   e. all of the above

6. In what document are patients able to request the type and amount of artificial nutritional and life-sustaining treatments that should or should not be used to prolong their life?
   a. Uniform Anatomical Gift Act
   b. a patient's bill of rights
   c. living will
   d. standard of care
   e. none of the above

7. The patient's obligations include
   a. honesty about past medical history.
   b. payment for medical services.
   c. following treatment recommendations.
   d. a and c only
   e. a, b, and c

8. Exceptions to informed consent include
   a. telling the patient about the risk involved in not having the procedure.
   b. the discussion of sensitive sexual matters.
   c. not having to explain risks that are commonly known.
   d. all of the above
   e. none of the above

9. The doctrine of informed consent
   a. can be delegated by the physician to a trusted assistant.
   b. may have to be waived in the event of an emergency situation.
   c. does not have to be signed by every patient.
   d. could result in a lawsuit for assault and battery if not performed.
   e. b and d only

10. A newspaper reporter seeks information from a receptionist about a prominent personality who has been hospitalized. What information can be given to the reporter?
    a. none
    b. the basic fact that the person is a patient
    c. the name and phone number of the attending physician
    d. a very brief statement about the person's medical condition
    e. there are no restrictions

Discussion Cases

1. Madison O'Rourke, a 25-year-old patient of Dr. Williams, refuses to take her medication to control diabetes and is not following her dietary plan to control her disease. After repeated attempts to help this patient, Dr. Williams has decided that she can no longer provide care for Madison. The office staff have been advised not to schedule Terry for any more appointments.

   a. Is there an ethical and/or legal concern regarding this situation?

   _____

   b. Is there anything else that either Dr. Williams or her staff should do to sever the patient relationship with Madison?

   _____
   _____

   c. Is this a breach of contract on the part of Dr. Williams? Explain your answer.

   _____
   _____

2. Dr. Williams has been treating a popular performer who has just died by suicide.

   a. What statement can Dr. Williams or her staff give to reporters when they call Dr. Williams's office?

   _____
   _____

   b. What can Dr. Williams or her staff say to the mother of the deceased patient when she calls for information?

   _____
   _____

Put It Into Practice

Interview someone you know who has recently been in the hospital. Ask that person to tell you what they believe are the patient's responsibilities. Do these statements agree with those in the textbook? How do they differ?

Web Hunt

Search the website of the American Hospital Association (**https://www.aha.org/other-resources/patient-care-partnership**). What does the document have to say about the confidentiality of health information?

Critical Thinking Exercise

What should you do if you know that your employer owns an MRI facility along with two other persons and your patients are being referred to this facility?

Bibliography

Allen v. Harrison, OK 44, Case Number: 111877 9 (2016). https://law.justia.com/cases/oklahoma/supreme-court/2016/111877.html

American Hospital Association. (2023). *The patient care partnership.* https://www.aha.org/other-resources/patient-care-partnership

Beaman, N., Routh, K.S., Papazian-Boyce, L., et al. (2017). *Pearson's comprehensive medical assisting: Administrative and clinical competencies* (4th ed.). Pearson.

Brotherton, S., Kao, A., & Crigger, B.J. (2016). Professing the values of medicine: The modernized AMA Code of Medical Ethics. *JAMA,* 316(10):1041–1042. DOI:10.1001/jama.2016.9752

DeGrazia, D., Mappes, T., & Ballard, J. (2010). *Biomedical ethics* (7th ed.). McGraw-Hill.

Fletcher, J. 1966. *Situation ethics: The new morality.* Westminster John Knox Press.

Garner, B. 2019. *Black's law dictionary* (11th ed.). Thomson Reuters.

Hall, M., & Orentlicher, D. 2020. *Health care law and ethics in a nutshell* (4th ed.). West Academic Publishing.

Munson, R. & Lauge, I. (2016). *Intervention and reflection: Basic issues in medical ethics* (10th ed.). Cengage Learning.

National Health Law Program. (2023). *Federal laws and policies to ensure access to health care services for people with limited English proficiency.* https://healthlaw.org/wp-content/uploads/2018/09/Federal-Language-Access-Laws.pdf

Rodziewicz, T.L., Houseman, B., & Hipskind, J.E. (2023). Medical error reduction and prevention. *StatPearls.* https://pubmed.ncbi.nlm.nih.gov/29763131/

Teo, W.Z.W., Brenner, L.H., & Bal, B.S. (2018). Medicolegal sidebar: Who should obtain informed consent? *Clinical Orthopaedics and Related Research.* Aug;476(8):1566-1568. DOI: 10.1097/CORR.0000000000000351

United States Attorney's Office, Northern District of Texas. (2021). *14 defendants sentenced to 74+ years in Forest Park healthcare fraud* [Press release]. https://www.justice.gov/usao-ndtx/pr/14-defendants-sentenced-74-years-forest-park-healthcare-fraud

Veatch, R.M., & Guidry-Grimes, L.K. (2019). *The basics of bioethics* (4th ed.). Routledge.

Professional Liability and Medical Malpractice

Key Terms

Affirmative defense

Alternative dispute resolution (ADR)

Arbitration

Arbitrator

Assumption of risk

Borrowed servant doctrine

Breach

Claims-made insurance

Comparative negligence

Compensatory damages

Contributory negligence

Damages

Defensive medicine

Dereliction

Direct cause

Duty

Feasance

Federal Rules of Evidence

Fraud

Law of agency

Liable

Malfeasance

Malpractice

Mediation

Misfeasance

Negligence

Nominal damages

Nonfeasance

Occurrence insurance

Product liability

Proximate

Punitive damages

Res ipsa loquitur

Res judicata

Rider

Settlement

Strict liability

Tort

Tort reform

Learning Objectives

After completing this chapter, you will be able to:

6.1 Define the key terms.

6.2 Define the four Ds of negligence for the physician.

6.3 Discuss the meaning of *respondeat superior* for the providers and employees.

6.4 Discuss the meaning of *res ipsa loquitur*.

6.5 Explain the term *liability* and what it means for physicians and other healthcare professionals.

6.6 List ten ways to prevent malpractice.

6.7 State two advantages of arbitration.

6.8 Discuss three types of damage awards.

6.9 Describe two types of malpractice insurance.

6.10 Explain the law of agency.

The Case of John F. and the HMO

John F., a 34-year-old father of two children, is a member of a health maintenance organization (HMO) in Texas. John has made several trips to an area clinic recommended by his HMO to seek medical attention since finding blood in his bowel movements. He has been taking large amounts of aspirin for persistent headaches but did not realize that this could cause internal bleeding. John was always seen at the clinic by a physician assistant, Robert M., who didn't ask John about taking any nonprescription medications. John didn't realize that he should mention his over-the-counter medication (aspirin) consumption. Robert tells John to take an antacid preparation to control the bleeding, but he does not order any tests. He tells John to return if he is not any better. Two days later, John is rushed to the area emergency department with a bowel hemorrhage.

1. What responsibility, if any, does Robert have for John's emergency condition?

2. Does the clinic have a responsibility to provide its HMO members with the services of a physician?

3. What responsibility, as a healthcare consumer, does John have for his own medical condition?

Introduction

Even when procedures or treatments are conducted with the best intentions and skill, they don't always turn out as expected. Unfortunately, we are living in a litigious society, and when medical accidents happen, the patients and their families may look for someone to blame.

Healthcare professionals need to be on constant alert for practices that could result in injury to the patient. Not only is the injury a painful process, it can also be a life-threatening one. All healthcare professionals must realize that they are responsible for their actions. The physician/employer also assumes responsibility for the employees through the doctrine of *respondeat superior*. While people have always been liable for their own conduct, the courts are now finding that everyone associated with negligent actions is liable for damages (monetary award to the plaintiff) (Figure 6.1).

The topics of negligence and malpractice are briefly discussed in Chapter 2. This chapter concentrates on professional liability and how to prevent malpractice from happening. Included in this chapter are numerous examples of court cases to illustrate the wide variety of lawsuits and negligence cases that name physicians and hospitals as defendants. While most of the cases reflect legal actions against physicians, all people working in the healthcare professions can be sued. Examples are also provided of other healthcare professionals who have been named in lawsuits, such as advance practice providers, nurses, medical assistants, dental assistants, laboratory technicians, nursing assistants, paramedics, pharmacists, physical therapists, and respiratory therapists.

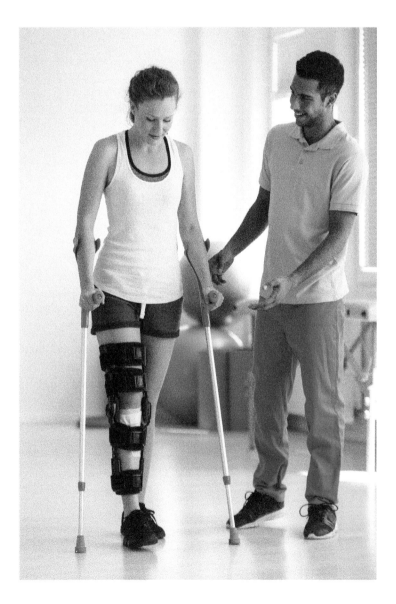

Figure 6–1 All healthcare professionals need to put safety first

Source: Photographee.eu/Shutterstock

Med Tip

All healthcare workers are responsible for their actions even though the doctrine of *respondeat superior* states that an employer is also liable for injury to a patient.

Professional Negligence and Medical Malpractice

Professional misconduct, including incorrect or negligent treatment of a patient by persons responsible for that patient's healthcare, such as physicians, dentists, nurses, and other allied health professionals, or a demonstration of an unreasonable lack of skill with the result of injury, loss, or damage to the patient, is considered malpractice. **Malpractice** is negligence or other wrongdoing committed by a professional person, such as a healthcare professional. Malpractice acts consist of professional misconduct, improper discharge of professional duties, and failure to meet professional standards of care that result in harm to another person. A physician is held to a different but not higher standard of care than a nurse, medical assistant, physician assistant, or phlebotomist. In the United States, physicians and most licensed professionals such as nurse practitioners, physician assistants, and nurses are held to a national standard of care. This standard is set by observing what a competent peer in another location would do in a similar circumstance. It is important to note that this high level of practice and "standard of care" is actually the minimum that is considered acceptable.

Some malpractice is relatively clear and easy to determine, such as when a surgical instrument left in a patient during an operation shows up on X-ray. However, many cases are not as clear. There are cases in which the physician or other healthcare professional has performed a procedure that would normally be beneficial but does not have the expected outcome. Because each patient is unique, each may react differently to medical treatment. If there is a negative result, the patient and family are naturally upset. But is this malpractice? A court of law is often asked to determine the answer.

Negligence is a form of malpractice that occurs when a healthcare professional either performs an action a reasonable professional *would not have* performed or fails to perform an action a reasonable professional *would have* performed in a similar situation. For example, two of the most common errors resulting from negligence in healthcare facilities are medication errors and patient falls. Both of these errors are preventable by double-checking all orders and using caution.

Med Tip

A person who is injured sues under tort law ("a wrongful act against another person"). Negligence is categorized as an *unintentional* tort. That is, the healthcare professional did not intend to do the wrong thing. (A wrong done deliberately would be categorized as an *intentional* tort.) The unintentional tort of negligence is the most common basis of lawsuits against healthcare professionals.

Injury to a patient is not the only cause of negligence suits. In addition, charges of negligence against a physician or other healthcare professional often arise because the patient or family is not happy with the outcome of the treatment or procedure. A jury in a negligence trial would have to determine if a reasonable professional person would have done the same action or would have treated the patient in the same way.

Med Tip

Healthcare professionals are expected to use "reasonable skill" when providing care and treatment to patients. Not everyone will perform an action in exactly the same way, as each person's skill level will vary by small degrees from the skill levels of others in the same profession or position. However, an "unreasonable lack of skill" is unacceptable because it can be concluded that the person did not have even the minimum required skill level or has simply been careless in performing the skill. This lack of skill or unacceptable performance of the skill can result in injury to the patient.

Many people consider the tort (civil wrong) of negligence and the tort of malpractice to be the same thing. The difference is that malpractice is a broader concept that encompasses both negligence, which is unintentional, and deliberate or intentional wrong acts. However, not every mistake or error constitutes negligence or malpractice. When a treatment or diagnosis does not turn out well, the physician or advanced practice provider has not necessarily been negligent. Rather, they must act within the standard of care appropriate for their profession, with attention to their special field or their particular level of medicine. All healthcare providers are held to this same standard in their field of practice. Physicians and healthcare workers who fail to act reasonably in the same circumstances are negligent. Medical malpractice often involves more than just a poor outcome for the patient. It may reflect an inexcusable lapse in judgment by a healthcare professional that results in serious injury and even death for the patient.

There is a lot of debate about the number of preventable deaths in hospitalized patients. The Agency for Healthcare Research and Quality states "The number of deaths due to preventable harm is controversial. Although some analyses claim that hundreds of thousands of patients may die every year in the U.S. due to medical errors, these estimates rely on flawed methodology and are not supported by more rigorous studies. . . . At a national level, the toll is clearly in the tens of thousands of deaths per year, perhaps more." Medication errors are one of the leading types of medical errors. Medical malpractice claims may arise when a physician acts in an unacceptable manner when compared with how other physicians with similar training would act. However, as already noted, an unsuccessful or unanticipated result from a surgical procedure or medical treatment does not, in itself, mean that malpractice has been committed.

Med Tip

The best way for you as a healthcare professional to avoid errors is to always double-check all orders and healthcare decisions that physicians and other healthcare professionals make. If you don't understand the physician's orders or if they seem improper, convey your questions to the physician immediately, before carrying out the orders. Technology is also helping by providing electronic prescriptions in place of handwritten ones; this has eliminated many medication errors. Most important, never perform a procedure for which you are not trained.

The Tort of Negligence

A **tort** is a breach of duty that causes injury, damage, or a wrong to a person or property, excluding breach of contract. Chapter 2 discusses the many injuries that are covered under tort law, including assault, battery, false imprisonment, defamation of character, fraud, and invasion of privacy. As healthcare professionals, many of us have observed serious torts occurring among friends and our own families by the negligent behavior of other healthcare professionals, including doctors.

The discussion about torts is important for us to thoroughly understand because, as healthcare professionals, we cannot even imagine causing injury to our patients.

Both actions and inactions (omissions) can be considered negligence. Failure to provide clear instructions regarding treatment or a medication's use is an omission that could result in a disastrous outcome for the patient. Providing incorrect information is also considered negligence.

Med Tip

Remember that you can be sued even if you are right. Patients can be injured through no fault of the medical personnel. The lawsuit brought by the injured patient may or may not be successful.

Professional liability malpractice claims are classified in three ways: *malfeasance, misfeasance,* and *nonfeasance.* These terms all stem from the word **feasance**, which means doing an act or performing a duty.

- **Malfeasance** refers to performing a wrong or illegal act. For example, it is malfeasance for a nurse or medical assistant to prescribe a medical treatment or medication. Only the physician or advance practice provider can prescribe medications and treatments. Medical personnel must be especially aware of malfeasance when they offer advice, such as "Try giving your child aspirin to bring down the fever." The term *malfeasance* is often used when a public official has done something illegal.

- **Misfeasance** is the improper performance of an otherwise proper or lawful act. An example of misfeasance occurs when a poor technique is used by a nurse, medical assistant, or phlebotomist to perform a venipuncture and the patient suffers nerve damage.

- **Nonfeasance** is the failure to perform a necessary action. For instance, it would be nonfeasance if a medical assistant or nurse is trained in cardiopulmonary resuscitation (CPR) but does not administer this life-saving technique when a patient collapses in the physician's waiting room and requires CPR.

In order to obtain a judgment for negligence against a physician (defendant), the patient (plaintiff) must be able to show all four of what are called the "four Ds"—duty, dereliction or breach of duty, direct or proximate cause, and damages or injuries.

Duty

Duty is the responsibility established by the provider–patient relationship. It is the obligation that one person has to another person—for instance, not to perform a medical procedure that is known to be harmful to a patient. The patient must prove that a relationship had been established. When the patient has made an appointment and has been seen by the provider, a relationship has been established. Further office visits and treatment also establish that the provider has a duty or obligation to the patient (Figure 6.2). There is also a duty to warn the patient of problems that could be associated with treatments or medications. A special type of duty arises, for example, when a patient tells a psychiatric counselor they intend to harm another person. In this situation, the psychiatric counselor has a duty to warn the other person.

The duty of "due care" uses the reasonable person standard, which means that everyone has a duty to act as a reasonable, prudent person of average intelligence would under the same or similar circumstances. Those in special professions, such as physicians, physician assistants, nurses, and medical

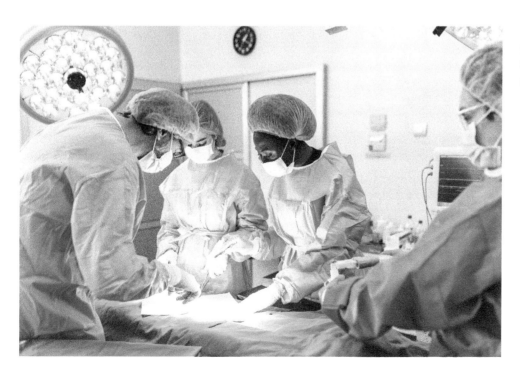

Figure 6–2 Healthcare professionals have a duty or obligation to their patients

Source: Photoroyalty/Shutterstock

assistants, are held to a standard of care exercised by similar professionals in the same or a similar community or geographic area. This standard never varies for a particular professional, so a physician is held to the same standard as another reasonable and prudent physician, a nurse is held to the same standards as other nurses, and so on.

There is a duty to care for a hospitalized patient after the patient enters the nursing floor. A phone call from admitting or the emergency department, stating "You are getting a new patient," usually precedes the patient's arrival. If all the beds are filled on the nursing unit, the nurse may state, "We don't have room for a new patient." But after the patient arrives on the nursing unit, there is an obligation, or legal duty, to care for that patient. You should identify the patient both by stating their name and by examining any other identification, such as an arm band or a driver's license. Patients also need to state their names if they are able to. Be cautious because patients with dementia, older adults, or those with whom you don't share a language may just agree with what you are saying. Use discretion with patient sign-in sheets to protect confidentiality.

Dereliction of Duty or Breach of Duty

Breach, or neglect, of duty (also called **dereliction** of duty) is a provider's failure to act as any ordinary and prudent provider (a peer) would act in a similar circumstance. To prove dereliction or neglect of duty, a patient would have to prove that the provider's performance or treatment did not comply with the acceptable standard of care. For example, if a surgeon does not properly inform patients about all the risks associated with surgical procedures, then the surgeon has neglected, or breached, their duty to the patients. If the outcome of a procedure is one that the patient did not anticipate or was not informed about, then this may constitute grounds for a lawsuit claiming dereliction of duty.

Direct or Proximate Cause

Direct cause is the continuous sequence of events, unbroken by any intervening cause, that produces an injury and without which the injury would not have occurred. Direct or **proximate** cause means that the injury was proximately or closely related to the physician's (defendant's) negligence. It does not necessarily mean the closest event in time or space to the injury, and it may not be the event that set the injury in motion. Proximate cause means that there were no intervening forces between the defendant's action(s) and the plaintiff's (patient's) injury—hence a cause-and-effect relationship. Proximate cause of injury requires the patient to prove that the provider's or agent's (such as a nurse's) dereliction of duty was the direct cause for the injury that resulted.

An example of proximate cause would be if a phlebotomist or laboratory technician, who works under the direct supervision of a doctor, performs a venipuncture on a patient to obtain a blood sample, and subsequently the patient complains of a loss of feeling in the arm that was used for the venipuncture. To prove proximate cause, the plaintiff (patient) would have to prove that there was no intervening cause, such as a tennis injury or damage from an accident, that occurred between the time the blood was drawn and the time the nerve damage happened.

Med Tip

Proximate cause refers to the *last* negligent act that contributed to a patient's injury, without which the injury would not have resulted.

Preponderance of Evidence

One side of a case must demonstrate a greater weight of evidence than the other side. The plaintiff must prove that it is more likely than not that the defendant, for example, the physician, has caused the injury. If the defendant demonstrates more convincing evidence than does the plaintiff, then the case will be found for the defendant. If both sides demonstrate equally convincing evidence, then the case will usually be found in favor of the defendant. Remember that the burden of proof remains on the plaintiff (also defined in Chapter 2).

> ### Med Tip
> To have a preponderance of evidence to find in favor of the plaintiff, the jury believes that it is at least 51 percent likely the defendant caused the injury.

Res Ipsa Loquitur

The doctrine of *res ipsa loquitur*, meaning "the thing speaks for itself," applies to the law of negligence. This doctrine tells us that the breach (neglect) of duty is so obvious that it doesn't need further explanation, or it "speaks for itself." For instance, leaving a sponge in the patient during abdominal surgery, dropping a surgical instrument onto the patient, and operating on the wrong body part are all examples of *res ipsa loquitur*. None of these would have occurred without the negligence of someone. *Res ipsa loquitur*, often called *res ipsa* or RIL, is so obvious that expert witnesses are usually not necessary.

Under the doctrine of *res ipsa loquitur*, an exception to the burden of proof rules occurs because the burden of proof now falls to the defendant, who must prove that, based on evidence, the patient's injury was not caused by negligence. The judge decides in pretrial hearings if a case can be tried on the basis of *res ipsa*. Three conditions must be present:

- The injury could not have occurred without negligence.
- The defendant had total and direct control over the cause of injury, and the duty was within the scope of the duty owed to the patient or injured party.
- The patient did not, and could not, contribute to the cause of the injury.

For example, a patient under anesthesia when the alleged injury occurred could not have contributed to the cause of the injury. However, if, before receiving the anesthetic, the patient neglected to inform the surgeon about a condition that could be adversely affected by the procedure or anesthesia, such as a diabetic condition or eating a full meal, then this may rule out *res ipsa loquitur* because the patient may have contributed to the cause.

- In order to have a civil malpractice lawsuit, the plaintiff (patient) must show that
- a relationship had been established between the patient and the provider,
- this relationship established a duty of the provider to the patient,
- this duty required the provider to perform at a particular standard of care,
- the duty was breached by the provider,
- the patient received an injury as a result of the provider's breach of duty, and
- the provider's breach of duty was the proximate cause of injury to the patient.

Damages

Damages refers to compensation awarded to the plaintiff for any injuries caused by the defendant. Patients may seek damages (recovery or compensation) for a variety of injuries, including the following:

- Permanent physical disability
- Permanent mental disability
- Loss of enjoyment of life
- Personal injuries
- Past and future loss of earnings
- Medical and hospital expenses
- Pain and suffering

If the patient does not receive any injury, then there is no negligence case. For example, if the risks involved in having a particular surgical procedure, such as the risk of infection, were not explained to a patient and the patient did not suffer an injury (infection, in this case), then there is no negligence case.

The court may award compensatory damages to pay for the patient's injuries. Other monetary awards fall into the categories of special compensatory, punitive, and nominal damages. Some states have placed a limit, or cap, on the amount of money that can be awarded in a medical malpractice case.

Compensatory damages are payments intended to compensate (make up) for the actual loss of income, emotional pain and suffering, or injury suffered by the patient. These losses are past, current, and future and include lost wages and profits. The court will consider the amount of physical disability, loss of earnings to date, and any future loss of earnings to determine the amount of the monetary award. *Special compensatory damages* refers to a monetary award to compensate the patient for losses that were not directly caused by the negligence. For example, the patient might incur additional medical expenses for physical therapy to regain strength after being bedridden because of the original injury. Noneconomic reasons include disfigurement, disability, and loss of consortium (loss of ability to have normal sexual intercourse).

In some states, the plaintiff's attorney may receive as much as one-third of the payment, plus expenses. In some states, where there is no cap, or limit, on the amount of money that can be awarded, the plaintiff may receive millions. In some cases, these large payments have meant that physicians' medical malpractice insurance premiums have increased to a point where physicians cannot afford them and, thus, have had to leave their practices.

Punitive damages, also called *exemplary damages*, are monetary awards by a court to a person who has been harmed in an especially malicious or willful way. This monetary award is not always related to the actual cost of the injury or harm suffered. Its purpose is to serve as punishment to the offender and a warning to others not to engage in malicious behavior. Punitive damages can result in a large cash award. The punitive awards have been growing substantially over the past decade and may reach into the millions. For example, a person who practices medicine without a license may receive punitive damages in order to serve as a warning to that person and others that this is an especially harmful practice.

Nominal damages refers to a slight or token payment to a patient to demonstrate that, while there may not have been any physical harm done, the patient's legal rights were violated. The award may be as little as one dollar. However, most states currently require actual damages in the form of compensatory payments rather than just nominal damages or payments.

Wrongful Death Statutes

If a patient's death has been caused by the provider's negligence, the deceased person's dependents and heirs may sue for wrongful death. Some states have wrongful death statutes that allow the deceased person's beneficiaries (estate) and dependents to collect money from the offender to compensate for the loss of future earnings to the estate. A plaintiff in a wrongful death suit does not have to prove that he or she was completely dependent on the deceased person for support but only that the death resulted in a financial loss. To win such a case, the plaintiff must prove that the defendant's actions were the "proximate," or immediate, cause of death.

Medical malpractice cases are state specific. Some states, such as Iowa, Missouri, and Pennsylvania, allow the surviving spouse and children of a wrongful death victim to sue for compensatory damages for the pain and suffering they experienced upon the death of their loved one. However, many states have placed a cap on the amount of money that can be awarded in wrongful death cases.

There are no federal malpractice laws. In common law practice, the government is immune from wrongful death suits, although some state governments now allow suits brought against state employees.

Fraud

Unlike negligence, which is an unintentional action that could lead to patient injury, **fraud** is the deliberate concealment of the facts from another person for unlawful or unfair gain. Healthcare fraud includes a wide range of illegal actions: illegal billing for services that may or may not have been rendered; receiving kickbacks for making referrals for Medicare and Medicaid patients; dishonesty when conducting medical research; embezzlement, particularly in the medical office; and the illegal sale of drugs.

Healthcare fraud is one of the most rapidly expanding illegal industries. This is especially true in the medical office. Therefore, it is paramount that medical assistants remain vigilant when performing their duties. There have been many medical office cases in which medical assistants were requested by their physician/employers to perform fraudulent acts. In every case, the medical assistant could have refused to perform the actions that were either beyond their scope of practice or obviously fraudulent.

The civil fraud section of the Department of Justice allows provisions under the False Claims Act (FCA) for the government to recover funds in the healthcare area. The government need only prove a deliberate false claim and may obtain fines and penalties as well as damages. The FCA states that the perpetrator must have knowledge of what they have done, although it does not clearly define how to determine the "knowledge."

Med Tip

"We become the choices that we make." — St. Thomas Aquinas

In the ongoing case of *United States v. Jamil, et al.*, the U.S. Department of Justice reported in February 2023 that two people from Oakland County, Michigan, who owned and operated several home health agencies in the Detroit area, submitted approximately $50 million in fraudulent claims for home healthcare services to Medicare. They also paid bribes to co-conspirators. A total of 23 people were allegedly involved in billing Medicare for unnecessary medical services and for services that were never provided. One was a registered nurse who fraudulently billed Medicare for services he had not provided, and he falsely certified patients as "homebound."

In another wide-ranging case concluded in 2022, *United States of America v. Steven Monaco, Daniel Osw Ari, Michael Goldis, and Aaron Jones*, two physicians, a physician assistant, and a medical assistant (among many others) pled guilty or were convicted of an elaborate plan to fill prescriptions for unnecessary compound medications that cost thousands of dollars per month. The medical assistant, who was 25 at the time of the charges, was sentenced at age 28 to two years in prison. The medical assistant was paid by a pharmaceutical sales rep to identify patients whose insurance would cover the expensive compound drugs. He would then forge the physician's names on the unnecessary prescriptions. The physician assistant was convicted of signing off on prescriptions for people who had not consulted with himself or the physician.

Med Tip

Rationalizing (wrongly justifying) unethical behavior can take the form of convincing yourself that it's not really illegal . . . or that no one will find out . . . or that the organization (your employer) will protect you. This type of rationalization is not only wrong, it can get you into deep trouble.

Some of the most frequently cited areas of medical-related fraud include the following:

- Billing fraud, which includes billing for services not needed, billing for nonexistent patients, or billing for products not needed or supplied
- Overutilization of services such as treatments, including office visits, laboratory tests, therapy, and prescriptions that are not necessary
- Pharmacy fraud of billing for prescriptions and supplies that were not delivered or providing lower-priced generic medications and billing for higher-priced medications
- Durable equipment and supplies, which includes billing the patients for equipment, such as wheelchairs and other devices, and unnecessary supplies
- Legal scams such as workers' compensation fraud and false injury claims
- Kickbacks, which are improper payments in order to induce physicians and other healthcare professionals to refer patients to a facility such as a hospital or insurance company

Med Tip

An allied health professional must use caution when submitting patient claims for medical reimbursement. Filing a false claim for programs such as Medicare or Medicaid is a federal crime. The employee's physician/employer could be severely fined and even lose their license for this type of fraudulent act.

Office of the Inspector General

One of the major players in the war against healthcare fraud, such as false insurance claims, is the Office of the Inspector General (OIG). This office was created to protect the programs under the Department of Health and Human Services (HHS), such as Medicare and Medicaid, from fraudulent activities. For example, healthcare payers will use the diagnosis and procedure codes submitted by billing and coding personnel when making a decision to pay or deny a claim. It is important to determine if an incorrect coding is the result of an error or a deliberate fraud. In a case such as this the OIG, if consulted, would provide an advisory opinion. If the coding was found to be in error, then it would have to be corrected. The party requesting the OIG's opinion could be prosecuted if the error is not corrected. The OIG reports problems with healthcare programs to the secretary of state and Congress and makes recommendations on how to correct them. The Office of Counsel to the Inspector General

- provides legal services to the OIG,
- represents the OIG in civil cases tried under the False Claims Act,
- imposes financial penalties on healthcare providers found guilty of fraud, and
- issues fraud alerts.

There are numerous federal statutes to avoid waste, fraud, and abuse in the healthcare industry. The major areas of concern are the following:

- Additional costs to federal healthcare programs such as Medicare and Medicaid
- Quality of patient care
- Access to care
- Freedom of choice
- Competition
- Healthcare providers' abuse of professional judgment

In general, most of the federal cases revolve around money—wrongful receipt of state or federal funds, presenting false claims for reimbursement, or improper referral relationships (kickbacks and discounts). In many cases there have been stiff fines and/or criminal penalties. False claims, which result in the loss of billions of dollars each year, carry a stiff fine. In addition, the provider can be found liable for up to three times the amount lawfully claimed. Because office staff, including nurses, are often the persons designated to submit the insurance claims for payment, they need to be fully aware of the consequences of providing false information.

The federal government's definition of what constitutes a "false claim" includes the following:

- A claim for payment for services or supplies that were never provided
- A claim using a diagnosis code other than the true diagnosis code to obtain reimbursement for services
- A claim indicating a higher level of service than that which was provided
- A claim for a service that the provider knew was not necessary
- A claim for services provided by an unlicensed individual

An example of a false claim is a podiatrist who knowingly submitted claims to Medicare and Medicaid for "nonroutine" surgical procedures when what he had actually done was trim the toenails and remove corns and calluses.

The OIG accepts public comments relating to alerts. The address is Department of Health and Human Services, Office of Inspector General, 330 Independence Avenue SW, Room 5246, Washington, DC 20201.

Med Tip

Remember that every person has the right to say "no" when asked to perform an activity that is unethical, illegal, or against his or her own value system.

Violation of Statutes

Every medical provider, including physicians, hospitals, nursing homes, and pharmacists, should be familiar with statutes that affect their particular discipline. For example, in the case of Osborne v. McMasters, a drugstore clerk employed by McMasters sold a bottle without a "poison" label to Osborne who then unknowingly took the poison and died. The poison label was required by law (statute). A verdict was returned against the defendant who then appealed the decision. The original judgment was held (affirmed) because the statute required McMasters to use reasonable care to protect customers from taking the wrong drug. This was found to be a breach of statutory duty that resulted in injury to the plaintiff and was the proximate cause of death to Osborne (*Osborne v. McMasters*, 41 N.W. 543 Minn. 1889). This example, while quite dated, is an excellent example of the need to always use extreme care when dispensing medications to patients.

Immunity for Charitable Organizations

In the past, under common law, tort immunity was granted to all charitable organizations on the theory that the charity was only working for the public good and not for profit. However, this immunity has now been rejected in almost all states. The more current belief is that charity is now a large-scale operation and should also include the expense of liability insurance as part of doing business.

Defense to Malpractice Suits

After the plaintiff's case has been presented, the defendant can put forward a defense, called an **affirmative defense**, which allows the defendant (usually a physician or hospital) to present evidence that the patient's condition was the result of factors other than the defendant's negligence. The attorney for the physician will suggest defenses grounded on law and truth that can be used to support the physician's side in a lawsuit relating to negligence. The most frequently used defense to negligence is denial. Other defenses include assumption of risk, contributory negligence, comparative negligence, borrowed servant, statute of limitations, and *res judicata*.

Med Tip

It is easier to prevent negligence than it is to defend it.

Denial Defense

The burden of proof, with the exception of *res ipsa loquitur*, is on the plaintiff (patient), who must prove that the defendant (provider) did the wrongful or negligent action. Therefore, the most common defense in a malpractice lawsuit is denial on the part of the provider. A provider may deny that they performed a procedure. In some cases, patients are upset about the side effects of a treatment and will sue for negligence. Even though unexpected side effects are undesirable, they are not generally the result of negligence. Signed informed consent documents can assist a provider in proving that they did explain potential side effects. It is up to a jury to determine if the plaintiff proved the defendant most likely caused the injury. The provider may bring in expert witnesses to substantiate that the standard of care was met.

Assumption of Risk

Assumption of risk is the legal defense that prevents a plaintiff from recovering damages if the plaintiff voluntarily accepts a risk associated with the activity. For example, when people continue to smoke after reading health warnings found on cigarette packaging or they are advised not to smoke by a physician, then they accept the risk when they smoke. A healthcare professional who agrees to treat a person with a communicable disease knows and assumes the risk of contracting the disease. A patient who understands the risks associated with open-heart surgery and signs a consent form has assumed those risks from complications of the surgery (but not because of negligence).

In order for this defense to be valid, the plaintiff must know and understand the risk that is involved, and the choice to accept that risk must be voluntary. Patients should be asked to sign an authorization for all procedures indicating that they understand the risks involved, accept those risks, and give their consent for treatment.

Med Tip

The physician or advanced practice provider is solely responsible for explaining the risks of a treatment or procedure to patient.

Contributory Negligence

Contributory negligence refers to conduct or unreasonable behavior on the part of the plaintiff that is a contributing cause of an injury. If it is determined that the patient was fully, or in part, at fault for the injury, the patient may be barred from recovering monetary damages, depending on how the state allocates damages. The concept is that the plaintiff's negligence *in combination* with the defendant's negligence is the cause of the plaintiff's injuries or damages.

For example, in *Jenkins v. Bogalusa Community Medical Center*, a patient being treated for arthritis was told not to get out of bed without ringing for assistance. He nonetheless attempted to get out of bed and fell, fracturing his hip; he subsequently died from an embolism following hip surgery. The court ruled that he contributed to his own death by failing to follow instructions (*Jenkins v. Bogalusa Comm. Medical Ctr.*, 340 So.2d 1065, La. Ct. App. 1976).

Med Tip

The *Jenkins v. Bogalusa Community Medical Center* case illustrates the importance of specific and timely charting. Instructions given to the patient should always be noted in the patient's record.

Comparative Negligence

Comparative negligence is a defense very similar to contributory negligence in that the plaintiff's own negligence helped cause the injury. However, unlike contributory negligence, which is a complete bar to recovery (meaning the plaintiff will recover nothing), comparative negligence allows the plaintiff to recover damages based on the amount of the defendant's fault. For instance, if a provider is 60 percent at fault and the patient is 40 percent at fault and the patient suffers $100,000 in damages, the physician will be required to pay $60,000.

A defense of comparative negligence has been used in cases in which the provider may be proven negligent, but the patient, in failing to continue with follow-up care by the provider, was also negligent, which added to the patient's injury.

Med Tip

To be "grossly negligent" requires that a person intentionally fails to perform a necessary duty.

Borrowed Servant

The **borrowed servant doctrine** is a special application of *respondeat superior*. This occurs when an employer lends an employee to someone else. The employee remains the "servant" of the employer, but under the borrowed servant doctrine, the employer is not liable for any negligence caused by the employee while in the service of a temporary employer.

An example of a "borrowed servant" occurs when a hospital or nursing home hires a nurse or assistant from an agency. Some courts have stated that the borrowed servant doctrine is in effect and the employer of the nurse, the agency, cannot be held liable. Other courts have used a "dual agency doctrine" stating that the nurse is an agent of both the agency and the hospital or nursing home and, thus, both are liable for his or her actions. In the case of an agency nurse or aide who goes into a patient's home to provide care, the agency and the employee are both liable.

Med Tip

A healthcare professional should have an understanding of what is right and wrong under the law. Arguing that a negligent act was unintentional is not a defense. Remember that ignorance of the law is not a defense.

Statute of Limitations

The statute of limitations protects a healthcare provider by limiting the time frame for a lawsuit to be filed. As discussed in Chapter 3, all states have statutes of limitations. In most states, the statute of limitations begins to run when the injured patient becomes aware of the injury. Different causes of action have different statutes of limitations. In some states, the statute of limitations for negligence is longer than that for malpractice. If too many years have passed since the events causing the injury, it is difficult to gather witnesses, and the witnesses may have difficulty in correctly recalling what happened. In general, the statute of limitations for negligence is from one to three years, depending on the state. Healthcare professionals and their employees must be aware of the statute of limitations in their state relating to retention of medical records.

An exception to the statute of limitations is the rule of discovery. The statute of limitations does not begin to "run" until the injury is discovered. In addition, it will not begin to "run" if fraud is involved. In a Michigan case, a patient who had a thyroidectomy suffered paralyzed vocal cords after the surgery. He was told it was because of a calcium deficiency when, in fact, the vocal cords had been accidentally cut during surgery. The statute of limitations would have run out in this case, but because fraud (hiding the presence of the cut vocal cords) occurred, the statute did not begin to "run" until the patient discovered the fraud (*Buchanan v. Kull*, 35 N.W.2d 351, Mich. 1949).

Res Judicata

The term *res*, by itself, means "a thing, an object, or subject matter" such as the contents of a will. *Res judicata* means "the thing has been decided" or "a matter decided by judgment." Thus, if a court decides a case, then the case is firmly decided between the two parties, and the plaintiff cannot bring a new lawsuit on the same subject against the same defendant. For example, according to *res judicata*, when a patient has sued a hospital and won the case for an injury caused by a medication error, then that patient cannot sue that hospital again for the same error.

Professional Liability

In the largest sense of the term, everyone is legally responsible or **liable** for their own actions. All home-owners, business owners, and healthcare employers are responsible for accidents and other harmful acts that take place on their property or premises.

Civil Liability Cases

As already discussed, physicians and other healthcare professionals may be sued under a variety of legal theories, including negligence and *respondeat superior*. Unfortunately, a fear of such lawsuits has influenced the practice of medicine. Some physicians and hospitals have been reluctant to withdraw or withhold treatment at the specific directive of the patient or family. A clearly stated refusal for continued treatment by an informed patient should relieve the physician and hospital of the duty to continue treatment. In fact, if treatment is continued after it has been refused by the patient, the healthcare provider could be liable for battery. In a 1990 case, a federal appellate court ruled that a physician who implanted a Hickman catheter into a minor child, based on a court order, could be sued for the death of the child two weeks later from a massive pulmonary embolus. The court ruled that the physician committed battery because the court order was not properly obtained and, therefore, was invalid. The father of the child, who had opposed the Hickman implant, was eventually awarded $2 million (*Bendiburg v. Dempsey*, 19 F.3d. 557, 11th Cir. 1994).

Med Tip

Medical personnel must listen to and respect the patient's wishes.

Physical Conditions of the Premises

Medical offices, clinics, and hospitals are required to exercise the same standard of care as any other business that has a public facility and grounds. An institution may be liable when regulatory standards have been violated, such as when an accident occurs in a clinic that has not followed regulations for maintaining a safe environment for patients. The institution may not be liable, however, if the plaintiff was aware of a situation that could cause an injury and then chose to ignore it. For example, if someone walks on a wet floor in spite of the caution sign, it is at their own risk.

Med Tip

Lawsuits involving the physical condition of hospitals and other medical facilities have involved such cases as broken steps, malfunctioning elevators and doors, and defective carpets. Every staff member must take responsibility for reporting and correcting defects that could cause injury.

In the case of *Rowland v. Christian*, the plaintiff was injured by a cracked water faucet handle on Christian's property. The issue in this case was to determine if an owner, who is aware of a concealed condition that presents an unreasonable risk of harm to others, must warn of the danger or repair the condition. The court found in favor of the plaintiff by ruling that a landowner owed a duty of ordinary care to any persons who are invited onto the property as well as trespassers. The result of this case encourages owners of buildings, such as hospitals, medical offices, and clinics, to warn of conditions, such as wet floors or construction (*Rowland v. Christian*, 443 P.2d 561, 1968).

Illegal Sale of Drugs

In most healthcare settings, access to controlled substances such as morphine and fentanyl may be available. One of the reasons to carefully screen all healthcare employees before employment is to determine if there is any history of drug possession or abuse. There are documented instances of physicians and employees, ranging from nurses to housekeeping personnel, who have been found guilty of stealing narcotic drugs from the workplace and either using them personally or selling them. Easy access to narcotics, coupled with a lack of proper security measures, can result in the loss of a license, severe penalty, and even prison for the offender.

In some cases, narcotics that were meant for an ill patient have been stolen and then documented as having been administered to the patient. The patient suffers as a result of this deception.

Med Tip

It's important to always be alert for any indications of drug misuse among coworkers. Even though it may be difficult to report a coworker's drug use, it is necessary in order to get help for them and to protect patients and the reputation of the facility.

Promise to Cure

A promise to cure a patient with a certain procedure or form of treatment is considered under contract law rather than civil law (Figure 6.3). In a Michigan case, a physician promised to cure a bleeding ulcer, and even though the physician was not negligent in the care of the patient, he was found liable for breach of contract when the treatment was unsuccessful. After this case, many states passed laws requiring that all promises to cure must be in writing (*Guilmet v. Campbell*, 385 Mich. 57, 188 N.W.2d 601, 1971).

Med Tip

Always use caution when speaking to patients. A comment such as "I'm sure you'll be fine" could be taken as a verbal contract.

Law of Agency

The **law of agency** governs the legal relationship formed between two people when one person agrees to perform work for another person. For instance, in a physician-owned office, the list of agents for the physician includes physician assistants, nurses, medical assistants, technicians, and even the cleaning staff if they are hired and paid directly by the physician. In order to protect the physician/employer from liability for negligence under the doctrine of *respondeat superior*, every healthcare professional should do the following:

- Have a written job description that clearly defines their responsibilities, duties, and skills necessary for the job; if there is no job description in place, ask for one to be written
- Use extreme care when performing their job
- Carry out only those procedures for which they are trained
- Be honest about any errors or inability to perform a procedure

One exception to the law of agency is the relationship between the pharmacist and the physician. A pharmacist is *not* an agent of the physician because the pharmacist is not hired, fired, or paid directly by the physician. Therefore, in this case the law of agency, or *respondeat superior*, has not been established.

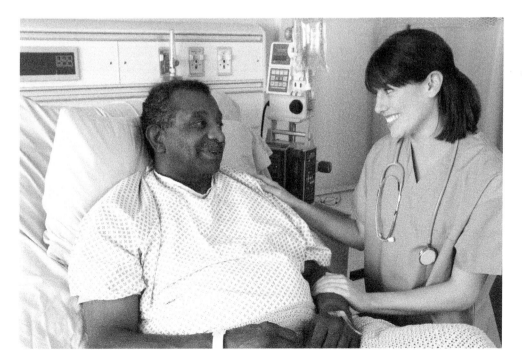

Figure 6–3 Choose your words carefully when speaking with patients

Source: Shutterstock

Altered Medical Records

The **Federal Rules of Evidence** allow paper medical records and electronic health records (EHRs) into courts as evidence under the Uniform Business Records Act. Any time that a medical record has the appearance of being altered or changed, it causes suspicion about the defendant's motives. The defendant, at the advice of their attorney, may end by settling a lawsuit in which there was no malicious intent to lie but simply a poor charting technique. A **settlement**, or agreement between both parties outside of the courtroom, may result in a payment or other form of satisfaction. A settlement does not indicate the guilt or innocence of the defendant. It usually indicates that the defendant believes that they may not win the lawsuit.

Med Tip

When charting in an electronic health record, follow your agency's protocols. When charting on paper, never completely obliterate any notation on a chart. If a chart note is placed on an incorrect chart, then cross through the notation with one line and state "Incorrect Chart." Always add your name after the correction.

It is poor technique to leave spaces on paper charts so that another person can add statements later. While this may be done simply because another staff member was not ready to chart, it gives the appearance that information was added back into the chart at a later date in order to attempt to deceive. Many electronic health records have protective barriers to help eliminate this problem.

Deliberate attempts to alter the medical record, to fabricate a medical record with someone else's name, or to lose a medical record can result in a defendant, such as a physician or hospital, losing a negligence case. In some of these cases, the physician or hospital had no knowledge that the record was being altered. However, under the principle of *respondeat superior*, the employer is held responsible for the employee's action. Note that radiology information systems are part of the medical record, and they should never be altered in any way.

Some lawyers, especially after losing a case, have been known to go back several weeks later to request another copy of the medical records. They will check to see if the record has been altered in any way since the trial ended. In one case, an LPN was found not to be negligent in the first case, but was found guilty upon appeal when the attorneys noted that the medical record had been changed after the trial ended. Even though the LPN had not made any of the changes, and was apparently not guilty of the original charges, nevertheless, upon appeal the original decision was overturned. The judge wonders "why alter the record if you are innocent?"

Med Tip

NEVER alter a medical record.

Who Is Liable?

Under the doctrine of *respondeat superior*, or "let the master answer," discussed in Chapter 3, the employer is liable for the consequences of the employee's actions committed in the scope of employment. The employer may not have done anything wrong yet still is liable. For example, if a medical assistant in a physician's office injures a patient while taking a blood sample, the physician/employer can be liable for the action even if the medical assistant was properly selected, well trained, and suitably assigned to the task. *Respondeat superior* does not assign responsibility to anyone other than the employer. Therefore, the immediate supervisor of the medical assistant is not the responsible party; the employer of both the medical assistant and the supervisor is responsible.

The doctrine of *respondeat superior* was implemented for the benefit of the patient, not the employee. It is not meant to protect the employee. Thus, the patient can sue both the physician and the employee. If both are found liable by the court, the plaintiff may seek to collect money from either party; however, the plaintiff cannot collect twice. The employer, if not at fault but forced to pay the plaintiff, can turn around and sue the employee for those damages (*St. John's Reg. Health Ctr. v. American Cas. Co.*, 980 F.2d 1222, 8th Cir. 1992).

Strict liability, in law, is the concept that a person is liable for consequences flowing from an activity even if the person doing the activity is not at fault. **Product liability** is a type of strict liability in which the manufacturer or seller may be liable for any injury caused by a defective or hazardous product it makes or sells. However, in a hospital case in which a patient was injured when his hospital gown caught fire, the court found the hospital also liable because it introduced the harmful product into the stream of commerce.

Liability Insurance

In order to protect against the risk of being sued and ultimately held liable for the plaintiff's injuries, most physicians and advance practice providers carry liability and malpractice insurance. Liability insurance is a contract by which one person promises to compensate or reimburse another person who suffers a loss from a specific cause or a negligent act. Many insurance plans are contingent on the insured person's practicing good safety habits. For example, liability coverage for buildings may be contingent on having a good fire alarm system.

In most cases, employers have a general liability policy to cover acts of their employees during the course of carrying out their duties. Some physicians carry a **rider**, or addition, to the policy that covers any negligence on the part of their assistants. For example, if a patient falls and breaks a bone while getting off the exam table, even though a medical assistant had warned the patient to sit up slowly and use the footstool, the insurance company might settle, or come to an agreement about the case, even though negligence was not found.

The two major types of liability insurance are claims-made insurance and occurrence insurance.

- **Claims-made insurance** covers the insured party for only the claims made during the time period the policy is in effect (or policy year). For example, if an injury occurred in one year but the claim for liability insurance coverage was made a year later, then the claim would be denied. It is, therefore, important with claims-made insurance to file claims reports in a timely manner, especially by the time of the policy's year end.

- **Occurrence insurance** (also called claims-incurred insurance) covers the insured party for all injuries and incidents that occurred while the policy was in effect (policy year), regardless of when they are reported to the insurer or the claim was made. Under this type of policy, if an injury occurred in one year when the policy was in effect, but the claim against the physician was made two years later, the occurrence liability insurance would cover the claim. With occurrence insurance, it is important to clearly document when an event took place.

Malpractice Insurance

Because physicians and advance practice providers treat the human body, not all medical outcomes are predictable or desirable—sometimes through no fault of the provider. Therefore, healthcare providers carry malpractice insurance to cover any damages they must pay if they are sued for malpractice and lose. All licensed healthcare professionals, such as nurses and pharmacists, should also carry malpractice insurance. Unlicensed healthcare personnel, such as medical assistants, are usually covered under their physician/employer's policy. However, because of the litigious nature of today's medical practice, many medical assistants also carry their own malpractice insurance coverage. Most states require that physicians carry malpractice insurance. In addition, nurses and other healthcare employees may be required to have their own individual coverage.

Physicians' malpractice insurance is expensive, and the cost varies widely depending on the medical specialty and the state in which the physician practices. For example, in 2020, annual premiums for internal medicine specialists ranged from $8,000 (in California) to $51,000 (in Florida). For obstetrician/gynecologists, rates in those same two states were $49,000 and $200,000, respectively. As already mentioned, some physicians carry a rider to these policies that covers malpractice suits based on injuries caused by employees and assistants during the course of carrying out their duties. Such coverage is important, again, because of the doctrine of *respondeat superior*.

Med Tip

Malpractice is professional misconduct or a demonstration of an unreasonable lack of skill with the result of injury, loss, or damage to the patient.

Practicing Defensive Medicine

Unfortunately, many physicians find themselves in the position of practicing a type of medicine that will help to protect them from lawsuits. This is referred to as **defensive medicine**. It means that more and more tests and procedures will be ordered for each patient in order to avoid a lawsuit. The result of this practice is twofold: The patient will have to undergo additional, and often painful, tests and procedures, and the cost of healthcare will increase. In addition, the use of specialists has greatly increased. Some medical specialties such as orthopedics and obstetrics are especially prone to litigation. The result is that, in some parts of the country, there is now a lack of specialists, such as obstetricians, because the cost of their malpractice insurance has become too expensive. The use of specialists has also meant that, in some cases, there is a reduced relationship between the primary care provider and the patient, resulting in a greater propensity for patients to sue if displeased with their medical outcomes.

Defensive medicine becomes problematic if a physician becomes reluctant to attempt some of the more risky, yet potentially effective, procedures for fear of a lawsuit. A more conservative approach might result in a poor outcome, and even death, of the patient.

A 1997 study by Levinson et al. attempted to determine whether any communication behaviors by physicians were associated with the frequency of malpractice claims. They found that primary care physicians who communicated well with their patients were much less likely to be sued. Specifically, these physicians spent time orienting their patients so they would know what to expect, used laughter and humor, solicited patients' opinions and feedback, checked their understanding, and encouraged them to talk.

Physicians are aware of the need to hire employees who are skilled in their professional duties as well as able to project a warm and caring attitude toward their patients. In some cases, an unhappy employee will reflect negatively on a patient's attitude toward the physician even if they are quite competent.

While it is usually a physician who practices defensive medicine, it can often be another healthcare professional who documents what has been done. Narrative documentation that is performed once a shift in either a hospital or nursing home does not always convey exactly what was done for the patient. For example, stating in the medical record "Patient required one-on-one monitoring" is clearly inaccurate because it is not possible unless there is a person assigned to only that patient.

Med Tip

Although there is not a law that states, "If you didn't document it, you didn't do it," it's difficult to defend a practice that isn't documented.

Alternative Dispute Resolution

Using methods other than going to court to solve civil disputes is called **alternative dispute resolution** (ADR). The process of **arbitration**, which involves submitting a dispute to a person other than a judge, is becoming a popular means for resolving a civil dispute. This third person, called an **arbitrator**, issues a binding decision after hearing both sides present witnesses and facts or evidence relating to their cases. However, for the arbitrator's decision to be binding, both parties (the patient and provider) must agree ahead of time to accept the decision of the arbitrator. The selection of an arbitrator must be agreed upon by both sides. This can be a time-consuming process.

In addition to arbitration, other methods include mediation and a combination of the two methods referred to as med-arb. **Mediation** involves using the opinion of a neutral third person for a nonbinding decision. The mediator listens to both sides of the dispute and then assists the parties in finding a solution. Using arbitration, mediation, or a combination of the two methods for deciding a civil case can save money and time.

Liability of Other Health Professionals

Not all cases of employee negligence are covered under the doctrine of *respondeat superior*. Also, physicians are not the only medical professionals liable for negligence—nurse practitioners and physician assistants work independently in many states, and they are also liable for negligence. It is important to note that physicians retain responsibility for the mid-level healthcare professionals working for them. The following discussion summarizes some cases illustrating negligence lawsuits against other healthcare professionals.

Physician Assistants

The role of the physician assistant, as determined in the 1970s, was meant to assist a physician in the primary care of a patient. Today, many physicians hire a licensed PA to help them with their patient care. The physician (employer) provides oversight of the PA's practice. The PA is able to legally perform more procedures than a registered nurse, but PAs cannot perform all the duties of a physician. A PA, in most states, is able to assess and evaluate patients' conditions, perform physical examinations, suture wounds, change dressings, and prescribe and administer medications. However, a problem can result when there is no physician oversight, such as when an HMO or a prison hires only a PA.

In the case of *Mandel v. Doe*, the county entered into a "Memo of Understanding" with its health department to provide medical care to the inmates of the county prison. This plan called for the PA to be supervised by a doctor, but the practice developed to the point where the PA was subject to no supervision or review. The court found that there was no final review of the PA's actions, therefore, the county was liable for any negligence on the part of the PA as it had given the PA the power to act (*Mandel v. Doe*, 888 F.2d 783, 11th Cir., Cal. 1989).

In November 2022, $27 million was awarded to a man who went to an urgent care clinic with symptoms of high fever, disorientation, an abnormal heart rate, and irregular breathing. The physician assistant in charge diagnosed him with the flu, despite testing negative for flu, and sent him home with Tamiflu and pain relievers. When the patient went to the emergency department a few days later, he was diagnosed correctly with bacterial meningitis, which should have been diagnosed by the physician assistant earlier. The patient was admitted to the ICU, put in an induced coma, suffered multiple strokes, and was left with permanent hearing loss, nerve damage, and brain damage (*Joseph Dudley, et al. v. Central Iowa Hospital Corp, et al.*).

Nurse Practitioners

As discussed in Chapter 3, nurse practitioners have varying scopes of practice depending on the state in which they are licensed to practice. Some states allow full practice; others allow reduced or restricted practice. Nurse practitioners need to be very careful not to exceed the scope of practice in their state.

A woman in Pennsylvania was awarded $18 million after a nurse practitioner failed to diagnose her breast cancer. After finding a lump in her breast, the patient saw a nurse practitioner twice in March 2018 but was told that it was benign and was not sent for further testing or imaging. Nine months later, she was diagnosed with aggressive breast cancer that had spread to her lymph nodes. The patient had a bilateral mastectomy and chemotherapy. If she had been diagnosed when she first saw the nurse practitioner, she would likely have been treated with a lumpectomy and would have had much better long-term survival prospects. The nurse practitioner was held to be negligent for not ordering breast imaging, leading to a delay in treatment and a much worse outcome for the patient (*Downes v. Carpenter*, No. 2019-12863-PL (Pa. Ct. Com. Pl. Chester County)).

Nurses

When nurses exceed their scope of practice, they violate their nursing license and may be performing tasks that are reserved by statute for another healthcare professional, such as a physician. Because of the shortage of nurses, their responsibilities are ever-increasing, which may lead to actions that result in malpractice. However, nurses have not generally been involved in lawsuits for exceeding their scope of practice, or license, unless they also acted negligently.

There have been many lawsuits against hospitals in which nurses were cited for errors, failing to perform CPR, and failing to alert the physician regarding their patient's condition. A research study of 43,329 nurses conducted by the University of Pennsylvania found that, in many cases, nurses felt overwhelmed and worried about the quality of care they provided to their patients. Some of this "burnout" is blamed on the shortage of nurses.

Nursing supervisors have been found negligent for not establishing procedures for the nursing staff that are designed to protect patients. In an Illinois case, the director of nursing was found negligent for failing to develop standards to prevent accidents involving excessive temperatures while bathing patients (*Moon Lake Convalescent Center v. Margolis*, 435 N.E.2d 956, Ill. App. Ct. 1989).

In *Quinby v. Morrow*, a patient recovered damages against a surgeon, the instrument nurse, and the hospital for a burn suffered when a hot metal gag was placed in the patient's mouth, causing third-degree burns (*Quinby v. Morrow*, 340 F.2d 584, 2d Cir. 1965).

A nurse was held liable in a Massachusetts case in which a patient who had received a strong sleeping medication fell out of the hospital bed, fracturing her hip. The nurse had left the bedside rails down and thus had failed to exercise due care (*Polonsky v. Union Hospital*, 418 N.E.2d 620, Mass. App. Ct. 1981).

Allied Health Professionals

Dental Assistants

In a South Carolina case, a patient sued a dental clinic and a dental assistant after the assistant, who was not supervised by the dentist, cut the patient's tongue with a sharp instrument. The court held that the dental assistant performed a breach of duty to the patient. The clinic was also held liable (*Hickman v. Sexton Dental Clinic*, P.A. 367 S.E.2d. 453, S.C. CT. App. 1988).

Laboratory Technicians

Healthcare employees who make repeated errors are not only liable for their errors but also subject to discharge. For instance, in Barnes Hospital v. Missouri Commission on Human Rights, a hospital fired a laboratory technician for inferior work performance when he mismatched blood on three occasions. The employee alleged that racial discrimination was the reason for his dismissal. The Supreme Court of Missouri determined that the evidence did not support racial discrimination and upheld the lower court's finding that he was justly discharged (*Barnes Hospital v. Missouri Commission on Human Rights*, 661 S.W.2d 534, Mo. 1983).

Using improper techniques or reagents to conduct laboratory tests can be a breach of duty. In *Insurance Company of North America v. Prieto*, a federal appellate court found a hospital liable when a laboratory technician used sodium hydroxide instead of sodium chloride to perform a gastric (stomach) cytology (cell) test (*Insurance Co. of N. Am. v. Prieto*, 442 F.2d 1033 6th Cir. 1971).

Medical Assistants

In the case of *Landau v. Medical Board of California*, Dr. Landau appealed a lower court's decision to remove her medical license. The lower court found her guilty of allowing her medical assistant to evaluate and remove lesions for biopsy from patients. Dr. Landau was found guilty of gross negligence by allowing an untrained and unlicensed medical assistant to remove tissue, such as moles, from patients for biopsy purposes. The court stated that Dr. Landau's failure to follow up with two of the patients constituted an extreme departure from the standard of care and had serious consequences— one of the patients died. Dr. Landau's license to practice medicine was revoked. The medical assistant was not charged (*Landau v. Medical Board of California*, 71 Cal. Rptr. 2d 54, Cal. App. 1998). In this case, the medical assistant did not refuse to perform the task given to her by Dr. Landau. However, she was, in fact, named in the litigation, although the principle of *respondeat superior* was ultimately followed.

In South Carolina in 2018, a medical assistant administered a tetanus shot to a patient who then suffered joint effusion, supraspinatus tendinopathy, a subchondral bone cyst to her shoulder, and arm muscle tears. Her left upper extremity was permanently impaired. The woman alleged that the medical assistant's negligence caused these injuries. She also claimed negligent supervision against the urgent care clinic. The jury awarded her a $62,500 verdict.

Med Tip

Medical assistants can be named or prosecuted in a lawsuit.

Nursing Assistants

A nursing assistant in a Mississippi nursing home was attempting to lift a patient into a whirlpool bath using a hydraulic lifting device. The seat on the device became disconnected, causing the patient to fall and fracture a hip. The nursing assistant was found negligent for improperly connecting the seat to the lift device (*Kern v. Gulf Coast Nursing Home, Inc.*, 502 So.2d 1198, Miss. 1987).

Paramedics

In 2023, a paramedic supervisor was sentenced to three years in federal prison. In the plea agreement Christopher Pattinson, age 41, admitted to tampering with approximately 1900 vials of fentanyl from the paramedic department, and he altered the hospital's narcotics logs and made false entries in the hospital's records. He also would remove vials of fentanyl from the locked narcotics supply cabinet and replace the drug with saline. He would then return the tampered vials to the locked supply cabinet. Pattinson will serve three years of supervised release after his incarceration, and he has been ordered to pay restitution to the hospital.

Most states have statutes that provide civil immunity for paramedics and other EMS providers who provide emergency life-saving care. In Morena v. South Hills Health Systems, the Pennsylvania Supreme Court held that paramedics were not negligent when they transported a shooting victim to the nearest hospital rather than to a hospital five miles away that had a thoracic surgeon. The court stated that paramedics were not capable of determining the extent of the patient's injury (*Morena v. South Hills Health Systems*, 462 A.2d 680, Pa. 1983).

Pharmacists

In 2015, the California Board of Pharmacy sought to hold a pharmacist-in-charge liable, for a technician who had stolen over 200,000 tablets of controlled substances, even though the pharmacist was unaware of the theft. The tech would order six bottles of 500 tablets for delivery, check in the drugs away from the pharmacist on duty, and secretly move three bottles at a time to her car. The board held the pharmacist liable and revoked his license, a district court affirmed the board's decision, and the pharmacist appealed. The court affirmed the board's decision arguing that the pharmacist could have restricted access to who orders controlled substances. He could have checked selected containers being checked in, or he could have checked the invoices (*Sternberg v. California State Board of Pharmacy,* (2015) 239 Cal.App.4th 1159).

Physical Therapists

In 2022, the United States Attorney's Office for the District of Colorado Dynamic Physical Therapy, LLC, and its owner agreed to pay $400,000 to the United States because they violated the False Claims Act by billing Medicare, Medicaid, and Tricare for individual aquatic therapy services when they had actually attended group sessions. A former employee of the company was the whistleblower.

A physical therapist who refused to allow an 82-year-old nursing home resident to use the bathroom before beginning a therapy session, resulting in the patient urinating during the session, was found by the court to be negligent. The therapist appealed the decision, claiming that her refusal to allow the patient to use the bathroom was a mere error in judgment regarding whether the patient really needed the bathroom break, and thus was not negligence. The state supreme court upheld the lower court's ruling, finding that the nursing home had a clear policy, known to and followed by other employees, of allowing patients to use the bathroom whenever they expressed a need, and therefore the therapist was negligent of the patient's health and welfare (*Zucker v. Axelrod*, 527 N.Y.S.2d 937, 1988).

Radiologic Technologists

In 2008, a 2-year-old boy named Jacoby Roth was taken to Mad River Community Hospital in California after he fell out of bed. A CT was ordered to check for possible head injuries. Jacoby was kept in the CT machine for 65 minutes and the technologist activated the CT scan 151 times. A normal test involves 25 images. Jacoby's parents stopped the test because they were worried it was taking too long. Jacoby developed radiology burns on his face. The hospital did not report the radiation overdose, but Jacoby's parents did, prompting an investigation by the California Department of Public Health. The licensed radiological technologist was fired, and her state license was suspended later that year. The parents filed a civil suit against the technologist and a settlement was reached. The hospital was fined, the fines were dismissed because authorities found that the incident was due to operator error, not negligence by the hospital.

Respiratory Therapists

All healthcare professionals are required to report unusual situations to their supervisors. If they do not, they are negligent in their duties. In an Indiana case involving an inhalation therapist and a nurse, the court found the two negligent in failing to report to their supervisor that an endotracheal tube had been left in a patient longer than the usual three to four days. The patient suffered injury from the tube and needed several surgical procedures to remove scar tissue and open her voice box. Subsequently, the patient required a tracheotomy to breathe and was only able to speak in a whisper at the trial (*Poor Sisters of St. Francis v. Catron*, 435 N.E.2d 305, Ind. Ct. App. 1982).

The lesson learned from these examples cautions healthcare professionals to only practice within their scope of practice, to scrupulously adhere to all safety precautions, and to ensure that their work is patient-centered. Occasionally, a healthcare worker must decline to carry out a task.

It's wise to talk to the risk management team about the need to complete an incident report whenever an unusual situation occurs. This report, which accurately reflects the time, date, and facts of the situation, can be subpoenaed by the court in the event of a negligence lawsuit.

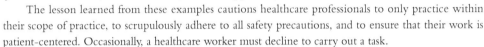

Med Tip

Be aware that any written records that you personally keep at home, such as a journal, can also be subpoenaed.

Tort Reform

Malpractice reform, also referred to as **tort reform**, is a controversial issue. According to the National Conference of State Legislatures, 35 states have passed reforms in which some of them limit an injured person's ability to sue. In some states, there is a cap on damage awards. Physicians, insurance companies, and other business interests want reform that will help to shield them from the high costs of lawsuits. On the other hand, patient advocate groups believe that entering into a lawsuit is the only choice left for many people who have been harmed by the healthcare they received. Some of the tort reforms have resulted in jury awards that are too small to make the lawsuit worthwhile for the patients or their families by the time the attorneys have been paid.

In the United States, punitive damages are rarely awarded—although they are available and are sometimes quite staggering in amount (millions of dollars). For example, in 1999, a Los Angeles county jury awarded $4.8 billion in punitive damages against General Motors to a group of six burn victims whose 1979 Chevrolet Malibu was rear-ended by a drunk driver, causing it to catch fire. This was later reduced to $1.2 billion by the judge.

Tort compensation more easily applies to property damage where the value can be assessed. However, it is difficult to quantify damages to a person's body and mind—so there is no fixed dollar amount that the court can relate to the severity of injury. Also, it is difficult to place a dollar amount on a person's pain and suffering.

Malpractice cases have caused some physicians to leave their practice of medicine even though they were not found to be negligent. It may take years before a malpractice case makes it into a courtroom or settlement. One physician writes about a lawsuit in which she was sued by the patient's family after the mother's death from an aggressive colon cancer that was unexpected and very fast. The physician states that she treated the patient as she would wish to be treated. She believes that the patient's children were coping with many emotions over their mother's death and that filing a malpractice suit helped them cope with their anger and frustration. This physician said, "I loved my patients and my practice, but this made me wary and mistrustful of them—and myself." Even though her insurance company would likely cover any settlement, the experience was devastating for this physician. A trial date was scheduled four years after the patient's death occurred. During the intervening four years, this physician closed her primary care practice of almost 30 years. Eleven days before the trial, the plaintiff's lawyers asked to withdraw from the case. The family asked for a continuance of the case, which the judge denied. Finally, the family agreed to drop the case because it appeared unlikely that they would win. This physician cited all the wasted time in the more than four years since the death occurred, the emotional anguish, and the $150,000 spent by her insurance company in the run-up to the trial. Not to mention giving up her 30-year practice.

Guidelines for Malpractice Prevention

You have a legal duty not to inflict harm to a patient. Take everything that you do seriously even when you think it is not an issue. And always be careful what you say in front of a patient.

General Guidelines

General guidelines for malpractice prevention also include concerns for safety, communications, and documentation.

- Always act within your scope of practice; never attempt to provide care beyond the scope of your training or experience.
- Make certain that all staff have a clear understanding of what conduct is unlawful.
- Provide in-service training on what is meant by the standard of care and professional conduct.
- Do not make promises of a cure or recovery.
- Treat all patients with courtesy and respect.
- Try to avoid having patients spend more than 20 minutes in the waiting room. Explain the reason for any delays in treatment.
- Always use two methods to identify the patient before beginning treatment. When a patient identification bracelet is available, use that to identify the patient as well as calling the patient by name.
- Physicians and advance practice providers should avoid diagnosing and prescribing medications over the telephone whenever possible.
- Physicians should provide ongoing continuing education and training for all staff.
- Do not criticize other staff members or your employer in public areas where patients could overhear your comments.

Safety

- Always make sure that patients use their assistive devices, such as canes and walkers, when they are in your facility. Don't let them leave these devices in the waiting room.
- Have periodic inspections of all equipment.
- Check electrical cords to make sure they are grounded.
- Keep all equipment in safe condition and ready to use.
- Keep floors clear and clean.
- Open doors carefully to avoid injuring someone on the other side of the door.
- Provide a mechanism to ensure that all doors and windows, and drawers if necessary, are locked.
- Lock up all controlled substances (narcotics).
- Follow fall prevention guidelines in facilities.
- Place warning signs regarding wet floors, fresh paint, construction, and other slippery or unsafe conditions.

- Handle biohazardous waste and sharps such as needles by placing them in the correctly labeled containers.
- Know and follow Occupational Safety and Health Administration (OSHA) safety guidelines.
- Have a disaster plan and provide periodic drills, including fire, for the staff.

Communication

- Use clear and direct language. For example, say "This does not seem to be the correct dose" rather than "This does not seem right."
- Maintain confidentiality concerning all patient information and conversations and never discuss within hearing distance of other patients.
- Return telephone calls to patients as soon as possible.
- Refrain from criticizing other medical professionals.
- Discuss all fees before beginning treatment.
- Provide emergency telephone numbers for patients to use when the office is closed.
- Take all patient complaints seriously.
- Use a coding system, such as the last four digits of the patient's Social Security number, on the patient registration log rather than the patient's name.
- Listen carefully to all the patient's remarks. Communicate the patient's concerns to the entire healthcare team.
- If the provider must withdraw from a case, fully inform the patient of the withdrawal in writing and provide enough notice (30 to 60 days) for the patient to acquire another physician.
- Call patients at home, either the afternoon of outpatient (day) surgery or the following day, to check on their progress. Document this phone call.
- Follow up on all missed and canceled appointments.
- Inform patients of all risks associated with any treatment and ensure they understand and, in writing, agree to accept the risks.
- Place all special instructions for patients in writing and maintain one copy for the medical record.

Documentation

- Prepare an incident report to document any unusual occurrence in the medical office, clinic, laboratory, or hospital.
- Maintain an accurate log in the patient's chart of all telephone conversations.
- Carefully document in the patient's medical record all prescription and refill orders.
- Make sure that signed consent forms are obtained before beginning any treatment or procedure.
- Document all missed appointments and cancellations in the patient's medical record.
- Document whenever it is necessary to withdraw from caring for a patient.
- Keep all paperwork current.
- Make sure that the provider has read and initialed all diagnostic test reports before filing them.
- Do not do "blame charting" by including criticism of a physician or other staff member in the patient's medical record.
- NEVER alter the medical record! If using an electronic medical record, make corrections according to the standards set by your physician/employer. If the medical record is maintained by pen and paper, NEVER use "white-out" or any other type of correction liquid or tape. Make any corrections by the acceptable method of drawing a single line through the error, writing the correction above the error, dating the change, and initialing it.
- Do not delete or alter what another person has charted in the medical record, even if it is clearly incorrect. Contact the supervisor or risk manager with this information.

- Enter all telephone orders from physicians on the patient's chart. If there is a concern that the physician may not countersign the order, then have another staff nurse on the phone line who will then sign the chart as a witness.

- Carefully document patient discharge notes on the medical chart. Give the patient a written copy of all discharge instructions.

- Never leave any spaces for a "late entry" in the medical record. It is a better practice to actually write a late entry when time allows and mark it as such. Remember to accurately note the time and date when the late entry was made. Never add personal notes such as "Too busy to chart yesterday."

- Don't just document, "Dr. called . . . " Be sure to include the physician's name such as "Dr. Nduku called . . . "

Chapter 6 Review

Points to Ponder

1. Is it true that if a patient is injured through no fault of yours, you could still be sued for negligence?

2. If you are trained in CPR and fail to use it on a patient in your facility, could you be sued for malpractice (nonfeasance)?

3. Do all four Ds of negligence need to be present in order to obtain a judgment of negligence against a physician?

4. Does the doctrine of *res ipsa loquitur* apply to all healthcare professionals or only to physicians?

5. Can an employee be sued even if the employer (physician) is liable under the doctrine of *respondeat superior*?

Discussion Questions

1. List five ways to prevent malpractice based on good communication.

2. Give examples of malpractice cases involving healthcare workers, other than physicians, as discussed in this chapter. Discuss the main issues in the case. It is not necessary to memorize the case citations.

3. Name and discuss the four Ds of negligence.

4. Discuss the *law of agency* and why it is an important concept for the healthcare worker to understand.

5. Explain the difference between malfeasance, misfeasance, and nonfeasance.

6. What is an exception to the statute of limitations?

7. Why do you need a thorough understanding of the law as it impacts your employer's practice?

8. State ten steps that may protect a physician and staff from liability.

Review Challenge

Short Answer Questions

1. What are the six guidelines for malpractice prevention relating to safety?

2. What is the difference between claims-made and occurrence insurance?

3. Give two examples of assumption of risk.

_____

_____

_____

_____

4. Is the rule of discovery an exception to the statute of limitations?

_____

_____

_____

5. Discuss the difference between comparative negligence and contributory negligence.

_____

_____

_____

_____

6. What is the role of the Office of Inspector General?

_____

_____

7. What are six examples of fraud in medical practice?

_____

_____

_____

_____

8. You drop a sterile packet of gauze on the floor. The inside of the packet is still considered sterile; however, the policy in your office is to re-sterilize anything that drops on the floor. This is the last sterile packet on the shelf, and the physician is waiting for it. The chances are very slight that any infection would result from using the gauze within the packet. What do you do?

_____

_____

_____

_____

Matching

Match the responses in column B with the correct term in column A.

COLUMN A

_____ 1. liable

_____ 2. rider

_____ 3. tort

_____ 4. proximate

_____ 5. misfeasance

_____ 6. nonfeasance

_____ 7. *res ipsa loquitur*

_____ 8. *res judicata*

_____ 9. cap

_____ 10. dereliction

COLUMN B

a. "the thing has been decided"

b. improper doing of a lawful act

c. legally responsible for one's actions

d. "the thing speaks for itself"

e. neglect

f. add-on to an insurance policy

g. failure to perform a necessary action

h. limit

i. a civil wrong

j. direct cause of injury

Multiple Choice

Select the one best answer to the following statements:

1. Bryce Simon, a pharmacy technician, fills a prescription for war-farin, a blood-thinning agent, for Nancy Whelan. He hands Nancy the prescription without giving her any instructions. Nancy has been taking large doses of aspirin for arthritis. The combination of aspirin and warfarin could cause excessive bleed-ing when Nancy takes them together. What is the legal term to describe a potential liability that Bryce may have committed?

   a. malfeasance

   b. misfeasance

   c. nonfeasance

   d. arbitration

   e. standard of proof

2. Emily King mistakenly administers syrup of ipecac, which causes vomiting, instead of syrup of cola, which soothes the stomach lining, to William Warfield. William immediately begins to vomit. Which term could be used to describe Emily's action?

   a. *res judicata*

   b. *res ipsa loquitur*

   c. nonfeasance

   d. misfeasance

   e. rider

3. Which of the four Ds is violated when a physician fails to inform the patient about the risks of not receiving treatment?

   a. duty

   b. dereliction

   c. direct cause

   d. damages

   e. None of the above is correct.

4. A phlebotomist draws blood from Sam Rodas' right arm. Sam experiences pain and numbness in that arm immediately after the blood is drawn. This is an example of what legal doctrine?

   a. duty

   b. feasance

   c. *res judicata*

   d. proximate cause

   e. rider

5. Amir Fayed continues to smoke after his physician warns him that smoking carries the risk of lung cancer. His physician documents this admonition in Amir's medical record. When Amir develops lung cancer, he sues his doctor for malpractice. Amir states that he did not know about the risk of continued smoking. What malpractice defense might apply in this case?

   a. denial

   b. assumption of risk

   c. contributory negligence

   d. borrowed servant

   e. b and c both apply.

6. Once the court has decided a case and the appeals process is over, there can be no new lawsuit on the same subject between the same two parties. This is referred to as

   a. statute of limitations.

   b. *res ipsa loquitur.*

   c. *res judicata.*

   d. contributory negligence.

   e. comparative negligence.

7. To cover their employees, some physicians carry additional insurance that is added onto the physician's liability insurance. This is called a

   a. liability.

   b. rider.

   c. tort.

   d. cap.

   e. standard of proof.

8. In a medical office, the list of agents for the physician includes the

   a. nurse, medical assistant, and LPN.

   b. technicians.

   c. cleaning staff.

   d. a and b only.

   e. a, b, and c.

9. The doctrine of *respondeat superior* does not apply between the physician and the

   a. nurse.

   b. medical assistant.

   c. phlebotomist.

   d. pharmacist.

   e. physical therapist.

10. Using a third person to help settle a dispute in a nonbinding decision is called

    a. mediation.

    b. arbitration.

    c. malpractice lawsuit.

    d. civil lawsuit.

    e. none of the above

Discussion Cases

1. Latoya Turner, a phlebotomist, drew a blood sample from Liam, a 30-year-old patient of Dr. Wright, to test for hepatitis. As Liam was leaving the office, his friend Harry came in and they greeted each other. Jessica took Harry into an exam room, and in the course of making conversation, he told her that he was a good friend of Liam's. He asked Latoya why Liam was seeing the doctor. Latoya responded that it was just for a test for hepatitis.

   When Harry arrived back home, he called Liam and told him what the phlebotomist had said. Liam called Dr. Wright and complained about Latoya's action and said that he planned to sue Dr. Wright. Dr. Wright dismissed Latoya. Dr. Wright told Latoya that if Liam did bring a lawsuit against her and she lost, then she would sue Latoya.

   a. What should Latoya have done or said when Harry asked about Liam's reason for being in the office?

   _____

   _____

   b. Would Dr. Wright have a legal right to sue Latoya if she was sued and lost?

   _____

   _____

   c. What important right did Latoya violate?

   _____

   _____

2. Denise, an LPN, works in a nursing home on the 3:00 to 11:00 pm shift. She is instructed to prepare medications to give to her own patients as they eat their evening meal. She is also told that it is the policy of the nursing home that she will also prepare all the medications to be distributed in the morning by the LPN who will pass medications at both breakfast and lunch the next day. Denise is told that the reason for doing this is because she will have more time, as the evening shift is not as busy as the morning shift. Denise does not want to object because she really needs the job.

   a. What are the potential problems with this policy?

   _____

   _____

   b. What should Denise do?

   _____

   _____

   c. If a patient is harmed by receiving the incorrect medicine, who would be charged with negligence?

   _____

   _____

3. David, an 89-year-old war hero with no living relatives, drove himself at night to a local hospital when he experienced shortness of breath and a headache. When he entered the emergency department (ED) he was placed in a wheelchair and briefly seen by an ED doctor. He was told that he could not be admitted because he was a veteran and had to go to a VA hospital, which was 90 minutes away, for treatment. David was wheeled into the hallway to wait for transportation to a VA hospital. The night shift was very busy. After sitting in the hall for five hours, David complained that he needed to lie down. The ED staff, who had been trying to move him to a VA hospital with no luck, finally transferred him by ambulance to a local nursing home. David had a massive stroke shortly after being admitted to the nursing home and died six weeks later.

   a. Does there appear to be negligence in this case?

   _____

   _____

   b. In your opinion, who might have acted on behalf of David?

   _____

   _____

   c. In your opinion, would contributory negligence be a defense if there is a malpractice lawsuit relating to David's death?

   _____

   _____

Put It Into Practice

Call an insurance company that handles malpractice insurance. Inquire about the cost and coverage for someone in your profession. Request an informational brochure. Write a summary of the information and report back to your class or your instructor.

Web Hunt

Using the website for the Institute for Healthcare Improvement (www.ihi.org) under Resources, go to Case Studies, and examine one of the latest studies on the website. State what, in your opinion, went wrong.

Critical Thinking Exercise

What would you do if you observed the physician you work for exhibiting signs of carelessness when treating patients and documenting the treatment?

Bibliography

Aiken, T.D. (2008). *Legal and ethical issues in health occupations* (2nd ed.). Saunders.

Beaman, N., Routh, K.S., Papazian-Boyce, L., et al. (2017). *Pearson's comprehensive medical assisting: Administrative and clinical competencies* (4th ed.). Pearson.

Becker, A. (2009). State disciplines hospital. *Hartford Courant* (May 28), 1, 3.

Bonner, L. 2008. Report rips N.C. hospital staff. *Chicago Tribune* (August 20), 9.

Courtroom View Network. (2022). *Iowa jury returns $27M malpractice verdict over delayed meningitis diagnosis, beating $250k settlement offer.* https://blog.cvn.com/iowa-jury-returns-27m-malpractice-verdict-over-delayed-meningitis-diagnosis-beating-250k-settlement-offer

Domino, D. (2009). California blames operator for CT incident. *Diagnostic Imaging*, 31(1). https://www.diagnosticimaging.com/view/california-blames-operator-error-ct-incident

Garner, B. 2019. *Black's law dictionary* (11th ed.). Thomson Reuters.

Glannon, J.W. (2020). *Examples & explanations: The law of torts* (6th ed.). Aspen Publishing.

Guido, G.W. (2019). *Legal and ethical issues in nursing* (7th ed.). Pearson.

Hall, M., & Orentlicher, D. 2020. *Health care law and ethics in a nutshell* (4th ed.). West Academic Publishing.

Levinson, W., Roter, D.L., Mullooly, J.P., Dull, V.T., & Frankel, R.M. (1997). Physician-patient communication. The relationship with malpractice claims among primary care physicians and surgeons. *JAMA.* 277:553–559.

Malnic, E. 2000. GM files appeal of 1.2 billion verdict, calling trial unfair. *Los Angeles Times* (December 7), 1.

Orem, T. (2022). *How much is malpractice insurance?* https://www.nerdwallet.com/article/small-business/how-much-is-malpractice-insurance

Ranji, S. (2016). Measuring and responding to deaths from medical errors. *The PSNet Collection.* https://psnet.ahrq.gov/perspective/measuring-and-responding-deaths-medical-errors

Savitsky, J. 2009. A patient dies, and then the anguish of litigation. *New York Times* (December 29), D5.

Schmalleger, F. (2018). *Criminal justice today: An introductory text for the 21st century* (15th ed.). Pearson.

United States Attorney's Office, District of Colorado. (2023). *Supervisory paramedic sentenced to three years in federal prison for stealing fentanyl and tampering with drugs intended for patients.* https://www.justice.gov/usao-co/pr/supervisory-paramedic-sentenced-three-years-federal-prison-stealing-fentanyl-and

United States Attorney's Office, District of Colorado. (2022). *Colorado Springs company and owner pay $400,000 to resolve allegations that they submitted false claims for aquatic therapy.* https://www.justice.gov/usao-co/pr/colorado-springs-company-and-owner-pay-400000-resolve-allegations-they-submitted-false

United States Attorney's Office, District of New Jersey. (2019). *Four people charged, fifth pleads guilty, in $4.5 million health care fraud conspiracy targeting state health benefits programs.* https://www.justice.gov/usao-nj/pr/four-people-charged-fifth-pleads-guilty-45-million-health-care-fraud-conspiracy-targeting

Venes, D. (2021). *Taber's cyclopedic medical dictionary* (24th ed.). F.A. Davis.

Public Duties of the Healthcare Professional

Learning Objectives

After completing this chapter, you will be able to:

7.1 Define the key terms.

7.2 Describe the public duties of physicians, nurses, and allied health professionals.

7.3 Discuss the guidelines that should be used when completing a legal record or certificate.

7.4 List the information that must be included on a death certificate.

7.5 List ten reportable communicable diseases.

7.6 Discuss the Child Abuse Prevention and Treatment Act of 1974.

7.7 Describe eight signs that indicate a child, spouse, or older adult may be abused.

7.8 List and explain the five schedules of drugs.

7.9 List ten signs that a healthcare worker may be misusing substances.

Key Terms

Autopsy

Bureau of Narcotics and Dangerous Drugs (BNDD)

Compounding

Controlled Substances Act of 1970

Coroner

Dispensing

Drug Enforcement Administration (DEA)

Elder abuse

Employee Assistance Program (EAP)

Food and Drug Administration (FDA)

Forensic medicine

Habituation

Inquest

Intimate partner violence (IPV)

Medical examiner

Morbidity rate

Mortality rate

Opioids

Postmortem

Probable cause

Public duties

Restraining or protective order

Retailing

Safety data sheet (SDS)

Vital statistics

The Case of Olivia and the Pediatrician's Office

Olivia, age 38 months, is brought to the pediatrician's office by her mother, and is taken to an exam room by Monica, a medical assistant. Mother states that Olivia is complaining that her left arm hurts, and she has been irritable for three days, which Monica documents as the chief complaint. Monica proceeds to take Olivia's vital signs. Her temperature and pulse are normal; her blood pressure is a little high. She is of average height, but weighs less than Monica expected. During Monica's assessment, Olivia starts to fidget, and her mother says sternly "Sit still, or else." Monica is startled because Olivia's behavior is normal for a 3-year-old and she wasn't impeding the examination. Monica leaves the room, telling Olivia and her mother that the nurse practitioner will be in soon. Once in the hallway, Monica goes to find the NP, Khalilah. Monica tells Khalilah that

she is concerned about Olivia and reports her findings. Khalilah enters the room, introduces herself, and asks Olivia what hurts. Olivia says nothing and just looks at her mother. Khalilah begins her examination with the right arm, to put Olivia at ease, and then moves to the left arm. She immediately notes that the elbow is partially dislocated (nursemaid's elbow). She also notices small round bruises on Olivia's forearm.

1. What would be the best way for Monica to document her interaction with Olivia and her mother?

2. Was Monica correct to share her concerns with Khalilah?

3. How might Khalilah approach a conversation with the mother about the nursemaid's elbow and the bruises on Olivia's forearm?

Introduction

In order to protect the health of all citizens, each state has passed public health statutes requiring that certain information be reported to state and federal authorities. These statutes help protect the public from unsanitary conditions in public facilities such as restaurants and restrooms, and they require the examination of water supplies. Physicians and other healthcare workers must inform the government when a situation may affect public health, such as in the case of communicable diseases.

Public Health Records and Vital Statistics

Important events, or **vital statistics**, in a person's life, such as birth and death dates, are used by the government, public health agencies, and other institutions to determine population trends and needs. The reporting agencies and services include the Department of Health and Human Services (DHHS), Centers for Disease Control and Prevention (CDC), the National Center for Health Statistics (NCHS), and the Public Health Service. The **mortality rate**, also called the death rate, is the ratio of the number of deaths to total population in a given location. The **morbidity rate** is the number of sick people or cases of disease in relationship to a specific population. The *Mortality and Morbidity Weekly Report*, a list of illness and death rates for a variety of illnesses, is published every week by the CDC in Atlanta, Georgia. The CDC is always on the lookout for outbreaks of disease in major cities and all the states. Therefore, the CDC needs to have accurate input from physicians and healthcare officials of statistics relating to deaths and illness.

The healthcare team's duty to report these events falls in the category of **public duties**—that is, duties owed to the public. These duties include reports of births, stillbirths, and deaths; communicable illnesses or diseases; drug misuse; certain injuries, such as rape, gunshot, and knife wounds; animal bites; and abuse of children, spouses, and older adults. Additional information includes data such as marriages, divorces, and induced termination of pregnancies.

Office personnel, such as medical assistants, and school nurses may carry out many of these reporting duties. The collection of this information should be taken seriously. The data—or facts, figures, and statistics—represent information about the individual patient's life. In addition, some of the data are of a highly sensitive nature, such as the facts concerning rape, abuse, and death.

Births

Physicians and midwives issue the certificates of live birth that will be maintained during a person's life as proof of age. A valid birth certificate is required to receive many government documents such as a Social Security card, passport, driver's license, and voter registration.

The rules and regulations regarding birth certificates vary by state. In all states, physicians can sign certificates for live births, and in some states midwives can as well (Figure 7.1). For a hospital birth, the certificate is filed by the hospital at the county clerk's office in the state in which the birth took place. If the birth occurs at home, the midwife or person in attendance at the birth can file the birth certificate at the county Public Health Department. For unattended births, a local health officer attempts to verify the facts regarding the birth. While the time frame to submit a birth certificate varies somewhat from state to state, in most cases it must be done within the first week of the baby's life. Some states impose a criminal penalty if the birth and death certificates are not properly completed and handled. If the birth has not been registered within a year, then the physician, midwife, or any other person in attendance at the birth may have to go to court to provide proof of the birth.

Physicians and others who attend a birth, such as midwives, are required to report certain diseases in newborns. Ophthalmia neonatorum is a serious eye condition present at birth that causes inflammation, swelling, redness, and an unnatural discharge in an infant's eyes. If untreated, it may result in blindness. Evidence of this disease must be reported within 12 hours after birth. A test for the condition of phenylketonuria (PKU) is another test required by state health departments on newborns. PKU can be treated with dietary restrictions. In addition, some states also require testing for sickle cell disease.

Med Tip

Some states impose a criminal penalty if a birth or death certificate is not handled correctly.

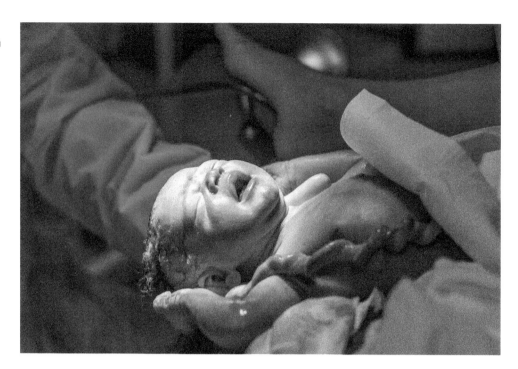

Figure 7–1 Physicians (and midwives in some states) sign certificates of live births

Source: Sopotnicki/Shutterstock

Deaths

Physicians sign a certificate indicating the cause of a natural death in all states, and nurse practitioners and physician assistants can do so in some states. The Department of Public Health in each state provides the specific requirement for that state. For example, in the case of a stillbirth before the twentieth week of gestation, the physician must file both a birth and death certificate in some states. In other states, neither is required if the fetus has not reached the twentieth week of gestation. And in some states, only a death certificate is required for a stillbirth after the twentieth week. In the case of a live birth with a subsequent death of the infant, both a birth certificate and a death certificate are necessary in all states.

The physician who had been attending the deceased person usually signs the death certificate, stating the time and cause of death. The physician must include the following information on the certificate:

- The date and time of death
- The cause of death: diseases, injuries, or complications
- How long the deceased person was treated for the disease or injury before dying
- The presence or absence of pregnancy (for female decedent)
- If an autopsy took place

In most states, a death certificate must be signed within 24 to 72 hours after the patient's death. After the physician has signed the certificate, it is given to the mortician, who files it with the state or county clerk's office (Figure 7.2).

Med Tip

Because funeral arrangements and burial cannot take place until the death certificate is signed, it is important that the healthcare provider sign as soon as possible.

The death certificate provides proof that a death has occurred. It is often required to confirm information concerning veteran's benefits, Internal Revenue Service (IRS) information, insurance benefits, and other financial information when settling an estate. If a funeral home provides the burial, they will often obtain copies of the death certificate for the family to submit to agencies, such as the IRS or credit card companies. The death certificate must be signed as soon as possible after a person's death. The time and date of the death are important facts and must be accurate.

Figure 7–2 Death certificates need to be completed and signed within 24 to 72 hours

Source: JohnKwan/Shutterstock

A **coroner** is the public health officer who holds an investigation, or **inquest**, if the death is from an unknown or violent cause. The coroner or medical examiner completes the death certificate if the deceased has not been under the care of a physician. In some states, the coroner will also investigate an accidental death, such as one resulting from a fall. A **medical examiner** is a physician, usually a pathologist, who can investigate an unexplained death and perform autopsies. An **autopsy**, which is a **postmortem** or after-death examination of the organs and tissues of the body, may have to be performed to determine the cause of death.

In some deaths, a coroner or health official must sign a death certificate. This applies, for example, to deaths in nursing homes, assisted living facilities, and home health nurses, where a nurse may be in charge when a death occurs. Cases needing a coroner's signature include the following:

- No physician present at the time of death
- A violent death, including homicide, suicide, or accident
- Death as a result of a criminal action
- An unlawful death such as assisted suicide
- Death from an undetermined cause (unexpected or unexplained)
- Death resulting from chemical, electrical, or radiation injury
- Death caused by criminal abortion, including self-induced
- Death occurring less than 24 hours after hospital admission
- No physician attending the patient within 36 hours preceding death
- Death occurring outside of a hospital or licensed health care facility
- Suspicious death, such as from a fall
- Death of a person whose body is not claimed by friends or relatives
- Death of a person whose identity is unknown
- Death of a child under the age of two years if the death is from an unknown cause or if it appears the death is from sudden infant death syndrome (SIDS)
- Death of a person in jail or prison

Unless the death results from suspicious causes, such as a homicide, an autopsy cannot be performed on a body without the consent of the surviving person who has the "first right" to the body. This person is usually a family member who is responsible for burying the deceased person.

Communicable Diseases

Physicians and advance practice providers must report all diseases that can be transmitted from one person to another and are considered a general threat to the public. The report can be made to the public health authorities by phone or mail. The communicable disease report should include the following:

- Name, address, age, and occupation of the patient
- Name of the disease or suspected disease
- Date of onset of the disease
- Name of the person issuing the report

The list of reportable diseases differs from state to state, but all states require reports of tuberculosis, rubeola, rubella, tetanus, diphtheria, cholera, poliomyelitis, acquired immunodeficiency syndrome (AIDS), meningococcal meningitis, and rheumatic fever. In addition, some diseases, such as influenza, need to be reported if there is a high incidence within a certain population. Sexually transmitted infections (STIs), such as syphilis, gonorrhea, and genital warts, must also be reported to protect the public. Employees in food service, day care, and healthcare occupations are more carefully monitored for contagious diseases by public health departments.

Vaccine requirements for children can vary by state, and they are typically determined by state laws and regulations rather than federal law. However, there are some vaccines that are recommended by the CDC and the Advisory Committee on Immunization Practices (ACIP) for all children, and many states have adopted these recommendations into their vaccination requirements. These vaccines include the following:

- Measles, mumps, and rubella (MMR) vaccine
- Diphtheria, tetanus, and pertussis (DTaP) vaccine
- Polio vaccine
- Hepatitis B vaccine
- *Haemophilus influenzae* type b (Hib) vaccine
- Varicella (chickenpox) vaccine
- Pneumococcal conjugate vaccine (PCV)
- Rotavirus vaccine
- Hepatitis A vaccine
- Meningococcal conjugate vaccine

The specific requirements for these vaccines, as well as the age at which they are required, can vary by state. Additionally, some states may have exemptions or allowances for medical, religious, or philosophical reasons, which can further complicate the requirements.

It's important to check with your state's health department or a healthcare provider to understand the specific vaccination requirements in your area, as they can change over time and may differ from state to state. Schools and childcare facilities often require proof of vaccination compliance, so parents should be aware of the requirements in their state to ensure their children are up to date on their vaccinations.

The National Childhood Vaccine Injury Act, passed by Congress in 1986, requires a physician or healthcare administrator to report all vaccine administrations and adverse reactions to vaccines and toxoids. In addition, the name and address of the person administering the vaccine and the date of administration should be documented in the patient's record.

Med Tip

Healthcare providers must report information directly relating to the vaccine and toxoid, such as the manufacturer and lot number.

All states have statutes or regulations that require healthcare providers to report cases of AIDS to the local or state department of health. The reporting of HIV test results varies from state to state. HIV reporting laws are generally intended to monitor the prevalence of HIV and improve public health responses. While many states do have mandatory reporting of positive HIV test results, the specifics can differ, including whether the names or personally identifiable information of individuals are included in the reports.

All states have voluntary HIV testing for all healthcare workers. However, reporting a positive HIV test result is not required throughout the country.

Many states have partner-notification laws that require the patient or the provider to tell the patient's sex or needle-sharing partners that they are at risk of the infection. A physician who wishes to notify a contact person under one of these laws should always discuss such plans with the patient first. The physician may wish to remind the patient of the moral obligation to others. Patients should always be informed that there are some statutes that impose criminal liability on someone who is an HIV carrier and knowingly engages in activities that could spread the virus to others (Fla. Stat. §Ann. 384.24.).

Med Tip

It is the duty of the healthcare provider to report communicable diseases, such as HIV and AIDS. However, patients often feel more comfortable sharing personal information with nurses, medical assistants, or laboratory technicians. These healthcare professionals have a duty to report this information to the provider.

Child Abuse

The first child protective agency in the world was established in 1874 when a little 10-year-old girl, Mary Ellen McCormack, explained to the court how her mother beat and abused her. The New York Society for the Prevention of Cruelty to Children began as a result of her story. She became known as "the child who put a face on abuse."

The Child Abuse Prevention and Treatment Act of 1974 requires reporting of all child abuse cases. All states have statutes that define child abuse and require that all abuse must be reported. To begin to investigate questions of neglect and child abuse, the state must have **probable cause**, which is a reasonable belief that something improper has happened. Many states list personnel who are required by law to make an immediate report of any suspected child abuse. These personnel include teachers; health professionals such as physicians, advance practice providers, emergency room staff, nurses, and medical assistants; law-enforcement personnel; daycare personnel; and social service workers. Neglect, or the failure to provide for a child's basic care, such as food, shelter, and medical care, are also considered to be abuse. Questionable injuries of children, including bruises, fractured bones, and burns, must be reported to local law-enforcement agencies.

Med Tip

Parents may have to be asked to leave the exam room while their child is questioned about suspicious bruises and injuries. See Child Abuse Prevention and Treatment Act in Chapter 12.

The term *battered child syndrome* is sometimes used by healthcare professionals to describe a series of injuries, including fractures, bruises, and burns, done to children by parents or caregivers. This is not a legal term but, rather, a description of injuries (Figure 7.3). Signs of neglect such as malnutrition, poor growth, and lack of hygiene are reportable in some states. In a Minnesota case, the court ruled that the Minnesota Board of Psychology acted correctly when it revoked the license of a psychologist who failed to report the sexual abuse of a child (*In re Schroeder*, 415 N.W.2d 436, Minn. Ct. App. 1987).

Physicians have been held liable if they do not report cases of child abuse. For example, in *Landeros v. Flood*, the state Supreme Court ruled that the physician should not have returned a battered child to the parents after he treated the child for intentionally inflicted injuries. The court held that "battered child syndrome" was a legitimate medical diagnosis and the physician should have suspected that the parents would inflict further injury on the child (*Landeros v. Flood*, 551 P.2d 389, Cal. 1976).

Any person who suspects that child abuse is taking place can report the abuse to local authorities without fear of liability. This includes teachers, nurses, and other healthcare personnel. It can sometimes be difficult to determine if a child's injury is accidental or intentional. The persons reporting these cases, acting in the best interests of the child, are protected by law from being sued by parents and others. In the case of *Satler v. Larsen*, a pediatrician reported a case of possible child abuse concerning a four-month-old comatose infant to the Bureau of Child Welfare. There was not enough evidence to demonstrate that the parents were at fault, and they subsequently sued the physician for defamation. The defamation lawsuit was dismissed because the physician reported the suspected abuse in good faith (*Satler v. Larsen*, 520 N.Y.S.2d 378, App. Div. 1987).

Most state statutes require that an oral report of suspected abuse be made immediately, followed by a written report. The written report should include the following:

- Name and address of the child as well as persons(s) responsible for the care of the child
- Child's age
- Description of the type and extent of the child's injuries
- Identity of the abuser, if known
- Photographs, soiled clothing, or any other evidence that abuse has taken place

Med Tip

The person reporting a suspected case of child abuse is protected from civil and criminal liability unless that person is the abuser. However, failure to report a suspected case of child abuse may result in a charge of misdemeanor.

Parental neglect can be perpetrated by parents, legal guardians, or caregivers. It is a broad concept that includes child abandonment and failure to provide medical care, food, housing, and proper clothing. Some other indicators of neglect could be the child has low body weight or bad hygiene. An example of parental neglect is when parents have a religious belief that does not allow medical treatment for their children. States refrain, as much as possible, from interfering with parental rights because the parents are the decision makers for their children. However, the state may have to step in when there is intentional neglect such as when a child is not receiving the medical care that could their life. For example, members of some religious denominations do not allow blood transfusions. If a child is diagnosed with leukemia, a type of cancer of the blood, they may need frequent blood transfusions in order to live. A full court hearing may be required to temporarily remove the child from the parent's custody in order to obtain treatment. There have been cases in which parents were charged with murder, manslaughter, or negligent homicide when a child died because of apparent parental neglect.

Elder Abuse

Elder abuse is defined in the amendment to the Older Americans Act (1987). It includes physical abuse, neglect, exploitation, and abandonment of adults 60 years and older and is reportable in most states. The reporting agency varies by state but generally includes social service agencies, welfare departments, and nursing home personnel. As in the case of child abuse, the person reporting the abuse is, in most states, protected from civil and criminal liability.

Residents of nursing home facilities must be protected from abusive healthcare workers. To do so, some states have made "resident abuse" a crime. In the case of *Brinson v. Axelrod*, a nurse's aide was prosecuted for resident abuse for causing injuries to the hands and face of an elderly resident (*Brinson v. Axelrod*, 499 N.Y.S.2d 24, App. Div. 1986). Another medical employee in a New York case was found guilty of resident abuse when she "held the patient's chin and poured the medication down her throat" after the patient had refused medication (*In re Axelrod*, 560 N.Y.S.2d 573, App. Div. 1990).

Older adults are also protected by the Older Americans Act from financial abuse or exploitation. This is considered a crime in many states.

Intimate Partner Violence

Intimate partner violence, also known as IPV, is defined by the CDC as physical violence, sexual violence, stalking and psychological aggression by a current or former intimate partner. Laws governing the reporting of IPV vary from state to state. The local police may have to become involved when IPV is suspected, and in some cases, a court will issue a **restraining or protective order** prohibiting the abuser from coming into contact with the victim. Questions that are frequently asked of a suspected abused partner include the following:

- Are you or your children afraid of your spouse?
- Does your partner threaten, grab, shove, or hit you?
- Does your partner prevent you from spending time with your family or friends?
- Do you stay with your partner because you are afraid of what they would do if you broke up?
- Has your partner ever abandoned you in a dangerous place?

Abused partners are warned that in most relationships the cycle of abuse happens many times. The abuse does not stop.

Med Tip

It is routine in many medical offices and hospitals to ask all patients if they feel safe at home. If the answer is "no," providers and nurses should follow up with more conversation; medical assistants and other allied health professionals should report the information to the provider.

Signs of Abuse

Healthcare workers, social workers, teachers, daycare personnel, and nursing home staff should all be on the lookout for signs of abuse. However, physical signs in children, partners, older adults, and persons with cognitive impairment can vary. Signs of abuse include the following:

- Repeated injuries
- Bruises such as blackened eyes and unexplained swelling
- Unexplained fractures
- Bite marks
- Unusual marks, such as those occurring from a cigarette burn
- Bruising, swelling, or pain in the genital area
- Signs of inadequate nutrition, such as sunken eyes and weight loss
- Sexually transmitted infection or genital abrasions
- Makeup used to hide bruises
- Sunglasses worn inside a building or hospital to hide blackened eyes

Healthcare workers must do everything possible to gain the victim's confidence. However, it is not possible to assure the victim that all information will be held in confidence, as abuse cases are reportable by law. This should be clearly explained to the victim at the time of the initial visit.

It is difficult to discuss the abuse with the victim when the suspected abuser is present. Always attempt to speak to the victim in private. If possible, have another healthcare professional present during the interview to act as a witness.

Med Tip

Those persons who are unable to protect themselves, such as children, must be protected by healthcare workers and caregivers who become aware of abusive situations. However, take care not to conclude too quickly that abuse has occurred when one or more of these signs are present. For example, some people, especially children, are simply prone to accidents.

Gathering Evidence in Cases of Abuse

Gathering evidence from abuse victims usually takes place in a hospital or emergency department setting. However, a physician, advance practice provider, or nurse may see an abused patient in the office. Precise documentation of all injuries, bruises, and suspicious fluid deposits in the genital areas of children is critical. The court may subpoena these records at a later date. The physician may also be asked to testify in court and offer observations.

Evidence in abuse cases includes the following:

- Photo of bruises and other signs of abuse
- Female child's urine specimen (containing sperm) or laboratory report indicating the presence of sperm in the urine
- Body fluids, such as semen, vomitus, or gastric contents such as found on clothing
- Various samples, such as blood, semen, and vaginal or rectal smears
- Foreign objects such as bullets, hair, and nail clippings

Evidence should be handled as little as possible, and by only one employee, to prevent damaging it. All evidence in abuse cases should be clearly labeled and protected with sealed plastic bags or covers.

It is important to maintain a clear chain of custody for evidence to verify that the specimen has been handled correctly. All evidence must be clearly labeled with the name of the patient, date, and time when the specimen was obtained, and all information regarding evidence should be carefully documented in the patient's medical record. In addition to the time and date, the medical record should include complete documentation of the patient's condition as well as the treatment that was provided. All photographs and X-rays should be carefully labeled with the patient's name, patient registration number, time, and date. Items such as clothing, including underwear, must be retained as evidence and not handled excessively or washed. All evidence should be kept in a locked storage area until it is required.

Care must be taken when turning evidence over to a third party. Always request identification and authorization of the person as well as a receipt, which can then be placed into the medical record.

Other Reportable Conditions

Many states require healthcare providers to file a report of certain medical conditions in order to maintain accurate public health statistics. These conditions include cancer, epilepsy, and congenital disorders such as PKU of the newborn that can cause cognitive impairment if untreated. Because the testing for many of these conditions occurs in the hospital, the reporting responsibility rests on the hospital.

Gunshot Wounds

Gunshot wound laws require reports when injuries are inflicted by lethal weapons or by unlawful acts. In addition, every case of a bullet wound, powder burn, or any other injury arising from the discharge of a gun or firearm must be reported to the police authorities of the city or town where the person reporting is located. The report must be made by the healthcare provider treating the patient or an administrative person in charge of a hospital or other institution.

Animal Bites

Most states require that healthcare personnel who treat a patient with a dog bite report the incident to the local animal control office. The report usually needs to be made within 12–24 hours of seeing the patient, and usually includes their name, age, address, contact information, and gender, along with their location when the bite occurred (Figure 7.3). Some states also ask for the type of dog, the name and age of the dog, and a brief description of the incident.

Forensic Medicine

Forensic medicine is that branch of medicine concerned with the law, especially criminal law, such as in gunshot cases resulting in death. A forensic pathologist is a physician who specializes in the examination of bodies when there are circumstances indicating that the death was unnatural, such as in suicide, accident, or homicide. Their examination usually includes an assessment of the time of death (from data such as the temperature of the corpse and decomposition) and a determination of the cause of death

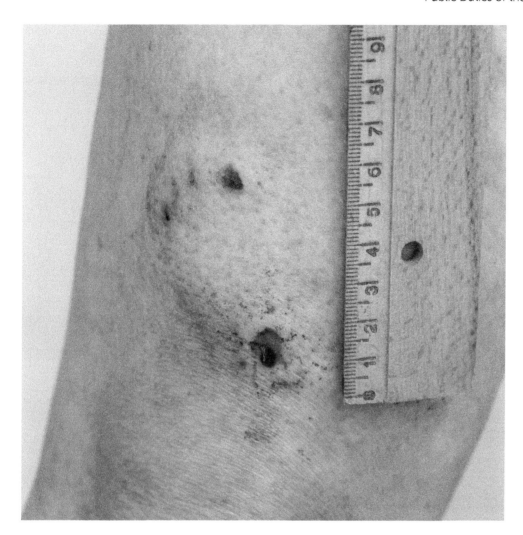

Figure 7–3 Puncture wounds on a leg, caused by a dog bite

Source: sima - Zoran Simin/ Shutterstock

(based on a study of the injuries). They also examine blood, hair, and skin from the victim with those on any weapons found in automobiles or on the clothing of suspects.

Forensic pathologists also examine victims of sexual and child abuse. In addition, they consult in cases of attempted poisoning and drug abuse. They are called upon to advise on blood grouping in cases of disputed paternity.

Controlled Substances Act and Regulations

The **Food and Drug Administration**, also known as FDA, an agency within the Department of Health and Human Services, ultimately enforces drug (prescription and over-the-counter) sales and distribution. The FDA came into existence with the passage of the Food, Drug, and Cosmetic Act of 1938, which sought to ensure the safety of those items sold within the United States.

Drugs that have a potential for addiction, an acquired physical or psychological dependence on a drug, **habituation**, the development of an emotional dependence on a drug because of repeated use, or misuse, abuse, excessive use, or improper use, are also regulated. The **Drug Enforcement Administration**, also known as DEA, of the Department of Justice controls these drugs by enforcing the Comprehensive Drug Abuse Prevention and Control Act of 1970, more commonly known as the **Controlled Substances Act of 1970**. This act regulates the manufacture and distribution of the drugs that can cause dependence and places controlled drugs into five categories that are called schedules: I, II, III, IV, and V. The **Bureau of Narcotics and Dangerous Drugs**, also known as BNDD, is the agency of the federal government authorized to enforce drug control.

Physicians (and advance practice providers in some states) who administer controlled substances, also called narcotics, must register with the DEA in Washington, DC, and the registration must be renewed every three years. A DEA registration number is assigned to each physician. A physician who leaves the practice of medicine must return the registration form and unused narcotic order forms to the nearest DEA office.

An accurate count of all narcotics must be kept in a record such as a narcotics log, and all narcotics records must be kept for two years. The date and the name of the person to whom the drug was administered, along with the signature of the person administering the drug, are recorded. In some states, physicians who prescribe narcotic drugs but do not administer them, such as dentists and psychiatrists, are also required to maintain narcotics logs and inventory records.

Most states limit the administration of narcotics to physicians and nurses. States may be more restrictive, but not less, than the federal government when regulating the administration of controlled substances. For example, a state may require physicians to keep controlled substances records for a longer period of time than the federal regulations require.

All narcotics must be kept under lock and key. According to the FDA, because of environmental concerns, *controlled* (narcotic) drugs should only be "wasted" or destroyed down a toilet or drain if there are specific instructions on the packaging to do this. Two people should be present when controlled substances are destroyed. Non-narcotic drugs should be removed from their original containers and properly disposed of with other medical waste.

As of 2023, 36 of the 50 states have enacted mandates for the use of Electronic Prescriptions for Controlled Substances (EPCS). And as of January 1, 2023, all Medicare Part D and Medicare Advantage prescription drug plans were required to be transmitted electronically. The use of EPCS is intended to overcome many of the problems associated with paper prescriptions. Electronic prescriptions are more legible and trackable for providers and pharmacists. They are intended to reduce the problem of stolen prescription pages and reduce the risk of medication errors.

The *controlled drugs* are classified into five schedules based on the potential for abuse, which are summarized in Table 7.1.

A violation of the Controlled Substances Act is a criminal offense that can result in a fine, loss of license to practice medicine, and a jail sentence. Medical office personnel can assist providers in maintaining compliance with the law by

- alerting the provider to license renewal dates;
- maintaining accurate inventory records; and
- keeping all controlled substances in a secure cabinet.

Table 7–1 Schedule for Controlled Substances

Level	Description	Comment
Schedule I	Highest potential for addiction and abuse. Not accepted for medical use. May be used for research purposes. Examples: heroin or LSD.	Cannot be prescribed.
Schedule II	High potential for addiction and abuse. Accepted for medical use in the United States. Examples: codeine, morphine, oxycodone, and secobarbital.	A DEA-licensed provider must prescribe through EPCS or complete the required triplicate prescription forms entirely in their own handwriting. The prescription must be filled within seven days, and it may not be refilled. In an emergency, the physician may order a limited amount of the drug by telephone. These drugs must be stored under lock and key if they are kept on the office premises. The law requires that the dispensing record of these drugs be kept on file for two years.
Schedule III	Moderate-to-low potential for addiction and abuse. Examples: butabarbital, anabolic steroids, and APC with codeine.	A DEA number is not required to prescribe these drugs, but the provider must prescribe through EPCS or handwrite the order. Five refills are allowed during a six-month period, and this must be indicated on the prescription form. Only a provider may telephone the pharmacist for these drugs.
Schedule IV	Lower potential for addiction and abuse than Schedule III drugs. Examples: chloral hydrate, phenobarbital, and diazepam.	The prescription must be prescribed through EPCS or signed by the provider. Five refills are allowed over a six-month period.
Schedule V	Low potential for addiction and abuse. Examples: cough medications containing codeine, lomotil.	Inventory records must be maintained on these drugs.

Prescriptions for Controlled Drugs

Physicians (and advance practice providers in some states) with a DEA registration number may issue a prescription for narcotics. This registration number must appear on all prescriptions for controlled substances. Schedule I drugs require approval by the FDA and the DEA for use in research. The sale of these drugs is forbidden. Schedule II drugs require a special DEA order form. Because there is a high potential for abuse and addiction with these drugs, the prescription cannot be refilled. Providers must take a written inventory of their drug supply every two years. All narcotics-dispensing records must be kept for a two-year period. It requires careful communication between the provider and patient to ensure that the patient is not seeking narcotics prescriptions from multiple physicians. In some instances, pharmacies that maintain careful records have been able to pinpoint abuse.

The compounding, dispensing, and retailing of drugs is controlled by the Controlled Substances Act. **Compounding** is the combination and mixing of drugs and chemicals. For example, a pharmacist compounds a drug by filling a physician's prescription that involves preparing and mixing medications. In general, most medications are compounded by the pharmaceutical companies. Hospital-based pharmacists may have to compound certain medications such as children's dosages. **Dispensing** is defined as distributing, delivering, disposing, or giving away a drug, medicine, prescription, or chemical. Most state statutes authorize professionals, such as nurses, nurse practitioners, or physician assistants, to dispense drugs. For example, hospital-based nurses may dispense to their patients medications that have been prepared by a pharmacist, if they have a physician's order. However, nurses may not enter a hospital pharmacy and remove drugs/medications from the hospital's floor stock in order to carry out a physician's orders. **Retailing** is the legal act of selling or trading a drug, medicine, prescription, or chemical.

The term "drug," in most state statutes, is similar to the definition found in the Federal Food, Drug, and Cosmetic Act. This states that a drug is intended to affect the structure or function of the body of man or other animals. When applying this definition, the courts have decided that aspirin, laxatives, vitamin and mineral capsules, and whole human blood can be considered drugs under certain circumstances. Therefore, when handling these drugs, even aspirin, nurses and other professionals must be aware that they cannot be compounded or retailed. And a nurse can only dispense these drugs with a physician's order. This means that if a hospitalized, nursing home, or home health patient asks a nurse for an aspirin, it cannot be dispensed without a prescription from the physician (Figure 7.4).

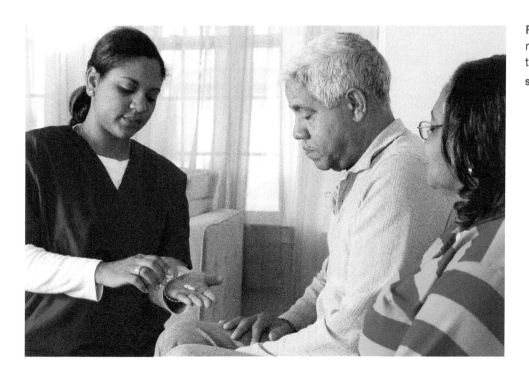

Figure 7–4 A home health nurse explaining drug safety to a patient and his wife

Source: Rob Marmion/Shutterstock

Substance Misuse

Misuse of prescription drugs is reportable immediately, according to the law. Such misuse can be difficult to determine, as the patient may seek prescriptions for the same drug from different providers. A provider will want to see a patient before prescribing medication. A violation of controlled substances laws is a criminal offense. For providers working in states that have not adopted EPCS, prescription pads and blanks should always be kept locked up when not in use.

Med Tip

All healthcare workers should be familiar with the laws relating to controlled substances. Violation of the laws can result in fines, imprisonment, and a loss of license to practice medicine.

Substance Misuse by Healthcare Personnel

Physicians, advance practice providers, nurses, and allied health professionals are as susceptible as any other individuals to misusing drugs or developing a substance use disorder (SUD). They often work in highly stressful work settings with easy access to drugs. It is estimated that 10–15 percent of healthcare workers misuse drugs or alcohol at some time in their career. Healthcare professionals who feel they are developing a substance abuse problem are ethically required to seek help in order to prevent mistakes in the workplace. Impaired healthcare professionals not only pose a potential threat to their patients, but they also tend to neglect their own health and well-being. Likewise, colleagues of impaired professionals are ethically required to report impaired colleagues to their superiors. Warning signs of impaired healthcare personnel in the workplace are outlined in Table 7.2.

Table 7–2 Warning Signs of Impaired Healthcare Personnel in the Workplace

Situation	Warning Signs
Poor work performance	• Frequent absences or late arrivals • Unorganized or erratic behavior • Errors in patient care • Poor charting or hygiene practices • Frequent trips to the bathroom • Unexplained absences from the unit
Easy access to prescription drugs	• Missing drugs • Inaccurate narcotic counts • Patient complaints of ineffective pain control • Judgment errors • Always volunteering to distribute medication to patients
Changes in mood	• Unable to concentrate • Irritable • Abrupt mood swings • Apathetic or depressed • Erratic behavior • Unkempt appearance
Signs of drug or alcohol use	• Breath smells of alcohol • Overuse of perfume, mouthwash, or mints • Slurred speech • Unsteady gait • Flushed face or reddened eyes • Wearing long sleeves in hot weather

If you suspect a colleague of misusing substances:

- Do not ignore their poor performance.
- Do not lighten or change their patient assignment.
- Do not accept excuses for their behavior.
- Do not allow yourself to be manipulated or fear confronting a professional if patient safety is in jeopardy.

Instead, you should do the following:

- Educate yourself on the signs and symptoms of substance misuse.
- Know your organization's policies and procedures concerning impaired workers.
- Document the facts that are concerning you (see Table 7.2 for examples).
- Urge the colleague to seek help (if you feel comfortable doing so).
- Submit your concerns and documentation to your superior.

Physicians with SUD are usually assigned to a physician health program (PHP) that provides coordination, monitoring, and expertise in the care of impaired physicians. Since 1982, the American Nurses Association (ANA) has stressed the need for peer assistance programs to support nurses who misuse substances. These programs offer comprehensive monitoring and support services to reasonably ensure the safe rehabilitation and return of the nurse to the professional community. See the following section on Employee Assistance Programs.

The Opioid Crisis

Opioid abuse is a relatively new problem that quietly entered the healthcare scene but has now become a full-blown crisis. When used correctly, in small dosages, opioids can be useful to help control pain. **Opioids** are synthetic products that are not derived from opium but have the same opiumlike effect, acting on the brain to decrease the sensation of pain. However, these drugs can also cause the breathing reflex and heartbeat to shut down in some people. It is important to remember that opioids are pain killers that can be addictive and do require a prescription. Unfortunately, a widespread black market has developed in which people can obtain opioids without a prescription. Opioid drugs include codeine, fentanyl, heroin, hydrocodone, hydromorphone, methadone, morphine, oxycodone, paregoric, sufentanil, and tramadol.

Med Tip

Addiction is an acquired dependence on drugs of abuse, such as narcotics, or alcohol. Addictions can affect the brain, cause dangerous behavior, and sometimes lead to overdose and death.

According to recent statistics, the drug overdose problem in America is a leading cause of death for Americans who are under the age of 50. The drug overdoses are especially severe when they occur along with the use of alcohol. Some studies suggest that up to one-third of the users of opioids for chronic pain will misuse them. In addition, 10 percent may even become addicted. According to recent literature, there is an added risk of addiction if the person has received the opioids illegally (without prescription) because they may be able to buy more pills than the physician would have ordered.

Some of the physical signs that a person is misusing opioids include the following:

- Confusion
- Physical agitation
- Unexplained or sudden drowsiness
- Withdrawal from others
- Unexpected vomiting and/or diarrhea
- Poor decision making
- Lying or making excuses for mood changes

- Dramatic mood changes
- Slow or shallow breathing
- Sudden dramatic behavior changes
- Poor coordination
- Unexpected depression
- Slurred speech

Given the current increasing numbers of opioid users, it is important to know how opioids act in the body and how they can be used safely. Opioids have the ability to affect a person's thinking as well as judgment. They are considered to be addictive, as well as dangerous, drugs if not used correctly. As they travel with the blood throughout the body, they release signals to the brain. Lower doses of this medicine can make the patient sleepy; unfortunately, higher doses may severely affect a patient with a slowing down of their heart rate and breathing, which can even lead to death. Because drugs sometimes interact with or boost another drug's effects, it is important for patients to discuss with their physicians all the medications they are using.

The CDC provides guidance to healthcare providers for safe prescribing of opioid medications. The CDC's recommendations include the following:

- Prescribe only the lowest effective dose, for the shortest period of time, whenever treating acute pain.
- Avoid or even delay prescribing opioids for chronic pain.
- Work with patients to create realistic treatment goals.

Med Tip

Opioid use should not be stopped suddenly. A healthcare provider needs to oversee the gradual process.

Protection for the Employee and the Environment

Employee Assistance Programs

An **Employee Assistance Program**, also known as EAP, may be defined as a management-financed and confidential counseling and referral service. It is designed to help employees and/or their family members assess a problem, such as alcoholism or marital strife, develop a plan to resolve personal problems, and determine the appropriate resources to assist in the resolution process. An EAP is a service provided by many institutions, such as hospitals and corporations, for all of their employees and employees' family members. The EAP is geared toward helping employees maintain their job performance while attempting to resolve the difficulty. It is generally administered and staffed by experienced professionals who are trained to understand personal problems and their relation to job performance.

It is estimated that employee health-related problems cost the U.S. economy $260 billion annually. Over $80 billion is related to alcohol and/or drug misuse and the resulting loss of productivity.

A "troubled" employee may need additional support from his or her supervisor. In addition, productivity may be affected for both employee and supervisor. The types of problems that an EAP can help with are substance abuse (alcoholism and drug abuse), stress-related (depression and anxiety) issues, family and marital problems, psychological troubles, and job-related (interpersonal and burnout) stress.

Med Tip

It is important to remember that only trained, objective professionals should counsel employees regarding their personal problems.

Without an effective way to deal with employee problems, a healthcare supervisor may confront the employee, accept continued excuses, provide inadequate counseling, reassign tasks, give verbal warnings, demote or transfer the employee, give a final warning, and eventually resort to termination of the employee. By using an effective EAP, the supervisor

- continues to supervise the employee's job performance;
- receives feedback from the first appointment from the EAP (subsequent appointment counseling sessions are not reported back to the supervisor because of confidentiality issues);
- notes improved performance or states the consequences of poor performance;
- consults the EAP counselor for suggestions on how to work with a difficult employee;
- does not diagnose;
- follows disciplinary documentation procedures;
- is free to focus on job performance; and
- continues to talk with the employee, but does not provide counseling.

Confidentiality is essential for the success of any EAP. Employees who have confidence in the medical staff may discuss personal problems with physicians and nurses. Many of these problems are those that an EAP staff is especially trained to handle, such as alcoholism, drug abuse, and marital problems. If it is necessary for a medical unit, such as in a hospital setting, to receive feedback on the employee's condition, then the employee must sign a release allowing the EAP counselor to communicate with the medical unit.

While it is preferable that employees leave their personal problems outside of the workplace, this is often difficult to do. All healthcare workers must have empathy for each other, while still respecting an individual's privacy.

Medical Waste

Hospitals in the United States generate almost 6 million tons of hazardous medical waste each year. And that number does not include dental practices, veterinary clinics, laboratories, nursing homes, medical offices, and other healthcare facilities. Much of this waste is dangerous, especially when it is potentially infectious or radioactive. There are four major types of medical waste: solid, chemical, radioactive, and infectious.

- *Solid waste* is generated in every area of a facility, including administration, cafeterias, patient rooms, and medical offices. It includes trash such as used paper goods, bottles, cardboard, and cans. Solid waste is not considered hazardous, but it can pollute the environment. Mandatory recycling programs have assisted in reducing some of the solid waste in the United States.
- *Chemical waste* includes germicides, cleaning solvents, and pharmaceuticals. This waste can create a hazardous situation—a fire or explosion—for the institution or community. It can also cause harm if ingested, inhaled, or absorbed through the skin or mucous membranes. Chemotherapeutic waste can be picked up only by a licensed chemotherapeutic waste transporter. Anyone handling chemotherapy waste, such as bedside nurses, home health aides, and family caregivers, should wear latex gloves when handling soiled bedding or clothing, bedpans, urinals, emesis basins, and diapers. After the caregiving tasks are complete, the gloves should be removed and the hands should be washed with soap and water.

Medical personnel have a duty to refrain from pouring toxic, flammable, or irritating chemicals down a drain. These chemicals should be placed in sturdy containers or buckets and then removed by a licensed removal facility. Chemical wastes must be documented on a **safety data sheet**, also known as SDS, which also provides specific information on handling and disposing of chemicals safely. Clinical laboratories, such as those used by nursing and medical assistant students, must also document their use of chemicals.

Med Tip

Don't flush medications down a toilet unless specifically instructed on the label to do so. Drugs can kill bacteria in septic systems and pass largely untouched through sewage treatment plants. After arriving in the landfills, drugs can trickle into groundwater.

Figure 7–5 Used syringes must be deposited in a sharps container

Source: Thom Hanssen Images/Shutterstock

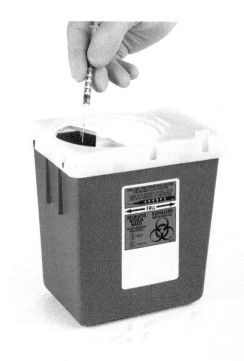

- *Radioactive waste* is any waste that contains or is contaminated with liquid or solid radioactive material. This waste must be clearly labeled as radioactive and never placed into an incinerator, down the drain, or in public areas. It should be removed by a licensed removal facility.

- *Infectious waste* is any waste material that has the potential to carry disease. Between 10 and 15 percent of all medical waste is considered infectious. This waste includes laboratory cultures as well as blood and blood products from blood banks, operating rooms, emergency departments, doctor and dentist offices, autopsy suites, clinical training laboratories, and patient rooms. All needles and syringes must be placed in a specially designed medical waste container (Figure 7.5). The three most dangerous types of infectious pathogens (microorganisms) found in medical waste are hepatitis B virus (HBV), hepatitis A virus (HAV), and HIV. Infectious waste must be separated from other solid and chemical waste at the point of origin, such as the medical office. It must be labeled, decontaminated onsite, or removed by a licensed removal facility for decontamination.

Med Tip

All healthcare personnel have an ethical responsibility to protect the public from harm caused by medical waste.

Chapter 7 Review

Points to Ponder

1. Is it only the responsibility of the physician to report child abuse cases? To whom, in your community, should such a report be made?

2. How soon after death does a death certificate have to be signed?

3. Does a woman have to report a stillbirth if it happens at home?

4. Who signs a death certificate in a death resulting from a fall from a window?

5. Does the healthcare provider have to report a case of genital warts, or can this information be kept confidential?

6. Is "battered child syndrome" a legitimate medical diagnosis?

7. Can a physician who, in good faith, reports a suspected case of child abuse be sued by parents?

8. Can a "wasted" controlled substance be poured down a sink?

9. Wouldn't it be better for a person who has personal problems to be counseled by a supervisor or employer who knows him or her than to be counseled by a stranger in EAP? Why or why not?

10. Should healthcare workers be tested to see if they are HIV-positive?

Discussion Questions

1. What drugs fall under each of the five categories (Schedules) of controlled substances?

2. To what does the term *public duties* refer?

3. What are the physician's public duties?

4. What records must physicians keep if they dispense or administer controlled substances?

5. What is the healthcare worker's responsibility for medical waste?

6. What are some conditions surrounding death that require an autopsy?

Review Challenge

Short Answer Questions

1. What are the four categories of medical waste?

2. What are some of the events that a healthcare provider has a duty to report?

3. In a case of child abuse, what does the requirement that the state must have probable cause mean?

4. In your opinion, should patients be told if their physician is HIV-positive?

5. What is a potential legal charge for a person who fails to report child abuse?

6. Violations of laws relating to controlled substances can result in what type(s) of legal action?

7. What can medical office personnel do to assist the physician in maintaining compliance with the Controlled Substances Act?

8. How could noncontrolled drugs be wasted?

Matching

Match the responses in column B with the correct term in column A.

COLUMN A

_____ 1. data
_____ 2. coroner
_____ 3. Schedule II drug
_____ 4. postmortem
_____ 5. Schedule I drug
_____ 6. addiction
_____ 7. inquest
_____ 8. DPT
_____ 9. STIs
_____ 10. public duty

COLUMN B

a. after death
b. statistics
c. physical dependence
d. diphtheria, pertussis, tetanus toxoid vaccine
e. public health official who investigates cause of death
f. report child abuse
g. LSD
h. codeine
i. sexually transmitted infections
j. investigation to determine cause of death

Multiple Choice

Select the one best answer to the following statements.

1. Vital statistics from a person's life include all of the following except
   a. pregnancies.
   b. marriages and divorces.
   c. animal bites.
   d. sensitive information such as rape and abuse.
   e. All of the above are considered to be vital statistics.

2. A coroner does not have to sign a death certificate in the case of
   a. suicide.
   b. death of older persons over the age of 90.
   c. death occurring less than 24 hours after hospital admission.
   d. death from electrocution.
   e. death of a prison inmate.

3. All of the following vaccines and toxoids are required for children by law except
   a. measles.
   b. polio.
   c. hepatitis.
   d. a and b only.
   e. a, b, and c are all required.

4. The Controlled Substances Act is also known as the
   a. Drug Enforcement Administration Act.
   b. Food and Drug Administration Act.
   c. Comprehensive Drug Abuse Prevention and Control Act.
   d. Bureau of Narcotics and Dangerous Drugs Act.
   e. none of the above

5. Schedule III drugs
   a. can be refilled by an order over the phone from the office assistant.
   b. are allowed only five refills during a six-month period.
   c. require the DEA number of the physician on the prescription.
   d. require the order to be typed on the prescription form.
   e. all of the above

6. An EAP program may help an employee cope with
   a. marital problems.
   b. alcoholism and drug abuse.
   c. criminal charges.
   d. a and b only
   e. a, b, and c

7. Infectious waste
   a. should be separated from chemical waste at the site of origin.
   b. can be safely removed by a licensed removal facility.
   c. consists of blood and blood products.
   d. may contain HIV and hepatitis A and B viruses.
   e. all of the above

8. Phenobarbital is an example of a
   a. Schedule I drug.
   b. Schedule II drug.
   c. Schedule III drug.
   d. Schedule IV drug.
   e. Schedule V drug.

9. The best method to "waste," or destroy, a narcotic is to
   a. place it in a medical waste container that is clearly marked.
   b. return it to the pharmaceutical company.
   c. flush it down a toilet only if instructed to do so on the packaging.
   d. do it without any witnesses.
   e. none of the above

10. Elder abuse is clearly defined in the

   a. Food and Drug Administration Act.

   b. Controlled Substances Act of 1970.

   c. amendment to the Older Americans Act of 1987.

   d. amendment to the Older Americans Act of 1974.

   e. none of the above

Discussion Cases

1. A pharmaceutical salesperson has just brought in a supply of nonprescription vitamin samples for the physicians in your practice to dispense to their patients. These vitamins are a new, expensive variety that is being given away to patients who are on a limited income and cannot afford to buy them. The other staff members take the samples home for their families' personal use. They tell you to do the same as the samples will become outdated before the physicians can use all of them. It would save you money.

   a. What do you do?

   b. Is your action legal? Why or why not?

   c. Is your action ethical? Why or why not?

   d. Does your physician/employer have any responsibility for the dispensing of these free nonprescription vitamins? Explain your answer.

   e. What precautions should be taken when storing nonprescription medications?

2. One of your coworkers recently told you that his partner is very ill with Covid. You observe, while this man is talking to you, that he is coughing. You are concerned about his health and caution him to be careful. The next day you see that he is on a list of CPR instructors who will be testing employees. Your facility still uses an older version of CPR in which there is mouth breathing performed on the "Annie."

   a. Who should you notify about your concerns?

   b. Should you approach your coworker and tell him about your concerns?

   c. What legal recourse does your coworker have if he is required to quarantine because of his medical condition?

Put It Into Practice

Find a newspaper article that discusses an abusive situation (spousal, child, elder, or drugs). Write your thoughts on what could have been done to prevent this from happening. Discuss the role of the healthcare team in reporting abuse cases.

Web Hunt

Search the website for the Centers for Disease Control and Prevention (**www.cdc.gov**). Provide a definition for the morbidity and mortality tables using the CDC's definition as stated on its website.

Critical Thinking Exercise

What would you do if you saw a fellow employee taking home non-narcotic medication samples from your employer's office?

Bibliography

Baldisseri, M.R. (2007). Impaired healthcare professional. *Critical Care Medicine*. Feb;35(2 Suppl):S106-16. DOI: 10.1097/01.CCM.0000252918.87746.96. PMID: 17242598.

Beaman, N., Routh, K.S., Papazian-Boyce, L., et al. (2017). *Pearson's comprehensive medical assisting: Administrative and clinical competencies* (4th ed.). Pearson.

Brotherton, S., Kao, A., & Crigger, B.J. (2016). Professing the values of medicine: The modernized AMA *Code of Medical Ethics*. *JAMA*, 316(10):1041–1042. DOI:10.1001/jama.2016.9752

Food & Drug Administration. (2020). How to safely dispose of unused or expired medicine. Video: https://www.fda.gov/drugs/safe-disposal-medicines/disposal-unused-medicines-what-you-should-know. Transcript: https://www.fda.gov/drugs/ensuring-safe-use-medicine/how-safely-dispose-unused-or-expired-medicine-video-transcript#:~:text=The%20best%20option%20is%20to,take%2Dback%20location%20near%20you.

Food & Drug Administration. (2023). All opioid pain medicines: Drug safety communication – FDA updates prescribing information to provide additional guidance for safe use. https://www.fda.gov/safety/medical-product-safety-information/all-opioid-pain-medicines-drug-safety-communication-fda-updates-prescribing-information-provide#:~:text=If%20the%20patient's%20pain%20is,risks%20associated%20with%20these%20products.

Harvard Health Publishing. (2017). *Working on addiction in the workplace*. https://www.health.harvard.edu/blog/working-on-addiction-in-the-workplace-2017063011941

Jain, N. & LaBeaud, D. (2022). How should the US health care lead global change in plastic waste disposal? AMA Journal of Ethics. https://journalofethics.ama-assn.org/article/how-should-us-health-care-lead-global-change-plastic-waste-disposal/2022-10

Markel, H. 2009. The child who put a face on abuse. *New York Times* (December 15), D5.

Merlo, L.J. & Teitelbaum. S.A. (2023). Substance use disorders in physicians: Epidemiology, clinical manifestations, identification, and engagement. *UptoDate*. https://www.uptodate.com/contents/substance-use-disorders-in-physicians-epidemiology-clinical-manifestations-identification-and-engagement#H1714180602

National Institute on Drug Abuse. (2020). *Misuse of prescription drugs research report*. https://nida.nih.gov/publications/research-reports/misuse-prescription-drugs/overview

Mitchell, R.J., & Bates. P. (2011). Measuring health-related productivity loss. *Population Health Management*. 14(2):93–8. DOI: 10.1089/pop.2010.0014.

Osmani, F., Arab-Zozani, M., Shahali, Z., & Lotfi, F. (2023). Evaluation of the effectiveness of electronic prescription in reducing medical and medical errors (systematic review study). *Annales Pharmaceutiques Francaises*. May;81(3):433–445. DOI: 10.1016/j.pharma.2022.12.002. Epub 2022 Dec 10. PMID: 36513154; PMCID: PMC9737496.

Workplace Law and Ethics

Key Terms

Affirmative action programs

Age Discrimination in Employment Act (ADEA)

Americans with Disabilities Act (ADA)

Americans with Disabilities Act Amendments Act of 2008 (ADAAA)

At-will employment

Clinical Laboratory Improvement Amendments (CLIA)

Consolidated Omnibus Budget Reconciliation Act (COBRA)

Credit Card Accountability Responsibility and Disclosure Act of 2009

Drug-Free Workplace Act

Emergency Medical Treatment & Labor Act (EMTALA)

Employee Retirement Income Security Act (ERISA)

Equal Credit Opportunity Act

Equal Employment Opportunity Act (EEOA)

Equal Employment Opportunity Commission (EEOC)

Equal Pay Act

Fair Credit Reporting Act

Fair Debt Collection Practices Act

Fair Labor Standards Act (FLSA)

Family and Medical Leave Act (FMLA)

Federal Insurance Contribution Act (FICA)

Federal Wage Garnishment Law

Free Appropriate Public Education (FAPE)

Individuals with Disabilities Education Act (IDEA)

Just cause

National Labor Relations Act (NLRA)

Occupational Safety and Health Act (OSHA)

Preempt

Pregnancy Discrimination Act

Probable cause

Rehabilitation Act

Sexual harassment

Social Security Act

Title VII of the Civil Rights Act

Truth in Lending Act (TILA)

Unemployment compensation

Wrongful discharge

Workers' Compensation Act

Learning Objectives

After completing this chapter, you will be able to:

8.1 Define the key terms.

8.2 Discuss the regulations concerning equal employment opportunity and employment discrimination.

8.3 Describe the regulations affecting employee health and safety.

8.4 Discuss the regulations affecting employee compensation and benefits.

8.5 Give examples of regulations affecting consumer protection and collection practices.

8.6 Describe accommodations that can be made in the workplace for persons with disabilities.

8.7 List several legal questions that may be asked during an employment interview and several questions that are illegal to ask during an interview.

8.8 Discuss guidelines for good hiring practices.

The Case of Janet K. and Epilepsy

Janet K. was diagnosed with epilepsy as an infant. Her condition was well controlled as she entered adulthood, and she was able to complete a nursing program in good health. She particularly enjoyed working as a scrub nurse in the operating room. Upon graduation she applied at the large university teaching hospital where she had performed her clinical work during her nursing program. The hospital knew of her medical history and offered her a job in their medical records department. Janet petitioned to be able to work in surgery, but the hospital administrators felt that it was too dangerous for Janet and for the surgical patients if she should have a seizure there.

While working in medical records, Janet's seizures began to return. She would have a seizure at least every month even though her medications had been changed. Janet noticed that some of her fellow medical records technicians would stay away from her for fear of not knowing how to help her during a seizure. One afternoon, a physician was dictating his case records in a cubicle next to Janet's when she had a seizure. He helped her and then went to the hospital administrator and told her that Janet should not be allowed to work in a hospital because it gave the hospital, with its image of healing, a bad reputation.

Janet, at the age of 27, was the only one terminated because of departmental downsizing.

1. Are there some physical or mental conditions that should prevent a person from working in a hospital or other healthcare setting? If so, what are they?

2. What should have been done when Janet's coworkers shunned her?

3. Was the physician who helped Janet when she had a seizure correct in asking the hospital administrator to dismiss (fire) her?

4. Should Janet have been given the opportunity to work in surgery? Why or why not?

Introduction

Applied ethics in healthcare always involve people—whether they are in a hospital, healthcare office, clinic, ambulance, nursing home, hospice, or agency. Workplace ethics refers to the moral standards that ought to direct the actions and choices made by both employers and employees. While it is common sense to treat employees, colleagues, and patients well, it is often in the workplace where people suffer discrimination, harassment, and other unethical practices. Many of our workplace and employment laws were established as far back as the 1930s. They are some of the reasons that we have fair standards and protection in the workplace today.

Professionalism in the Workplace

The profession of healthcare, whether practiced by a physician, advanced practice provider, nurse, medical assistant, or other healthcare professional, is inherently meaningful. A medical or health-related career usually requires several years of education to achieve competence, and, in many cases, it is a career that a person selects for all of their working years. Healthcare professionals can justifiably find pride in their achievements.

Healthcare professionals do not enter their field of study with the expectation that they will have to compromise their professional behavior. However, it has become increasingly difficult to provide the level of care and concern for patients given the elements of increased documentation and sicker patients staying fewer days in a hospital to recover from illness or surgery. In some cases, very ill patients are being seen in healthcare offices, emergency department settings, or clinics because they do not have insurance to pay for a hospital stay.

In today's world of specialization, patients may have several physicians managing their care. This can result in the patient's spending less time with any one healthcare professional. In fact, many patients feel that the care they receive has become depersonalized as they never get to know any one caregiver very well. The reverse is also true, as healthcare professionals become frustrated that they do not have enough time to really get to know and understand their patients.

The case of Libby Zion illustrates this point. Libby was an 18-year-old college student who was treated in a large, busy New York teaching hospital. She entered the hospital's emergency department with moderate aches and pains suggesting influenza. Libby also exhibited agitated behavior but did not tell the emergency department physician that she was taking a number of prescription drugs. She was given a sedating medication as well as physical restraints to control her agitated movements. Libby died eight hours after she was admitted. In retrospect, Libby's death was caused by a fatal drug interaction that was not well recognized at the time. Her parents and several journalists investigated the competence and amount of time spent by the healthcare personnel who cared for Libby. They also examined information about the long hours that interns and residents work in a teaching hospital. The results of the parents' crusade, media coverage, and a resulting court case meant that there is now a closer look at accountability and supervision in teaching hospitals. Interns and residents now have mandatory rest periods and days off work as a result of the Libby Zion case. Another important lesson from her death is to always ask patients what medications they are currently taking and to be on the lookout for drug interactions. Forty years after Libby's death, her legacy lives on in the important changes made in the care of patients.

Professionalism means that each healthcare professional will monitor the time and care that each patient receives so that the care is effective as well as efficient. Ideally, attention should be paid to persons who appear agitated to determine if drug use may be involved. In addition, screenings should always take place for individuals who appear agitated. Professionalism means that we treat all patients with the same standards regardless of race, color, religion, gender, or national origin. This responsibility should not be left to others.

Med Tip

Efficiency is getting the job done; effectiveness is doing the job right! This is especially true in healthcare.

Discrimination in the Workplace

In spite of knowledge about good healthcare habits, people working in the healthcare field often suffer from many of the same problems that affect their patients. For example, overweight doctors, nurses, and allied health professionals may experience discriminatory behavior because of their weight. In some cases, overweight or obese healthcare professionals are either not hired or else they are placed in an unpopular work setting where they will not be seen or promoted. It is an injustice to discriminate against either a fellow employee or a patient because of their weight.

Some companies and hospitals have implemented wellness programs, including weight loss, with the belief that healthy employees are more productive. Ethical concerns about privacy issues arise even from well-meaning wellness programs when electronic data records are kept to track the employee's weight loss.

Med Tip

As simple as this sounds, always treat a coworker as you wish to be treated.

Privacy and the Workplace

The federal government has taken an active role in attempting to prevent violations of a patient's privacy. The Health Insurance Portability and Accountability Act of 1996 (HIPAA), discussed in Chapter 10, includes stiff fines and other penalties if a patient's privacy is violated. However, in spite of federal regulations, some healthcare workers are still invading a patient's privacy, often just to satisfy curiosity.

For example, seven-year-old Nixzmary Brown was found beaten and starved and left to die in a small room that her brothers and sisters called "the dirty room." Her mother and stepfather were both charged with the crime. According to New York's Health and Hospitals Corporation, dozens of workers, including doctors, nurses, technicians, and clerks, opened the patient's computer file even though they had nothing to do with the case. There were several employees who had a legitimate reason to view the file on a "need-to-know" basis, but investigators believed that 39 employees opening the file were just too many. It was determined that "sheer curiosity" had driven many of the healthcare workers to open Nixzmary's file. The 39 hospital employees who violated the child's privacy were suspended for 30 to 60 days without pay and received privacy training before returning to work.

Opening a patient's medical file should always be on a "need-to-know" basis. Any other reason may constitute an illegal action. In addition, photos of patients cannot be taken, either for teaching purposes or for personal use, without the patient's permission. It is just as inappropriate to look at a coworker's personnel file as it is to illegally examine a patient's file. A coworker's personnel evaluations and salary levels are privileged information. Viewing personnel records without a "need to know" could result in dismissal from a job.

Cultural Considerations in Healthcare Practice

In the world of modern healthcare, the importance of cultural considerations cannot be overstated. As healthcare professionals strive to provide the best care for patients from diverse backgrounds, understanding and respecting the cultural beliefs, values, and practices of each patient and colleague is crucial.

Figure 8–1 Healthcare professionals must respect the cultural needs of their patients

Source: Prostock-studio/Shutterstock

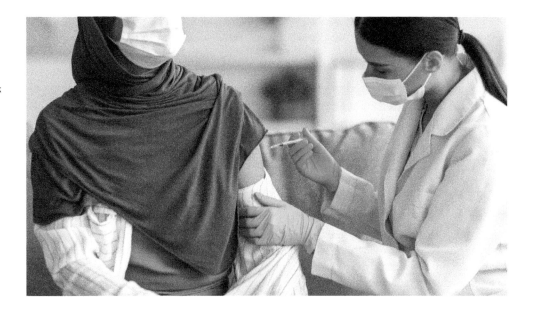

This is not only an ethical imperative but also a key factor in ensuring the effectiveness of medical treatment and promoting better health outcomes.

Cultural diversity is a hallmark of our globalized world, and it is reflected in the patient populations seen in healthcare settings. In any given hospital or clinic, one can find patients from different socioeconomic, cultural, ethnic, and religious backgrounds. These differences can greatly influence a patient's health beliefs, expectations, and responses to medical treatment. To provide high-quality care, healthcare professionals must navigate this cultural landscape with sensitivity and awareness.

One of the fundamental principles of cultural competence in healthcare is recognizing that culture encompasses not only race or ethnicity but also factors such as religion, language, gender, sexual orientation, age, socioeconomic status, and more (Figure 8.1). Each of these elements can shape a person's health perceptions and behaviors. It's essential for healthcare providers to move beyond stereotypes and assumptions to understand each patient's unique cultural context.

Language is a primary consideration in cultural competence. Language barriers can lead to misunderstandings, misdiagnoses, and nonadherence to treatment plans. Healthcare professionals should have access to interpreters or translation services when needed, but they should also take the time to learn common medical terms in the languages spoken by their patients. Effective communication is essential for informed consent, symptom description, and follow-up care.

Med Tip

It is wise to keep in mind how you would wish to be treated if you were a patient in another country where you couldn't speak the primary language.

Religion and spirituality are also integral components of culture that can profoundly influence healthcare decisions. For example, some religious groups may refuse certain medical interventions, while others may have specific rituals or dietary restrictions that impact their treatment plans. Healthcare providers need to be sensitive to these beliefs and collaborate with patients and their families to find treatment options that respect their religious values while addressing their health needs.

There are some beliefs that do not allow a person to receive a blood transfusion. When such a situation occurs, a physician may seek a court order for a child to receive blood over the objections of the parent. Used frequently, the case of *Prince v. Commonwealth of Massachusetts* reasoned that "Parents may be free to be martyrs themselves. But it does not follow that they are free in identical circumstances to make martyrs of their children" (*Prince v. Commonwealth of Massachusetts*, 321 U.S. 158 1944). Prince was upheld by the U.S. Supreme Court in 1968 (*Jehovah's Witnesses v. King County Hospital* 278 F. Supp. 488 (W.D. Wash. 1967) aff'd 390 U.S. 598 (1968)), saying "the right to practice religion freely does not include liberty to expose . . . the child . . . to ill health or death." However, a number of states, such as

Pennsylvania and Illinois, have "mature minor" doctrines that recognize that mature minors have a common law right to refuse medical treatment.

From an ethical perspective, the principle of patient autonomy, or independence for their beliefs, is always an important consideration. However, all of these, sometimes conflicting, conditions can result in confusion for the healthcare professional. As long as a person is competent, they have the right to make their own decisions. Bioethical and legal issues arise when a person is called upon to make decisions for another person such as a child or an older or cognitively impaired adult. In these cases, a guardianship may have to be established by the courts so that the best interests of the patient are observed. There will always be ethical discussions about where religious boundaries should be drawn and when the state should step in to protect individuals.

Med Tip

It is never appropriate to judge, with either verbal or nonverbal criticism, another person's religious customs and beliefs. An exception occurs when there is evidence of abuse as a result of a religious practice.

Cultural considerations extend to the understanding of pain, its expression, and its management. Different cultures may have varying norms for expressing pain or may view stoicism as a virtue. Misinterpretation of a patient's pain can lead to suboptimal pain management. Additionally, cultural practices and beliefs about pain management, including the use of alternative therapies like acupuncture or herbal remedies, should be explored and respected where appropriate.

Cultural beliefs also influence preventive care and health promotion. For example, some cultures may place a strong emphasis on holistic well-being and preventive measures, while others may rely more on medical intervention. Understanding these differences can help healthcare professionals tailor their recommendations and education to each patient's cultural context.

Moreover, cultural considerations impact end-of-life care and decision-making. Different cultures have diverse approaches to death and dying, including religious rituals, views on life support, and organ donation. Healthcare professionals should be aware of these differences to assist patients and their families in making decisions that align with their cultural values.

Med Tip

Healthcare professionals must be ready to help people regardless of their income levels, cultural origins, or attitudes.

Implicit bias, or unconscious prejudices, can also interfere with culturally competent care. Physicians, nurses, and allied health professionals must be aware of their own biases and actively work to counteract them. Cultural competence training and diversity education can help healthcare professionals develop self-awareness and the ability to provide more equitable care. As an example, different cultures have their own practices for personal hygiene. A bias occurs when a healthcare professional doesn't pay attention to a person who displays poor hygiene or has a body odor.

Med Tip

It is always wise to keep one's opinions about the use of deodorants, clean clothing, and frequency of bathing to oneself, unless the patient's health is suffering as a result of their hygiene. Slang terms for dealing with bodily functions should never be used. It's perfectly acceptable to ask a patient if they need to use the bathroom.

In addition to individual patient care, healthcare institutions themselves must consider cultural competence in their policies and practices. This includes hiring diverse staff, providing training in cultural competence, and making sure that patient populations are represented in clinical trials and research studies. Ensuring that diverse perspectives are integrated into the healthcare system at all levels is crucial for addressing health disparities.

Cultural competence is not a static skill; it is an ongoing process of learning and adaptation. Healthcare professionals should continually seek to expand their cultural knowledge and stay informed about the changing demographics and cultural dynamics of their patient populations.

Effective Hiring and Managing Practices

There are many examples of lawsuits relating to hiring practices that would not have happened if the employer had acted within the confines of the law. Fairness is one of the most important elements when supervising employees. In addition, employers can improve the quality of their employees by using an effective screening process before the actual hiring takes place. It is imperative to perform thorough background checks on applicants in the healthcare field because they may not have listed their criminal record on an application form. Employers are at risk of lawsuits when they hire employees who are a foreseeable danger to others. Some recommendations for good hiring practices include the following:

- Develop clear policies and procedures on hiring, discipline, and termination of employees.
- Effectively screen potential employees' backgrounds.
- Clearly state in all written materials, such as employee handbooks, memos, and manuals, that an employee handbook is not a contract.
- Use a two-tier interview screening process. Have candidates interviewed both by healthcare professionals who will supervise or work with the new employee and by trained human resource or personnel department employees.
- Carefully assess the applicant's skill level by having them perform some of the position requirements (i.e., drawing blood samples, teaching, performing surgical setups).
- Develop an application form that asks for appropriate information about the applicant's qualifications.
- Provide a job description to every employee.
- Develop a progressive disciplinary procedure and make the policy known to all employees and supervisors.
- Whenever possible, have human resource personnel present during the firing process. Document what is said during this process.
- Provide in-service training to supervisors on how to conduct job interviews and motivate and discipline employees.
- Become familiar with the legal and illegal questions that can be asked in an employment interview.

Legal and Illegal Interview Questions

The Equal Employment Opportunity Commission (EEOC) has strict guidelines on the types of questions that can be asked during a job interview. These questions have both ethical and legal considerations. Questions that may be interpreted as discriminatory cannot be asked. In some cases, a question may be legal but still inadvisable for an interviewer to ask. For example, while it is legal under the law to ask if an applicant is married, it is inadvisable because it may be discriminatory. Marriage has nothing to do with job performance. If an unmarried applicant is hired, a married applicant may believe that they were not given the job based on marital status. Table 8.1 contains a list of questions you can and cannot ask during an interview.

Med Tip

In an interview, always stop to remember what you *cannot* ask. If in doubt, don't ask!

Table 8-1 Legal and Illegal Questions

Questions	Legal	Illegal
Age?	It is legal to ask applicants if they are between the ages of 17 and 70, but not to ask their specific age. If their age falls outside these boundaries, then it is legal to ask their birth date.	
Birthplace?	It is legal, but inadvisable to ask where the applicants, their parents, spouse, or children were born.	It is illegal to ask about their national heritage or nationality or that of their spouse.
Address?	It is legal to ask, along with how long the applicant has lived there.	
Married?	It is legal to ask, but inadvisable.	
Maiden name?	It is legal to inquire if reference information (educational, employment, license) is under a different name.	It is illegal as this could indicate a marriage.
Children?		It is illegal to ask. It is also illegal to ask any questions relating to childcare arrangements.
Height and weight?		It is illegal to ask unless it relates to the job requirements.
Race or color?		It is illegal to ask.
Religion or creed?	It is legal to ask if working on a particular day, such as a Saturday or Sunday, would interfere with applicant's religious practices.	It is illegal to ask about an applicant's religion.
Ever been arrested?	It is legal to ask if the applicant has ever been convicted of a crime or has any pending felony charges. For example, "Have you been convicted within the past year on drug-related charges?"	It is illegal to ask if they've been arrested because an arrest does not indicate guilt.
Citizenship?	It is legal to ask, "Are you a citizen of the United States?"	
Disabilities?	It is legal to ask if the applicant has any physical impairment that would affect their ability to do the job.	It is illegal to ask if an applicant has a disability or a disease.
Organizations you belong to?	It is legal to ask applicants if they belong to any organizations.	Illegal to ask about membership in any specific organization or to require applicants to list the organizations to which they belong.
Languages?	It is legal to ask what languages a person can speak or write.	Note, however, it can be perceived as discriminatory and a method to determine a person's national origin.
Military experience?	It is legal to ask if the person has been a member of the armed forces, type of training, and when discharged.	Illegal to ask what type of discharge was received (honorable, dishonorable, medical, etc.).

The Employee Handbook

The employee handbook usually explains behaviors, such as sleeping on the job, that can cause an employee's termination. Management needs to use care when issuing a handbook. Statements in employee handbooks have been interpreted as "implied contracts" in a court of law. In *Watson v. Idaho Falls Consolidated Hospitals, Inc.*, a nurse's aide claimed wrongful discharge and sued her employer, a hospital, for violating provisions in the employee handbook when it terminated her. Employees had been asked to read and sign a revised handbook to show that they understood hospital policies regarding counseling, discipline, and termination. The court stated that management and the employees were under an obligation to follow the policies stated in the handbook. Because it was proved in court that the hospital violated the stated policy in the handbook when it terminated her, Watson won her suit (*Watson v. Idaho Falls Consol. Hosp. Inc.*, 720 P.2d 632, Idaho 1986).

In another case, a Minnesota court held, in a wrongful discharge suit, that the hospital's employee handbook was clearly an employment contract. The handbook contained detailed statements on conduct and procedures for discipline, which the hospital violated when it fired the plaintiff (*Harvet v. Unity Medical Ctr.*, 428 N.W.2d 574, Minn. Ct. App. 1988). These cases indicate that the employee handbook must be carefully examined for any erroneous or misleading statements.

In addition, when there is a dispute, employees should be given opportunities to speak and present evidence on their own behalf. Employees should be allowed to see, comment on, or copy anything affecting them in written reviews and personnel file memos.

Federal Regulations Affecting Professionals

Both state and federal laws regulate the employer (physician) and employee (staff) relationship. In some cases, local laws in a particular city or county may also regulate a healthcare practice. Therefore, healthcare facilities and medical practices must remain current on regulations affecting employment practices, such as health, safety, compensation, workers' compensation, unions, and discrimination laws. Generally, federal laws apply only to those businesses or organizations that employ a declared number of employees (such as 15, 20, 50, or more) and who work a minimum number of weeks in a period of a year. It is always wise to seek advice from legal counsel or a corporate attorney, if the organization has one on staff, concerning specific cases.

Med Tip

It is a widely accepted policy that all employees, whether working in the healthcare field or elsewhere, should receive time away from their workstation for a lunch break (½ hour) and two 15-minute breaks during an eight-hour workday. These breaks may be required as part of a union agreement if employees are unionized. These policies may be established in individual states by the Department of Labor.

In most situations, federal laws **preempt**, or overrule, state laws. However, there are some exceptions. One occurs when there is not a federal law relating to a topic, in which case the states can then regulate it. A second exception occurs if the court has already ruled that state law does not conflict with federal law, in which case the state law is enforced. Another exception is called a complete preemption, in which Congress prohibits states from regulating a particular area of law. An example of this is the Employment Retirement Income Security Act (ERISA), which is discussed later in this chapter.

The major categories of federal laws regulating the employer–employee relationships include equal employment opportunity and employment discrimination; employee health and safety; compensation and benefits regulations; consumer protection and collection practices; and federal labor acts. In discussing these regulations, many of the legal terms, such as a law and an act, are interchangeable. The cases discussed in this chapter illustrate the variety of lawsuits relating to these regulations.

Med Tip

Each state has its own individual state and local laws. Always determine the local laws that pertain to your particular area. Local county health departments are a good source of information.

Equal Employment Opportunity and Employment Discrimination

The government regulates many aspects of the employment relationship, with laws that affect recruitment, placement, pay plans, benefits, penalties, and terminations. The basic assumption of the law is that, in the workplace, people must be judged primarily by their job qualifications and performance. A discussion of these laws should be prefaced with a look at the historical doctrine of employment-at-will.

At-Will Employment

The common-law doctrine of at-will employment has historically governed the employment relationship. **At-will employment**, in which there is *no* contract of employment, means that employment takes place at the will of either the employer or the employee. Thus, the employer may terminate a person's employment at will, without notice, at any time, and without a reason. Conversely, the employee may quit at any time, without notice and without a reason. The exception to this occurs when there is a specific employment contract between the employer and employee, specifying the duration and terms of employment. Then the relationship *cannot* be terminated during the contract period unless some provision of the contract has been violated by the employer or employee. The only protection afforded at-will employment is that employees cannot be fired for an illegal reason—for example, because of the color of their skin or their age.

This concept of termination for any reason without incurring liability when there is at-will employment has been widely accepted. However, at-will employment has begun to lose favor. **Wrongful discharge** lawsuits, in which the employee believes the employer does not have a **just cause**, or legal reason, for firing the employee, have become more common. An example of this occurs when the employer asks employees to perform procedures for which they are not trained or that are not within the scope of their license. Even if employers win a wrongful discharge lawsuit, they may ultimately be the losers because of the negative publicity and effect on employee morale. The following sections cover equal employment opportunity and employment discrimination laws.

Title VII of the Civil Rights Act of 1964, Amended in 1991

Title VII of the Civil Rights Act prohibits discrimination (unfair or unequal treatment) in employment based on five criteria: race, color, religion, gender, or national origin. This strongly worded act means that employers may not refuse to hire, unlawfully discharge, or in any other way discriminate against employees based on these five criteria. This Kennedy administration initiative, which was implemented under the Johnson administration, is regarded as one of the most significant pieces of law because it governs job discrimination and regulates opportunity. This act applies to all organizations that have 20 or more employees working 20 weeks or more during a year.

Title VII affects all aspects of patient care in institutions that receive government funding, such as Medicare and Medicaid. In addition, Title VII created the U.S. Equal Employment Opportunity Commission (EEOC). The EEOC enforces provisions under Title VII. These include the Age Discrimination in Employment Act, the Equal Pay Act, and a section of the Rehabilitation Act.

> ### Med Tip
>
> Some of the most frequent violations in the healthcare employment field are related to Title VII issues.

The **Equal Employment Opportunity Commission**, also known as EEOC, monitors Title VII, and the Justice Department enforces the statute. In some cases, the EEOC defers enforcement to local and state agencies. Employees must exhaust all administrative remedies offered by the EEOC before they can sue their employer under Title VII. The Equal Employment Opportunity Act, the Pregnancy Discrimination Act, and the Civil Rights Act of 1991 have further amended this act.

Title VII also makes sexual harassment a form of unlawful sex discrimination. **Sexual harassment** is defined as "unwelcome sexual advances, requests for sexual favors, and other verbal or physical conduct of a sexual nature." The Civil Rights Act makes it illegal for employers to allow anyone to be sexually harassed at work by anyone else, regardless of sex, gender, or orientation. An employee who quits a job because sexual harassment created an offensive or hostile work environment may sue the employer for damages. For example, in 2022, AMG Specialty Hospital was fined by the EEOC for subjecting a female employee to a sexually hostile work environment. The woman, who was the director of case management, was being harassed by the male chief clinical officer of AMG. The hospital failed to make a timely response to her complaint, and they failed to prevent or remedy the harassment, which forced the woman to resign. AMG was required to pay the woman over $80,000 in back pay and damages, and requires AMG to make affirmative steps to prevent sexual harassment in the future.

Affirmative action programs to remedy discriminatory practices in hiring historically marginalized populations are also covered under Title VII. These programs, required by federal statute, require that positive steps, such as hiring diverse personnel, be taken to remedy past discrimination and to take steps to prevent future discrimination. Courts may mandate that affirmative action programs be implemented if there is evidence that an employer has intentionally discriminated against a particular marginalized group.

Defining Employees and Employers Under Title VII

If an employer withholds employment taxes from a person's income, then that person is considered an employee. While some cases are less clear, in general, if the employer can control the details of that person's work, then the person is considered to be an employee. In some cases, physicians who have lost medical staff memberships and thus hospital admitting privileges have been able to sue the hospital under Title VII.

A person who employs the services of another and provides payment for those services is considered an employer. An employer has the right to control the physical conduct of the employee in performing the service. The statute does not apply to independent contractors. A coworker is not an employer and, thus, is not liable under Title VII. The courts have also found that a parent company of the employer is not liable as the employer under Title VII (*Garcia v. Elf Atochem*, N. Am., 28 F.3d 446, 5th Cir. 1994).

The employment status of travel nurses is interesting. Travel nurses are employed by the agency they work for, but the hospital where they are assigned has control over their schedule, assignments, uniforms, breaks, and work protocols, so is controlling the physical conduct of the employee. This level of control by hospitals has been the basis for some lawsuits brought by travel nurses seeking to hold both the agencies and the healthcare facilities responsible for wage and hour violations (*Grande v. Eisenhower Medical Center* (2020) 44 Cal.App.5th 1147, 1162–1163).

Filing with the EEOC

Most EEOC actions begin with the filing of a charge of discrimination by an individual who believes they have been discriminated against. A charge of discrimination must be filed within 180 days following the incident unless the facts warrant an exception that extends the period to 300 days. After a charge of discrimination is filed, the EEOC will conduct an investigation. If the EEOC finds **probable cause** that Title VII may have been violated, attempts are made to mediate the matter.

Title VII directs the EEOC to (1) undertake studies and provide information and technical assistance to employers, labor organizations, and the general public concerning effective means available to implement this act; and (2) carry on a continuing program of research, education, and technical assistance with specified components related to the purposes of this act.

Civil Rights Act of 1991

Congress amended Title VII by passing the Civil Rights Act of 1991. Wrongful discharge suits fall under this law. The Civil Rights Act of 1991 permits the court to award both compensatory damages (for the loss of income or emotional pain and suffering) and punitive damages (to punish the defendant) to mistreated employees. Before this amendment, only compensatory damages were awarded.

Title VII provides that a hospital must treat physicians, nurses, other employees, and patients in a nondiscriminatory manner. It also prohibits hospital employees, such as nurses, from discriminating against patients, physicians, or fellow employees.

Equal Employment Opportunity Act (EEOA) of 1972

The **Equal Employment Opportunity Act**, also known as EEOA, authorizes the EEOC to sue employers in federal court on behalf of a class of people or an individual whose rights under Title VII have been violated.

Pregnancy Discrimination Act of 1978

Under the **Pregnancy Discrimination Act**, employers must treat pregnant women as they would any other employee, providing they can still do the job. This act has saved jobs for women and allowed them to advance even if they became pregnant or had to take a short leave for childbirth. An employer cannot force a woman to quit her job because she is pregnant. In addition, under this law, a woman cannot be refused a job because she has had an abortion. The pregnant woman is assured of equal treatment in such areas as disability, sick leave, and health insurance. The employer's healthcare plan must cover pregnancy in the same way it would cover other medical conditions. If the worker is unable to work because of the pregnancy, then she qualifies for sick leave on the same basis as all the other employees.

If the employer offers employee leaves for disabilities, then a similar leave must be offered for pregnancy. Mandatory maternity leaves violate Title VII, because the Pregnancy Discrimination Act of 1978 is an amendment to that statute. In addition, the employer's health plan must provide coverage for the dependent spouses of employees.

A federal district court found that a hospital had violated the Pregnancy Discrimination Act when it fired an X-ray technician upon learning that she was pregnant. The court felt that while it was necessary for the X-ray technician to avoid working in some areas of the X-ray department because of her condition, there were less discriminatory alternatives that the hospital could have used (*Hayes v. Shelby Memorial Hosp.*, 726 F.2d 1543, 11th Cir. 1984).

This statute has many aspects that require special considerations. For instance, one federal court held that an employee who had job absences because of infertility treatments was not protected under this act (*Zatarain v. WDSU-Television, Inc.,* WI 16777 E.D., La. 1995). In a 1994 case, a federal appellate court ruled that a pregnant home-health nurse who refused to treat an AIDS patient could be discharged under this statute (*Armstrong v. Flowers Hosp.*, 33 F.3d 1308, 11th Cir. 1994).

Age Discrimination in Employment Act (ADEA) of 1967, Amended in 1991

The **Age Discrimination in Employment Act**, also known as ADEA, protects persons 40 years or older against employment discrimination because of age. This law applies to employers who have 20 or more employees working for them 20 or more weeks during a year. The employer will not be liable for violation of this law if there are extenuating circumstances, such as if the person does not have the ability to perform the job. If two people are up for hiring or a promotion and one of them is over 40, then the employer must be able to show (in writing) why the younger person, if hired or promoted, is more qualified. Education and performance, in addition to other factors, count toward qualification. Mandatory retirement is prohibited under this law except for certain exempt executives.

> ### Med Tip
>
> Note that all persons over 40 are protected by both Title VII and the Age Discrimination in Employment Act.

Employers must be cautious about what they say or put into writing in the event that they must terminate a person's employment. For example, in a 1985 age discrimination suit, a 62-year-old supervisor nurse resigned and then sued the hospital because its administration had told her "new blood" was needed and made comments about her "advanced age." She believed these statements made working conditions intolerable. The nurse supervisor won the suit (*Buckley v. Hospital Corp. of America, Inc.*, 758 F.2d 1525, 11th Cir. 1985).

Rehabilitation Act of 1973, Amended in 1974

The **Rehabilitation Act** prohibits employment discrimination against people with disabilities. This act prohibits discrimination based on disability in any institution that receives federal financial assistance.

Therefore, a hospital or agency that receives Medicare and Medicaid reimbursement must comply with this law. However, courts have held in favor of plaintiffs, such as hospitals and nursing homes, that are not equipped to care for a special-needs patient such as a violent or aggressive patient who abuses the staff (*Grubbs v. Medical Facilities of America, Inc.*, 879 F. Supp. W.D., Va. 1995).

This act had a major influence on the Americans with Disabilities Act of 1990 because it included a very broad definition of "handicapped." It included people with physical or mental impairment, people who have had an impairment, and people who currently have an impairment. This definition protected people with a recognizable disability, such as a physical disability that requires the person to use a wheelchair, and opened many doors for people with disabilities such as mental health diagnoses who were formerly forgotten. In addition, this law was the beginning of a legal means for people to challenge their denial of employment for physical or mental reasons.

Americans with Disabilities Act (ADA) of 1990, Amended in 2008

There are about 43 million disabled persons (13 percent of the population) in the United States, including people with vision, hearing, cognitive, walking, self-care, and independent living abilities. The **Americans with Disabilities Act**, also known as ADA, prohibits employers who have more than 15 employees from discriminating against such individuals. Persons with AIDS are also covered under this act. In order to comply with this act, the employer must make reasonable accommodations, such as lowering telephones, installing ramps, and making elevator floor numbers accessible to persons who use wheelchairs. The exception to this occurs if the accommodations would be an undue hardship for the employer, such as the significant difficulty of installing an elevator in an old building. The term *undue hardship* has caused problems, as there is no clear definition of the term *hardship* or a dollar amount that constitutes *hardship*. There is a two-year implementation window for employers who must comply with this law. Patients, as well as employees, are protected under this statute.

Private physicians can be held liable under the ADA for acts that take place in their offices. For example, in 1995 a federal appellate court upheld a lower court decision that an HIV-positive patient could sue his primary care physician for allegedly failing to treat or refer him to another physician (*Woolfolk v. Duncan*, 872 F. Supp. 1381, E.D., Pa. 1995).

In *Tugg v. Towney*, a federal court ruled that the ADA requires a state to provide counselors who use sign language to counsel Deaf patients in state mental facilities. According to the court, the facility did not satisfy the ADA statute by merely providing mental health services through the use of interpreters (*Tugg v. Towney*, 864 F. Supp. 1201, S.D. Fla. 1994). The ADA addresses the law as it affects Deaf individuals. Other regulations, such as **Individuals with Disabilities Education Act**, also known as IDEA, and **Free Appropriate Public Education**, also known as FAPE, address the rights of the Deaf and hard of hearing.

Basic accommodations that can be made for persons with disabilities include the following:

- Parking spaces, clearly marked for those with disabilities, near an accessible doorway
- Inclined ramps into buildings or over curbs in parking lots
- Elevator floor numbers that are accessible to patients and employees who use wheelchairs
- Handicap-accessible bathrooms with handrails
- Hallways with at least 36 inches of clearance for wheelchairs
- Desks and counters that accommodate a wheelchair
- Telephone adapters for the hearing impaired
- Allowing a medically fragile child to carry a cell phone
- Permitting the use of tape recorders or laptop computers in class
- Allowing extra time for a student with a difficulty in movement or walking to move between classrooms

Under Title III, the ADA also prohibits discrimination against students with disabilities in private schools that are considered public accommodations.

Americans with Disabilities Act Amendments Act (ADAAA) of 2008

The **Americans with Disabilities Act Amendments Act of 2008**, also known as ADAAA (Public Law, ADAAA), is an Act of Congress that became effective on January 1, 2009. This law amended the Americans with Disabilities Act of 1990.

The ADAAA was signed into law by President George W. Bush on September 25, 2008, as a response to decisions made by the Supreme Court. This Court had interpreted the original text of the ADA. However, members of the U.S. Congress believed that the original decisions were limiting the rights of persons with disabilities. Therefore, the ADAAA reversed those decisions by changing the law.

The ADAAA made changes to what the term *disability* meant by broadening and clarifying this definition, resulting in an increase in the number and types of persons who are now protected under this law. This act focuses not on whether the person with a "disability" has an impairment that limits a life activity, but rather, whether a "covered entity," such as an employer, has discriminated against the employee.

National Labor Relations Act (NLRA) of 1935, Amended in 1947

The **National Labor Relations Act**, also known as NLRA, or the Wagner Act, established some of the most basic union rights. It guarantees the basic rights of employees in the private sector to organize trade unions, to bargain collectively, and, when necessary, to take collective action including to strike. This act prohibits employer actions such as attempting to force employees to stay out of unions, and it labels these actions as "unfair labor practices." This act set up the National Labor Relations Board (NLRB) to enforce labor law in relation to collective bargaining and unfair labor practices. The NLRB conducts elections when employers are expected to collectively bargain with labor unions.

Employee Health and Safety

Both state and federal laws regulate issues affecting an employee's health and safety. While a state law may be stricter than the federal law, it cannot be more lenient. The following sections cover employee health and safety laws.

Occupational Safety and Health Act of 1970

Under the **Occupational Safety and Health Act**, which is administered by the Occupational Safety and Health Administration (OSHA), an employer is required to provide a safe and healthy work environment and protect the worker against hazards. OSHA regulations preempt all other state and local regulations regarding employee safety and health, meaning that states may *not* pass any laws concerning the working environment. In addition, there are right-to-know laws in many states that give employees access to workplace safety information such as information about the use of hazardous or toxic substances.

Employers and office managers should become familiar with OSHA regulations as they apply to their specific fields, not only to protect employees but also to avoid fines for OSHA violations, which can be severe. In addition, poor publicity and public relations resulting from a serious OSHA violation can damage an office or company's reputation.

Med Tip

In a healthcare workplace, additional safety issues may arise that are not found elsewhere, including protecting individuals against bloodborne pathogens.

In 1991, OSHA developed rules to protect healthcare workers from bloodborne diseases. These are known as OSHA Occupational Exposure to Bloodborne Pathogens Standards (29 CFR 1910.1030). OSHA also established penalties, which in 2023 are up to $15,625 per violation of a serious requirement, $15,625 per day for failure to abate the problem, and $156,259 for willful or repeated violations of these standards by employers. These standards apply to any employee who has occupational exposure to infectious material. This is defined as a reasonable anticipation that the employee's duties will result in skin, mucous membrane, eye, or parenteral (a medication route, such as by injection, other than through the digestive tract) contact with bloodborne pathogens (disease-producing microorganisms) or other potentially infectious material (OPIM), such as visible blood (https://www.osha.gov/bloodborne-pathogens). Healthcare workers, including physicians, nurses, medical assistants, laboratory workers, and housekeeping personnel, have occupational exposure. The OSHA standards mandate that each employee with occupational exposure must be offered the hepatitis B vaccination at the expense of the employer.

Med Tip

Note that an employee may decline, in writing, to receive the hepatitis B vaccine.

The OSHA standards refer to urine, stool, sputum, nasal secretions, vomitus, and sweat only if there is visible evidence of blood. The OSHA compliance checklist for healthcare facilities and offices includes eyewash stations, fire extinguishers, first-aid kits, written training programs, labels for chemical and hazardous waste, sharps containers, exit signs, spill kits, accident report forms, and chemical inventory lists.

The Hazard Communication Standard (HCS) from OSHA is meant to reduce injuries and illnesses in the workforce by alerting healthcare employees to potential dangers and risks when using hazardous chemicals and materials (29 CFR 1910.1200). Safety data sheets (SDS) must be easily accessible wherever hazardous materials are used. Employees are instructed to read the sheets and know how to handle all hazardous products, such as blood and chemicals.

Med Tip

OSHA guidelines are available at https://www.osha.gov/laws-regs.

Clinical Laboratory Improvement Amendments (CLIA) of 1988, Amended in 2012

The federal government now requires that all clinical laboratories that test human specimens must be controlled (see Figure 8.2). The **Clinical Laboratory Improvement Amendments**, also known as CLIA, establishing minimum quality standards for laboratories, has been amended several times. The CLIA 1992 standards mandate that there must be written policies and procedures for a comprehensive quality assurance program that will evaluate the overall ongoing quality of the testing process. The regulations require that laboratories

- evaluate the effectiveness of their policies and procedures,
- identify and correct problems,
- ensure the competence and adequacy of staff,
- take corrective action if errors are found,
- integrate corrective procedures into future policies and procedures,
- document employee training and assess competency after the first year,
- maintain the identity and integrity of patient samples during the entire testing process, and
- are subject to inspection every two years if performing moderate or high complexity tests.

CLIA testing regulations are mandated for most tests conducted in laboratories. However, there are certain tests that are waived if they are simple to run, almost foolproof, and if an erroneous result would not result in a negative impact on the patient. The Food and Drug Administration (FDA) has the responsibility for categorizing the tests and allowing the waiver (exemption) of testing. In general, tests

Figure 8–2 Laboratory technologist

Source: Wichudapa/Shutterstock

approved by the FDA for home use are usually waived, although the manufacturer must request the waiver. Tests that require a microscope, calculations, or a judgment call are not waived and must meet CLIA standards. It is always advisable to search the CLIA website at https://www.cdc.gov/clia/index .html for a complete list of waived tests. If the laboratory test is not on this list, then it is not waived and must meet all CLIA requirements.

Health Maintenance Organization (HMO) Act of 1973, Amended in 1996

The Health Maintenance Organization (HMO) Act requires any company with at least 25 employees to provide an HMO alternative to regular group insurance for their employees if an HMO is available in the area.

Many new HMOs were formed in response to this law. HMOs have been able to cut healthcare costs in some areas by focusing on wellness such as well-baby physicals and mammograms. Under an HMO, the patient does not have the same wide choice of doctors as under a traditional healthcare plan. In addition, a patient may have to get a second opinion and permission from the HMO before having a major procedure performed. The HMO may make use of the concept of a primary care provider (PCP) (often referred to as a gatekeeper) as a method of controlling costs. In a gatekeeper situation, all medical care sought by a client must be channeled through the PCP, and any referrals are made within the HMO provider list.

Consolidated Omnibus Budget Reconciliation Act (COBRA) of 1985

The **Consolidated Omnibus Budget Reconciliation Act**, also known as COBRA, is an important act that covers a wide range of federal government financing for health insurance coverage continuation *after* an employee has been laid off or left a job.

Every year, millions of Americans are left without any healthcare coverage, many because of job loss. COBRA has helped to decrease this number of uncovered Americans. Under COBRA, a company with 20 or more employees must provide extended healthcare insurance to terminated employees for as long as 18 months—usually, but not always, at the employee's expense. This insurance may be costly, but for some people it's the best way to have current insurance. COBRA has enforcement power as all federal funding may be lost for noncompliance.

Healthcare COBRA also contains an amendment called EMTALA (Emergency Medical Treatment and Labor Act), which prohibits "patient dumping" from one hospital to another if the patient does not have health insurance. EMTALA is more fully discussed later in the chapter.

Drug-Free Workplace Act 1988

Employers have become increasingly aware of how expensive drug-using employees are in terms of decreased productivity, workplace accidents, and increased healthcare costs. Even under the best security conditions, the nature of some healthcare organizations, such as hospitals, healthcare offices, and clinics, allows for employee access to various drugs.

Med Tip

To prevent drug abuse, some organizations, such as hospitals, require drug testing as a condition of employment.

Under the **Drug-Free Workplace Act**, employers contracting to provide goods or services to the federal government must certify that they maintain a drug-free workplace. The employer must inform the employee of the intent to maintain a drug-free workplace and of any penalties, such as discharge, that the employee would incur for violation of the policy.

Compensation and Benefits Regulations

Several laws influence the compensation (salary) and benefits provided to employees. The following sections cover these laws.

Social Security Act of 1935, Amended in 1983

The **Social Security Act** is a federal law that covers all private and most public sector employees. This act laid the groundwork for unemployment compensation in the United States. Social Security is paid by the employer and the employee in equal payroll taxes and Medicare participant premiums. Social Security is composed of several different, but related, programs: retirement, disability, dependent and survivor's benefits, as well as health benefits under Medicare. The amount paid to the retiree or disabled person or dependent survivor is calculated based on the worker's average wages earned during their working life.

Fair Labor Standards Act (FLSA) of 1938, Amended in 2010

This is the main statute regulating employee benefits. The **Fair Labor Standards Act**, also known as FLSA, establishes the minimum wage, requires payment for overtime work, and sets the maximum hours employees covered by the act may work. The act covers all non-management employees in both for-profit and not-for-profit institutions.

The employer must pay one and one-half times the regular hourly pay rate for any work the employee performs over 40 hours in a seven-day (one-week) period. FLSA uses the single workweek to compute the hours of overtime. The law does not permit averaging hours over two or more weeks. Thus, an employee who works 35 hours one week and 45 hours the next—for a weekly average of 40 hours for the two weeks—must still be paid the overtime rate for five hours.

One exception allows hospitals to negotiate an agreement with their employees to establish a work period of 14 days. In this case, overtime pay would go into effect for employees who work more than 80 hours in the 14-day period. It is also acceptable to require fewer than 40 hours a week to qualify for overtime payment or a higher rate than one and one-half times the regular hourly pay, but the employer cannot require more hours or pay less than the law requires.

This law affects full-time and part-time hourly employees. Some workers, such as management or salaried employees, are exempt from the minimum wage and overtime requirement of the FLSA. In addition, part-time employees and employees who are part of a time-sharing program generally do not benefit from this law.

The Wage and Hour Division of the United States Department of Labor has established a number of criteria under the FLSA, including the following:

- The federal minimum wage has been set at $7.25 per hour effective July 2009.

- Covered nonexempt employees must be paid overtime for hours worked over 40 hours per week at not less than one and one-half times their regular pay.

- Employers must display a FLSA poster outlining the requirements of the FLSA and they must maintain employee time and pay records.

- Child labor provisions were established to protect the education opportunities and to provide safe working conditions for young people.

Equal Pay Act of 1963

The **Equal Pay Act**, an amendment to the Fair Labor Standards Act, makes it illegal for an employer to discriminate on the basis of gender in the payment to people who are performing the same job. Equal work means work that requires equal skill, responsibility, and effort under the same or similar working conditions. For example, male orderlies cannot be paid more than female orderlies (*Odomes v. Nucare, Inc.*, 653 F.2d 6th Cir. 1981).

Unemployment Compensation

The Social Security Act was the origin of this insurance program. Today, employers pay taxes into a state unemployment compensation plan that covers employees who are unable to work through no fault of their own. The **unemployment compensation** laws provide for temporary weekly payments for the unemployed worker. State unemployment compensation insurance taxes for individual employers vary from state to state according to state laws and the turnover experience of the business.

In order to receive unemployment insurance, the employee must have worked for an employer who has paid, or was required to pay, unemployment compensation taxes. However, certain types of employers are exempt, such as employers for religious, educational, or charitable organizations; employers for small farming operations; employers of family members; and employers who use federal government labor.

While state unemployment insurance law provides temporary payments for those who lose their jobs, if an employee is fired for good cause, the employee is not entitled to unemployment benefits. In the case of *Love v. Heritage House Convalescent Center*, the court found that a nursing assistant was properly denied unemployment benefits because she was terminated for poor work attendance. According to the employee's personnel record, the convalescent center had already shown great tolerance in allowing the employee to continue working as long as it had (*Love v. Heritage House Convalescent Ctr.*, 463 N.E.2d 478, Ind. Ct. App. 1983).

Unemployment compensation was also denied in a case in which a nurse's aide was discharged for leaving a resident unattended and unrestrained on a commode and for using the medication of one patient (a medicated cream) on another patient (*Starks v. Director of Div. of Employment Section*, 462 N.E.2d 1360, Mass. 1984).

Federal Insurance Contribution Act (FICA) of 1935

The **Federal Insurance Contribution Act**, also known as FICA, is the oldest act relating to compensation. Under FICA, employers are required to contribute to Social Security plans for their employees. There is a severe fine if the payment by the employer is not made on time. This act also requires detailed record-keeping documenting the employer's payment. The key to the proper implementation of this act is to hire a trusted office manager.

Workers' Compensation Act

The **Workers' Compensation Act** protects workers and their families from financial problems resulting from employment-related injury, disease, and even death. Under the law, employers typically pay into a fund to help cover costs when an employee is hurt or sustains an injury arising in the course of employment. Examples include a back injury or a work-related disease, such as carpal tunnel syndrome from improper or prolonged computer keyboard usage.

The goal of workers' compensation is to get the employee back to work as soon as possible. COBRA may allow for a retraining opportunity if the injury results in permanent inability to work in the same job. If there is a health problem within the first three months of employment on a new job, the previous employer may have to pay the workers' compensation, as most of the benefits were paid into the employee's fund by that employer. Some healthcare practices only handle patients with workers' compensation injuries. Workers' compensation programs are administered at the state level with no federal involvement or mandatory standards.

Under the Workers' Compensation Act, an employee must submit a written notice of the injury to the employer. Generally, an employee will receive only a partial salary, such as two-thirds of salary, as compensation.

Workers' compensation benefits are generally available even if the employee is at fault for their injury, but an employee who has violated hospital policy is not eligible to receive benefits. In a seminal case, *Fair v. St. Joseph's Hospital*, the hospital employee was disqualified from receiving compensation because he violated the policy by fighting with a coworker (*Fair v. St. Joseph's Hosp.*, 437 S.E.2d 875, N.C. App. 1933).

Even if an employee is covered by workers' compensation, the employee may still sue and recover for injuries caused by nonemployees. For example, in a 1994 case in California, a psychiatric nurse sued a psychiatric patient who kicked her in the abdomen, causing injury to her unborn child. The court ruled that the workers' compensation law did not bar this lawsuit (*Agnew-Watson v. County of Alameda*, 36 Cal. Rptr. 2nd 196, CT. App. Cal. 1994).

Employee Retirement Income Security Act (ERISA) of 1974

The **Employee Retirement Income Security Act**, also known as ERISA, regulates employee benefits and pension plans. Before the passage of ERISA, widespread abuse of pension plans led to their collapse, leaving retired employees without the pension benefits their companies had promised. ERISA responded to this problem by requiring employers to put aside money that can be used only to pay future benefits. ERISA also guarantees vesting of pension plans.

Vesting refers to a certain point in time—such as after ten years of employment—when an employee has the right to receive benefits from a retirement plan. Under ERISA, employees who stay with a company for ten years are entitled to 50 percent of the employer's retirement plan even if they leave the company and take another job. Employees are entitled to 100 percent of the employer's pension contribution after 15 years of employment, when they become fully vested. In some cases in the past, employees had been laid off just before they became vested. ERISA now prohibits this practice.

Family and Medical Leave Act (FMLA) of 1994

The **Family and Medical Leave Act**, also known as FMLA, allows eligible employees to take unpaid, job-protected leave from work for specified family and medical reasons. While on leave, their group health insurance coverage continues under the same terms and conditions. According to the Department of Labor (https://www.dol.gov/agencies/whd/fmla), eligible employees are entitled to the following:

- Twelve workweeks of leave in a 12-month period for
  - the birth of a child and to care for the newborn child within one year of birth;
  - the placement with the employee of a child for adoption or foster care and to care for the newly placed child within one year of placement;
  - to care for the employee's spouse, child, or parent who has a serious health condition;
  - a serious health condition that makes the employee unable to perform the essential functions of their job; or
  - any qualifying exigency arising out of the fact that the employee's spouse, child, or parent is a covered military member on "covered active duty."
- Twenty-six workweeks of leave during a single 12-month period to care for a covered service member with a serious injury or illness if the eligible employee is the service member's spouse, child, parent, or next of kin (military caregiver leave).

The leave does not have to be taken consecutively. When it is necessary, employees make take FMLA leave intermittently. This includes taking time off in separate blocks (for chemotherapy, for example), or having a reduced work schedule (working fewer days or fewer hours/day). When leave is needed for medical treatment, the employee should make an effort to disrupt the work schedule as little as possible.

The company must maintain the employee's health coverage while the employee is on a family medical leave. The employee must be returned to the original or equivalent position they held before going on leave. In addition, there cannot be any loss of employment benefits that accumulated before the start of the leave.

Consumer Protection and Collection Practices

The consumer protection and collection practices laws serve to protect the consumer from unfair practices. The following sections cover laws about consumer protection and collection practices.

Emergency Medical Treatment & Labor Act (EMTALA) of 1986

The **Emergency Medical Treatment & Labor Act**, also known as EMTALA, is a section of the COBRA that ensures public access to emergency services regardless of the ability to pay. It involves dealing with *patient dumping*, a slang term for transferring emergency patients from one hospital to another if the patient does not have health insurance or is unable to pay for services.

Patients entering a hospital emergency department must now be stabilized before they can be transferred to another facility. If the patient cannot be stabilized then they can be transferred to a regional trauma center without incurring an EMTALA violation. According to this law, if a hospital is reported for patient dumping, the person doing the reporting (the whistleblower) may not be penalized. The government may impose stiff fines and even terminate Medicare agreements if the hospital is determined to have violated EMTALA. In addition, the patient can also sue the hospital. Physicians may also be at risk for legal action if they misrepresent the patient's condition. However, EMTALA does not apply to health maintenance organizations, private clinics, or private physicians' offices. The practice of patient dumping has significantly diminished since the passage of EMTALA.

Fair Credit Reporting Act of 1971

The **Fair Credit Reporting Act** (which is Title VI of the Consumer Credit Protection Act), amended by the **Credit Card Accountability Responsibility and Disclosure Act of 2009**, establishes guidelines for use of an individual's credit information. If a patient has been denied credit based on a poor rating from a credit agency, the patient must be notified of this fact and given the name and address of the reporting agency. The agency must disclose the credit information to the consumer, who may correct and update this information.

Equal Credit Opportunity Act of 1975

The **Equal Credit Opportunity Act** (Title VII of the Consumer Credit Protection Act) prohibits businesses, including hospitals and healthcare offices, from either granting or denying credit based on the applicant's race, color, religion, national origin, sex, marital status, age, or receipt of public assistance. This law mandates that all people must be issued credit if they qualify for it, based on the premise that if credit is given to one person, it should be given to all persons who request it and are qualified.

Truth in Lending Act (TILA) of 1968

The **Truth in Lending Act**, also known as TILA, requires a full written disclosure about interest rates or finance charges concerning the payment of any fee that will be collected in more than four installments. This is also called Regulation Z of the Consumer Protection Act. Installment payments are often used for orthodontia, obstetrical care, and surgical treatment. It is legal to include a finance charge if a patient pays the bill in installments. However, few physicians and dentists require this charge.

Fair Debt Collection Practices Act of 1978, Amended in 2010 and 2021

Healthcare offices and hospitals would not be able to remain in business if patients didn't pay their bills for medical care. However, fair collection practices must be honored. The **Fair Debt Collections Practices Act** prohibits unfair collection practices by creditors (institutions or persons who are owed money). For example, the Federal Communications Commission (FCC) has issued guidelines for the specific times that credit collection phone calls can be made. It also prohibits telephone harassment and threats, and consumers have the right to cease all collection communications from debt collectors. Under this law, telephone calls for purposes of collections can only be made daily between the hours of 8:00 am and 9:00 pm, and consumers cannot be called more than seven times within a period of seven days for a particular debt (Figure 8.3). Debt collectors are allowed to use email and text messages to contact consumers, but they are not allowed to use social media platforms.

Med Tip

Personnel involved in the billing and collections operations of any facility must have a full understanding of the laws regulating the collection process.

Using a Collection Agency

Professional collection agencies are available when all other attempts to collect unpaid bills fail. The account should always be reviewed with the physician or head of the healthcare practice before turning it over for collection. After the patient is told the account is going to a collection agency, it must, by law, go. After the

Figure 8–3 Collection calls are made between 8:00 am and 9:00 pm

Source: Cathy Yeulet/123RF

account has been turned over, no further collection attempts can be made by the physician's office or hospital—that would be considered harassment. If the patient should contact the office or hospital after the account has been turned over for collection, the patient should be referred to the collection agency.

Bankruptcy

When patients become unable to pay their debts, they may file for bankruptcy. Bankruptcy is a legal method for providing some protection to individual debtors who owe money by establishing a fair method for distribution of the debtor's assets to all the creditors. If a patient files for bankruptcy, a court-appointed trustee may place the patient's assets in a special fund, and then distribute the funds according to a predetermined method. After a debtor files for bankruptcy, a creditor may no longer seek payment from the patient. Instead, the creditor must file a claim in bankruptcy court at a later date.

Federal Wage Garnishment Law of 1970

Garnishment refers to a court order that requires an employer to pay a portion of an employee's paycheck directly to one of the employee's creditors until the debt is resolved. The **Federal Wage Garnishment Law** restricts the amount of the paycheck that can be used to pay off a debt.

Claims against Estates

When a patient dies, a bill should be sent to the estate of the deceased. There is generally a specific time limit allowed when filing a claim against an estate. The probate department of the superior court in the county that is handling the estate can provide information on the time limits and also the name of the administrator of the estate.

The Statute of Limitations

This statute defines how long a healthcare practice has to file suit to collect on a past-due account. Because the time limit varies from state to state, an attorney should be consulted to determine the particular state's law. Because there is a statute of limitations on collecting a debt, it is important to attempt any debt collection as soon as possible.

Chapter 8 Review

Points to Ponder

1. Why did the federal government enact laws such as Title VII, the ADA, and COBRA?
2. How do you respond to an illegal interview question?
3. Isn't it important for an employer to know if a potential employee has a disability? Why or why not?
4. In your opinion, does the Family and Medical Leave Act of 1994 discriminate against working persons who do *not* have children or older parents?
5. Are you entitled to take off a couple of days to reenergize yourself if you do not use up all of your sick days during the year?

Discussion Questions

1. Identify the principal kinds of illegal discrimination that result in unequal employment opportunities.
2. What amendments to Title VII are discussed within this chapter?
3. What are considered potentially infectious materials under OSHA guidelines?
4. What regulation assists terminated employees in obtaining extended healthcare coverage?
5. What does the Fair Labor Standards Act of 1938 control?
6. Who is eligible to receive a leave of absence under the Family and Medical Leave Act of 1994?
7. What does ERISA control?

Review Challenge

Short Answer Questions

1. What law protects employees from being sexually harassed in the workplace?

   _____

   _____

   _____

   _____

   _____

2. What do the initials EMTALA stand for and who does this law protect?

   _____

   _____

   _____

   _____

   _____

3. As a healthcare worker, is it legal for your employer to ask you to provide a urine sample for a drug test? Why or why not?

   _____

   _____

   _____

   _____

   _____

4. Under what federal regulation(s) are Deaf children offered interpreters?

   _____

   _____

   _____

   _____

5. Give examples of efficiency and effectiveness. Why is effectiveness more important?

   _____

   _____

   _____

   _____

   _____

6. What does the term "just cause" mean?

   _____

   _____

   _____

   _____

   _____

7. What are six illegal interview questions?

   _____

   _____

   _____

   _____

8. Discuss the Fair Pay regulation under FLSA and what it means for overtime payments to healthcare employees such as RNs and LPNs.

   _____

   _____

   _____

   _____

Matching

Match the responses in column B with the correct term in column A.

COLUMN A

_____ 1. creditor

_____ 2. preempt

_____ 3. vesting

_____ 4. discrimination

_____ 5. just cause

_____ 6. at-will employment

_____ 7. OSHA

_____ 8. ADA

_____ 9. Title VII

_____ 10. debtors

COLUMN B

a. Civil Rights Act of 1964

b. Occupational Safety and Health Act

c. having a legal reason

d. overrule

e. one who owes money to another

f. one to whom a debt is owed

g. unfair treatment

h. employee gains the rights to receive benefits

i. Americans with Disabilities Act of 1990

j. employment can be terminated

Multiple Choice

Select the one best answer to the following statements:

1. In most cases, federal laws
   a. are better than state laws.
   b. are not followed as closely as state laws.
   c. preempt state laws.
   d. are used when state laws are not effective.
   e. none of the above

2. Title VII of the Civil Rights Act of 1964 prohibits discrimination based on
   a. color, race, and national origin.
   b. religion.
   c. gender.
   d. income level and education.
   e. a, b, and c only.

3. The following acts are covered as amendments under Title VII with the exception of the
   a. Pregnancy Discrimination Act of 1978.
   b. Drug-Free Workplace Act of 1988.
   c. Equal Employment Opportunity Act of 1972.
   d. Civil Rights Act of 1991.
   e. Age Discrimination in Employment Act of 1967.

4. The Occupational Safety and Health Act (OSHA) developed standards in 1991 stating that infectious materials include
   a. any unidentified body fluid.
   b. amniotic fluid.
   c. saliva in dental procedures.
   d. cerebrospinal fluid.
   e. all of the above.

5. The most important act covered under compensation and benefits regulations is said to be the
   a. Workers' Compensation Act.
   b. Social Security Act of 1935.
   c. Federal Insurance Contribution Act of 1935.
   d. Fair Labor Standards Act.
   e. Family and Medical Leave Act of 1994.

6. Regulation Z of the Consumer Protection Act is also referred to as
   a. Equal Credit Opportunity Act of 1975.
   b. Fair Credit Reporting Act of 1971.
   c. Truth in Lending Act of 1969.
   d. Employee Retirement Income Security Act of 1974.
   e. Workers' Compensation Act.

7. When making a claim for payment after a patient has died, the claim (or bill) must be
   a. sent in the name of the deceased person to his or her last known address.
   b. sent to the administrator of the estate of the deceased person.
   c. sent to a collection agency with specific instructions to collect the payment from the next of kin.
   d. waived.
   e. none of the above.

8. When using a collection agency to collect outstanding debts (unpaid bills) from a patient,
   a. allow the collection agency to continue pursuing collection.
   b. stay closely involved in the process and make frequent follow-up phone calls to the delinquent patient.

c. it is wise to first threaten the patient that you will send the unpaid account to a collection agency and then give the patient a second chance.

d. review the delinquent account with the physician or office manager before turning over the account to the agency.

e. all of the above

9. ERISA

a. controls employee benefit plans.

b. controls employee pension plans.

c. determines eligibility.

d. determines vesting.

e. all of the above

10. Under the Workers' Compensation Act,

a. employers must pay into a fund to help cover costs when an employee is hurt.

b. the previous employer never has to pay for workmen's compensation.

c. workers' compensation is only administered at the federal level.

d. employees may not sue nonemployees.

e. there is a guarantee of receiving a full salary while on workers' compensation.

Discussion Cases

1. Analyze *"The Case of Janet K. and Epilepsy"* (found at the beginning of the chapter) using the three-step ethics model (Blanchard-Peale model found in Chapter 1).

   a. _____
   _____

   b. _____
   _____

   c. _____
   _____

2. You and your friend Jayden both work as technologists in the imaging department of the local community hospital. The department is short-staffed, and Jayden agreed to work extra shifts during the past week to help out. He tells you, "Now I'm taking two days off as sick days. I've earned them, and I need the rest."

   a. Can your friend use his sick days for this purpose?
   _____
   _____

   b. What is your advice to Jayden?
   _____
   _____

   c. Do you need to do anything else?
   _____
   _____

3. Kelly Block, a registered nurse, is assisting Dr. Brown while he performs a minor surgical procedure. Dr. Brown is known to have a quick temper, and he becomes very angry if a surgical procedure is delayed for any reason. As Kelly is handing a needle with suture thread to Dr. Brown, she feels a slight prick in her sterile gloves. She tells Dr. Brown about this and explains that she will have to be excused from the procedure for a few minutes while she changes gloves. He becomes angry and tells her to "forget about it and help me finish."

   a. Will it be harmful to anyone if Kelly wears the gloves during the rest of the procedure, as it was just a slight prick and the patient's wound does not appear to be infected?
   _____
   _____

   b. Who is at fault if the patient does develop an infection?
   _____
   _____

   c. What recourse does Kelly have if she develops a blood-borne pathogen infection, such as hepatitis, from the small hole in her gloves?
   _____
   _____

   d. Is this an ethical or a legal issue, or both?
   _____
   _____

   e. Are there any federal regulations that might help Kelly in the event of an injury or infection? If so, what are they?
   _____
   _____

Put It Into Practice

Write a letter of application for a position you may wish to seek upon graduation from your program of study. Submit this letter, along with an updated résumé, to your instructor for comments. Using Table 8.1 as a guide, review the personal information you provided in your cover letter and résumé. Have you given any information that is not required? Are there any gaps in your employment record? If so, why? How will you answer any of the questions in Table 8.1 if you are asked them during an interview?

Web Hunt

Search the website of the Occupational Safety and Health Administration Act (**www.osha.org**) to find an article that relates to OSHA or workers' compensation. Summarize the article.

Critical Thinking Exercise

What would you do if you overheard your manager state that she didn't want to hire a new employee who was 58 years old because it would take too long to train the person on the electronic medical record system because she was "older and might not catch on quickly"?

Bibliography

Beaman, N., Routh, K.S., Papazian-Boyce, L., et al. (2017). *Pearson's comprehensive medical assisting: Administrative and clinical competencies* (4th ed.). Pearson.

Garner, B. (2019). *Black's law dictionary* (11th ed.). Thomson Reuters.

Lerner, B. (2009). A life-changing case for doctors in training. *New York Times* (March 3), D5, D7.

Perez-Pena, R. (2006). City seeks action against 39 in case of "Nixzmary" prying. *New York Times* (September 23), B5.

Phelan, S.M., Burgess, D.J., Yeazel, M.W., Hellerstedt, W.L., Griffin, J.M., & van Ryn, M. (2015). Impact of weight bias and stigma on quality of care and outcomes for patients with obesity. *Obesity Reviews*, 16(4):319–26. DOI: 10.1111/obr.12266.

Rosenbaum, L. & Lamas, D. (2012). Residents' duty hours—toward and empirical narrative. *New England Journal of Medicine*, 367:2044–2049. https://www.nejm.org/doi/full/10.1056/NEJMsr1210160

Schmalleger, F. (2018). *Criminal justice today: An introductory text for the 21st century* (15th ed.). Pearson.

U.S. Equal Employment Opportunity Commission (EEOC). (2022). AMG Specialty Hospital to pay $82,481 to settle EEOC sexual harassment case. *Press Release.* https://www.eeoc.gov/newsroom/amg-specialty-hospital-pay-82481-settle-eeoc-sexual-harassment-case

Woolley, S. (2005). Children of Jehovah's Witnesses and adolescent Jehovah's Witnesses: What are their rights? *Archives of Disease in Children,* DOI: 10.1136/adc.2004.067843

The Medical Record

Learning Objectives

After completing this chapter, you will be able to:

9.1 Define the key terms.

9.2 List five purposes of the medical record.

9.3 List five requirements for maintaining medical records as recommended by The Joint Commission.

9.4 Discuss what is meant by timeliness of charting and why it is important in a legal context.

9.5 Describe ways to protect patient confidentiality that relate to the use of fax, copiers, email, and computers.

9.6 Discuss the time periods for retaining adults' and minors' medical records, fetal heart monitor records, and records of birth, death, and surgical procedures.

9.7 Explain the guidelines to follow when a subpoena *duces tecum* is in effect.

9.8 Describe confidentiality obligations using electronic health records.

Key Terms

Credibility gap
Credible
Disclosed
Doctrine of professional discretion
Electronic health record (EHR)
Electronic medical record (EMR)
Encryptions
Firewalls
Health record
Medical record
Open-record laws
Personal health record (PHR)
Privileged communication
The Joint Commission
Timeliness of documentation

The Case of Jason and the Ransomware Attack

Jason was diagnosed with stage III colorectal cancer. After surgery, he was prescribed chemotherapy and then radiation, which was administered daily. But one day, he received a call from the hospital telling him not to come in for his appointments until further notice. The hospital had been hit by a cyberattack. A ransomware gang had taken control of the hospital network and was demanding a ransom to unlock the files.

The hospital staff no longer had access to electronic health records, imaging files, lab results, and communication links with other departments. The hospital was unprepared for the attack, but quickly developed manual workarounds. For example, administrators were put to work carrying lab results from the lab to the health providers on the floors. Staff were sent out to buy walkie-talkies so that teams could communicate.

The ransomware attack didn't affect just Jason's hospital. Because his hospital could no longer accept emergency patients, other area emergency departments became overcrowded. The U.S. Department of Health and Human Services declared in 2023 that cyberattacks are the single largest threat to American hospitals, and they deserve immediate attention because of the threat to life. The cyberattack on Jason's hospital lasted almost a month and cost more than $50 million in damages, mostly in lost revenue.

Jason and all of the hospital's patients had their treatment severely disrupted. Jason's radiation treatments were cancelled for a week. He and his wife were fearful that his tumors would grow aggressively during that week. Luckily, Jason's oncologist was able to get Jason's radiation therapy moved to another hospital.

It turned out that the malware had gotten into the hospital's system when an employee used a hospital laptop to access personal email, one of which came from a company that had been hacked. When that laptop was connected back to the hospital's system, it launched the network-wide attack. The hospital was relieved that the hackers only wanted money; in other ransomware attacks, the hackers have stolen patient data such as Social Security numbers, insurance information, and medical records.

1. If you were the one to call Jason and tell him his appointments were canceled for the week, what would you say?

2. What steps do you think were taken by the IT department to prevent further ransomware attacks.

3. How can you help prevent ransomware attacks?

Introduction

The **medical record**, also called the **health record**, is all of the written or electronic documentation relating to a patient. It includes past history information, current diagnosis and treatment, and correspondence relating to the patient. Billing information is often maintained in a separate accounting record. It is important to remember that the medical record is a legal document. Various laws cover the reporting, disclosure, and confidentiality of medical records. Thus, medical record management requires attention to accuracy, confidentiality, and proper filing and storage. Proper management is also necessary because the records may be subpoenaed, or ordered by the court, during a malpractice case.

Each patient's medical record contains essentially the same categories of material but with information unique to that patient. For example, not every patient has a consultation report from another physician or a surgical report. The format for the medical record reflects the physician's specialty. An orthopedic surgeon, for instance, uses a format that includes questions pertaining to the patient's mobility and pain level.

Purpose of the Medical Record

Medical records serve multiple purposes. They provide a medical picture and record of the patient from birth to death. It is an important document for the continual management of a patient's healthcare and furnishes documentary evidence of the course of evaluation and treatment. The patient record, which can result from a lifetime of healthcare visits, can assist the healthcare team in diagnosing, treating, and tracking the patterns of the patient's health. It also provides data and statistics on health matters such as births, deaths, and communicable diseases. The healthcare team can track the ongoing patterns of the patient's health through the medical record. Since 2014, as part of the American Recovery and Reinvestment Act, federal law requires that all medical records be kept in electronic format in order to be eligible for Medicaid and Medicare reimbursements (Figure 9.1).

In electronic form, a medical record is known as an **electronic medical record**, also known as an EMR, or an **electronic health record**, also known as an EHR. Most healthcare professionals use these terms interchangeably, but technically there is a slight difference between the EMR and the EHR that is discussed later in the "Electronic Health Records" section.

Med Tip

Remember that the primary purpose of the medical record or chart is to assist with making the diagnosis, treatment, and patient care.

Figure 9–1 All medical records must be kept in an electronic form

Source: John Giustina/The Image Bank/Getty Images

The medical record is invaluable in an ambulatory healthcare or hospital setting as it provides the base for the management of the patient's care, alerts the physicians and staff to patterns and changes in patient responses, and provides data for research and education.

In addition, because this legal document contains an objective, factual record of a patient's medical condition and treatment, either the patient or the physician in a malpractice suit may use this information. Finally, the medical record is a legal document and, as such, should not contain flippant or unprofessional comments.

Med Tip

The medical record is a document that records both the care and treatment that a patient did and did not receive. The terms "medical record" and "medical chart" are used interchangeably.

The medical record serves as an important path for communication among healthcare personnel. In a case briefly discussed in Chapter 3, *Norton v. Argonaut Insurance Company*, the medical record played a key role in documenting a medication error. A physician prescribed 2.5 mL of Elixir Pediatric Lanoxin, used to treat heart conditions, to be given orally to the baby by the infant's mother while the baby was hospitalized. The doctor increased the baby's Lanoxin dosage to 3.0 mL and told the mother about the new dosage. He signed a chart order that read, "Give 3.0 mL Lanoxin today for one dose only." The mother gave the baby 3.0 mL as she was told to do by the doctor. A nurse, who was not familiar with the fact that the doctor allowed the mother to give the baby her medication, read the doctor's order for 3.0 mL of Lanoxin to be given today. She then gave an injection of the drug to the baby not knowing that the mother had already administered the dose orally. This overdose of medication caused the baby's death. In this case, the parents sued the doctor, the nurse, and the hospital. In this landmark case, the nurse was held responsible for the infant's death because of injecting a potentially lethal dose of a heart medication without questioning the prescribing physician. The physician's order was unclear because he did not state that the mother would administer the 3.0 mL of Lanoxin orally (*Norton v. Argonaut Ins. Co.*, 144 So. 2d 249, La. App. 1962). The nurse also has a responsibility to make the proper inquiry if there is any question or uncertainty about an order. This was a case of negligence.

Contents of the Medical Record

The medical record contains both personal information about the patient and medical or clinical notations supplied by the physician and other healthcare professionals caring for the patient. Personal patient information includes full name, address, telephone number, date of birth, marital status, employer, and insurance information. The clinical data or information includes all records of medical examinations, including X-rays, laboratory reports, and consent forms. The medical record will also contain any correspondence between the healthcare team and the patient such as letters of withdrawal and consultation reports from other physicians. If a patient has provided informed consent for a procedure or test that has been explained to them, then a record of this explanation and the oral consent must be documented in the medical record.

Med Tip

Document patient comments such as "I'm all alone" or "I just feel I can't go on." Any comments of this nature should be relayed to the physician or advance practice provider because they may indicate an emotional problem in addition to the physical one for which the patient is seeking treatment.

As a legal document, both the defendant (physician) and plaintiff (patient) in a lawsuit can use the medical record. Because of its importance, some states have passed statutes that define what must be contained in the record. Many of these statutes reflect the accreditation requirements of **The Joint**

Commission, an agency that oversees hospital accreditation standards, or Medicare requirements as the minimum standard. Under these requirements, the medical record must include the following information:

1. Personal information such as name, address, date of birth, phone number, medical record number for the patient, emergency contact information, and marital status
2. Past significant medical history, surgeries, allergies, and current medications
3. Family background, encompassing husband and offspring. adherence to a particular religion or set of beliefs
4. Living wills, advanced medical directives, or DNRs
5. Dated medical records that are signed by every healthcare professional who treats the patient. Every entry needs to have a distinct number that is time-stamped in the patient's medical record.

The medical record should never contain irrelevant material—material that is not related to the patient or the patient's care. All healthcare personnel who provide care must document that care or treatment and then sign their name to the documentation. EHR systems provide various ways to sign or attest to the identity of the person who has made an entry. These may be digital signatures, biometric identifiers (such as a fingerprint), or a code or PIN assigned to the individual entering the information. No personnel may sign any name or provide any other identifying information other than their own. In addition, not all healthcare professionals will be empowered to chart information on a patient's medical record.

Med Tip

In healthcare today, there is far less manual charting and far more computer-based charting (electronic health records [EHRs]).

Corrections and Alterations

Some medical record errors are unavoidable. These might include errors in spelling, transcription, or inadvertently omitting information or test results. Occasionally, an error occurs when patient information is written in or added to the wrong chart. It is perfectly acceptable to correct these errors as long as this is done properly. Nothing should be deleted. All corrections on paper files should be made by drawing a single line through the error, writing the correction above the error, dating the change, and then initialing it. Do not erase or use correction fluid. The original statement or error should *never* be obliterated. Many healthcare professionals will also note in the margin of the record why the change was made, as for example, "incorrect chart." No changes to a patient's chart should ever be made after a reasonable period of time following discharge.

Med Tip

Use the ink color specified by your agency when manually charting or making a medical record entry. Never use pencil.

EHR corrections are handled very differently from paper record corrections. Each facility, depending on its software program, will have its own guidelines, or protocol, for correcting errors. One example occurs when an addendum, or revision, must be added after the date of the original entry. For example, in a healthcare office, if a patient is unable to provide a urine sample on the day of their exam but brings one in the following day, a CMA or RN can draft a temporary revision or addition to the medical record, such as a test result, along with the notation "revision" and their name. Any time this record is examined, the word "revision" will show up. All entries should be double-checked before transmitting the information. The user should sign out of all electronic patient records when not in use.

While it is acceptable to make an immediate correction in a medical record, it should never be altered. In one case, the plaintiff's attorney waited several weeks after the defendant was found not guilty and requested the medical record a second time. He noted that it had been altered after the case was closed. Upon review of the case, the judge ordered punitive damages.

Falsification of medical records is grounds for criminal indictment. In a New York case, two orthopedic surgeons performed a procedure on a patient that required implanting a prosthetic device into the hip joint. The salesman of the prosthetic device was in the operating room when the patient had to be reopened in order to correct the placement of the device. One of the surgeons left the operating room to return to his office and agreed that the salesman could assist the remaining surgeon. The salesman assisted by removing the prosthesis from the patient and preparing it for the surgeon to re-implant. The surgeon who left the operating room was sued for malpractice because the surgical record did not show that he had been replaced with a nonphysician during the surgery. The hospital and surgical nurse were also indicted for violating a duty imposed on them by the nature of their profession (*People v. Smithtown Gen. Hosp.* 736, 402 N.Y.S.2d 318, Sup. Ct. 1978).

Normal, as well as abnormal or negative, findings should all be noted in the medical record. Some doctors and staff become hurried and document only the abnormal. This can result in a problem if the medical record becomes part of a court record. If a jury does not see a test or procedure documented, then they tend to assume that it was not done no matter how strongly the physician or healthcare provider asserts that it was.

Med Tip

It is almost impossible to hide a change in a paper medical record, as handwriting, type of ink, and paper used can all be detected through scientific testing. Electronic systems are programmed to prevent disguising a correction made after the original information is saved.

Timeliness of Documentation

Medical records must be accurate and timely. **Timeliness of documentation** means that all entries should be made as they occur or as soon as possible afterward. Federal reimbursement guidelines mandate that all medical records should be completed within 30 days following the patient's discharge from a hospital. The Joint Commission has issued guidelines for timeliness in charting.

Late entries into the medical chart mean that, even for a brief period of time, the medical record is incomplete. This can cause a serious problem if the incomplete record is subpoenaed for a malpractice suit. Any entry made into a medical record after a lawsuit is threatened or filed is suspect. Also, if the medical record is not updated promptly, there could be a lapse of memory about what actually occurred.

Completeness of Entries

The medical record may be the most important document in a malpractice suit because it documents the type and amount of patient care that was given. If the medical record is incomplete, the physician or other healthcare provider may be unable to defend allegations of malpractice, even if there was no negligence (Figure 9.2). For instance, in a 1985 Missouri case, a physician ordered that a patient be turned every two hours. The attending nurses, however, failed to note in the patient's record when they turned her. The patient claimed that she had not been turned as ordered and that this caused her to develop serious pressure injuries, which led to the amputation of one leg. The nurses presented an expert witness who testified that in some instances nurses become so busy that they place the needs of the patient, such as turning, before the need to document. The court eventually dismissed this case. However, not all such cases are dismissed (*Hurlock v. Park Lane Med. Ctr. Inc.*, 709 S.W.2d 872, Mo. Ct. App. 1985).

Med Tip

The medical record is a legal document and, as such, can be subpoenaed into court as evidence in a malpractice case.

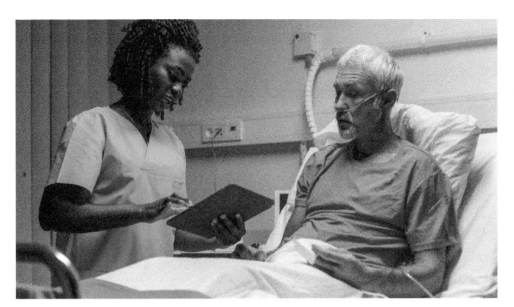

Figure 9–2 Medical assistant gathering information from patient admitted to the emergency department
Source: Gorodenkoff/Shutterstock

In a California case, an appeals court ruled that the physician's inability to provide the patient's medical record created the inference of guilt (*Thor v. Boska*, 113 Cal. Rptr. 296, Ct. App. 1974). This is an example of a situation in which the physician may not have been at fault. However, the fact that he was unable to provide any documentation about his treatment of the patient meant that even at the appeals court level, he did not win his case.

Med Tip

Remember that in the eyes of the court, if it's not documented, it wasn't done.

Credibility of the Medical Record

For something to be **credible** it must be believable or worthy of belief, trustworthy, and reliable. This is asking a lot of brief statements written in a medical record. However, credibility is exactly what is necessary for everyone, including lawyers, to acknowledge that the medical record is an accurate picture of what happened to the patient. A **credibility gap** exists if there is an apparent disparity between what is said or written and the actual facts. This gap results in a failure to accept one's statements as factual, or a person's professed motives as the true ones. For example, if a hospital record concerning a patient's fall from a hospital bed includes an inserted statement such as "side rails were up," a lawyer and jury may believe otherwise. If X-rays or other important medical records are missing, an assumption may be made that this was purposely done to hide something. Even a documented fire or flood can cause a credibility gap to occur.

Med Tip

Opinion and speculation do not belong in the medical record. Statements such as "It appears the mother hit the child," while based on physical evidence, are not acceptable in the medical record. In this case, it is correct to describe the injury and the child's statement.

One physician may be asked by an attorney to review a medical record pertaining to a medical malpractice case of another physician to help determine if there is evidence of malpractice. The second physician will be looking for gaps or other problems with the record such as illegible handwriting, delays in placing X-ray and laboratory reports into the file, altered records, or any contrived or invented documentation. Medical records are frequently examined during Medicaid or Medicare fraud cases in which a physician has falsely claimed payment for services that were never rendered.

Med Tip

Anyone processing medical billing records must be conscientious about the accuracy of names, dates, and services rendered. Careless documentation for claims of insurance payments can result in healthcare providers being brought up on charges of fraud.

Ownership of the Medical Record

In most states, the general rule is that the physician or owners of a healthcare facility, such as a hospital or nursing home, own the medical records, but patients have the legal right of **privileged communication** (confidential information told to their healthcare team) and access to their medical records. Therefore, patients must authorize the release of their records in writing.

The Health Insurance Portability and Accountability Act (HIPAA) is a landmark piece of legislation in the United States that was enacted in 1996 to safeguard the privacy and security of individuals' medical information. One of the key provisions of HIPAA is the right of patients to access their medical records. This right empowers individuals to take control of their healthcare, make informed decisions, and ensure the accuracy of their medical information.

HIPAA grants patients several essential rights when it comes to accessing their medical records. These rights are grounded in the principle that individuals should have control over their health information and include the following:

- *Right to inspection and copy*—HIPAA allows patients to request access to their medical records and obtain copies. This means that individuals can review their medical history, diagnoses, treatment plans, and any other information in their records. This right promotes transparency and empowers patients to actively participate in their healthcare.

- *Requesting amendments*—If a patient believes that their medical record contains inaccurate or incomplete information, HIPAA permits them to request corrections or amendments. This ensures that the information within their records is both accurate and relevant to their healthcare decisions.

- *Timely access*—HIPAA mandates that healthcare providers must respond to requests for access to medical records within 30 days. This ensures that patients can promptly access their health information when needed.

- *Protection of privacy*—HIPAA safeguards patients' privacy by requiring healthcare providers to maintain the confidentiality and security of medical records. Patients can rest assured that their information is not being inappropriately disclosed.

- *Electronic access*—In today's digital age, HIPAA also acknowledges the importance of electronic access to medical records. Many healthcare providers now offer online portals where patients can access their records securely, making it more convenient for individuals to keep track of their health information.

The rights afforded by HIPAA are significant for several reasons. First, they empower patients to take a more active role in their healthcare. By having easy access to their medical records, patients can better understand their conditions, treatment plans, and any potential risks or side effects. This promotes informed decision-making and enhances the quality of healthcare. Second, these rights enhance the overall trust in the healthcare system. Patients can have confidence that their sensitive medical information is being handled with care and respect for their privacy. HIPAA establishes a clear framework for maintaining the confidentiality and security of medical records, which is crucial in an era where data breaches and privacy concerns are on the rise.

The process of accessing medical records under HIPAA is relatively straightforward. Patients typically need to submit a written request to their healthcare provider or facility. This request should include specific details, such as the records they want to access and whether they want physical or electronic copies.

While HIPAA grants patients the right to access their medical records, it's essential to note that there may be some limitations. For instance, certain psychotherapy notes and information related to pending legal actions may not be accessible. Also, under the **doctrine of professional discretion**, a healthcare provider may determine, based on their best judgment, if a patient with mental health issues should view the medical record. However, even in such cases, patients have the right to challenge these decisions and seek resolution.

Because the medical record is a written or electronic documentation of the contract established between the physician or healthcare provider and the patient, it must be retained for legal purposes. There is often a need for a healthcare provider, such as hospital personnel and consulting physicians, to view a patient's medical record. However, when the need no longer exists, then the right to view the medical record, or access to it, stops.

Med Tip

- ALWAYS sign out of a laptop or computer system when leaving the patient's room.
- NEVER leave an EHR open. It directly violates HIPAA regulations by granting the patient complete access to the data of other patients.

Confidentiality and the Medical Record

To protect patient confidentiality, medical records should not be released to third parties without the patient's written consent. If an attorney obtains a subpoena for the medical records, only the specific records that are requested, such as the surgical notes, should be copied and sent. For example, the fact that a patient is HIV-positive or has been seen in an emergency department after an auto collision may have no bearing on a malpractice suit relating to a surgical procedure.

Taking photographs or other visual images of patients, such as videotapes, without the proper patient consent is an invasion of the patient's privacy. The patient must sign an authorization form in order for photos and films, such as mammograms and digital or radiographic images, to be used or released outside of the healthcare facility.

Confidential material should not be transmitted by fax. A fax transmission is not acceptable when an original is required. Guidelines for maintaining patient confidentiality when using a fax machine, copy machine, email, or computer are listed in Table 9.1.

Table 9–1 Maintaining Patient Confidentiality When Using Fax (Facsimile) Machines, Copy Machines, or Email

Mechanism of Delivery	Guidelines
Fax machines	• Send patient information via fax only when absolutely necessary.
	• Verify the fax telephone number of the receiver before sending the fax.
	• Make sure the intended receiver is there before sending confidential records by fax.
	• Shred confidential fax papers that are no longer needed. Do not place them in the trash.
	• Use a fax cover sheet that states "Confidential. Please return if received in error."
	• Only fax the specific documents requested, not the entire medical record.
	• Do not leave confidential material unattended on a fax machine.
	• Ideally, the fax machine should be located in a restricted access area.
Copy machines	• Never leave medical records unattended on a copy machine where others may read them.
	• Shred all discarded copies.
	• Be diligent about removing all papers caught in a paper jam.
	• Do not print confidential medical information on a printer that is shared with another department or person.
Email	• Avoid using email to send confidential information.
	• Do not allow other patients or unauthorized staff members to view a computer screen with confidential patient information.
	• Screen savers should be used to prevent confidential patient information being viewed by others.
	• Computer screens should be out of view of the general public.
	• Passwords should be changed on a regular basis and not shared with others.

> ## Med Tip
>
> Many healthcare facilities require all employees to sign a confidentiality agreement. Failure to honor this agreement can result in dismissal and possible legal action.

Release of Information

Insurance companies often have a desire to examine the medical records before they issue a reimbursement for a procedure. Only the specific information that is requested, not the entire medical chart, should be sent to the insurance company.

> ## Med Tip
>
> Never send the entire medical chart unless it is requested. Send out only the exact material or portion of the medical record that is requested.

An *original* version of a medical record should never be sent to anyone. A copy should be made of the original, and the copy sent to the patient who has requested the record in writing. In the case of X-rays, the healthcare provider or institution may allow the original to be sent, with the stipulation that it be returned. Document when and where the file was sent.

In addition, patients must always sign a release form when they request to have their medical records and films sent to another physician. This often occurs when the primary care provider (PCP) has requested that the patient have a consultation with another physician or specialist.

In general, only a patient can authorize the release of their own medical records. However, there are some exceptions to the rule, which include the following:

- Parents of minor children
- Legal guardian
- An agent (someone the patient selects to act on his or her behalf in a Healthcare Power of Attorney). Under some circumstances, such as with an emancipated minor, the minor (not the parent) must sign the release.

> ## Med Tip
>
> Because patients have a legal right to their medical records, it is never acceptable to refuse to turn over a copy on the grounds that the patient has not paid their bill.

State hospital licensing regulations typically stipulate that the medical record is the property of the hospital and should not be removed from the premises unless there is a court order. Under the law, access to mental health records is more limited than is access to general medical records. See Chapter 10 for a further discussion of release of patient information under HIPAA regulations.

State Open-Record Laws

Some states have freedom of information laws, called **open-record laws**, that grant public access to records maintained by state agencies. However, medical records are generally exempt from this statute, so the public cannot obtain such information. In some cases, though, if the private patient's interest in confidentiality is outweighed by the benefit of disclosure for the public interest, then disclosure is allowed. For example, in the case of *Child Protection Group v. Cline*, the court allowed personal information about a bus driver's psychiatric records to be **disclosed**, or made known, to parents of schoolchildren when there was a concern that he would not be able to drive the school bus safely (*Child Protection Group v. Cline*, 350 S.E.2d 541, W. Va. 1986).

Retention and Storage of Medical Records

Retention of Records

Each state varies on the length of time for which medical records and documents must be kept. It also varies by state depending on whether it is the record of a minor or adult. However, most states require that medical records should be stored for ten years from the time of the last entry. These requirements apply to both paper medical records and electronic health records. Most healthcare facilities store medical records permanently because malpractice suits can still be filed within two years from the date that the occurrence or alleged malpractice event became known.

Using the statute of limitations as a guide for retaining records, the medical record of a minor would be kept until the patient reaches the age of maturity plus the period of the statute. As an example, in a state where the age of maturity is 21 and the statute of limitations for torts is two years, the retention period for a newborn's record would be 23 years.

Med Tip

Remember that the statute of limitations can be extended for many reasons. It is always better to err on the side of retaining medical records too long, rather than not long enough. Check your own state to determine the statute of limitations for record keeping.

Because of limited storage space, paper medical records may have to be destroyed after a period of time has elapsed. State laws should always be checked before destroying any records. The courts take the requirement to retain records seriously. An Illinois appeals court declared that a patient could sue when a hospital failed to retain her X-rays (*Rodgers v. St. Mary's Hospital*, 556 N.E.2d 913, Ill. App. Ct. 1990). In a Florida case, a woman whose husband died during the administration of anesthesia was unable to present expert testimony because her husband's anesthesiology records were missing. The court ruled that she could sue the hospital because it was the hospital's duty to make and maintain medical records (*Bondu v. Gurvich*, 473 So. 2d 1307, Fla. Dist. Ct. App. 1984). Table 9.2 describes time period recommendations for retaining medical records as adopted by the American Health Information Management Association (AHIMA).

In the event that a healthcare facility cannot retain patients' records beyond a ten-year time frame, there are certain considerations for the methods of destruction:

- Maintain careful records relating to when a record can be destroyed.
- Designate a person to be responsible for deciding, based on established policies, what records to keep and what to purge.
- Define which records are kept on-site and which are off-site.
- Maintain a log that details which records have been destroyed as well as when and how this was done.
- Provide a method for disposal (e.g., shred, pulp, or incinerate) that destroys all information in the record. Some facilities hire a service that handles the destruction of medical records. This service must abide by HIPAA guidelines. (See Chapter 10 for more information about HIPAA.)

Table 9–2   Time Periods for Retaining Medical Records

Type of Record	Time Period
Adult patient records	Ten years after the most recent encounter
Minor's health records	Age of maturity plus statute of limitations
Fetal heart monitor records	Ten years after infant reaches maturity
Medicare and Medicaid records	Five years
Register of birth	Permanently
Register of death	Permanently
Register of surgical procedures	Permanently
Immunization records	Permanently
Chemotherapy records	Permanently

Storage of Records

Manual records of current patients are usually kept within the healthcare office for easy access. Older records of former patients do not need to be kept in the office where they will take up valuable space. Healthcare facilities often rent storage space. It is important to use a clean, dry warehouse space for storage. If records that are needed in court have been destroyed in a warehouse fire or flood, the court may believe that it was a deliberate attempt by the facility to avoid the truth. Previously, some facilities used microfiche for storage, which results in a space-saving, miniaturized film of the medical record. Practices with microfiche records need to have microfiche readers available. Currently, manual records are more often scanned and converted to digitized files. Today, most medical records are maintained electronically. This provides for greater efficiency, improved accuracy, and easier storage. However, the previous paper medical records *must* still be retained in accordance with legal requirements.

Electronic Health Records

Benefits of EHRs

For many years medical records were paper records maintained by the healthcare provider. This meant that, as a patient relocated, large amounts of paper records would be filed and maintained in numerous medical facilities for just that one patient. The historical paper records of a patient can now be scanned or otherwise brought onto an electronic system. This has the advantage of making them more readily accessible to the healthcare providers.

As noted earlier, the *electronic health record,* also referred to as an *electronic medical record,* in which all patient-related data are computerized into one record, is an electronic or digital documentation of a patient's medical history. It is maintained by the healthcare provider and includes the clinical information relative to the patient's care. The distinction between an EHR and an EMR is that an EMR is a digital version of the paper charts in a clinician's office that contain the medical and treatment history of one patient in one practice. EHRs do all that EMRs do and more. EHRs focus on the total health of the patient and are meant to share information with other healthcare providers. They contain information from all the healthcare providers involved in the patient's care. EHRs may also contain statistical information about multiple patients.

The benefits of EHRs include the following:

- Make health information more available, reduce delays in treatment, reduce duplication of tests, and assist patients in being better informed about their health.
- Provide better organization and accuracy of patient information.
- Allow access to evidence-based tools so providers can use them to make decisions about patient care.
- Reduce the incidence of medical error by improving the accuracy and clarity of medical records.
- Bring information relating to the patient's health into one place.
- Contain information about a patient's medical history, such as diagnoses, medications, allergies, laboratory data and test results, radiology reports, past medical history, vital signs, immunizations, progress notes, and treatment plans as well as any healthcare problems.
- Be created, managed, and consulted by authorized healthcare providers.
- Have the ability to provide "real-time" patient-centered medical records.

Electronic health records allow patient records to be modified, authenticated, stored, and retrieved by the computer. Many hospitals use "computers on wheels" known as COWs or COW carts, which can be wheeled from room to room for charting at the point of care (Figure 9.3). A key feature is that it can be consulted by authorized providers and staff across more than one healthcare organization. This has made record maintenance and retrieval much more efficient and effective in healthcare offices, clinics, laboratories, and hospitals. However, it has resulted in increased concerns about patient privacy as so many more healthcare professionals may now be able to view a patient record unless precautions are taken. A well-designed computerized system may offer better protection than a "file-drawer" storage system because there are passwords, **encryptions** (scrambling and encoding information before sending it electronically), and the use of **firewalls** (software to prevent unauthorized users) to maintain security.

Figure 9–3 COW carts are used in many hospitals
Source: Denise Lett/Shutterstock

As part of the American Recovery and Reinvestment Act, all public and private healthcare providers and other eligible professionals (EP) were required to adopt and demonstrate "meaningful use" of EHRs by January 2014, in order to maintain their existing Medicare and Medicaid reimbursement levels. "Meaningful use," as defined by HealthIT.gov, consists of using digital medical and health records to do the following:

- Improve quality, safety, and efficiency and reduce health disparities.
- Maintain privacy and security of patient health information.
- Improve care coordination.
- Engage patients and families in their healthcare.

Physical storage space is not a problem for electronic health records, which are generally stored digitally in a secure computer database maintained by the organization or healthcare system to which the medical practice belongs.

Challenges with EHRs

Electronic health records have revolutionized the healthcare industry by digitizing patient information, streamlining medical processes, and improving patient care. However, the adoption of EHRs has also given rise to significant security concerns. Protecting sensitive health data from unauthorized access and breaches is crucial to ensure the confidentiality and integrity of patient information. Some of the challenges that come with EHRs include the following:

- ***Data breaches***—One of the most pressing security concerns regarding EHRs is the potential for data breaches. When EHR systems are compromised, it can lead to the exposure of sensitive patient information, including medical histories, treatment plans, and personal identifiers. These breaches can occur through cyberattacks, such as hacking, malware, and phishing attempts, or due to human errors like misconfigured access permissions.

- ***Identity theft***—EHRs contain personal information, making them a prime target for identity theft. Attackers can use stolen medical records to commit identity fraud, gaining access to financial accounts, medical services, and more, all under the victim's identity.

- ***Unauthorized access***—In healthcare settings, numerous individuals require access to EHRs, including physicians, advance practice providers, nurses, allied health professionals, and administrative staff. The challenge lies in ensuring that only authorized personnel can access these records. Unauthorized access can lead to privacy violations, misuse of information, and potentially harmful actions.

- *Insider threats*—While external threats are a significant concern, insider threats are equally troubling. Disgruntled employees, whether through negligence or malice, can exploit their access to EHRs to steal or manipulate patient data. Security measures must address these internal vulnerabilities.

- *Ransomware attacks*—Ransomware attacks have become increasingly prevalent in healthcare. In these attacks, cybercriminals encrypt EHRs and demand a ransom for their release. Hospitals and healthcare providers are often forced to pay, as they cannot afford to have critical patient data held hostage.

- *Interoperability challenges*—EHRs are most effective when they can share information across different healthcare systems and providers. However, this interoperability introduces security challenges. Data must be protected during transmission to prevent eavesdropping, and secure data sharing standards must be established to ensure that information is not compromised during exchange.

- *Inadequate encryption*—Data encryption is a critical security measure for EHRs, yet it is not always implemented effectively. Inadequate encryption can leave data vulnerable, as attackers can intercept and decode the information during transmission.

- *Legacy systems*—Many healthcare institutions still use outdated EHR systems that may lack modern security features. These legacy systems can be particularly vulnerable to attacks, as they often do not receive the necessary security updates and patches.

- *Patient consent*—Patient consent is a complex issue in EHR security. Patients may not always fully understand or consent to how their data is being used or shared. Proper informed consent procedures and mechanisms for patients to control their data are necessary to maintain trust and security.

- *Third-party vendors*—Healthcare providers often rely on third-party vendors for EHR solutions, which can introduce additional security concerns. These vendors may have access to sensitive patient data, making it essential to vet their security practices thoroughly.

- *Social engineering*—Attackers may use social engineering techniques to gain unauthorized access to EHRs. This can involve manipulating healthcare staff into revealing login credentials or other sensitive information.

- *Data retention and disposal*—Proper data retention and disposal practices are crucial to EHR security. Old or redundant records must be securely archived and eventually destroyed to prevent unauthorized access.

Addressing these security concerns is imperative for maintaining patient trust and the overall success of EHR systems. Healthcare providers and agencies should adopt a comprehensive security strategy that includes robust encryption, regular security assessments, employee training, and ongoing monitoring of EHR systems. Additionally, regulatory bodies like HIPAA play a crucial role in setting standards and enforcing security measures for EHRs to protect patient data effectively. As EHR technology evolves, staying vigilant in the face of new threats and vulnerabilities is essential to ensure the privacy and security of patient information in the digital age of healthcare.

Personal Health Record

A **personal health record**, also known as a PHR, is a record of information, often in the patient's own words, that is controlled by the patient or the patient's family. This personal health record may be shared with caregivers and family members. This allows the family members and healthcare providers to have a record of the patient's medical history. A PHR provides family members and caregivers with accurate, current information to assist them in caring for the patient and making decisions for further medical care and treatment.

Med Tip

Ideally, a personal health record will have a summary of an individual's health and medical history based on data from many healthcare sources, including information that is entered by the individual patient.

Loss of Medical Records

The loss of manual medical records can result in a deadly outcome if vital information relating to the patient is gone. Whether a medical record is lost through careless filing of the record or as a result of a deliberate attempt to prevent litigation, it is always preventable. There are many safeguards that a health-care office, clinic, and even a hospital can implement to prevent the loss of paper records:

- All records removed from files should be listed in a journal. The person to whom the file was given and the date should be recorded.

- Place some indication in the file cabinet that a file has been removed. Many offices use a color-coded insert to alert personnel about the file removal.

- If possible, designate one person responsible for maintaining a list of all records removed from files. That person then collects all files and returns them to the proper location.

- Digitizing paper records is an excellent way to safeguard against record loss.

Juries tend to be unsympathetic in a court case that revolves around a lost medical document or record. For example, during the discovery phase in the case of *Keene v. Brigham & Women's Hospital,* the plaintiff was told that the hospital had lost his medical records. A default judgment for the plaintiff was entered at the appeals court level and upheld at the Supreme Court level. The courts maintained that, without the medical record containing evidence relating to the medical malpractice claim against the hospital, it was impossible to make a determination of guilt or innocence of the defendant (*Keene v. Brigham & Women's Hosp., Inc.* 439 Mass. 223, 2003).

Reporting and Disclosure Requirements

State laws require the disclosure of some confidential medical record information, such as birth and death records, without the patient's consent. These items are discussed in Chapter 7, Public Duties of the Healthcare Professional.

Med Tip

Laws regarding medical records vary from state to state. Healthcare professionals who have any involvement with the medical record should learn what the statutes in their own state require.

Use of the Medical Record in Court

Improper Disclosure

Healthcare providers and institutions such as hospitals and clinics may face civil and criminal liability for releasing medical records without the proper patient authorization. Private citizens can institute a civil lawsuit to recover damages if their records are released inappropriately. Wisconsin statutes provide for compensatory as well as punitive damages for improper disclosure (Wis. Stat. § 252.15(8)). Many of the cases that have been tried for improper disclosure relate to HIV and AIDS patients. While disclosure of a patient's HIV and AIDS status to the health department is required by state statute, disclosure to any other person or organization is not allowed.

Subpoena *Duces Tecum*

A subpoena *duces tecum* (Latin for "under penalty, take with you") is a written order requiring a person to appear in court, give testimony, and bring the particular records, files, books, or information that are described in the subpoena. The court issues a subpoena for records that document patient care and, in some instances, billing and insurance records. The purpose of issuing a subpoena for a patient's medical record is to receive written evidence of the patient's medical condition and the care that was received. All copying or printing costs associated with subpoenaed records must be borne by the attorney requesting the subpoena.

Med Tip

Ordinarily, a medical record cannot be sent to anyone without consent in writing from the patient and the physician's approval. One exception to this is when a record is subpoenaed.

A local sheriff or federal marshal often serves a subpoena, but many state statutes allow anyone over the age of 18 to serve a subpoena. The subpoena may be served either by certified mail or in person, depending on the state requirement. In general, only the person who is named on the subpoena can accept it. The subpoena can then be said to "have been served."

When a medical record is subpoenaed, only the parts of the record requested should be provided to the requesting attorney. For manual records, unless the original document is subpoenaed, a certified photocopy may be sent. If the original record is subpoenaed, a photocopy is marked COPY and placed in the file along with a note about the location of the original copy. Until the original is returned, a receipt for the subpoenaed record should be placed in the file, and the patient or the patient's attorney should be notified that the record has been subpoenaed. Any notice relating to subpoenaed records should be sent to the patient by certified mail.

If a medical record has been subpoenaed, or requested by the court, certain guidelines should be followed:

- Notify the physician that a subpoena has been received. In the case of an institution, such as a hospital, a "custodian of the record" such as a hospital records administrator will be appointed to receive a subpoena for hospital medical records.

- Notify the patient that their record has been subpoenaed. If the patient is represented by an attorney and suing the physician, then the physician and their staff cannot contact the patient except via the attorney.

- Notify the physician's attorney that a subpoena has been received.

- Verify that all the information on the subpoena is correct. Pay particular attention to identification numbers such as the Social Security number. In some cases, patients may have the same name, and a subpoena is sent to a physician in error.

- Carefully make sure that the requesting attorney's name and phone number as well as the court case (docket) number are listed on the subpoena.

- Review the records to make sure that all the records requested are available. No attempt should be made to alter, delete, or add any information to the record.

- Make sure that a copy of the medical record is acceptable. In some cases, only the original record will be accepted. Most physicians do not want their original records to leave their possession.

- Photocopy the original record and number all the pages. Place the total number of pages on the front of the file folder. Prepare a cover list of the contents and place that in the file folder along with the medical documents.

- Turn over only the specific materials that have been requested.

- If an EHR is requested, send a labeled disc containing only the requested material.

- After the medical record materials relating to the subpoena have been compiled, lock the file in a secure place.

- Turn the records directly over to the judge on the due date. The materials should not be left with a clerk or receptionist.

- The healthcare professional who takes the records to court should be prepared to be sworn in to make the records admissible as evidence.

- Check with the court to make sure that the trial date is the same as the date listed on the subpoena.

Chapter 9 Review

Points to Ponder

1. Do you agree with the statement, "If it's not documented, it wasn't done"? Why or why not?

2. In order to protect your physician/employer, should you "hide" to avoid receiving a subpoena *duces tecum*? Why or why not?

3. As a healthcare professional, are you permitted to read the medical record of a person you know? Why or why not?

4. Would it be helpful to other healthcare professionals who will be using the same patient's medical record to document that

patient's poor attitude by including a statement such as "bad attitude?" Why or why not?

5. Can you be liable if you or your staff lose or delete a patient's medical record?

6. A patient requests her healthcare facility to change her diagnosis in her medical record from R/O (rule out) bladder infection to "bladder infection" because her insurance will not pay for an R/O diagnosis. Should the record be changed?

Discussion Questions

1. What is the significance of the medical record for the physician? For the healthcare professional? For the patient?

2. Who owns the medical chart?

Review Challenge

Short Answer Questions

1. How long should a medical record be kept for a one-year-old child who resides in a state with a statute of limitations of two years for a tort offense?

2. What does a subpoena *duces tecum* request the subpoenaed person to provide?

3. Exactly what does "timeliness in documentation" mean?

4. What are some of the precautions to follow when using electronic health records?

5. What would you say to a patient who demands his digital image and says, "It's my digital image. I paid for it"?

6. What is the doctrine of professional discretion?

_____

_____

_____

_____

_____

7. What are some examples of a "custodian of the record"?

_____

_____

_____

_____

_____

8. Who can serve a subpoena?

_____

_____

_____

_____

_____

9. Explain the precautions that must be taken when faxing medical records.

_____

_____

_____

_____

10. Explain the precautions that must be taken when using a computer in a healthcare setting.

_____

_____

_____

_____

_____

_____

Matching

Match the responses in column B with the correct term in column A.

COLUMN A

_____ **1.** firewall

_____ **2.** credible

_____ **3.** disclosed

_____ **4.** The Joint Commission

_____ **5.** microfiche

_____ **6.** privileged communication

_____ **7.** EHR

_____ **8.** timeliness

_____ **9.** encryptions

COLUMN B

a. made known

b. scrambling and encoding information before sending it electronically

c. electronic health record

d. software to prevent unauthorized users

e. an agency that oversees hospital accreditation standards

f. reliable

g. miniaturized photographs of records

h. no late entries on medical chart

i. confidential information that has been told to a physician (or attorney) by the patient

Multiple Choice

Select the one best answer to the following statements.

1. Medicare and Medicaid records should be retained for
   a. one year.
   b. five years.
   c. ten years.
   d. the lifetime of the patient.
   e. an indefinite period of time.

2. The contents of the medical record include all of the following except
   a. past medical problems.
   b. informed consent documentation.
   c. patient's income level.
   d. family medical history.
   e. none of the above

3. Medical record entries should be made
   a. within 60 days of the patient's discharge.
   b. at the physician's discretion.
   c. after the patient gives consent.
   d. as soon as possible.
   e. ten days after the procedure.

4. The patient
   a. has the legal right of privileged communication.
   b. owns the medical record.
   c. cannot have any portion of the medical record.
   d. a and c only
   e. a, b, and c

5. When correcting a written medical error, one should
   a. use a professional brand of error correction fluid to make the correction.
   b. erase the error and make the correction.
   c. draw a line through the error, write the correction above the error, and initial the change.
   d. never make any corrections on the medical record.
   e. none of the above

6. The medical record is legally owned by the
   a. patient.
   b. physician.
   c. state.
   d. lawyer.
   e. no one.

7. Medical records
   a. provide a record from birth to death.
   b. provide statistics on health matters.
   c. are legal documents.
   d. a and c only
   e. a, b, and c

8. All of the following are guidelines to use when sending medical records by fax except
   a. make sure there is a receiver waiting for the fax.
   b. use a cover sheet marked "confidential."
   c. send the entire medical record via fax.
   d. do not place the original fax in a trash container.
   e. All of the above are correct.

9. An exception, or exceptions, to the open-record laws in some states is/are
   a. psychiatric history.
   b. confidential medical record information such as HIV test results.
   c. safety and criminal records of persons involved in the education of children.
   d. all of the above
   e. none of the above

10. The records of all adult patients should be kept a minimum of
   a. two years.
   b. five years.
   c. ten years.
   d. 20 years.
   e. They should be kept permanently.

Discussion Cases

1. Mary Smith has been a patient of Dr. Williams from 1985 to the present time. During that time, she has had three children and been treated for a variety of conditions, including depression in 1986 and herpes in 1990. Mary and her husband, George, have filed for divorce. George wants custody of the children and is claiming that Mary has a medical condition that makes her an unfit mother. An attorney, acting on George's behalf in the divorce proceedings, has obtained a subpoena for Mary's medical records for the years 1995 to the present. Dr. Williams's assistant, who is a medical records technician, copies Mary's entire medical record from 1985 to the present and sends it to the attorney.

   a. What negative effects for Mary might this error cause?

   b. Is there a violation of confidentiality? Why or why not?

   c. Do you believe that this is a common or uncommon error?

   d. Was it appropriate for the assistant to make a copy of any part of Mary's medical record?

2. Peter B. is admitted to a local hospital emergency department (ED) suffering from an anxiety attack. He tells the ED physician that he is anxious about a job promotion for which he is being considered. Peter's secretary is worried about him and asks her father, Dr. K., who is on the medical staff at the hospital, to go to the ED and see how Peter is doing. Dr. K., who is often in the ED, knows all the staff and they willingly give him access to Peter's medical record when he asks for it. Dr. K. calls his daughter to tell her that Peter is

being treated for anxiety with an antidepressant medication and will probably be discharged. She relays this encouraging message to Peter's boss. Peter does not receive the promotion.

a. Will it be an easy matter for Peter to prove that the ED staff caused Peter to lose his promotion? Explain your answer.

_____

_____

b. What precautions can be taken to avoid giving confidential information to healthcare personnel who have no need to see it?

_____

_____

c. In your opinion, should a diagnosis of anxiety be a concern for an employer? Why or why not?

_____

_____

d. Note that while the previous case is obviously illegal, it is based on a true event. Please comment.

_____

_____

3. Demi Daniels calls to ask you to change her diagnosis in her medical record from R/O (rule out) bladder infection to "bladder infection" because her insurance will not pay for an R/O diagnosis. In fact, she tested negative for an infection, but the physician placed her on antibiotics anyway.

a. What do you do?

_____

_____

b. Is this a legal question? Why or why not?

_____

_____

c. Is this an ethical question? Why or why not?

_____

_____

d. What could happen to the physician you work for if you make a mistake?

_____

_____

Put It Into Practice

Request a copy of your medical record from your primary care provider or access your medical record through your facility's portal. Examine the contents to determine how well they document your medical history.

Web Hunt

Using the website of the American Health Information Management Association (www.ahima.org), provide a description of the organization. Visit the patient resource center of the site and summarize the statement concerning who owns the medical record.

Critical Thinking Exercise

What would you do if you saw a nurse making a change in a patient's medical chart after receiving a subpoena *duces tecum* for that medical record?

Bibliography

American Hospital Association. (2020). Ransomware attacks on hospitals have changed. *AHA Center for Health Innovation*. https://www.aha.org/center/cybersecurity-and-risk-advisory-services/ransomware-attacks-hospitals-have-changed

Beaman, N., Routh, K.S., Papazian-Boyce, L., et al. (2017). *Pearson's comprehensive medical assisting: Administrative and clinical competencies* (4th ed.). Pearson.

Office of the National Coordinator for Health Information Technology (ONC). (2023). Benefits of EHRs. *HealthIT.gov.* https://www.healthit.gov/topic/health-it-and-health-information-exchange-basics/benefits-ehrs

The Joint Commission. (2023). *Comprehensive accreditation manual for hospitals.* Joint Commission Resources.

U.S. Department of Health and Human Services. (2022). *Individual's right under HIPAA to access their health information 45 CFR 164.524.* https://www.hhs.gov/hipaa/for-professionals/privacy/guidance/access/index.html

Venes, D. (2021). *Taber's cyclopedic medical dictionary* (24th ed.). F.A. Davis.

Patient Confidentiality and HIPAA

Learning Objectives

After completing this chapter, you will be able to:

10.1 Define the key terms.

10.2 Identify the problems associated with patient confidentiality

10.3 Describe the information to which the Privacy Rule refers and how it applies to your profession

10.4 Discuss the purpose of the Health Insurance Portability and Accountability Act (HIPAA) of 1996.

10.5 List which entities are affected by HIPAA.

10.6 Discuss the penalties for noncompliance with HIPAA.

10.7 List the patients' rights under the Privacy Standards.

10.8 Discuss the ethical issues concerning information technology.

Key Terms

Clearinghouse

Covered entities

Covered transactions

Deidentifying

Electronic protected health information (EPHI)

Employer Identification Number (EIN)

Employer Identifier Standard

Facial recognition technology

Healthcare plan

Health Insurance Portability and Accountability Act of 1996 (HIPAA)

Health Information Technology for Economic and Clinical Health (HITECH) Act

HIPAA-defined permission

Medical informatics

Minimum necessary standard

Notice of Privacy Practices (NPP)

Office of Civil Rights (OCR)

Privacy Act of 1974

Privacy Rule

Protected health information (PHI)

State's preemption

Telehealth

Treatment, payment, and healthcare operations (TPO)

Voice recognition technology

Wireless local area networks (WLANs)

The Case of the New Minister

Dawn is an ordained minister in a little church located in a small Midwest community. She has had to overcome some discrimination as the first female clergy member in the town. However, Dawn feels that her church congregation and other members of the community have finally started to accept her in this new role. Dawn was recently diagnosed with irritable bowel syndrome by a gastroenterologist in the next town. He performed a colonoscopy on Dawn to rule out cancer of the bowel and found nothing more than a few benign polyps, which he removed. He told Dawn that he wanted her to start taking amitriptyline for three months to see if that would solve her irritable bowel problem. He said that he had success using this antidepressant, also known as Elavil, to treat irritable bowel syndrome. He said he would call the prescription in to Dawn's local pharmacy.

When Dawn went in to pick up her prescription, she met two members of her congregation who were also picking up their prescriptions. The pharmacist leaned over the front counter and said to Dawn, "Do you know that this is an antidepressant?"

1. What rights of Dawn's were violated?

2. Were any laws broken by the pharmacist's statement? If so, what are they?

3. How could Dawn's reputation suffer from this brief comment by the pharmacist?

Introduction

Patients have two major expectations when they visit a healthcare provider: quality care and confidentiality. They have a right to expect both. However, with the advent of modern technology, including the Internet, email, and EHRs, the number of people who have access to patient information has increased at a rapid rate. In order to address the concern for patients' privacy, especially via electronic transmissions, Congress mandated that the **Health Insurance Portability and Accountability Act of 1996**, also known as HIPAA, enforce its privacy provision by April 14, 2003. This law, while somewhat complicated and expensive for providers to implement, has meant more careful attention to issues of patient privacy.

Confidentiality

One version of the Hippocratic Oath states, "What I see or hear in the course of the treatment . . . , which on no account must be spread abroad, I will keep to myself . . . ." Historically, physicians were expected to maintain all confidences concerning their patients, and patients took this confidentiality for granted. However, the image of one patient sharing their health information with only one provider is no longer applicable in today's world. A dozen or more physicians, advance practice providers, nurses, and allied health professionals may be involved in a patient's care along with multiple institutions, including hospitals, MRI testing centers, rehabilitation centers, and skilled nursing facilities. Today, there is widespread use of electronic record keeping and electronic transmission of medical records. For example, information needs to be transmitted to third-party providers, such as insurance companies, to arrange for payment of the patient's medical services.

Modern healthcare and technology have meant that patient privacy issues have become of paramount concern among patients, healthcare professionals, and ethicists. In many cases, patients have become fearful of admitting to what could be embarrassing information, such as past drug use, abortions, and mental health problems. When patients fail to convey this information to their healthcare providers, it creates a difficult environment for the healthcare team that is treating the patients without the benefit of complete medical information.

Confidentiality about sensitive information is necessary to preserve the patient's dignity. However, in order to receive payment from third-party payers such as insurance companies, Medicare, and Medicaid, the patient's diagnosis may have to be revealed, no matter how embarrassing it is for the patient. But patients want to be assured that the information relayed about them to a third party is

Figure 10–1 Nurse reviewing form with patient

Source: Prostock-studio/Shutterstock

limited to just the **minimum necessary standard** in order to carry out the request. In addition, patients expect to be told when information about them is being relayed to a third party such as an insurance company.

The healthcare community has been conscientious about having patients sign an approval form granting permission for the release of their medical records (Figure 10.1). However, patients' confidentiality and privacy have become more difficult with the advent of digital technologies in every healthcare office. Unfortunately, the creation of new laws has become necessary as a result of the unethical violation of patients' privacy.

Med Tip

A notice should be posted in the reception area of all healthcare providers explaining the HIPAA policy on confidentiality.

U.S. Supreme Court Justice Louis Brandeis defined our right to privacy as "the right most valued by civilized men." While we realize that much has changed since 1928 when Justice Brandeis wrote these words, we still believe that this is a precious right that needs to be protected. Our right to privacy is not protected specifically by the Bill of Rights or any portion of the Constitution. However, many legal scholars believe that the right to privacy is found in some of the constitutional amendments, such as the First, Fourth, Fifth, Ninth, and Fourteenth Amendments.

There are numerous court cases, creating case law, which defend our constitutional rights to privacy. These decisions have then become precedents for future cases. Unfortunately, new technology, especially computer data banks, since Justice Brandeis, has allowed personal patient information to become public. For example, testing for the presence of drugs and alcohol in some business areas such as transportation and private industry may infringe on individual rights.

Med Tip

Personal and confidential information about patients should be limited to conveying it to the absolute minimum number of healthcare employees.

Privacy Act of 1974, Amended in 1988

The **Privacy Act of 1974** provides private citizens some control over information that the federal government collects about them by limiting the use of information for unnecessary purposes. Under this 1974 law, an agency may maintain only the information that is relevant to its authorized purpose. Additionally, under this law, citizens have the right to gain access to their records and to copy any of the records, if necessary. Under the Privacy Act individuals were given the right to

- find out what information is collected about them by the government,
- see and have a copy of that information,
- correct or amend their information, and
- exercise control over the disclosure of that information.

The Privacy Act applies only to federal agencies and government contractors. However, hospitals that are operated by the federal government, such as Veterans' Affairs hospitals, are bound by the act to make their records available for public disclosure.

It is sometimes necessary for confidential information to be shared without the knowledge or consent of the person. Thus, this law also permits federal agencies to collect, maintain, use, or disseminate any record of identifiable personal information but only in a manner that ensures that

- such action is for a necessary and lawful purpose,
- the information is current and accurate for its intended use,

- adequate safeguards are provided to prevent misuse of such information, and
- the information is used only in those cases where there is an important public policy need that has been determined by a specific statutory authority.

Health Insurance Portability and Accountability Act of 1996, Updated in 2013

The Health Insurance Portability and Accountability Act was passed and signed into law by Congress on August 21, 1996, and was fully implemented in 2005. HIPAA was designed to regulate issues relating to the privacy and confidentiality of patient health information. This law was passed in an effort to reduce the costs of healthcare and streamline a fragmented and complicated healthcare system. The law also established a set of national standards for the protection of health information. This includes identifying privacy procedures and standards to be used for electronic transmissions as well as for the storage of healthcare records.

The rationale for the passage of HIPAA included a concern that healthcare had become a complicated and difficult process to understand for many people and institutions, including businesses. There was less time available for evaluating patient care and delivery needs due to the intricacy of billing codes, keeping up with many software applications for managing the storage of different records, and reviewing board information. This sweeping reform law affects virtually everyone included in the U.S. healthcare system—patients, providers, payers, and intermediaries such as hospitals, healthcare offices, pharmacies, and medical device companies.

The objectives of HIPAA are to

- protect the privacy of healthcare information;
- improve the portability of health insurance;
- combat fraud, abuse, and waste in healthcare;
- promote the expanded use of medical savings accounts;
- simplify the administration of health insurance; and
- protect the privacy of healthcare insurance.

The Essential Elements of HIPAA

HIPAA consists of five titles, or main sections, each with its own overall purpose:

- *Title I* protects health insurance coverage for workers and their families when they change or lose their jobs.
- *Title II*, known as the Administrative Simplification provisions, requires national standards for electronic healthcare transactions and national identifiers for providers, health insurance plans, and employers. (More about Title II follows.)
- *Title III* sets guidelines for pre-tax medical spending accounts.
- *Title IV* sets guidelines for group health plans.
- *Title V* governs company-owned life insurance policies.

Title II

Title II, Administrative Simplification, is the section of HIPAA that affects most healthcare providers, insurance companies, and clearinghouses. A healthcare **clearinghouse** is a private or public entity that processes or facilitates the processing of nonstandard electronic transactions into HIPAA transactions. Thus, a clearinghouse may also refer to a billing service. Title II provisions were meant to make it easier and cheaper to electronically transmit health information. However, Congress realized that widespread electronic transmission of a patient's health information could affect a patient's privacy. Subsequently, Congress mandated that the Department of Health and Human Services (HHS) be responsible for developing detailed Privacy Standards.

The overall objectives of Title II are the following:

- Improve efficiency and effectiveness of the healthcare system via electronic exchange of administrative and financial information.
- Protect security and privacy of this stored patient medical information.
- Reduce high transaction costs in healthcare, which include paper-based transactions, multiple healthcare data formats, misuse, errors, and the loss of healthcare records.
- Standardize electronic patient health records; administrative and financial data, including healthcare claims, healthcare payments, and remittance advice; healthcare claims status; enrollment and disenrollment in a healthcare plan; eligibility in a healthcare plan; and healthcare premium payments.
- Establish unique identifying codes for all healthcare providers, healthcare plans, employers, and individuals.
- Ensure the security of electronic health information with standards protecting the confidentiality and integrity of individually identifiable health information, past, present, or future.

To achieve these overall objectives, Title II contains five rules that healthcare facilities were required to implement within a certain time frame

1. *Privacy Rule.* The **Privacy Rule** protects the confidentiality, integrity, and privacy of patient-identifying information that is being distributed. (See more about the Privacy Rule below.)

2. *Transactions and Code Sets Rule.* The primary goal of this rule is administrative simplification through simplification and uniformity of billing and coding for healthcare services. This requires the use of standard formats and data content for electronic transmission.

3. *Security Rule.* While the Privacy Rule applies to all **protected health information**, also known as PHI, the Security Rule deals specifically with **electronic protected health information**, also known as EPHI, laying out administrative, physical, and technical safeguards for electronic health information. Some methods include use of antivirus software; password protection; and firewalls. According to HIPAA, healthcare plans and providers can use and disclose EPHI but only if they have permission or a "need-to-know reason" for each use of the information. (See more about PHI and EPHI below.)

4. *Unique Identifiers Rule (National Provider Identifier).* This rule mandates that covered healthcare providers must use the National Provider Identifier (NPI) to identify themselves and others for all electronic transactions. The four identifiers are the provider, the health plan, the employer, and the individual.

5. *Enforcement Rule.* This rule set the date when compliance with the HIPAA law would become enforceable and established penalties and procedures for investigating violations.

(For specific information on HIPAA rules, go to the government website: https://www.hhs.gov/hipaa/for-professionals/index.html.)

The Privacy Rule

The HIPAA law went into effect on April 14, 2001, and required that all "covered entities" must be in compliance with the privacy, security, and electronic-data provisions by April 14, 2003. **Covered entities** are healthcare plans, health clearinghouses, and all healthcare providers using electronic transactions including hospitals, nursing homes, physician practices, pharmacies, laboratories, and allied health practices.

The Privacy Rule does the following:

- Limits how personal health information can be used
- Provides training to employees on issues of security
- Provides "patient privacy notices" to patients and personnel
- Allows patients to have a copy of their health records
- Requires security of health records in paper, electronic, or other forms
- Obtains patient consent before disclosing patient information to persons outside of the healthcare field

Med Tip

There is uncertainty in the healthcare community regarding many of the HIPAA privacy provisions. The original document began as a 337-word guideline, but the final regulation expanded to 101,000 words, or more than 500 pages.

While it is true that the Privacy Rule is concerned with confidentiality, that is not the basis for this rule. As medical records expanded into electronic format and were transmitted electronically, it became critical to protect patient privacy. The Privacy Rule lays down the standards that should be followed to become HIPAA compliant.

Most laws will permit certain practices unless there is a specific provision or rule *against* doing it. However, HIPAA is just the opposite. You can only use and disclose patient information if there is a reason for each disclosure. The foundation of the Privacy Rule is that any use and disclosure of patient information must have a legitimate purpose or permission from the patient. For example, permissions or reasons include disclosure to the patient, required disclosures, and payment for treatment.

Med Tip

A guideline to follow is to disregard whatever you see or hear at work if you know the patient or someone who does. This ensures patient privacy and compliance with HIPAA regulations.

Protected Health Information

As noted above, the Privacy Rule applies to PHI, which refers to any individually identifiable information that relates to all past, present, and future physical or mental conditions or the provision of healthcare to an individual. For example, information such as a patient's name, age, gender, Social Security number, ZIP Code, email, test and laboratory results, medical diagnosis, and insurance information are all PHI.

The PHI information needs to be protected because hackers and cybercriminals can sell it or hold it hostage through ransomware attacks. On the other hand, PHI is valuable to clinical and research scientists to create large databases of patient information for population health management. There are many reasons for obtaining health information in which the patient does not need to be identified. For instance, health statistics relating to communicable diseases can be obtained by **deidentifying**, or removing, descriptive information about the patient. The following information must be removed to deidentify PHI:

- Patient's name
- Address, including zip code
- Social Security number
- Telephone and fax numbers
- All dates, including birth (except year), admission, discharge, and death
- Other identifying numbers or characteristics such as birth certificate, photos, and fingerprints
- Email and website address
- Medical records numbers
- Healthcare insurance and beneficiary numbers
- License numbers
- Motor vehicle registration numbers
- Facial photographs, such as those found on driver's license

Cautions for healthcare professionals to use when handling PHI include the following:

- Do not leave your laptops or other information-gathering equipment unattended while any patient information is on the screen.
- When you are not using your laptop, log off of the system.

- Do not give out your password to anyone.
- Develop automated replies to acknowledge that you have received an email.
- Avoid using email if you require an urgent reply.
- Do not use email without the patient's or client's consent.
- Use caution when giving out your email address.
- Do not forward email without permission.
- Change passwords frequently.

Compliance with HIPAA

To comply with HIPAA regulations, a healthcare practice must appoint a person to be their official representative to draft private HIPAA policies and procedures as well as to implement a program to educate and train all providers and employees on the mandates required by HIPAA.

These policies should become part of the organization's procedures manual. Policies relating to confidentiality and privacy should be included in the manual as well.

Some state laws require that health information be released "for the good of society." Decisions on what information to release would be made by healthcare administrators with assistance from other healthcare specialists. All employees assisting with this function must understand the seriousness of their role.

Examples of statistics (not names of individuals) that might be released under these state laws include the following:

- Births, stillbirths, and deaths
- Child or elder abuse or neglect
- Spousal rape
- Incest
- Assault or abusive conduct
- Suspicious wounds
- Suspected drug use
- Injuries inflicted by a knife, gun, or other deadly weapon
- Certain communicable, infectious, or contagious diseases

Med Tip

A yearly review of HIPAA is always worthwhile, in both large and small facilities.

Release of Information

Both state and federal laws exist protecting the release of medical records. HIPAA regulations state that the patient has a right to know how, when, and why their medical information is used. Also, a patient's written request for their own medical record is usually honored, unless there is a concern that the disclosures of medical or technical information will cause distress or harm to the patient. Many physicians, as well as other healthcare providers, believe that it becomes easier for patients to participate effectively in their own healthcare when they see their medical records (Figure 10.2).

There is a general authorization for a healthcare provider or hospital to release information to insurance companies about third-party payment claims. In fact, the claims for payment may not be paid without the authorization and information provided by the healthcare provider or hospital. Patients may be refused treatment if they refuse to grant consent for their records to be released. There are three exceptions when consent may not be necessary:

- When there is an emergency situation and the patient is unable to provide a signature (However, this must be obtained as soon as the patient is able.)
- When there is a language barrier, the consent may be implied.
- When the person is a prison inmate.

Figure 10–2 Healthcare professional explaining HIPAA document to patient
Source: Shutterstock

In some cases, healthcare providers have prohibited the release of psychiatric records to the patient. The belief is that reading the records could be detrimental to the patient.

There are laws regulating who may sign a release of information for persons who are underage or unable to sign for themselves. These include the following:

- If the patient or client is a minor, then the parent or legal guardian may sign the release form.

- If the parents are legally separated or divorced, the parent who has legal custody of the minor must sign all release forms.

- If the patient or client is incompetent, a court-appointed guardian will sign the release form.

- If the patient or client is deceased, then the legal representative of the estate signs the release form.

The HITECH Act

The **Health Information Technology for Economic and Clinical Health Act**, called the HITECH Act, was signed into law in 2009. This law expands HIPAA by including business functions, such as billing, accounting, and others. It was enacted as a part of The American Recovery and Reinvestment Act (ARRA) of 2009.

The HITECH Act includes measures to modernize the nation's use of technology when handling private health information. It is meant to promote the adoption and "meaningful use" of health information technology. This act addresses privacy and security concerns that are associated with the electronic transmission of health information and also addresses the civil and criminal enforcement of the HIPAA rules. The HITECH Act further elaborates on the complex use of electronic health information including enforcement, accountability, penalty, and prosecution guidelines for those involved in accessing private health information.

The HITECH Act has had a role in defining requirements relating to security and privacy regulations of the Privacy Rule. The Privacy Rule sets the standards that should be followed to become HIPAA compliant. The HITECH Act also encourages initiatives that assist in adopting electronic health records (EHRs).

The use of EHRs requires careful protection of patient information. For example, if a healthcare professional wishes to place patient information on the Internet, then several precautions must be taken to protect the patient's privacy. To address this concern, the HITECH Act recommended imposing data breach notification requirements for any unauthorized uses and disclosures of "unsecured private health information (PHI)."

Eligible hospitals and professionals must become "meaningful users" of the certified EHR to qualify for incentive payments through the state Medicare Incentive Program. Uses for electronically captured health information include tracking clinical conditions, reporting clinical quality measures, and the use of this information to include the patient and their family in their care. This is more comprehensive than the electronic medical record (EMR).

HIPAA requires the covered entities to limit the disclosures to only the *minimum* information necessary to carry out the medical treatment. Under HIPAA, this information can be conveyed to vendors, such as health insurance carriers, if they have obtained a written assurance (contract) from the vendor that the information will be protected. These standards to protect the PHI are in effect even if the patient is deceased. The five forms required by HIPAA to protect a patient's privacy include the following:

1. The privacy notice
2. Acknowledgment that the notice was received
3. Authorization, or consent, from the patient to provide information to others
4. An agreement reached with a healthcare professional's business associates
5. A trading partner agreement

Under HIPAA, patients must grant written consent or permission to disclose their PHI for treatment, payment, and other healthcare purposes. A **Notice of Privacy Practices**, also known as NPP, a legal, written statement that details the provider's privacy practices, must be distributed to every patient. The patient is requested to read the document and then sign it. This signed form, or acknowledgment, is then placed into the patient's medical record.

Sometimes, patients refuse to sign the NPP. If that happens, take the following steps:

- Indicate the patient's decision and date on an acknowledgment form or log.
- Include the reason for the patient's decision, if known.
- Place a copy of this documented unsigned acknowledgment form in the patient's record.
- Assure the patient that a refusal to sign the NPP does not mean that they cannot exercise their rights.
- No healthcare provider or institution can refuse to treat the patient based solely on refusal to sign the NPP.
- The patient may still request a copy of the NPP even if they refuse to sign it.

Covered Entities

Public health authorities, healthcare clearinghouses, private health insurers, self-insured employers, information systems vendors, various service organizations, and universities, are all included under HIPAA. These organizations are referred to as covered entities. A healthcare clearinghouse is a private or public entity that processes or facilitates the processing of nonstandard electronic transactions into HIPAA transactions. Thus, a clearinghouse may also refer to a billing service.

In other words, if a provider, such as a physical therapist, submits a bill or receives payment for healthcare or treatment, this healthcare professional would most likely be considered to be a covered entity under HIPAA.

Med Tip

Note that patients, whose healthcare information is protected under HIPAA, are not considered covered entities.

Under HIPAA, a **healthcare plan** is an individual or a group insurance plan that provides or pays for medical care. Healthcare plans include group health plans, health maintenance organizations (HMOs), the Medicare program parts A and B, the Medicaid program, and employee welfare benefit plans. Thus, there are few, if any, healthcare providers that are not affected by this law.

Treatment, payment, and healthcare operations, also referred to as TPO, is the term used to indicate that a healthcare provider is qualified to provide care or *treatment,* may reveal a patient's PHI in order to obtain *payment* for healthcare, and can provide functions or *healthcare operations* such as quality assurance.

Covered Transactions

Certain types of electronic transactions for the transmission of healthcare information, called **covered transactions**, are mandated under HIPAA regulations. Covered transactions are defined as those taking place between two covered entities, such as the following examples:

- A physician or healthcare provider sending any PHI to another provider
- A healthcare provider submitting an electronic claim to an insurance company or healthcare plan
- A healthcare provider sending any PHI to a billing service

Remember that because patients are not included as covered entities, they can send electronic requests (email) to their healthcare providers requesting information about their personal health records. However, many healthcare providers are reluctant to send information via email to their patients because of privacy concerns.

Med Tip

To safeguard vulnerable populations (such as a nursing home resident with dementia) there are exceptional cases where patient information exchange may be prohibited.

State's Preemption

There are some situations in which a state's privacy laws are stricter than the Privacy Standards established by HIPAA. In this case, the state's laws would take precedence over the federal HIPAA regulation. This is referred to as a **state's preemption**. There are situations in which state laws will require the release of information for the good of society. For example, when a state law requires a disclosure, such as reporting an infectious disease outbreak to the public health authorities, the federal privacy regulations would not preempt the state law.

Standard Identifiers

In the past, healthcare organizations used multiple identification formats when doing business with each other. This resulted in confusion and errors. Standard identifiers are now being used in an attempt to reduce these problems. The **Employer Identifier Standard**, which was published in 2002, uses an employer's tax ID number or their **Employer Identification Number**—also known as an EIN—as the standard code number for all electronic transmissions.

Patient Considerations under HIPAA

The healthcare provider, such as a physician or advance practice provider, has several confidentiality obligations to the patient. These include the obligation to obtain patient consent and authorization for any disclosures of medical information and permitting patient access to medical information. In addition, the provider must obtain patient authorization before disclosing PHI for purposes other than medical treatment, such as payment collection or a disclosure of psychotherapy notes.

The provider has a requirement to provide only the minimum necessary standard information for any disclosure about the patient. This standard means that the provider must make a reasonable effort to limit the disclosure of patient information to only the *minimum* that is necessary to accomplish the purpose of the request. The minimum necessary standard does not apply when a provider is submitting information to the patient, the HHS, or another provider, such as a physician or hospital, for the purpose of treatment.

The minimum necessary standard requirements do not apply to any health information disclosures that are required by law. For example, a physician, as a covered entity, is still required to disclose PHI that is requested in a subpoena.

> ## Med Tip
>
> The minimum necessary standard is important to remember when supplying a request for patient information. Never send a copy of the patient's entire medical record when only *specific* information is requested.

Permitted Incidental Disclosures

When the Privacy Rule became effective in 1996, there was confusion as to what could and could not be disclosed about the patient. In response to this confusion, the Department of Health and Human Services (DHHS) released a guidance document in 2002 that clarified the "permitted incidental disclosures." Examples of permitted disclosures include the following:

- Healthcare staff at a nursing station can coordinate patient care if they speak in a low voice.
- Nurses and other staff members can talk to a patient by phone or discuss the treatment of a patient with another provider if the discussions are conducted in low voices and away from listeners.
- Laboratory results can be discussed with patients or other healthcare professionals in a treatment area if privacy precautions are taken.
- A message can be left for a patient on an answering machine or with family members, but the amount of information must be limited to just the purpose of the call.
- Patients can be asked to sign in and be called by name in the waiting room, but they should not sign the reason for their visit.
- The patient's name can be announced in the waiting room or a public address system can be used to page the patient to come to a particular location.
- A lighted X-ray board can be used in a nursing station if it is not publicly visible.
- Patient charts can be placed outside of exam rooms if reasonable precautions are used. The charts should be placed with the name facing the wall or a cover should conceal the chart.

Patients' Rights

Patients have many rights under HIPAA. Healthcare providers have the additional responsibility of alerting patients to their own rights under this law. Under the Privacy Standards, patients have the right to the following:

- A copy of the privacy notice provided by the healthcare provider
- Access to their medical records, copies of their medical records, the right to restrict access by others, and to learn how their records have been accessed
- Request that amendments or changes be made to the record
- Ask the provider to limit how healthcare information is shared and to keep disclosures to the minimum needed for treatment and business operations
- Ask to whom the healthcare information was given
- Ask to be contacted in a special way, such as by mail or at work
- Ask to be contacted in a place other than home or work
- Examine and copy the health information the provider has recorded
- Complain to the covered entity and the Department of Health and Human Services if the patient believes there is a violation of their privacy

HIPAA-Defined Permissions

HIPAA defines ten areas in which permission must be granted in order to use or disclose PHI. **HIPAA-defined permission** is based on the reason for knowing, or use of, the information. Only two disclosures are *required* by HIPAA: for DHHS requests and to honor patient requests. All ten permissions are described in Table 10.1.

Table 10–1 HIPAA-Defined Permissions

Disclosure	Condition
1. Required disclosures	a. Health and Human Services (HHS) can view accounts, records, and other financial documents.
	b. Patient requests to view their personal medical records
2. Valid patient authorization	a. Allows for PHI to be disclosed
3. Patient requests for disclosure	a. May view own records
	b. May discuss treatment and medical condition with a physician or other healthcare provider
4. For the treatment, payment, and healthcare operations (TPO) of other covered entities	a. The patient's written permission is needed for other covered entities, such as attorneys and insurance plans, to have access to PHI covered entities.
5. For patient representatives such as family	a. Must present a legal document, such as Medical Power of Attorney, before granting access to PHI by family or friend
6. Qualified disaster relief organizations	a. Used to provide notification regarding disaster relief
	b. May be provided unless the patient objects
7. Incidental disclosures about patients without their authorization	a. Nurses and healthcare professionals may discuss patient cases when they are out of hearing distance of others.
	b. Healthcare professionals may discuss laboratory results with patients and others if they are out of hearing distance of others.
	c. Healthcare professionals may leave limited telephone messages for patients; it is always preferable to ask the patient if this is acceptable.
	d. May call a patient by name in a waiting room or over a public address system
	e. May leave patient chart outside an exam room if the patient's identity is not visible
8. For public purposes	a. When the PHI disclosure is required by law such as with a request by the court
	b. Public health departments are authorized to collect data relating to communicable diseases, births, and deaths.
	c. In all cases of abuse or neglect
	d. Disclosure necessary to prevent serious harm, such as when a patient threatens another person or makes a suicide threat; healthcare professionals must notify the patient that this disclosure has been made
	e. The Food and Drug Administration (FDA) can collect PHI relating to the safety of drugs and products.
	f. PHI may be disclosed to notify people at risk of a communicable disease.
	g. May release PHI in case of subpoena; consult with privacy official to determine specific criteria that apply
	h. Law enforcement has the right to PHI in cases of abuse, neglect, gunshot wounds, suspicious death, identifying a suspect, or medical emergency.
	i. Coroners and funeral directors may receive PHI to be able to perform their functions.
	j. Organ and tissue donation agencies may receive PHI to facilitate the donation process.
	k. Researchers may receive PHI under certain conditions; consult with the privacy officer.
	l. State workers' compensation programs may need PHI.
	m. Government agencies and facilities, such as prisons and the military, may receive PHI under certain conditions.
9. When deidentification has occurred (i.e., when patient identifiers have been removed)	

(Continued)

Table 10–1 *(Continued)*

Disclosure	Condition
10. In a limited data set in which certain identifiers, such as patient's, relative's, and employer's names have been removed, patients do not have the right to access	a. Psychotherapy notes b. Certain laboratory tests, under the Clinical Laboratory Improvement Act of 1988 (CLIA), may only be given to the person who authorized the test—usually a physician or advance practice provider. c. If they are prison inmates d. Certain research projects in which limited access has been granted in advance e. If the PHI is part of a government record f. If the PHI was obtained under a promise of confidentiality

Special Rules Relating to Research

HIPAA regulations also relate to medical information that is compiled and used for research purposes. Providers and other covered entities that wish to use individually identifiable patient information that is related to treatment, such as for cancer patients, must perform a very detailed authorization check or fill out a detailed authorization form. The researchers must obtain

- a patient authorization that complies with the rules set by HIPAA; or
- a waiver of authorization from a privacy board or an institutional review board, such as is found in a teaching hospital or university. The waiver must include extensive documentation as required by HIPAA.

This regulation also covers information used for research from records of a deceased patient.

Maintaining Privacy of Health Records

The privacy of health records is a constant concern of patients as well as healthcare providers. Every year, many people are taken advantage of by healthcare fraud schemes. Breaches of health information can lead to identity theft, credit card fraud, and Medicaid and Medicare fraud (Figure 10.3).

Figure 10.3 Make sure screens in reception areas can't be seen by patients

Source: vinnikovayana/123RF

Patients will often ask their doctors and caregivers for advice about the protection of their records. Healthcare providers are becoming more cautious about the handling and storage of medical records. Both healthcare providers and patients share some of the same concerns.

In addition to the precautions healthcare practices take, there are several methods healthcare consumers can use to protect themselves from fraudulent use of their healthcare information. These include the following:

- Make sure you understand all the information on every form that you sign. If not, then ask for clarification from the person presenting the document to you.

- Do not give out personal or medical information over the phone or through the mail unless you are sure who you are communicating with. Avoid including medical information in an email or via websites, as email and Internet communications can be hacked.

- Be cautious about responding to unsolicited offers of any "free" health service or information.

- Make sure that healthcare records and insurance cards are carefully secured. Review all medical bills to make sure that the claim for payment matches the care you received.

For more information on how medical practices can protect against fraudulent use of health records, go to the Federal Trade Commission's Medical Identity Theft website.

For more information on how consumers can protect their medical information, go to the AARP site, "How Private Is Your Medical Information?" at https://www.aarp.org/caregiving/health/info-2017/how-private-is-medical-information.html.

Implementing HIPAA's Privacy Rules

HIPAA is misunderstood. New studies are finding that some healthcare providers are being too overzealous in applying this law, leaving family members, caregivers, public health personnel, and law enforcement officers without the necessary information to care for the patients. This results in frustration and delays in the treatment of patients. HIPAA was passed by Congress in 1996 to allow patients easier access to their medical records, while limiting this access to others. Unfortunately, this has not always happened.

HIPAA regulations have made many healthcare agencies, such as hospitals, reluctant to release any information about their patients because of fear of civil or criminal penalties under HIPAA. This is particularly true when a patient refuses to be listed on the hospital's patient directory. In certain situations, some healthcare providers, trying to avoid any error under HIPAA by disclosing PHI inappropriately, refuse to provide medical records to anyone except the patient. For instance, some state workers' compensation programs, which are exempted under HIPAA, have had difficulty receiving the medical information they require for the purpose of providing financial assistance for the patient.

Reports of problems with accessing patient information have been filed by nonmedical persons. For example, human resource departments often require medical information to be able to administer the Family and Medical Leave Act (FMLA), facilitate return-to-work policies, assist in Americans with Disabilities Act (ADA) accommodation discussions, and obtain results from drug testing. In addition, lawyers working with workers' compensation claims, medical malpractice, and personal injury litigation need access to medical records. And members of the clergy complain that the privacy rules keep them from visiting the sick members of their congregations when they are hospitalized. They complain that the law is being too narrowly interpreted.

Police are also confronting problems because of HIPAA. The law requires hospitals to report to the police when a patient comes in with a gunshot wound or there is a suspected case of child abuse or neglect. According to some police officials, compliance with HIPAA is slowing police investigations and even impeding the prosecution of crimes. Police officers have noted that they are being denied access to anyone who has opted not to be listed in hospital directories—including crime victims and persons previously reported as missing. Although HIPAA makes exceptions for criminal investigations, some hospitals, concerned with violating the law, err on the side of caution and refuse to release any information. Under HIPAA, hospitals must allow police to interview patients and must provide information about their condition when a serious crime has been committed.

When the HIPAA regulations are not correctly interpreted, major issues have arisen. For example, a patient with suicidal ideation in Chicago was released from the hospital into the care of his friend to recuperate. Within a week Charlie was dead after jumping to his death from his friend's balcony.

The friend did not know that Charlie was suicidal when he was admitted to the hospital. The hospital did not release that information to the friend because they believed they could not under HIPAA regulations. The friend said he would have monitored Charlie better if only he had been told about his condition.

Educational facilities are coping with the task of gaining access to information about the mental stability of their students after the horrendous killing of 32 students and faculty at Virginia Tech. Many mental health professionals believe their patients' records are protected from disclosure under HIPAA. However, other experts believe that information about mentally disturbed students, who indicate that they would use harmful behavior against others, should be made known to the authorities.

In another case, a California mother was unable to get the hospital to produce a key medical record documenting her son's blood pressure in his final hours. The young man had died from an overdose just hours after she was told that he was stable. The record finally arrived six years later and indicated that her son had been in mortal danger for several hours while awaiting care. The medical record arrived too late under state law to file a civil lawsuit.

Med Tip

A violation of HIPAA, a federal law, is a criminal offense. Therefore, fear of violating this law has caused an overreaction to it among many healthcare professionals. According to Dr. William Kobler, former president of the Illinois State Medical Association, physicians have become excessively cautious about releasing patient information out of fear that they will be charged with a large fine.

Misconceptions about HIPAA

The DHHS states that the law requires "reasonable safeguards" be taken to protect patient privacy. The privacy provision applies to physicians, advance practice providers, pharmacists, and insurers. It was originally intended to protect computerized medical records and billing and to allow patients easier access to their own medical records. However, the purpose has been interpreted much more broadly. According to the HHS, many misconceptions about HIPAA are slowly being cleared up. Note the following clarifications to the privacy law:

- Does not prevent healthcare providers or hospitals from sharing patient information with other physicians or hospitals in order to treat patients.
- Does not prevent hospitals from disclosing names of patients to clergy or from keeping patient directories. It does not require that patients sign in to be included in the hospital directory of patients, only that they can opt out and not be included.
- Allows hospitals or healthcare providers to share information with the patient's spouse, family members, friends, or anyone whom the patient has identified as involved in their care.
- Does not apply to most police or fire departments. The hospital may release names and information about homicides, accident victims, and other incidents. However, HIPAA does limit the information that emergency medical technicians (EMTs) may disclose.

Office personnel, acting on behalf of healthcare providers and dentists, can still send out reminders about appointments and leave messages on patients' answering machines.

Med Tip

The HIPAA law, as it is currently written, prohibits patients/consumers from suing over privacy violations. Instead, patients/consumers must register their complaints with the Department of Health and Human Services.

Recommendations for Implementing HIPAA

Following are some practical recommendations for healthcare providers to follow when implementing HIPAA:

- Appoint and train a privacy officer to receive complaints and provide information concerning the provider's privacy notice materials.
- Conduct an internal assessment of existing policies, procedures, and practices for collecting and handling medical records and patient information to determine where the deficiencies in privacy may occur.
- Enter into written agreements with all nonemployee service providers who may have access to PHI.
- Adopt procedures for handling patient requests.
- Implement a Notice of Privacy Practices.
- Revise employee manuals regarding HIPAA standards. These personnel policies must reflect the organization's handling of employees who use or disclose PHI in violation of HIPAA. The **Office of Civil Rights**, also known as the OCR, would likely ask for a copy of these policies during an investigation of violations.
- Train all employees on policies and procedures regarding HIPAA.
- Retain signed authorizations, copies of notices of privacy practices, and any agreements with patients restricting disclosure of PHI. This documentation should be retained for a period of six years from the date it was created or the date when they were last in effect.
- Implement and enforce sanctions (penalties) for violations of provider policies and procedures.
- Establish a complaint process for noncompliance with the privacy regulation.

Noncompliance with HIPAA

Noncompliance with HIPAA can result in serious penalties for healthcare providers such as physicians, dentists, and hospitals. The penalties for violating HIPAA include civil penalties and criminal penalties (see Table 10.2).

Healthcare fraud, especially relating to Medicare and Medicaid programs, has been increasing during the past decade. Fraud alerts issued by the Inspector General's Office of the DHHS concerning suspicious

Table 10–2 Penalties for Noncompliance with HIPAA Regulations

Violation	Penalty
Civil Violations (Enforced by Office for Civil Rights)	
Unknowing penalty	$100–$50,000 per violation Annual maximum of $25,000 for repeat violations
Reasonable cause penalty	$1,000–$50,000 per violation Annual maximum of $100,000 for repeat violations
Willful neglect, but the violation is corrected	$10,000–$50,000 per violation Annual maximum of $250,000 for repeat violations
Willful neglect that is not corrected	$50,000 per violation Annual maximum of $1.5 million
Criminal Violations (Enforced by the Department of Justice)	
Knowingly obtaining or disclosing PHI	Fines up to $50,000 Imprisonment up to 1 year
Offenses committed under false pretenses	Fines up to $100,000 Imprisonment up to 5 years
Offenses committed with intent to sell, transfer, or use PHI	Fines up to $250,000 Imprisonment up to 10 years

practices can alert providers and the public to the potential for medical privacy abuse. Also, the DHHS has the authority to exclude covered entities from Medicare if they are not compliant with HIPAA.

Examples of sanctions against covered entities who violated HIPAA include the following:

- Advocate Health, based in Illinois, paid a fine of $5.5 million to settle their case related to PHI violations. Their subsidiary, Advocate Health Group, had three separate data breaches that affected 4 million patients. The OCR found that Advocate failed to assess the vulnerabilities of their EPHI system, failed to limit access to electronic information, did not ensure in writing that associated businesses would safeguard the EPHI, and failed to safeguard and unencrypted laptop that was left overnight in an unlocked vehicle.

- Cignet Health, based in Maryland, paid a fine of $4.3 million for violating the Privacy Rule. Cignet violated the rights of 41 patients by denying them access to their medical records. Cignet also refused to respond to OCR's repeated demands to produce the records and failed to cooperate with the OCR investigation.

- Anthem Inc. is one of America's largest health insurers. In December 2014, cybercriminals breached Anthem's system. The breach was discovered in January 2015. During that time, they gained access to the data on 78.8 million plan members. Anthem agreed to pay the OCR $16 million and undertook a corrective action plan to address their compliance issues.

Ethical Concerns with Information Technology

Medical Informatics

Medical informatics is the application of communication and information to healthcare practice, research, and education. Many hospitals and healthcare institutions are able to link together diverse areas such as pharmacy, laboratories, administrative, and medical records through the use of informatics. For example, many hospital pharmacies have implemented a fully computerized medication ordering system to lower the incidence of medication errors because of the inability to correctly interpret handwritten orders.

Informatics presents a multitude of ethical issues, especially with the use of the Internet by healthcare providers and patients. Healthcare providers have expressed concerns about security when patient data, such as that contained in medical records, is transmitted via the Internet. A report on confidentiality and security issues by the Computer Based Patient Record Institute, based in Schaumburg, Illinois, states, "Breaches of confidentiality can lead to loss of employment and housing, health and life insurance problems, and social stigma. . . . Formal information security programs must be established by each organization entrusted with healthcare information."

Med Tip

Because the amount of medical information available is said to double every five years, computerized systems have become indispensable.

Clinical Decision Support Systems

Clinical decision support systems (CDSS) are powerful tools that have revolutionized the way healthcare professionals make clinical decisions. These systems integrate patient data, medical knowledge, and information technology to provide real-time guidance and recommendations, enhancing the quality of care, reducing errors, and improving patient outcomes.

At the heart of a CDSS is a vast database that stores medical knowledge, guidelines, and best practices. This knowledge is continually updated to keep pace with the ever-evolving field of healthcare. CDSS analyzes patient-specific data, such as medical history, diagnostic test results, and medication records, and matches this information with the vast knowledge repository to generate patient-specific recommendations. These recommendations can range from drug interaction alerts and diagnostic suggestions to treatment options and preventive care guidelines.

One of the primary benefits of CDSS is its ability to improve the accuracy of diagnoses and treatment plans. By cross-referencing patient data with the latest medical knowledge, CDSS helps healthcare providers identify potential problems or suggest alternative treatments, ultimately reducing medical errors and adverse events. This results in safer and more effective patient care. Another advantage of CDSS is its capacity to streamline healthcare workflows. These systems assist in managing patient records, automating administrative tasks, and enhancing communication among healthcare professionals.

However, there are challenges associated with CDSS. There are concerns about the potential for information overload, where clinicians may become overwhelmed by the sheer volume of alerts and recommendations. Also, decisions by healthcare professionals are often made during direct patient contact, which means that many decisions are made in a matter of seconds or minutes and are still strongly determined by the experience and knowledge of the professional.

Data security and privacy are also critical issues in the context of CDSS. The vast amount of sensitive patient data stored and processed by these systems makes them attractive targets for cyberattacks. Ensuring robust security measures and strict adherence to data protection regulations is essential.

Despite these challenges, the future of CDSS looks promising. As artificial intelligence and machine learning technologies continue to advance, CDSS is poised to become even more intelligent and adaptive. These systems will increasingly incorporate predictive analytics, allowing for the early detection of diseases and personalized treatment plans. Additionally, the integration of CDSS with wearables and mobile health applications will make healthcare more patient-centric and convenient.

Furthermore, CDSS has the potential to support global healthcare initiatives. In remote and underserved areas, CDSS can extend the reach of healthcare expertise, offering guidance to healthcare providers who may have limited access to specialized knowledge. Telehealth, in combination with CDSS, can bridge the gap between patients and healthcare professionals, making quality care more accessible.

Wireless Local Area Networks

Wireless local area networks, also known as WLANs, are used by healthcare providers to access patient records from central databases while they are conducting patient rounds (bedside visits), adding observations and patient assessments to the databases, checking on medications, and completing a variety of other functions. The use of wireless networks by healthcare professionals presents ethical challenges and dilemmas. There can be a trade-off between quick access to the patient's medical records and the security of those records. Decisions relating to the use of WLANs must take into account the impact they have on the patient's privacy as mandated by HIPAA. HIPAA requires that there be safeguards in place to protect the privacy of electronic and nonelectronic protected health information. The HIPAA security rules that were issued in final form on February 20, 2003, apply to PHI in *electronic* form only.

Voice Recognition Technology

With the advent of voice recognition, doctors are now able to verbally chart their patient's records using **voice recognition technology**. This allows more immediate and thorough documentation. New technology enables a healthcare provider to input information by voice in real-time on mobile devices as they talk with the patient. Some devices can actually highlight and validate medical facts, as well as spot inconsistencies in dictation. Most providers are already skilled in using dictation devices in hospital medical record systems. The new technology takes this a step further and allows dictation and data storage as well as "intelligence" software. For example, the software can prompt the doctor to add more information if some clarification is missing, such as the patient's blood pressure or heart rate.

Facial Recognition Technology

Public facilities, such as schools and hospitals, are becoming more aware of the need for better security systems. Included in this category is **facial recognition technology**. This technology can check each face coming into a building against a database of persons who may be dangerous to a particular group of people or a person who is a known threat. The major advantage of facial recognition technology is the ability to quickly recognize persons such as angry or disgruntled employees, sex offenders, expelled students, and others who may be seen as a threat. Security can then be alerted to determine if the person standing in front of a facial recognition camera is a risk to others.

This same technology can be used to help identify an individual, such as a patient. While this technology is now in limited use in healthcare settings, its potential is great. As more useful applications are developed, facial recognition will no doubt become more widely used in hospitals and other healthcare facilities.

While facial recognition can be a very powerful new tool, it can also present some serious risks. There have been questions about a person's right to privacy as well as information security. There must be efforts made to balance the benefits of facial recognition with a concern for privacy. The system is not foolproof. It will not be able to give a warning against someone who is not a known threat. Some officials are warning that facial recognition will not automatically warn everyone about a potential attack, or even stop an attacker from entering a building or a school.

HIPAA has a requirement that healthcare organizations must secure access to PHI data in order to protect patient privacy and to protect against data breaches that can lead to fraud and medical identity theft.

Telehealth

Telehealth, also called *telemedicine,* or the use of communication and information technologies to provide healthcare services to people at a distance, is seen as the future of healthcare. Modern technology has the ability to provide health services for homebound and rural patients via telephone and the Internet. These methods have also been used to provide continuing healthcare education for many years. During the COVID-19 pandemic, DHHS expedited the use of telehealth for Medicare, and many of these uses have since been made permanent. Medicare patients can now use telehealth for behavioral and mental healthcare, and there are no geographic restrictions for receiving mental health services.

The Centers for Disease Control and Prevention is developing programs that use telehealth to help improve the health of people living in rural areas. Telehealth can reduce barriers to care, including giving access to specialists for those who have time or access restrictions, or transportation or mobility issues.

Telehealth raises legal issues, such as concerns about practicing healthcare across state lines, that must be addressed. Provider reimbursement for these types of consultations is uncertain. Also, the credentials of the person giving healthcare advice over the Internet are open to both legal and ethical discussion. And last, but very important, is the issue of maintaining privacy during telehealth visits. If you are receiving a telehealth visit or initiating one with a patient, keep these parameters in mind:

- Providers should make their calls from a private setting such as their office or an appointment room (Figure 10.4). Only other members of the patient's healthcare team can be in the room.

- Patients should choose a private location, such as a private room in their house, their car, or outdoors away from other people, for the appointment setting.

- Patients should take steps to protect their identity and data: use antivirus software, avoid using public Wi-Fi, and protect your wireless connection with a password.

Figure 10–4 Telehealth visits should be conducted in a private space

Source: VesnaArt/Shutterstock

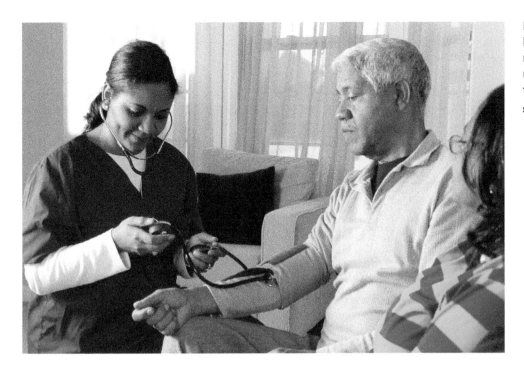

Figure 10–5 When providing healthcare in the home, maintain the patient's privacy unless they have authorized family members to attend

Source: Rob Marmion/Shutterstock

Home Care

Nurses and allied healthcare professionals who work in patients' homes are employees of a covered entity, and therefore are required to comply with the Privacy Rule. This can be challenging in the home setting where family members and other professionals may be nearby. Sometimes, that patient will authorize family members to participate in the visit, but there are times when a patient expressly states that they do not want a particular person to be made aware of their condition (Figure 10.5).

Similar to staff working in healthcare centers, visiting nurses and allied health professionals have to use discretion before disclosing the PHI of patients to third parties without the written authorization of the patients or a person appointed with durable power of attorney for healthcare. Third parties can include people such as family members, friends, and members of the clergy, all of whom will likely have genuine concern for the well-being of the patient.

Technology Technicians

The advent of new technology has resulted in a need for new categories of health technicians:

- **Health Information Administrator:** Must have the ability to work with electronic health records technology and have a clear understanding of the requirements under HIPAA as well as the HITECH Act. This person oversees personnel who are responsible for the use and collection of electronic health records.

- **Health Information Technician:** Works with electronic health records in positions such as medical records, coding, collecting, and supervising the use and collection of electronic health records.

These positions require college degrees and certification in healthcare privacy and security.

Pending Updates to HIPAA

In 2023, there were proposed updates to the HIPAA Privacy Rule. The updates include items such as allowing patients to inspect PHI in person and takes notes of photographs; changing the time to provide access to PHI from 30 days to 15 days, restricting the right of individuals to transfer EPHI to a third party to only PHI that is maintained in an EHR, and requiring covered entities to post a fee schedule for PHI access and disclosures. Updates would also include that covered entities would no longer be required to obtain written acknowledgment from individuals that they have received a Notice of Privacy Practices.

These updates, if enacted, are designed to ease the administrative burden of compliance with HIPAA. However, the updates will require changes to procedures and policies and the retraining of staff, all of which will be challenging for agencies.

Chapter 10 Review

Points to Ponder

1. Will it be possible to balance the wealth of medical information available to the patient via the Internet with the loss of a personal relationship between the patient and caregiver?

2. How can a patient's PHI be maintained when medical information is being faxed from one location to another?

3. Is the high cost of implementing HIPAA in a small healthcare practice worth the expense?

4. In your opinion, will HIPAA make it more or less difficult for public services such as police, fire, and ambulance services to administer to patients? Explain your answer.

Discussion Questions

1. Why has patient confidentiality become more difficult in the present healthcare environment?

2. Why is the implementation of the new Privacy Rule so expensive?

3. Should family members, and even friends, have access to a patient's medical record? Why or why not?

4. Should patients be treated via telehealth? Why or why not?

Review Challenge

Short Answer Questions

1. What is the Privacy Rule and why is it important?

2. What is a covered transaction? Give an example of one.

3. What are some examples of forms of identity that must be deidentified when health statistics are obtained?

4. What are some of the misconceptions about HIPAA?

5. What are some of the benefits of telehealth?

6. What might be some of the ethical concerns with WLANs?

7. What are some privacy precautions to use when taking care of patients?

_____

_____

_____

_____

8. Who should patients contact if they wish to register a complaint about a potential privacy violation?

_____

_____

_____

9. What does "minimum necessary standard" mean and why is it important?

_____

_____

_____

_____

10. Explain the quote from Justice Brandeis, found in this chapter, relating to our right to privacy.

_____

_____

_____

_____

Matching

Match responses in column B with the correct term in column A.

COLUMN A

_____   1. Privacy Rule

_____   2. WLANs

_____   3. HIPAA

_____   4. EIN

_____   5. clearinghouse

_____   6. healthcare plan

_____   7. PHI

_____   8. telehealth

_____   9. Employer Identifier Standard

_____   10. DHHS

COLUMN B

a. number assigned to an employer

b. individually identifiable information

c. wireless systems to send and receive data

d. based on employer's tax ID or on their EIN

e. all covered entities must be in compliance

f. Department of Health and Human Services

g. a billing service

h. use of information technologies to treat people at a distance

i. Health Insurance Portability and Accountability Act of 1996

j. individual or group that provides or pays for healthcare

Multiple Choice

Select the one best answer to the following statements.

1. The Privacy Rule is meant to ensure
   a. standardization of health data.
   b. standardization of financial data.
   c. standardization of medical care.
   d. a and b only
   e. a, b, and c

2. An example of a clearinghouse is
   a. PHI.
   b. a skilled nursing facility.
   c. a billing service.
   d. a government regulation.
   e. EIN.

3. The government organization that investigates a violation of a patient's medical privacy is called
   a. OSHA.
   b. OCR.
   c. PHI.
   d. HIPAA.
   e. none of the above

4. A network of wireless communication systems used to access patient records is
   a. HIPAA.
   b. PHI.
   c. WLAN.
   d. EIN.
   e. ADA.

5. The privacy law
   a. prevents hospitals from sharing medical information with other facilities.
   b. prevents hospitals from sharing registered patient names with the clergy.
   c. does not apply to most police and fire departments.
   d. allows unlimited information to be shared by EMTs.
   e. none of the above

6. A violation of HIPAA
   a. is a criminal offense.
   b. does not carry any financial penalty at present.
   c. is not reportable.
   d. does not affect a physician's reputation, as it is just a document.
   e. may have a fine of under $100 for all offenses.

7. When implementing HIPAA, healthcare providers and physician groups should
   a. hire a privacy officer.
   b. implement a Notice of Privacy Practices.
   c. retain signed authorizations for at least six years.
   d. enter into written agreements with nonemployee service providers.
   e. all of the above

8. Covered entities include all of the following except
   a. hospice programs.
   b. medical device companies.
   c. clinical laboratories.
   d. police departments.
   e. skilled nursing facilities.

9. Patients' rights under HIPAA include the ability to
   a. examine their medical records.
   b. have a full copy of their medical record.
   c. complain to the HHS if they believe there is a violation of privacy.
   d. a and c only
   e. a, b, and c

10. When patient information is requested via a subpoena, you must
    a. comply and send the entire record immediately.
    b. provide only the minimum necessary standard even if more is requested in the subpoena.
    c. provide all PHI that is requested in the subpoena.
    d. provide PHI only with the consent of the patient.
    e. None of the above are correct.

Discussion Cases

1. Chee Vonghas just reported for duty and is reviewing the patients she will have during the evening shift. One of them, Ida Monroe, is in isolation for an infectious disease. Dr. Jerome comes into the nursing station around 9:00 PM after making hospital rounds to see his patients. He tells Chee that he noticed that one of his neighbors, Ida Monroe, is a patient, and he would like to review her medical record. Chee starts to give him access to the medical record and then realizes that Dr. Jerome is not Ida's physician. Dr. Jerome says not to worry about that, as he has taken care of the rest of Ida's family for years and is sure that Ida will want him to consult on her case. When Chee hesitates to give him access to the medical record, Dr. Jerome says that he will report her to her nursing supervisor.

   a. Should Chee give Ida's medical record to Dr. Jerome? Why or why not?

   b. What should Chee say to Dr. Jerome?

   c. What should Chee do if Dr. Jerome continues to insist on seeing Ida's medical record?

   d. What ethical principles are involved in this case?

   e. What legal regulations are involved in this case?

2. You are a CMA working in the office of a physician who performs major surgical procedures on hospitalized patients. A patient, who is the father of a friend of yours, comes in for a pre-surgery exam. You happen to know that this man is an alcoholic. You also know that the surgeon you work for does not like to perform surgery on alcoholic patients, as he believes they have difficulty healing and often have excessive bleeding after surgery. You wish to tell the surgeon about the man's drinking problem, but you are afraid that it would be a HIPAA violation.

a. What do you do?

_____

_____

b. Is this a legal and/or ethical problem?

_____

_____

c. Should you discuss your concerns with your friend?

_____

_____

d. What is your first responsibility?

_____

_____

3. An older patient has approached you in the healthcare office where you work. He is very distressed at having to read and sign a HIPAA document. He asks you the following questions. What do you say?

a. "Why am I getting so many of these privacy notices every time I go into a healthcare office or hospital? Why can't you use one that I already signed before for another doctor?"

_____

_____

b. "Can I see my medical record?"

_____

_____

c. "I live with my daughter. Can she see my medical record if she asks for it?"

_____

_____

d. "I want to file a complaint. Where can I do that?"

_____

_____

Put It Into Practice

Request a copy of a notice of privacy from your primary care provider's office. What does this notice state about filing a complaint?

Web Hunt

Look under the official government website relating to HIPAA (www.hhs.gov/hipaa/index.html) to find the answers to frequently asked questions about HIPAA. Describe five questions and answers that you believe all healthcare professionals should know.

Critical Thinking Exercise

What would you do if, as part of your job in handling the office mail, you came across a consultation report from a psychiatrist about one of your family members?

Bibliography

American Medical Association. (2023). *HIPAA violations & enforcement*. https://www.ama-assn.org/practice-management/hipaa/hipaa-violations-enforcement

Bryant, M. (2016). Advocate Health pays whopping $5.55M to settle alleged HIPAA violations. *HealthCareDive*. https://www.healthcaredive.com/news/advocate-health-pays-whopping-555m-to-settle-alleged-hipaa-violations/423926/

Centers for Disease Control and Prevention. (2022). *Health Insurance Portability and Accountability Act of 1996 (HIPAA)*. https://www.cdc.gov/phlp/publications/topic/hipaa.html

Centers for Disease Control and Prevention. (2022). *Telehealth in rural communities*. https://www.cdc.gov/chronicdisease/resources/publications/factsheets/telehealth-in-rural-communities.htm

Nguyen, K-L. (2019). HIPAA: At what cost? *Medical Economics*. https://www.medicaleconomics.com/view/hipaa-what-cost

Sutton, R.T., Pincock, D., Baumgart, D.C. et al. (2020). An overview of clinical decision support systems: benefits, risks, and strategies for success. *npj Digital Medicine*, 3, 17. https://doi.org/10.1038/s41746-020-0221-y

The HIPAA Journal. (2017). *HIPAA compliance for visiting nurses.* https://www.hipaajournal.com/hipaa-compliance-for-visiting-nurses/

The HIPAA Journal. (2018). *$16 million Anthem HIPAA breach settlement takes OCR HIPAA penalties past $100 million mark.* https://www.hipaajournal.com/16-million-anthem-hipaa-breach-settlement-takes-ocr-hipaa-penalties-past-100-million-mark/

The HIPAA Journal. (2023). *HIPAA training requirements.* https://www.hipaajournal.com/hipaa-training-requirements/

U.S. Department of Health & Human Services. (1995). *Case example Cignet Health.* https://www.hhs.gov/guidance/document/case-example-cignet-health

U.S. Department of Health & Human Services. (2023). Telehealth policy changes after the COVID-19 public health emergency. *Telehealth.HHS.gov.* https://telehealth.hhs.gov/providers/telehealth-policy/policy-changes-after-the-covid-19-public-health-emergency

U.S. Department of Health & Human Services. (2023). Telehealth privacy for patients. *Telehealth.HHS.gov.* https://telehealth.hhs.gov/patients/telehealth-privacy-for-patients

U.S. Department of Health & Human Services. (2022). *Summary of the HIPAA Privacy Rule.* https://www.hhs.gov/hipaa/for-professionals/privacy/laws-regulations/index.html

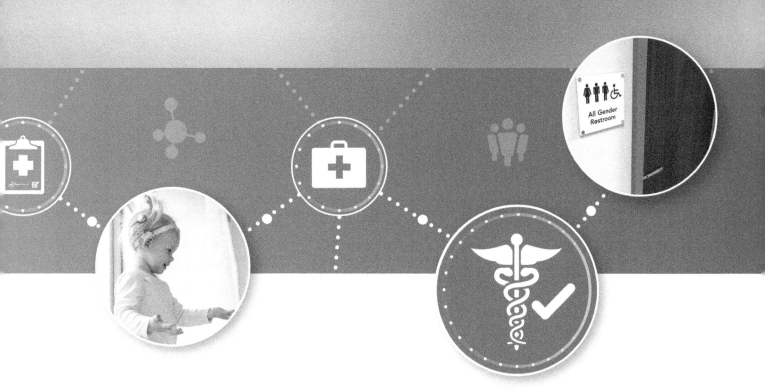

Part 3

Healthcare Ethics

Chapter 11   Ethical and Bioethical Issues in Healthcare

Chapter 12   Ethical Issues Related to the Beginning of Life

Chapter 13   Ethical Issues Related to the End of Life

Chapter 14   Ethical Issues in Healthcare Trends

Ethical and Bioethical Issues in Healthcare

Learning Objectives

After completing this chapter, you will be able to:

11.1 Define the key terms.

11.2 Discuss the importance of codes of ethics such as the Nuremberg Code.

11.3 Summarize the ethical issues related to organ transplantation.

11.4 Discuss ethical issues relating to end-of-life issues and medical aid-in-dying.

11.5 Describe the types of therapeutic research.

11.6 Discuss the issues relating to embryonic stem cell research.

Key Terms

Censure

Cloning

Control group

Double-blind test

Embryonic stem cells

Euthanasia

Expulsion

Harvested

Human genome

Human Genome Project

Institutional review board (IRB)

Medical aid-in-dying

National Organ Transplant Law of 1984

Nontherapeutic research

Placebo group

Randomized study

Revocation

Therapeutic research

Uniform Anatomical Gift Act

United Network for Organ Sharing (UNOS)

The Case of the COVID-19 Vaccine Line Jumpers

In 2020, as the world grappled with the unprecedented COVID-19 pandemic, the race to develop and distribute vaccines brought to light a significant ethical dilemma: line jumping. Line jumping refers to the practice of individuals, often privileged or well-connected, getting access to COVID-19 vaccines ahead of those in priority groups, such as healthcare workers, people living in group homes, older adults, and those with compromised immune systems.

There were documented incidents of people dressing up to look older than 65. A casino executive and his wife flew to a remote community of the White River First Nation in Canada, pretended to be local motel employees, and received vaccinations. In Florida, a paramedic stole three doses of vaccine that were meant for first responders. Several concierge doctors (who run private practices for a select group of clients) were offered $10,000 and more from wealthy patients for early vaccines. Even within hospitals, there were administrators and people who were able to work from home who jumped ahead of front-line workers. These attempts (and successes) at line jumping raised a host of ethical concerns.

The primary ethical concern was the glaring lack of equity and fairness. Vulnerable populations, particularly those most at risk from the virus, were often marginalized as the wealthy and influential secured early access to vaccines. This reinforced existing social and economic disparities, as those with means were able to protect themselves while others faced heightened risks. Line jumping also had broader implications for resource allocation. Limited vaccine supplies meant that giving doses to individuals outside of priority groups could hinder the goal of achieving herd immunity and exacerbate the global public health crisis.

Those who engaged in line jumping faced questions about their moral responsibility to the wider community. Prioritizing personal interests over collective welfare raised moral concerns about one's social and civic duty during a public health crisis. The casino executive and his wife were fined around

$800 each, and the executive wound up resigning from his position.

Efforts to address line jumping included increased transparency in vaccine distribution, implementing strict eligibility criteria, public education campaigns, and addressing root causes of vaccine inequality.

Ultimately, the line-jumping issue underscored the importance of ethics and social responsibility during crises. It highlighted the need for transparent, equitable vaccine distribution, and the significance of cooperation among governments, pharmaceutical companies, and the global community to combat a pandemic effectively. As the world continues to grapple with COVID-19 and future health crises, these ethical lessons are invaluable in shaping an ethical, equitable response.

1. Do you agree or disagree with the casino executive and his wife being fined for line jumping?

2. If you agree, do you think the penalty was appropriate?

3. If you got the COVID-19 vaccine, did you wait your turn or try to jump the line?

Introduction

Healthcare ethics, bioethics, and healthcare law are intertwined out of necessity. When ethical principles are violated, a civil lawsuit often follows. As we have explained throughout this textbook, ethics, that branch of philosophy relating to morals or moral principles, involves the examination of human character and conduct, the distinction between right and wrong, and a person's moral duty and obligations to the community.

Ethics, as discussed in the healthcare professions, is applied ethics. In other words, while theoretical concepts involving ethics are important for the student to know, the basis for study involves *applying* one's moral and value system to a career in healthcare.

Ethics involves more than just common sense, which is an approach for making decisions that most people in society use. Ethics goes way beyond common sense: It requires a critical-thinking approach that examines important considerations such as fairness for all consumers, the impact of the decision on society, and the future implications of the decision.

An example of ethical critical thinking is whistleblowing, which occurs when an employee publicly reports a potentially dangerous situation in their organization to authorities who can take corrective action. The employee must

- exhaust all other channels for correcting the situation within the organization,

- have documented evidence that would convince an impartial and reasonable observer, and

- have good reason to believe that by "blowing the whistle" and going public, the necessary changes will be made to prevent harm and injury.

The ethical justification for whistleblowing is evident as it is a service to protect others. This is often done at great personal risk to the whistleblower. Often whistleblowers are subject to harsh treatment by others within their organization, even coworkers. Before a decision is made to "go public" with information, it is wise to consider all other alternatives. An anonymous complaint can be made to a regulatory agency such as the Environmental Protection Agency (EPA). The Occupational Safety and Health Act (OSHA) of 1970 prohibits any retaliation against an employee who files a complaint with OSHA. Whistleblowers who work for the federal government are protected by law from losing their jobs.

Even though the lives of many whistleblowers have been negatively affected, most say that they could not have lived with themselves if they had remained silent.

Med Tip

The dignity of the individual, whether it is the patient or a member of the healthcare team, must always be of paramount concern when discussing ethics and bioethics.

Figure 11–1 Hippocrates

Source: NJphoto/Alamy Stock Photo

Bioethics concerns ethical issues discussed in the context of advanced medical technology. The somewhat new field of bioethics requires the healthcare professional to ask whether a practice such as gene therapy or **cloning** can be morally justified. In addition, physicians must ask themselves if these practices are compatible with the character traits of a good physician.

Med Tip

Remember that, as discussed in Chapter 1, an illegal act, or one that is against the law, is almost always unethical. However, an unethical act may not be illegal. For instance, providing medical treatment, such as an organ transplant, to a celebrity and denying the same treatment to an indigent "street person," while legal, is clearly unethical.

Ethics has been a part of the medical profession since the beginning of medical practice. In 400 B.C., Hippocrates, a Greek physician referred to as "the father of medicine," wrote a statement of principles for his medical students to follow that is still important in medicine (see Figure 11.1). Called the Hippocratic Oath, the code reminds students of the importance of their profession, the need to teach others, and the obligation to never knowingly harm a patient or divulge a confidence. The principles stated in the oath are found today in many of the professional codes of ethics, such as that of the American Medical Association (AMA), which is found in Appendix A.

Ethical Standards and Behavior

All healthcare professions have ethical standards and behaviors that are set by the corresponding professional organization. Some examples of professional organizations with stated ethical standards are the American Medical Association, American Nurses Association, American Academy of Physician Associates, and American Association of Nurse Practitioners. Healthcare providers need to know the standards to which they are held, along with general ethical concepts such as autonomy, nonmaleficence, and beneficence.

While some associations can sanction healthcare providers for ethical violations, it is up to the state licensing departments to limit, suspend, or revoke a healthcare provider's license to practice. For example, a physician who is accused of unethical behavior or conduct in violation of these standards can be issued a warning or **censure** (criticism) by the AMA. The AMA Board of Examiners may recommend the **expulsion** (being forced out) or suspension of a physician from membership in the medical association. Expulsion is a severe penalty because it limits the physician's ability to practice medicine. Even if the AMA censors a member, it does not have the authority to bring legal action against the physician for unethical behavior. If someone alleges, or declares without proof, that a physician has committed a criminal act, the AMA is required to report it to the state licensing board or governmental agency. Violation of the law, followed by a conviction for the crime, may result in a fine, imprisonment, or **revocation** (taking away) of the physician's license.

Codes of Ethics

People's behavior must match their set of values. For example, it is not enough to believe that patient confidentiality is important if one then freely discusses a patient's personal information with a coworker or friend. In this case, the healthcare professional's values and behavior are at odds. Professional organizations have developed codes of ethics that summarize the basic principles and behavior that are expected of all practitioners in that discipline. These codes, also known as statements of intent, are meant to govern the conduct of members of a given profession, such as medicine.

Some codes of ethics were developed as a direct response to atrocities that occurred during wartime, especially in response to the medical experimentation in Nazi concentration camps during World War II (WWII). Public awareness of the ethical and legal problems associated with medical research, such as experimenting on human subjects, gained prominence in the post-WWII trials at Nuremberg, Germany. In these trials, more than 25 Nazi medical personnel were accused of committing war crimes against involuntary human subjects. The most infamous experimenter, Josef Mengele, was also known as the "angel of death." What became known as the Nuremberg Code developed after these trials made public what the Nazis had done under the guise of medical research. This code became a forerunner for the subsequent codes and guidelines that were adopted by healthcare and research organizations and agencies. The Nuremberg Code reminds us that basic ethical principles must be followed when conducting medical research, or any research involving human beings. The Nuremberg Code is found in Appendix A.

American Medical Association Principles of Medical Ethics

The current AMA Principles of Medical Ethics discuss human dignity, honesty, responsibility to society, confidentiality, the need for continued study, patient autonomy, a responsibility of the physician to improve the community, a responsibility to the patient, and access to medical care. They are regularly updated by the Council on Ethical and Judicial Affairs (CEJA) of the AMA. This version was first adopted in 1957, revised in 1980, and revised again in 2001. The Code was revised again in 2016, after eight years of work by the CEJA. The latest version covers topics such as patient privacy, patient autonomy, and the ethical management of medical records. The basic principles are summarized as follows:

1. Physicians should be dedicated to providing competent medical care, with compassion and respect for human dignity and rights.

2. Physicians will uphold the standards of professionalism, be honest in all professional interactions, and strive to report physicians deficient in character or competence, or who are engaging in fraud or deception, to appropriate entities.

3. Physicians should respect the law and recognize a responsibility to seek changes in those requirements that are contrary to the best interests of the patient.

4. Physicians will respect the rights of patients, colleagues, and other health professionals, and will safeguard patient confidence and privacy within the constraints of the law.

5. Physicians will continue to study, apply, and advance scientific knowledge; maintain a commitment to medical education; make relevant information available to patients, colleagues, and the public; obtain consultation; and use the talents of other health professionals when indicated.

6. Physicians are, in the provision of appropriate patient care—except in emergencies—free to choose whom to serve, with whom to associate, and the environment in which they provide medical care.

7. Physicians should recognize a responsibility to participate in activities contributing to the improvement of their community and the betterment of public health.

8. Physicians will, while caring for a patient, regard responsibility to the patient as paramount.

9. Physicians should support access to medical care for all people.

Med Tip

Every healthcare professional who interacts with patients, such as medical receptionists, medical assistants, nurses, physician assistants, and pharmacy technicians, must be familiar with the Principles of the AMA.

The Council on Ethical and Judicial Affairs of the AMA is comprised of nine members who interpret the Principles of Medical Ethics. The council's interpretation or clarification is then published for AMA members. All members of the medical team are expected to cooperate with the physician in upholding these principles. For example, just as physicians cannot refuse to treat patients based on race or color, neither can their staff. Their behavior can reflect either negatively or positively on their employer/physician. A few of the opinions of the Council on Ethical and Judicial Affairs are adapted and summarized in Table 11.1.

Table 11–1 Summary of Opinions of the Council on Ethical and Judicial Affairs of the AMA

Issue	Opinion
Abuse	Physicians who are likely to detect abuse in the course of their work have an obligation to familiarize themselves with protocols for diagnosing and treating abuse and with community resources for battered women, children, and older persons. If it were not reported, it might mean further abuse or even death for the victim.
Accepting patients	A physician may decline to accept a patient if the medical condition of the patient is not within the area of the physician's expertise and practice. However, a physician may not decline a patient because of race, color, religion, national origin, or any other basis for discrimination.
Allocations of health resources	Physicians have a duty to do what they can for the benefit of the individual patient. Physicians have a responsibility to participate and to contribute their professional expertise in order to safeguard the interests of patients in decisions made at the societal level regarding the allocation or rationing of health resources. The treating physician must remain a patient advocate and, therefore, should not make allocation decisions.
Confidential care of minors	Physicians who treat minors have an ethical duty to promote the autonomy of minor patients by involving them in the medical decision-making process to a degree equal with their abilities.
Equitable care	In 2023, the Code was updated to focus on "the social forces that drive how and to whom health care is provided." It states that it is the joint responsibilities of individual physicians and healthcare institutions to ensure that all members of communities receive "safe, effective, patient centered, timely, efficient, and equitable care."
Euthanasia	Euthanasia is the administration of a lethal agent by another person to cause the patient's death and thereby relieve the patient's suffering. Instead of engaging in euthanasia, physicians must aggressively respond to the needs of patients at the end of life. Patients should not be abandoned after it is determined that a cure is impossible.
Fee splitting	The practice of a physician accepting payment from another physician for the referral of a patient is known as fee splitting and is considered unethical.
Financial incentives for organ donation	The voluntary donation of organs in appropriate circumstances is to be encouraged. However, it is not ethical to participate in a procedure to enable a donor to receive payment, other than for the reimbursement of expenses necessarily incurred in connection with the removal of any of the donor's nonrenewable organs. In addition, when death of the donor has occurred, the death must be decided by a physician other than the donor patient's physician.
Gene therapy	The Council's position is that gene therapy, the replacement of a defective or malfunctioning gene, is acceptable as long as it is used for therapeutic purposes and not for altering human traits.

Table 11–1 *(Continued)*

Issue	Opinion
Ghost surgery	A surgeon cannot substitute another surgeon to perform a procedure without the consent of the patient.
HIV testing	Physicians should ensure that HIV testing is conducted in a way that respects patient autonomy and assures patient confidentiality as much as possible.
Mandatory parental consent to abortion	Physicians should ascertain the law in their state on parental involvement in abortion to ensure that their procedures are consistent with their legal obligations.
Physician-assisted suicide	Instead of assisting patients in committing suicide, physicians must aggressively respond to the patient at the end of life.
Quality of life	In making decisions for the treatment of seriously disabled newborns or of other persons who are severely disabled by injury or illness, the primary consideration should be what is best for the individual patient and not the avoidance of a burden to the family or to society.
Withholding or withdrawing life-prolonging treatment	Patients must be able to make decisions concerning their lives. Physicians are committed to saving lives and relieving suffering. When these two objectives are in conflict, the wishes of the patient must be given preference.

Source: Adapted from the American Medical Association, Code of Medical Ethics © 2008–2009.

American Nurses Association Code of Ethics

The American Nurses Association (ANA) has developed a code for nurses that discusses their obligation to protect patients' privacy, respect patients' dignity, maintain competence in nursing, and assume responsibility and accountability for individual nursing judgments. This code is found in Appendix A.

Code of Ethics of the American Association of Medical Assistants

Medical assistants may not be faced with the life-and-death ethical decisions that face the physician, but they will encounter many dilemmas regarding right and wrong on an almost daily basis. For example, how would you handle a situation in which another employee violates confidentiality or uses foul language in front of a patient? How do you treat a patient whose body smells of urine and alcohol? What do you do if you make an error? What do you do if you observe a coworker making an error? These are issues involving ethics and doing the right thing at the right time. To provide guidance for this category of allied health professional, the American Association of Medical Assistants (AAMA) has developed a Code of Ethics for Medical Assistants. This code is found in Appendix A.

Other professional organizations, including the American Dietetic Association, the American Health Information Management Association, the American Occupational Therapy Association, the American Society for Medical Technology, and the American Society of Radiologic Technologists, have developed codes of ethics.

Med Tip

Know the code of ethics that relates to your professional practice. Many healthcare professionals keep a framed copy near their place of work to remind them of this responsibility.

Bioethical Issues

Bioethical issues, resulting from advances in medical technology, are reported in newspapers and journals almost daily. Debates about cloning, harvesting embryos, and in vitro fertilization were unknown four or five decades ago.

There is a real concern that expensive biotech treatments will be used for chronic illness when a more reasonably priced product is available. Patients may not be able to afford the co-pay or their out-of-pocket share. An ethical dilemma arises when the patient is no longer able to afford the treatment and the insurance company refuses to pay. The patient with a chronic disease may decide that "enough is enough" and decide not to take medication.

Current bioethics topics include many facets of organ transplantation, maternal–fetal conflict, parental decision making, end-of-life issues and medical aid-in-dying, among many others. Selected topics are addressed in detail here.

Organs and Tissue for Transplantation

Many more people need organs than in the past because dialysis and other medical advances are able to keep them alive longer as they wait for transplants (Figure 11.2). The **United Network for Organ Sharing** system, established in 1999—also known as the UNOS—contains a database relating to every organ donation and transplant event occurring in the United States since 1986. Current estimates of people waiting for a transplant in the United States are estimated as high as 400,000. In late 2023, there were more than 103,000 people listed on the UNOS waiting list, and many of these people will die before they can receive an organ. The most needed organs are kidneys (Figure 11.2).

Organ Donation

The United States and Great Britain are among the countries that are committed to the donation model for organs. Under the donation model, organs may be taken, or **harvested**, only with the consent of the donor (or the donor's surrogate representative). The **Uniform Anatomical Gift** which has been adopted in all states, permits competent adults to either allow or forbid the posthumous (after death) use of their organs through some type of written document, including a donor card. See Figure 11.3 for a sample donor card. Organs and tissues such as corneas, hearts, and lungs, can be donated posthumously (after death). Other organs such as kidneys, bone marrow, and partial livers can be donated by living people.

In the United States, people may voluntarily donate their organs and tissues to others. They can indicate their desire to do this in their advance directives or, in some states, on their driver's license. The most commonly donated organs and tissues are the eyes (usually the cornea), heart, kidneys, skin, bone marrow, blood, liver, and lungs. In addition, the long bones of the body (tibia, fibula, femur, humerus, radius, and ulna) can also be transplanted. There is a law in the United States that prohibits the sale of organs. The only payment allowed is to cover the medical costs for the donor of the transplant.

Because of a severe shortage of donor organs, patients have resorted to going onto the Internet to search for living donors, and have even used ads, public broadcasts, and billboards to advertise their need, particularly for bone marrow.

Figure 11–2 Patients undergoing hemodialysis while waiting for a kidney transplant

Source: mailsonpignata/Shutterstock

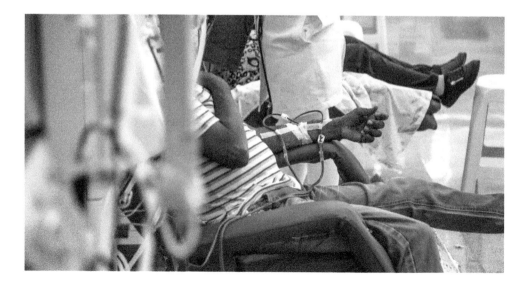

Organ Donor Card

I, ________________________, hereby make the following anatomical gift, if medically acceptable, to take effect upon my death.

_______Any organs or parts _______Entire body

Only the following specific organs or parts:

____

Limitations or special wishes if any:

____

(Signatures of donor and witnesses appear on reverse side.)

Front of card

Organ Donor Card (side two)

Signed by the donor and the following two witnesses in the presence of each other.

Donor Signature: ______________________________

Date of Birth: ______________ Date signed: __________

City and State:________________________________

Witness Signature:_____________________________

Witness Signature:_____________________________

This is a legal document under the Uniform Anatomical Gift Act or similar laws.

Back of card

Figure 11–3 Organ donor card

Source: Bonnie F. Fremgen

Organ Trafficking

Most people agree that selling organs is morally objectionable. The **National Organ Transplant Law of 1984** forbids the sale of organs in interstate commerce in the United States. This law seeks to protect the poor from being exploited, as they may be tempted to earn money by selling what they believe to be an unneeded organ, such as a kidney. Iran is the only country in the world that allows living donors to be compensated, and those organs are supposed to stay in the country and be transplanted into other Iranians.

Therefore, a brisk market exists for organs on the black market. It is estimated that 10 percent of all transplants worldwide are illegal. This involves people voluntarily selling a kidney, for example, or being coerced or kidnapped and forced to give up an organ to an organ trafficking ring. A common scenario involves a refugee or migrant who is desperate for money. They are lured by the promise of a new job, trafficked to another country, and taken to a hospital where doctors perform illegal surgery removing a kidney or other tissue. This means that there are medical professionals who are part of the problem.

Transplant Rationing

UNOS is the legal entity in the United States responsible for allocating organs for transplant. They use a formula that gives half the weight to considerations of medical utility or need, and the other half to considerations of justice.

One of the most discussed bioethical issues is who shall receive an organ transplant. These procedures are some of the most expensive of all medical procedures. For example, liver transplants cost over $800,000. In addition, the follow-up care to aid the transplant by suppressing the immune system can be more than $30,000 a year. In the United States, the allocation of transplanted organs is managed by UNOS, a nonprofit organization that operates under contract with the federal government. UNOS is responsible for overseeing the organ transplant system and ensuring that donated organs are distributed fairly and equitably. The process of allocation includes the following:

- **Waitlist Registration**: Patients in need of a transplant must be evaluated by a transplant center to determine their eligibility for transplantation. If deemed suitable, they are placed on the national transplant waiting list maintained by UNOS. Each patient's medical condition, blood type, and other factors are taken into consideration when determining their position on the list.

- **Organ Matching:** When a donated organ becomes available, UNOS uses a sophisticated computer system to match the organ with a recipient. The matching process considers factors such as the recipient's medical urgency, time spent on the waiting list, blood type compatibility, tissue compatibility, and geographic proximity.

- **Local, Regional, and National Allocation:** Organs are initially offered to potential recipients within the local area where the organ is donated. If no suitable recipient is found locally, the organ is then offered to candidates in the broader regional and national allocation pools, increasing the chances of finding a suitable match. The goal is to ensure that organs are distributed fairly and that they go to the patients who are in the greatest need.

- **Medical Urgency:** Some organs, such as hearts and lungs, are allocated based on medical urgency, with the sickest patients receiving the highest priority. For other organs like kidneys and livers, the allocation algorithm takes into account both the medical urgency and time on the waiting list.

- **Geographic Considerations:** Geographic considerations are also taken into account in organ allocation to minimize transportation time, as some organs have limited viability outside the body. However, efforts are made to balance the need for local distribution with the goal of ensuring fairness.

- **Pediatric Priority:** There is a priority system in place for pediatric candidates, ensuring that children receive organs that are appropriately sized for their age and weight.

- **Exception Cases:** In certain cases, patients may receive exceptions to the standard allocation rules if they have special medical needs or other compelling factors.

It is important to note that the allocation process aims to be as fair and transparent as possible, and it undergoes continuous refinement to adapt to changing medical and ethical considerations. UNOS regularly reviews and updates its policies and procedures to improve the organ transplant system in the United States. Additionally, potential donors and recipients should be aware that living organ donation, such as kidney or partial liver donation, follows a different process that is typically coordinated through transplant centers.

Unfortunately, in some cases, transplant departments have exaggerated the severity of their patient's condition in order to have them jump ahead on the UNOS list. UNOS has recently made changes in its allocation system to prevent this type of abuse. From an ethical perspective, the transplant surgeon still may have to make the life-or-death decision about who receives the first available organ.

Medicare fully funds kidney transplants and also funds heart transplants after all other medical treatments have been tried. Most insurance plans also fund kidney and heart transplants. Many liver transplant centers require patients who have alcohol use disorder to stop drinking alcohol for six months in order to be eligible for a liver transplant. But for patients with alcohol-related hepatitis, a six-month wait may be too long, and they will die before they can make it onto the transplant list. Some hospitals now try to identify patients who are least at risk for relapse.

A dramatic example of the painful decisions surrounding the issue of organ transplants is the situation that the state of Oregon faced in the 1980s. The state could either fund Medicaid coverage for 1,500 additional patients or continue to fund its organ transplant program for an anticipated 34 patients. Between 1985 and 1987, the state funded 19 transplants at a cost of $1 million; only nine of these patients survived the transplant. Cost estimates for transplants in Oregon for the years 1987 to 1989 were $2.2 million. Because the amount was expected to double during the next two years, voters in Oregon believed that it was more cost-effective to fund Medicaid, which provides basic healthcare for many, rather than fund transplants for the few patients who would require them. The public response to this new plan was slow. However, there was a nationwide response when a seven-year-old boy died without receiving a needed bone marrow transplant to treat leukemia. The new law resulted in several lawsuits as well as fundraising for transplants in Oregon. The lessons learned from Oregon's plight are many:

- Medical resources are limited in all states.
- The need for acute care, such as for transplants, is more visible than preventive care, such as prenatal care.
- New medical discoveries and treatments, with their enormous costs, are likely targets for cost containment rather than older, more basic, medical treatments.
- For new treatments to be funded, they must replace older, ineffective treatments.

These difficult issues mean that policymakers will have to examine all treatments on a cost/benefit basis and be ready to eliminate outdated and ineffective medical treatments.

Maternal–Fetal Conflict

Ethics and maternal–fetal conflicts are complex issues that arise in the field of healthcare, where the interests and well-being of a pregnant woman clash with those of her developing fetus. These conflicts can manifest in various medical scenarios, such as when a pregnant woman's health is at risk due to a condition or treatment that may harm the fetus, or when the woman refuses medical interventions that are deemed necessary to protect the fetus.

Ethical considerations in such cases often center on the principle of autonomy, where the pregnant woman has the right to make decisions about her own body and health. At the same time, ethical principles of beneficence and nonmaleficence require healthcare professionals to act in the best interest of both the pregnant woman and the fetus.

Balancing these ethical principles can be challenging. Healthcare providers must engage in open and empathetic communication with the pregnant woman to ensure her autonomy is respected, while also considering the potential consequences for the fetus. This may involve exploring alternative treatments or interventions that minimize harm to either party.

Furthermore, legal and cultural factors can influence how maternal–fetal conflicts are resolved. Legal frameworks and societal attitudes toward abortion, for example, can play a significant role in decision-making.

End-of-Life Issues and Medical Aid-in-Dying

End-of-Life Issues

Ethical issues at the end of life are complex and multifaceted, touching upon the intersection of medicine, autonomy, and compassion. These challenges often arise in the context of advanced illness, where patients and their families must make difficult decisions about treatment, quality of life, and the timing of death.

One central ethical concern is the principle of autonomy. Patients have the right to make decisions about their own care, including whether to continue or discontinue life-sustaining treatments, even if those decisions may hasten their death. However, respecting autonomy can clash with the moral duty of healthcare professionals to preserve life. Striking a balance between these values requires thoughtful communication, informed consent, and advance care planning.

Another significant issue is the appropriate use of palliative care and hospice services. Some patients may not have access to these vital resources, while others may be referred too late in their illness. Providing equitable access to palliative care is a matter of justice and compassion, ensuring that patients receive comprehensive end-of-life support.

End-of-life ethical issues require careful consideration, emphasizing the importance of open and honest communication, patient-centered care, and respect for individual values. Ethical frameworks must evolve to address the changing landscape of healthcare and the diverse perspectives of patients and families facing the end of life.

Medical Aid-in-Dying

Medical aid-in-dying, also called physician aid-in-dying, physician-assisted suicide, or **euthanasia**, is a contentious and ethically complex issue in the realm of healthcare. This practice involves a physician providing a terminally ill patient with the means to end their own life, typically through a prescription for a lethal dose of medication. The ethical considerations surrounding medical aid-in-dying are multifaceted.

As with end-of-life care, one of the primary ethical principles at the heart of this issue is autonomy. Advocates argue that individuals who are suffering from terminal illnesses should have the right to make decisions about the timing and manner of their death, as a manifestation of their personal autonomy. They contend that this choice allows patients to maintain control over their suffering and maintain their dignity.

On the other hand, opponents of medical aid-in-dying raise concerns about the potential for abuse, coercion, and the devaluation of human life. They argue that physicians, whose primary role is to preserve life, should not participate in actions that intentionally end it. The slippery slope argument suggests that once medical aid-in-dying is accepted, it may expand to include individuals who are not terminally ill, leading to unintended consequences.

Ethical debates on this topic also involve considerations of beneficence and nonmaleficence. Supporters argue that medical aid-in-dying can be an act of mercy, relieving a patient's unbearable suffering. Opponents assert that it is a violation of the medical profession's commitment to "do no harm."

The legality and practice of medical aid-in-dying vary by country and state, reflecting differing societal and ethical views. Ethical debates continue, highlighting the need for thoughtful deliberation and robust safeguards to protect vulnerable individuals while respecting personal autonomy in end-of-life decisions.

Rationing Medical Care

Rationing medical care in the United States is a complex and ethically charged issue that stems from the challenges of resource allocation, access disparities, and the high cost of healthcare. While the United States does not have a formal, centralized rationing system like some countries with universal healthcare, several implicit forms of rationing exist.

One of the most significant implicit methods of rationing medical care in the United States is financial means. The country's predominantly private healthcare system, coupled with the absence of universal coverage, means that individuals' access to care often depends on their ability to pay. This can lead to inequities, as those with better insurance or personal wealth can receive more comprehensive and timely medical care than those without adequate financial resources.

Insurance coverage also plays a role in rationing. Insurance companies make decisions about which treatments, medications, and procedures they will cover, and these decisions can limit what is accessible to patients. Moreover, patients who are uninsured or underinsured may face barriers to care, making access to medical services contingent on coverage and affordability.

Geographic location is another implicit factor in rationing. Access to medical care varies significantly based on where individuals live. Rural areas often have limited healthcare facilities and specialists, leading to challenges in accessing advanced or specialized treatments. This can result in delayed or suboptimal care for those in underserved areas.

Wait times and availability of healthcare services, especially for elective or nonurgent procedures, can be a form of rationing. In some cases, patients may need to wait for extended periods to receive certain treatments or surgeries, potentially impacting their health outcomes.

Ethical dilemmas surround rationing medical care, as healthcare providers must balance the principles of justice, fairness, and the duty to prioritize patient well-being. Resource allocation committees or ethics boards within healthcare institutions often grapple with making difficult choices, particularly during public health crises or when resources are limited.

Efforts to mitigate the implicit rationing of medical care in the United States include expanding insurance coverage through initiatives like the Affordable Care Act, promoting preventive care to reduce the burden of costly treatments, and investing in telehealth and technology to improve access to care, especially in underserved areas.

It is understandable that when unexpected situations occur, it is necessary to ration healthcare services because of limited medications and vaccines, service providers, and treatments. For example, during the COVID-19 pandemic, there were shortages of N-95 masks for healthcare workers, swabs for COVID tests, and hospital beds for the sickest patients. All of these issues had to be managed logistically and ethically. The Centers for Disease Control and Prevention issued guidelines outlining a phased approach to vaccine distribution, with an initial focus on priority groups. The phases included healthcare workers, residents of long-term care facilities, essential workers, individuals aged 65 and older, and those with underlying health conditions. Unfortunately, many people "jumped the line" as described in the chapter opening case.

The Ethics of Biomedical Research

The relief of pain and suffering, the restoration of body functions and health, and the prevention of disability and death are all aims of healthcare. Human experimentation is considered necessary for medical progress to occur. Both animal testing and human testing have been used successfully to further medical knowledge and conquer disease.

Medical research always carries with it some degree of risk. Human beings cannot be used for testing purposes unless they consent to participate. Obtaining informed consent is particularly important in **nontherapeutic research**, or research that will not directly benefit the research subjects. There are additional protections for children who participate in research: One or both parents must consent, and if the child is over age 7, they must assent to the study. The justification for all medical research is that the benefits must outweigh the risks. Many consider that this utilitarian, or benefit/cost, approach to decision-making is a good model to use when examining medical research. Merely increasing knowledge is not considered an adequate justification for taking a risk with a human life.

Medical researchers must abide by the standards for testing that have been established by the Nuremburg Code (see Appendix A) and their medical associations, such as the AMA and the ANA. The Nuremburg Code is one of the most influential documents in this history of clinical research.

In the United States, healthcare researchers also need to follow the Belmont Report. The Belmont Report was written by the National Commission for the Protection of Health Subjects of Biomedical and Behavioral Research, after a number of unethical research projects came to light. The Belmont Report, published in 1979, describes the basic ethical principles, such as respect for persons, beneficence, and justice, that all research must be based on. The Belmont Report also discusses the boundaries between healthcare practice and healthcare research along with the process of informed consent, assessment of risks and benefits, and selection of subjects.

The Department of Health and Human Services (DHHS) implements government standards for research, and their Office for Human Research Protections provides regulations and guidance. The government requires that all institutions that receive federal research funds, such as hospitals and universities, establish an **institutional review board**, also called IRB, that oversees any human research in that facility. In 1991 the Federal Policy for the Protection of Human Subjects (also known as the Common Rule) for research was adopted by 15 federal departments and agencies. In 2017 this policy was revised. Not all federal agencies have adopted the Common Rule. In particular, while the Food and Drug Administration is part of HHS, it has its own regulations for human subject research.

Privacy is another major concern when dealing with technological advancements. For example, scientists are now able to decode our genetic composition through the human genome project. But this also means that information about a person's future health, such as a five-year-old child's future tendency for serious heart disease, may become available to others, including insurance companies. The question arises about to whom our health information should be made available.

Many scientists and politicians have examined the potential loss of lives in the case of a terrorist attack. The federal government established Project BioShield in 2004 to promote the development of vaccines and preventive medications in quantities that can protect a large number of people. Economists and ethicists are concerned that the amount of money spent on these items will leave less for diseases that are becoming more prevalent. On the other hand, the Strategic National Stockpile was instrumental in the COVID-19 pandemic, when it was used as part of Project BioShield, to coordinate, procure, and deliver millions of vaccine ancillary kits and other supplies throughout the country.

Therapeutic Research

Informed consent (as discussed in Chapter 5) is necessary when a patient is involved in therapeutic research. **Therapeutic research** is a form of medical research that may directly benefit the research subject. The research subject must be made aware of all the risks involved with the research. In addition, the subject must be informed about the type of research design that is used. The research design will be one of these:

- **Control group** who receive no treatment
- **Randomized study** in which the subject is assigned at random to either the control or experimental treatment group (who receive treatment)
- **Placebo group** in which an inactive substance or an alternative type of treatment is given

The healthcare provider conducting the research must explain all the facts relating to the research, even if this means that the patient may decide not to participate. While the provider is responsible for explaining to the patient all the risks involved in a research project, other healthcare professionals, such as nurses, pharmacists, and medical assistants, may become aware of information relating to a research project that needs to be conveyed to the attending researcher. An example would be a patient who tells the nurse that he is taking a medication prescribed by another attending healthcare provider at the same time that he is taking an experimental drug from a medical researcher.

Many ethicists believe that it is unethical to use a control group when conducting medical experiments, as this group has no hope of benefiting from the experimental drug.

In a **double-blind test**, neither the experimenter nor the patient knows who is getting the research treatment. This is considered to be an objective means of gathering test data because it eliminates any bias, or preference, the researcher may have toward a specific research method or treatment. An ethical question arises with double-blind tests about the *process* of informed consent. Are the patients fully aware that they may not be receiving any treatment whatsoever? In some research situations, in which the physicians discover an immediate positive effect of an experimental drug on the test group, the project will be adjusted so that the control group can also receive the treatment.

Clinical trials are organized medical studies to provide large amounts of clinical data used to evaluate medical treatments. The studies are funded by drug companies, medical device manufacturers, and the government to test new treatments on volunteers. The overall objective is to determine if the product is safe and effective to use on patients. The treatments must be approved by an independent safety panel, with the oversight of the FDA or the Office for Human Protections. All of the research subjects must be fully informed of any potential ill-effects or hazards.

Many patients who participated in clinical trials have received benefits for illnesses such as stroke, multiple sclerosis, and cancer. However, in some cases, not all clinical trials have a positive outcome; some have ended in permanent life-altering disabilities, diseases, or even death.

Med Tip

Some medical ethicists have concluded that, in some cases, the risk to human life is too great in clinical trials.

A Black woman, Henrietta Lacks, unknowingly gave an incredible gift to research when a strain of cancer cells was saved from a tumor that was removed from her in 1951. Mrs. Lacks died a few months later from a virulent strain of cervical cancer. The tumor was sent to a researcher at Johns Hopkins where he was trying to find cells that would live indefinitely so that researchers could experiment on them. Mrs. Lacks' cancer cells were perfect as they multiplied rapidly and did not die in the lab. A cell line from these cells, called HeLa (named after Henrietta Lacks), has become immortal and is still used by researchers (Figure 11.4). This cell line was used to develop the first polio vaccine, and helped produce medications for numerous diseases including Parkinson's, leukemia, and the flu. Millions and millions of these cells have been produced and are now sold to researchers, and they have generated millions of dollars in profit. However, the Lacks family was not informed of the use of the cells and did not benefit from them during Lacks' life. Henrietta Lacks died in poverty. In 2023, the Lacks family settled a lawsuit with the biotechnology company Thermo Fisher Scientific, which they said had been "unjustly enriched" by the

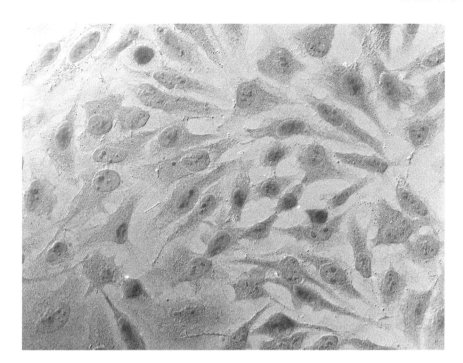

Figure 11–4 HeLa cervical cancer cells stained with Coomassie blue under a microscope

Source: Heiti Paves/123RF

use of the cells. Even though rules about informed consent have changed in the last 70 years, patients still do not have much control over tissues and organs that are removed during surgery.

Conflicts of Interest

Conflict of interest in medicine refers to situations where a healthcare professional's personal or financial interests may compromise their objectivity and ability to make decisions solely in the best interests of their patients. It's a complex ethical issue that can arise in various aspects of healthcare. Here are some examples:

- *Research and Clinical Trials:* Researchers who have financial ties to a pharmaceutical or biotech company might be inclined to prioritize the interests of their sponsor over the well-being of their study participants. This can result in biased research outcomes and a lack of transparency.

- *Pharmaceutical and Medical Device Industry:* Healthcare providers may receive payments, gifts, or speaking fees from pharmaceutical companies, potentially influencing their prescribing habits. This can lead to the overuse of certain medications or devices, which may not be the best option for patients.

- *Personal Investments:* Healthcare professionals may have personal investments in healthcare-related companies, making it challenging to remain impartial when making decisions about treatments, tests, or referrals for patients.

To address conflicts of interest in medicine, there is a growing emphasis on transparency and disclosure. Many professional organizations and regulatory bodies require healthcare providers to disclose their financial relationships with outside entities. However, managing conflicts of interest effectively may involve more robust policies and regulations, ethical education, and a commitment to patient-centered care, with decisions made based on the best interests of the patient rather than financial gain. This is essential to maintain trust in the healthcare system and ensure that patients receive the most appropriate and unbiased care.

Human Genome Project

The **Human Genome Project** was begun in the early 1990s as a research program by the federal government. The purpose was to determine or "map" the sequence of the total number of genes, estimated at 100,000, each of us has within the 23 pairs of human chromosomes. This complete set of genes is known as the **human genome**. It resembles a set of blueprints for the human being that is stored in the nucleus of each cell.

Med Tip

A genome linkage map is similar to a roadmap in that it provides the location of where a particular gene (genetic material) is located on the chromosomes.

The goal of the Human Genome Project, which is supported by scientists in several countries, is to provide a map of where each gene is located on the 23 pairs, or 46 chromosomes. The U.S. portion of the genome project was divided between scientists in nine centers at both national laboratories and universities. It was estimated that this important project would cost between $3 and $5 billion and take 15 to 20 years to complete. However, the project was completed ahead of time in the year 2003, and it has provided important information for both biological and medical researchers.

The Human Genome Project provides a better understanding of the process of human evolution. The most important information for medical researchers relates to an improved understanding of the relationship between certain genes and particular diseases. The hope is that this genome information will result in the eventual elimination or control of genetic diseases such as cystic fibrosis and sickle-cell anemia. Ultimately, a test for a gene could actually diagnose a medical condition before any symptoms even appear. The "maps" that have been created by this project make it ten times quicker to locate a particular gene on a linkage map.

While the Human Genome Project has provided valuable insights into human genetics, it has also raised issues that need to be resolved. The vast amount of genetic data collected has raised significant privacy concerns. Ensuring the security of this data and protecting individuals' genetic privacy is an ongoing challenge. As the Project advances, it raises ethical questions about the potential for genetic discrimination. The knowledge of a person's genetic makeup could be used to deny insurance coverage or employment, and there is a need for new laws and regulations to protect individuals from such discrimination. Finally, the Project has led to the development of personalized medicine, but this can be expensive and inaccessible for many people. It has raised concerns about healthcare disparities, where only those with the means to afford genetic testing and tailored treatments can benefit.

Embryonic Stem Cell Research

Embryonic stem cells are derived from the inner cell mass of a blastocyst, which is an early stage of embryo development. Human embryos reach the blastocyst stage 4–5 days post fertilization, at which time they consist of 50–150 cells. Scientists regard these cells as the building blocks of a new era of regenerative medicine in which the body can eventually heal itself.

Isolating the inner cell mass using immunosurgery results in destruction of the blastocyst, a process which raises ethical issues and has resulted in intense criticism from several fronts because the embryos used in the research are destroyed. Embryonic stem cell research forces a fundamental discussion about the moral status of an embryo. It often hinges on when one believes personhood or moral value begins, which varies among individuals and cultures.

One of the most significant ethical concerns is the source of embryos for research. Typically, embryonic stem cells are derived from surplus embryos created during in vitro fertilization procedures. Critics argue that using embryos for research purposes raises moral questions about the status of these embryos and whether they have a right to life. There are further concerns about the "slippery slope" effect, where the acceptance of embryonic stem cell research could lead to further ethically questionable practices, such as human cloning or the creation of designer babies.

Researchers are currently focusing on the therapeutic potential of embryonic stem cells, with clinical use being the goal for many laboratories. Potential uses include the treatment of diabetes and heart disease. The cells are being studied to be used as clinical therapies, models of genetic disorders, and cellular/DNA repair.

Ethical debates surrounding embryonic stem cell research highlight the importance of balancing scientific progress with ethical considerations, respecting the diverse beliefs and values held by society, and advocating for transparent, regulated research practices. These discussions continue to evolve as research and technological advances raise new ethical questions.

Chapter 11 Review

Points to Ponder

1. Why do students still learn about codes of ethics such as the Nuremberg Code?

2. Do all physicians follow the guidelines relating to euthanasia as discussed in the Opinions of the Council on Ethical and Judicial Affairs of the AMA? If not, why not?

3. What would you do if you knew that a patient diagnosed with cancer was part of a control group of research patients who were not receiving a drug that could benefit them?

4. What do you do when you observe unethical behavior by a coworker?

5. What do you do when you make a mistake?

6. In your opinion, what criteria should be used for selecting the recipient of a scarce organ such as a heart or liver? Would you include such factors as the patient's medical need, chance for success of the procedure, and the patient's responsibility for causing the illness? Why or why not?

Discussion Questions

1. Explain what the AMA Principles of Medical Ethics statement on "improvement of the community" means.

2. Discuss the freedom of choice that a physician has about accepting patients, as stated in the AMA's Principles of Medical Ethics.

3. What should healthcare professionals do if their ethical values differ from those of their employer? Discuss several options.

4. Describe several bioethical issues that modern-day healthcare professionals have to face.

5. Why are bioethical issues discussed in codes of ethics?

6. Describe a situation in which the "slippery slope" of ethics may be a concern.

7. Should whistleblowers be protected by law from losing their jobs if they "blow the whistle" about an illegal or unethical action in their organization?

Review Challenge

Short Answer Questions

1. Describe equitable care and why it is included in the AMA Code of Ethics.

_____

_____

_____

_____

2. Describe three of the considerations that UNOS uses for the allocation of scarce organs.

_____

_____

_____

_____

3. Describe medical aid-in-dying and explain why it is controversial.

_____

_____

_____

_____

4. Describe five reasons why informed consent is needed in all research.

_____

_____

_____

_____

5. What is whistleblowing? What federal laws might protect a whistleblower?

_____

_____

_____

6. Describe a double-blind research study.

_____

_____

_____

_____

7. Explain some clinical uses of the Human Genome Project.

_____

_____

_____

_____

8. Explain the Nuremburg Code and why it is important.

_____

_____

_____

_____

9. What is UNOS and what does it do?

_____

_____

_____

_____

10. Marion is blind and Deaf as a result of a childhood ailment. She is now 45. She is very independent but does require some assistance with grocery shopping and other activities. She is single, and her family of siblings and relatives live in another state. How might Marion be given some assistance without being intrusive to her?

_____

_____

_____

_____

Matching

Match the responses in column B with the correct term in column A.

COLUMN A

_____ 1. revocation

_____ 2. expulsion

_____ 3. censure

_____ 4. placebo group

_____ 5. posthumous

_____ 6. embryonic stem cells

_____ 7. euthanasia

_____ 8. ghost surgery

_____ 9. double-blind test

_____ 10. harvesting

COLUMN B

a. condemn

b. remove organs or embryos

c. after death

d. research design

e. take away; recall

f. one physician substituting for another

g. force out

h. cells from a blastocyst

i. those who don't receive a drug

j. aiding in the death of another person

Multiple Choice

Select the one best answer to the following statements.

1. Nontherapeutic research

    a. will always benefit the research subject.

    b. does not directly benefit the research subject.

    c. is unethical.

    d. should be justified with the benefits outweighing the risks.

    e. b and d only

2. A double-blind test means that

    a. neither the patient nor the researcher knows who is getting the treatment.

    b. the participants are visually impaired.

    c. the results will not be gained from an objective method for testing.

    d. the control group will eventually benefit from being in the experiment.

    e. there is an unethical practice taking place.

3. Many professional codes of ethics are based on

    a. current laws.

    b. mandates from the government.

c. early writings of Hippocrates.

d. outdated value systems.

e. none of the above.

4. Embryonic stem cells are

a. genetically identical cells from a single common cell used to create an identical organism.

b. master cells in the body that can generate specialized cells.

c. the same as chromosomes.

d. the same as gene markers.

e. none of the above.

5. Which of the following are factors that UNOS considers when allocating organs for transplant?

a. geographic considerations

b. medical urgency

c. pediatric priority

d. geriatric priority

e. organ matching

6. The Summary of Opinions of the Council on Ethical and Judicial Affairs of the AMA

a. describes fee splitting as an acceptable practice.

b. admonishes the surgeon against "ghost surgery."

c. admonishes the physician to be sensitive to the need to assist patients in suicide.

d. describes gene therapy as acceptable as long as it is for the purpose of altering human traits.

e. all of the above

7. Taking away a license to practice medicine is called

a. revocation.

b. censure.

c. expulsion.

d. a and c only

e. a, b, and c

8. Medical issues relating to maternal–fetal conflict include

a. nonmalfeasance.

b. the mother refusing treatment to protect the fetus.

c. abortion.

d. the mother's health being at risk and possible harm to the fetus.

e. all of the above

9. Conflicts of interest occur

a. when there are financial interests present.

b. if stock is owned by the physician in the company that sponsors the research.

c. if the researcher can control the results of the research.

d. if the patient's needs are not considered.

e. all of the above

10. Embryonic stem cells

a. are derived from blastocysts.

b. consist of 250–500 cells.

c. are used in regenerative medicine.

d. are taken 7–9 days post fertilization.

Discussion Cases

1. Mickey Mantle, Baseball Hall of Fame center fielder for the New York Yankees, received a liver transplant in 1995, after a six-hour operation. It took only two days for the Baylor Medical Center's transplant team to find an organ donor for the 63-year-old former baseball hero when his own liver was failing because of cirrhosis and hepatitis. Mantle was a recovering alcoholic who also had a small cancerous growth that was not believed to be spreading or life threatening.

There is usually a waiting period of about 130 days for a liver transplant in the United States. A spokesperson for the United Network for Organ Sharing, located in Richmond, Virginia, stated that there had been no favoritism in this case. She based her statement on the results of an audit conducted after the transplant took place. However, veteran transplant professionals were surprised at how quickly the transplant liver became available.

Doctors estimated that, because of Mantle's medical problems, he had only a 60 percent chance of a three-year survival. Ordinarily, liver transplant patients have about a 78 percent three-year survival rate. There are only about 4,000 livers available each year, with 40,000 people waiting for a transplant of this organ. According to the director of the Southwest Organ Bank, Mantle was moved ahead of others on the list because of a deteriorating medical condition. The surgery was uneventful, and Mantle's liver and kidneys began functioning almost immediately. His recovery from the surgery was fast.

There were mixed feelings about speeding up the process of an organ transplant for a famous person. However, Kenneth Mimetic, an ethicist at Loyola University in Chicago, stated, "People should not be punished just because they are celebrities." The ethics of giving a scarce liver to a recovering alcoholic was debated in many circles. University of Chicago ethicist Mark Siegler said, "First, he had three potential causes for his liver failure. But he also represents one of the true American heroes. Many people remember how he overcame medical and physical obstacles to achieve what he did. The system should make allowances for real heroes."

"Mickey Mantle died two months later from cancer."

a. As in the case of the liver transplant for Mickey Mantle, should the system make allowances for "real heroes"? Why or why not?

_____

_____

b. Some ethicists argue that patients with alcohol-related, end-stage liver disease should not be considered for a liver transplant because of the poor results and limited long-term survival. Others argue that because alcoholism is a disease, these patients should be considered for a transplant. What is your opinion, and why?

_____

_____

c. Analyze this case using the Blanchard-Peale three-step model in Chapter 1.

_____

_____

2. The Tuskegee Syphilis Study, conducted between 1932 and 1972 by the United States Public Health Service, is one of the most infamous instances of unethical human experimentation in medical history. This study focused on the natural progression of syphilis in a group of Black men in Macon County, Alabama. The researchers initially enrolled 600 men, including 399 with syphilis and 201 without the disease, to investigate the effects of untreated syphilis.

The most egregious ethical violation in the Tuskegee Study was the withholding of treatment for the participants. Even after penicillin became a widely recognized and effective treatment for syphilis in the 1940s, the researchers deliberately withheld it from the subjects, allowing the disease to progress, leading to severe health complications and death for some.

In 1972, the study came to light, leading to public outrage and ethical reform in medical research. The U.S. government formally apologized for the study, and in 1974, the National Research Act was passed, creating Institutional Review Boards (IRBs) to protect human research subjects.

Compensation for the victims and their families came in 1974 when a class-action lawsuit resulted in a $10 million settlement. The surviving patients received an out-of-court settlement of $37,500 for the infected men and $16,000 for the men in the control group. The families of men who had died also received compensation of $15,000 for the infected men and $5,000 for the uninfected men. This settlement provided lifetime medical care for surviving participants and their families and established the Tuskegee Health Benefit Program. Additionally, in 1997, President Bill Clinton issued a formal apology to the survivors, calling the study "shameful."

a. Could this type of research study be conducted today? Why or why not?

_____

_____

b. Taking into account an average annual inflation rate of 5 percent over a period of 37 years, the settlement of $37,500 would now be approximately $240,000, the $16,000 settlement would be $100,000, the $15,000 settlement would be $94,000, and the $5,000 settlement would be $32,000. In your opinion, was this a fair settlement? Why or why not?

_____

_____

c. The public knew about the study, so what should they have done?

_____

_____

d. Many scientists believe that using data from this type of experiment indirectly condones the experiments. Others believe that the suffering should not be in vain and, thus, the data should be used for the good of others. In your opinion, how should the data be used that is obtained from an unethical experiment and how can we prevent this from happening again?

_____

_____

Put It Into Practice

Select a newspaper article relating to a medical ethics or bioethical issue. Explain the ethical issue and summarize the article. Discuss the people who could be adversely affected by this issue.

Web Hunt

Using the website of the Department of Health and Human Services (**www.hhs.gov**), examine the statement on "National Organ and Tissue Donation Initiative." Click on the site for organ donation and discuss the steps that you would need to take in order to become an organ and tissue donor.

Critical Thinking Exercise

What would you do to correct the imbalance in healthcare for people who lack resources?

Bibliography

Administration for Strategic Preparedness & Response. (2023). Project BioShield. https://aspr.hhs.gov/AboutASPR/ProgramOffices/BARDA/Pages/Project-Bioshield.aspx

Administration for Strategic Preparedness & Response. (2023). Strategic National Stockpile role in the federal vaccination program. https://aspr.hhs.gov/SNS/Pages/SNS-Role-Federal-Vaccination-Campaign.aspx

American Medical Association. (2016). *Code of medical ethics, current opinions on ethical and judicial affairs.* Chicago: American Medical Association.

American Medical Association. (2023). *Council on Ethical & Judicial Affairs (CEJA) reports by year.* https://www.ama-assn.org/councils/council-ethical-judicial-affairs/council-ethical-judicial-affairs-ceja-reports-year

Emanuel, E.J., Persad, G., Upshur, R., et al. (2020). Fair allocation of scarce medical resources in the time of Covid-19. *New England Journal of Medicine,* 382:2049-2055. https://www.nejm.org/doi/full/10.1056/NEJMsb2005114

Goldstein, J. (2021). Hospital workers start to "turn against each other" to get vaccine. *The New York Times.* https://www.nytimes.com/2020/12/24/nyregion/nyc-hospital-workers-covid-19-vaccine.html

Gonzalez, J., Garijo, I., & Sanchez, A. (2020). Organ trafficking and migration: A bibliometric analysis of an untold story. *International Journal of Environmental Research and Public Health.* 5;17(9):3204. DOI: 10.3390/ijerph17093204. PMID: 32380680; PMCID: PMC7246946.

Hall, M., & Orentlicher, D. (2020). *Healthcare law and ethics: A nutshell* (4th ed.). West Academic Publishing.

Hauck, G. (2021). Cutting, bribing, stealing: Some people get COVID-19 vaccines before it's their turn. *USA Today.* https://www.usatoday.com/story/news/health/2021/02/03/covid-vaccine-some-people-cutting-bribing-before-their-turn/4308915001/

Hernandez, J. (2023). Henrietta Lacks' descendants reach a settle over the use of her 'stolen' cells. *National Public Radio.* https://www.npr.org/2023/08/01/1191283359/henrietta-lacks-descendants-settlement-stolen-cells

Jamusik, N. (2019). The Nuremburg Code and its impact on clinical research. *MASSDEVICE.* https://www.massdevice.com/the-nuremberg-code-and-its-impact-on-clinical-research/

Munson, R., & Lague, I. (2016). (2016). *Intervention and reflection: Basic issues in medical ethics* (10th ed.). Cengage Learning.

Rothberg, M.B., Class, J., Bishop, T.F., Friderici, J., Kleppel, R., & Lindenauer, P.K. (2014). The cost of defensive medicine on 3 hospital medicine services. *JAMA Internal Medicine.* 174(11):1867–1868. DOI:10.1001/jamainternmed.2014.4649

Shaw, B., & Barry, V. (2015). *Moral issues in business* (13th ed.). Cengage Learning.

U.S. Department of Health & Human Resources. (2018). *The Belmont report.* https://www.hhs.gov/ohrp/regulations-and-policy/belmont-report/read-the-belmont-report/index.html

U.S. Department of Health & Human Resources. (2022). *Federal policy for the protection of human subjects ('common rule').* https://www.hhs.gov/ohrp/regulations-and-policy/regulations/common-rule/index.html

U.S. Department of Health & Human Resources. (2023). *Office for Human Research Protections.* https://www.hhs.gov/ohrp/index.html

Veatch, R.M., & Guidry-Grimes, L.K. (2019). *The basics of bioethics* (4th ed.). Routledge.

Warsi, A. (2023). *In Nepal's "kidney valley," poverty drives an illegal market for human organs. PBS News Hour.* https://www.pbs.org/newshour/world/in-nepals-kidney-valley-poverty-drives-an-illegal-market-for-human-organs

Ethical Issues Related to the Beginning of Life

Learning Objectives

After completing this chapter, you will be able to:

12.1 Define the key terms.

12.2 Describe the ethical considerations relating to artificial insemination.

12.3 Describe the ethical considerations relating to surrogate motherhood.

12.4 List several ethical issues surrounding sterilization and contraception.

12.5 Outline current regulations of abortion in your state.

12.6 Describe the ethical considerations related to genetic testing.

12.7 Describe the ethical considerations related to wrongful life.

Key Terms

Abortion

Amniocentesis

Artificial insemination

Assisted reproductive technology

Child Abuse Prevention and Treatment Act

Contraception

Embryo

Emergency contraception

Fetus

Gestational period

Induced abortion

In vitro fertilization (IVF)

Preimplantation genetic diagnosis

Safe Haven Laws

Selective fetal reduction

Spontaneous abortion

Sterilization

Surrogacy

Therapeutic sterilization

Viable

The Case of the OB/GYN and Olivia M.

Olivia M, a nurse who is 16 weeks into her first pregnancy, lives in Texas, which now bans abortion. When she woke up to find her bed soaking wet, she realized her water had broken, and she and her husband headed to her local emergency department. Olivia knew that she was at high risk for infection or hemorrhage, and she understood that at 16 weeks' gestation, her baby wasn't viable. Olivia requested to be induced right away. The emergency physician asked the hospital administration for guidance and was told to do nothing until the patient developed an infection. The physician sent Olivia home, telling her to monitor her temperature and watch for bleeding, and that she should return to the hospital when those symptoms occurred. Olivia called in sick to work and returned to her home. Olivia sent her husband off to his job and called her mother and some friends for support; they came bringing supplies to handle the leaking fluids as well as food. They developed a schedule to have someone stay with Olivia until her status changed. Two days later, Olivia woke up with a fever of 101 degrees F. She returned to the hospital, and since she now had an infection, labor was induced. Olivia labored for over 24 hours with no progression, and it was then determined that she needed a dilation and evacuation. Therapeutic abortion is the most common treatment for women who are miscarrying in their second trimester. The procedure was performed successfully. But after having an infection for two days, experiencing labor for a day, and undergoing surgery, Olivia was exhausted emotionally and physically. She wound up staying home from work for two weeks.

1. Do you think the physician handled this case in the best way?

2. Do you think the hospital was correct to delay Olivia's procedure?

Introduction

Issues related to the beginning of life are especially challenging because they carry the extra burden of each person's personal values. There is widespread disagreement on when life begins and ends. However, all healthcare professionals must be willing to understand the topics and issues discussed by patients and their healthcare providers, and have knowledge of the federal court system and laws pertaining to reproduction, which are ever changing.

Fertility Treatments and Assisted Reproductive Technology

Some people desire children but are unable to achieve pregnancy. These people often seek medical assistance from their primary care provider or a fertility expert.

Fertility Treatments

Infertility is defined as a lack of conception despite having unprotected sexual intercourse for at least 12 months. Fertility treatments include procedures such as removing blockages in the reproductive system, prescribing medication to stimulate the ovaries to produce more eggs, and inseminating sperm directly into the uterus.

Fertility Drugs

Fertility drugs increase female hormones and the production of ova, thus enhancing the ability to conceive a pregnancy. However, the use of fertility drugs also increases the woman's chance of having a multiple birth. While the birth of twins to a woman who has taken fertility drugs is not unusual, there is also a chance that more eggs may be fertilized, resulting in more **embryos** (the stage is of pregnancy between the second and eighth week). There are cases where women have given birth to seven or eight children in one pregnancy.

Because there is little chance that all the babies of a multiple pregnancy will be healthy and/or survive, physicians may recommend that some of the embryos be removed through a procedure called **selective fetal reduction**. It is performed by entering the uterus and removing some of the embryos, leaving only one, two, or three (Figure 12.1). The removed embryos are usually destroyed, although there have been some attempts to freeze discarded embryos for later use in stem cell research.

Figure 12–1 Most triplets born in the United States are the result of the use of fertility drugs

Source: digitalskillet/Shutterstock

Artificial Insemination

Artificial insemination is the injection into the female's vagina of seminal fluid that contains male sperm from the woman's partner or from a donor. Artificial insemination is done for a variety of reasons such as when the male's sperm has a low count or the female has unreceptive cervical mucus.

Artificial insemination is a common practice, resulting in thousands of babies being conceived. There are few legal problems if the husband's or partner's semen is used. However, in some cases, women have used their deceased husband's semen, which has caused problems concerning the child's rights in relation to the father. For instance, should the child be entitled to receive Social Security benefits from the deceased father's Social Security account? In a 1995 case, a federal administration law judge ruled that a child conceived from frozen sperm and born more than 11 months after her father's death was entitled to receive Social Security benefits.

A donor is a person who donates his semen for the insemination of a woman who is not his wife. If the woman is married, problems may arise because the donor is unrelated to the woman. In response, many states have passed laws to address such issues, but none of these laws have prohibited the use of a donor's sperm.

Oklahoma was the first state to pass sperm donor legislation that provides guidelines for both the physician and the hospital regarding the issue of consent. The 1967 Oklahoma statute specifies that both the husband and wife must consent in writing to the procedure. The reasons for this strict mandate are twofold. First of all, if the physician touches the woman without her consent, it could result in a charge of battery. Second, the husband might claim that the wife had committed adultery because the semen was not his.

The most common legal and ethical concerns surrounding artificial insemination relate to the legitimacy of the child and the determination of who is responsible for the child's support. Several state statutes suggest that a child is legitimate if the husband consents to the use of donor sperm. These statutes also state that the donor is not responsible for the child's support.

The Oklahoma statute also clarifies that a child conceived through artificial insemination is legitimate and entitled to all the rights of a naturally conceived child. Thus, a child born as a result of a donor insemination must receive support from the nondonor husband. Similarly, California holds the husband responsible for child support, as if he were the natural father, if he consented in writing to the insemination procedure.

Assisted Reproductive Technology

Assisted reproductive technology is defined as fertility treatments in which either eggs or embryos are handled. In vitro fertilization and surrogate motherhood are two commonly used methods of assisted reproductive technology.

In Vitro Fertilization

Some couples have viable reproductive cells (ovum and sperm), but conception does not occur for them using the natural means of sexual intercourse. In this situation **in vitro fertilization**, also called IVF, has been helpful. In this process, ovum and sperm cells are combined outside of the woman's body (Figure 12.2). These cells are grown in a laboratory and later implanted into the woman's uterus. Until the early 1990s, this procedure was considered experimental, but this attitude has changed, and several insurers now pay for the procedure.

The physician needs to carefully explain the entire procedure to the couple. The process is quite invasive for the woman, involving daily injections or drugs, multiple imaging appointments, and surgery to remove the eggs. The couple should also be informed about what happens to the unused cells. In most cases, the unused cells, even when they are fertilized embryos, are destroyed. In some cases, the fertilized cells are not destroyed but frozen for possible future implantation.

Another potential issue in IVF is pregnancy with multiples, as described in the section on Fertility Treatments. Most IVF clinics advise implanting only one or two embryos, while others allow the parents to choose.

Surrogacy

Surrogacy is an arrangement between a woman who agrees to carry and birth a child for another person or couple. Most surrogacy arrangements are supported by a legal agreement.

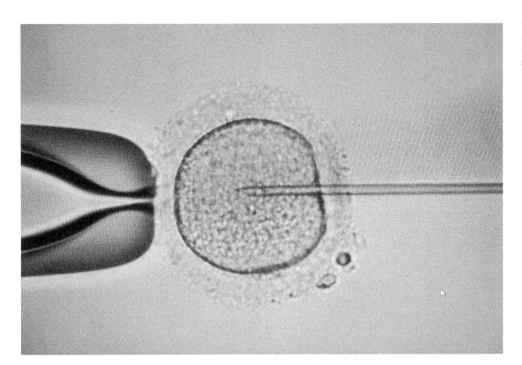

Figure 12–2 Sperm being injected into an ovum

Source: Martchan/Shutterstock

Surrogacy laws are generally divided into two categories: gestational surrogacy and traditional surrogacy. In gestational surrogacy, the surrogate mother is not genetically related to the child she carries, as the embryo is created using the intended parents' genetic material or donor gametes. Traditional surrogacy involves the surrogate providing her own egg and, therefore, a genetic connection to the child.

Laws governing surrogacy are primarily determined at the state level, and they can vary significantly from one state to another. Some states have clear and supportive surrogacy laws, making the process relatively straight-forward for intended parents and surrogates. Others may have more restrictive laws or lack specific legislation on surrogacy.

In states with clear surrogacy laws, surrogacy contracts are typically enforceable, and the intended parents are recognized as the legal parents from the moment of birth. In states without such laws, the legal process can be more uncertain and complicated, potentially requiring court orders to establish parentage. Surrogacy laws also address compensation for surrogates. Some states allow for reasonable compensation to cover a surrogate's expenses and inconvenience, while others have restrictions on the amount that can be paid to surrogates.

In states with supportive surrogacy laws, orders can be obtained that establish the intended parents as the legal parents before the child's birth. This can help streamline the administrative and legal processes following the birth. In states with restrictive surrogacy laws, intended parents may need to pursue adoption proceedings after the child's birth to establish their legal parentage, which can be a more complex and time-consuming process.

A problem can arise if the surrogate mother changes her mind when the baby is born, as occurred in the famous Baby M case. Most surrogacy agreements now stipulate that the woman who carries the baby cannot also donate the egg.

THE BABY M CASE

The Baby M case resulted from a surrogate parenting contract between Mary Beth Whitehead and Mr. and Mrs. Stern. Initially, Mrs. Whitehead had agreed to a surrogate motherhood arrangement with the Sterns —in which she would give up the child at birth—in return for $10,000. A Michigan attorney and a New York infertility clinic handled this agreement. Mrs. Whitehead was then inseminated with Mr. Stern's sperm in 1985. On March 7, 1986, Baby M was born. She was named Sarah Elizabeth by the Whiteheads and Melissa Elizabeth by the Sterns. The baby was turned over to the Sterns on March 30. The next day, the Sterns temporarily returned the baby when Mrs. Whitehead threatened suicide. On May 5, Mr. Stern went to the Whitehead residence with a court order to return the baby to his custody. However, Richard Whitehead had escaped to Florida with the child. Three months later, both the

Whiteheads and the child were located by a private detective, and Baby M was returned to the Sterns on July 31. Mrs. Whitehead was allowed visitation rights pending the outcome of the trial.

The New Jersey Supreme Court eventually granted parental rights to the natural mother, who had since remarried. However, the court granted the Sterns continuing custody of the baby, saying it was in the best interests of the child. The decision allowed overnight stays and vacations with the natural mother. The Sterns did not appeal this decision (*In re Baby M,* 537 A.2d 1227, N.J. 1988).

Legal and Ethical Considerations Regarding Fertility Treatments and Assisted Reproductive Technology

The ethical principles of beneficence and nonmaleficence, that is to do no harm or minimize harm, should be carefully observed and balanced in fertility treatments because of the risk of multiple pregnancy, especially when fertility drugs and artificial insemination are combined. The ethical as well as the legal duty is to ensure that patients give fully informed consent to the risks of multiple pregnancy and understand the risks of selective fetal reduction, which can include inadvertent loss of the entire pregnancy.

Many moral and ethical problems surround the issue of donor insemination. Records that contain the identity of the sperm donor are considered confidential and handled in the same manner as adoption papers; thus, they are not made a part of a public record. However, with the advent of consumer DNA kits, it is now impossible for sperm banks to keep donors' identities secret. Some clinics are revising their policies to make it clear that they won't share a donor's name, but they cannot guarantee anonymity. Other clinics are starting to offer "open ID" donor systems where donors are told that potential offspring may contact them when they turn 18.

While most states require that only a licensed physician should perform artificial insemination, this does not guarantee that it will be done in an ethical manner. In one famous case, a fertility physician was convicted for using his own sperm (*James v. Jacobson,* 6 F.3d 233, 4th Cir. 1993).

Med Tip

If the information is available, it is important to document in a child's health record if the child's conception involved artificial insemination. In some cases, the medical history of the donor is known and can be added to the child's record. However, the topic should never be discussed in front of the child. It is up to the parents to determine if they wish to talk to the child about their heritage.

While many babies have been born using frozen embryos, this procedure has created legal and ethical problems. Custody battles have challenged the "ownership" of the frozen embryos. In a 1989 divorce case, a Tennessee couple contested the ownership of frozen embryos in their divorce proceedings. The trial judge ruled that the embryos were children, and he awarded custody to the mother. However, the appellate court granted joint custody. The case then went to the Supreme Court in Tennessee, which ruled that if the parties did not agree, the embryos should be destroyed. In this case, the couple did not agree, and the embryos were destroyed (*Davis v. Davis,* 842 S.W.2d 588, Tenn. 1992).

Some attorneys suggest that a married couple should place their wishes in writing about what should happen to their embryos in the case of death or divorce. But there is still no guarantee that a court would accept the couple's decision, or that one partner could enforce an agreement, even if written, against the wishes of the other partner. Thus, the legal status of these embryos remains unclear.

There are moral and ethical issues involved in assisted reproductive technology. Many religions oppose selected technologies including IVF and surrogacy. Others accept technologies that use the eggs and sperm of married couples, but do not accept donor eggs or donor sperm.

And there can be mechanical issues that have to be resolved by the law. In 2023, a settlement was made in a suit against Chart, Inc., a manufacturer of cryopreservation tank that was being used by the Pacific Fertility Center in San Francisco. The tank held more than 2500 embryos and 1500 eggs at almost 200 degrees below zero Celsius. In 2018, the tank malfunctioned, and many of the embryos and eggs were damaged when they quickly thawed. The case, which was brought by three women and one couple, was settled for $15 million, with Chart liable for 90 percent and the fertility clinic liable for 10 percent.

Other issues that have reached the court include fertility clinics that have used the wrong sperm or embryos, with the parents finding out later that they are not biologically related to their child.

Ethical and legal problems surround surrogacy as well. Is it right to ask a surrogate mother to give up all rights to a baby she has carried for nine months? Does, or should, the child have an emotional or physical link to the surrogate mother? Can the contract between the surrogate mother and the parents be enforced?

There are two very strong opinions regarding surrogacy. Opponents of the practice state that they have a moral objection to commercial surrogacy. They believe it to be the equivalent of baby selling because the mother is often paid a fee over and above the costs of the delivery. However, there are many people who believe that surrogacy is a viable alternative for people who want to grow their family that way. For some people who want children, age restrictions and a limited number of adoptable children have limited their ability to have a family. In addition, infertility treatments can take both an emotional and a financial toll on those who use IVF.

Contraception and Sterilization

Contraception

Contraception is the prevention of the sperm from fertilizing the egg, which in turn, leads to pregnancy. A variety of methods are used by the male (such as condoms) and by the female (such as birth control pills), or both (use of multiple methods or fertility awareness). The decision for which contraception methods to use is a personal choice that may be influenced by health conditions, religious beliefs, and lifestyle. Therefore, contraception is any action taken to prevent pregnancy from occurring. Birth control drugs, intrauterine devices, condoms, a tubal ligation of the female, and a vasectomy of the male are all forms of contraceptive techniques. Abstinence from sexual intercourse and noncoital sex are also means of avoiding pregnancy.

Ethical considerations surrounding contraception often revolve around issues related to personal autonomy, religious beliefs, the sanctity of life, and societal values. One of the primary ethical arguments in favor of contraception is the principle of personal autonomy. This viewpoint emphasizes an individual's right to make decisions about their own body and reproductive choices.

Ethical concerns about contraception often intersect with religious beliefs. Many religious traditions hold diverse views on contraception, with some endorsing its use and others condemning it. For example, some branches of Christianity and Islam promote natural family planning methods while discouraging artificial contraceptives. Some ethical concerns about contraception are grounded in the belief that life begins at conception. Individuals who hold this view argue that certain contraceptive methods, such as the intrauterine device or the morning-after pill, may interfere with a fertilized egg's ability to implant in the uterus, effectively causing the termination of a potential life.

Society's values and priorities can also influence ethical considerations regarding contraception. On one hand, advocates argue that widespread access to contraception can lead to lower rates of unintended pregnancies, reduce the number of abortions, and contribute to overall family planning and socioeconomic stability. On the other hand, critics worry that easy access to contraception might encourage promiscuity or undermine traditional family structures.

Equity and justice issues play a significant role in ethical discussions around contraception. Access to contraception is not uniform, and disparities exist, often disproportionately affecting marginalized communities. Ethical considerations revolve around ensuring that everyone has equal access to contraception, regardless of their socioeconomic status, ethnicity, or geographic location.

The right to contraception is protected by two Supreme Court decisions: *Griswold v. Connecticut* and *Eisenstadt v. Baird*. In 1965, Connecticut's law banning contraceptives was challenged in a case known as *Griswold v. Connecticut*. Before 1965, Connecticut imposed a criminal penalty on any physician who prescribed contraceptives for a married woman whom the physician believed would be harmed by a pregnancy. The U.S. Supreme Court struck down the Connecticut law, declaring that it was the woman's constitutional right to privacy to use contraceptives if she wished (*Griswold v. Connecticut*, 381 U.S. 479, 1965). Justice William O. Douglas, who wrote the majority opinion, asked the question, "Would we allow the police to search the sacred precincts of marital bedrooms for telltale signs of the use of contraceptives?" This case effectively entitled married couples to use contraception legally.

In 1972, Massachusetts charged William Baird for giving away contraceptive vaginal foam to women at Boston University following a lecture on overpopulation. He was charged with a felony for giving contraception to unmarried women. In *Eisenstadt v. Baird,* the U.S. Supreme Court struck down the Massachusetts law because the distinction between married and unmarried women did not satisfy the "rational bases test." Writing for the majority opinion, Justice William J. Brennan, Jr. said "If the right of privacy means anything, it is the right of the individual, married or single, to be free from unwarranted governmental intrusion into matters so fundamentally affecting a person as the decision whether to bear or beget a child" (*Eisenstadt v. Baird.* 405 U.S. 438 (1972).

Emergency Contraception

Emergency contraception, also called the "morning-after pill" or "Plan B" contains a high dose of a contraceptive that can prevent a pregnancy if taken within 72 hours following intercourse. It works by releasing hormones that prevent ovulation and the implantation of a fertilized egg. There is divided opinion about the use of this pill by religious organizations and rape crisis counselors. Many will only allow the drug to be administered to nonovulating women. In most states, there is a requirement that all pharmacies carry this drug and allow it to be sold "over the counter," without a prescription. In some states, such as Arkansas, lawmakers passed a law that protects pharmacists from having to fill the prescription for the "morning-after pill" based on moral reasons. Rape crisis counselors believe that it is morally indefensible to deny this pill to rape victims.

The same drugs used for emergency contraception are used for a medical abortion, which is discussed in the "Abortion" section of this chapter.

Sterilization

Sterilization is the process of medically altering reproductive organs so as to terminate the ability to produce offspring. It may be the result of surgical intervention such as a vasectomy (surgical removal or tying of the vas deferens to prevent the passage of sperm) in the male or a tubal ligation (tying the uterine tubes) in the female. While sterilization is usually considered an elective or voluntary procedure, it can also be therapeutic, incidental, or involuntary. Sterilization can be incidental if the procedure is performed for another purpose, such as in the case of a hysterectomy for uterine carcinoma. It can also be a side effect of treatments such as chemotherapy.

Voluntary Sterilization

Voluntary or elective sterilization of competent persons presents few legal problems—although there are religions that oppose sterilization. Sterilization is the most popular method of contraception, or birth control, in the United States for married couples. However, the failure of sterilization procedures to prevent births is the most common reason for "wrongful conception" or "wrongful pregnancy" cases.

Sterilization is sought for a variety of reasons: economic, personal, therapeutic, and genetic. Some people, for economic reasons, do not want to assume the additional expense of raising a child. Others do not want any, or more, children. Sterilization may be sought if the mother's health is in danger. Genetic reasons for sterilization include the knowledge or potential of having a child with a genetic condition.

For most surgical operations, the patient's written consent is all that is necessary. Without consent, this procedure, or operation, could be considered battery. Because sterilization procedures are permanent, consenting individuals must be at least 21 years of age. Currently, no federal or state laws require consent from one spouse for another spouse's sterilization. But in cases of sterilization, many hospitals and physicians have policies that also require the consent of the spouse. However, in most cases, performing sterilization without spousal consent has presented very little legal risk. In a case in Oklahoma, a husband sued his wife's physician for performing sterilization without his consent. The court dismissed the suit and stated that he had not been legally harmed, because his marital rights do not include a childbearing wife (*Murray v. Vandevander,* 522 P.2d 302, Okla. Ct. App. 1974).

Therapeutic Sterilization

Therapeutic sterilization may be necessary if the mother's life or mental health is threatened. In some cases, it is necessary to remove a diseased organ, such as when a woman has uterine or ovarian cancer, in order to preserve the patient's life. This operation would result in sterilization, but it would be incidental and thus would not be classified as a sterilization procedure.

Involuntary Sterilization

In the United States, involuntary sterilization was practiced often in the past, targeting individuals with disabilities, mental illnesses, or those considered unfit to reproduce according to eugenic ideologies. However, such practices have been largely abandoned, and laws have been reformed to protect the rights and autonomy of most individuals. However, 31 states still have laws that allow forced sterilization in specific cases, some states allow children to be sterilized, and only two states have laws banning involuntary sterilization. Most of the people impacted by forced sterilization are under guardianship, or conservatorship, because they are intellectually disabled. For example, Idaho's Title 39, Chapter 39, Sterilization, states that a person who is functionally incapable of giving or withholding informed assent but for whom sterilization is in their best interest can be involuntarily sterilized based on the "nature and extent of the person's disability."

Negligence Suits Related to Sterilization

Many negligence claims involve cases in which a woman has become pregnant after a sterilization procedure. In an Oklahoma case, a physician assured his patient that she was sterile after he performed such a procedure in August 1980. She subsequently became pregnant and delivered a baby in October 1981. She successfully argued that because of the physician's negligence in performing the operation, she incurred $2,000 in medical expenses and would require $200,000 to raise the child. This case went to an appeals court, which ruled that parents could not recover the expenses for raising a healthy child, but they were entitled to the expenses resulting from the unplanned pregnancy (*Goforth v. Porter Med. Assoc., Inc.,* 755 P.2d 678, Okla. 1988).

In some cases, the negligence occurs during the sterilization procedure. For example, in *McLaughlin v. Cooke,* a physician was found negligent for mistakenly cutting an artery while performing a vasectomy. This error resulted in excessive bleeding and tissue necrosis, and the testicle eventually had to be removed. The physician was found to be negligent because he did not intervene soon enough to prevent the necrosis from happening (*McLaughlin v. Cooke,* 774 P.2d 1171, Wash. 1989).

Legal and Ethical Questions Regarding Contraception and Sterilization

Birth control is legal everywhere in the United States, but some states, such as Arizona, Georgia, and South Dakota, allow pharmacists to refuse to dispense contraceptives, 12 states allow some healthcare providers to refuse to provider services related to contraception, and 18 states allow some healthcare providers to refuse to provide sterilization procedures.

Regardless of one's religious beliefs, healthcare professionals must realize that sterilization and birth control present ethical issues because of the risks surrounding these procedures. The ethical issues surrounding contraception and sterilization include the following:

- Is it morally acceptable for public schools, receiving federal and state funding, to dispense contraceptive devices, such as condoms, and information?

- Some courts suggest that habitual and violent sex offenders should be ordered to undergo sterilization. Is this morally and ethically acceptable?

- Some people believe that women who receive public funds such as Medicaid should not continue to have children and thus increase the welfare rolls. Is it ethical and morally acceptable to require these women to seek sterilization before they are allowed benefits?

- Many hospitals refuse to allow sterilization procedures on their premises. What is the ethical implication of this restriction if this is the only hospital in the area?

- Some people believe that intellectually disabled women should be sterilized to prevent a pregnancy from occurring if they have sexual intercourse. Is this a violation of a woman's rights?

These are some of the questions and issues that patients, physicians, other healthcare professionals, and policymakers are considering. There are no easy answers. Some people refuse the use of any contraceptive method for any reason, based on their religious beliefs. Others believe that women should have complete autonomy over their reproductive choices. Some people fall in the middle.

Abortion

An issue that causes great controversy is the question of when life begins. Many people and various religions believe that life takes place at the moment of conception; therefore, any interference with this process, such as emergency contraception or abortion, is the wrongful taking of another's life. Others believe that life does not begin until 14 days after the egg and sperm unite to form an embryo. During this time, the embryo is attached to the uterine wall. Some claim that life begins when the embryo becomes a **fetus** at about the third month of development, or around the ninth week of pregnancy. At this time, the fetus starts to develop organs and has a pronounced heartbeat and a functioning brain. Many feel that life does not begin until the fetus is **viable** (able to survive outside the uterus), which is generally understood to mean between 22 and 24 weeks of pregnancy. Still others claim that life does not begin until birth occurs. There are perhaps as many claims about when life begins as there are weeks in the time before birth occurs, or the **gestational period**, which is usually around 40 weeks.

This controversy has created an ethical dilemma for many medical professionals. Physicians and other healthcare workers whose religious or personal beliefs lead them to oppose abortion cannot counsel women on ending a pregnancy, assist at abortions, or in any way terminate a pregnancy. Their religious beliefs must be respected by coworkers.

Abortion is the termination of a pregnancy. An abortion may be spontaneous or induced. A **spontaneous abortion** is one that occurs naturally without any interference. It is also referred to by the layperson as a *miscarriage*. A spontaneous abortion can result from an illness or injury of the mother, her physical inability to bear a child, or other causes. An **induced abortion**, or one that is caused by artificial means such as medications (often called Plan B) or surgical procedures, is used to save the life of the mother and/or to end the pregnancy.

The History of Abortion Law in United States

Under common law in the 19th century, abortions performed before the first fetal movements, which occur at or about six weeks, were not illegal. However, legal and illegal abortions were being performed that were painful and often resulted in the mother's death. The AMA adopted an antiabortion position in 1959, which was quite influential and resulted in political action to control abortions. States began passing statutes that made induced abortions a crime, whether they occurred before or after fetal movements, unless they were performed to save the mother's life.

In the 1960s and 1970s, states amended these laws to permit induced abortion only if the physical or mental health of the mother was threatened, if the child was at serious risk of congenital anomalies, or when the pregnancy was the result of a rape or incest. The "pro-choice" and "pro-life" movements emerged, with activists advocating for and against abortion rights.

Roe v. Wade and Subsequent Rulings

In 1973, the case of *Roe v. Wade* reached the U.S. Supreme Court. The decision declared a Texas criminal abortion law, which prohibited all abortions not necessary to save the life of the mother, to be a violation of the woman's right to privacy under the Fourteenth Amendment of the Constitution (*Roe v. Wade*, 410 U.S. 113, 1973). Jane Roe (a pseudonym), a single pregnant woman, challenged the District Attorney of Dallas County, Henry Wade, when she believed that her "right to privacy" under the Fourteenth Amendment was violated by a Texas antiabortion statute. This 1973 case gave strength to the argument that a woman should be allowed the right to have privacy over matters that relate to her own body, including pregnancy. While the Supreme Court refused to determine when life begins, it did recognize that states would have an interest in protecting the potential lives of their citizens. Therefore, the Court tried to clarify the extent to which states can regulate and even prohibit abortion. To set up guidelines, the Supreme Court adopted a three-step process relating to the three trimesters of pregnancy:

1. ***First trimester***—During the first three months of pregnancy, the decision to have an abortion is between the woman and her physician. The state may, however, require that the physician be licensed in that state. During the first trimester, the fetus is generally not viable, or able to live outside of the uterus.

2. ***Second trimester***—During the second three months of pregnancy, the court determined, "the State, promoting its interest in the health of the mother, may, if it chooses, regulate the abortion procedure in ways that are reasonably related to maternal health." If the fetus is viable, which occurs at around six months, the Supreme Court believes the states have a compelling interest in the life of the unborn child, and so abortions could be prohibited at this stage except when necessary to preserve the life or health of the mother.

3. ***Third trimester***—The Supreme Court determined that by the time the final stage of pregnancy (seventh through the ninth month) has been reached, the state has a compelling interest in the unborn child. This interest would override the woman's right to privacy and, therefore, justify stringent regulation of and even prohibit *all* abortions except to save the life of the mother or to protect maternal health.

Dobbs v. Jackson Women's Health Organization and Current Changes to State Laws

On June 24, 2022, the United States Supreme Court announced its decision in the case of *Dobbs v. Jackson Women's Health Organization*. The case concerned the constitutionality of a 2018 Mississippi state law that banned most abortion operations after the first 15 weeks of pregnancy. The court upheld the ruling, which effectively overturned *Roe v. Wade* and the constitutional right to abortion that had taken precedence for 50 years.

After that ruling, the states now decide their own positions on abortion. Some states have enacted new restrictions and bans, and others have continued to affirm the right of women to privacy in medical decisions. As of late 2023, states range from having no restriction on abortion (e.g., Oregon, Vermont, and Alaska), to restrictions from 22 weeks to viability (e.g., California, Wyoming, Pennsylvania, Maine), to restrictions from 6–18 weeks, which includes the use of emergency contraception for a medical abortion (e.g., Utah, Arizona, North Carolina, Florida), to a complete ban on abortion (e.g., Idaho, Texas, both Dakotas, Mississippi, Tennessee, West Virginia). All states in the last category allow for exceptions to save the life of the mother, and some allow abortion if the pregnancy is the result of rape or incest.

Overall, elective abortions are now illegal in almost a third of the U.S. states. Healthcare for pregnant patients and their healthcare providers in these states has become difficult. The standard of care for pregnancy complications such as ectopic pregnancy, premature rupture of membranes, and spontaneous miscarriage is being scrutinized, resulting in delays or denials of care. There have been cases where women experiencing pregnancy complications have been turned away by hospitals for fear of litigation. Others have had to wait until they or their pregnancy has deteriorated further to receive an abortion. Exceptions to the abortion bans are not clear, and many providers are concerned that if they provide a medically indicated abortion, they will be sued, lose their medical license, or even be charged with a felony.

Med Tip

If you work with women of child-bearing age, it is wise to have a fundamental understanding of your state's laws about abortion.

It is difficult to track the number of abortions in the United States. In 2020 (before the *Dobbs* decision), the CDC estimated there were around 620,000 abortions, while the Guttmacher Institute estimated 930,000. Since the *Dobbs* ruling, it appears as though the number of legal abortions increased in the United States as a whole, but it has decreased sharply in states with strict limits or total bans on abortion.

Additional Issues Concerning Abortion

Incompetent Persons

Difficult issues surround situations in which incompetent persons may be subjected to unplanned or unwanted pregnancies. Many believe that if the incompetent person were able to speak for herself, she would not wish to be pregnant as a result of incest or rape. In some of these cases, abortions have been performed using a welfare agency as the *guardian ad litem* (a guardian appointed by the court to speak on behalf of the incapacitated party). In a 1987 case, a profoundly cognitively impaired woman became pregnant as a result of a sexual attack while she was a resident in a group home. The attacker was unknown. In this case, the *guardian ad litem*, rather than the girl's mother, spoke on behalf of the patient because the mother and daughter had little contact. The family court authorized an abortion in this case (*In re Doe*, 533 A.2d 523 R.I., 1987).

Legal Standing of the Fetus

In 2004, the U.S. Congress passed a law called the Unborn Victims of Violence Act. This law is designed to provide legal penalties for any harm that is done to an unborn child at federal facilities such as military bases or in crimes that cross state lines. The law treats all unborn life as a person.

Almost 40 states have statutes that grant varying degrees of legal standing to a fetus. These are statutes that relate to criminal matters, such as murder and homicide, and permit civil wrongful-death suits.

Employees' Right to Refuse to Participate in Abortions

Hospital employees have the right to refuse to participate in performing an abortion, and a hospital cannot dismiss the employee for insubordination. An employee can abstain from assisting in an abortion procedure as a matter of conscience or religious conviction.

Med Tip

Healthcare professionals must keep in mind that people have very strong, and often differing, viewpoints about abortion. Their viewpoints must be respected even when they differ from the employee's viewpoint. However, no one should be required to participate in an action, such as abortion, if it is against their beliefs.

EMTALA

An issue for hospitals in states with abortion bans is the Emergency Medical Treatment and Labor Act (EMTALA), a federal law that requires hospitals to treat people with emergent conditions or risk losing funding from federal programs such as Medicare and Medicaid. Some physicians have urged their hospitals to evoke EMTALA when a pregnant women's health is in jeopardy.

Ethical Issues Regarding Abortion

Abortion raises a multitude of ethical issues, even for those who believe abortion, in general, should be legal. Two seminal cases are presented, along with a discussion of the conscience clause when applied to abortion services.

Baby Doe Regulations

In the 1980s, a tiny baby in Bloomington, Indiana, was born with Down syndrome and other disabilities. This baby, known as Baby Doe, was born with a hole between the trachea and the esophagus, which made normal feeding impossible. The parents refused to grant consent for surgery that would correct the blockage. The hospital went to court to get permission to perform life-saving surgery on the baby's esophagus. The court refused to grant the request, stating that it was the parents' right to make medical decisions for their baby. However, the court did appoint a public guardian who could appeal the ruling on behalf of the baby. Baby Doe died before the public guardian was able to take the case to the Supreme Court.

This was considered to be a case of withholding treatment rather than of mercy killing or euthanasia, because food, water, and repair of the medical condition were withheld. The belief is that the treatment would not have been withheld if the baby had been less disabled.

The Baby Doe case became national news. The public protested about withholding treatment from a disabled (Down syndrome) infant. As a result, Congress enacted legislation, the **Child Abuse Prevention and Treatment Act** of 1987, which prohibited the withholding of medical treatment solely because the infant was disabled. The government entered the picture with legislation preventing any healthcare providers, such as hospitals, from receiving federal financial aid if they discriminated against infants with disabilities. In other words, the same medical treatment that is given to nondisabled infants must also be given to disabled infants. Because most, if not all, hospitals receive some government aid, this law went into effect in virtually all hospitals. Notices about the Baby Doe regulation must now be posted in all maternity and pediatric wards as well as in neonatal intensive care units. In addition, a hotline telephone number is also posted so that anyone can call with information about life-saving measures being withheld from a baby.

This law has been changed slightly to allow parents to have some say in the medical treatment of their infant with disabilities.

There are many ethical questions that arise out of Baby Doe regulations, such as the following examples:

- Should strangers become the advocates for disabled infants' medical treatments if they are in disagreement with the parents' decisions?
- Would it be better to spare the infant a life that may include suffering and future surgical procedures?
- Should all modern technology that is available to save life be used no matter what the consequences are for the child?

In a more positive outlook, it should be noted that there are thousands of children born with Down syndrome who are able to live a full and meaningful life.

In the Matter of Baby K

Baby K was born with anencephaly (missing a brain and spinal cord), and her mother requested that her baby daughter receive a mechanical ventilator to assist with breathing. The doctors had recommended that life-saving measures not be used because the infant could not see, hear, or interact with her environment. They further recommended that Baby K only be given nutrition, in fluid forms, and kept warm. Baby K survived longer than other infants with anencephaly, and even though unconscious, she was kept alive in a nursing home. She had several episodes of difficulty breathing and was transferred to a hospital for treatment. Both the hospital and Baby K's father joined in a lawsuit against the mother to request that aggressive life-saving measures be discontinued for the child.

Baby K's mother disagreed with the hospital's wishes to withhold life-saving measures such as respiratory assistance. She requested that the hospital follow the guidelines of the federal law, Emergency Medical Treatment and Active Labor Act (EMTALA), which prohibited hospitals from "dumping" patients who are unable to pay for their care. The court upheld the mother's request. It stated that, while they understood the physicians' dilemma when faced with having to provide medical care that they consider to be morally and ethically incorrect, nevertheless, the statute (EMTALA) had to be upheld (*Matter of Baby K,* 16 F.3d 590, 4th Cir. 1994).

Conscience Clause in Contraception and Abortion

Some healthcare professionals have embraced a conscience clause by refusing to provide medication or care when their religious beliefs are challenged. In Texas, a pharmacist refused to sell the morning-after pill to a rape victim. In Chicago, an ambulance driver refused to drive a patient for an abortion. And in California, a gay woman seeking artificial insemination was turned away by fertility specialists. These cases have caused legal and even political battles. The patients filed lawsuits and complaints, and the workers cited religious discrimination after being fired or disciplined. Patient advocates, and some members of the general public, point out that medicine has a long tradition of healers putting the needs of their patients first. There is no simple answer to this dilemma.

Some anesthesiologists are refusing to assist in sterilization procedures. Occasionally a respiratory therapist has refused to remove ventilators from terminally ill patients. Some gynecologists refuse to prescribe contraceptives. In every case, there is some other healthcare professional who can provide the patient service. But hospital administrators, providers, lawyers, ethicists, and patient advocates are all trying to balance each person's conflicting rights as well as defuse this contentious situation. There are many observers who say that a patient's needs must come first. On the other hand, the rights of employees to practice their religion are also of paramount importance. At present, there is no easy or clear answer to this dilemma.

Med Tip

Always clarify your own values and beliefs with your employer when you are hired. Everyone has the right to religious freedom. Most employers want to know ahead of time if they need to make adjustments to assignments.

Genetic Disorders

The science of genetics is the study of heredity and its variations. It describes the biological influence that parents have on their offspring. Genetic disorders are caused by changes in the normal DNA sequence. Genetic disorders can be caused by a mutation in one gene, multiple genes, or by environmental factors. Some genetic mutations can be inherited from one or both parents. Other mutations are acquired during a person's life either randomly or due to environmental exposure (such as to cigarette smoke). Many cancers are caused by genetic mutations, only a few of which have been identified so far, such as the *BRCA1* and *BRCA2* mutations that cause an increased likelihood of breast and ovarian cancer in women.

Over 10,000 human diseases have been identified as being caused by single defective gene. These include Tay-Sachs disease, sickle-cell disease, and cystic fibrosis. In these recessive diseases, each parent must pass on a copy of the single defective gene for the child to inherit the disease (Figure 12.3). If only one copy of the defective gene is passed on, then the child will be a carrier of the defective gene but will not have clinical symptoms of the disorder. Statistically, 24 percent of offspring will be affected by the disorder. Therefore, persons who carry the recessive gene for these disorders can be tested before having children so they can make decisions accordingly. Other conditions for which genetic testing is available include Huntington's disease, retinoblastoma, Down syndrome, and phenylketonuria (PKU). These and other hereditary disorders are described in Table 12.1.

Genetic counseling is usually performed by geneticists who have a master's or higher degree, or by physician geneticists who are medical doctors with special training in genetics. Genetic counselors meet with prospective parents before pregnancy occurs to discuss the potential for passing on a defective gene (see Figure 12.3).

Patients can use the results of genetic testing to plan a pregnancy that will not result in a child with an inherited disorder. Patients with familial diseases can use IVF combined with **preimplantation genetic diagnosis**, also called PGD, to screen for certain diseases. Doctors examine several of the parents' embryos to determine which ones do not carry the familial disorder. An embryo without the defective gene is implanted in the mother and the pregnancy hopefully develops normally and results in the birth of a healthy child.

There are a growing number of parents who are electing to use PGD to test for genes that cause diseases that are either untreatable or severe. Diseases that can be detected with PGD include cystic fibrosis, sickle-cell disease, and Huntington's disease.

Prenatal Testing

The most common means of genetic testing during a pregnancy is through **amniocentesis**. During an amniocentesis, the pregnant patient is scanned by ultrasound to find a pocket of amniotic fluid. A needle

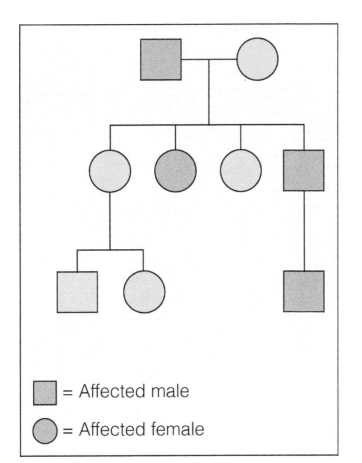

Figure 12–3 Inheritance of recessive genetic disorders

Source: PEARSON, NURSING: A CONCEPT-BASED APPROACH TO LEARNING, VOLUME 1, 4th Ed., ©2023, Figure 19-14, pg. 1524.

■ = Affected male

● = Affected female

Table 12–1 Genetic Disorders

Disorder	Characteristics
Cooley's anemia	Rare form of anemia or reduction of red blood cells. More common in people of Mediterranean origin.
Cystic fibrosis	Disorder of exocrine glands causing an excessive production of thick mucus. Affects the respiratory system and organs such as the pancreas.
Down syndrome	A condition that causes moderate to severe cognitive impairment. The child may have a sloping forehead, flat nose, low-set eyes, and general short stature. More commonly seen when the mother is over 40.
Duchenne muscular dystrophy	A progressive wasting-away of muscles. May also have heart and respiratory problems. Caused by a recessive gene and is more common in boys.
Huntington's disease	A condition in which there are bizarre involuntary movements. May have progressive mental and physical disturbances.
Phenylketonuria (PKU)	A metabolic disorder in infants that, if untreated, can result in cognitive impairment. Is treated with a special diet. Most states require a screening test for PKU. Affects mainly people of European heritage.
Retinoblastoma	A cancerous tumor of the eye that is fatal if untreated.
Sickle-cell disease	Severe, chronic, incurable disorder that results in anemia and causes joint pain, chronic weakness, and infections. Occurs more commonly in people of Mediterranean and African heritage.
Tay-Sachs disease	A deficiency of an enzyme that leads to cognitive impairment and blindness. Transferred by a recessive gene and more commonly found in families of Eastern European Jewish descent. Death generally occurs before the age of 4.

Figure 12–4 Amniocentesis

Source: PEARSON, NURSING:
A CONCEPT-BASED APPROACH
TO LEARNING, VOLUME 2, 4th Ed.,
©2023, Figure 33-32 pg. 2270.

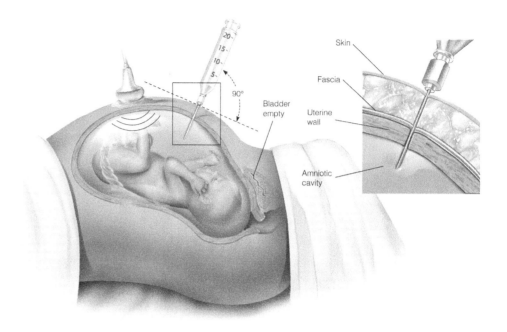

is then inserted into the uterine cavity to withdraw amniotic fluid (Figure 12.4). This fluid is tested for the presence of genetic defects such as Tay-Sachs disease and Down syndrome. Before the procedure, physicians must discuss all the risks with the patient, such as the risk of damage to the fetus and of causing early labor. A consent form must be signed, as the procedure is invasive.

Med Tip

Genetic testing is not always performed for the purpose of termination of a pregnancy. In many cases, parents are better able to plan for the care of the child if they have advanced information about the potential for genetic disorders.

Savior Siblings

Savior siblings are children who are conceived specifically to provide tissue (usually umbilical cord blood or bone marrow) to save the life of an older sibling who has a genetic disorder. Now that IVF and PGD are widely available, most parents who want a savior sibling are able to determine which embryos to use for conception. Prior to the advent of PGD, there were cases where amniocentesis was used to determine whether the fetus had the familial disorder, and abortion was used if the fetus tested positive.

The Uniform Anatomical Gift Act has implemented legal safeguards to prevent women from becoming pregnant with the specific purpose of aborting the fetus to sell the fetal tissues or organs or donate them to a relative. (See Chapter 5 for more information on the Uniform Anatomical Gift Act.)

Genetic Testing of Newborns

It is estimated that between 3 and 5 percent of all newborns have a hereditary or congenital disorder, and one-fourth of all hospitalizations and deaths among babies are because of these disorders. Routine genetic screening on newborns has become standard in many hospitals.

Almost all states have passed laws requiring PKU testing on infants immediately after birth so that treatment, such as dietary restrictions, can begin right away. PKU is a relatively rare (5.4 per 100,000 infants) metabolic disease that accounts for only 0.8 percent of all intellectually disabled people. Without this treatment, babies with PKU face cognitive impairment, and even death.

In addition, federally funded voluntary screening centers exist to screen for sickle-cell disease. Donors of semen for artificial insemination are routinely screened to rule out genetic diseases.

Ethical Questions Regarding Genetic Testing

Genetic testing and counseling have provided assistance for parents who wish to make rational decisions regarding their family planning. Medical researchers believe that if all people who are carriers of diseases caused by a dominant gene, such as Huntington's disease, produced no children with the disease, then the disease would become eradicated. Many ethical and moral questions arise when examining these issues:

- Do parents have the right to be informed of all the results of a genetic test? The duty of the physician *is* to inform the patient of all the results of testing. This is especially difficult for some physicians who oppose abortion, because they know that there is a likelihood the parents may seek an abortion if the testing indicates a baby with a genetic disorder.

- It is now almost routine to tell patients that genetic testing might uncover unexpected unpleasantness, such as the discovery that they might be at risk for Alzheimer's disease, but that they will be given all the information if they ask. Occasionally, a case of "misidentified paternity" (incorrect identity of the father) is discovered in this type of testing.

- Does a person have a right to have children who are likely to be impaired? For example, after having a series of tests, including an amniocentesis, a woman may be informed that the baby she is carrying will be born with a neural tube defect such as spina bifida. Because this child will have a difficult life, including painful surgeries, the mother may be advised to abort. But many people who are opposed to abortion would elect to deliver the baby and spend the time during pregnancy preparing to care for their child. There is no legal sanction either for or against abortion in this case. Each decision must be based on the free choice of the parents depending on the state in which they live.

- Is society ever justified in requiring people to submit to genetic screening and counseling?

- Do a small number of people with the potential for a disease or genetic condition, such as PKU, justify the expense of testing all babies?

- Should public funds be used to pay for genetic testing when the parents are unable to pay? Many people believe that indigent patients should have the same access to genetic testing that the rest of the population has. However, if genetic problems are discovered, according to the Hyde Amendment, public funds cannot be used to pay for an abortion.

- Should we limit the types of diseases or disorders that can be tested for, using a test such as PKU? For example, is using the test to determine a predisposition for cancer of the same importance as testing for mild skin conditions and obesity?

- These and other difficult questions face the parents and physicians every time genetic testing is performed.

Wrongful-Life Suits and Safe Haven Laws

Wrongful Life

In some cases, a baby is born with severe anomalies that greatly affect the quality of life of the child. A wrongful-birth claim or lawsuit is often brought against a physician or laboratory by the parents of a child born with these genetic defects. The parents may claim that they were not informed in a timely fashion that their child might have defects. They believe that this lack of information meant that they did not have the option of deciding whether to abort the child.

Some lawsuits are also brought when sterilization has failed. Parents have brought lawsuits against a physician or laboratory for breach of duty when they negligently failed to inform the parents of a failed sterilization. In general, the courts have rejected wrongful-life lawsuits brought against hospitals or physicians by children with genetic defects who claim they were injured by the action of being born.

The courts reason that it is impossible to assess a dollar amount of damages for being alive as opposed to being dead.

Smith v. Cote is an example of such a case. The court awarded damages for wrongful birth but not for wrongful life. The court ruled that the physician was negligent by failing to test for the mother's exposure to rubella and to inform her of the potential for congenital anomalies. Rubella in pregnant women during the first trimester can cause disorders, such as deafness, in the fetus. In this case, the mother claimed that she might have sought an abortion if she had known all the facts surrounding her pregnancy. However, the court refused to award the child damages for the "wrong" of being born (*Smith v. Cote*, 513 A.2d 341 N.H., 1986).

Med Tip

It is important for all healthcare workers to take the issue of their own health seriously. They need to alert their employer if they contract a contagious disease such as rubella, which could cause serious complications if a pregnant patient or coworker were to become infected.

Wrongful Conception/Wrongful Pregnancy

In 2011, a woman in Washington went to a federally funded healthcare clinic for her contraceptive shot of DepoProvera. The clinic mistakenly gave her a flu shot instead of the contraceptive shot, and she gave birth to a child with a condition that causes cognitive delays, epilepsy, vision problem, and speech/language delays. After a trial in 2020, a U.S. District Judge awarded the $7.5 million to the child and $2.5 million to the parents for medical and educational expenses, damages for the parents, and other expenses. In 2022, the Washington Supreme Court stated that under the law, it was correct for the district judge to award extraordinary damages in this case of wrongful life (*Pacheco v. United States*, 21 F.4th 1183 (9th Cir. 2022).

A 1991 case in New Mexico presented many ethical concerns. In this case, the parents of a healthy baby were awarded the cost of raising the child to adulthood when they conceived a child after an unsuccessful tubal ligation (sterilization). The physician ligated (tied) only one of the mother's tubes and failed to inform her of this negligence (*Lovelace Medical Ctr. v. Mendez*, 805 P.2d 603, N.M. 1991).

In another case, a mother of *advanced maternal age* (a medical term for a pregnant woman over age 35), who was not advised by her doctor that her age put her unborn child at a greater risk for genetic disorders, sued when she gave birth to a child with Down syndrome. The court found in favor of the family to seek financial damages for the added cost of raising a child with a disability. Wrongful-birth lawsuits are increasingly awarding financial damages to parents. But wrongful-life lawsuits, in which the disabled children sue the physicians, have generally been rejected by the courts.

Med Tip

The best method to avoid a wrongful conception/wrongful pregnancy lawsuit is for the physician to advise the parents, in writing, that there are always a small number of failures in these procedures.

Safe Haven Laws

Safe Haven Laws create a safe alternative to leaving unwanted babies in unsafe places such as on doorsteps and in dumpsters. All 50 states have these laws, which allow a parent to voluntarily give up custody of an infant 31 days or younger to a hospital emergency department (ED) or a police or fire station. For example, in Connecticut an ED nurse will talk to the parent about the child's medical history. The ED will also give the parent information on how to contact the Department of Children and Families (DCF) services. The infant is then turned over to DCF who are required by law to contact both parents of its intent to keep custody of the child and seek termination of parental rights. If the parents' names or

Figure 12–5 Safe Haven Baby Box installed at an Indiana fire station

Source: Richard Ellis/Alamy Stock Photo

addresses are unknown then DCF will place a newspaper notice. The parent(s) can change their mind and try to regain custody, but they must act quickly and make a request to the court for an attorney to represent them. The court will schedule a hearing within 30 days of DCF's application, and the termination of parental rights can be granted at the first hearing. DCF will attempt to place the child for adoption within 30 days. Thirteen states also allow mothers to surrender their babies anonymously in Safe Haven Baby Boxes. These are installed mostly at fire stations (Figure 12.5).

These laws are meant to protect babies whose parent(s) are unable to care for them. The laws do not provide protection to parents if abuse or neglect has already occurred. It also does not allow for the abandonment of older children. States vary on administration of these laws.

Med Tip

It's important to know the Safe Haven Law in your state. These laws vary somewhat from state to state.

Chapter 12 Review

Points to Ponder

1. What do you say to a patient who asks for family planning advice?

2. How would you react to a coworker who tells you she has recently had an abortion?

3. Can you relate to the dilemma faced by a surrogate mother who is giving up her baby to the contractual parents? Why or why not?

4. What would you say to a person who does not share your religious or moral views concerning abortion?

5. What are some of the daily issues faced by parents who have children born with hereditary disorders?

6. In your opinion, should cells or tissue from aborted fetuses be used in the treatment of diseased or disabled persons? Why or why not?

Discussion Questions

1. Discuss the ethics of minors having the same access to contraceptives as adults.

2. Should there be mandatory testing for genetically transmitted diseases? Why or why not?

3. Discuss the effects of U.S. Supreme Court decisions relating to abortion since *Dobbs v. Jackson Women's Health Organization.*

4. What are the ethical implications relating to abortion?

5. What are some of the ethical implications relating to fertility drugs?

6. Discuss the ethical implications relating to an artificial insemination donor.

7. How is the traditional notion of family challenged by the new reproductive technologies?

8. Should genetic counseling include recommendations by the medical personnel?

Review Challenge

Short Answer Questions

1. What might you say to parents who are going through IVF and ask to have four embryos implanted?

2. What are some of the ethical issues surrounding sterilization?

3. What consent is required for sterilization?

4. Why is selective reduction or the "harvesting" of embryos used?

5. What are some of the considerations when using a surrogate mother?

6. Explain the difference between contraception and emergency contraception.

7. What is the difference between an embryo and a fetus?

8. What are the current laws in your state regarding abortion?

9. In your opinion, is it ever proper to hasten the death of a severely disabled baby? Explain your answer.

_____

_____

_____

_____

10. Discuss the ethics of parents having a savior sibling.

_____

_____

_____

_____

_____

Matching

Match the responses in column B with the correct term in column A.

COLUMN A

_____ **1.** fetus

_____ **2.** embryo

_____ **3.** in vitro fertilization

_____ **4.** anencephaly

_____ **5.** genetics

_____ **6.** amniocentesis

_____ **7.** SFR

_____ **8.** surrogate

_____ **9.** gestation period

_____ **10.** viable

COLUMN B

a. time before birth during the development of the fetus

b. test for genetic disorders

c. born without a brain and spinal cord

d. able to survive

e. biological influence of parents on their offspring

f. second to twelfth week of development

g. selective fetal reduction

h. ovum and sperm combined outside of the mother's body

i. substitute

j. third month of development until birth

Multiple Choice

Select the one best answer to the following statements.

1. The current laws relating to artificial insemination
   a. do not forbid artificial insemination.
   b. state that the donor father must provide a portion of the child's support.
   c. provide for the records that relate to the donor to remain open.
   d. clarify the child's legitimacy.
   e. all of the above

2. The Baby M case is an example of
   a. problems encountered with fertility drugs.
   b. problems relating to the practice of eugenics.
   c. problems encountered as a result of the use of a surrogate.
   d. problems encountered because of involuntary sterilization.
   e. problems encountered as a result of genetics.

3. An ethical issue or issues relating to contraception is/are
   a. dispensing contraceptives in schools receiving federal funds.
   b. requiring sex offenders to undergo sterilization.
   c. providing contraceptives for women on Medicaid.
   d. sterilization of intellectually disabled women.
   e. all of the above

4. A miscarriage is the same thing as a/an
   a. induced abortion.
   b. spontaneous abortion.
   c. drug-induced abortion.
   d. conscience clause.
   e. therapeutic abortion.

5. A genetic disorder that causes severe joint pain, chronic weakness, and infections and is more prevalent in people of African heritage is
   a. Tay-Sachs disease.
   b. retinoblastoma.
   c. cystic fibrosis.
   d. sickle-cell disease.
   e. Cooley's anemia.

6. Genetic testing of the newborn is required by law for
   a. Tay-Sachs disease.
   b. phenylketonuria.
   c. retinoblastoma.
   d. Down syndrome.
   e. Cooley's anemia.

7. A disease that could cause serious birth anomalies in an unborn child if the pregnant mother is exposed to it during her pregnancy is

   a. Down syndrome.

   b. Huntington's disease.

   c. cystic fibrosis.

   d. rubella.

   e. retinoblastoma.

8. Withdrawing a small amount of amniotic fluid from the uterus for genetic testing is called

   a. induced abortion.

   b. eugenics.

   c. amniocentesis.

   d. spontaneous abortion.

   e. drug-induced abortion.

9. A person who is appointed by the court to defend a lawsuit on behalf of an incapacitated person is a/an

   a. donor.

   b. surrogate.

   c. district attorney.

   d. savior sibling.

   e. *guardian ad litem.*

10. Tay-Sachs disease

   a. results from an enzyme deficiency.

   b. is more common among people of Eastern European descent.

   c. is curable if diagnosed early.

   d. a, b, and c

   e. a and b only

Discussion Cases

1. Between the years 1956 and 1970, 10,000 children were admitted to Willowbrook State Hospital, an institution for cognitively impaired children on Staten Island in New York. The hospital experienced a large number of infectious diseases among its patients. Conditions at the hospital were not good, and most children suffered from hepatitis, measles, and parasitic and respiratory infections. Hepatitis, in particular, was a problem as many of the children were not toilet-trained and the disease was spread through an oral–intestinal route. Researchers determined that nearly all susceptible children became infected with hepatitis during their first year at the hospital.

   Almost 800 were entered into a research project to gain information about hepatitis with the hopes of eventually developing an immunization against the disease. All the parents of the children in the research project granted written consent. The children were injected with the same strain of hepatitis that was already prevalent in the hospital.

   The physician-researchers in charge of the project received intense criticism for subjecting the children to the research. The researchers defended their actions by stating the following:

   a. The children that were used as subjects were unharmed or, at least, not made any more ill than they already were.

   b. The children may have even benefitted because they were placed on an isolated unit and thus were not exposed to the other infectious diseases.

   c. The children in the study may have had a subclinical infection, which would render them immune to the hepatitis virus.

   d. The children may have been better off as a result of the research because the study added to the growth of information about the disease.

   e. All the parents had given their informed consent.

The medical community was outraged about the experiment and raised the following objections:

   a. Cognitively impaired persons, especially children, should not be used for research experimentation.

   b. The children are unable to defend or speak for themselves.

   c. There is a greater possibility of abuse with children than with adults.

   d. The parents may have been coerced to grant consent, as the hospital was full and there was only space to admit children into the hepatitis unit.

   e. The experiment did not appear to be therapeutic.

   f. The benefits to the hospital and the community at large were minimal.

   g. The experiments were designed to confirm *existing* studies about the effects of gamma globulin immunization for hepatitis.

   h. Researchers withheld from the nonresearch children (control group) an inoculation that may have been effective against hepatitis.

Because the 800 children were isolated from other children, they did not acquire infectious diseases prevalent at the time. Ultimately, the claim that the children in the research study benefited from the project was upheld in court.

   a. What are the pros (positives) of this study?

   _____

   _____

   b. What are the cons (negatives) of this study?

   _____

   _____

c. Is society ever justified in permitting this type of research when the outcome benefits only some members of society? Why or why not?

_____

_____

d. Should public funds be used to pay for this type of research on children? Why or why not?

_____

_____

e. Some say that the final outcome of the Willowbrook case falls into a "gray area" of ethics in which there is no one clear answer. If this is the case, then, in your opinion, where do we draw the line on testing children?

_____

_____

Source: Summarized from G. Pence. Classic Cases in Medical Ethics. New York: McGraw Hill Publishing Company, 1990.

2. Your sister and her husband are having difficulty becoming pregnant. She comes to you as a healthcare professional and asks your thoughts on what they might do to conceive a child.

a. What are some topics that you might discuss with your sister and her husband?

_____

_____

b. Who would you recommend that they speak with about this problem?

_____

_____

c. Is there an ethical problem in giving medical advice to a family member? Why or why not?

_____

_____

3. Your neighbor's 18-year-old daughter has just given birth to a baby boy. The neighbor is concerned that neither she, nor her daughter, can take care of this baby. She asks you about the Safe Haven Law.

a. What can you tell her about the Safe Haven Law in your state?

_____

_____

b. In your opinion, is giving her advice about this law within the code of ethics of your chosen healthcare profession?

_____

_____

c. Is this a legal and/or ethical problem?

_____

_____

Put It Into Practice

Contact your local chapter of Planned Parenthood and a Right-to-Life organization and request information on their organization and services. Compare the philosophies and missions of the two organizations as stated in their published materials. What do they have in common? What are the differences?

Web Hunt

Using the website of the National Institutes of Health (**www.nih.gov**), click on the "Office of Rare Diseases" heading. Using the list provided by the office, determine which of the hereditary disorders in Table 12.1 is considered a rare disease.

Critical Thinking Exercise

What would you do if your best friend's daughter comes into the office where you work seeking birth control pills? You know that her mother does not know that she is sexually active.

Bibliography

Bernstein, L. (2023). One of the largest fertility clinic mishaps in U.S. settled out of court. *The Washington Post*, March 15. https://www.washingtonpost.com/health/2023/03/15/chart-industries-pacific-fertility-center-settlement/

Balch, B. (2023). What doctors should know about emergency abortions in states with bans. *Association of American Medical Colleges*. https://www.aamc.org/news/what-doctors-should-know-about-emergency-abortions-states-bans

Dimant, J. & Mohamed, B. (2023). What the data says about abortion in the U.S. *Pew Research Center*. https://www.pewresearch.org/short-reads/2023/01/11/what-the-data-says-about-abortion-in-the-u-s-2/

Guttmacher Institute. (2023). *Refusing to provide health services*. https://www.guttmacher.org/state-policy/explore/refusing-provide-health-services

Haines, J., Hubbard, K., & Wolf, C. (2023). Where state abortion laws stand without Roe. *U.S. News and World Report*, October 6. https://www.usnews.com/news/best-states/articles/a-guide-to-abortion-laws-by-state

Idaho Legislature. (2023). Title 39, Health and Safety, Chapter 39, Sterilization. https://legislature.idaho.gov/statutesrules/idstat/title39/t39ch39/sect39-3909/

Johnson, G. (2022). Court: Extraordinary damages OK in "wrongful life" case. *The Associated Press*. https://apnews.com/article/health-seattle-washington-birth-defects-supreme-court-879ad1efcff52e71571b489799549549

Jones, R.K., Kirstein, M., & Philbin, J. (2022). Abortion incidence and service availability in the United States, 2020. Guttmacher Institute. https://www.guttmacher.org/article/2022/11/abortion-incidence-and-service-availability-united-states-2020#

Keshavan, M. (2019). Consumer DNA tests negate sperm-bank-donor anonymity. *Scientific American*, Sept 12. https://www.scientificamerican.com/article/consumer-dna-tests-negate-sperm-bank-donor-anonymity/

Kortsmit, K., Nguyen, A. T., Mandel, M.G., et al. (2022). Abortion surveillance—United States, 2020. *Morbidity and Mortality Weekly Report*, 71(10):1–27. https://www.cdc.gov/mmwr/volumes/71/ss/ss7110a1.htm

Library of Congress. (1972). *Eisenstadt, Sheriff, v. Baird*. https://tile.loc.gov/storage-services/service/ll/usrep/usrep405/usrep405438/usrep405438.pdf

Millman, J. (2023). Abortions increased the year after Roe was overturned. *Axios*. https://www.axios.com/2023/10/24/abortion-increase-roe-wade-state-ban

National Constitution Center. (2023). *Supreme Court Case: Griswold v. Connecticut*. https://constitutioncenter.org/the-constitution/supreme-court-case-library/griswold-v-connecticut

National Women's Law Center. (2022). *Forced sterilization laws in each state and territory*. ƒ.NWLC_SterilizationReport_2022_Appendix.pdf

Rubin, B., & Lourgos, A. 2013. Couple battle over frozen embryos. *Chicago Tribune* (September 18), Sec. 1.

Ethical Issues Related to the End of Life

Key Terms

Active euthanasia

Assisted suicide

Brain death

Cardiac death

Comatose

Curative care

Euthanasia

Healthcare proxy

Hospice

Hypothermia

Life-support systems

Medical aid-in-dying

Palliative care

Passive euthanasia

Persistent vegetative state (PVS)

Principle of double-effect

Quality of life

Respite care

Rigor mortis

Substitute judgment rule

Surrogate

Terminally ill

Uniform Determination of Death Act

Viatical settlements

Withdrawing life-sustaining treatment

Withholding life-sustaining treatment

Learning Objectives

After completing this chapter, you will be able to:

13.1 Define the key terms.

13.2 Discuss the difference between cardiac death and brain death.

13.3 Describe the ethical issues in caring for terminally ill patients.

13.4 Provide examples of ordinary versus extraordinary means used in the treatment of terminally ill patients.

13.5 List and discuss the various models of stages of grief.

13.6 Discuss quality-of-life issues and the dying person's bill of rights.

13.7 Compare and contrast hospice care and palliative care.

The Case of Marguerite M. and the Angiogram

Marguerite M., an 89-year-old widow, is admitted into the cardiac intensive care unit in Chicago's Memorial Hospital at 3:00 AM on a Sunday morning with a massive heart attack (myocardial infarction). Her internist, Dr. K., who is also a close family friend, has ordered an angiogram to determine the status of Marguerite's infarction. Dr. K. knows that the angiography and resulting treatment need to be done within the first six hours after an infarction in order to be effective. Therefore, the procedure is going to be done as soon as the on-call surgical team can set up the angiography room. The radiologist, who lives 30 minutes from the hospital, must also be in the hospital before the procedure can begin. At 4:30 AM the team is ready to have Marguerite, who is barely conscious, transferred from the intensive care unit (ICU) to the surgical suite.

Coincidentally, at 4:30 AM Sarah W., an unconscious 45-year-old woman, is brought in by ambulance with a massive heart attack. The emergency department (ED) physicians,

after conferring with her physician by phone, conclude that she will need a balloon angiography (dilating an obstructed blood vessel by threading a balloon-tipped catheter into the vessel) to save her life. When they call the surgical department to have the on-call angiography team brought in, they are told that the room is already set up for Dr. K.'s patient. They do not have another team or surgical room for Sarah. A decision is made that because Sarah needs the balloon angiography in order to survive, they will use the angiography team for her.

Dr. K. is called at home and told that his patient, Marguerite, will not be able to have the angiography. The hospital is going to use the angiography team for Sarah, because she is younger than Marguerite and has a greater chance for recovery. Unfortunately, it took longer than expected to stabilize Sarah before and after the procedure and the six-hour "window" when the procedure could be performed on Marguerite passed. Marguerite died the following morning.

1. Do you believe that this case presents a legal or an ethical problem, or both?
2. What do you believe should be the criteria for a healthcare provider to use when having to choose a solution that will benefit one patient at the expense of another?
3. How can Dr. K. justify this decision when speaking to the family of Marguerite M.?
4. What options does a member of the angiography team or a caregiver for Marguerite have if they disagree with this decision?

Introduction

Issues relating to death and dying are especially sensitive, as they are topics that are ultimately faced by everyone. The questions are difficult to contemplate, even though they are critical. For example, should a feeding tube be inserted when a patient can no longer be fed by mouth? Should a ventilator be attached when the patient can no longer breathe independently? Should CPR be attempted when the heart stops beating? There are no definitive agreements within the healthcare profession on many of the issues relating to death and dying. The one point of agreement is that the dying patient must be treated with dignity.

Death is inevitable for everyone. Modern medicine has enabled people to live longer and survive diseases such as pneumonia that once caused people to die quickly. Infections can be treated and eliminated. Older adults, who may welcome death at the end of a long life or illness, can now be kept alive by medical technology. This has caused ethical and moral dilemmas for the healthcare profession. It is important to remember that professional codes of ethics usually include a statement about the healthcare professional's duty to preserve the dignity and life of the patient.

Legal Definition of Death

Determining when a person has died is important for a variety of reasons. Obviously, the most important reason is that no one wants to make the mistake of treating living patients as though they were dead. A person who has died is no longer treated the same way as a living human. This in no way means that the body of a deceased person, also known as a corpse, can be handled disrespectfully.

The actual determination of death has also become critical in the past few decades because of advances in medicine such as organ transplantation and life-support systems. **Life-support systems**, such as ventilators/respirators and feeding tubes, allow healthcare practitioners to sustain for additional weeks, months, or even years a person who, according to all traditional standards, has died. The classic case is that of Karen Ann Quinlan.

The Karen Ann Quinlan Case

On April 15, 1975, 21-year-old Karen Ann Quinlan was admitted to a New Jersey hospital after becoming unconscious from taking a combination of a prescription drug and alcohol. She suffered cardiopulmonary (heart and breathing) arrest and was placed on a respirator after her pulse was restored. She received a tracheotomy (a surgical incision into the trachea to assist in ventilation), and had a nasogastric (NG) feeding tube inserted through her nose and into her stomach to receive nourishment. At that point, she was considered to be comatose, that is, in a deep state of profound unconsciousness from which she could not be awakened. Her electroencephalogram (EEG), which measured brain activity, was abnormal, but a brain scan showed her brain activity to still be within normal limits. Months passed with no change in Quinlan's **comatose** condition, but her physical condition continued to deteriorate. She lost weight, dropping from 115 to 70 pounds by September, and her body became rigid. When many months went by with no signs that Karen would ever recover from the coma, her condition was considered to be irreversible.

Karen's father appealed to the court to appoint him as guardian, which it ultimately did. He requested that the extraordinary procedures, such as the respirator, be discontinued. The Superior Court denied this request. Many other legal battles took place, and eventually the respirator was discontinued. However, Quinlan continued to breathe on her own even after the respirator was discontinued. The hospital continued to feed Karen by artificial means, and she lived in a coma for ten years before she died on July 11, 1985. The Quinlan case was groundbreaking because it represented the first time a family had requested a court to approve the removal of a respirator from a permanently comatose patient and won the case (*In re Quinlan*, 355 A.2d 647, N.J. 1976).

The insertion of a feeding tube is a serious decision when the patient is comatose. Feeding tubes are a life-extending treatment as they will continue to provide nutrition and hydration long after a patient is able to take nourishment on their own. An incompetent person, one who is unable to make decisions on their own behalf, raises one of the most difficult ethical problems for those persons who must decide whether to withdraw nutrition and hydration. The reason for this is that there is no one clear definition of incompetence. In fact, *competence* is a legal term, and incompetence can only be declared in a court of law.

Although a healthcare provider cannot legally declare a patient mentally incompetent, they may recognize when a patient does not have the capacity to make decisions regarding their own care. But this medical judgment is often not enough when determining to withdraw life support measures. Healthcare providers must decide based on mental capacity, physical condition, and the possibility of recovery. If the patient has periods of mental incapacity as well as lucid moments, then the courts will want decisions followed that are made during the patient's lucid moments. The family will also have to be consulted. Thus, there is not a simple answer to when to remove a feeding tube or withhold nutritional or other life-support measures.

Med Tip

The right to accept or reject medical treatment is each person's fundamental right.

Criteria for Death

Certain criteria or standards assist in the determination that death has occurred. Some indications, in addition to the loss of a heartbeat, include a significant drop in body temperature, no pupil response to light, loss of body color, no response to pain, **rigor mortis** (stiffness that occurs in a dead body), and biological disintegration. However, these symptoms may not appear until several hours after death, or not at all if life-support equipment is used.

While the criteria for death vary, this becomes problematic when a general consensus for the definition of *death* is needed. For instance, because a deceased person's organs can be removed for transplantation into a living body, if permission has been granted by the deceased before death or by the deceased's relatives, it is important to determine if and when death has occurred.

In one unusual case, an emergency department doctor pronounced a 20-month-old little girl, Mackayala Jespersen, dead after drowning in her backyard swimming pool. The doctor made this pronouncement based on the flat-line heart and brain tracings taken after she had been given CPR for an hour. As a police detective was photographing her dead body for record-keeping purposes, she took a deep breath. This occurred 39 minutes after being pronounced dead. Other children have survived **hypothermia** (the state in which body temperature is below normal range) when they fell into ice-cold water. But this little girl's case is unusual because all of the proper procedures to determine death were followed, and the criteria used to define death were met. However, she was still alive.

There is a continuing controversy over whether to use a cardiac definition of death or a brain-oriented definition of death. Even then, in some cases it is difficult to determine if someone is alive or dead.

Cardiopulmonary Death

Traditionally, death was defined as **cardiac death**, or death in which the heart has stopped functioning. The definition for a cardiac death means that there is an irreversible loss of all cardiac function. The cessation of breathing is another important criterion for determining death. If a person's respiratory system fails and cannot be revived, it is a significant indicator of death. Heartbeat and breathing are interdependent. When the heart stops functioning, breathing will also stop; conversely, if breathing stops, the heart will soon stop beating. If no assistance is given, such as CPR, the patient is unlikely to recover. A person who suffered an irreversible cessation of respiratory and circulatory functions was considered dead. Healthcare personnel can make this determination based on lack of pulse or breathing. A cardiac death is considered a legal death.

In most situations, the cardiac determination of death is effective. However, using only the cardiac definition of death creates some problems. For example, it is now possible to live for months or even years with a total artificial heart (TAH). A TAH is usually implanted when a patient needs a heart transplant, but a donor heart is not available. The TAH is temporary.

Also, in some cases, the cessation of breathing and pulse are reversible, such as in a drug overdose or hypothermia. This prolonged absence of oxygen can result in neurological damage. A patient who has suffered a cardiac arrest and is "clinically dead" may successfully be resuscitated with CPR. This person cannot be considered dead because the cessation of breath and pulse is not irreversible.

Med Tip

Cardiac death (cessation of heart function) and *cardiopulmonary death* (cessation of heart and lung function) are interchangeable as legal definitions of death.

Another serious problem with using only the cardiac-oriented definition of death involves organ transplantation. In many cases, if the surgeon waits until all cardiac function has ceased, many of the potential donor's organs are useless as transplants. Obviously, it is not ethical or moral to change the definition of death in order to increase the number of organs available for transplant. However, many people believe that a cardiac-oriented definition of death is inadequate.

Brain Death

Brain death, meaning complete and irreversible cessation of all brain function, has gained favor as the definition of death in many countries, including the United States. *Death by Neurologic Criteria* is the proper term, though *brain death* is used widely. Using brain death as the criterion for declaring death is based on the premise that the brain is responsible for all bodily functions, and once the brain stops functioning, all other bodily functions will stop. In most states, if the whole brain is determined to be dead (with no remaining brain function), then the person is considered deceased.

Med Tip

Modern technology has made it possible to maintain heart and lung function for hours, and even days, after all brain function has stopped.

The criteria for brain death determination varies by hospital, region, and state. In 2023, a consensus guideline for pediatric and adult brain death/death by neurologic criteria was endorsed by the American Academy of Neurology, the American Academy of Pediatrics, and the Society of Critical Care Medicine as an attempt to standardize the criteria. A dilemma occurs in the case of a patient whose heart and respiratory functions are maintained by mechanical means, such as a ventilator, but who has no brain activity. The patient's brain is dead, but because technology is sustaining cardiopulmonary functioning, the body is still alive. Discontinuing the ventilation support for a patient would result in the cardiac death of the patient. A moral dilemma confronts healthcare providers when they have to determine definitely whether such a person has died.

There is a checklist to assist healthcare providers in determining brain death/death by neurological criteria. There are prerequisites before the clinical examination, the actual clinical examination (which demonstrates no brainstem activity to support life), and an apnea test.

A **persistent vegetative state**, or PVS, is a long-lasting brain condition in which the patient is in a state of deep unconsciousness, although there may be some responses such as yawning or grunting. The diagnosis of PVS is usually made by a neurologist and confirmed by two consulting neurologists after a brain-injured patient has been in a coma for at least six months. Although the definitions overlap, distinctions may be made between a vegetative state and a coma. Yawning/grunting-type activity often occurs in a vegetative state, whereas a coma is generally characterized by no responses at all. On the other hand, most comas are temporary and the patient usually "wakes up" after several weeks, although possibly with residual mental damage. A vegetative state is more severe and far less likely to result in recovery. If a vegetative state persists for a few months, it is almost always irreversible.

To protect the patient, and also protect healthcare providers against malpractice suits, an outside medical opinion should be sought before terminating life support. This issue has actually had a bearing in a criminal case. In Arizona, a murder defendant argued that it was not his criminal action that caused the death of the victim, but rather the actions of the physician who discontinued the life-support system. In this case, the court rejected the defendant's argument, holding that brain death was the valid test for death in Arizona. The court found that the victim's brain function had ceased as a result of the defendant's criminal action before the life support was discontinued (*State v. Fierro*, 603 P.2d 74, Ariz. 1979).

Uniform Determination of Death Act

In the 1980s, the American Bar Association, the American Medical Association, the Uniform Law Commissioners, the American Academy of Neurology, and others approved a **Uniform Determination of Death Act**, also called UDDA. As of 2023, this law has been adopted by 37 states and the District of Columbia. It says the following:

> An individual, who has sustained either (1) irreversible cessation of circulatory and respiratory functions, or (2) irreversible cessation of all functions of the entire brain, including the brain stem, is dead.

Source: National Conference of Commissioners on Uniform State Laws

Some people, such as some Orthodox Jews, Catholics, and right-to-life proponents, object to the brain death criteria. These groups believe acceptance of the brain death criteria in all circumstances would legitimize practices they consider immoral, such as euthanasia and abortion.

Med Tip

Many phrases are used to refer to a deceased person, such as *passed away, passed on, departed,* and *left this world*. It is important to know which one is used in a particular family so as to be as compassionate as possible when discussing the death of a family member or loved one.

Ethical Issues in Caring for Terminally Ill Patients

In caring for the critically ill or those patients who are considered to be **terminally ill**, where death is inevitable, there are several ethical considerations: (1) withdrawing versus withholding treatment, (2) active euthanasia versus passive euthanasia, (3) direct versus indirect killing, and (4) ordinary versus extraordinary means.

Withdrawing versus Withholding Treatment

Withdrawing life-sustaining treatment, such as artificial ventilation, means to discontinue it after it has been started. **Withholding life-sustaining treatment** means never starting it. Healthcare practitioners often find it more difficult to withdraw treatment after it has been started than to withhold treatment. However, many people believe that both are ethically wrong.

Starting a life-sustaining treatment, even on a temporary basis, allows the healthcare provider more time to evaluate the patient's condition. The healthcare provider may believe that if the treatment is ineffective, it can be stopped. However, in some cases, it has been necessary to get a court order to discontinue a treatment, such as a respirator, that has already been started.

Active Euthanasia versus Passive Euthanasia

The word **euthanasia** literally means "good death" from the Greek word *eu* meaning "good" and *Thanatos*, the ancient Greek personification of death. However, interpretations of the meaning of euthanasia have become much more complicated than simply that someone has or is allowed to have a "good death."

Most people equate the term euthanasia with "actively doing something" to create that good death. Other terms that people use instead of the term euthanasia are assisted suicide, right to die, and medical aid-in-dying (as described in Chapter 11). There are differing viewpoints on whether euthanasia is ethical or unethical. Many people believe that euthanasia is a humane treatment of terminally ill patients in order to put an end to their suffering and pain. At the present time, euthanasia in the sense of killing someone to spare them suffering is illegal in all states. **Assisted suicide**, or **medical aid-in-dying**, meaning helping someone to kill themselves, is legal in ten states and illegal in 40. Keep in mind that this list can change whenever the law is changed in any individual state.

Most people believe that there is a distinction between actively killing a patient (active euthanasia or assisted suicide) and allowing a patient to die by forgoing treatment (passive euthanasia). This moral distinction is approved by the AMA and the President's Commission for the Study of Ethical Problems in Medicine and Biomedical and Behavioral Research. It is not accepted by Orthodox Judaism.

Active euthanasia, the intentional killing of the terminally ill, involves a second party directly introducing a lethal dose of medication, such as by injection, into the dying person. As already noted, active euthanasia is illegal in all jurisdictions in the United States.

While active euthanasia is illegal, and medical aid-in-dying is legal in only ten states, **passive euthanasia**, or allowing a patient to die naturally, is legal everywhere. Passive euthanasia involves withholding medical interventions that would only serve to sustain life. This includes hydration (supply of fluids) and nutritional feeding. The patient is to be kept clean, warm, and protected from infection and pain as much as possible. The dying patient is medicated to be pain free, but no lethal doses are administered. The dying process is neither inhibited nor accelerated.

There is always the concern that chronically ill and dying patients may be pressured to choose euthanasia in order to spare their families further emotional or financial strain. Any pressure of this type can lead to serious ethical and moral questions.

The three cases presented below brought national attention to the concept of medical aid-in-dying.

The Nancy Cruzan Case

The Nancy Cruzan case is an example of a situation in which the removal of a feeding tube was a form of active euthanasia *within* the law.

On January 11, 1983, 25-year-old Nancy Cruzan was involved in an automobile crash that left her in a vegetative state. A feeding tube was implanted in her in a Missouri hospital. Three years after the collision, her parents, who had been granted guardianship, believed that she would never regain consciousness. The family sought legal assistance from the American Civil Liberties Union and requested that the feeding tube be removed. The judge ruled in favor of the Cruzans, but the case was appealed. The U.S. Supreme Court overturned the judge's decision and ruled against the Cruzans because under Missouri law, hydration or nutritional support could not be withdrawn from an incompetent patient unless clear evidence demonstrated that this is what the patient would have requested. Several years later, new evidence became known when two of Cruzan's former coworkers came forward. They both stated that she had said she would not wish to be maintained like Karen Quinlan. In December 1990, a judge complied with the Cruzans' wish to have their daughter's feeding tube removed. In reaction to this verdict, right-to-life protestors demonstrated outside the rehabilitation center where Cruzan was being kept alive. The feeding tube was removed on December 14, 1990, and she was pronounced dead 12 days later on December 26, 1990 (*Cruzan v. Director, Missouri Dep't. of Health*, 497 U.S. 261, 1990). In 1996, the Cruzan family went through another tragedy when Nancy's father, Joe Cruzan, hanged himself in the family home. His family and friends believed that he was unable to emotionally recover from his daughter's long, drawn-out death.

Both the Karen Quinlan and the Nancy Cruzan cases are considered to be landmark cases in medical law and ethics because they established an individual's right to refuse to receive medical care. Because both these cases lasted over a period of several years, the cases also illustrated the need for people to let family members know both verbally and particularly in writing what their wishes are for life-sustaining medical care if they become incompetent.

Terri Schiavo: "The Face That Moved a Nation"

The Terry Schiavo case is another example of well-known case where Terry's husband and parents fought over whether to remove her feeding tube. They each won multiple court cases, resulting in Terry's feeding tube being being removed and reinserted many times.

In October 2003, the face of Terri Schiavo smiling at her mother caught the interest of the U.S. public and the governor of Florida, Jeb Bush. Terri had been in a persistent vegetative state since 1990. Her husband, Michael, and her parents were friendly until a jury awarded $1 million to Terri, under Michael's control, in a medical malpractice lawsuit. The parents contend that Michael stopped his wife's therapy and used the money to pay lawyer's fees in an attempt to have his wife's feeding tube removed. Terri's husband stated that he wanted to fulfill his wife's wishes that she not be kept living in a comatose or vegetative state. Her parents opposed having the tube removed, declaring that she is not comatose, but rather appears to smile, blink, and is able to follow balloons and her parents as they move about her room.

Healthcare providers who examined Terri over the years indicated that she could respond to pain, blink her eyes, and raise her leg when asked to do so. In 2003, a speech pathologist stated that Terri uttered "stop" in response to a medical procedure that was being done to her. One doctor stated that she was not in a "persistent vegetative state," based on the evidence he found when he examined her.

Terri's feeding tube was removed as ordered by the court. There was a great amount of media attention over her case, including a photo of Terri Schiavo smiling up at her mother on the front page of many national newspapers, and many protests were held (Figure 13.1). One week after the feeding tube was removed, Governor Jeb Bush and the Florida legislature ordered that the feeding tube be reinserted. It was. In fact, Terri's feeding tube was removed and reinserted three times before the final removal. She died 13 days after the feeding tube was removed, which was 15 years after her collapse from cardiac arrest at the age of 26, and seven years after her court battle began.

The Brittany Maynard Case

Brittany Maynard was a young woman whose case garnered widespread attention and ignited a national debate on the topic of assisted suicide. Diagnosed with terminal brain cancer in 2014, Maynard faced the harsh reality of a limited lifespan filled with unbearable pain and suffering. Frustrated by the lack of legal options for assisted dying in her home state of California, she made the difficult decision to relocate to Oregon, where the Death with Dignity Act allowed terminally ill patients to end their lives through prescribed medication.

Maynard's decision to share her story publicly through videos and interviews brought attention to the ethical and moral dilemmas surrounding assisted suicide. Supporters hailed her bravery in choosing to die on her own terms, emphasizing the importance of individual autonomy and the right to a dignified death. Critics, however, raised concerns about the potential slippery slope of legalizing assisted suicide, fearing it could lead to abuse and undermine the sanctity of life.

Figure 13–1 Protesters outside Terri Schiavo's hospice in 2003

Source: Matt May/Getty Images News/Getty Images

The Brittany Maynard case reignited conversations about end-of-life care, the right to die with dignity, and the need for comprehensive legislation addressing these complex issues. Her advocacy contributed to increased awareness and discussions about the importance of compassionate and humane end-of-life options for individuals facing terminal illnesses. The case underscored the ongoing need for society to grapple with the ethical, legal, and emotional dimensions of assisted suicide in order to provide compassionate choices for those in the most challenging circumstances.

Arguments in Favor of Euthanasia

Arguments in favor of euthanasia include the following:

- *Mercy and compassion:* Euthanasia allows individuals to end their lives with dignity and avoid unnecessary suffering. It is seen as a compassionate and merciful act to help someone in extreme pain or with a terminal illness.

- *Autonomy and personal freedom:* Advocates argue that individuals have the right to make decisions about their own lives, including when and how they die. Euthanasia is seen as an extension of personal autonomy and freedom.

- *Quality of life:* Euthanasia can be seen as a way to improve the quality of life for individuals facing unbearable pain or a terminal illness. It allows them to avoid a prolonged, agonizing death.

- *Relief for families:* Euthanasia may provide emotional relief for family members who are witnessing their loved ones suffer. It can spare them from the distress of seeing a family member in pain.

Arguments in Opposition to Euthanasia

Arguments against euthanasia include the following:

- *Sanctity of life:* Many religious and ethical beliefs emphasize the sanctity of human life, arguing that intentionally ending a life is morally wrong and goes against the principles of respecting life.

- *Slippery slope:* Critics of euthanasia express concerns about a potential "slippery slope," where the practice could be extended beyond terminally ill patients to other vulnerable populations or situations.

- *Healthcare ethics:* The healthcare profession's ethical principles often emphasize the preservation of life and the duty of healthcare professionals to do no harm. Euthanasia can be viewed as a violation of these principles.

- *Potential for abuse:* There are concerns about the potential for abuse in implementing euthanasia, including coercion or pressure on individuals to choose death due to financial or other reasons.

- *Advances in palliative care:* Some argue that advances in palliative care and pain management can address the suffering of terminally ill patients without resorting to euthanasia. Therefore, the focus should be on improving end-of-life care rather than providing the option of assisted death.

Direct versus Indirect Killing

In some situations, an action can lead to two effects: one that is intended and even desirable, and another that is unintended and undesirable.

A person's death may result from another person's intended action or inaction. For instance, if a nurse intentionally ignores a patient who is choking because they want the patient to die, that person has killed the patient.

However, death may be an unintentional result of another person's action. For example, if a high-risk patient dies during surgery, the patient's death was not intended or desired. A surgeon who is morally opposed to abortion may have to remove a cancerous uterus in a pregnant woman; the death of the fetus is not intended or desired, but it is the indirect result of treating the disease.

These actions fit within the **principle of double-effect**, which recognizes that an action may have two consequences: one desired (and intended or morally good) and one undesired (and unintended). Some organizations oppose direct killing but accept undesired and unintended deaths. The courts generally make the same distinctions.

Ordinary versus Extraordinary Means

Another important distinction concerns the difference between ordinary and extraordinary means. This distinction is important for determining which treatments are morally required. To do this, we cannot simply separate common means, such as fluids and feeding tubes, from uncommon means, such as ECMO, because in some situations even common procedures or treatments may be considered extraordinary. Many believe that it is inappropriate to use the complexity of technology to determine what treatment to use or not use. For example, is it morally right to force a nasogastric feeding tube into a 90-year-old patient with pneumonia who does not wish to have this treatment? In another situation, it may be considered an ordinary means of treatment to temporarily use a respirator on a 90-year-old patient who is recovering from a choking episode.

The term *ordinary* refers to a treatment or procedure that is morally required, such as fluids and comfort measures. *Extraordinary measures* refer to those procedures and treatments that are morally expendable. Some professionals use the terms *appropriate* and *inappropriate* instead of *ordinary* and *extraordinary*. A treatment is considered morally expendable, or inappropriate, if it does not serve any useful purpose. For example, a commonsense judgment would determine that chemotherapy would be useless in the final days of life of a patient with cancer.

These are difficult issues to encounter. The administration of fluids, nutrition, and routine nursing procedures such as turning a patient may result in what the patient believes is a grave burden. These treatments may cause further pain and discomfort. In addition, they may actually be useless to recovery, but, as in the case of turning bedridden patients, they are considered necessary nursing care or ordinary means of care.

Right to Refuse Treatment

The right to refuse healthcare treatment is a fundamental aspect of individual autonomy and the right to control one's own body. Rooted in the principle of bodily integrity, this right empowers individuals to make decisions about their healthcare based on personal values, beliefs, and preferences. Respecting a patient's autonomy is a cornerstone of healthcare ethics and is enshrined in various legal frameworks.

One key aspect of this right is the concept of informed consent, where individuals have the right to be fully informed about their medical condition, the available treatment options, and the potential risks and benefits associated with each option. Armed with this information, individuals can make autonomous decisions about whether to accept or reject healthcare interventions. On the other hand, the first step in any refusal of care is determining the patient's capacity to do so. For example, patients who are under the influence of alcohol or other substances lack the capacity to make their own healthcare decisions.

This right has gained increasing recognition in healthcare practice and legal systems worldwide, acknowledging that individuals have the right to shape their medical destinies in alignment with their values and personal circumstances. As healthcare ethics and legal norms continue to evolve, the right to refuse medical treatment remains a crucial element in upholding the dignity and self-determination of individuals in the realm of healthcare.

In extreme cases in which the patients' refusal places their lives in danger, legal action sometimes results. The following is an example of such a case.

In January 1978, the Tennessee Department of Human Services filed a lawsuit seeking to have a *guardian ad litem* appointed to care for 72-year-old Mary Northern, who had no living relatives and suffered from gangrene of both feet. This condition required removing both her feet in order to save her life. During the court hearings, even though she was alert and lucid, Northern did not have the capacity to understand the severity or the consequences of her disease process, as demonstrated by her insistence that her feet were black because of dirt and that her physicians were incorrect about the seriousness of her infection. The court determined that she was in imminent danger of death without the amputation and authorized the state's commissioner of human services to act on her behalf in consenting for the surgery. However, on May 1, 1978, before Mary could be stabilized for surgery, she died of a blood clot from the gangrenous tissue (*State Dep't. of Human Services v. Northern*, 563 S.W.2d 197, Tenn. Ct. App. 1978).

Stages of Grief

The stages of grief when facing impending death have been widely studied and conceptualized through various theories, offering insights into the emotional and psychological processes individuals undergo. One well-known model is the Kübler-Ross model, introduced by psychiatrist Elisabeth Kübler-Ross in 1969 (Figure 13.2).

Dr. Kübler-Ross devoted much of her life to working with terminally ill patients and their families. She divided the process of grief associated with dying into five stages that she believes the patient, family members, and caregivers all go through. The five stages are denial, anger, bargaining, depression, and acceptance. According to Kübler-Ross, these stages overlap and may not be experienced by everyone in the stated order, but all are present in the dying patient. The five stages of grief are summarized in Table 13.1.

Figure 13–2 Kübler-Ross's five stages of grief

Source: marekuliasz/Shutterstock

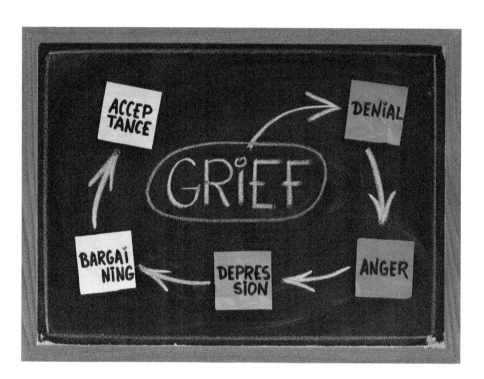

Table 13–1 Kübler-Ross five stages of grief

Stages	Definition
Denial	A refusal to believe that dying is taking place. This may be a time when the patient (or family member) needs time to adjust to the reality of approaching death. This stage cannot be hurried.
Anger	The patient may be angry with everyone and may express an intense anger toward God, family, and even healthcare professionals. The patient may take this anger out on the closest person, usually a family member. In reality, the patient is angry about dying.
Bargaining	This involves attempting to gain time by making promises in return. Bargaining may be done between the patient and God. The patient may indicate a need to talk at this stage.
Depression	There is a deep sadness over the loss of health, independence, and eventually life. There is an additional sadness of leaving loved ones behind. The grieving patient may become withdrawn at this time.
Acceptance	This stage is reached when there is a sense of peace and calm. The patient makes comments such as, "I have no regrets. I'm ready to die."

Another perspective comes from J. William Worden, who proposed the "Tasks of Mourning" model. Worden identifies four tasks: (1) accepting the reality of death, (2) processing the pain of grief, (3) adjusting to a world without the deceased, and (4) finding a way to maintain a connection while moving forward.

Bowlby and Parkes reformulated the Kübler-Ross model to emphasize that the grieving process is not linear. They described four stages of grief: shock and disbelief, searching and yearning, disorganization and repair, and rebuilding and healing.

The Dual Process model, developed by Margaret Stroebe and Henk Schut, emphasizes the oscillation between confronting the reality of loss and avoiding the emotional pain associated with it. This model recognizes the importance of balancing grieving activities with activities that provide a respite from grief.

These theories collectively underscore the dynamic and individualized nature of the grieving process when confronted with one's impending death. While these models provide valuable frameworks, it's crucial to recognize the unique and personal nature of grief, with individuals navigating their own emotional landscapes as they cope with the prospect of dying.

Quality-of-Life Issues

Quality of life refers to more than just what a person experiences at one moment in time. It includes many dimensions such as physiological status, emotional well-being, functional status, and satisfaction with life in general. A medical procedure or intervention, such as aggressive treatment for a terminal illness, will have an impact on the physical, social, and emotional well-being of a patient. This impact can be measured to assess the intangible costs and consequences of the disease or illness. These quality-of-life measurements can assist with making healthcare decisions based not only on clinical factors and costs but also on issues that the patient believes are important. Measures used to assess quality of life include the following:

- General health
- Physical functioning
- Role limitations, such as within the family structure
- Pain
- Social function
- Vitality
- Mental health

Questions are asked relating to each of these dimensions by the healthcare professional to create a patient's health profile. Two useful quality-of-life measurement instruments are the Functional Living Index: Cancer (FLIC) and the Arthritis Impact Measurement Scale (AIMS). The results of these measurement tests can aid the practitioner and the patient in making quality-of-life decisions, such as whether to extend life with the use of support systems.

The Dying Person's Bill of Rights

The Dying Person's Bill of Rights reflects the needs of individual patients during the dying process. Note that this document reflects the dying individual's need for a combination of physical comfort, emotional support, personal autonomy, and respect from those caring for the individual and their family.

- I have the right to be treated as a living human being until I die.
- I have the right to maintain a sense of hopefulness, however changing its focus may be.
- I have the right to express my feelings and emotions about my approaching death in my own way.
- I have the right to participate in decisions concerning my care.
- I have the right to expect continuing medical and nursing attention even though cure goals must be changed to comfort goals.
- I have the right not to die alone.

- I have the right to be free from pain.
- I have the right to have my questions answered honestly.
- I have the right not to be deceived.
- I have the right to have help from and for my family in accepting my death.
- I have the right to die in peace and with dignity.
- I have the right to retain my individuality and not be judged for my decisions that may be contrary to the beliefs of others.
- I have the right to be cared for by caring, sensitive, knowledgeable people who will attempt to understand my needs and will be able to gain some satisfaction in helping me face my death.

Source: Barbus, A. J. (1975). *The dying person's bill of rights*. South Western Michigan Inservice Education Council.

Managing Pain

Controlling pain in individuals who are dying is a critical aspect of end-of-life care, aiming to enhance their quality of life and provide comfort. Palliative care, which focuses on relieving symptoms and improving the overall well-being of individuals with life-limiting illnesses, plays a central role in pain management during the dying process.

The World Health Organization's (WHO) pain relief ladder is a widely used framework for managing pain in cancer and other terminal illnesses (Figure 13.3). It advocates for a stepwise approach to pain management, starting with non-opioid analgesics and progressing to weak opioids and then strong opioids as needed. This ladder also emphasizes the importance of adjuvant medications and non-pharmacological interventions to address pain comprehensively.

Intravenous or oral administration of opioids, such as morphine, remains a cornerstone in managing severe pain. However, individualized care is crucial, considering factors such as the patient's tolerance, preferences, and potential side effects.

Multidisciplinary collaboration is key in pain management for those nearing the end of life. A team comprising physicians, nurses, pharmacists, psychologists, and other healthcare professionals can tailor interventions to meet the unique needs of each patient.

Ultimately, the goal is not just pain relief but optimizing the individual's overall well-being, allowing them to face the end of life with dignity and as much comfort as possible. Open communication between healthcare providers, patients, and their families is essential to ensure that the pain management plan aligns with the patient's values and goals for their remaining time.

Figure 13–3 The World Health Organization's pain relief ladder

Source: PEARSON, NURSING: A CONCEPT-BASED APPROACH TO LEARNING, VOLUME 1, 4th Ed., ©2023, Figure 3-7 pg. 190.

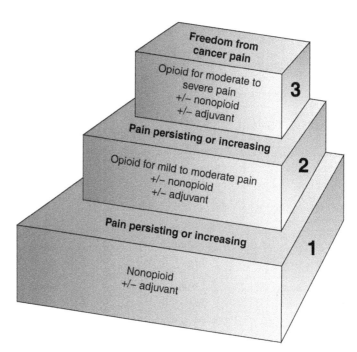

Hospice Care

Hospice, a multidisciplinary, family-centered care, is a system that is designed to provide care and supportive services to terminally ill patients and their families. The hospice movement, which originated in France, has a commitment to keep patients with a terminal illness as pain-free as possible. Our modern-day hospice is modeled after Saint Christopher's Hospice in London, which was started by Dr. Cicely Saunders in 1966. She established a facility with a homelike atmosphere where terminally ill patients, both young and old, find comfort until death. Hospices, based on Dr. Saunders's model, are found throughout the world. The hospice service is available both in a facility such as Dr. Saunders's model and also in the patient's own home, where a hospice worker provides daily care if needed.

There is mounting evidence that hospice care can provide "death with dignity." Hospice care is focused on providing comfort measures, emotional support, and a final environment as pain-free as possible for the patient. There is now a much greater understanding of the use of narcotics for terminally ill cancer patients.

Med Tip

In previous decades many physicians and nurses were concerned that a high dose of narcotic medication to alleviate pain would result in respiratory failure and addiction. There is new evidence that patients can be kept almost pain-free at the end of their life with carefully managed medication control.

Whenever possible, patients are kept awake and alert so that they can spend some of their last moments with their family members. Additional services, such as pastoral and respite care for the family, are part of the hospice philosophy. The staff consists of specially trained personnel who have experience and interest in caring for the dying patient. The patient is usually only hospitalized in a hospice unit during the final weeks of life.

Hospice care is meant to liberate patients from their pain and suffering so that they can truly live until they die.

Med Tip

Because most of the hospice care is now provided in the patient's home, this can be a burden on the patient's family with the result that the family may require **respite care** (relief time from the responsibilities of patient care).

Palliative Care

Palliative care is the total care of patients whose disease is no longer responsive to curative therapy. This type of care, consisting of comfort measures, is meant to provide relief of pain and suffering so the patient can die with dignity. Comfort measures include frequent turning and bathing, gentle massage, providing oral fluids, and listening to the patient. Palliative care emphasizes symptom control, such as for pain, shortness of breath, and supportive therapy for depression. Palliative care is not euthanasia, nor do the healthcare professionals giving this type of care passively allow people to die. There are eight domains of palliative care.

1. Structure and processes of care
   - Identify patients' and their family's values and goals.
   - Provide an interprofessional team knowledgeable about palliative care.
2. Physical aspects of care
   - Administer pharmacologic and nonpharmacologic interventions as needed to provide comfort.
   - Provide hygiene care (e.g., oral care, skin care, change of bed linens).

3. Psychologic and psychiatric aspects of care
   - Systematically assess and address psychological and psychiatric services for patient.
   - Provide grief counseling and emotional and informational support for family.

4. Social aspects of care
   - Assess and address patient and family social needs, through cultural humility and using trauma-informed practice.
   - Refer to social services (e.g., hospice care).

5. Spiritual, religious, and existential aspects of care
   - Facilitate visits with clergy, spiritual leaders, and healers.
   - Allow practice of cultural, spiritual, and religious rituals.

6. Cultural aspects of care
   - Encourage cultural and traditional practices to be carried out by involving the patient and family in care planning.
   - Administer care that is culturally sensitive.

7. Care of the imminently dying patients
   - Communicate signs of impending death to family.
   - Provide comfort to patients and family during their final days and weeks of life.

8. Ethical and legal aspects of care
   - Consider legal and ethical aspects of care, such as advance directives and DNR orders.
   - Respect patient and family wishes within the legal and ethical constraints of practice.

Palliative care, which is the opposite of **curative care** in which we attempt to cure the patient's disease, requires healthcare professionals who understand the need for compassion, rather than surgical or medical interventions. What palliative care can do is to make the end-of-life period a meaningful experience for the patient, rather than something of which to be frightened.

Some critics of modern-day healthcare believe that our culture has a built-in bias that "everything that can be done will be done" for the dying patient. Some physicians have stated that aggressive treatment for older adults, such as chemotherapy at acute care hospitals, can be inhumane. And once they are started they cannot be withdrawn. Many dying patients do not wish to lose the opportunity to make decisions about their quality of life and give up control over their care. But this may not mean that they wish to have extraordinary measures taken to prolong their life. Dr. Dennis McCullough uses the term "slow medicine" meaning that a compassionate approach to caring for aging loved ones does not require aggressive and even painful procedures. He believes that because nine out of ten people who live into their 80s will be unable to care for themselves at a certain point, they must make their choices clear to their caregivers ahead of time. If they do not wish heroic measures, such as CPR, to be taken, then this must be stated in writing.

Viatical Settlements

Viatical settlements allow people with terminal illnesses, such as amyotrophic lateral sclerosis, to obtain money from their life insurance policies by selling them. The term *viatical* comes from the Latin term *viaticum*, the money and supplies given to Roman officials before taking on a risky journey for the empire. (*Viaticum* is also the Roman Catholic sacrament given to the dying patient.) A viatical settlement means that in exchange for a 20 to 50 percent discount on the face value of the patient's insurance policy, they can have immediate access to the money. The patient names the settlement company as the recipient of the death benefit. In return, the viatical settlement company assumes complete responsibility for the insurance policy, including making all the premium payments. The owner then receives no further benefits from the insurance. At the time of the patient's (viator's) death, the viatical settlement company receives the death benefit from the policy.

Terminally ill patients can use the money to provide for medical and nursing care during their final illness or use the money to enjoy a vacation with family members or to pay for experimental medical treatments that health insurance companies will not cover.

There are problems with viatical settlements, including tax liabilities and a potential loss of means-based entitlements such as Medicaid. Because the payment to the patient is less than the face value of the insurance policy, the patient could be "giving away" a significant amount of money to the settlement company. In addition, terminally ill patients often live much longer than they expected with their illness, and the small payment by the settlement company may not be enough to help them.

Advance Directives

The Federal Patient Self-Determination Act of 1991 mandates that adult patients admitted into any healthcare facility that receives funding from either Medicare or Medicaid must be asked if they have an advance directive or wish to have information about these self-determination directives. An advance directive is a document that directs a **surrogate** (a person who is replacing another person) to represent them. Ideally, people make decisions about advance directives before they are in a situation in which they are being admitted to a hospital or nursing home. If these documents—such as a living will, durable power of attorney for healthcare, Uniform Anatomical Gift Act, or do not resuscitate (DNR) order—have to be drawn up after a patient has entered a facility, then it should be done in a non-stressful manner.

Advance directives are popularly known as living wills. These documents became popular about 30 years ago when medical technology made it possible for people to be kept alive in unpleasant and fragile conditions for long periods of time. An advance directive is a statement or declaration by a patient that they do not want to be connected to life support equipment if they become terminally ill without hope of recovery. The document should be signed and witnessed and may serve as a "living will," depending on the current law in the person's state. Advance directives limit the type and amount of medical care and treatment that patients will receive if they should become incompetent and have a poor prognosis. It is important that directives are placed in writing; it is not sufficient for a person to just tell someone what his or her wishes for treatment are. The courts typically enforce written advance directives. For additional discussion about advance directives, see Chapter 5.

Med Tip

All healthcare professionals should be aware that it is also acceptable for a patient to write an advance directive asking to receive *maximum* care and treatment for as long as possible.

The **substitute judgment rule** is used when decisions must be made for people who cannot make their own decisions. Under this rule, a person, committee, or institution will attempt to determine what the person would do if they were competent to make their own decisions. However, there is always speculation about what decision the patient would actually make if they were competent, even though they may have indicated their wishes to another person at an earlier time. Therefore, when there is a lack of an advance directive, most decision makers will rule in favor of using all interventions such as tube feedings. This is a case in which the principle of beneficence is followed because it operates in the interests of the patient. A subjective judgment of a committee or institution may or may not be what the patient would request if able to do so. Therefore, an advance directive is clearly the recommended document to advise the best course of treatment for the patient.

Without an advance directive from the individual patient, treatments that might be ordered for patients include CPR, mechanical breathing or respirator, tube feedings, kidney dialysis, chemotherapy, intravenous therapy, surgery, diagnostic tests, antibiotics, and transfusions.

Med Tip

It is recommended that all persons over the age of 18 place in writing their wishes about what type of treatment they should receive if they become incompetent. The advance directive should be specific about treatments such as CPR, tube feeding, and ventilators.

Healthcare Proxy

In some cases, a person can sign a **healthcare proxy** appointing another person to act for them in making healthcare decisions on their behalf. Each state has passed laws to allow a healthcare proxy to be signed that authorizes the person appointed to make such healthcare decisions. Healthcare proxies may place specific limitations on the authority of the authorized person. Such proxies can be revoked either orally or in writing.

Ethical Dilemmas

Suicide

Suicide is a major *preventable* health problem in the United States, where over 49,000 people died by suicide in 2022. There are an estimated 11 attempted suicides for every completed suicide death. People who die by suicide often have feelings of isolation, helplessness, and self-loathing. They can't see any way out of their suffering other than suicide. According to studies, most people who die by suicide don't want to die—they just want to stop hurting. Talking openly about suicidal thoughts and feelings may save a life.

Suicide is a complex behavior pattern, with the risk factors varying by gender, age, and ethnic group. Men are at a higher risk of suicide than women. Suicide is the eighth leading cause of death for men and the 15th for women. Adults ages 3–64 account for 46.8 percent of suicides in the United States. Older adults, especially White men of European ancestry, have the highest rate of suicide at 50.1 per 100,000 people. People who identify as LGBTQIA+, those who are veterans, and people who live in rural areas all are at increased risk for suicide.

Med Tip

A suicidal person may not ask for help, but don't assume that it isn't wanted. If a suicide attempt is impending, immediately dial 911, call a local crisis center, or, if possible, take the person to an emergency department. A suicidal person should never be left alone!

The ethical landscape surrounding suicide is complex and varies across different cultures and belief systems. Open dialogue, empathy, and comprehensive mental health support are crucial components of addressing the ethical dimensions of suicide.

- *Autonomy vs. preservation of life:* Some argue that individuals have the right to autonomy, including the right to make decisions about their own lives, even if it involves ending their lives. Others emphasize the ethical duty to preserve life and argue that society has a responsibility to intervene and prevent suicide, viewing it as a tragedy that can often be prevented.

- *Mental health and decision-making capacity:* The ethical dilemma arises when individuals struggling with mental health issues may not have the full capacity to make rational decisions. Balancing respect for autonomy with the duty to protect those who may be vulnerable due to mental health challenges is a complex ethical consideration.

- *Impact on others:* Suicide can have profound and lasting effects on family, friends, and the broader community. The ethical question arises about the responsibilities of individuals to their social networks and the potential harm caused by their decision.

- *Cultural and religious perspectives:* Cultural and religious beliefs often shape attitudes toward suicide. In some cultures and religions, suicide may be considered morally unacceptable, while in others, it may be viewed with more understanding or empathy.

- *Prevention and intervention:* Ethical questions arise regarding the role of society and healthcare professionals in preventing suicide. This includes the development of mental health support systems, access to treatment, and responsible reporting in the media to avoid sensationalizing suicide.

- ***Stigmatization and mental health advocacy:*** Addressing the stigma associated with mental health issues is an ethical imperative. Promoting mental health awareness and advocacy can contribute to a more compassionate and understanding society.

The Case of the Conjoined Twins

A marathon 50-hour operation to separate 29-year-old Iranian twins joined at the head resulted in their deaths during the surgical procedure in July 2003. The twins, Ladan and Laleh Bijani, made a desperate plea to surgeons to give them a chance at living independent lives. The twins knew that the operation carried deadly risks, but knowingly accepted the risks, according to their physicians. Many of their physicians and relatives tried to talk the twins out of having the procedure. But the women gave instructions to their next-of-kin that they wished to be separated under all circumstances, no matter what the surgeons encountered during the surgery. Dr. Benjamin Carson, who was a part of the neurosurgical team to separate the twins, said that he was persuaded to proceed with the operation based on the medical evidence and the strong desire of the twins to be separated. He stated, "These were individuals who were absolutely determined to be separated. The reason I felt compelled to become involved is because I wanted to make sure they had their best chance."

Source: Dr. Benjamin Carson

However, during the operation, the surgeons found that contrary to their first impression, the twins' brains were fused together, and a vein graft failed, causing the twins to hemorrhage and die. After the death of the twins, Dr. Carson said that in hindsight he believes it was unwise for the medical team to tacitly agree to continue with the surgery to separate the twins no matter what they encountered during the surgery.

There have been many ethical debates about the separation of conjoined twins, such as Ladan and Laleh, who have little chance of both surviving such a surgery. Michael Grodin, director of medical ethics at the Boston University School of Medicine, stated, "The key issue is that they were adults and could understand the risks and benefits and make decisions on their own." He went on to say, "Obviously, if the chances were 100 percent that the twins were going to die, then the surgeons shouldn't have offered it. To do so would have been akin to participating in an assisted suicide." Grodin and other ethicists agree that no one knows exactly where the ethical cut-off point should be for an operation or procedure in which the odds for recovery are poor.

Source: Michael Grodin

Some parents have opted not to have their conjoined twins separated because one would ultimately die during the separation if they share key organs. In the case of each twin receiving a kidney or a limb, the surgeons will often recommend separation. In the case of a shared heart, the decision becomes an ethical dilemma because both twins may die during the separation.

Mechanical Heart Recipient

The first implanted mechanical heart, a grapefruit-sized plastic and titanium four-pound heart called an AbioCor, was implanted into a 59-year-old man, Robert Tools, in July 2001. This patient did quite well with his mechanical heart until he suffered a severe stroke from a blood clot that was believed to be caused by the mechanical device. Mr. Tools was unable to take anticoagulant medications to reduce the risk of blood clots forming. He spent the final days of his life partly paralyzed and breathing through a ventilator. Before he had the mechanical heart transplant, Mr. Tools had been on the brink of death with end-stage heart failure and had been given little chance of surviving more than 30 days. Up until the time of his stroke, he expressed gratitude after the surgery and said that he had no regrets. Robert Tools lived for five months with his mechanical heart. The manufacturers of the mechanical heart said the success of the AbioCor is measured by how well it extends life and restores life's quality.

Chapter 13 Review

Points to Ponder

1. What do you say to a dying patient who asks you, "Why me?"

2. What are some major concerns of family members of a dying patient?

3. Does an individual have the right to determine when they wish to die? Why or why not?

4. What are the benefits of hospice care for the terminally ill?

5. Why is the ability to determine when death has occurred so critical in today's healthcare environment?

6. What is cardiac death?

7. Can a patient write an advance directive requesting maximum care?

Discussion Questions

1. Explain the statement, "Healthcare practitioners often find it more difficult to withdraw treatment after it has started than to withhold treatment."

2. Describe a situation in which passive euthanasia might be acceptable.

3. Discuss the cases of Nancy Cruzan, Terri Schiavo, and Brittany Maynard and how they advanced the narrative on medical aid-in-dying.

4. What are the pros and cons of a viatical settlement?

Review Challenge

Short Answer Questions

1. Explain the substitute judgment rule.

2. What does palliative care include?

3. Explain some of the arguments surrounding assisted suicide.

4. What is the difference between withdrawing and withholding life-sustaining treatment?

5. Do you think the courts acted properly in granting Michael Schiavo control over his wife's feeding tube?

6. How might the Schiavo case affect future court decisions of the same nature?

_____

_____

_____

_____

_____

7. Describe the differences between ordinary and extraordinary means to keep a person alive.

_____

_____

_____

_____

_____

8. What are the three steps of pain management according to the World Health Organization?

_____

_____

_____

_____

_____

_____

Matching

Match the responses in column B with the correct term in column A.

COLUMN A

_____ **1.** proxy

_____ **2.** expired

_____ **3.** medical aid-in-dying

_____ **4.** comatose

_____ **5.** rigor mortis

_____ **6.** hypothermia

_____ **7.** deep unconsciousness

_____ **8.** cardiac death

_____ **9.** brain death

_____ **10.** active euthanasia

COLUMN B

a. body temperature is below normal

b. person acting on behalf of another person

c. legal definition of death

d. euthanasia

e. stiffness that occurs in death

f. vegetative condition

g. illegal act in all states

h. died

i. death by neurologic criteria

j. persistent vegetative state

Multiple Choice

Select the one best answer to the following statements.

1. The practice of allowing a terminally ill patient to die by forgoing treatment is called
   a. active euthanasia.
   b. passive euthanasia.
   c. medical aid-in-dying.
   d. a and c
   e. b and c

2. An electroencephalogram is used to
   a. reverse a coma patient's condition.
   b. measure cardiopulmonary function.
   c. measure brain function.
   d. reverse the condition of hypothermia.
   e. reverse the condition of rigor mortis.

3. The Uniform Determination of Death Act
   a. provides a definition of active euthanasia.
   b. provides a definition of brain death.
   c. is also called the doctrine of double-effect.
   d. mandates that every patient entering a nursing home must provide a written document stating the care they wish to receive.
   e. discusses the treatments that might be used for a comatose patient.

4. Criteria or standards for death include
   a. rigor mortis.
   b. hypothermia.
   c. loss of body color.
   d. biological disintegration.
   e. all of the above

5. What is the ethical term used to morally justify the removal of a cancerous uterus from a pregnant patient?

   a. mercy killing

   b. extraordinary means

   c. ordinary means

   d. doctrine of double effect

   e. advance directive

6. Another term meaning death is

   a. comatose.

   b. expired.

   c. proxy.

   d. terminally ill.

   e. hypothermia.

7. A hospice provides for

   a. palliative care.

   b. pain medications.

   c. in-patient care.

   d. home care.

   e. all of the above

8. Extraordinary care means that when caring for a comatose patient, one should include

   a. CPR and mechanical breathing.

   b. chemotherapy.

   c. turning and hydration.

   d. a and b only

   e. a, b, and c

9. The Karen Ann Quinlan case involved

   a. mercy killing.

   b. removal of hydration from a comatose patient.

   c. removal of a respirator from a comatose patient.

   d. a heart transplant.

   e. court order for a surgical procedure on an incompetent patient.

10. Terms referring to heart and pulmonary function include

   a. cardiac.

   b. comatose.

   c. hypothermia.

   d. cardiopulmonary.

   e. none of the above

Discussion Cases

1. Analyze the Marguerite M. case discussed at the beginning of this chapter using the Seven-Step Decision model found in Chapter 1.

   a. _____

   b. _____

   c. _____

   d. _____

   e. _____

   f. _____

   g. _____

2. Donald Hamilton, an alert 55-year-old man, was diagnosed with inoperable pancreatic cancer. His prognosis was poor; he was given about six months to live. He underwent several series of chemotherapy treatments, but they were of no benefit. He continued to lose weight, suffered from nausea, and became weaker. After three months of chemotherapy treatments, he stated that he wanted no further treatment. He became bedridden and was admitted into a nursing home for terminal care. Donald's son, who lived in another state, arrived at the nursing home and demanded that his father's healthcare provider be called immediately. The son wanted his father to be hospitalized and placed on chemotherapy. When the provider explained that there was little hope for the father's recovery, the son threatened to sue the provider for withdrawal of care.

   a. Identify the ethical issues in the case.

      _____

      _____

   b. In your opinion, does the son have a legitimate reason to sue the provider? Why or why not?

      _____

      _____

   c. What are the possible solutions to this case?

      _____

      _____

   d. What might the provider have done to prevent the confrontation with Donald's son?

      _____

      _____

3. Lois, who is in the last stages of breast cancer, was recently admitted into a hospice program. Her husband, Henry, is relieved to have a hospice nurse come into their home and help with the care of his wife. After Lois had been receiving care for a week, Henry asked when he should take Lois into the hospital out-patient department for more chemotherapy. The hospice nurse said, "I thought that you understood

that since treatments would no longer help Lois and she would ultimately die, that she would not receive any more treatments once she entered the hospice program." Henry said he did not understand this and insisted that he wanted everything done to save Lois.

a. How could this misunderstanding have been avoided?

_____

_____

b. What discussions should Lois and Henry have had with each other before Lois went into a hospice program?

_____

_____

c. What could hospice programs do to better inform the general public of their purpose?

_____

_____

Put It Into Practice

Look for a recent obituary in your area. What information does it give about the deceased person? What would you like to read about yourself if you could write your own obituary?

Web Hunt

Visit the website of the National Hospice and Palliative Care Organization (**www.nhpco.org**) and look under "Help Me Find a Provider." Using this listing, find a hospice in your area.

Critical Thinking Exercise

What would you say if you were asked for your opinion on who in our society has the right to determine who should and should not live?

Bibliography

American Medical Association. 2016. *Code of medical ethics: Current opinions on ethical and judicial affair.* Chicago: American Medical Association.

Barbus, A. J. (1975). *The dying person's bill of rights.* Lansing: South Western Michigan Inservice Education Council.

Bell, M. 2004. Judge in Florida voids Terri's Law. *Chicago Tribune* (May 7), 4.

Bor, J., & Niedowski, E. 2003. A great emptiness: The deaths of conjoined twins. *Hartford Courant* (July 9), 1, A4.

Brown, D. 2001. Surgeon in doomed operation on twins speaks out. *Hartford Courant* (July 12), A5.

Caplan, L., McCartney, J., & Sisti, D. 2006. *The case of Terri Schiavo.* Amherst, NY: Prometheus Books.

Centers for Disease Control and Prevention. (2023). *Facts about suicide.* https://www.cdc.gov/suicide/facts/index.html

Centers for Disease Control and Prevention. (2023). *Disparities in suicide.* https://www.cdc.gov/suicide/facts/disparities-in-suicide.html

Greer, D. M., Kirschen, M. P., Lewis, A., et al. (2023). Pediatric and Adult Brain Death/Death by *Neurologic* Criteria Consensus Guideline. Report of the AAN Guidelines Subcommittee, AAP, CNS, and SCCM. Neurology, Oct 2023, 10.1212/WNL.0000000000207740; DOI: 10.1212/WNL.0000000000207740

Kampert, P. 2003. The face that moved a nation. *Chicago Tribune* (October 23), 1, 25.

McCullough, D. 2009. *My mother, your mother: Embracing slow medicine, the compassionate approach to caring for your aging loved one.* New York: HarperCollins.

Nutt, A. (2018, June 7). Suicide rates rise sharply across the United States, new report shows. *Washington Post.* Available at https://www.washingtonpost.com/news/to-your-health/wp/2018/06/07/u-s-suicide-rates-rise-sharply-across-the-country-new-report-shows/?utm_term=.100f2de869c1.

Pirotte, B. D., & Benson, S. (2023). Refusal of care. *StatPearls.* https://www.ncbi.nlm.nih.gov/books/NBK560886/

Quill, T. 2005. Terri Schiavo: A tragedy compounded. *New England Journal of Medicine,* 352, 1630–1633.

Spears, W., Mian, A., & Greer, D. (2022). Brain death: A clinical overview. *Journal of Intensive Care,* 10: 26. https://jintensivecare.biomedcentral.com/articles/10.1186/s40560-022-00609-4

Tyrell, P., Harberger, S., Schoo, C., & Siddiqui, W. (2023). Kubler-Ross stages of dying and subsequent models of grief. *StatPearls.* https://www.ncbi.nlm.nih.gov/books/NBK507885/

Uniform Law Commission. (2023). *Determination of death act.* https://www.uniformlaws.org/committees/community-home?CommunityKey=155faf5d-03c2-4027-99ba-ee4c99019d6c

USAFACTS. (2023). *What are the leading causes of death in the US?* https://usafacts.org/articles/americans-causes-of-death-by-age-cdc-data/

Ethical Issues in Healthcare Trends

Learning Objectives

After completing this chapter, you will be able to:

14.1 Define the key terms.

14.2 Describe the systemic problems with healthcare in the United States.

14.3 Explain the ethical implications of maternal mortality, healthcare-associated infections, multidrug-resistant organisms, and the opioid crisis.

14.4 Discuss disparities in healthcare including the social determinants of health, health literacy, and food insecurity.

14.5 Describe how to communicate better with patients who are Deaf, have hearing loss, or have impaired vision.

14.6 Describe the challenges facing older adults and people with intellectual and physical disabilities in the healthcare system.

Key Terms

American Deaf culture

American Sign Language

Americans with Disabilities Act

Artificial intelligence

Blindness

Concierge healthcare

Food insecurity

Fraud

Healthcare-associated infections

Maternal mortality

Multidrug-resistant organisms

Opioid crisis

Protocol

Robotics

Robotic-assisted surgery

Social determinants of health

Triage

Visual impairment

Case of Anne and the Runaway Stroller

Anne, a 75-year-old woman with late-stage Alzheimer's disease, was walking to a neighborhood restaurant holding on to the arms of her husband and a friend. Suddenly, a young woman, talking on her cell phone as she was jogging while pushing a stroller containing a young baby, ran toward Anne, veering to the side at the last second and then continued on her run. The quick movement of the stroller startled Anne, who then fell onto the cement sidewalk. Her friend, a nurse, could tell by the angle of her leg that Anne had probably broken her hip. Her husband called an ambulance, which arrived in 10 minutes. Anne was taken to a new city hospital where she was diagnosed in the emergency department with a broken hip.

Anne was immediately admitted to a room across from the nursing station, which had an open design, allowing her to be observed at all times. The nurses were frequently in her room to assess her condition. In addition, her room contained a built-in bed for close relatives to stay overnight.

Anne had surgery the day after she was admitted. Her family came to take turns in spending time with her in the room so that Anne was never alone. The **protocol** (clinical plan of treatment) that the hospital used for all hip surgery patients was started immediately. She was up in a chair the day after surgery and started walking with assistance a short time later. The nursing staff and a discharge planner met with Anne's husband and family, explaining the care she would need. Four days after surgery, Anne was discharged to a nursing home where she spent a week until her insurance coverage ran out. She then went home and received home healthcare a few hours a day for several weeks. However, her husband and children did provide much of the care when she was sent home.

A month after surgery, Anne was walking with some assistance—but without a limp or pain. In other words, a patient with late-stage Alzheimer's had the same care and good results as other patients with hip fractures have come to expect.

1. Do you believe that a patient with late-stage Alzheimer's disease should have expensive hip replacement surgery? Or would it be more practical for a patient at her age and mental condition to have her hip immobilized instead of repairing it with surgery?

2. Do you believe that having Anne released from the hospital so early was an undue burden on her family?

3. What do you think about the care given to Anne, as well as the design of the hospital, in this case?

4. Do you believe that the woman who startled Anne and caused her to fall bears any responsibility for Anne's injury?

Introduction

Healthcare is an ever-changing field. There are new advances in treatments, medications, and surgical procedures. Patients are receiving better care in many healthcare settings than they were 50 years ago. As with all issues relating to healthcare, we will be faced with new ethical dilemmas. It might be useful to remember these wise words of the general counsel for a major service organization: "The best way to avoid litigation is to do it right in the first place."

Selected Issues in the Current Healthcare System

Systemic Problems in Healthcare

First, Do No Harm

According to the Agency for Healthcare Research and Quality, medical errors are killing tens of thousands of Americans every year. These patients are dying from preventable medical errors including incorrect diagnoses, drug mix-ups, needle infections, and surgical mishaps. Medication errors are one of the leading types of medical errors. Another preventable error is healthcare-acquired infections. Every day, 1 in 31 patients in U.S. facilities acquires an infection while being treated. The Centers for Medicare and Medicaid Services no longer reimburses hospitals for the cost of preventable complications such as wrong-type blood transfusions and patients who have developed pressure injuries. Ethically and legally, the healthcare profession needs to do a better job of keeping patients safe.

Cost of Healthcare

The cost of healthcare in the United States has long been a topic of intense debate and scrutiny, with ethical implications that extend far beyond the financial realm. At the heart of the matter lies a complex web of factors, including the structure of the healthcare system, the role of insurance companies, pharmaceutical pricing, and the overall approach to healthcare delivery. Examining the ethical dimensions of these issues reveals a landscape fraught with challenges and moral dilemmas.

One of the most glaring ethical concerns is the accessibility of healthcare services. The exorbitant costs associated with medical care in the United States create a significant barrier for a substantial portion of the population. This results in a two-tiered system where those with financial means can access the best treatments and services, while others are left grappling with limited options or, in some cases, forgoing essential care altogether. The principle of justice is compromised when individuals' access to healthcare is determined by their economic status rather than their medical needs.

Furthermore, the profit-driven nature of the healthcare industry in the United States raises ethical questions about prioritizing financial gain over the well-being of patients. Pharmaceutical companies, for example, often set prices for life-saving medications at levels that are financially burdensome for patients. This practice can lead to a moral conflict between the duty to provide effective healthcare and the desire for corporate profit. The tension between capitalism and the ethical obligation to prioritize public health underscores the need for systemic reforms.

The role of health insurance companies adds another layer to the ethical discourse. While insurance is designed to mitigate the financial burden on individuals, the intricate policies, exclusions, and high premiums often result in coverage gaps and denied claims. This creates a situation where individuals are paying into a system that fails to provide the promised security when they need it most. The ethical principle of beneficence, which emphasizes the obligation to promote well-being, is compromised when insurance structures contribute to individuals' inability to access necessary medical care.

The ethical implications of the cost of healthcare in the United States also extend to healthcare providers. The pressure to generate revenue can lead to over-treatment, unnecessary procedures, and the prescription of expensive medications when more cost-effective alternatives may exist. This not only inflates healthcare costs but also raises concerns about the integrity of medical decision-making. The Hippocratic Oath's directive to "do no harm" may be strained when financial considerations are given undue weight in healthcare practice.

In conclusion, the ethical implications of the cost of healthcare in the United States are multifaceted and deeply rooted in systemic issues. As a society, addressing these ethical concerns requires a commitment to reevaluating the values that underpin the healthcare system. Prioritizing accessibility, promoting justice, and placing the well-being of patients above financial interests are essential steps in fostering a healthcare system that aligns with ethical principles and serves the needs of all individuals, regardless of their economic standing.

Med Tip

Healthcare office personnel must treat all patients with the same consideration for the patient's dignity regardless of their ability to pay.

Lack of Healthcare Providers

The United States faces a pressing challenge in the form of a significant shortage of healthcare providers, a situation with far-reaching implications for public health and well-being. This shortage encompasses various healthcare professionals, including physicians, advance practice providers, nurses, and allied health professionals, and is particularly pronounced in rural and underserved urban areas.

One key factor contributing to the shortage is the increasing demand for healthcare services, driven by an aging population with complex medical needs. As the population ages, the demand for healthcare professionals rises, leading to a strain on the existing workforce. Additionally, the Affordable Care Act (ACA) expanded access to healthcare for millions of Americans, further intensifying the need for healthcare providers.

Moreover, the lengthy and rigorous education and training required to become a healthcare professional contribute to the shortage. The time and financial commitment involved in obtaining a medical degree or other healthcare qualifications can deter potential candidates, limiting the pool of individuals entering the field.

In rural areas, the lack of infrastructure and resources poses a unique set of challenges. Healthcare providers may be hesitant to practice in these areas due to limited professional support, reduced access to advanced medical facilities, and lower compensation. This leaves vast swaths of the population with inadequate access to essential healthcare services.

The shortage of healthcare providers also has significant implications for the quality of care delivered. Overburdened healthcare professionals may experience burnout, impacting their ability to provide optimal care. The COVID-19 pandemic increased stress across the healthcare workforce. Lisa Rotenstein, a primary care physician and assistant professor, analyzed burnout, feelings of being overworked, and intent to leave the profession in healthcare workers. Her team found that 50 percent of the respondents experienced burnout. A feeling of being overworked was reported by 37 percent of physicians and 47 percent of other clinical staff. The intent to leave the profession was reported by 28 percent of the healthcare workers surveyed, including 41 percent of nurses.

Addressing the shortage of healthcare providers requires a multifaceted approach. This includes increasing funding for medical education programs, implementing policies to incentivize healthcare professionals to practice in underserved areas, and leveraging technology to extend the reach of healthcare services. A comprehensive strategy is essential to ensure that all Americans have timely access to quality healthcare, regardless of their geographic location or socioeconomic status. The shortage of healthcare providers is a critical issue that demands immediate attention and innovative solutions to safeguard the health and well-being of the nation's population.

Allocation of Scarce Time and Resources

The allocation of scarce time and resources in healthcare is a critical and complex ethical challenge that requires careful consideration of priorities, equity, and the overall well-being of the population. In the realm of healthcare, time and resources are finite, and decisions must be made to ensure that they are used efficiently and ethically.

One key ethical principle guiding the allocation of resources is distributive justice, emphasizing fair and equitable distribution. This principle is especially relevant in healthcare, where decisions about resource allocation can have life-altering consequences. In a system with limited resources, determining how to prioritize treatments, interventions, and access to healthcare services becomes paramount.

Triage, a common practice in emergency medicine, exemplifies the ethical challenges of resource allocation. Healthcare providers must make rapid decisions about who receives immediate care based on the severity of their condition. In hospital emergency departments, this process requires balancing the need for efficiency with the ethical imperative to provide care to those who are most critically ill. Those with little or no obvious illness or injury have to wait until patients with a serious or life-threatening injury or illness have been cared for.

The concept of "resource stewardship" underscores the responsibility of healthcare providers and institutions to use resources judiciously and avoid unnecessary waste. This involves making informed decisions about diagnostic tests, treatments, and interventions, considering both the potential benefits and costs. Striking a balance between providing quality care and avoiding unnecessary expenses is crucial in a healthcare landscape with limited resources.

Furthermore, the allocation of time in healthcare settings poses ethical dilemmas. Healthcare professionals must manage their time efficiently to address the needs of all patients under their care. This requires thoughtful prioritization, effective communication, and a commitment to providing compassionate and patient-centered care.

In conclusion, the ethical allocation of scarce time and resources in healthcare is a dynamic and ongoing challenge. Striking a balance between distributive justice, resource stewardship, and the need for efficiency is essential for ensuring that healthcare systems effectively meet the needs of diverse patient populations. Ethical decision-making in resource allocation is fundamental to providing high-quality, equitable, and accessible healthcare to individuals and communities, even in the face of limitations.

Fraud

Unfortunately, the healthcare system still has issues with **fraud**, which is an intentional deception or injury to another person. Injury, in the case of fraud, is a wrongful act that results in damage to a person's reputation or property. Examples of fraud consist of misrepresentation, concealment, or nondisclosure of a fact or misleading conduct. Therefore, a person who represents themself as a nurse must have a nursing license that is registered in the state where they are practicing nursing. If there is no current license, then a fraudulent action has occurred. In that case, misuse of the title "Registered Nurse" is considered an unclassified felony. In addition, if this person has signed a document, such as a medication record, with an "RN" after their name, this may be considered a forgery under the law, and that person may also be arrested for committing a felony.

Other instances of fraud consist of falsifying medical documents such as a patient's medical chart, an application for a medical license, or a medical diploma. Recall the cases presented in Chapter 6.

Healthcare fraud can take many forms. The government is able to perform "real-time" analysis of all Medicare and Medicaid billings to obtain information on payments for care. This helps to ensure that healthcare facilities such as hospitals, laboratories, physicians' offices, and other healthcare organizations are complying with all billing and healthcare service requirements. Commissions of healthcare fraud, including false billing schemes, pharmacy fraud, and kick-back schemes for unnecessary health referrals, are crimes that can result in prison time.

The cost to the country from fraudulent claims relating to Medicare billings are said to be in the millions. These false billings, as already noted, range from charging for a false diagnosis, kickbacks for referrals, and providing medical procedures and services that are not needed. In some cases of fraud, the medical provider has split reimbursement for a false billing with the patient.

Recall the case presented in Chapter 6, *United States of America v. Steven Monaco, Daniel Osw Ari, Michael Goldis, and Aaron Jones,* where two physicians, a physician assistant, and a medical assistant (among many others) pled guilty or were convicted of an elaborate plan to fill prescriptions for unnecessary compound medications that cost thousands of dollars per month. They charged insurance carriers for New Jersey's state employees for the very expensive and medically unnecessary medications.

Examples of Conditions and Situations with Ethical Implications

Maternal Mortality

The World Health Organization defines **maternal mortality** as the death of a woman while pregnant or within 42 days of termination of the pregnancy. Maternal mortality is considered a general indicator of the overall health of a population. International data show the maternal mortality rate in the United States exceeds the rate in other high-income countries. In 2020, the maternal mortality rate in the United States was 24 deaths per 100,000 live births—more than three times the rate in most other high-income countries. The U.S. maternal mortality rate is exceptionally high for Black women, with 69.9 Black women dying per 100,000 live births—a rate 2.6 times higher than that of White women—in 2020 (Figure 14.1). The U.S. maternal mortality rate continued to increase in 2021. There were 1205 maternal deaths in 2021 compared with 658 in 2018.

Thus, maternal mortality in the United States raises profound ethical concerns, shedding light on systemic issues within the healthcare system that disproportionately affect pregnant women. Several ethical issues contribute to the alarming rates of maternal mortality, prompting calls for comprehensive reform and increased attention to maternal health.

- *Disparities in access to care:* One of the primary ethical concerns is the glaring disparity in access to prenatal and postpartum care. Women from marginalized communities, including those of lower socioeconomic status and marginalized groups, often face barriers such as lack of insurance, transportation issues, and inadequate healthcare facilities. The ethical principle of justice is compromised when certain populations are disproportionately affected, highlighting a systemic failure to provide equitable access to essential maternal healthcare.

- *Implicit bias and cultural competency:* Implicit bias within healthcare systems can contribute to delays in diagnosis and treatment, affecting maternal outcomes. If healthcare providers hold unconscious biases, it may impact the quality of care provided to certain groups. Ensuring cultural competency and addressing biases in medical care are ethical imperatives to uphold the principles of autonomy, dignity, and equality in maternal healthcare.

Figure 14–1 Black women have the highest maternal mortality rates in the United States

Source: Shutterstock

- *Postpartum care deficiencies:* The limited focus on postpartum care contributes to the ethical concerns surrounding maternal health. More than 50 percent of pregnancy-related deaths in the United States occur in the postpartum period. The transition from pregnancy to postpartum is a vulnerable period, and inadequate support during this time can lead to complications. Addressing the ethical imperative of continuity of care requires a shift in healthcare policies and practices to prioritize postpartum health and well-being. Another postpartum factor is the lack of a mandate for paid maternity leave in the United States. All high-income countries except for the United States mandate at least 14 weeks of paid leave.

- Addressing these ethical concerns necessitates a comprehensive and multifaceted approach. Healthcare policy reforms, increased education and awareness, cultural competency training for healthcare professionals, and a commitment to addressing systemic inequities are imperative to improving maternal outcomes and ensuring ethical standards in maternal healthcare in the United States.

Healthcare-Associated Infections

Healthcare-associated infections, also called HAIs, are infections that patients get in a healthcare facility while receiving medical care. Every day, 1 in 31 patients in U.S. healthcare facilities contracts an HAI, which equals over 1 million people per year. The most common HAIs include catheter-associated urinary tract infections, central line-associated bloodstream infections, pneumonia, and surgical site infections.

Healthcare professionals are required to prioritize patient well-being. HAIs jeopardize patient safety, causing harm that is preventable with proper infection control measures. In addition, vulnerable populations may be disproportionately affected by HAIs due to factors such as socioeconomic status, access to healthcare, and underlying health conditions. Ethical considerations demand a commitment to minimizing risks and ensuring that healthcare environments prioritize patient safety.

Healthcare institutions have an obligation to be transparent about HAI rates, take responsibility for preventable infections, and implement measures to improve patient safety. Addressing the issue of HAIs requires a comprehensive approach that includes rigorous infection prevention protocols, transparent communication, patient education, and ongoing efforts to promote a culture of safety and accountability within healthcare institutions.

Multidrug-Resistant Organisms

Multidrug-resistant organisms, known as MDROs, are germs that are resistant to many antibiotics, which makes the use of the drugs less effective or even not effective at all. MDROs are a critical global health challenge, raising significant concerns within the realm of healthcare. Among others, MDROs include the following:

- **MRSA**, or methicillin-resistant *Staphylococcus aureus*, is a bacterium responsible for several hard-to-treat infections in humans. It can cause serious skin and soft-tissue infections in patients in hospitals and nursing homes. It is a strong bacterium that is resistant to penicillin-type antibiotics as well as cephalosporins.

- **VRE**, or vancomycin-resistant Enterococcus, is a type of Enterococci that has become resistant to the drug vancomycin. Enterococci are naturally present in the intestinal tract, but VRE infections can occur in patients with serious underlying illnesses.

- **C. diff**, or *Clostridium difficile* infections, cause diarrhea and colitis (an infection of the colon) to over half a million people each year.

The responsible use of antibiotics is an ethical imperative to address the rising threat of MDROs. Overprescribing or misusing antimicrobial agents contributes to the development of resistance, compromising the effectiveness of these drugs. Healthcare providers have a duty to practice antimicrobial stewardship, ensuring judicious use to protect both individual patients and public health.

All healthcare workers must also prioritize robust infection prevention and control measures to mitigate the spread of MDROs. Adhering to stringent hygiene protocols, surveillance, and isolation practices are essential professional and ethical obligations.

Opioid Crisis

The **opioid crisis** describes a rapid rise in overdose deaths starting in the 1990s in the United States. The first wave began when providers began prescribing both natural and semi-synthetic opioids to manage patients' pain. The second wave began in 2010, with a rapid increase in opioid overdose deaths, primarily involving heroin. The last wave began in 2013 with significant increases in overdose deaths, particularly involving illicit fentanyl (a synthetic opioid). The number of people who died from an overdose in 2021 is over six times the number of people who died from overdose in 1999 (Figure 14.2).

The healthcare community faced challenges in recognizing and addressing signs of opioid addiction promptly. This delay in identifying and responding to the emerging crisis allowed it to escalate, impacting individuals from all walks of life. The role the healthcare system in the opioid epidemic is multifaceted, encompassing both beneficial pain management practices and unintentional contributions to the crisis. Physicians and advanced practice providers, acting with the intention of relieving patients' suffering, prescribed opioids at high rates, underestimating the risk of addiction. Patients adhered to their provider's prescription and became addicted.

The pharmaceutical industry, in turn, played a role in aggressively marketing opioid medications, contributing to the widespread availability of these drugs. In 2020, the U.S. Department of Justice settled a criminal and civil investigation in Purdue Pharma LP and individual shareholders from the Sackler family, when they pleaded guilty in federal court. The company paid a criminal fine of over $3.5 billion and another $2.8 billion for its civil liability. The Sackler family agreed to pay $225 million in damages to resolve its civil False Claims Act liability. In addition, four more U.S. companies will pay $26 billion to settle thousands of civil lawsuits claiming their business practices helped to create and fuel the opioid crisis.

Healthcare is now at the forefront of mitigating the epidemic. Healthcare providers are increasingly advocating for responsible prescribing practices, enhanced medical education on pain management alternatives, and greater awareness of the potential risks associated with opioids. Furthermore, medical professionals play a pivotal role in treating individuals with opioid use disorder, emphasizing harm reduction, and promoting evidence-based interventions to address addiction and prevent overdoses. By acknowledging medicine's dual role in the opioid epidemic, the healthcare industry is working toward responsible solutions to curb the crisis while ensuring effective pain management.

Figure 14–2 Almost 80,000 Americans died from opioid overdose in 2022

Source: Sipa USA/Alamy Stock Photo

Diversity and Equity in Healthcare

Disparities in Healthcare

Disparities in healthcare refer to differences in access to, quality of, and outcomes from healthcare services among various population groups. These disparities can be influenced by a complex interplay of social, economic, cultural, and structural factors, creating unequal healthcare experiences for individuals based on characteristics such as race, ethnicity, socioeconomic status, gender, geographic location, and more.

One of the prominent aspects of healthcare disparities is the unequal distribution of health resources and services. Access to medical facilities, preventive care, diagnostic services, and treatment options can vary significantly across different demographic groups. Socioeconomic factors play a crucial role in shaping these disparities, with individuals of lower income facing challenges in accessing timely and appropriate healthcare.

Moreover, racial and ethnic minorities often experience disparities in healthcare outcomes. Factors such as discrimination, cultural differences, and limited health literacy contribute to these disparities. Additionally, geographic disparities highlight variations in healthcare access and outcomes based on geographical location, with rural areas often facing challenges in healthcare infrastructure and service availability compared to urban areas.

Addressing healthcare disparities is a multifaceted challenge that requires a comprehensive approach. Strategies may include improving healthcare access, increasing cultural competence among healthcare providers, addressing social determinants of health, and promoting policies that ensure equitable distribution of resources. Recognizing and addressing healthcare disparities is crucial for achieving health equity and ensuring that all individuals have the opportunity to attain their highest level of health. Some of the disparities in healthcare in the United States today are described below.

Social Determinants of Health

According to Healthy People 2030, **social determinants of health** (SDH) are the conditions in which people are born, grow, live, work, and age, and they play a critical role in influencing health outcomes (Figure 14.3). In the field of healthcare, understanding and addressing social determinants is essential for providing holistic and effective healthcare. These determinants encompass a range of factors, including socioeconomic status, education, employment, social support networks, and the physical environment.

Socioeconomic status, a key social determinant, significantly influences health. Individuals with lower income may face challenges in accessing healthcare services, affording medications, and maintaining a healthy lifestyle. Education level is another crucial determinant, as it often correlates with health literacy and the ability to make informed healthcare decisions.

Employment conditions contribute to health disparities, with factors such as job stability, workplace safety, and access to benefits impacting overall well-being. Social support networks, including family and community relationships, play a protective role in health by influencing stress levels and mental well-being.

The physical environment, encompassing factors like housing, access to nutritious food, and exposure to pollutants, also shapes health outcomes. For instance, individuals in neighborhoods with limited access to fresh produce may face challenges in maintaining a healthy diet.

Healthcare professionals increasingly recognize the importance of considering social determinants in patient care. Integrating this understanding into healthcare practice involves identifying and addressing the underlying social factors that contribute to health disparities. By acknowledging and addressing social determinants of health, healthcare providers can contribute to more comprehensive and equitable healthcare, ultimately improving health outcomes for diverse patient populations.

Health Literacy

The National Assessment of Adult Literacy Survey found that 36 percent of U.S. adults had basic or below-basic health literacy. A 2010 study commissioned by the Institute of Medicine noted that, in general, a significant number of Americans are functionally illiterate and only 12 percent of adults are proficient in

Figure 14–3 The Healthy People 2030 Social Determinants of Health include healthcare access and quality, neighborhood and built environment, social and community context, economic stability, and education access and quality

Source: Data from U.S. Department of Health and Human Services

Social Determinants of Health

Social Determinants of Health
Copyright-free

Healthy People 2030

health literacy. This means that many people have difficulty using information on a medication label or even understanding the definition of a medical term. Healthy People 2030 identifies health literacy as a central focus to help eliminate health disparities. This communication gap has meant that healthcare reform must address policies that mandate how medically related descriptions are presented to patients. For example, information on drug labels and written health information that is given to patients must be in clear and easy-to-understand wording. The Agency for Healthcare Research and Quality found that low reading ability and health literacy were linked to poorer health and a higher risk of death. They also found a link between low reading ability including health literacy and more frequent use of hospital emergency departments.

Strategies that healthcare workers can use to assist patients to achieve health literacy include the following:

- Help patients to navigate healthcare facilities and websites. Advocate for good signage and excellent usability of patient portals.

- Make sure all patients feel comfortable from the reception area to the examination room or hospital room.

- Listen carefully and communicate clearly. Do not interrupt patients when they are talking. Ask questions if you are unclear about what they are describing.

- Simplify health information as much as possible: Use plain language (e.g., *itching* instead of *pruritus*) and use visual cues when possible (e.g., a visual pain measurement scale [Figure 14.4]).

- Use the teach-back method to confirm that patients understand instructions. This method involves asking patients to repeat what you've taught them by using a realistic scenario such as "tell me how you'll take your medication tomorrow" or "how will you explain your diagnosis to your family."

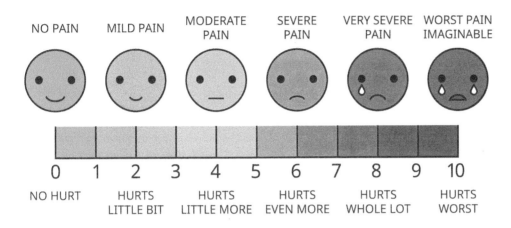

Figure 14–4 Visual pain measurement scale

Source: lukpedclub/Shutterstock

- Help patients manage their health by suggesting guidelines, strategies, and self-management practices. For example, there are excellent medication apps for smartphones that help patients remember when to take their drugs.

Food Insecurity

In the United States, 20 percent of children and a total of 44 million people experience **food insecurity**, meaning they don't have enough food to eat or have access to healthy food. In 2022, 49 million people requested assistance with getting adequate amounts and types of food. Food insecurity affects people all over the United States, but is more prevalent in rural areas, in the southern states, in the very young and the very old, and in families of color.

Individuals experiencing food insecurity often struggle to maintain a balanced and adequate diet, leading to nutritional deficiencies and a higher risk of chronic health conditions. Insufficient access to nutritious food contributes to malnutrition, affecting physical and mental health, especially in vulnerable populations such as children and pregnant women. Food insecurity is associated with a higher prevalence of conditions like obesity, diabetes, cardiovascular disease, and developmental issues in children. Additionally, the stress and anxiety related to uncertain access to food can impact mental health. Addressing food insecurity is crucial for promoting overall well-being and preventing a range of health issues, emphasizing the interconnectedness of nutrition, socioeconomic factors, and health outcomes.

Strategies to combat food insecurity include the following:

- Screen patients for food insecurity at wellness visits and check-ups.
- Learn about federal nutrition programs so that you can educate patients about them.
- Discover local resources for food so you can direct patients and families to them.

Healthcare for Patients with Disabilities

Healthcare for people with disabilities is a critical and multifaceted aspect of public health, emphasizing the need for inclusive and accessible healthcare services. Individuals with disabilities often face unique health challenges, requiring tailored approaches to address their diverse needs. Access barriers, both physical and systemic, can impede timely and appropriate healthcare for this population. Moreover, people with disabilities may experience higher rates of chronic conditions, necessitating comprehensive and coordinated healthcare strategies. Inclusive healthcare involves not only accommodating physical disabilities but also considering communication methods, cognitive differences, and social support systems. Ensuring equitable access to healthcare services for individuals with disabilities is essential for promoting their overall health, quality of life, and societal participation. Recognizing and addressing these challenges is pivotal in advancing healthcare equity and fostering a healthcare system that serves the diverse needs of all individuals, regardless of their abilities.

Deaf Patients

The culture and language of the Deaf tend to meld together or intertwine. To better understand the **American Deaf Culture**, it is important to understand their language. American Sign Language (ASL) is used by Deaf people to communicate with both the Deaf population and the hearing population. ASL is considered to be a complete language. It has its own grammar, different from English grammar, with its own rules, idioms, jokes, and poetry. The Deaf culture prefers to always have the word "Deaf" capitalized.

Sources of information about laws and resources for the Deaf include the **Americans with Disabilities**, abbreviated as ADA, passed by Congress in 1990 to ensure the rights of persons with disabilities. It prohibits discrimination in employment, public services, transportation, communication, and other areas. The National Association of the Deaf is also an excellent resource for information. In addition, each state has a commission for the Deaf.

AMERICAN SIGN LANGUAGE

American Sign Language, abbreviated as ASL, is often the first language of the Deaf or hard-of-hearing person. ASL is often more effective than writing everything down on paper. Healthcare professionals do not always understand ASL. However, interpreters, using sign language, are available to facilitate communication. They sign everything that is voiced and they voice everything that is signed. Thus, they can communicate with the patient, the hearing family, and the healthcare professionals. Many hospitals have an employee who, while possibly also having other duties, can communicate in ASL.

Because English may not be the first language of a Deaf person, it may mean that the person's understanding of written English is at a lower level than that of a hearing person of the same age. Schools and organizations need to take this into consideration when communicating with the Deaf.

American Sign Language is not considered a universal language. Other countries have their own sign languages. ASL is designed to assist the American Deaf culture but does not exactly copy American English. Therefore, persons who wish to communicate with the Deaf regularly should become knowledgeable and adept at using sign language. Relying totally on pen and paper to communicate with the Deaf is not as effective. "Lip reading" is not considered to be very effective because only 30 to 35 percent of spoken words can be understood.

Considering the serious nature of healthcare appointments, procedures, and discussions, it is always wise to have an ASL interpreter for a Deaf patient. This can help to avoid misunderstanding of important medical issues, instructions, and treatments. Situations in which an interpreter may be needed for effective communications include the following:

- When discussing a patient's symptoms, concerns, medications, and medical history
- When explaining or describing medical diagnoses, conditions, tests and treatment options, surgery, and procedures
- When giving a diagnosis, recommended treatment, and the prognosis

COCHLEAR IMPLANTS

Cochlear implants can improve hearing in some people. It involves an electrical device surgically implanted into the cochlea of the patient's ear to transmit sound to the Deaf individual (Figure 14.5). It allows the person to hear some sounds that they would otherwise not hear. A tool for the Deaf, it is much like a hearing aid. However, the implant can change the way sound is heard, and some people in the Deaf culture do not support the use of an implant.

Some implants work very well, but some people believe that the implant may reduce any residual hearing they may have. Twenty-five percent of the Deaf do not use a cochlear implant at all.

Patients with Hearing Loss

Hearing loss refers to a partial or complete inability to perceive sounds in one or both ears. It can vary in degree, ranging from mild to profound, and may affect one's ability to hear and comprehend speech,

Figure 14–5 Young child with a cochlear implant
Source: Best smile studio/Shutterstock

environmental sounds, and other auditory stimuli. Hearing loss can result from various causes, including age-related factors (presbycusis), exposure to loud noises, genetic predisposition, infections, diseases, or damage to the ear structures. The condition can be temporary or permanent, and it may impact different frequency ranges of sounds. Hearing loss is often categorized based on its onset (congenital or acquired), the affected ear or ears (unilateral or bilateral), and the degree of impairment (mild, moderate, severe, or profound). Treatment options vary and may include hearing aids, cochlear implants, or other assistive devices, depending on the nature and severity of the hearing loss.

Hearing loss significantly impacts overall health, extending beyond the obvious challenge of impaired auditory function. Social isolation, communication difficulties, and diminished quality of life are common consequences. Hearing loss is linked to cognitive decline and an increased risk of conditions like dementia. Mental health issues such as depression and anxiety can arise due to the strain of coping with communication challenges. Additionally, untreated hearing loss may contribute to reduced work productivity and employability, affecting economic well-being. Physical health is also at risk, as hearing loss has been associated with a higher incidence of falls and accidents. Timely intervention through the use of hearing aids or other assistive devices is crucial not only for improving auditory function but also for mitigating the broader health implications associated with hearing loss, ultimately enhancing overall well-being.

Hearing loss comes on gradually, and many people don't realize its impact until their hearing loss is quite advanced. According to the National Council on Aging, 28 million adults age 20–69 need hearing aids, but only 16 percent who need them actually use them. However, people over age 70 are using hearing aids at an increasing rate. Income level has a major impact on the use of hearing aids. Hearing aids are expensive, and Medicare and many other insurance programs don't cover them. However, some Medicare Part C Advantage plans do cover hearing aids. Medicare does cover visits to audiologists if the patient is referred by a provider as part of a diagnosis, or if a hearing loss or balance issue has existed for more than 12 months.

When communicating with a patient with hearing loss, do the following:

- Ask the patient what you can do to help the communication process.
- Make sure the environment is quiet with no background noise.
- Get the patient's attention before you start talking.
- Face the patient directly when speaking; do not cover your mouth in any way.
- Pronounce your words clearly but without exaggeration.
- If there is more than one provider in the room, speak one at a time.

Patients with Vision Disorders

There are many degrees of **visual impairment**, up to and including **blindness**. Vision terms listed by the American Foundation for the Blind include the following:

- *Low vision:* A permanent vision loss that interferes with activities of daily living that cannot be corrected by regular eyeglasses, contact lenses, medicine, or surgery.
- *Moderate visual impairment:* Visual acuity on a Snellen eye chart (Figure 14.6) of 20/70 to 20/160.
- *Severe visual impairment:* Visual acuity on a Snellen eye chart of 20/200 to 20/400 or a visual field of 20 degrees or less.
- *Profound visual impairment:* Visual acuity on a Snellen eye chart of 20/500 to 20/1000 or a visual field of 10 degrees or less.
- *Legal blindness:* A definition used by the U.S. government to determine eligibility for benefits. In the United States, this means a medically diagnosed central visual acuity of 20/200 or less in the better eye.

Figure 14–6 Snellen eye chart used to measure visual acuity

Source: MisterEmil/Shutterstock

E	1	20/200
F P	2	20/100
T O Z	3	20/70
L P E D	4	20/50
P E C F D	5	20/40
E D F C Z P	6	20/30
F E L O P Z D	7	20/25
D E F P O T E C	8	20/20
L E F O D P C T	9	
F D P L T C E O	10	
P E Z O L C F T D	11	

General guidelines for assisting patients who are blind include the following:

- When meeting a patient who is blind, speak to them directly, identify yourself with your name and title, even if you've met them before, and feel free to use words like "look" and "see."

- Ask patients to let you know what they need in the way of assistance.

- Orient patients to the physical environment by describing the room, where they are sitting, and where you will be.

- Explain what you are going to do before touching them.

- Offer alternatives to printed educational material or discharge instructions such as large print, electronic, or Braille copy. Or you can offer to read the material aloud.

Patients with Intellectual Disabilities

Providing healthcare to patients with intellectual disabilities requires a thoughtful and person-centered approach to ensure that their unique needs are addressed effectively. Healthcare providers should receive training in intellectual and developmental disabilities to enhance their understanding and competence.

Here are some key considerations for healthcare providers:

- Use clear and simple language and allow extra time for communication and understanding. Use alternative communication methods, such as visual aids or communication boards.

- Develop personalized care plans that consider the specific health needs and challenges of each individual. Involve family members, caregivers, and support staff in care planning to ensure a comprehensive approach.

- Ensure that healthcare facilities are physically accessible, considering mobility issues and sensory sensitivities. Provide accommodations for individuals with communication or behavioral challenges.

- Emphasize preventive care to address potential health issues before they become more significant problems.

- Recognize and respect the diverse cultural backgrounds and values of individuals with intellectual disabilities and their families.

Legal and ethical considerations include being familiar with relevant laws and regulations, including those related to informed consent and guardianship; upholding ethical standards in providing care and respecting the autonomy of individuals with intellectual disabilities; and advocating for the rights and inclusion of individuals with intellectual disabilities in healthcare decision-making and policy development. By adopting a patient-centered and inclusive approach, healthcare providers can contribute to improving the health outcomes and overall well-being of individuals with intellectual disabilities.

Patients with Physical Disabilities

Delivering healthcare to patients with physical disabilities requires an individualized approach to address their unique needs and ensure equitable access to quality care. Here are key considerations for healthcare providers:

- Ensure physical accessibility to healthcare facilities and equipment, including ramps, elevators, restrooms, examination tables, scales, and other medical equipment (Figure 14.7).

- Communicate directly with the patient, even if they have a caregiver or support person.

- Recognize and respect the autonomy and preferences of individuals with physical disabilities. Involve patients in their care planning and decision-making processes.

- Be knowledgeable about and supportive of assistive technologies that patients may use for communication, mobility, or activities of daily living.

- Consider the unique health risks associated with specific physical disabilities and emphasize preventive care and screenings to address potential health issues proactively.

- Be prepared to assist with transfers and mobility as needed, providing appropriate equipment and trained staff.

- Be attentive to pain management strategies, as individuals with physical disabilities may experience chronic pain related to their condition.

- Recognize and respect the diverse cultural backgrounds and values of individuals with physical disabilities and their families.

Figure 14–7 All aspects of healthcare facilities should be accessible for all patients

Source: ciud/Shutterstock

By prioritizing accessibility, communication, and individualized care, healthcare providers can contribute to improving the health outcomes and overall well-being of patients with physical disabilities. Collaborative and patient-centered approaches are essential for ensuring that healthcare services are inclusive and responsive to the diverse needs of this population.

Healthcare for Older Adults

The ethical and legal healthcare landscape for older adults presents unique challenges due to the complexities associated with aging, the potential for cognitive decline, and the presence of chronic health conditions. Here are some of the key challenges:

- *Informed consent:* Older adults may face challenges in providing informed consent, especially if they have cognitive impairments such as dementia. Healthcare providers must navigate the balance between respecting autonomy and ensuring the individual's best interests.

- *End-of-life decision-making:* Decisions about end-of-life care, advance directives, and do-not-resuscitate (DNR) orders can be ethically and emotionally challenging for both healthcare providers and families. Ensuring that the wishes of the older adult are respected requires clear communication and sensitivity.

- *Polypharmacy and medication management:* Older adults often take multiple medications for various chronic conditions, increasing the risk of polypharmacy. Balancing the benefits and risks of medications while considering individual goals of care is a complex ethical challenge.

- *Quality of life vs. length of life:* Healthcare providers must consider the balance between prolonging life and maintaining or improving the quality of life for older adults. Discussions around the goals of care and the potential benefits and burdens of medical interventions are crucial.

- *Elder abuse and neglect:* Older adults may be vulnerable to abuse or neglect, either in healthcare settings or within their homes. Recognizing and addressing elder abuse poses legal and ethical challenges, particularly when the older adult has diminished capacity.

- *Resource allocation:* Allocating healthcare resources, such as organ transplants or intensive care, may raise ethical dilemmas. Decisions about resource allocation must consider factors such as age, comorbidities, and life expectancy while avoiding ageism.

- *Cognitive impairment and decision-making capacity:* Determining an older adult's decision-making capacity, especially in cases of cognitive impairment, poses ethical challenges. Healthcare providers must balance respect for autonomy with the need to protect individuals who may not fully understand the consequences of their decisions.

- **Cultural competence and diversity:** Older adults come from diverse cultural backgrounds, and providing culturally competent care is essential. Ethical considerations include respecting cultural values, preferences, and beliefs in the provision of healthcare.

- **Access to palliative and hospice care:** Ensuring timely access to palliative and hospice care can be challenging, with potential barriers including lack of awareness, limited availability, and reluctance to discuss end-of-life care options.

- **Healthcare proxy and surrogate decision-making:** Identifying and involving appropriate healthcare proxies or surrogates raises ethical questions, particularly if conflicts arise among family members or if the designated surrogate's decisions may be perceived as against the patient's best interests.

Navigating these ethical and legal challenges in the healthcare of older adults requires a patient-centered and multidisciplinary approach. Healthcare providers must be equipped to address the unique needs and preferences of older individuals while respecting their autonomy and promoting their well-being. Regular communication with patients, their families, and interdisciplinary teams is crucial in ensuring ethically sound and legally compliant healthcare for older adults.

Ethical Issues Regarding Selected Advances in Healthcare

Telehealth

While telehealth has been applauded as an advancement in healthcare, it comes with some disadvantages as well. Building and maintaining a strong provider–patient relationship may be challenging in a virtual setting, as nonverbal cues and personal interactions are limited. Remote consultations lack the hands-on physical examination that is crucial for certain healthcare assessments, potentially impacting diagnostic accuracy. Limited access to technology or low digital literacy may hinder some individuals, particularly older adults, from utilizing telehealth services. Finally, technical glitches, such as Internet connectivity problems or platform malfunctions, can disrupt telehealth appointments and affect the quality of the consultation.

Ethical challenges include socioeconomic disparities that may contribute to the digital divide, limiting access to telehealth services for certain populations. Rural populations in particular, who already lack access to healthcare in general, may lack the Internet connection or the smartphones needed for telehealth visits.

Other challenges include credentialing and licensing of telehealth providers, which varies widely from state to state, and reimbursement for telehealth visits. Medicaid now reimburses in all 50 states for live telehealth visits, but only 34 states cover remote patient monitoring.

Use of Robotics

Robotics in medicine is the use of machines that have the capacity to perform human tasks. Many hospitals now use robots to deliver supplies such as linens, as well as medications and meals to patient care floors. They have not replaced healthcare personnel but have made their work more efficient.

Robotic-assisted surgery is a method of performing surgery using very small tools attached to a robotic arm (Figure 14.8). The surgeon sits at a computer station in the operating room and controls the robotic arm via the computer. The robotic arm containing a small knife makes a small incision into the anesthetized patient. Then a thin tube with a camera attached to the end (endoscope) allows the surgeon to view very large three-dimensional images of the body as the surgery takes place. The surgeon manipulates the robot's movements to perform the surgery.

Challenges with the use of robotic-assisted surgery include the following:

- There is no standardized training or credentialing for robotic-assisted surgery.

- Patients need to be fully aware of the technology's potential risks in order to give informed consent.

- There are multiple stakeholders—the surgeon, the hospital, and the manufacturer—in the functioning of the robotic systems, which makes legal liability complex.

Figure 14–8 Robotic-assisted surgery

Source: Terelyuk/Shutterstock

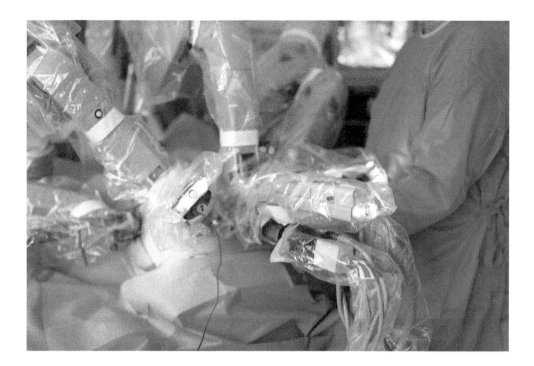

Concierge Healthcare

Concierge healthcare, also known as concierge medicine or boutique medicine, is a healthcare model in which patients pay a membership or retainer fee to access enhanced medical services and personalized care. This model aims to provide a more exclusive and personalized experience for patients, often involving increased access to the healthcare providers, longer appointment times, and a focus on preventive care. Concierge healthcare is not a substitute for health insurance. Patients are still advised to maintain traditional health insurance for coverage of major medical expenses and emergencies.

While concierge healthcare offers personalized and convenient services, it has been a subject of debate regarding potential impacts on healthcare equity, as the model's exclusive nature limits access for individuals who cannot afford the membership fees. It is essential to weigh the benefits and drawbacks of concierge healthcare in the context of broader healthcare accessibility and affordability considerations.

According to the *AMA Journal of Ethics,* concierge healthcare creates several dilemmas:

* It reinforces existing social inequities, particularly racism and classism, through unequal tiers of care.

* It contributes to the unequal distribution of resources in a resource-limited setting.

* While it is more expensive for patients and profitable for facilities than traditional healthcare delivery, it has not been shown to produce better outcomes.

Artificial Intelligence

Artificial intelligence is the use of computer science, robust datasets, machine learning, and deep learning to solve problems. These disciplines are used to create AI algorithms to make predictions or classifications based on input data.

The use of artificial intelligence (AI) in medicine presents various ethical considerations that need careful attention. Some of the key ethical issues include the following:

* ***Patient data protection:*** AI systems in medicine often rely on large datasets, including sensitive patient information. Ensuring the privacy and security of this data is crucial to prevent unauthorized access or misuse.

- *Informed consent:* Patients may not fully understand the implications of their data being used in AI applications. Obtaining informed consent becomes challenging, especially when the potential uses of the data are not well-understood or predictable.

- *Informed decision-making:* Patients should have the right to understand how AI is used in their healthcare and be involved in decisions about its implementation. The role of AI in diagnosis and treatment should complement, not replace, the provider-patient relationship.

- *Data bias:* If the training data used to develop AI algorithms is biased, the resulting models may also exhibit biases. This can lead to unfair or discriminatory outcomes, particularly if the training data does not represent diverse populations.

- *Health disparities:* AI applications may inadvertently exacerbate existing health disparities if they are not designed and implemented with a focus on equitable healthcare delivery.

- *Legal and ethical responsibility:* Determining responsibility when an AI system makes a mistake or produces an adverse outcome can be complex. It raises questions about who is accountable—developers, healthcare providers, or the AI system itself.

- *Medical liability:* If an AI system contributes to a medical error, there may be challenges in assigning liability, especially if the decision-making process of the AI is not fully understood.

- *Job displacement:* The integration of AI into healthcare may lead to concerns about job displacement among certain healthcare professionals. Striking the right balance between automation and the human touch is crucial.

- *Ethical training:* Healthcare professionals need training to understand and use AI ethically. The use of AI should enhance, rather than replace, the ethical decision-making capabilities of healthcare providers.

- *Access to technology:* Ensuring that AI-driven medical advancements are accessible to all, regardless of socioeconomic status, is essential. Failure to address this issue could exacerbate existing healthcare inequalities.

- *Unintended consequences:* Introducing AI into healthcare may have unintended consequences, and ethical considerations should extend beyond immediate benefits to anticipate and mitigate potential risks.

Addressing these ethical concerns requires collaboration among healthcare professionals, technologists, policymakers, and the public to develop guidelines, regulations, and best practices that promote the responsible and ethical use of AI in medicine.

Chapter 14 Review

Points to Ponder

1. In your opinion, what health services should be available for patients with Alzheimer's disease?

2. Why are MDROs a major concern for hospitals?

3. Discuss the roles that pharmaceutical companies and healthcare providers played in the opioid crisis.

4. Discuss the impact that the high cost of healthcare has had on our country.

Discussion Questions

1. Discuss how the statement, "First, do no harm" impacts your chosen profession.

2. Explain the impact of the lack of healthcare providers.

3. Discuss the ethics regarding the use of robotic-assisted surgical procedures.

4. Discuss why healthcare professionals should study Deaf culture.

Review Challenge

Short Answer Questions

1. Describe the five components of the social determinants of health.

_____

_____

_____

_____

2. Describe the disparities of maternal mortality in the United States.

_____

_____

_____

_____

3. What are healthcare-associated infections and why are they important?

_____

_____

_____

_____

4. What are some examples of fraud as discussed in this chapter?

_____

_____

_____

_____

5. What is concierge healthcare?

_____

_____

_____

_____

6. List five ways you can support patients with disabilities in your practice area.

_____

_____

_____

_____

_____

Matching

Match the responses in column B with the correct term in column A.

COLUMN A

_____   1. blindness

_____   2. protocol

_____   3. fraud

_____   4. robotics

_____   5. triage

_____   6. fentanyl

_____   7. MRSA

COLUMN B

a. deception or injury

b. machines performing human tasks

c. antibiotic-resistant bacterium

d. clinical plan

e. determining the order in which to treat patients

f. legal term

g. a synthetic opioid

Multiple Choice

Select the one best answer to the following statements:

1. VRE is
   a. a bacterium.
   b. a standard of measurement for healthcare costs.
   c. difficult to treat with standard types of antibiotics.
   d. a and c
   e. all of the above

2. Factors involved in the cost of healthcare in the United States include
   a. the role of insurance companies.
   b. the price of medications.
   c. structure of the healthcare system.
   d. maternal mortality.
   e. a, b, and c

3. Fraud is an intentional deception or injury to another person that results in damage to a person's reputation or property. Examples of fraud in the healthcare field include

 a. a doctor or nurse practicing without a license.

 b. false Medicare billing.

 c. drinking while driving.

 d. conducting drug tests on groups of people without their knowledge.

 e. a and b

4. Types of fraud in healthcare include

 a. having a license to practice in the state where you work.

 b. using a title that you haven't earned.

 c. taking kickbacks for referrals.

 d. filling prescriptions for unnecessary drugs.

 e. b, c, and d only

5. Common MDROs include

 a. C. diff

 b. MRSA

 c. VRE

 d. all of the above

 e. none of the above

6. Which are components of social determinants of health?

 a. socioeconomic status

 b. employment

 c. physical environment

 d. social support network

 e. all of the above

7. Which are good techniques for communicating with patients who have hearing loss?

 a. Have only one person speak at a time.

 b. Speak loudly.

 c. Ask the patient how to help the process.

 d. Exaggerate your words.

 e. a and c only

Discussion Cases

1. Tony, a 91-year-old veteran of World War II, has lived in a big city his entire life and has used Veteran Affairs (VA) facilities for healthcare that are free under his VA coverage. He also has a small home in a nearby state where he spends weekends. One weekend, while in this nearby state, Tony fell, cut his arm, and hit his head. A neighbor applied a pressure dressing to his bleeding arm and then took him to a nearby emergency department. The ED started an IV and sutured the cut on his arm. The ED also performed an ECG, which detected a heart problem. Tony was then admitted to the hospital. When the neighbor returned home, she noticed that she had blood on her clothing.

 When the neighbor visited Tony the next day in the hospital, she found that he was in isolation and all visitors had to wear gowns and masks. She asked his nurse why he was in isolation. The nurse asked for, and Tony gave, permission to discuss his situation with the neighbor. The nurse then told the neighbor that Tony had tested positive for MRSA.

 a. Did the nurse do anything wrong by telling the neighbor about Tony's condition as the patient did give his permission?

 _____

 _____

 b. Should the ED nurse have cautioned the neighbor about the possibility of MRSA when she saw blood on the neighbor's clothing?

 _____

 _____

2. Tony, who was discussed in the previous case, returns to a VA hospital in the city for his preventive care exam. He is supplied with samples of medications to use for various medical conditions. He does not take his records from his doctor or ED visit in the nearby state to the VA medical center. Nor does he take his VA records to the nearby state to show to his doctor and hospital located there.

 a. What are the risks of this behavior?

 _____

 _____

 b. Could the excellent care he received at both hospitals actually harm Tony in any way?

 _____

 _____

Put It Into Practice

Look for a recent article about the use of artificial intelligence in medicine. Evaluate the information in the article using what you have learned in your healthcare class.

Web Hunt

Search the website of the Department of Health and Human Services (**www.HHS.gov**) and discuss the mission of the organization.

Critical Thinking Exercise

How would you deal with the disparities, or differences, in healthcare for some people?

Bibliography

Agency for Healthcare Research and Quality. (2019). Health care-associated infections. *PSNet.* https://psnet.ahrq.gov/primer/health-care-associated-infections

Agency for Healthcare Research and Quality. (2023). Personal health literacy. *PSNet.* https://psnet.ahrq.gov/primer/personal-health-literacy

American Foundation for the Blind. (2023). *Blindness and low vision.* https://www.afb.org/blindness-and-low-vision

American Foundation for the Blind. (2021). Serving the needs of individuals with visual impairments in healthcare settings. *Best practices guide for hospitals interacting with people who are blind or visually impaired.* https://www.afb.org/research-and-initiatives/serving-needs-individuals-visual-impairments-healthcare-setting

American Medical Association. (2020). *7 things about EHRs that stress out doctors.* https://www.ama-assn.org/practice-management/digital/7-things-about-ehrs-stress-out-doctors

Centers for Disease Control and Prevention (CDC). (2022). *Current HAI progress report.* https://www.cdc.gov/hai/data/portal/progress-report.html

Centers for Disease Control and Prevention (CDC). (2023). *Provisional data shows U.S. drug overdose deaths topped 100,000 in 2022.* https://blogs.cdc.gov/nchs/2023/05/18/7365/

Centers for Disease Control and Prevention (CDC). (2023). *Understanding the opioid overdose epidemic.* https://www.cdc.gov/opioids/basics/epidemic.html

Coughlin, S.S., Vernon, M., Hatzigeorgiou, C., & George, V. (2020). Health literacy, social determinants of health, and disease prevention and control. *Journal of Environmental Health Science and Engineering.* 6(1):3061. Epub 2020 Dec 16. PMID: 33604453; PMCID: PMC7889072.

Douthard, R.A., Martin, I.K., Chapple-McGruder, T., Langer, A., & Chang S. (2021). U.S. maternal mortality within a global context: Historical trends, current state, and future directions.

Journal of Women's Health (Larchmont). Feb;30(2):168–177. DOI: 10.1089/jwh.2020.8863. Epub 2020 Nov 18. PMID: 33211590; PMCID: PMC8020556.

Everett, C. (2023). Only 1 in 6 Americans with hearing loss wears hearing aids—here's why. *National Council on Aging.* https://www.ncoa.org/adviser/hearing-aids/low-hearing-loss-treatment-reasons/

Feeding America. (2023). *Hunger in America.* https://www.feedingamerica.org/hunger-in-america

Harris, E. (2023). US maternal mortality continues to worsen. *JAMA.* 329(15):1248. DOI:10.1001/jama.2023.5254

Healthy People 2030. (2023). *Social determinants of health.* https://health.gov/healthypeople/priority-areas/social-determinants-health

Healthy People 2030. (2023). *Health literacy in Healthy People 2030.* https://health.gov/healthypeople/priority-areas/health-literacy-healthy-people-2030

Marks, J., Predescu, I., & Dunn, L.B. (2021). Ethical issues in caring for older adults. *Focus.* Jul;19(3):325–329. DOI: 10.1176/appi.focus.20210011. Epub 2021 Jul 9. PMID: 34690601; PMCID: PMC8475933.

Marquez, R.M., & Lever, H. (2023). Why VIP services are ethically indefensible in health care. *AMA Journal of Ethics.* 25(1): E66–71. https://journalofethics.ama-assn.org/article/why-vip-services-are-ethically-indefensible-health-care/2023-01

Melillo, G. (2020). US ranks worst in maternal care, mortality compared with 10 other developed nations. *The American Journal of Managed Care,* December 3. https://www.ajmc.com/view/us-ranks-worst-in-maternal-care-mortality-compared-with-10-other-developed-nations

Nijor, S., Rallis, G., Lad, N., & Gokcen, E. (2022). Patient safety issues from information overload in electronic medical records. *Journal of Patient Safety.* Sep 1;18(6):e999–e1003. DOI: 10.1097/

PTS.0000000000001002. Epub 2022 Apr 7. PMID: 35985047; PMCID: PMC9422765.

NPR. (2022). *4 U.S. companies will be $26 billion to settle claims they fueled the opioid crisis.* https://www.npr.org/2022/02/25/1082901958/opioid-settlement-johnson-26-billion

Pai, S.N., Jeyaraman, M., Jeyaraman, N., Nallakumarasamy, A., & Yadav, S. (2023). In the hands of a robot, from the operating room to the courtroom: The medicolegal considerations of robotic surgery. *Cureus.* Aug 17;15(8):e43634. DOI: 10.7759/cureus.43634. PMID: 37719624; PMCID: PMC10504870.

Patil, S.P., Craven, K., Kolasa, K. (2018). Food insecurity: How you can help your patients. *American Family Physician.* 98(3): 143–145. https://www.aafp.org/pubs/afp/issues/2018/0801/p143.html

Podgorica N, Flatscher-Thöni M, Deufert D, Siebert U, Ganner M. (2021) A systematic review of ethical and legal issues in elder care. *Nurs Ethics.* Sep;28(6):895–910. DOI: 10.1177/0969733020921488. Epub 2020 May 29. PMID: 32468910.

Ranji, S. (2016). Measuring and responding to deaths from medical errors. *The PSNet Collection.* https://psnet.ahrq.gov/perspective/measuring-and-responding-deaths-medical-errors

Rural Health Information Hub. (2023). *Barriers to telehealth in rural areas.* https://www.ruralhealthinfo.org/toolkits/telehealth/1/barriers

The Commonwealth Fund. (2020). *Maternal mortality and maternity care in the United States compared to 10 other developed countries.* https://www.commonwealthfund.org/publications/issue-briefs/2020/nov/maternal-mortality-maternity-care-us-compared-10-countries

The Harvard Gazette. (2023). *Doctors nor the only ones feeling burned out.* https://news.harvard.edu/gazette/story/2023/03/covid-burnout-hitting-all-levels-of-health-care-workforce/

U.S. Department of Justice, Office of Public Affairs. (2020). *Justice Department announces global resolution of criminal and civil investigations with opioid manufacturer Purdue Pharma and civil settlement with members of the Sackler family.* https://www.justice.gov/opa/pr/justice-department-announces-global-resolution-criminal-and-civil-investigations-opioid

Appendix A: Codes of Ethics

The Nuremberg Code

1. The voluntary consent of the human subject is absolutely essential. This means that the person involved should have legal capacity to give consent; should be so situated as to be able to exercise free power of choice, without the intervention of any element of force, fraud, deceit, duress, over-reaching or other form of constraint or coercion; and should have sufficient knowledge and comprehension of the elements of the subject matter involved as to enable him to make an understanding and enlightened decision. This latter element requires that before the acceptance of an affirmative decision by the experimental subject there should be made known to him the nature, duration and purpose of the experiment; the method and means by which it is to be conducted; all conveniences and hazards reasonable to be expected; and the effects upon his health or person which may possibly come from his participation in the experiment. The duty and responsibility for ascertaining the quality of the consent rests upon each individual who initiates, directs, or engages in the experiment. It is a personal duty and responsibility which may not be delegated to another with impunity.

2. The experiment should be such as to yield fruitful results for the good of society, unprocurable by other methods or means of study, and not random and unnecessary in nature.

3. The experiment should be so designed and based on results of animal experimentation and knowledge of the natural history of the disease or other problem under study that the anticipated results will justify the performance of the experiment.

4. The experiment should be so conducted as to avoid all unnecessary physical and mental suffering and injury.

5. No experiment should be conducted where there is an *a priori* reason to believe that death or disabling injury will occur; except, perhaps, in those experiments where the experimental physicians also serve as subjects.

6. The degree of risk to be taken should never exceed that determined by the humanitarian importance of the problem to be solved by the experiment.

7. Proper preparations should be made and adequate facilities provided to protect the experimental subject against even remote possibilities of injury, disabilities, or death.

8. The experiment should be conducted only by scientifically qualified persons. The highest degree of skill and care should be required through all stages of the experiment of those who conduct or engage in the experiment.

9. During the course of the experiment the human subject should be at liberty to bring the experiment to an end if he has reached the physical or mental state where continuation of the experiment seems to him to be impossible.

10. During the course of the experiment the scientist in charge must be prepared to terminate the experiment at any stage, if he has probable cause to believe, in the exercise of good faith, superior skill, and careful judgment required of him that a continuation of the experiment is likely to result in injury, disability, or death to the experimental subject.

Source: Reprinted from *The Trials of War Criminals before the Nuremberg Military Tribunals.* Washington, DC: U.S. Government Printing Office, 1948.

Nurses' Code of Ethics (American Nurses Association)

The American Nurses Association (ANA) has developed a code for nurses that discusses the nurses' obligation to protect the patient's privacy, respect the patient's dignity, maintain competence in nursing, and assume responsibility and accountability for individual nursing judgments. This code states the nurses' ethical responsibilities and is summarized here:

1. The nurse practices with compassion and respect for inherent dignity, worth, and unique attributes of every person.

2. The nurse's primary commitment is to the patient, whether an individual, family, group, community, or population.

3. The nurse promotes, advocates for, and protects the rights, health, and safety of the patient.

4. The nurse has authority, accountability, and responsibility for nursing practice; makes decisions; and takes action consistent with the obligation to promote health and to provide optimal care.

5. The nurse owes the same duties to self as to others, including the responsibility to promote health and safety, preserve wholeness of character and integrity, maintain competence, and continue personal and professional growth.

6. The nurse, through individual and collective effort, establishes, maintains, and improves the ethical environment of the work setting and conditions of employment that are conducive to safe, quality health care.

7. The nurse, in all roles and setting, advances the profession through research and scholarly inquiry, professional standards development, and the generation of both nursing and health policy.

8. The nurse collaborates with other health professionals and the public to protect human rights, promote health diplomacy, and reduce health disparities.

9. The profession of nursing, collectively through its professional organizations, must articulate nursing values, maintain the integrity of the profession, and the integrate principles of social justice into nursing and health policy.

Source: © American Nurses Association. Reprinted with permission from American Nurses Association. All rights reserved.

AAMA Code of Ethics for Medical Assistants

The AAMA Code of Ethics for Medical Assistants sets forth principles of ethical and moral conduct as they relate to the medical profession and the particular practice of medical assisting.

Members of the AAMA dedicated to the conscientious pursuit of their profession, and thus desiring to merit the high regard of the entire medical profession and the respect of the general public which they serve, do pledge themselves to strive always to:

A. Render service with full respect for the dignity of humanity.

B. Respect confidential information obtained through employment unless legally authorized or required by responsible performance of duty to divulge such information.

C. Uphold the honor and high principles of the profession and accept its disciplines.

D. Seek to continually improve the knowledge and skills of medical assistants for the benefit of patients and professional colleagues.

E. Participate in additional service activities aimed toward improving the health and well-being of the community.

Source: Copyright by the American Association of Medical Assistants, Inc. Reprinted by permission.

Appendix B: Case Citations

Agnew-Watson v. County of Almeda, 36 Cal. Rptr. 2d 196 Ct. App. (Cal. 1994).

Allen v. Harrison, OK 44, Case Number: 111877 9 (2016).

Armstrong v. Flowers Hosp., 33 F.3d 1308 (11th Cir. 1994).

In re Axelrod, 560 N.Y.S.2d 573 (App. Div. 1990).

In re Baby M, 537 A.2d 1227 (N.J. 1988).

Barnes Hospital v. Missouri Commission on Human Rights, 661 S.W.2d 534 (Mo. 1983).

Bendiburg v. Dempsey, 19 F.3d 557 (11th Cir. 1994).

Big Town Nursing Home v. Newman, 461 S.W.2d 195 (Texas Civ. App. 1970).

Bondu v. Gurvich, 473 So. 2d 1307 (Fla. Dist. Ct. App. 1984).

Brinson v. Axelrod, 499 N.Y.S.2d 24 (App. Div. 1986).

Buchanan v. Kull, 35 N.W.2d 351 (Mich.1949).

Buckley v. Hospital Corp. of America, Inc., 758 F.2d 1525 (11th Cir. 1985).

Canterbury v. Spence, 464 F.2d 772 (D.C. 1972).

Child Protection Group v. Cline, 350 S.E.2d 541 (W. Va. 1986).

Cline v. Lund, 31 Cal. App. 3d 755 (1973).

Cruzan v. Director, Missouri Dep't of Health, 497 U.S. 261 (1990).

Darling v. Charleston Community Mem. Hosp., 211 N.E. 2d 253 (1965).

Davis v. Davis, 842 S.W.2d 588 (Tenn. 1992).

DeMay v. Roberts, 9 N.W.146 (Mich. 1881).

In re Doe, 533 A2d 523 (R.I. 1987).

Downes v. Carpenter, No. 2019-12863-PL (Pa. Ct. Com. Pl. Chester County).

Eisenstadt v. Baird. 405 U.S. 438 (1972).

Erickson v. Dilgard, 252 2d 705 (N.Y.S. 1962).

Estate of Berthiaume v. Pratt, 365 QA.2d 792 (Me. 1976).

Fair v. St. Joseph's Hosp., 437 S.E.2d 875 (N.C. App. 1933).

Garcia v. Elf Atochem, N. Am., 28 F.3d 446 (5th Cir. 1994).

Goff v. Doctors General Hospital, 333 P.2d 29 (Cal. Ct. App. 1958).

Goforth v. Porter Med. Assoc., Inc., 755 P.2d 678 (Okla. 1988).

Grande v. Eisenhower Medical Center (2020) 44 Cal.App.5th 1147, 1162–1163.

Grijalva v. Shalala, 946 F. Supp. 747 (Ariz. 1996).

Griswold v. Connecticut, 381 U.S. 479 (1965).

Grubbs v. Medical Facilities of America, Inc., 879 F. Supp. W.D. (Va. 1995).

Guilmet v. Campbell, 385 Mich. 57, 188 N.W.2d 601 (1971).

Harvet v. Unity Medical Ctr., 428 N.W.2d 574 (Minn. Ct. App. 1988).

Hayes v. Shelby Memorial. Hosp., 726 F.2d 1543 (11th Cir. 1984).

Hickman v. Sexton Dental Clinic, P.A. 367 S.E.2d 453 (S.C. Ct. App. 1988).

Hurlock v. Park Lane Med. Ctr. Inc., 709 S.W.2d 872 (Mo. Ct. App. 1985).

Insurance Co. of N. Am. v. Prieto, 442 F.2d 1033 (6th Cir. 1971).

James v. Jacobson, 6 F.3d 233 (4th Cir. 1993).

Jeczalik v. Valley Hosp., 434 A.2d 90 (N.J. 1981).

Jehovah's Witnesses v King County Hospital 278 F. Supp. 488 (W.D. Wash. 1967) aff'd 390 U.S. 598 (1968).

Jenkins v. Bogalusa Comm. Med. Ctr., 340 So.2d 1065 (La. Ct. App. 1976).

Joseph Dudley, et al. v. Central Iowa Hospital Corp, et al. (2022).

Keene v. Brigham & Women's Hosp., Inc. 439 Mass. 223 (2003).

Kern v. Gulf Coast Nursing Home, Inc., 502 So.2d 1198 (Miss. 1987).

Korman v. Mallin, 858 P.2d 1145 (Alaska 1993).

Landau v. Medical Board of California, 71 Cal. Rptr. (Cal. App. 1998).

Landeros v. Flood, 551 P.2d 389 (Cal. 1976).

Love v. Heritage House Convalescent Ctr., 463 N.E.2d 478 (Ind. Ct. App. 1983).

Lovelace Medical Ctr. v. Mendez, 805 P.2d 603 (N.M. 1991).

Mandel v. Doe, 888 F.2d. 783 (11th Cir. 1989).

Matter of Baby K; 16 F.3d, 590 (4th Cir. 1994).

McLaughlin v. Cooke, 774 P.2d 1171 (Wash. 1989).

Moon Lake Convalescent Center v. Margolis, 435 N.E.2d 956 (Ill. App. Ct. 1989).

Morena v. South Hills Health System, 462 A.2d 680 (Pa. 1983).

Morrison v. MacNamara, 407 A.2d 555 (D.C. 1979).

Murray v. Vandevander, 522 P.2d 302 (Okla. Ct. App. 1974).

Norton v. Argonaut Ins. Co., 144 So.2d 249 (La. App. 1962).

Odomes v. Nucare, Inc., 653 F.2d (6th Cir. 1981).

O'Neill v. Montefiore Hosp., 202 N.Y.S2d, 436 (App. Div. 1960).

Osborne v. McMasters, 41 N.W. 543 (Minn. 1889).

Pacheco v. United States, 21 F.4th 1183 (9th Cir. 2022).

People v. Smithtown Gen. Hosp., 736, 402 N.Y.S.2d 318 (Sup. Ct. 1978).

Polonsky v. Union Hospital, 418 N.E.2d 620 (Mass. App. Ct. 1981).

Poor Sisters of St. Francis v. Catron, 435 N.E.2d 305 (Ind. Ct. App. 1982).

Prince v. Commonwealth of Massachusetts, 321 U.S. 158 (1944).

Quinby v. Morrow, 340 F.2d 584 (Cir. 1965).

In re Quinlan, 355 A.2d 647 (N.J. 1976).

Rodgers v. St. Mary's Hospital, 556 N.E.2d 913 (Ill. App. Ct. 1990).

Roe v. Wade, 410 U.S.113 (1973).

Rowland v. Christian, 443 P.2d. 561 (Cal. 1968).

Satler v. Larsen, 520 N.Y.S.2d 378 (App. Div. 1987).

In re Schroeder, 415 N.W.2d 436 (Minn. Ct. App. 1987).

Smith v. Cote, 513 A.2d 341 (N.H. 1986).

Starks v. Director of Div. of Employment Section, 462 N.E.2d 1360 (Mass. 1984).

State v. Fierro, 603 P.2d 74 (Ariz. 1979).

State Dep't. of Human Services v. Northern, 563 S.W.2d 197 (Tenn. Ct. App. 1978).

Sternberg v. California State Board of Pharmacy, (2015) 239 Cal.App.4th 1159.

St. John's Reg. Health Ctr. v. American Cas. Co., 980 F.2d 1222 (8th Cir. 1992).

Swanson v. St. John's Lutheran Hosp., 597 P.2d 702 (Mont. 1979).

Teeters v. Currey, 518 S.W.2d 512 (Tenn.1974).

Thompson v. Brent, 245 So.2d 751 (La. App. 1971).

Thor v. Boska, 113 Cal. Rptr. 296, Ct. App. (1974).

Tugg v. Towney, 864 F. Supp. 1201, S.D. (Fla. 1994).

United States of America v. Steven Monaco, Daniel Osw Ari, Michael Goldis, and Aaron Jones (2022).

Watson v. Idaho Falls Consol. Hosp., Inc., 720 P.2d 632 (Idaho 1986).

Williams v. Summit Psychiatric Ctrs., 363 S.E.2d 794 (Ga. App. 1987).

Wis. Stat., §252.15(8).

Woolfolk v. Duncan, 872 F. Supp. 1381, E.D. (Pa. 1995).

Zatarain v. WDSU-Television, Inc., WI 16777 E.D. (La. 1995).

Zucker v. Axelrod, 527 N.Y.S.2d 937 (1988).

Glossary

Abandonment Withdrawing medical care from a patient without providing sufficient notice to the patient.

Abortion The termination of a pregnancy.

Accreditation A voluntary process in which an agency is requested to officially review healthcare institutions—such as hospitals, nursing homes, and educational institutions—to determine compliance.

Active euthanasia Actively ending the life of, or killing, a patient who is terminally ill.

Administrative law A branch of law that covers regulations set by government agencies.

Advance directive The various methods by which a patient has the right to self-determination prior to a medical necessity; includes living wills, healthcare proxies, and durable power of attorney.

Advanced practice providers A term that encompasses physician assistants (PAs), nurse practitioners (NPs), and other providers such as certified nurse midwives (CNMs), clinical nurse specialists (CNSs), and certified registered nurse anesthetists (CRNAs), all of whom have advanced education and clinical training and practice medicine with or without the supervision of a physician, depending on the state in which they practice.

Affirmative action programs To remedy discriminating practices in hiring minority group members. Also covered under Title VII.

Affirmative defense A defense that allows the defendant (usually a physician or hospital) to present evidence that the patient's condition was the result of factors other than the defendant's negligence.

Against medical advice When a noncompliant patient leaves a hospital without a physician's permission.

Age Discrimination in Employment Act Act that protects persons 40 years or older against employment discrimination because of age.

Agent Person authorized to act on behalf of a patient.

Alternative dispute resolution (ADR) Methods for resolving a civil dispute that do not involve going to court.

American Deaf Culture The culture and language of the Deaf population in America.

American Sign Language Often the first language of Deaf or hard-of-hearing persons.

Americans with Disabilities Act Act that prohibits employers who have more than 15 employees from discriminating against disabled individuals.

Americans with Disabilities Act Amendments Act of 2008 This act broadened and clarified the definition of "disability."

Amniocentesis A test for the presence of genetic defects in which a needle is used to withdraw a small amount of the amniotic fluid that surrounds the fetus in the uterus.

Amoral Lacking or indifferent to moral standards.

Applied ethics The practical application of moral standards to the conduct of individuals involved in organizations.

Arbitration Submitting a dispute for resolution to a person other than a judge.

Arbitrator A person chosen to decide a disagreement between two parties.

Artificial insemination The injection of seminal fluid that contains male sperm into a female's vagina from her husband, partner, or donor by some means other than sexual intercourse.

Artificial intelligence The use of computer science, robust datasets, machine learning, and deep learning to solve problems.

Assault Imminent apprehension of bodily harm.

Assisted reproductive technology Fertility treatments in which either eggs or embryos are handled.

Assisted suicide Suicide committed by a person with the assistance of someone else; a form of euthanasia that concerns some ethicists because it could lead to a form of legalized murder.

Associate practices A legal agreement in which physicians agree to share a facility and staff but do not, as a rule, share responsibility for the legal actions of each other.

Assumption of risk A legal defense that prevents a plaintiff from recovering damages if the plaintiff voluntarily accepts a risk associated with the activity.

At-will employment Employment that takes place at either the will of the employer or the employee.

Autopsy A postmortem examination of organs and tissues to determine the cause of death.

Battery Bodily harm and unlawful touching (touching without consent of patient).

Beyond a reasonable doubt Evidence that supports an almost absolute certainty that a person did commit a crime.

Bioethicists Persons who specialize in the field of bioethics.

Bioethics Also called biomedical ethics, the moral dilemmas and issues of advanced medicine and medical research.

Blindness The most advanced degree of visual impairment.

Bonding A special type of insurance that covers employees who handle financial statements, records, and cash.

Borrowed servant doctrine A special application of *respondeat superior* in which an employer lends an employee to someone else.

Brain death Complete and irreversible cessation of all brain function.

Breach Neglect of an understanding between two parties; failing to perform a legal duty; also known as *dereliction*.

Breach of contract The failure, without legal excuse, to perform any promise or to carry out any of the terms of an agreement; failure to perform a contractual duty.

Bureau of Narcotics and Dangerous Drugs An agency of the federal government responsible for enforcing laws covering statutes of addictive drugs.

Capitation rate A fixed monthly fee paid by an HMO to healthcare providers for providing medical services to patients who are members of that HMO.

Cardiac death Death in which the heart has stopped functioning.

Case law Law that is based on decisions made by judges; also called *common law*.

Censure To find fault with, criticize, or condemn.

Certification A voluntary credentialing process usually offered by a professional organization.

Checks and balances System designed by the framers of the Constitution so that no one branch of government would have more power than another and so that each branch of government is scrutinized by other branches of government.

Child Abuse Prevention and Treatment Act Act that prohibited withholding of medical treatment solely because the infant is disabled.

Civil law Relationships between individuals or between individuals and the government, which are not criminal.

Claims-made insurance Liability insurance that covers the insured party for only the claims made during the time period the policy is in effect (or policy year).

Class action lawsuit Lawsuit filed by one or more people on behalf of a larger group of people who are all affected by the same situation.

Clearinghouse A private or public healthcare entity that facilitates the processing of nonstandard electronic transactions into HIPAA transactions (e.g., a billing service).

Clinical Laboratory Improvement Amendments Act that established minimum quality standards for laboratories.

Cloning Generating a group of identical matching cells that come from a single common cell.

Closing arguments Closing speech or summary made by the attorneys for both the plaintiff and the defendant.

Coding up A form of medical fraud; billing for a diagnosis with a higher compensation rate than the actual diagnosis.

Comatose Being in a vegetative condition.

Common law Law that is based on decisions made by judges; also called *case law*.

Comparable worth Also known as pay equity, the theory that extends equal pay requirements to all persons doing equal work.

Comparative negligence A defense, similar to contributory negligence, that the plaintiff's own negligence helped cause the injury; not a complete bar to recovery of damages but only damages based on the amount of the plaintiff's fault.

Compensatory damages An amount of money awarded by the court to make up for loss of income or emotional pain and suffering.

Competent Capable of making a decision without mental confusion due to drugs, alcohol, or other reasons.

Compounding The combination and mixing of drugs and chemicals.

Concierge healthcare A healthcare model in which patients pay a membership or retainer fee to access enhanced medical services and personalized care.

Confidentiality This term refers to keeping private all information about a person (patient) and not disclosing it to a third party without the patient's written consent.

Conscience clause Legislation or regulation stating that hospitals and healthcare professionals are not required to assist with such procedures as abortion and sterilization.

Consent The voluntary agreement that a patient gives to allow a medically trained person the permission to touch them, examine them, and to perform a treatment.

Consideration In contract law, consideration is something of value given as part of the agreement.

Consolidated Omnibus Budget Reconciliation Act Act that offers government financing for health insurance coverage continuation after an employee has been laid off a job.

Constitutional law The inviolable rights, privileges, or immunities secured and protected for each citizen by the Constitution of the United States or by the constitution of each state.

Contraception Birth control.

Contract law That division of law that includes enforceable promises and agreements between two or more persons to do or not to do a particular thing.

Contributory negligence Conduct on the part of the plaintiff that is a contributing cause of injuries; a complete bar to recovery of damages.

Control group Research subjects who receive no treatment.

Controlled Substances Act of 1970 A federal statute that regulates the manufacture and distribution of drugs that are capable of causing dependency.

Copayment An agreed-upon fee paid by the insured for certain medical services; usually $10 to $20.

Coroner A public health officer who holds an investigation (inquest) if a person's death is from an unknown or violent cause.

Corporation A type of medical practice, as established by law, which is managed by a board of directors.

Cost/benefit analysis Also called utilitarianism, an ethical approach in which the benefit of the decision should outweigh the costs.

Covered entities Healthcare organizations covered under HIPAA regulations such as public health authorities, healthcare clearinghouses, self-insured employers, life insurers, information systems vendors, and universities.

Covered transactions Certain electronic transactions of healthcare information that are mandated under HIPAA.

Credibility gap An apparent disparity between what is said or written and the actual facts.

Credible Believable or worthy of belief.

Credit Card Accountability Responsibility and Disclosure Act of 2009 This act established guidelines for use of an individual's credit information.

Criminal law Set up to protect the public from the harmful acts of others.

Curative care When an attempt is made to cure the patient; the opposite of palliative care.

Damages Any injuries caused by the defendant; usually a monetary award is given as compensation.

Defamation of character Making false and/or malicious statements about another person; includes libel and slander.

Defendant Person or group of people sued civilly or prosecuted criminally in a court of law.

Defensive medicine Ordering more tests and procedures than are necessary in order to protect oneself from a lawsuit.

Deidentifying Removing descriptive information about a patient.

Delegation The transfer of responsibility for a patient's care from one caregiver to another.

Deposition Oral testimony that is made before a public officer of the court to be used in a lawsuit.

Dereliction Neglect of an understanding between two parties; failing to perform a legal duty; also known as *breach*.

Diagnostic related groups Designations used to identify reimbursement per condition in a hospital; used for Medicare patients.

Direct cause The continuous sequence of events, unbroken by any intervening cause, that produces an injury and without which the injury would not have occurred.

Disclosed Made known.

Discovery The legal process by which facts are discovered before a trial.

Discovery rule Legal theory that provides that the statute of limitations begins to run at the time the injury is discovered or when the patient should have known of the injury.

Dispensing Distribution, delivery, disposing, or giving away a drug, medicine, prescription, or chemical.

Do not resuscitate A designation placed on a patient's medical record indicating that in the case of cessation of circulation and breathing, artificial resuscitation (CPR) is not to be done.

Doctrine of professional discretion This principle declares that a physician or advanced practice provider may determine, based on their best judgment, if a patient with mental or emotional problems should view the medical record.

Double-blind test A research design in which neither the experimenter nor the patient knows who is getting the research treatment.

Drug Enforcement Administration A division of the Department of Justice that enforces the Controlled Substances Act of 1970.

Drug-Free Workplace Act Act that established the requirement that employers must certify that they maintain a drug-free workplace.

Due process The entitlement of all employees to have certain procedures followed when they believe their rights are in jeopardy.

Durable power of attorney A legal agreement that allows an agent or representative of the patient to act on behalf of the patient.

Duty Obligation or responsibility.

Duty-based ethics Focusing on the performance of one's duty to various people and institutions.

Elder abuse Form of abuse that includes physical abuse, neglect, exploitation, and abandonment of adults 60 years and older and is reportable in most states.

Electronic health record Electronically captured health information that includes tracking clinical conditions, reporting clinical quality measures, and using this information to include patients and their families in their care.

Electronic medical record Fully computerized method of medical record keeping.

Electronic protected health information Information protected under the Security Rule of HIPAA setting the administrative, physical, and technical safeguards for electronic health information.

Embezzlement The illegal appropriation of property, usually money, by a person entrusted with its possession.

Embryonic stem cells Cells that are derived from the inner cell mass of a blastocyst, which is an early stage of embryo development; currently used in research, focusing on therapeutic potential.

Embryos The stage of prenatal development between the second and eighth week of pregnancy.

Emergency contraception Medication that contains a high dose of a contraceptive that can prevent a pregnancy if taken within 72 hours following intercourse; also called the *morning after pill* and *plan B*.

Emergency Medical Treatment & Labor Act A section of COBRA dealing with patient dumping.

Employee Assistance Program A management-financed, confidential counseling referral service designed to help employees and/or their family members assess a problem such as alcoholism.

Employee Retirement Income Security Act Act that regulates employee benefits and pension plans.

Employer Identification Number A number assigned to an employer for purposes of identification.

Employer Identifier Standard A standard number based on an employer's tax ID number or EIN that is used for all electronic transmissions.

Encryptions Scrambling and encoding information before sending it electronically.

Endorsement An approval or sanction.

Equal Credit Opportunity Act Act that prohibits businesses (including hospitals) from denying or granting credit based on race and gender, referred to as discrimination.

Equal Employment Opportunity Act Act that authorizes the EEOC to sue employers in federal court on behalf of people whose rights have been violated under Title VII.

Equal Employment Opportunity Commission The group that monitors Title VII of the Civil Rights Act.

Equal Pay Act Act that makes it illegal for an employer to discriminate on the basis of gender in payment to men and women who are performing the same job.

Estate court Handles cases involving estates of the deceased.

Ethics The branch of philosophy relating to morals and moral principles.

Euthanasia The administration of a lethal agent by another person to a patient for the purpose of relieving intolerable and incurable suffering.

Exclusive provider organization A type of managed care that combines the concepts of the HMO and PPO.

Expert witness A medical practitioner or other expert who, through education, training, or experience, has special knowledge about a subject and gives testimony about that subject in court, usually for a fee.

Expressed contract An agreement that is entered into orally or in writing.

Expulsion The act of forcing out.

Facial recognition technology A technology that has the ability to check each face entering a building against a database of known dangerous persons.

Fair Credit Reporting Act Act that established guidelines for use of an individual's credit information.

Fair Debt Collections Practices Act Act that prohibits unfair collection practices by creditors.

Fair Labor Standards Act Act that established the minimum wage, required payment for overtime work, and set the maximum hours employees covered by the act may work.

False imprisonment This occurs in healthcare when a medical professional, or a person hired by that professional, takes an action to confine a patient.

Family and Medical Leave Act Act that allows both the mother and the father to take a leave of absence for up to 12 weeks, in any 12-month period, when a baby is born.

Feasance Doing an act or performing a duty.

Federal Insurance Contribution Act Act that requires employers to contribute to Social Security for employees.

Federal Rules of Evidence Rules that govern the admissibility of evidence into federal court.

Federal Wage Garnishment Law Law that restricts the amount of the paycheck that can be used to pay off a debt.

Fee splitting An agreement to pay a fee to another physician or agency for the referral of patients; this is illegal in some states and is considered to be an unethical medical practice.

Felony A serious crime that carries a punishment of death or imprisonment for more than one year. Examples are murder, rape, robbery, and practicing medicine without a license.

Fetus Stage of prenatal development following the embryonic stage; begins at the ninth week of pregnancy.

Firewalls Software to prevent unauthorized users.

Fixed-payment plan A payment plan for medical bills that offers subscribers (members) complete medical care in return for a fixed monthly fee.

Food and Drug Administration An agency within the Department of Health and Human Services that ultimately oversees and enforces laws regarding drug sales and distribution.

Food insecurity When a person or family does not have enough food to eat or have access to healthy food.

Forensic medicine Branch of medicine concerned with the law, especially criminal law.

Fraud The deliberate concealment of the facts from another person for unlawful or unfair gain.

Fraudulent Deceitful.

Free Appropriate Public Education The provision that requires school districts to provide free appropriate public education to each qualified person with a disability.

Gatekeeper The person, such as a primary care physician, or entity, such as an insurance company, that approves patient referrals to other physicians or services.

Gestational period Time before birth during which the fetus is developing, usually nine months.

Good Samaritan laws State laws that help protect healthcare professionals and ordinary citizens from liability while giving emergency care to accident victims.

Group practices Three or more physicians who share the same facility and practice medicine together.

Guardian ad litem Court-appointed guardian to represent a minor or unborn child in litigation.

Habituation The development of an emotional dependence on a drug due to repeated use.

Harvested Removed organs or embryos.

Health Care Quality Improvement Act This act provides for peer review of physicians by other physicians and healthcare professionals.

Health Information Technology for Economic and Clinical Health Act The HITECH Act expands HIPAA by including business functions, such as for billing, accounting, and others, and also includes measures to modernize the nation's use of technology when handling private health information.

Health Insurance Portability and Accountability Act of 1996 Act that regulates the privacy of patients' health information.

Health maintenance organization A type of managed care plan that offers a range of health services to plan members for a predetermined fee per member by a limited group of providers.

Health record All written and computer-generated documentation relating to the patient.

Healthcare ethics Moral conduct based on principles regulating the behavior of healthcare professionals.

Healthcare plan An individual or group plan that provides or pays for medical care.

Healthcare proxy A document signed by a person appointing another person to act for them in making healthcare decisions on their behalf.

Healthcare-associated infections Infections that patients get in a healthcare facility while receiving medical care.

HIPAA-defined permission Permission to use information based on the reason for knowing, or use of, the information.

Hospice Multidisciplinary, family-centered care designed to provide care and supportive services to terminally ill patients and their families.

Human genome The complete set of genes within the 23 pairs of human chromosomes.

Human Genome Project A research program funded by the federal government to "map" and sequence the total number of genes within the 23 pairs, or 46 chromosomes.

Hypothermia State in which body temperature is below normal range.

Implied consent The assumption that a person has given permission for an action, which is inferred from their actions, rather than from verbal agreement.

Implied contract An agreement that is made through inference by signs, inaction, or silence.

In loco parentis Latin for "in place of a parent"; a person assigned by a court to act *in loco parentis* stands in place of a child's parent or parents and possesses parental legal rights and responsibilities toward the child.

In vitro fertilization The process of combining ovum and sperm outside of a woman's body.

Incident report A means of documenting problem events within a hospital or other medical facility.

Incompetent patient One who is determined to be unable to provide for their own needs and protection.

Indictment A written charge presented to the court by the grand jury against a defendant.

Indigent A person who is impoverished and without funds.

Individuals with Disabilities Education Act The reauthorized and revised Americans with Disabilities Act to align with the No Child Left Behind Act.

Induced abortion An abortion caused by artificial means such as medications or surgical procedures.

Informed—or expressed—consent Consent granted by a person after the patient has received knowledge and understanding of potential risks and benefits.

Inquest An investigation held by a public official, such as a coroner, to determine the cause of death.

Institutional review board A hospital or university board of members who oversee any human research in that facility.

Intentional torts These occur when a person has been intentionally or deliberately injured by another.

Intimate partner violence Physical violence, sexual violence, stalking and psychological aggression by a current or former intimate partner.

Invasion of privacy The unauthorized publicity of information about a patient.

Jurisdiction The power to hear a case.

Just cause Legal reason.

Justice-based ethics Based on the moral restraint of "the veil of ignorance."

Law of agency The legal relationship formed between two people when one person agrees to perform work for another person.

Laws Rules or actions prescribed by a governmental authority that have a binding legal force.

Liable Legal responsibility for one's own actions.

Libel Any publication in print, writing, pictures, or signs that injures the reputation of another person.

Licensure A mandatory credentialing process that allows an individual to perform certain skills.

Life-support systems Systems such as ventilators/respirators and feeding tubes that allow medical practitioners to sustain a patient's life.

Litigation A dispute that has resulted in one party suing another.

Litigious Excessively inclined to sue.

Living will A legal document in which a person states that life-sustaining treatments and nutritional support should not be used to prolong life; a type of advance directive.

Malfeasance Performing an illegal act.

Malpractice Professional misconduct or demonstration of an unreasonable lack of skill with the result of injury, loss, or damage to the patient.

Managed care organizations A type of medical plan that pays for and manages the medical care a patient receives.

Maternal mortality The death of a woman while pregnant or within 42 days of termination of the pregnancy.

Mediation Using the opinion of a third party to resolve a civil dispute in a nonbinding decision.

Medicaid Federal program, implemented by the individual states, to provide financial assistance for the indigent.

Medical aid-in-dying Practice that involves a healthcare provider giving a terminally ill patient a prescription for a lethal dose of medication.

Medical examiner A physician, usually a pathologist, who can investigate an unexplained death and perform autopsies.

Medical informatics The application of communication and information to healthcare practice, research, and education.

Medical orders for life-sustaining treatment A document that outlines a patient's preferences for medical interventions in the event of a life-threatening situation.

Medical practice acts Laws established in all 50 states that define the practice of medicine as well as requirements and methods for licensure in a particular state.

Medical record All the written and computer-generated documentation relating to a patient.

Medicare Federal program that provides healthcare coverage for persons over 65 years of age as well as for disabled persons or those who suffer kidney disease or other debilitating ailments.

Minimum necessary standard The requirement that the provider must make a reasonable effort to limit the disclosure of patient information to only the minimum amount that is necessary to accomplish the purpose of the request.

Minor A person who has not reached the age of maturity, which in most states is 18.

Misdemeanor Less serious offenses than felonies; punishable by fines or imprisonment of up to one year. These include traffic violations and disturbing the peace.

Misfeasance The improper performance of an otherwise proper or lawful act.

Morality The quality of being virtuous or practicing the right conduct.

Morbidity rate The rate of sick people or cases of disease in relationship to a specific population.

Mortality rate Death rate.

Multidrug-resistant organisms Germs that are resistant to many antibiotics, which makes the use of the drugs less effective or even not effective at all; examples include MRSA, VRE, and C. diff.

Mutual recognition model A licensing system that allows a nurse to have a single license that confers the privilege to practice in other states that are part of the Nurse Licensure Compact.

National Labor Relations Act Act that prohibits employer actions, such as attempting to force employees to stay out of unions, and labels these actions as "unfair labor practices."

National Organ Transplant Law of 1984 Federal law that forbids the sale of organs in interstate commerce.

Negligence An unintentional action that occurs when a person either performs or fails to perform an action that a "reasonable person" would or would not have committed in a similar situation.

Nominal damages A slight or token payment awarded by the court.

Noncompliant patient One who fails, or refuses, to cooperate with the recommendations of a healthcare professional.

Nonfeasance The failure to perform an action when it is necessary.

Nontherapeutic research Research conducted that will not directly benefit the research subject.

Notice of Privacy Practices A written statement that details the provider's privacy practices.

Occupational Safety and Health Act Requires an employer to provide a safe and healthy work environment; the employer must protect the worker against hazards.

Occurrence insurance (also called claims-incurred insurance) covers the insured party for all injuries and incidents that occurred while the policy was in effect (policy year), regardless of when they are reported to the insurer or the claim was made.

Office of Civil Rights The federal office that investigates violations of HIPAA.

Open-record laws State freedom of information laws that grant public access to records maintained by state agencies.

Opioid crisis A rapid rise in overdose deaths from misuse of opioids that started in the 1990s in the United States.

Opioids Synthetic products that are not derived from opium but have an opium-like effect, acting on the brain to decrease the sensation of pain.

Palliative care Care for terminally ill patients consisting of comfort measures and symptom control.

Parens patriae Authority occurs when the state takes responsibility from the parents for the care and custody of minors under the age of 18.

Partnerships A legal agreement in which two or more physicians share the business operation of a medical practice and become responsible for the actions of the other partners.

Passive euthanasia Allowing a patient to die by forgoing treatment.

Patient Self-Determination Act Act that requires healthcare institutions to provide information to adult patients about advance directives.

Per diem Daily rate.

Persistent vegetative state An irreversible brain condition in which the patient is in a state of deep unconsciousness.

Personal health record A record of information, often in the patient's own words, that is controlled by the patient or the patient's family.

Placebo group Research in which an inactive or alternative type of treatment is given.

Plaintiff A person or group of people suing another person or group of people; the person who instigates the lawsuit.

Pleadings Formal written statements.

Postmortem After death.

Precedent A ruling of an earlier case that is then applied to subsequent cases.

Preempt Overrule.

Preferred provider organization A managed-care concept in which the patient must use a medical provider who is under contract with the insurer for an agreed-upon fee in order to receive copayment from the insurer.

Pregnancy Discrimination Act Mandates that employers must treat pregnant women as they would any other employee, providing they can still do the job.

Preimplantation genetic diagnosis Genetic testing on embryos for genes that cause untreatable or severe diseases.

Preponderance of evidence Evidence showing that more likely than not the incident occurred.

Primary care providers HMO-designated physician or advanced practice provider who manages and controls an enrolled patient's healthcare.

Principle of autonomy Right to make decisions about one's own life.

Principle of beneficence Action of helping others and performing actions that result in benefit to another person.

Principle of double-effect When an action can have two effects: one that is morally good or desirable and one that is not.

Principle of justice Warns us that equals must be treated equally.

Principle of nonmalfeasance Means "First, do no harm."

Privacy Act of 1974 Provides private citizens some control over information that the federal government collects about them by limiting the use for unnecessary purposes.

Privacy Rule A requirement that all covered entities under HIPAA must be in compliance with the privacy, security, and electronic-data provisions by April 14, 2003.

Privileged communication Confidential information that has been told to a physician (or attorney) by the patient.

Probable cause A reasonable belief that something improper has occurred.

Probate court Handles cases involving estates of the deceased.

Product liability A type of strict liability in which a manufacturer or seller may be liable for any injury caused by a defective or hazardous product.

Prosecutor A person who brings a criminal lawsuit on behalf of the government.

Prospective payment system The payment amount or reimbursement with a set rate for certain procedures is known in advance.

Protected health information Any individually identifiable information that relates to the physical or mental condition or the provision of healthcare to an individual.

Protocol A clinical plan of treatment.

Proximate The injury was closely (proximately) related to the defendant's negligence.

Proxy A person who acts on behalf of another person.

Prudent person rule Also called the responsible person standard, means a healthcare professional must provide the information that a prudent, reasonable person would want before making a decision about treatment or refusal of treatment.

Public duties Responsibilities that healthcare providers owe to the public.

Public law Concerns relationships between individuals and the government as well as relationships between individuals that are of concern to society as a whole.

Punitive damages Also called exemplary damages, monetary award by a court to a person who has been harmed in an especially malicious and willful way; meant to punish the offender.

Quality assurance Gathering and evaluating information about the services provided as well as the results achieved and comparing this information with an accepted standard.

Quality of life The physiological status, emotional well-being, functional status, and life in general of an individual.

Randomized study A form of therapeutic research in which the subject is assigned at random to either a control group or an experimental treatment group.

Reciprocity The cooperation of one state in granting a license to practice medicine to a physician already licensed in another state. Reciprocity can be applied to other licensed professionals such as nurses and pharmacists.

Registration This indicates that the person whose name is listed on an official record or register has met certain requirements in that particular profession.

Regulations Rules or laws made by agencies.

Rehabilitation Act Act that prohibits employers from discriminating against the handicapped.

Res ipsa loquitur Latin phrase meaning "the thing speaks for itself."

Res judicata Latin phrase meaning "the thing has been decided."

Respite care Providing the family with relief from the responsibilities of patient care.

Respondeat superior Latin phrase meaning "let the master answer"; means the employer is responsible for the actions of the employee.

Restraining or protective order Court order that prohibits an abuser from coming into contact with the victim.

Retailing The legal act of selling or trading a drug, medicine, prescription, or chemical.

Revocation The act of taking away or recalling, such as taking away a license to practice medicine.

Revoke Take away, as in revoke a license.

Rider Additional component to an insurance policy.

Rights-based ethics A natural rights ethical theory that places the primary emphasis on a person's individual rights.

Rigor mortis Stiffness that occurs in a dead body.

Risk management A practice to minimize the incidence of problem behavior that might result in injury to a patient and liability for the organization.

Robotic-assisted surgery A method of performing surgery using very small tools attached to a robotic arm.

Robotics In medicine, the use of machines that have the capacity to perform human tasks.

Safe Haven Laws Laws that provide safe and legal alternatives to leaving babies in unsafe places when a parent voluntarily gives up custody.

Safety data sheet Document that provides specific information on handling and disposing of chemicals safely.

Scope of practice The activities healthcare professionals are allowed to perform as indicated in their licensure, certification, and/or training.

Selective fetal reduction Procedure to remove some of the embryos from a multiple pregnancy, leaving only one, two or three.

Settlement The act of determining the outcome of a case outside a courtroom; settling a case is not an indication of legal wrongdoing.

Sexual harassment Unwelcome sexual advances or requests for sexual favors.

Slander Speaking false and malicious words concerning another person that brings injury to their reputation.

Social determinants of health The conditions in which people are born, grow, live, work, and age, which play a critical role in influencing health outcomes.

Social Security Act Federal law that covers all private-sector and most public-sector employees.

Sole proprietorship A type of medical practice in which one physician may employ other physicians.

Solo practices A medical practice in which a physician works alone.

Spontaneous abortion Termination of pregnancy that occurs naturally before the fetus is viable.

Standard of care The ordinary skill and care that medical practitioners use and that is commonly used by other medical practitioners in the same locality when caring for patients; what another medical professional would consider appropriate care in similar circumstances.

State's preemption When the state privacy laws are stricter than the privacy standards established by HIPAA.

Statute of limitations The period of time that a patient has to file a lawsuit.

Statutes Laws enacted by state and federal legislatures.

Sterilization The process of medically altering reproductive organs so as to terminate the ability to produce offspring.

Strict liability The concept, in law, that a person is liable for consequences flowing from an activity even if the person is not at fault.

Subpoena Court order for a person or documents to appear in court.

Substitute judgment rule This is used when decisions must be made for a person who cannot make their wishes known.

Summary judgment Judge's ruling to end a lawsuit without a trial based on a matter of law presented in pleadings.

Surrogacy An arrangement (usually a legal agreement) between a woman who agrees to carry and birth a child for another person or couple.

Surrogate A person who is replacing another person.

Telehealth The use of communications and information technologies to provide healthcare services to people at a distance.

Terminally ill One whose death is determined to be inevitable.

The Joint Commission An agency that oversees hospital accreditation standards.

Therapeutic research A form of medical research that might directly benefit the research subject.

Therapeutic sterilization Sterilization undertaken to save a mother's life or protect her health.

Third-party payers A party other than the patient who assumes responsibility for paying the patient's bills (e.g., an insurance company).

Timeliness of documentation All entries into a medical record should be made as soon as they occur or as soon as possible afterward.

Title VII of the Civil Rights Act Act that prohibits discrimination in employment based on five criteria: race, color, religion, gender, or national origin.

Tolling Also known as running of the statute of limitations, means the time has expired.

Tort A civil injury, or wrongful act, committed against another person or property that results in harm and is compensated in money damages.

Tort law Law that covers private or civil wrongful acts that result in harm to another person or that person's property.

Tort reform A controversial issue in which limits are placed on an injured person's ability to sue.

Treatment, payment, and healthcare operations Functions that a healthcare provider can perform.

Triage In emergency medicine, making rapid decisions about who receives immediate care based on the severity of their condition

Truth in Lending Act Act that requires a full written disclosure about interest rates or finance charges concerning the payment of any fee that will be collected in more than four installments; also known as Regulation Z.

Unemployment compensation This provides for temporary weekly payments for the unemployed worker.

Uniform Anatomical Gift A state statute allowing persons 18 years of age or older and of sound mind to make a gift of any or all body parts for purposes of organ transplantation or medical research.

Uniform Anatomical Gift Act A state statute allowing persons 18 years of age or older and of sound mind to make a gift of any or all body parts for purposes of organ transplantation or medical research.

Uniform Determination of Death Act This law has been adopted in 37 states. It says that an individual, who has sustained either (1) irreversible cessation of circulatory and respiratory functions, or (2) irreversible cessation of all functions of the entire brain, including the brain stem, is dead.

Unintentional torts Wrongful acts, such as negligence, that occur when a patient is injured as a result of a healthcare professional's not exercising the ordinary standard of care.

United Network for Organ Sharing The legal entity in the United States responsible for allocating organs for transplantation.

Utilitarianism An ethical theory based on the principle of the greatest good for the greatest number.

Viable In the case of a fetus, ability to survive outside the uterus.

Viatical settlements These arrangements allow people with terminal illnesses, such as AIDS, to obtain money from their life insurance policies by selling them.

Virtue-based ethics A character trait based on a concern for the person.

Visual impairment A category of vision deficit encompassing both those who are blind and those with low vision.

Vital statistics Major events or facts from a person's life, such as live births, deaths, induced termination of pregnancy, and marriages.

Voice recognition technology This enables doctors to verbally chart their patients' records to allow more immediate and thorough documentation.

Waive Give up a right.

Wireless local area networks A wireless system that is used by providers, nurses, and allied health professionals to access patient information.

Withdrawing life-sustaining treatment Discontinuing a treatment or procedure, such as artificial ventilation, after it has started.

Withholding life-sustaining treatment Failing to start a treatment or procedure such as artificial ventilation.

Workers' Compensation Act Act that protects workers and their families from financial problems resulting from employment-related injury, disease, and death.

Wrongful discharge When an employee believes that the employer does not have a just-cause or legal reason for firing the employee.

Index

A

Abandonment, of patients, 93–94
AbioCor, 293
Abortion, 262–266
    additional issues concerning, 264
    AMA judicial council opinion on, 239t
    Baby K, 265
    Conscience Clause in, 265–266
    defined, 262
    Dobbs v. Jackson Women's Health Organization, 263
    employee's right to refuse participation in, 264
    EMTALA, 264
    ethical issues, 264–266
    history of abortion law, 262–263
    incompetent persons and, 264
    induced, 262
    Plan B contraceptive pill and, 260
    Roe v. Wade, 262–263
    spontaneous, 262
Abuse
    AMA judicial council opinion on, 238t
    child, 147–148
    elder, 148
    gathering evidence in cases of, 150
    Older Americans Act and, 148
    reporting, 148
    Safe Haven Laws and, 271
    signs of, 149
    substance, 154–156, 154t
Acceptance stage, stages of grief, 286t
Accreditation, 56
Accreditation Review Commission on Education for
        the Physician Assistant (ARC-PA), 53
Accrediting Bureau of Health Education Schools
        (ABHES), 82
Acquired immunodeficiency syndrome (AIDS)
    Americans with Disabilities Act and, 174
    duty to report, 146
    improper disclosure and, 201
    Pregnancy Discrimination Act and, 173
Active euthanasia
    defined, 282
    pros and cons, 284
Activities of daily living (ADLs), 51
Administrative law, 38
Advance directives, 104–108, 104t
    defined, 104
    DNR order, 291
    durable power of attorney, 106, *107*
    frequently asked questions, 106, 108
    healthcare proxy, 292
    living will, 105, *105*
    medical orders for life-sustaining treatment, 106
    Patient Self-Determination Act, 104–105
    substitute judgment rule and, 291
    surrogate designation, 291
    Uniform Anatomical Gift Act, 106

Advanced practice providers, 6
Advanced practice registered nurse (APRN), 82, 83t
Affirmative action programs, 172
Affirmative defense, malpractice suits, 123
Against medical advice (AMA), 94
    hospitalization discharge, 94
Age Discrimination in Employment Act (ADEA), 173
Agent, of power of attorney, 106
Agnew-Watson v. County of Alameda, 180
Alleging, criminal act, 237
Allen v. Harrison, 103
Allied health professionals, 51, 55–56, 82, 83t–84t
    code of ethics, 239
    negligence lawsuits against, 131–134
Allied Health Professions, 83t–84t
Allocation, of resources
    angiogram, case of, 277–278
    of organs, 241–242
Alterations, to medical records, 191–192
Altered medical records, 128
Alternative dispute resolution (ADR), 130
Alzheimer's disease
    genetic testing and, 269
AMA. *See* Against medical advice (AMA); American
        Medical Association (AMA)
American Academy of Neurology, 281
American Academy of Orthopedic Surgeons
    medical errors and, 93
American Association for Respiratory Care
        (AARC), 51
American Association of Medical Assistants (AAMA),
        56, 79
    code of ethics, 239, 321
American Bar Association, 281
American Civil Liberties Union (ACLU), 282
American College of Physicians, 80
American College of Surgeons, 80
American Deaf culture, 308
    American Sign Language and, 308
    Americans with Disabilities Act (ADA) and, 308
    cochlear implants and, 308
    interpreters needed for, 308
    National Association of the Deaf and, 308
American Health Information Management
        Association (AHIMA), 197, 197t
American Hospital Association (AHA)
    The Patient Care Partnership, 99
    patient rights during hospitalization, 97
    truth telling *versus* maintaining confidentiality, 96
American Medical Association (AMA)
    AMA judicial council opinion on, 238t,
        238t–239t, 239t
    censure and, 237
    and ethical standards, 10
    and Hippocratic Oath, 236
    position on abortion, 262
    principles of medical ethics and, 237–238
    Uniform Determination of Death Act and, 281

American Medical Technologists (AMT), 56, 79
American Nurses Association (ANA), 54
    code of ethics, 239, 321
American Nurses Credentialing Center
        (ANCC), 54
American Occupational Therapy Association
        (AOTA), 51, 74
American Physical Therapy Association
        (APTA), 51
American Recovery and Reinvestment Act, 189,
        199, 215
American Sign Language (ASL)
    American Deaf culture and, 308
    lip reading and, 308
American Society of Clinical Pathology (ASCP), 55
American Society of Phlebotomy Technicians
        (ASPT), 51
Americans with Disabilities Act Amendments Act
        (ADAAA) of 2008, 175
Americans with Disabilities Act (ADA) of 1990, 174
    and accommodations for disabilities, 174
Amniocentesis, 266
Amorality, 7
AMT Institute for Education (AMTIE), 79
Amyotrophic lateral sclerosis (ALS), case of, 90
Analysis, cost-benefit, 8
Anencephaly, 265
Anger stage, stages of grief, 286t
Animal bites, 150
Anne and the Runaway Stroller, case studies, 298–299
Appellate court system, 44
Applied ethics, defined, 2
Aquinas, Thomas, 15
Arbitration, 130
Arbitrator, 130
Arizona, life-support case in, 281
Armstrong v. Flowers Hosp., 173
Arthritis Impact Measurement Scale (AIMS), 287
Artificial conception
    artificial insemination, 256
    ethical considerations, 258–259
    fertility drugs, 255
    in vitro fertilization, 256
    surrogacy, 256–258
Artificial insemination, 256
Artificial intelligence, 314–315
Assault, 33, 33t
Assisted conception. *See* Artificial conception
Assisted reproductive technology
    defined, 256
    ethical considerations, 258–259
    fertility treatments, 255–256
    legal, 258–259
Assisted suicide, 282
Associate practice, 77
Assumption of risk, malpractice suits defense,
        123–124
At-will employment, 171

Autonomy, 96, 167
    vs. preservation of life, 292
    principle of, 18
Autopsy, 145

B

Baby Doe regulations, 264–265
Baby K case, 265
Baby M case, 257–258
Bankruptcy, 183
Bargaining stage, stages of grief, 286*t*
Barnes Hospital v. Missouri Commission on Human Rights, 132
Battery, 33, 33*t*
Behavior ethics, 236–237
    ethics principles (values) and, 11–12
Bench trial, defined, 32
Bendiburg v. Dempsey, 126
Beneficence
    defined, 11
    principle of, 18
Benefits regulations. *See* Compensation and benefits (federal regulations)
Beyond a reasonable doubt, defined, 37
Bias, 167
Big Town Nursing Home v. Newman, 33
Bioethical issues, 239–245
    genetic information, 245
    organ donation, 240
    organ trafficking, 241
    transplant rationing, 241–243
Bioethicists, 19
Bioethics (biomedical ethics)
    and advanced medical technology, 236
    analysis principles, 18–19
    defined, 2
    reasons to study, 2–5
Biomedical research
    conflicts of interest, 247
    control group, 246
    double-blind tests, 246
    embryonic stem cell research, 248
    ethics of, 245–248
    Placebo group, 246
    randomized study, 246
    therapeutic research, 246–247
Birth and life issues. *See also specific issues*
    abortion and, 262–266
    assisted reproductive technology, 256–258
    conscience clause in, 265–266
    contraception, 259
    embryonic stem cells, 248
    ethical issues, 254–276
    fertility treatments, 255–256
    genetic disorders, 266–269
    hereditary disorder, 266
    Human Genome Project, 247–248
    Safe Haven Laws, 270–271
    and sterilization, 260
    wrongful conception/pregnancy, 270
    wrongful-life suits, 269–270
Birth certificates, 143
Birth control, ethical issues, 261
Blanchard-Peale three-step ethics model, 15
Blindness, 310
Bloodborne pathogens, 175, 176
BNDD. *See* Bureau of Narcotics and Dangerous Drugs (BNDD)
Board of nursing (BON), 50, 53
Bonding, insurance, 62

Bondu v. Gurvich, 197
Borrowed servant doctrine, 124
Brain death, 280–281
Brandeis, Louis, 210
Breach, 118
Breach of contract, 36
Breach of duty, 118
Brennan, William J., 260
Brinson v. Axelrod, 148
Buchanan v. Kull, 125
Buckley v. Hospital Corp. of America, Inc., 173
Burden of proof, 42
Bureau of Narcotics and Dangerous Drugs (BNDD), 151
Burke, Edmund, 20
Bush, Jeb, 283

C

CAAHEP. *See* Commission on Accreditation of Allied Health Education Programs (CAAHEP)
California
    artificial insemination case in, 265–266
    completeness of medical records case in, 193
    liability case in, 132
    workers' compensation case in, 180
Canterbury v. Spence, 96, 102
Capitation rate, in HMO, 74
Cap, on malpractice compensation, 120
Cardiac death, 279–280
Cardiopulmonary arrest
    cardiac death and, 279–280
    Karen Ann Quinlan and, 278–279
Cardiopulmonary death, 279–280
Cardiopulmonary resuscitation (CPR)
    abandonment and, 94
    advance directives and, 291
    do not resuscitate (DNR) orders and, 105
    failure to perform lawsuits, 132
    Good Samaritan law and, 59
    informed consent and, 33
Carson, Benjamin, 293
Case citations, 31
Case law, 30
    as category of governmental rules, 29
    list of citations, 322–323
    stare decisis origins from, 30
Case studies
    Anne and the Runaway Stroller, 298–299
    COVID-19 Vaccine Line Jumpers, 234–235
    David Z. and Amyotrophic Lateral Sclerosis (ALS), 90
    Janet K. and Epilepsy, 163–164
    Jason and the Ransomware Attack, 188
    John F. and the HMO, 113
    Marguerite M. and the Angiogram, 277–278
    Marion and the Pacemaker, 69–70
    the New Minister, 208
    of OB/GYN and Olivia M., 254
    Olivia and the Pediatrician's Office, 142
Censure
    by AMA, 237
    of physician, 237
Centers for Disease Control and Prevention (CDC)
    public health reporting and, 143
Centers for Medicare & Medicaid Services (CMS), 71
Certification, healthcare practitioners, 79
Certified nursing assistants (CNAs), 55
Certified Respiratory Therapist (CRT), 55
Charitable organizations, immunity for, 123
Charting, notations for corrections, 191

Checks and balances, government, 27
Chemical waste, 157
Child abuse, 147–148
    Child Abuse Prevention and Treatment Act of 1974, 147
    Child Abuse Prevention and Treatment Act of 1987, 265
    gathering evidence, 150
    Mary Ellen McCormack case of, 147
    Minnesota case of, 147
    probable cause to investigate, 147
    signs of, 149
Child Abuse Prevention and Treatment Act of 1974, 147
Child Abuse Prevention and Treatment Act of 1987, 265
Child Protection Group v. Cline, 196
Children's Health Insurance Program (CHIP), 71
Chromosomes, 247–248
Circuit courts. *See* Court of appeals
Civil (private) law, 31–35
    and class action lawsuits, 37
    components, *32*
    contract law, 32, 35–37
    defined, 31
    preponderance of evidence required in, 32
    tort law, 32–35
Civil liability cases, 125–126
Civil Rights Act of 1991, 172
Civil Rights Act of 1964, Title VII of, 171–172
    sexual harassment definition, 14
Civil trial, procedure for, *42*
Claims, against estates, 183
Claims-made insurance, 129
Class action lawsuit, 37
Clearinghouse, for HIPAA transactions, 216
Cline v. Lund, 61
Clinical decision support systems (CDSS), 224–225
Clinical Laboratory Improvement Act (CLIA) of 1988, 176–177, *177*
Cloning, 236, 239
Closing arguments, 42
Clostridium difficile infections, 303
Cochlear implants, 308
Codes of ethics, 320–321
Coding up, 33
Cognitive impairment
    and decision-making capacity, 312–313
    hereditary disorders and, 267*t*
    PKU testing and, 268
Collection agency, using, 182–183
Comatose state
    defined, 278–279
    Terri Schiavo case and, 283
Commission on Accreditation for Respiratory Care (CoARC), 55
Commission on Accreditation of Allied Health Education Programs (CAAHEP), 56, 82
Common law, 30
Communicable diseases, reporting cases of, 146–147
Communication, as malpractice prevention and, 136
Comparable worth, 14–15
Comparative negligence, malpractice suit defense, 124
Compassion, in workplace, 13
Compensation and benefits (federal regulations), 178–181
    Employee Retirement Income Security Act, 180
    Equal Pay Act, 179
    Fair Labor Standards Act (FLSA), 178–179
    Family and Medical Leave Act (FMLA), 180–181
    Federal Insurance Contribution Act, 179

Compensation and benefits (*Continued*)
  Social Security Act, 178
  unemployment compensation, 179
  Workers' Compensation Act, 179–180
Compensatory damages, 120
Competency, of parties in valid contracts, 35
Compounding, of medications, defined, 153
Comprehensive Omnibus Budget Reconciliation Act
      (COBRA), 93
Computers on wheels (COWs) carts, 198, 199
Conception, wrongful, 270
Concierge healthcare, 314
Confidentiality. *See also* Health Insurance Portability
      and Accountability Act (HIPAA)
  in AAMA code of ethics, 321
  AMA judicial council opinion on, 238*t*
  case of, 208
  computerized records and, 195–196
  Employee Assistance Programs and, 157
  medical records and, 195–196
  patient, 208–232
  patient rights and, 58, 98
  physician duty to respect, 95
  transmitting records and, 195*t*
Conflicts of interest, 247
Conjoined twins, 293
Connecticut
  contraception ban and, 259
  Safe Haven law and, 270
Conscience clause, 75–76
Consent, 100–104
  exceptions to, 103–104
  under HIPAA, 214
  implied, 103–104
  informed, 100–103, 245, 312, 315
  refusal to grant, 104
Consolidated Omnibus Budget Reconciliation Act
      (COBRA), 71, 177–178
  patient dumping and, 178
Constitutional law, 29
Consumer Protection Act, 181
Consumer protection and collection practices,
      181–183, *182*
  claims against estates, 183
  Emergency Medical Treatment and Active Labor
      Act, 181
  Equal Credit Opportunity Act, 181
  Fair Credit Reporting Act, 181
  Fair Debt Collection Practices Act, 182
  Federal Wage Garnishment Law, 183
  statute of limitations, 183
  Truth in Lending Act, 181–182
Continuing education (CE), 79
Contraception
  Conscience Clause in, 265–266
  defined, 259
  emergency, 260
  ethical considerations, 261–262
  legal, 261–262
  sterilization, 260–261
Contract law, 35–39
  as addressing a breach, 35
  breach of contracts in, 36
  competent parties in, 35
  consideration in, 35
  defined, 32
  expressed contracts, 36
  implied contracts, 36
  termination of contracts, 36–37
  types of contracts in, 36–37
  verbal contracts, 36

Contracts, 36–37
  breach of, 36
  expressed, 36
  implied, 36
  termination of, 36–37
  types of, 36–37
Contributory negligence, malpractice suit defense, 124
Control group, 246
Controlled substances, 151–156
  and addiction, 151
  Controlled Substances Act of 1970, 151
  prescriptions for, 153, *153*
  schedules for, 152, 152*t*
Cooley's anemia, hereditary disorder, 267*t*
Copayment, in PPO, 74
Coroner
  cases needed for, 145
  defined, 145
Corporation, 78
Corporation, professional, 78
Corrections, to medical records, 191–192
Cost/benefit analysis, 8
Council on Ethical and Judicial Affairs (AMA),
      opinions, 238*t*–239*t*
Court
  improper disclosure, 201
  subpoena *duces tecum*, 201–202
  use of medical records in, 201–202
Court of appeals, 39, 40
Court systems, 39–40
  appellate, 44
  estate, 40
  federal, 39
  probate, 40
  state, 40
  structure of federal, 29, 39
  testifying in, 43
  types of courts, 39–40
Covered entities, under HIPAA, 212, 216–217
Covered transactions, 217
COVID-19 pandemic, 74, 226, 245, 300
COVID-19 Vaccine Line Jumpers, 234–235
Credentialing, 54
Credibility gap, 193
Credibility of medical records, 193
Credit Card Accountability and Disclosure Act of
      2009, 181
Creditor, 183
Criminal case, defined, 37
Criminal law, 37
Cruzan, Nancy, 282
Cruzan v. Director, Missouri Dep't. of Health, 282
Cultural competence, 302, 313
Cultural diversity, 313
Cultural issues, 165–168
Curative care, 290
Cystic fibrosis, 266
  genetic disorders, 267*t*

D

Damages, 119–120
  cap, 120
  compensatory, 120
  nominal, 120
  punitive, 120
Darling v. Charleston Community Memorial Hospital, 61
Data bias, 315
Data breaches, 199
Data protection, patient, 314
Data, public health, 143

Data retention and disposal, 200
Davis v. Davis, 258
DEA. *See* Drug Enforcement Administration (DEA)
Deaf patients, 308
Death certificates, 144–145
Debtors, 183
Decision-making capacity, 292
Defamation of character, 33*t*, 34
  libel, 34
  slander, 34
Defendant, defined, 31, 40
Defensive medicine
  defined, 130
  practicing, 6, 130
Deidentifying, 213
Delegation, 84
DeMay v. Roberts, 97
Denial defense, malpractice suits, 123
Denial stage, stages of grief, 286*t*
Dental assistant
  negligence lawsuit against, 132
  occupation of, 83*t*
Deontological theory, 8
Department of Children and Families (DCF),
      Safe Haven laws and, 270
Department of Health and Human Services
  and administrative law, 38
  institutional review boards (IRBs) and, 245
  Office of Inspector General and, 122
  "reasonable safeguards" for patient privacy, 222
  rules for HMOs, 72
Deposition, 40
Depression stage, stages of grief, 286*t*
Dereliction, of duty, 118
Diagnostic related groups (DRGs), 72
Diphtheria, tetanus, and pertussis (DTaP) vaccine, 146
Direct cause, of negligence, 118–119
Direct killing *versus* indirect killing, 284
Disabilities
  accommodations for, 174
  Americans with Disabilities Acts, 174–175
  Baby Doe regulations, 264–265
  Baby K and, 265
  Child Abuse Prevention and Treatment Act of
      1987, 265
  expanded definition, 174
  hearing loss, 308–309
  Individuals with Disabilities Education Act
      (IDEA), 174
  intellectual disabilities, 311
  physical disabilities, 311–312
  Rehabilitations Act, 173–174
  undue hardship and, 174
  vision disorders, 310–311
Disclosure
  improper, 201
  medical records and, 201–202
  permitted incidental, 218
  state open-record laws and, 196
Discovery, 40
Discovery rule, 59
Discrimination
  in employment, 170–175
  of handicapped, 174
  Rehabilitation Act and, 173–174
  Title VII of the Civil Rights Act and, 171–172
  in workplace, 164
"Diseased Leg" case, 26–27
Disparities
  access to care, 302
  in healthcare, 305

Dispensing, of drugs, 153
District court, 40
Dobbs v. Jackson Women's Health Organization, 263
Doctorate of physical therapy (DPT), 55
Doctrine of professional discretion, 194
Documentation
    completeness of, 192
    malpractice prevention and, 136–137
    timeliness of, 192
Do not resuscitate (DNR)
    advance directives and, 291
    living wills and, 105
Double-blind test, 246
Double-effect principle, 284
Douglas, William O., 259
Downes v. Carpenter, 131
Down syndrome
    Baby Doe and, 264–265
    genetic disorders, 267*t*
    genetic testing and, 266
    wrongful conception/pregnancy, 270
Drug Enforcement Administration (DEA), 151
Drug-Free Workplace Act of 1988, 178
Drugs
    controlled, 153
    fertility, 255
    illegal sale of, 126
Duchenne muscular dystrophy, genetic disorders, 267*t*
Due process, in workplace, 13–14
Durable power of attorney
    agent, 106
    defined, 106
    proxy, 106
    sample, *107*
Duty
    dereliction of, 118
    negligence and, 117–118
    in provider–patient relationship, 117
Duty-based ethics, 9, 10*t*
Dying Person's Bill of Rights, 287–288

E

EIN. *See* Employer Identification Number (EIN)
Eisenstadt v. Baird, 259, 260
Elder abuse, 148
    and neglect, 312
Electroencephalogram (EEG), 278
Electronic health records (EHR), 72, 73
    American Recovery and Reinvestment Act, 199
    benefits of, 198–199
    challenges, 199–200
    defined, 189
    EHR and EMR distinctions, 198, 216
    encryptions, 198
    firewalls, 198
    Health Information Technology for Economic and Clinical Health (HITECH) Act, 215–216
    meaningful use requirement, 199
    Medicare Incentive Program requirement, 216
Electronic medical records (EMR)
    defined, 189
    EMR and EHR distinctions, 198, 216
Electronic protected health information (EPHI)
    disclosure "need-to-know" criterion, 212
    and HIPAA security rule, 212
Embezzlement
    bonding and, 62
    defined, 34
Embryo, in vitro fertilization, 255
Embryonic stem cells, 248

Emergencies (medical)
    duties during, 93
    informed consent and, 102
Emergency contraception, 260
Emergency medical technicians (EMT/paramedic), 60
    abandonment and, 94
    civil immunity finding, 133
    occupation of, 83*t*
Emergency Medical Treatment and Active Labor Act (EMTALA), 264
    Baby K and, 265
    "patient dumping" and, 93, 178, 181
Emotions *versus* ethics, 17
Empathy, defined, 11
Empathy, in workplace, 13
Employee Assistance Program (EAP), 156–157
Employee handbook, 169–170
Employee health and safety (federal regulations)
    Clinical Laboratory Improvement Act, 176–177, *177*
    Consolidated Omnibus Budget Reconciliation Act, 177–178
    Drug-Free Workplace Act, 178
    Health Maintenance Organization Act, 177
    Occupational Safety and Health Act, 175–176
Employee Retirement Income Security Act (ERISA) of 1974, 180
Employees
    abortion, right to refuse participation in, 264
    employer's duty to, 62
    protection for, 156–158
    respondeat superior and, 60–61
    safety, 175–178
    scope of practice for, 61–62
    under Title VII of Civil Rights Act, 171–172
    "troubled", 156
Employer Identification Number (EIN), 217
Employer Identifier Standard, 217
Employers
    duty to employees, 62
    liability and, 128–129
    Title VII of Civil Rights Act and, 172
Employer-sponsored health insurance, 71
Employment discrimination, 170–175
EMR. *See* Electronic medical records (EMR)
EMTALA. *See* Emergency Medical Treatment and Active Labor Act (EMTALA)
Encryptions, 198
End-of-life, 277–297
    active euthanasia *versus* passive euthanasia, 281–284
    brain death, 280–281
    cardiac death and, 279–280
    conjoined twins, 293
    criteria for death, 279
    decision-making, 312
    direct *versus* indirect killing, 284
    ethical issues related to, 277–297
    issues, 243
    Karen Ann Quinlan and, 278–279
    legal definition of death, 278
    ordinary *versus* extraordinary means, 285
    pain management, 288
    quality-of-life issues, 287–292
    right to refuse treatment, 285
    stages of grief, 286–287, 286*t*
    suicide, 292–293
    Uniform Determination of Death Act, 281
    withdrawing *versus* withholding treatment, 281
Endorsement, physician licensure and, 52
Environmental Protection Agency (EPA), 235
EPA. *See* Environmental Protection Agency (EPA)

Epilepsy, workplace ethics case, 163–164
Equal Credit Opportunity Act of 1975, 181
Equal employment opportunity (federal regulations)
    Age Discrimination in Employment Act, 173
    Americans with Disabilities Act, 174
    at-will employment, 171
    Civil Rights Act of 1991, 172
    Equal Employment Opportunity Act, 172
    National Labor Relations Act, 175
    Pregnancy Discrimination Act, 173
    Rehabilitation Act, 173–174
    Title VII of Civil Rights Act, 171–172
Equal Employment Opportunity Act (EEOA) of 1972, 172
Equal Employment Opportunity Commission (EEOC)
    enforcement of Title VII of Civil Rights Act, 171–172
    job interview guidelines, 169*t*
Equal Pay Act of 1963, 179
Erickson v. Dilgard, 104
ERISA. *See* Employee Retirement Income Security Act (ERISA) of 1974
Estate court, 40
Estate of Berthiaume v. Pratt, 34
Estates, claims against, 183
Ethical dilemmas
    conflicts between beliefs and health care roles, 70
    conjoined twins, 293
    cost of biotech medical care and, 240
    mechanical heart recipient, 293
    medical assistants and, 239
    organ donation and, 240
    suicide, 292–293
Ethical issues
    artificial intelligence, 314–315
    concierge healthcare, 314
    robotics, use of, 313
    telehealth, 313
Ethical responsibility, 315
Ethical training, 315
Ethics, 7–15
    abortion, 264–266
    allied health professionals codes of, 239
    applied in medicine, 234–253
    assisted reproductive technology, 258–259
    of biomedical research, 245–248
    birth and life issues, 254–276
    birth control and, 261
    Blanchard-Peale three-step ethics model, 15
    caring for terminally ill patients, 281–285
    codes of, 320–321
    committees, 19
    common sense approach to, 14–15
    conscience clause, 75–76
    contraception, 261–262
    defined, 7
    dilemmas in, 3–5
    duty-based, 9, 10*t*
    versus emotions, 17
    end of life, 277–297
    fee splitting, 75
    genetic testing and, 269
    healthcare, 7, 302–304
    Health Care Quality Improvement Act of 1986, 76
    Human Genome Project, 247–248
    information technology and, 224–227
    interpersonal, 12–15
    justice-based, 9, 10*t*
    Lo three-step clinical model, 16–17
    in managed care, 75

Ethics (*Continued*)
    medical record informatics and, 224
    models for analysis, 15–17
    physicians code of, 237–238
    principles or values driving behavior, 11–12
    reasons to study, 2–5
    versus religious beliefs, 17
    rights-based, 8, 10*t*
    seven-step decision model of, 16
    standards and behavior, 236–237
    sterilization, 260–262
    theories of, 8–10, 10*t*
    utilitarianism and, 8, 10*t*
    virtue-based, 9–10, 10*t*
Ethics, applied, 2
Ethics committees, 19
Etiquette, medical, 20
Euthanasia
    active *versus* passive, 281–284
    AMA judicial council opinion on, 238*t*
    Baby Doe and, 265
    defined, 244, 281
Evidence
    Federal Rules of Evidence, 128
    gathering in abuse cases, 150
    preponderance of, 32, 118
Examination for licensure, 51–52
Exclusive provider organization (EPO), 74
Expert witness, 43
Expressed consent. *See* Informed consent
Expressed contract, 36
Expulsion
    by AMA Board of Examiners, 237
    of physician, from American Medical
        Association, 237
Extraordinary *versus* ordinary means, 285

F

Facial recognition technology, 225–226
Fair Credit Reporting Act of 1971, 181
Fair Debt Collection Practices Act of 1978, 182
    bankruptcy and, 183
    collection agency, 182–183
Fair Labor Standards Act (FLSA) of 1938, 178–179
Fairness, in workplace, 13
Fair v. St. Joseph's Hospital, 180
False imprisonment, 33–34, 33*t*
Falsification, of medical records, 192
Family and Medical Leave Act (FMLA) of 1994,
        180–181
FDA. *See* Food and Drug Administration (FDA)
Feasance, 117
Federal Communications Commission (FCC),
        collection agency guidelines and, 182, *182*
Federal court system, 39
Federal Insurance Contribution Act (FICA) of
        1935, 179
Federal Licensing Examination (FLEX), 51
Federal organizations, 54
Federal Patient Self-Determination Act of 1991, 291
Federal programs, 71–73
    diagnostic related groups, 72
    meaningful use, 72–73
    Medicaid, 73
    Medicare, 71–72
Federal regulations
    compensation and benefits, 178–181
    consumer protection and collection practices,
        181–183, *182*

employee health and safety, 175–178
    medical professional employment and, 170
Federal Rules of Evidence, 128
Federal Wage Garnishment Law of 1970, 183
Federation of State Boards of Physical Therapy
        (FSBPT), 51
Fee-for-service (FFS) basis, 74
Fee splitting
    AMA judicial council opinion on, 238*t*
    ethics of, 75
Fellow of American College of Physicians (FACP), 80
Fellow of American College of Surgeons (FACS), 80
Felony
    case process, *38*
    defined, 37
Fertility drugs, 255
Fertility treatments
    artificial insemination, 256
    fertility drugs, 255
Fetal reduction, selective, 255
Fetus
    defined, 262
    legal standing of, 264
    as person, 264
Fidelity, defined, 11
Fifth Amendment and due process, 13
Firewalls, 198
First, Do No Harm, 299
Fixed-payment plan, defined, 70
FLEX. *See* Federal Licensing Examination (FLEX)
Florida, missing medical records case, 197
Food and Drug Administration (FDA), 151–152
    clinical laboratory standards and, 176
Food, Drug, and Cosmetic Act of 1938, 151
Food insecurity, 307
Forensic medicine, 150–151
Forensic pathologist, 151
Fourteenth Amendment and due process, 13
Fraud
    "coding up" and, 34
    defined, 34
    documentation and, 193
    embezzlement and, 34
    healthcare, 301–302
    as intentional tort, 33*t*, 34
    malpractice and, 120–121
    Medicaid and, 34
    Medicare and, 34, 120–121, 220–221
Fraudulent practices, 34
Free Appropriate Public Education (FAPE), 174
Functional Living Index: Cancer (FLIC), 287

G

Garcia v. Elf Atochem, 172
Garnishment, 183
Gatekeeper
    in managed care, 73
    primary care provider as, 177
Gender harassment, 14
Gene therapy, AMA judicial council opinion on, 238*t*
Genetics
    disorders, 266, 267*t*
    prenatal testing, 266–268
    savior siblings, 268
    testing of newborns, 268–269
Genetic testing
    Down syndrome and, 266
    ethical questions regarding, 269
    ethics and, 269

Huntington's disease, 266, 269
    of newborns, 268–269
    Phenylketonuria (PKU) and, 266
    prenatal, 266–268
    Retinoblastoma and, 266
    Tay-Sachs disease and, 266
Gentleness, defined, 11
Gestational period, 262
Ghost surgery, AMA judicial council opinion on, 239*t*
Goff v. Doctors General Hospital, 61
Goforth v. Porter Med. Assoc., Inc., 261
Good Samaritan laws, 59–60
Government programs, 71
Grande v. Eisenhower Medical Center, 172
Grand jury, 40
Grijalva v. Shalala, 72
Griswold v. Connecticut, 259
Grodin, Michael, 293
Group practices, 77–78
Grubbs v. Medical Facilities of America, Inc., 174
Guardian ad litem
    abortions and, 264
    defined, 59
    right to refuse treatment and, 285
Guilmet v. Campbell, 127
Gunshot wounds, reporting, 150

H

Habituation, 151
Haemophilus influenzae type b (Hib) vaccine, 146
Hardship, undue, 174
Harvesting organ, defined, 240
Harvet v. Unity Medical Ctr., 170
Hayes v. Shelby Memorial Hosp., 173
Hazard Communication Standard (HCS), 176
Healthcare
    allocation of scarce time and resources, 301
    concierge, 314
    cost of, 299–300
    disparities in, 305
    diversity in, 305–313
    equity in, 305–313
    ethical issues in, 298–319
    medical errors and, 299
    for older adults, 312–313
    for patients with disabilities, 307–312
    proxy, 313
    selected issues in current system, 299–304
    surrogate decision-making, 313
Healthcare-associated infections (HAIs), 303
Health care consumer, role of, 98
Healthcare environment
    exclusive provider organizations (EPOs), 74
    federal programs, 71–76
    healthcare practices, 77–79
    healthcare practitioners, 79–84
    Health Care Quality Improvement Act of 1986, 76
    health insurance, 70–71
    health maintenance organizations (HMOs), 70, 74
    managed care, 73–74
    managed care organizations (MCOs), 73–74
    preferred provider organizations (PPOs), 74
    telehealth, 74–75
Healthcare ethics, 7
Healthcare law, 5–7
Healthcare plan, under HIPAA, 216
Healthcare practices
    associate practice, 77
    group practices, 77–78

partnership, 77
professional corporations, 78, *78*, 79*t*
sole proprietorship, 77
Healthcare practitioners
advanced practice providers, 82
Allied Health Professionals, 82, 83*t*–84*t*
certification, 79
licensure, 79
nurses, 82, 83*t*
physicians, 80, 81*t*, 82*t*
registration, 79–80
Healthcare providers, lack of, 300
Healthcare proxy, 292
Health Care Quality Improvement Act (HCQIA) of
1986, 76
Health disparities, 315
Health Information Technology for Economic and
Clinical Health (HITECH) Act of 2009, 72,
73, 215–216
Health insurance, 70–71
Health Insurance Marketplace, 71
Health Insurance Portability and Accountability Act
(HIPAA), 96, 194
compliance with, 214
confidentiality and, 98, 208–232
covered entities, 212, 216–217
covered transactions, 217
Enforcement Rule, 212
five titles, 211
implementation of, 221–223
misconceptions about, 222
noncompliance, 223–224, 223*t*
Notice of Privacy Practices, 216
patient consent to release of records, 214–215
patient rights, 218
permissions, 219*t*, 220*t*
permitted incidental disclosures, 218
privacy and, 165, 210–211
Privacy Rule, 212–213
Privacy Rule clarification, 218
and protected health information, 212
recommendations for implementing, 223
release of information and consent, 214–215
release of medical records under, 196
rules relating to research, 220
Security Rule, 212
standard identifiers, 217
state law requirements, 214
state's preemption, 217
Title II, 211–212
Transactions and Code Sets Rule, 212
Unique Identifiers Rule, 212
updates, 227
Health literacy, 305–307
Health Maintenance Organization (HMO) Act of
1973, 177
Health maintenance organizations (HMOs)
capitation rate, 74
case of, 113
described, 74
as a group practice, 78
and physicians' charges, 91
Health record. *See also* Medical records
defined, 189
Internet issues and, 215, 221
maintaining privacy of, 220–221
mental, 196
personal, 200
privacy protection strategies, 220–221
Hearing loss, 308–309

Hepatitis A vaccine, 146
Hepatitis B vaccine, 146, 176
Hickman v. Sexton Dental Clinic, 132
H. influenzae type B vaccine (HiB), 146
HIPAA-defined permissions, 218, 219*t*, 220*t*
Hippocrates, 236
Hippocratic Oath, 209, 236
Hiring and managing practices, 168–170
legal and illegal questions, 168–170, 169*t*
HIV. *See* Human immunodeficiency virus (HIV)
HMO. *See* Health maintenance organizations
(HMOs)
Holistic care, defined, 11
Home care, 227
Honesty, in workplace, 13
Honor, in AAMA code of ethics, 321
Hospice care
access to, 313
model, 289
Human dignity, in AAMA code of ethics, 321
Human genome, 247
Human Genome Project, 247–248
Human immunodeficiency virus (HIV)
AMA judicial council opinion on, 239*t*
infectious waste disposal, 158
Humility, defined, 11–12
Huntington's disease, 267*t*
genetic testing and, 266
Hurlock v. Park Lane Med. Ctr., 192
Hyde Amendment, 269
Hyde, Henry, 269
Hypothermia, 279

I

Identity theft, 199
Illinois, retention of records case, 197
Immunity, for charitable organizations, 123
Implicit bias, 302
Implied consent, 103–104
Implied contract, 36
Improper disclosure, 201
Inadequate encryption, 200
Incident report, 64
Incompetent patients, 94
Incompetent persons, 264
Independent practice association (IPA), 78
Indian Health Service (IHS), 71
Indictment, defined, 40
Indigent
defined, 8
duty to treat, 93
Medicaid for, 73
Indirect killing *versus* direct killing, 284
Individuals with Disabilities Education Act
(IDEA), 174
Induced abortion, 262
Infectious materials, 176
Infectious waste, 158
Informatics, 224
Information technology (informatics), 224–227
Informed consent, 96, 100–103, 245, 312, 315
Informed decision-making, 315
Injury, fraud cases and, 301
Inquest, 145
Insider threats, 200
Institutional review board (IRB), 245
Instrumental activities of daily living (IADLs), 51
Insurance
claims-made, 129

fixed-payment plan, 70
liability, 129
malpractice, 129–130
occurrence, 129
private, 70
third-party payers, 70
Insurance Company of North America v. Prieto, 132
Integrity, in workplace, 12–13
Intellectual disabilities, 311
Intentional torts, 32–34
assault, 33, 33*t*
battery, 33, 33*t*
defamation of character, 33*t*, 34
false imprisonment, 33–34, 33*t*
fraud, 33*t*, 34
invasion of privacy, 33*t*, 34
Interoperability challenges, 200
Interpersonal ethics, 12–15
Interview questions, 168, 169*t*
Intimate partner violence (IPV), 148–149
Invasion of privacy, 33*t*, 34
In vitro fertilization, 256
Involuntary sterilization, 261

J

Jacob and the Diseased Leg, 26–27
James v. Jacobson, 258
Jeanette M. and the Phone Call, 1
Jeczalik v. Valley Hospital, 76
Jehovah's Witnesses v. King County Hospital, 166
Jenkins v. Bogalusa Community Medical Center, 124
Jespersen, Mackayala, 279
Job displacement, 315
The Joint Commission
accreditation of healthcare professionals, 79
timeless in charting guidelines, 192
The Joint Commission on Accreditation of
Healthcare Organizations (The Joint
Commission), 57, 56
*Joseph Dudley, et al. v. Central Iowa Hospital Corp,
et al.*, 131
Jurisdiction, defined, 39
Just cause, employment discharge and, 171
Justice
defined, 11
principle of, 18
Justice-based ethics, 9, 10*t*

K

Keene v. Brigham & Women's Hosp., Inc., 201
Keller, Helen, 2
Kern v. Gulf Coast Nursing Home, Inc., 133
Kobler, William, 222
Korman v. Mallin, 101
Kübler-Ross, Elisabeth, 286
Kübler-Ross five stages of grief, 286–287, 286*t*

L

Laboratory technician
negligence lawsuits against, 132
occupation of, 83*t*
Landau v. Medical Board of California, 132
Landeros v. Flood, 147
Latoya and the Physical Therapy Patient, 48
Law of agency, 127

Laws
    administrative, 38
    case (common), 30
    civil (private), 31–35
    class action lawsuit, 37
    classification of, 31–39
    common (case), 30
    constitutional, 29
    contract, 36–37
    criminal, 37
    defined, 5
    Good Samaritan laws, 59–60
    healthcare, 5–7
    public law designation, 30
    reasons to study, 2–5
    regulatory, 29–30
    right-to-know, 175
    sources of, 29–31
    state open-record, 196
    tort, 32–34
Legacy systems, 200
Legal blindness, 310
Legal responsibility, 315
Legal system, 27–29
    as branch of government, 27
    classification of laws in, 31–39
    federal and state court systems in, 27, 39
    federal court structure in, *29*
    separation of powers in, 28, *28*
    sources of law for, 29–31
    trial process, 40–44
Length of life *vs.* quality of life, 312
Liability insurance
    claims-made, 129
    occurrence, 129
Liability, professional, 125–130
    of allied health professionals, 131–134
    altered medical records, 128
    alternative dispute resolution, 130
    civil liability cases and, 125–126
    illegal sale of drugs, 126
    law of agency, 127
    liability insurance and, 129
    malpractice insurance and, 129–130
    physical conditions of premises, 126
    promise to cure, 127
    responsible party for, 128
Libby Zion case, 164
Libel, 34. *See also* Defamation of character
Licensed practical nurse (LPN), 50
Licensed Practice Nurses (LPNs), 82, 83*t*
Licensed vocational nurses (LVN), 50,
    82, 83*t*
Licensure
    accreditation and, 56
    of allied health professionals, 55–56
    defined, 79
    endorsement in, 52
    examination for, 51–52
    healthcare practitioners, 79
    of nurse practitioners, 53
    of nurses, 53–55
    physician assistants, 53
    for physicians, 51–56
    practicing without a license and, 52
    reciprocity and, 52
    registration in, 52
    revocation and suspension, 52, 236, 237
    revocation of licensure, 52
Life-support systems, 278

Litigation
    case citations, 31
    defined, 40
    trial process, 40–44
Litigious society, 2, 114
Living will, 105, *105*
    do not resuscitate (DNR) orders and, 105
    effective conditions, 105
    sample, *105*
Lo, Bernard, 16
In loco parentis, 99
Loss, of medical records, 201
Lo three-step clinical model for decision making,
    16–17
Lovelace Medical Ctr. v. Mendez, 270
Love v. Heritage House Convalescent Center, 179
Low vision, 310
Loyalty, in workplace, 13

M

Malfeasance, 117
Malpractice, 113–141
    communication as prevention, 136
    defined, 35, 115
    documentation as prevention, 136–137
    malfeasance classification, 117
    misfeasance classification, 117
    negligence, 115–120
    nonfeasance classification, 117
    not guilty verdicts, 42
    Office of Inspector General and, 122–123
    prevention, 135–137
    tort reform, 134–135
Malpractice insurance
    cost of, 129
    defensive medicine and, 130
    licensed healthcare professionals and, 129
Malpractice suits
    affirmative defense to, 123
    assumption of risk defense to, 123–124
    borrowed servant doctrine, 124
    comparative negligence defense to, 124
    contributory negligence defense to, 124
    denial defense to, 123
    res judicata decision in, 125
    statute of limitations and, 125
Managed care, 73–74
    ethical and legal considerations, 75
Managed care organizations (MCOs)
    ethical and legal considerations, 75
    operation, 73–74
Mandel v. Doe, 131
Massachusetts
    liability case in, 132
    religious beliefs case in, 166
Maternal–fetal conflict, 243
Maternal Mortality, 302–303
Matter of Baby K, 265
McCormack, Mary Ellen, child abuse case of, 147
McCullough, Dennis, 290
McLaughlin v. Cooke, 261
MCO. *See* Managed care organizations (MCOs)
Measles, mumps, and rubella (MMR) vaccine, 146
Mechanical heart recipient, 293
Mediation, 130
Medicaid
    advance directives and, 291
    confidentiality and, 209
    federal programs, 73

    fraud and, 34, 120–121, 220–221
    fraud cases and medical records, 193
    managed care ethics and, 75
    Office of Inspector General and, 122
    organ transplants and, 242–243
    Rehabilitation Act and, 174
    Title VII of the Civil Rights Act and, 171
    viatical settlements and, 291
Medical aid-in-dying, 244, 282
Medical assistants, 51, 56
    negligence lawsuit against, 132
    occupation of, 83*t*
Medical errors
    First, do no harm principle, 299
    Medicare/Medicaid reimbursement and, 299
Medical etiquette, 20
Medical examiner, 145
Medical informatics, 224
Medical liability, 315
Medical orders for life-sustaining treatment
    (MOLST), 106
Medical Patient's Rights Act, confidentiality and, 58
Medical practice
    group, 77–78
    group, as HMO, 78
    group, as independent practice association
        (IPA), 78
    professional corporations, 78, *79*
    types of, 78, 79*t*
Medical practice acts, 6–7, 49–50
Medical records, 188–202
    altered, 128
    birth certificates, 143
    case of ransomware attack, 188
    case of reporting public health issues, 143
    completeness of entries in, 192
    confidentiality and, 195–196
    contents of, 190–191
    corrections and alterations to, 191–192
    credibility of, 193
    death certificates, 144–145
    defined, 189
    electronic, 199
    falsification of, 192
    improper disclosure of, 201
    legal standing of, 189, 190
    loss of, 201
    ownership of, 194–195
    Privacy Act and, 210–211
    purpose of, 189–190
    release of information, 196
    reporting and disclosure requirements, 201
    retention and storage of, 197–198
    state open-record laws, 196
    storage of, 189
    subpoena *duces tecum*, 201–202
    timeliness of documentation, 192
    time periods for retaining, 197*t*
    use of in court, 201–202
Medical specialties, 81*t*
Medical waste, 157–158
Medicare
    accreditation and, 56
    advance directives and, 291
    card, example of, *72*
    confidentiality and, 209
    diagnostic related groups and, 72
    federal programs, 71–72
    fee splitting and ethics, 75
    fraud and, 34, 120–121, 220–221

fraud cases and medical records, 193
and HIPAA noncompliance, 223–224, 223*t*
managed care ethics and, 75
Office of Inspector General and, 122
rationing of health care and, 71
Rehabilitation Act and, 174
Social Security Act and, 178
Title VII of the Civil Rights Act and, 171
as utilitarian ethics, 8
Medicare Act, as ethical utilitarianism, 8
Medicare-Medicaid Antifraud and Abuse
    Amendments, 34
Medication management, 312
Mengele, Josef, 237
Meningococcal conjugate vaccine, 146
Mental health
    advocacy, 293
    and decision-making capacity, 292
Mentally challenged persons. *See* Cognitive
    impairment
Mercy killing. *See* Euthanasia
Michigan
    Baby M case, 257
    promise to cure case and, 127
Microfiche, 198
Minimum necessary standard, 210, 217
Minnesota
    child abuse case in, 147
    reporting laws in, 147
    wrongful discharge suit in, 170
Minors
    competencies of, 99*t*
    rights of, 99
Misdemeanor
    case process, 37, *39*
    defined, 37
Misfeasance, 117
Mississippi, liability case in, 133
Missouri
    completeness of medical records case, 192
    liability case in, 132
Model Occupational Therapy Practice Act, 51
Model Practice Act for Physical Therapy
    (MPA), 51
Moderate visual impairment, 310
Modified Rights of the Terminally Ill Act, 105
Moon Lake Convalescent Center v. Margolis, 31, 132
Morality, 7
Morbidity rate, 143
Morena v. South Hills Health Systems, 133
"Morning after" pill, "Plan B" contraceptive
    pill, 260
Morrison v. MacNamara, 35
Mortality rate, 143
MRSA (Methicillin-resistant *Staphylococcus
    Aureus*), 303
Multidrug-resistant organisms (MDROs), 303
Municipal ordinances, 30
Murray v. Vandevander, 260
Mutual recognition model, 54

N

National Association of the Deaf, 308
National Board for Certification in Occupational
    Therapy (NBCOT), 55
National Board for Respiratory Care (NBRC), 51, 55
National Board of Medical Examiners (NBME), 51
National Childhood Vaccine Injury Act of 1986, 146

National Commission of Certification of Physician
    Assistants (NCCPA), 53
National Council Licensure Examination for Practical
    Nurses (NCLEX-PN®), 54
National Council Licensure Examination for
    Registered Nurses (NCLEX-RN®),
    53–54
National Council of State Boards of Nursing
    (NCSBN), 53, 54, 82
National Healthcareer Association (NHA), 55
National Labor Relations Act of 1935, 175
National Labor Relations Board (NLRB), 175
National Organ Transplant Law of 1984, 241
National Physical Therapy Examination
    (NPTE), 55
NBME. *See* National Board of Medical Examiners
    (NBME)
Neglect of duty, 118
Negligence, 35, 115–120
    comparative, malpractice suit defense, 124
    contributory, malpractice suit defense, 124
    damages, 119–120
    dental assistant lawsuit, 132
    dereliction or breach of duty, 118, 132
    direct or proximate cause, 118–119
    duty and, 117–118
    as form of malpractice, 115–116
    laboratory assistant lawsuit, 132
    medical assistant lawsuit, 132
    nurse lawsuits, 131–132
    nurse practitioner lawsuits, 131
    nursing assistant lawsuit, 133
    paramedic/EMS provider lawsuit, 133
    pharmacist lawsuit, 133
    physical assistant (PA) lawsuit, 133
    physical therapist, 133
    respiratory therapist lawsuit, 134
    sterilization suits, 261
    tort of, 116–120
Negligent torts. *See* Unintentional torts
New Jersey, Baby M case, 258
New York
    Baby M case, 257
    falsification of medical records case in, 192
    Libby Zion case in, 164
Nixzmary's Law, 165
Nominal damages, 120
Noncompliance issues
    patients and, 94
    penalties under HIPAA, 223–224, 223*t*
Noncompliant patient
    abandonment and, 94
    defined, 94
Nonfeasance, 117
Nonmalfeasance, principle of, 18
Nontherapeutic research, 245
Norton v. Argonaut Insurance Company, 56–57, 190
Notations, chart, 191
Notice of Privacy Practices (NPP), 216
Nuremberg Code, 237, 320
    text of, 320
Nurse Licensure Compact, 54
Nurse practice act (NPA), 50, 53, 55
Nurse practitioner practice acts, 50
Nurse practitioners (NPs), 53, 82
Nurses, 82, 83*t*
    code of ethics, 239, 321
    negligence lawsuits against, 131–132
Nursing assistants, negligence lawsuit against, 133
Nursing Students, 54–55

O

OB/GYN and Olivia M. case study, 254
Occupational Safety and Health Act (OSHA) of
    1970, 175–176
    as rights-based ethics, 8
Occupational therapists (OTs), 51, 55
Occupational therapy assistants (OTAs), 51
Occurrence insurance, 129
OCR. *See* Office of Civil Rights (OCR)
Odomes v. Nucare Inc., 179
Office of Civil Rights (OCR), HIPAA policies
    and, 223
Office of Inspector General (OIG)
    false claims and, 122
    immunity for charitable organizations and, 123
    violation of federal statutes and, 123
Older Americans Act, 148
O'Neill v. Montefiore Hosp., 36
Open-record laws, 196
Opioid crisis, 155–156, 304
Opioids
    CDC guidance for prescribing, 156
    crisis, 155–156, 304
    defined, 155
    symptoms of abuse, 155–156
    symptoms of addiction, 156
Ordinary means *versus* extraordinary means, 285
Oregon, organ transplant case in, 242
Organ donation
    AMA judicial council opinion on, 238*t*
    as bioethical issue, 240
    organ donor card, *241*
Organ trafficking, as bioethical issue, 241
Organ transplants
    allocation of, 242
    and Medicaid, 242–243
    and National Organ Transplant Law of 1984, 241
Osborne v. McMasters, 123
OSHA. *See* Occupational Safety and Health Act
    (OSHA) of 1970
OSHA Occupational Exposure to Bloodborne
    Pathogens Standards rules, 175
OTC. *See* Over-the-counter medications (OTC)
Other Potentially Infectious Material (OPIM), 176
Over-the-counter medications (OTC)
    consumer role to declare use, 98
    harm from undisclosed use, 113
Ownership, of medical records, 194–195

P

Pacheco v. United States, 270
Palliative care, 289–290
    access to, 313
Paramedics. *See also* Emergency medical technicians
    (EMT/paramedic)
    civil immunity finding, 133
    occupation of, 83*t*
Parens patriae authority, 99
Parenteral, defined, 176
Partnership, 77, *77*
Passive euthanasia
    Brittany Maynard case, 283–284
    defined, 282
    Nancy Cruzan case, 282
    Terry Schiavo case, 282–283
Patient consent, 200
Patient data protection, 314

Patient dumping, 93, 178, 181
Patients
    abandonment of, 93–94
    accepting, AMA judicial council opinion on, 238t
    advance directives and, 104–108
    confidentiality and, 98–99, 208–232
    consent of, 100–104
    incompetent, 94
    noncompliant, 94
    physician duty to properly identify, 95
    physician duty to respect confidentiality and, 95
    physicians and, 90–108
    privacy and, 13, 14
    responsibilities, 97–98
    rights, 97–98, 218
    terminally ill, 281
Patient Self-Determination Act (PSDA),
        104–105, 108
Patient's Rights Act, 58
Pay equity, 14
Pennsylvania, liability case in, 133
People v. Smithtown Gen. Hosp., 192
Per diem, Medicaid payment, 73
Permissions
    HIPAA-defined, 218, 219t, 220t
    and HIPAA Title II, 212
Permitted incidental disclosures, 218
Perseverance, defined, 11
Persistent vegetative state (PVS)
    defined, 280
    Terri Schiavo case and, 283
Personal health record, 200
PGD. See Preimplantation genetic diagnosis
        (PGD)
Pharmacists
    negligence lawsuits against, 133
    occupation of, 84t
Pharmacy technician code of ethics, 13
Phenylketonuria (PKU)
    genetic disorders, 267t
    genetic testing and, 266
Phlebotomists, 51, 55
Physical disabilities, 311–312
Physical therapists (PTs), 51, 55
    negligence lawsuit against, 133
    occupation of, 84t
Physical therapy assistants (PTAs), 51
Physician assistant (PA), 50, 53
Physician Assistant National Certifying Examination®
        (PANCE), 53
Physician Assistant National Recertifying Exam
        (PANRE), 53
Physician assistants (PAs), 82
    occupation of, 84t
    practicing without oversight, 131
Physician-assisted suicide (PAS)
    AMA judicial council opinion on, 239t
    Oregon law right of conscience exemptions, 76
Physician-owned practices, 77–78
Physician–patient relationship, 90–108
    doctrine of informed consent and, 100–103
    minor rights and, 99
    professional practice responsibilities and, 92–96
    role of health care consumer in, 98
    standard of care and, 57
Physicians
    American College of Physicians, 80
    American College of Surgeons, 80
    duties of, 92t, 93–96
    licensure of, 51–56
    malpractice insurance and, 130

medical and surgical specialties, 80, 81t
physician abbreviations and, 82t
practicing medicine without license, 52
as primary care physician (PCP), 80
public duties of, 143–151
respondeat superior and, 60
standard of care and, 56, 57
Placebo group, defined, 246
Plaintiff, defined, 33, 40
Pleadings, 41
Pneumococcal conjugate vaccine (PCV), 146
Polio vaccine, 146
Polonsky v. Union Hospital, 132
Polypharmacy, 312
Poor Sisters of St. Francis v. Catron, 134
Posthumous, 240
Postmortem, 145
Postpartum care deficiencies, 303
PPO. See Preferred Provider Organizations
        (PPOs)
Precedent, 7
Preempting, federal versus state laws, 170
Preferred Provider Organizations (PPOs), 74
Pregnancy
    prenatal testing, 266–268
    wrongful-life, 269–270
Pregnancy Discrimination Act of 1978, 171, 173
Preimplantation genetic diagnosis (PGD), 266
Premises, physical conditions of and liability, 126
Prenatal testing, 266–268
Preponderance of evidence, 32, 118
Prescriptions, controlled drugs and, 153, 153
Primary care physician (PCP), 80
    transfer of records and, 196
Primary care providers, 73
Prince v. Commonwealth of Massachusetts, 166
Principle of beneficence, 96
Principle of double-effect, 284
Principles of Medical Ethics (AMA), 237–238
Privacy. See also Confidentiality
    defined, 13, 14
    health care workplace and, 165
    invasion of, 33t, 34
    maintaining of health records, 220–221
Privacy Act of 1974, 210–211
Privacy Rule
    under HIPAA Title II, 211–212
    implementation, 221–223
    permitted incidental disclosures and, 218
Privileged communication, 98–99, 194
Probable cause
    child abuse and, 147
    discrimination and, 172
Probate court, 40
Product liability, 129
Professional corporations, 78, 79
Professionalism, in health care, 164–165
Profound visual impairment, 310
Project Bioshield, 245
Promise to cure, 127
Prosecutor, defined, 40
Prospective payment system, Medicaid and, 73
Protected health information (PHI)
    deidentification of, 213
    HIPAA Privacy Rule and, 212
    subpoenaed, 217
Protocol, 298
Provider–patient relationship. See Physician–patient
        relationship
Provider's rights and responsibilities, 91–92
Proximate cause, of negligence, 118–119

Proxy
    healthcare, 313
    power of attorney, 106
Prudent person rule, 57–58
Public duties, of health care professionals, 143–151
Public health records. See Vital statistics and public
        health records
Public law
    administrative law branch of, 38
    classification, 31
    criminal law branch of, 37
    process of enactment, 30
    relevant to medical practice, 37
Punitive damages, 120

Q

Quality assurance (QA) programs, 19–20
    accreditation and, 56
Quality of life
    advance directives and, 291
    AMA judicial council opinion on, 239t
    Arthritis Impact Measurement Scale (AIMS), 287
    defined, 287
    Dying Person's Bill of Rights, 287–288
    Functional Living Index: Cancer (FLIC), 287
    healthcare proxy, 292
    hospice care, 289
    vs. length of life, 312
    measures of, 287
    palliative care, 289–290
    viatical settlements, 290–291
Quinby v. Morrow, 132
Quinlan, Karen Ann, 278–279
    landmark case, 282

R

Radioactive waste, 158
Randomized study, informed consent and, 246
Ransomware attacks, 200
Rationing medical care, 244–245
"Reasonable person standard,", 57
"Reasonable physician standard", 101
In re Axelrod, 148
In re Baby M, 258
Reciprocity, physician licensure and, 52
In re Doe, 264
Registered nurse (RN). See also Nurses
    negligence lawsuits against, 131–132
    occupation of, 84t
Registered Professional Nurses (RN), 82, 83t
Registered Respiratory Therapist (RRT), 55
Registration
    healthcare practitioners, 79–80
    for licensure, 52
Regulations, defined, 29
Regulation Z. See Truth in Lending Act (Regulation Z)
        of 1969
Regulatory law, 29–30
Rehabilitation Act of 1973, 173–174
Release of information, 196
    under HIPAA, 214–215
Religious beliefs versus ethics, 17
Religious issues
    conception and, 261, 266
    parental neglect and, 148
    patient autonomy and, 167
Reporting, medical records and, 201
In re Quinlan, 279
In re Schroeder, 147

Research
control group in, 246
nontherapeutic, 245
Placebo group, 246
rules relating to, 220
therapeutic, 246
Res ipsa loquitur (RIL)
doctrine of, 119
malpractice denial defense and, 123
Res judicata, malpractice suit decision, 125
Resource allocation, 312
Respect, in workplace, 12
Respiratory therapists (RTs), 51, 55
negligence lawsuits against, 134
occupation of, 84*t*
Respite care, 289
Respondeat superior
altered medical records and, 128
borrowed servant doctrine and, 124
civil liability cases and, 125, 128
doctrine of, 60
employer-employee responsibilities and, 60–61, 114
malpractice insurance and, 129
role of supervisor concerning liability, 128
scope of practice and, 60
Responsibility, defined, 12
Restraining (protective) order, 149
Retailing, of drugs, 153
Retinoblastoma
genetic disorders, 267*t*
genetic testing and, 266
Revocation, of licensure, 52, 237
Rider, 129
Rights
of minors, 99
of patients, 97–98
of physicians, 91–92
Rights-based ethics, 8, 10*t*
Right-to-know laws, 175
Right to refuse treatment, 285
Rigor mortis, 279
RIL. *See Res ipsa loquitur* (RIL)
Risk, assumption of, 123–124
Risk management, 62–63
falls and, 63
medication errors and, 63
"Seven Rights" of medicine administration, 63
Three Checks and, 63
Triple Check method and, 63
Robotic-assisted surgery, 313
Robotics, 313
Rodgers v. St. Mary's Hospital, 197
Roe v. Wade, 262–263
Rotavirus vaccine, 146
Rowland v. Christian, 126

S

Safe Haven Laws, 270–271
Safety, as malpractice prevention, 135–136
Safety Data Sheet (SDS), 157, 176
Saint Christopher's Hospice, London, 289
Sanctity of life, defined, 12
Satler v. Larsen, 148
Saunders, Cicely, 289
Savior siblings, 268
Schiavo, Terri, 282–283
Scope of practice, 61–62
Selective fetal reduction, 255
Settlement, in lawsuit, 128
Seven-step decision model, 16

Severe visual impairment, 310
Sexual harassment, 14, 171
Shinal v. Toms, 100
Sickle-cell disease, genetic disorders, 266, 267*t*
Slander, 34
Smith v. Cote, 270
Social determinants of health (SDH), 305
Social engineering, 200
Social Security Act of 1935, 178
Sole proprietorship, 77
Solo practice, 77
South Carolina, liability case in, 132
Specialties
medical, 81*t*
surgical, 81*t*
Spontaneous abortion, 262
Standard of care, 56–57
Standards of proof, 43
Stare decisis, 30
Starks v. Director of Div. of Employment Section, 179
State Board of Medical Examiners, 49
State Board of Registration, 49
State court system, 40
State Dep't. of Human Services v. Northern, 285
State laws, 96
State open-record laws, 196
State's preemption, 217
State v. Fierro, 281
Statute of limitations, 59–60
malpractice suits and, 125
past-due accounts and, 183
retaining records and, 197
Statutes
defined, 29
federal health care, 123
wrongful death, 120
Statutory law, 29–30
Stem cell research, embryonic, 248
Sterilization, 260–262
defined, 260
involuntary, 261
legal, 261–262
negligence suits related to, 261
therapeutic, 260–261
voluntary, 260
Sternberg v. California State Board of Pharmacy, 133
St. Francis v. Catron, 134
Stigmatization, 293
St. John's Reg. Health Center v. American Cas. Co., 129
Storage, of medical records, 197–198
Strict liability, 129
Subpoena, 40–41
of medical records, 189
Subpoena *duces tecum,* 41, 201–202
Substance abuse, 154–156, 154*t*
opioid crisis and, 155–156
Substitute judgment rule, 291
Suicide, 292–293
Summary judgment, 41
Surgical specialties, 81*t*
Surrogacy, 256–257
Surrogate, advance directives and, 291
Suspension, of licensure, 52
Swanson v. St. John's Lutheran Hospital, 76
Sympathy, in workplace, 13

T

Tarasoff v. Regents of the University of California, 97–98

Tay-Sachs disease
genetic disorders, 267*t*
genetic testing, 266
Technology access, 315
Technology technicians, 227
Teeters v. Currey, 59
Telehealth, 58, 74–75, 226
ethical issues, 313
Teleological theory, 8
Terminally ill, 281
Therapeutic research, 246
Therapeutic sterilization, 260–261
Third-party payers, 70, 74
Third-party vendors, 200
Thompson v. Brent, 57, 61
Thor v. Boska, 193
Timeliness of documentation, 192
Title VII of the Civil Rights Act of 1964, 171–172
Tolerance, defined, 12
Tolling, statute of limitations and, 59
Tools, Robert, 293
Tort, defined, 32
Tort law, 32–34
abandonment of patients, 93–94
assault and health care, 33, 33*t*
battery and health care, 33, 33*t*
defamation of character and health care, 33*t*, 34
embezzlement and, 34
false imprisonment and health care, 33–34, 33*t*
fraud and health care, 33*t*, 34
intentional torts, 33, 33*t*
invasion of privacy and health care, 33*t*, 34
malpractice and, 35
in medical practice, 33
negligence and, 35, 116–120
negligent torts, 35
standard of care and, 35
unintentional torts, 35
Tort reform, 134–135
Transplant rationing, as bioethical issue, 241–243
Treatment (medical)
right to refuse, 285
withdrawing life-sustaining, 281
withholding life-sustaining, 281
Treatment, payment, and health care operations (TPO), 217
Triage, 301
Trial process, 40–44
appellate court system, 44
burden of proof, 42
civil trial procedure, *42*
closing arguments, 42
deposition, 40
discovery, 40
examination of witnesses, 41
grand jury and, 40
jury selection, 41
opening statements, 41
pleadings, 41
presentation of evidence, 41
procedure, 40–42
settling out of court, 41
standards of proof, 43
subpoena, 40–41
subpoena *duces tecum,* 41
summary judgment, 41
testifying in court, 43
Truth in Lending Act (Regulation Z) of 1969, 36, 181–182
Truth telling, 95–96

Tubal ligation. *See* Sterilization
Tugg v. Towney, 174

U

UDDA. *See* Uniform Determination of Death Act
    (UDDA)
Unauthorized access, 199
Unborn Victims of Violence Act, 264
Undue hardship, 174
Unemployment compensation, 179
Uniform Anatomical Gift Act, 106, 240
    advance directives and, 291
    fetal harvesting and, 268
Uniform Business Records Act, 128
Uniform Determination of Death Act (UDDA), 281
Unintended consequences, healthcare, 315
Unintentional torts, 35
    malpractice and, 35
    negligence and, 35
United Network for Organ Sharing (UNOS), 240
United States of America v. Steven Monaco, Daniel Osw
    Ari, Michael Goldis, and Aaron Jones, 121
United States v. Beauchamp et al., 91
United States v. Jamil, et al., 121
UNOS. *See* United Network for Organ Sharing
    (UNOS)
U.S. Government
    branches of, 27, *28*
    checks and balances, system of, 27
U.S. Medical Licensing Examination (USMLE), 52
USMLE. *See* U.S. Medical Licensing Examination
    (USMLE)
Utilitarianism
    defined, 8
    as ethical theory, 8, 10*t*

V

Vaccines and Toxoids
    Diphtheria, tetanus, and pertussis (DTaP)
        vaccine, 146

Haemophilus influenzae type b (Hib) vaccine, 146
Hepatitis A vaccine, 146
Hepatitis B vaccine, 146, 176
    mandated by law, 146
    Measles, mumps, and rubella (MMR) vaccine, 146
    Meningococcal conjugate vaccine, 146
    National Childhood Vaccine Injury Act of
        1986, 146
    Pneumococcal conjugate vaccine (PCV), 146
    Polio vaccine, 146
    Rotavirus vaccine, 146
    Varicella (chickenpox) vaccine, 146
Vancomycin-resistant Enterococcus
    (VRE), 303
Varicella (chickenpox) vaccine, 146
Veracity, 96
Vesting, pension plans and, 180
Veterans Health Administration, 71
Viable, fetus, 262
Viatical settlements, 290–291
Virtue-based ethics, 9–10, 10*t*
Vision disorders, 310–311
Visual impairment. *See also* Vision disorders
    defined, 310
    legal blindness, 310
    moderate, 310
    profound, 310
    severe, 310
Vital statistics and public health records
    birth certificates, 143
    death certificates, 144–145
    defined, 143
Voice recognition technology, 225
Voluntary sterilization, 260

W

Waive, defined, 41
Watson v. Idaho Falls Consol. Hosp. Inc., 169
Whistleblowing, 181
Whitehead, Mary Beth, 257–258
Williams v. Summit Psychiatric Ctrs., 34

Wireless local area networks (WLANs), 225
Wisconsin, improper disclosure in, 201
Withdrawing life-sustaining treatment, 281
Withholding life-sustaining treatment, 281
Witness, expert, 43
WLAN. *See* Wireless local area networks
    (WLANs)
Woolfolk v. Duncan, 174
Work, defined, 12
Workers' Compensation Act, 179–180
Workplace
    compensation and benefits regulations,
        178–181
    consumer protection and collection practices,
        181–183
    cultural considerations, 165–168
    discrimination in, 164
    employee health and safety in, 175–178
    equal employment opportunity and employment
        discrimination, 170–175
    federal regulations affecting professional
        in, 170
    hiring and managing practices, 168–170
    interview questions in, 168
    privacy and, 165
    professionalism in, 164–165
    religious considerations in, 167
World Federation of Occupational Therapists
    (WFOT), 74
Wrongful death statutes, 120
Wrongful discharge, 171
    at-will employment, 171
    employment lawsuits, 172
Wrongful-life suits, 269–270
    wrongful conception/pregnancy, 270
    wrongful life, 268–269

Z

Zatarain v. WDSU-Television, Inc., 173
Zion, Libby, 164
Zucker v. Axelrod, 133